# Succession Chart

## U.S. Court of Appeals for the Second Circuit

| March 3, 1891<br>26 Stat. 826 | March 3, 1891<br>26 Stat. 826 | March 3, 1891<br>26 Stat. 826 | April 17, 1902<br>32 Stat. 106 | January 17, 1929<br>45 Stat. 1081 | May 31, 1938<br>52 Stat. 584 |
|---|---|---|---|---|---|
| WALLACE<br>William J.<br>1891 | LACOMBE<br>Emile H.<br>1891 | SHIPMAN<br>Nathaniel<br>1892 | COXE<br>Alfred C., Sr.<br>1902 | CHASE<br>Harrie B.<br>1929 | CLARK<br>Charles E.<br>1939 |
| WARD<br>Henry G.<br>1907 | HOUGH<br>Charles M.<br>1916 | TOWNSEND<br>William K.<br>1902 | MANTON<br>Martin T.<br>1918 | WATERMAN<br>Sterry R.<br>1955 | ANDERSON<br>Robert P.<br>1964 |
| MAYER<br>Julius M.<br>1921 | HAND<br>Augustus N.<br>1927 | NOYES<br>Walter C.<br>1907 | PATTERSON<br>Robert P., Sr.<br>1939 | OAKES<br>James L.<br>1971 | TIMBERS<br>William H.<br>1971 |
| HAND<br>Learned<br>1924 | HARLAN<br>John Marshall<br>1954 | ROGERS<br>Henry W.<br>1913 | FRANK<br>Jerome N.<br>1941 | PARKER<br>Fred I.<br>1994 | PRATT<br>George C.<br>1982 |
| MEDINA<br>Harold R.<br>1951 | LUMBARD<br>Joseph E.<br>1955 | SWAN<br>Thomas W.<br>1926 | MOORE<br>Leonard P.<br>1958 | HALL<br>Peter W.<br>2004 | LEVAL<br>Pierre N.<br>1993 |
| FRIENDLY<br>Henry J.<br>1959 | MULLIGAN<br>William H.<br>1971 | HINCKS<br>Carroll C.<br>1953 | MANSFIELD<br>Walter R.<br>1971 | | WESLEY<br>Richard C.<br>2003 |
| VAN GRAAFEILAND<br>Ellsworth A.<br>1974 | CARDAMONE<br>Richard J.<br>1981 | SMITH<br>John J.<br>1960 | WINTER<br>Ralph K., Jr.<br>1981 | | |
| ALTIMARI<br>Frank X.<br>1985 | CABRANES<br>José A.<br>1994 | MESKILL<br>Thomas J.<br>1975 | PARKER<br>Barrington D., Jr.<br>2001 | | |
| POOLER<br>Rosemary S.<br>1998 | | CALABRESI<br>Guido<br>1994 | CARNEY<br>Susan L.<br>2011 | | |
| | | DRONEY<br>Christopher F.<br>2011 | | | |

Organized by the year of commission.

| May 19, 1961<br>75 Stat. 80 | May 19, 1961<br>75 Stat. 80 | May 19, 1961<br>75 Stat. 80 | October 20, 1978<br>92 Stat. 1629 | October 20, 1978<br>92 Stat. 1629 | July 10, 1984<br>98 Stat. 333 | July 10, 1984<br>98 Stat. 333 |
|---|---|---|---|---|---|---|
| KAUFMAN<br>Irving R.<br>1961 | HAYS<br>Paul R.<br>1961 | MARSHALL<br>Thurgood<br>1961 | NEWMAN<br>Jon O.<br>1979 | KEARSE<br>Amalya L.<br>1979 | MINER<br>Roger J.<br>1985 | MAHONEY<br>J. Daniel<br>1986 |
| WALKER<br>John M., Jr.<br>1989 | GURFEIN<br>Murray I.<br>1974 | FEINBERG<br>Wilfred<br>1966 | KATZMANN<br>Robert A.<br>1999 | RAGGI<br>Reena<br>2002 | SACK<br>Robert D.<br>1998 | SOTOMAYOR<br>Sonia<br>1998 |
| LIVINGSTON<br>Debra A.<br>2007 | PIERCE<br>Lawrence W.<br>1981 | JACOBS<br>Dennis<br>1992 | | | CHIN<br>Denny<br>2010 | LOHIER<br>Raymond J., Jr.<br>2010 |
| | MCLAUGHLIN<br>Joseph M.<br>1990 | | | | | |
| | STRAUB<br>Chester J.<br>1998 | | | | | |
| | LYNCH<br>Gerard E.<br>2009 | | | | | |

### June 18, 1910
### 36 Stat. 539

KNAPP
Martin A.
1910

MACK
Julian W.
1929

The Commerce Court, created in 1910 and having jurisdiction to review decisions of the Interstate Commerce Commission, was made up of five Article III judges who had parallel assignments to the various circuit courts, and who continued to serve assignments to the circuits after the Commerce Court was dissolved in 1913. Judges Knapp and Mack were assigned to the Second Circuit in 1910 and 1929, respectively.

## Chief Judges

Learned Hand (1948-1951)
Thomas W. Swan (1951-1953)
Harrie B. Chase (1953-1954)
Charles E. Clark (1954-1959)
Joseph E. Lumbard (1959-1971)
Henry J. Friendly (1971-1973)
Irving R. Kaufman (1973-1980)
Wilfred Feinberg (1980-1988)
James L. Oakes (1988-1992)
Thomas J. Meskill (1992-1993)
Jon O. Newman (1993-1997)
Ralph K. Winter, Jr. (1997-2000)
John M. Walker, Jr. (2000-2006)
Dennis Jacobs (2006-2013)
Robert A. Katzmann (2013-present)

# THE JUDGES OF THE SECOND CIRCUIT

CORNELL LAW REVIEW

# AD HOC COMMITTEE ON THE 125TH ANNIVERSARY OF THE COURT OF APPEALS FOR THE SECOND CIRCUIT

Judge Richard C. Wesley, Chair
Karen Greve Milton, Circuit Executive & Secretary

*Judicial & Court Committee Members*

Judge José A. Cabranes
Judge Denny Chin
Judge Dennis Jacobs
Chief Judge Robert A. Katzmann
Luis M. Lopez, Circuit Librarian
Judge Jon O. Newman
Sally Pritchard, Senior Staff Attorney
Judge John M. Walker, Jr.
Catherine O'Hagan Wolfe, Clerk of Court

*Attorney Members*

Robert Anello, Morvillo Abramowitz Grand Iason & Anello, P.C.
Professor John Q. Barrett, St. John's University School of Law
Sheila S. Boston, Kaye Scholer LLP
Michael A. Cardozo, Proskauer Rose LLP
John Gordan, III
Bettina B. Plevan, Proskauer Rose LLP
Karen Patton Seymour, Sullivan & Cromwell LLP
Professor John F. Witt, Yale Law School

# THE JUDGES OF THE SECOND CIRCUIT

## THE CURRENT COURT



## FORMER MEMBERS

# FOREWORD

*Robert A. Katzmann**

With the enactment 125 years ago of the Evarts Act, a court of appeals was created in each of the nation's nine circuits. What we now call the United States Court of Appeals for the Second Circuit began as a three-judge court covering New York, Connecticut and Vermont, expanding over time to 13 active judges as docket pressures increased, with the indispensable support of senior judges. In that century and a quarter, the Second Circuit has adjudicated thousands upon thousands of cases. With the rarity of Supreme Court review, our court is the tribunal of last resort in some 99 percent plus of the cases it resolves. With its tradition of oral argument, the Second Circuit is open to litigants, regardless of status, economic or otherwise.

As chief judge, I have the great privilege of serving with extraordinary colleagues—judges and staffs—all of whom share the objective of adjudicating cases fairly and efficiently. We have benefitted from superior advocacy as we endeavor to resolve the matters before us. I launched the project for the 125th anniversary of our court, not for self-celebration, but because any institution, in the effort to do its work well, should on occasion reflect on its past, to better settle the present and meet the challenges of the future. To that end, I proposed, and my colleagues agreed to establish, a special committee to undertake a wide range of activities relating to that 125-year experience, as we had done some 25 years ago. That committee, very ably chaired by Judge Richard C. Wesley, consists of a dedicated group of judges, court staff, and members of the bar, whose names are listed in this volume.[1] The activities include: this biographical collection of the judges; exhibitions documenting the court's cases and history; reenactments of some of our notable cases; lectures on the history of the court; remembrances of some distinguished judges of the past, Learned Hand, Henry J. Friendly, and Thurgood Marshall;

reflections of four Supreme Court justices, Chief Justice John Roberts, Jr., Justice Ruth Bader Ginsburg, Justice Sonia Sotomayor, and Justice Elena Kagan; and a program on the certification of opinions from our court to state high courts.

A cornerstone of our anniversary celebration is this volume, which contains biographies of all 74 judges who have sat on the Second Circuit.

At my public induction ceremony in 1999, my longtime collaborator and friend, Judge Frank M. Coffin of the First Circuit, likened a great appellate court to a symphony orchestra. He said: "It is not like a string quartet or a brass symphony or a set of timpani. All the members of the symphony can read music that is given but each plays a slightly different or greatly different instrument. It is the difference in the instruments that accounts for the depth and richness of a symphony sound." If I might extend the metaphor, I have watched and listened with a sense of admiration as our symphony readied itself for its many performances. I have marveled at the quality of its musicians. The richness of the tone comes from the diversity of backgrounds and experiences, some from the world of practice, some from the world of academia, some from district court and some from politics. As Judge Guido Calabresi once observed, it is the diversity of background rather than difference in judicial philosophy, however different such approaches might be, that creates the court's character. That, in my view, accounts for the timbre of the sound.

A great orchestra, like a great court, depends on a shared sense of mission, a shared view of and a deep commitment to the values and purposes of the enterprise. Its players, though they come with different perspectives, labor in ongoing and noncompetitive relationships with one another, respect one another's strengths, forgo ego for the greater good, honor patience and compromise, and recognize that the excellence of the final product results from the combined energies, skills, experiences and insights of the full complement of players. Even if a prior life brought the satisfaction of the virtuoso performer, the players of court understand that the music would be jarring if such virtuosity were not submerged for the benefit of a collaborative sound. In the pages that follow, you will have a sense of the lives of the judges of the Second Circuit, their backgrounds and experiences, all of which have contributed to the Second Circuit sound.

Gratitude is due to the editors of the *Cornell Law Review* who volunteered to work on the biographies in addition to their regular editing duties. Special thanks go to Editors-in-Chief Mateo de la Torre and Amelia Hritz, who recruited their colleagues to work on the project and spent countless hours managing it. Court aficionados will enjoy Judge Wesley's "redux" of Judge Wilfred Feinberg's 1986 article, *Unique Customs and Practices of the Second Circuit*. As Judge Wesley explains, technology has changed the way we do things, but it has not changed our court's collegial culture. We are indebted to my colleague Judge José A. Cabranes, who chaired the biographies project with great care; and to Judges Jon O. Newman and Dennis Jacobs, who provided thoughtful edits and suggestions. Judge Newman's introduction elegantly traces the statutory origins of the federal appellate courts, and Judge John M. Walker's illuminating article on the life and work of Senator William Evarts discusses the public servant who wrote the statute that created the modern courts of appeals. The biographies in this volume would not have been possible without the court's fine librarians, Adriana Mark, Julie Jones, Carole Martin, Taryn Rucinski, Mark Schwartz, Carolyn Tanen, Eugene Hsue, and Douglas Tomasulo, who worked tirelessly to gather primary and secondary sources on the lives of all the judges.

Lastly, and most importantly, much gratitude is due to the Staff Attorney's Office: to David Byowitz, Lucas Buzzard, Greg Capobianco, Abby Maltz, Molly Manning, Dan Principato, Eva Saltzman, Rick Sawyer, Emily Seiderman, Emer Stack, and Stephen Strother, the staff attorney "historians" who wrote the biographies; to Emma Pletenycky and Jason Lebowitz, who, respectively, provided logistical support and wrote the historical introduction during a summer internship; to Liz Duwe and Cathy Minuse, supervisory staff attorneys who worked as both historians and guiding hands; and to Sally Pritchard, our director of legal affairs, who wrote several of the biographies and skillfully oversaw the project. I often say that the court would cease to function without our Staff Attorney's Office. That was particularly true here: this wonderful volume would not exist but for these attorneys' curiosity, diligence, and fine writing.

* Chief Judge, Court of Appeals for the Second Circuit.

# FEINBERG REDUX—AN INSIDE LOOK AT THE SECOND CIRCUIT

*Richard C. Wesley**

## INTRODUCTION

The biographies compiled in this volume present one of several stories of the Second Circuit over its 125-year history. My colleagues and I are grateful for the dedicated work of Sally Pritchard and the attorneys of the Staff Attorney's Office in creating those biographies and for the editing work performed by former Chief Judges Jon O. Newman and Dennis Jacobs along with Judge José A. Cabranes. Their efforts, in conjunction with the Editorial Board of the Cornell Law Review, have produced a document that gives detail and texture to those who have labored, or continue to labor, here as judges of this great Court. That labor, particularly the characteristics of it that are unique to the Second Circuit, constitutes a story in itself.

In 1986, then-Chief Judge Wilfred (Bill) Feinberg wrote an article published in the *Hofstra Law Review* entitled *Unique Customs and Practices of the Second Circuit.*[1] Chief Judge Feinberg made the case that the subject deserved attention, as "some, if not all, of these customs and practices are little known outside of the official family but are worthy of scrutiny and discussion."[2] During the intervening thirty-one years following the Feinberg article, changes in the docket, technology, and judicial resources have fostered modification of some past procedures and the introduction of new tools that facilitate the Court's work as it has evolved. Despite these changes, a good many of the customs and practices of the Second Circuit remain the same. More importantly, the culture of the Court—its abiding respect for the views of colleagues and its high premium on collegiality—has not changed and is a vital part of life at 40 Foley Square.

## CUSTOMS AND PRACTICES

### A. VOTING MEMOS

In 1986, Chief Judge Feinberg referred to the use of voting memos as "perhaps the most valuable Second Circuit practice."[3] At that time, when a panel agreed "in a brief discussion immediately after argument or submission of an appeal" that a case should be decided by an opinion, the judges of the panel would circulate voting memos that day or the next.[4] These memos would precede the end-of-week voting conference[5] and Judge Feinberg remarked that "[t]his preparation for the voting conference streamline[d] it and frequently [made] possible quick agreement on a common approach."[6]

Today, we continue to exchange memos, but in a more limited and focused manner. Panels are rarely made up of the same three judges for the entire week; this practice is of recent vintage[7]—begun only in the last ten years—and was instituted to give the judges more flexibility in scheduling sitting days. As a result, voting conferences are often held immediately following each day's oral arguments and submissions. Voting memos are now reserved for cases in which, at conference, the panel is unclear on how the case should be resolved, often because the case presents a difficult legal issue due to a complex record, an intricate legal scheme, or a combination of both. The post-conference memos seek to identify the issues open for discussion and to offer each judge's perspective on how those issues affect the resolution of the case. Much like the voting memos in 1986, voting memos today help the judges clarify their thinking on the case and serve as a blueprint for the opinion.[8]

In addition, there are occasions when colleagues elect to send memos after a voting conference to further explain their views on the case or to express a concern about the proposed disposition. Some judges also use emails to panel members to discuss troubling aspects of a case or to seek advice on problems with the resolution of a matter during the drafting of an opinion.[9] The deliberative process is perhaps a bit more ad hoc today than it was at the time of Chief Judge Feinberg's article, but the focus on "getting it right" remains the same.

The memoranda are stylized to a degree. Each has a courteous and somewhat formal tone. If written in response to a memo from a colleague, the memo generally begins with a note of thanks to the author for expressing his or her thoughts on the case. The memo almost always also ends with a note of thanks to panel colleagues for taking the time to read the memo and expresses an interest by the author to continue the exchange of viewpoints on the matter at hand. My clerks are often struck by the dynamic of the memos: the formality combined with an expression of thanks for the exchange of views, even if those views might differ significantly. The style of memoranda is definitely cultural; the tradition of mutual respect for the views of colleagues runs deep at the Circuit.[10]

### B. Oral Argument

With one notable exception discussed below, the Second Circuit continues to be the only circuit that does not employ a general screening procedure of the court's entire docket in order to identify cases that can be decided without oral argument.[11] Instead, we almost always allow oral argument if requested by the parties.[12] Under Federal Rule of Appellate Procedure 34, the panel may deny requested oral argument only if it unanimously agrees that oral argument is not necessary.[13] There are occasions where panels of this Court do deny oral argument,[14] but they are rare. Moreover, in response to anecdotal experience that an increasing number of lawyers were relying solely upon their briefs without providing adequate notice, the Court recently changed its local rules to require that oral argument must be requested.[15] The default rule prior to this change was that oral argument was granted in all cases unless counsel indicated that argument was not necessary.[16] The result has been an increase in number of cases taken on submission.[17]

In addition, the Second Circuit is the only federal court of appeals in the nation that allows *pro se* litigants to argue their appeals.[18] While some might question the wisdom of allowing non-lawyers to argue the merits of their cases—Mr. Lincoln's characterization of the man who represents himself comes to mind[19]—the longstanding view of the Court is that the Second Circuit is open for all business and the entreaties of those who choose to argue their own cases are as deserving as those offered up by the best lawyers in the land. As is the case in counseled matters,[20] the number of *pro se* appeals being argued has dropped over the last few years as a result of the change in the Local Rules that makes submission of appeals the default.[21]

## C. THE NON-ARGUMENT CALENDAR

The Non-Argument Calendar is an institutional response to unique circumstances that forced the Court to employ a case-screening device for one category of cases.

The Immigration and Nationality Act gives the circuit courts appellate jurisdiction over appeals of removal orders from the Board of Immigration Appeals ("BIA").[22] In 2002, in an attempt to relieve its backlog of 56,000 cases, the BIA began using summary procedures: authorizing single members (instead of three-member panels) to make decisions, including to summarily affirm or reject appeals.[23] The result was a catastrophic increase of cases on the Court's docket.[24] For the first few years, the Court was immersed in charting the law in this new area of endeavor. But ultimately immigration cases began to clog the Court's calendar: entire sitting dockets were almost entirely immigration cases. The Court was reluctant to employ a screening mechanism. As a result of the heroic efforts of former Chief Judge Newman, the Court created the Non-Argument Calendar ("NAC") for a limited set of immigration cases that ensures full, robust judicial review of each case individually.[25]

The NAC is based on a sequential-judging mechanism.[26] Each week, a group of cases (as few as three or as many as six, but always a multiple of three) are submitted to a NAC panel of three judges. The panel receives a packet that contains the briefs, the record from the BIA, and a bench memorandum prepared by a law clerk in the Staff Attorney's Office that contains a detailed analysis of the facts and legal issues involved in the case, along with a draft summary order proposing a resolution of the case.[27] A voting sheet accompanies each case and designates each of the three panel members as Judge No. 1, Judge No. 2, or Judge No. 3; each member of the panel is Judge No. 1 for at least one case and is responsible for beginning the review of the materials for that particular case. Upon completion of his or her Judge No. 1 duties—which includes voting on the disposition of the matter[28]—that judge sends the case on to the chambers of Judge No. 2, who completes his or her review, votes, and sends it along to the chambers of Judge No. 3. After the case has been reviewed and approved for disposition by Judge No. 3, the order or summary order is filed and the matter is closed.[29] Any judge on the panel can stop the process at any time by voting to send the matter to the Regular Argument Calendar ("RAC"). In each year from 2011 through 2014, the Court handled about 850 matters in the NAC.[30] While the process has not been without its critics,[31] the NAC has provided the Court with a fair and balanced way of dealing with a large portion of its docket[32] after many of the legal issues involved in those cases had already been settled at the circuit level. The NAC was a reluctant accommodation to monumental change in the Court's docket.

## D. THE IN BANC CULTURE AND PROCEDURES

The Circuit's well-known tradition of disfavoring in banc review of panel decisions has not changed one wit in the thirty years between Chief Judge Feinberg's 1986 article and today. Indeed, that tradition was so well documented[33] that the in banc section of this article is the shortest. The number of in banc matters heard annually has not changed in the last thirty years.[34] But the manner in which the in-banc process is carried out within the Court has changed significantly. In 2010, Chief Judge Jacobs commissioned a panel of judges to set out a series of in-banc protocols for the Court. The protocols are internal procedures that have provided a methodology for the consideration of a colleague's request for in banc review of an opinion. Such protocols had not previously existed and the absence of procedures had, on occasion, caused some concerns by colleagues because of the ad hoc way in which the in-banc request was considered. The protocols are specific; they detail the order in which memos are exchanged on the in-banc question, they govern the in-banc voting period, and they even set out the order of the speakers at the voting conference following the in-banc oral argument and voting among the members of the in-banc panel. I think it fair to say that the protocols have been well received by the members of the Court. As judges, we understand rules; requiring others to adhere to rules is what we do! But while the protocols have given each of us certainty as to the procedures of an in-banc poll and resolution of the in-banc appeal, they have not changed the longstanding tradition of disfavoring in-banc review.

## E. The Expedited Appeals Calendar

In the wake of the heightened pleading standard required by *Bell Atlantic Corporation v. Twombly*[35] and *Ashcroft v. Iqbal*,[36] in 2011 the Court instituted an Expedited Appeals Calendar ("XAC") to facilitate the prompt determination of appeals from district court orders that dismiss a complaint for: "(A) lack of subject matter jurisdiction under [Federal Rule of Civil Procedure] 12(b)(1); (B) failure to state a claim upon which relief may be granted under [Federal Rule of Civil Procedure] 12(b)(6); or (C) filing a frivolous complaint, or for any other ground specified in 28 U.S.C. § 1915(e)(2)."[37] If one of these grounds is cited by the lower court in dismissing the matter and the parties indicate that result on the appropriate form, the Clerk will notify the parties that the matter has been placed on the XAC and will set a briefing schedule that is substantially shorter than that employed for all other cases.[38] "A request to extend the briefing time is disfavored and is governed by Local Rule 27.1."[39] The XAC is directed at a set of cases that by their nature do not have large records on appeal and tend to involve only questions of law without a disputed factual background. Unless a party requests restoring the appeal to the RAC, a shortened briefing schedule is set, the appeal is scheduled for an early hearing, and panels endeavor to decide the appeal promptly. The XAC is one way in which the Court has attempted to meet the needs of both the Bar and the litigants without compromising the careful attention each case merits from the Court.

## F. "Tabs" and the Editing Process for Opinions

The use of "tabs" by colleagues to register their approval (or disapproval) of a proposed opinion has not changed since Chief Judge Feinberg's article with the exception that the "small, rectangular pieces of paper, one side of which, like a postage stamp, has a gummed substance on it"[40] have been replaced by a form that allows a judge to indicate: (1) approval of the opinion subject to "technical" suggestions from a chambers clerk (generally citation format concerns or typographical corrections); (2) approval with suggestions set out in an attached memo (typically proposing substantive, or even stylistic, changes to the opinion); (3) agreement with the result, but intention to file a concurrence;[41] or (4) down-right disagreement and a decision to write a dissent.[42] As one can see, we needed a form to allow more specific responses from the judges—the little sticky notes just would not do. But clinging to history, we have retained the word and thank a colleague for sending his or her "tab."

The "veritable minuet" described by Chief Judge Feinberg[43] continues today. If a panel member delivers a tab agreeing with the opinion but offering some suggestions, the tab gives the author the choice of not accepting the suggestions. But if the panel member sends a memo citing concerns with the opinion without a tab, the non-tabbing judge has indicated that failure to take the suggestions could be a deal breaker.[44] My clerks are always fascinated by this process and quickly take up the intrigue that accompanies it. They revel in sending a memo of suggestions without a tab, but hate it when the same is done to us. I confess I enjoy the process myself. We learn a great deal about colleagues through the tabbing process.

Any suggestions made by a colleague, whether stylistic or substantive, are almost always accompanied by proposed language.[45] In the past, when *all* memoranda were exchanged by fax, this could result in a tedious process for chambers clerks in adding the language. It also increased the potential for errors in transposing the material.[46] Today, we increasingly send any language suggestions via fax *and* email and include a "black-lined" copy of the opinion in which the non-author judge has inserted the proposed changes into the opinion for the author to review.[47] This process is efficient, reduces errors in transposing suggested changes, and provides a useful format for the authoring judge to evaluate the suggestions.

### G. TECHNOLOGY AND THE COURT

Technological advances have often been met with skepticism by judges and understandably so, as the danger of unauthorized disclosure of sensitive court information is a legitimate concern.[48] However, as noted above, the Court now uses word processing programs to make the distribution and editing of opinions less time-consuming and more efficient. The electronic filing of briefs and records is a national matter not unique to the Second Circuit.[49] In this Court, the increased use of technology by judges has significantly reduced the reliance on paper copies of briefs, records, bench memoranda from the Staff Attorney's Office, and inter-chambers communications. Thirty years ago when Chief Judge Feinberg wrote about the customs and practices of the Circuit, he carried a large briefcase filed with briefs and records of cases he was preparing with him whenever he traveled. Today, many of his successors travel with an electronic tablet, iPad, or laptop computer. They edit opinions, draft memoranda, and communicate with colleagues on devices that were unimaginable in 1986. Some of us even use them on the bench.

## THE "STORY" OF THE SECOND CIRCUIT

My task here has been to focus on some aspects of the Second Circuit that make it different from the other twelve circuits around the United States. The differences are of a general nature. Chief Judge Feinberg sought to focus on those general differences to give the public an insider's view of *how* we operate as a court. But there is more to this Court, more to our story.

We do our work with colleagues that we did not choose and often did not know prior to their arrival at Foley Square. We come from widely varying backgrounds, faiths, and world views. The common and often difficult task of appellate judging requires respect and careful attention to the views of others; the time together, the regular dialogue in seeking answers to legal issues of great significance, and the affinity we share for the law draw each of us closer to the others. To some extent, that aspect of the story of the Second Circuit will never be *fully* told, for much of it lies within the private chambers lives of colleagues past and present. A few will have testimonials to their time here, but for most of us, our legacy lies in the work we did here; and that is as it should be. The ultimate strength in what we do and have done is reflected in the clarity and soundness of the reasoning of our opinions.

* Judge, United States Court of Appeals for the Second Circuit. 2016 is the 125th anniversary of the birth of the Second Circuit. To mark that milestone, Chief Judge Robert A. Katzmann launched a year-long initiative, which I chair, to reflect on our past. While I am designated as the author of this article, its creation was dependent on the extraordinary efforts of my law clerk Katelyn Cannella. Katelyn's keen editor's eye and her dogged pursuit of sources made the task much easier and this article far more readable. I also wish to express my thanks to Judge Jon O. Newman; Catherine O'Hagan Wolfe, the Clerk of Court; and Michael Bierce, her able counsel, for their additional research and editing assistance. Lastly, thanks to Sally Pritchard for her helpful comments.

1. Wilfred Feinberg, *Unique Customs and Practices of the Second Circuit*, 14 HOFSTRA L. REV. 297 (1986).

2. *Id.* at 297. Judge Feinberg also indicated that "the subject of court administration is generally neglected," and "judicial administration continues to be the stepchild of the law," and that such "inattention is odd." *Id.* at 297–98.

3. *Id.* at 298.

4. *Id.* at 298–99.

5. At the time Judge Feinberg wrote his article, it was more common for the members of a panel to sit together for a whole week, which enabled those judges to hold a voting conference for the week's cases at that week's end. *See id.* at 301–02. *But see id.* at 301 n.14 (noting that "the same three judges do not *always* make up the panel for an entire week's sitting," and thus that "several short conferences involving the different panel members are often necessary" (emphasis added)).

6. *Id.* at 300.

7. An additional explanation for why we no longer circulate voting memos for every case that will be decided via a written opinion is that the caseload of the Court has increased significantly over the last thirty years. In the twelve-month period ending on June 30, 1986, the Court decided 1,214 cases on the merits. ADMIN. OFFICE OF THE U.S. COURTS, ANNUAL REPORT OF THE DIRECTOR OF THE ADMIN. OFFICE OF THE U.S. COURTS 1986, at 103 tbl.S-3 (1986). In contrast, in the calendar year 2014, the Second Circuit decided 2,900 cases on the merits. *Federal Court Management Statistics, December 2014*, ADMIN. OFFICE OF THE U.S. COURTS,http://www.uscourts.gov/statistics-reports/federal-court-management-statistics-december-2014 (last updated Dec. 31, 2014) [hereinafter *Federal Court Management Statistics*] (providing link to Federal Court Management Statistics Report–Summary).

8. *See id.* at 299 ( "[T]he act of recording one's views and then justifying them produces a sounder result."). And, as in 1986, "one persuasive memo . . . can change the vote of at least one, and perhaps both, of the other panel members." *See id.* at 300. Judge Feinberg noted that 93% of cases in which an opinion was written were disposed of unanimously. *Id.* The numbers are similar today, with roughly 90% of our cases decided by unanimous opinion, without a concurrence or dissent. The unanimity rate would be much higher if one were to look to all of our merits dispositions, including summary orders.

9. As the reader will see throughout this article, technology has had a decided impact on Court and how the Court does its work.

10. One other technique for administration continues since Judge Feinberg's era. The Second Circuit is the only court of appeals where, at court meetings, judges report on the status of all assigned opinions that have not been circulated to panel members 60 days after argument.

11. *See generally* LAURAL HOOPER, DEAN MILETICH & ANGELIA LEVY, FED. JUDICIAL CTR., CASE MANAGEMENT PROCEDURES IN THE FEDERAL COURTS OF APPEALS (2d ed. 2011), *available at* http://www.fjc.gov/public/pdf.nsf/lookup/caseman2.pdf/$file/caseman2.pdf (detailing for each circuit the "screening" procedures for argument and nonargument disposition). The relevant practices of each Circuit are found on the following pages: D.C. Circuit (pg 51), First Circuit (pg 64), Third Circuit (pg 89), Fourth Circuit (pg 101), Fifth Circuit (pg 110–11), Sixth Circuit (pg 123), Seventh Circuit (pg 137), Eighth Circuit (pg 151–52), Ninth Circuit (pg 173), Tenth Circuit (pg 187), and Eleventh Circuit (pgs 204–05). The "screening" procedures described for each circuit generally involve a review of the merits of the appeal and a decision of whether to move the case to an argument calendar or to decide the case on the briefs. In addition, in all circuits, a large number of cases—more than 17,000 nationwide in 2014—are resolved prior to argument as procedural dispositions, with or without judicial action. *See Federal Court Management Statistics*, *supra* note 7. Procedural dispositions by three judges are largely, but not exclusively, based upon: (1) motions by the Government for dismissal of criminal appeals in which the defendant waived the right to appeal; (2) dismissals of *pro se* appeals pursuant to 28 U.S.C. § 1915 following a merits review upon a motion, *see* Fed. R. App. 34(a)(2); or (3) *sua sponte* dismissals where the notice of appeal is untimely or taken from a non-final order.

12. The Court continues the practice Judge Feinberg noted of determining upon the submission of briefs, appeals brought by "incarcerated pro se prisoners, applications for mandamus, and criminal appeals in which counsel files a brief pursuant to *Anders v. California*, [368 U.S. 738 (1967)] and asks to be relieved." Feinberg, *supra* note 1, at 303.

13. The Rule provides: "Oral argument must be allowed in every case unless a panel of three judges who have examined the briefs and record unanimously agrees that oral argument is unnecessary for any of the following reasons:

> (A) the appeal is frivolous; (B) the dispositive issue or issues have been authoritatively decided; or (C) the facts and legal arguments are adequately presented in the briefs and record, and the decisional process would not be significantly aided by oral argument." FED. R. APP. 34(a)(2). Many circuits use screening panels to review cases for these three criteria.

Hooper, Miletich & Levy, *supra* note 11.

14. Local Rule 34.1(b) provides: "The court may determine to take a case on submission, without oral argument, in accordance with [Federal Rule of Appellate Procedure] 34(a)(2). If the court decides to take a case on submission, the clerk will notify the parties." 2D CIR. LR 34.1(b) (2010).

15. Local Rule 34.1(a) requires: "Within 14 days after the filing of the last appellee's brief, each party must file an Oral Argument Statement Form. *Failure to timely file the Oral Argument Statement Form signifies that the party does not seek oral argument.*" 2D CIR. LR 34.1(a) (2010) (emphasis added).

16. The old local rule's language tracked that of Federal Rule of Appellate Procedure 34, *see supra* note 13, and provided that, "Oral argument will be allowed in all cases except those in which a panel of three judges, after examination of the briefs and record, shall be of the unanimous view that oral argument is not needed for one of the following reasons: (i) the appeal is frivolous; (ii) the dispositive issue or set of issues has been recently authoritatively decided; or (iii) the facts and legal arguments are adequately presented in the briefs and record, and the decisional process would not be significantly aided by oral argument." THE ASS'N OF THE BAR OF N.Y.C., APPEALS TO THE SECOND CIRCUIT 105 (9th ed. 2007).

17. In calendar year 2014, the Court terminated 2,585 fully-briefed cases on the merits, after accounting for consolidated cases. Of these, 855 were terminated after oral argument (33.1%) and 1,730 were terminated after submission on the briefs (66.9%). U.S. Courts of Appeals Caseload Tables (December 2014) (transcript on file with the United States Courts Library for the Second Circuit). This is in contrast to the 77.1% of fully-briefed appeals that were argued in 1985. Feinberg, *supra* note 1, at 304. However, the Court's current practice is in line with the average of other circuits, other than the Federal Circuit, if a bit more generous with oral argument. The Court ranks second in terms of number of arguments heard. *See* U.S. Courts of Appeals Caseload Tables.

18. HOOPER, MILETICH & LEVY, *supra* note 11, at 16.

19. Abraham Lincoln is credited as saying, "He who represents himself has a fool for a client." Apparently the saying was actually first used in a Philadelphia magazine. FRED R. SHAPIRO, THE OXFORD DICTIONARY OF AMERICAN LEGAL QUOTATIONS 44 (1993). The maxim, as originally published, stated, "He who is always his own counselor will often have a fool for his client." *Id.*

20. *See supra* note 17. While 33.1% of fully-briefed cases were argued in 2014, the number was higher in 2007 when the Court terminated 2,800 cases on the merits, after accounting for consolidated cases, with 947 terminated after oral argument (33.8%) and 1,853 terminated after submission on the briefs (66.2%). ADMIN OFFICE OF U.S. COURTS, STATISTICAL REPORTS, *Table B-1: U.S. Courts of Appeals—Appeals Commenced, Terminated, and Pending, By Circuit, During the 12-Month Period Ending December 31, 2007*, http://jnet.ao.dcn/resources/statistics/caseload-tables/appeals-caseload-tables (transcript on file with the United States Courts Library for the Second Circuit).

21. The number of fully-briefed *pro se* appeals terminated on the merits in 2014 was 1,063, after accounting for consolidated cases. Of those, 69 were terminated after oral argument (6.5%) and 994 were terminated after submission on the briefs (93.5%). *See* U.S. Courts of Appeals Caseload Tables, *supra* note 17. In 2007, for example, before the change in the local rule, the number of *pro se* appeals terminated on the merits was 840, with 115 of those (or 13.7%) decided after oral argument. ADMIN OFFICE OF U.S. COURTS, STATISTICAL REPORTS, *Table B-9A: U.S. Courts of Appeals—Pro Se Cases Commenced, Terminated, and Pending, by Circuit, During the 12-Month Period Ending December 31, 2007*, http://jnet.ao.dcn/resources/statistics/caseload-tables/appeals-caseload-tables (transcript on file with the United States Courts Library for the Second Circuit).

22. Immigration and Nationality Act, ch. 477, 66 Stat. 163 (1952) (codified at 8 U.S.C. § 1101 *et seq.*); 8 U.S.C. § 1252.

23. John R. B. Palmer et al., *Why Are So Many People Challenging Board of Immigration Appeals Decisions in Federal Court? An Empirical Analysis of the Recent Surge in Petitions for Review*, 20 GEO. IMMIGR. L.J. 1, 4–5 (2005); *see also* Jon O. Newman, *The Second Circuit's Expedited Adjudication of Asylum Cases: A Case Study of a Judicial Response to an Unprecedented Problem of Caseload Management*, 74 BROOK. L. REV. 429, 430–31 (2009) ("In 2002, then-Attorney General John Ashcroft, concerned that the BIA had accumulated a backlog of 56,000 cases, announced a proposed regulation to expand the BIA's streamlining procedures and clear its backlog." (footnote omitted)).

24. "The impact of this flood of decisions was not distributed evenly among the courts of appeals. For example, in the summer of 2004 the Second and Ninth Circuits received about 70 percent of the petitions challenging BIA decisions." Newman, *supra* note 23, at 431 (footnote omitted).

25. The NAC applies to all cases involving a challenge to the BIA's denial of asylum or withholding of removal. 2D CIR. LR 34.2. "Cases on the NAC are submitted to panels of three judges, any one judge on a panel having the option of removing the case from the NAC and transferring it to the court's Regular Argument Calendar (the 'RAC')." Newman, *supra* note 23, at 433–34.

26. The Court borrowed this mechanism from the Eleventh Circuit, which employs sequential voting on most dispositive motions. Interview by Sally Pritchard with Judge Jon O. Newman, in New York, N.Y. (July 28, 2015).

27. Newman, *supra* note 23, at 434.

28. *Id.* "The voting options are: refer the petition to the RAC, deny, grant, remand, or other. The voting sheet provides blanks to be checked to indicate whether the proposed order from the [Staff Attorney's Office] is acceptable (either as submitted or as edited by the judges) or whether Judge No. 1 (or occasionally Judge No. 2 or No. 3) has proposed a substitute order." *Id.*

29. *Id.* "In the absence of exceptional circumstances, each judge is required to vote and send the voting sheet on in one week. Thus, the voting is normally concluded within three weeks of submission." *Id.*

30. Statistics on file with the United States Courts Library for the Second Circuit. From 2003 through 2013, the Court determined over 21,000 appeals from the BIA. *Id.*

31. Erick Rivero, Note, *Asylum and Oral Argument: The Judiciary in Immigration and the Second Circuit Non-Argument Calendar*, 34 HOFSTRA L. REV. 1497 (2006).

32. From 2003 to 2008, new immigration cases made up a third or more of the Court's filings. Statistics on file with the United States Courts Library for the Second Circuit. BIA decisions are still appealed to the federal courts at a rate 3.5 times higher than in 2002. *Id.*

33. *See* Wilfred Feinberg, *The Office of Chief Judge of a Federal Court of Appeals*, 50 FORDHAM L. REV. 369, 376–77 (1984); Jon O. Newman, *In Banc Practice in the Second Circuit: The Virtues of Restrain*, 50 BROOK. L. REV. 365 (1984).

34. The Court has gone in banc twice from 2009 to 2014. *Poventud v. City of New York*, 750 F.3d 121 (2d Cir. 2014) (*en banc*); *Arar v. Ashcroft*, 585 F.3d 559 (2d Cir. 2009) (*en banc*). We heard one case in banc in 2015. *United States v. Ganias*, No. 12–240–cr, 2015 WL 3939426 (2d Cir. June 29, 2015) (granting rehearing en banc). Judge Feinberg noted that there were three in bancs in this Court between 1982 and 1985. Feinberg, *supra* note 1, at 311 n.52.

35. 550 U.S. 544 (2007).

36. 556 U.S. 662 (2009).

37. 2D CIR. LR 31.2(b)(1).

38. 2D CIR. LR 31.2(b)(2), (3). "If an appeal remains on the XAC, the briefing schedule is 35 days for each party, compared to the normal schedule of up to 91 days for each party." Jon O. Newman, *The Second Circuit's Expedited Appeals Calendar for Threshold Dismissals*, 80 BROOK. L. REV. 429, 431 (2015) (footnote omitted).

39. *Expedited Appeals Calendar*, U.S. COURT OF APPEALS FOR THE SECOND CIRCUIT, http://www.ca2.uscourts.gov/clerk/case_filing/appealing_a_case/civil_case/expedited_appeals_calendar.html (last updated Dec. 5, 2013).

40. Feinberg, *supra* note 1, at 314.

41. A memo is often attached to such a tab, explaining why the judge is considering authoring a concurrence—a move that suggests that the author of the opinion may yet be able to change his or her analytic tack to accommodate, and thwart, the potential concurring judge's concerns.

42. Again, a memo is almost always attached explaining in some detail the nature of the colleague's disagreement.

43. Feinberg, *supra* note 1, at 314–15.

44. And of course in both instances the third judge is empowered to add fuel to the fire by opposing the tabbing judge's suggestions or agreeing with the judge who withheld his tab!

45. The same is true I am told for substantive suggestions at the Third Circuit. *See* Conversation between Judge Wesley and Justice Samuel Alito, *supra* note 41.

46. Though, unlike some other circuits, we line-number circulated opinions to facilitate the offering of suggestions.

47. Additions are indicated by underlining and deletions by strike-through.

48. The Supreme Court has similarly been hesitant to embrace the use of technology. The Chief Justice recently explained that "[t]he federal courts, including the Supreme Court, must often introduce new technologies at a more measured pace than other institutions, especially those in private industry." Adam Liptak, *Supreme Court, in Big Leap, Plans to Put Filings Online*, N.Y. TIMES (Dec. 31, 2014), http://www.nytimes.com/2015/01/01/us/politics/supreme-court-plans-to-provide-briefs-and-filings-electronically.html?_r=0. This allows time to "fairly consider[] how to keep the information . . . secure from foreign and domestic hackers, whose motives may range from fishing for secrets to discrediting the government or impairing court operations." *Id.* However, Justice Sotomayor has a different explanation. Reflecting on the Justices' use of paper memos, she attributed the practice to tradition and because "they don't know how" to use email. Adam Liptak, *Three Supreme Court Justices Return to Yale*, N.Y. TIMES (Oct. 25, 2014), http://www.nytimes.com/2014/10/26/us/three-supreme-court-justices-return-to-yale.html?_r=0.

49. HOOPER, MILETICH & LEVY, *supra* note 11, at 13 ("As of May 2012, all of the courts of appeals fully use electronic filing.").

# THE LIFE AND CAREER OF WILLIAM MAXWELL EVARTS

*John M. Walker, Jr.*[*]

The Court of Appeals for the Second Circuit owes its origin 125 years ago to the Evarts Act of 1891, which established the regional courts of appeals.[1] The Act was the last major public accomplishment of an iconic lawyer-statesman of the nineteenth century, William Maxwell Evarts, whose life and career are the subject of this essay.[2]

At the time the Act was passed, although he would live for another decade, Senator Evarts was nearly blind and in the twilight of a career in the law and public life that spanned fifty years.[3] He had been a successful New York litigator; attorney general of the United States; secretary of state; a founder and the first president of the Association of the Bar of the City of New York; chief counsel for President Andrew Johnson during his impeachment trial; and a diplomat who served as an American envoy to Europe during the Civil War, the time of the republic's greatest peril. He had distinguished himself as a brilliant legal mind, an eloquent orator, and a key player in many of the most important political moments of his era. Yet despite his consistent political engagement, Evarts was not a politician but rather a lawyer, legal scholar, and devoted public servant with a strong independent streak and highly-developed advocacy skills which, time and again, he was called upon to employ on behalf of his country. The Evarts Act was his last great act of public service — one final contribution to the nation he had served and helped to shape over his entire career.

## I. EARLY LIFE AND EDUCATION

Evarts was a Yankee patrician. He was born in 1818 in Boston to Jeremiah Evarts and Mehitabel Barnes Sherman.[4] Jeremiah was one of the leading lay religious leaders of the early nineteenth century whose ancestors had settled in Connecticut at the dawn of the colonial period.[5] Mehitabel was the daughter of Roger Sherman, the eminent Connecticut statesman who was one of only two men to have signed the Declaration of Independence, the Articles of Confederation, and the United States Constitution.[6]

Evarts was educated at the Boston Public Latin School before entering Yale College at the age of fifteen.[7] After completing college at age nineteen, Evarts spent a year in a law office and then studied for another year at the predecessor to the Harvard Law School under Judge Joseph Story.[8] (It was customary at that time for a young man entering the legal profession to prepare by "reading" under the instruction of an experienced attorney.[9])

His promise was evident. Following a student trial, one of Evarts' fellow students, Richard H. Dana, Jr., who would later author the classic memoir *Two Years Before the Mast,* extolled Evarts' performance as "the most complete, systematic, precise, and elegantly spoken law argument I have yet heard, including many arguments of our most distinguished counsel before our highest courts."[10] Judge Story, who presided over the trial, was similarly effusive in his praise of Evarts.[11]

Throughout his career, Evarts would be highly regarded by his peers and colleagues as a man possessed of superior intellect, personal charm, good humor, and a tireless work ethic. He would also be celebrated for his commanding and persuasive oratory, both in the courtroom and in the public arena.[12] In the nineteenth century—with radio broadcasts not even on the horizon—the great public issues of the day were aired in the press, but also at convocations, conventions and in the public spaces wherever a crowd could be assembled.[13] People appreciated great oratory, a form of genuine entertainment, both for its content and its artistry.[14] Evarts's mastery of the craft was apparent from even his early school days.[15]

## II. EARLY CAREER AND RISE

In 1839, at age twenty-one, Evarts departed from New England and all of his friends, relatives, and connections for New York to begin what would be a singular career in the law and public life.[16] He brought with him several letters of introduction, including the following glowing missive from Judge Story: "I think [Evarts] destined to take a very elevated rank in the profession, and he is one of the few to whom I am ready to confide the future advancement of the laws."[17]

In 1842, after two years working under Daniel Lord—one of New York's most prominent attorneys and the founder of Lord, Day & Lord—and a third year practicing on his own, Evarts joined Charles Butler to form a law firm that would be his professional home until his death in the early dawn of the next century.[18] Around this time, Evarts began to make a name for himself with the defense of Monroe Edwards, a notorious forger.[19] Although Edwards was convicted, Evarts's two-hour opening address to the jury yielded applause from the packed courtroom and lasting admiration from his colleagues.[20] From that case onward, Evarts was never for want of clients.[21]

In 1848, he was co-counsel with the United States Attorney for the Southern District of New York, B.F. Butler, in a prosecution of mutinous seamen.[22] The following year he became an Assistant United States Attorney under the new United States Attorney, J. Prescott Hall.[23] Together they confronted violations of the Neutrality Act of 1818, which prohibited the sale of military equipment to warring states, including, in an early case, the purchase of a ship fitted with armaments by the German Confederation at war with Denmark.[24] Much of Evarts's work in the office was devoted to arresting and seizing ships—together with their munitions and men—destined for conflicts by insurgents against Spanish Cuba and by Haiti against the Dominican Republic.[25]

By the time his term as an Assistant United States Attorney came to a close in 1853, Evarts, only thirty-five years old, had firmly established himself as a top-tier lawyer in New York.[26] He had been admitted to the bar of the Supreme Court of the United States and in 1848 had argued, in the inaugural term of the New York Court of Appeals, the first of many cases he would argue before that tribunal.[27] In 1857, Evarts argued his first case in the United States Supreme Court, where he would enjoy a similar burgeoning practice,[28] exemplified by the eight cases he argued before the Court in 1866 alone.[29] His junior partner Joseph H.

Choate—a noted lawyer in his own right and later the American ambassador to the United Kingdom—commented on Evarts's legal skills and, in particular "the extraordinary speed with which [Evarts] would make himself master of all the questions involved in a case to be tried."[30] Choate "had never seen anything like this mental action before" and remarked, "Taking him for all in all, [Evarts] was the quickest-witted man that I have ever known . . . . Nothing could possibly escape him, and his mind seemed to flash instantaneously, no matter what was the subject that engaged his attention.[31]

While his professional star continued to rise, Evarts did not neglect his personal life. He met Helen Wardner in her hometown of Windsor, Vermont, where he was studying law, and in 1843 they married.[32] Their marriage of more than fifty years produced twelve children.[33] They raised their copious family in New York and summered in Windsor.[34]

Evarts viewed politics as a means to remediate civil ills and was active throughout his life in the Republican Party beginning with the party's inception in the mid-1850s. His principled independence, however, did not always endear him to party leaders.[35] His earlier affiliation with the Whigs had led him to support the ticket of William Henry Harrison and John Tyler,[36] and he was an admirer of Daniel Webster, whom he had met while at Yale.[37] It was his involvement in the political campaign of Zachary Taylor in 1848 that had led to his appointment as an Assistant United States Attorney.[38] But with the advent of the Republican party of Lincoln and William H. Seward and its steadfast opposition to slavery, Evarts's political ties, particularly with Seward, deepened.

## III. COMPROMISE OF 1850 AND THE *LEMMON* CASE

Although an opponent of slavery, Evarts took what he believed to be a pragmatic approach to the question: he supported the Compromise of 1850, which included the controversial Fugitive Slave Act that required the return of slaves from free states to their owners.[39] In his first significant political speech, on October 30, 1850 at the old Castle Garden at the southern tip of

Manhattan, he characterized the Compromise as the lesser of two evils, the greater being the dissolution of the Union.[40]

A few years later, from 1857 to 1860, Evarts litigated the widely-followed *Lemmon* slave case.[41] Jonathan Lemmon and his wife, both citizens of Virginia, had traveled with their eight slaves to New York.[42] Upon their arrival, New York's Superior Court granted a writ of habeas corpus and released the slaves, who fled to Canada.[43] The State of Virginia took up Lemmon's case because the decision threatened the institution of slavery.[44] New York Governor John A. King appointed Evarts to represent New York's interest.[45] Evarts prevailed in the intermediate level Supreme Court and then squared off in the New York Court of Appeals against another famous New York attorney, Charles O'Conor, who represented Virginia.[46] Evarts's prevailing argument was that Virginia law, upholding the property rights of slave-owners, was of no moment in New York and that no applicable law—neither the laws of New York, the Constitution and laws of the United States, nor the principles of comity—authorized the restraint of the slaves.[47] Virginia did not pursue an appeal to the Supreme Court, likely because the Civil War was superseding the legal landscape of slavery.[48]

Following the completion of the case in the New York Court of Appeals, Evarts remarked to O'Conor, "[T]hey tell me that this has been the finest argument ever heard in this Court."[49] O'Conor responded, "I cannot speak for my own, but certainly yours was very fine, and not the least fine passages were where you hit me the hardest."[50]

## IV. ELECTION OF 1860

In the wake of his victory in *Lemmon*, Evarts turned his attention to the national election of 1860 and the presidential candidacy of New York Senator William H. Seward.[51] Evarts was a delegate to the Republican Convention in Chicago and fully expected the party's nomination to go to Seward.[52] Evarts placed Seward's name before the Convention without a speech, as was the custom, but gave numerous speeches to various state delegations on Seward's behalf.[53] According to James G. Blaine of Maine, "the great career of Mr. Seward was never so illuminated as by this brilliant painting of Mr. Evarts."[54] Seward's intense anti-slavery views, however, were too much for the Convention and, after Seward led in the first two ballots, the tide shifted to Abraham Lincoln.[55] After Lincoln's victory celebration had quelled, Evarts rose to extol Seward's virtues but then moved that Lincoln's nomination be unanimous.[56] Thereafter, Evarts delivered numerous campaign speeches in the state of New York in support of Lincoln and the Republican Party.[57]

When Seward took office in 1861 as Lincoln's secretary of state, Seward's Senate seat became vacant.[58] The candidates for the Republican Party were Evarts and the newspaperman Horace Greeley.[59] Because Republicans controlled the New York legislature then responsible for selecting the senator, the Evarts-Greeley contest would be determinative.[60]

Although Evarts had achieved public prominence with his anti-slavery advocacy in *Lemmon* and his staunch support of Seward at the Republican Convention, his advocacy at Castle Gardens for the Compromise of 1850 that included the Fugitive Slave Act impaired his chances.[61] Greeley also had problems: his anti-slavery position was so pronounced that many felt it would contribute to dissolving the Union, and Greeley seemed ready to acquiesce in secession.[62] After leading on the first ballot, Evarts fell slightly behind Greeley.[63] Successive ballots failed to garner a majority for either man, and it appeared that Greeley was on the verge of winning. At that point, party leaders, including Governor Edwin D. Morgan, determined that Evarts's support should be thrown to a "dark horse" candidate, former judge Ira Harris. Harris secured the nomination and was ultimately elected senator.[64]

## V. Civil War Years

At the outbreak of the Civil War, Evarts threw himself behind the Union cause. He served as a member of the Union Defense Committee of New York, charged with raising volunteers and providing the Union with equipment and supplies,[65] and he took on the role of special counsel for the United States on war-related matters as well as the role of a special agent of the State Department.[66] His oldest son, Charles, served in the Union Army.[67]

The early years of the war yielded a series of complex issues of constitutional, international, and maritime law with which Evarts the lawyer became engaged. In two important wartime cases, Evarts argued positions for the United States that were in tension with one another. The first arose from the Union's capture of the crew of the privately owned ship *Savannah* that had been commissioned by the Confederacy to take prizes of war.[68] The issue was whether the seamen should be held as enemy prisoners of war or criminally prosecuted as pirates. This issue raised the question of the legal status of the insurgency.[69] The defense team, including Daniel Lord, Evarts's former employer and mentor, argued that the defendants were prisoners of war and should be acquitted.[70] Evarts, brought in as special counsel to the United States Attorney for the Southern District of New York, argued that prosecution for piracy was proper because the Confederacy had no right of secession under the Constitution and thus the seamen were not enemy combatants to be held as prisoners of war but rather insurrectionists and pirates who could be prosecuted and, if convicted, executed.[71] The jury deadlocked 8-4 for conviction.[72] Soon thereafter, however, the government adopted the view that southern privateers were not pirates, and such prosecutions were discontinued.[73] The deeper question left unresolved was whether the Constitution was a compact between the states from which states could lawfully withdraw to create a new compact or whether the Constitution created a new unified nation such that secession was treason and those acting on its behalf traitors and pirates.[74]

Evarts argued the second case, consolidated with others as the *Prize Cases*, in the United States Supreme Court.[75] Here, the Union rather than the Confederacy had seized ships that violated the Union blockade of southern ports.[76] Under international law, such blockades and seizures were only lawful in wartime, but at the time of the blockade, Congress had not declared war and the position of the United States government was that the Confederacy was only a domestic insurrection.[77] Evarts, representing the United States, argued that the blockade was nonetheless lawful under international law because the insurrection and President Lincoln's justified military response had sufficient attributes of war, save the formal declaration, which was all that international law required.[78] By a 5-4 vote, the Court accepted Evarts's position and held that Lincoln had the authority to impose the blockade without congressional authorization.[79]

As the war progressed, Evarts assumed an equally prominent role as a diplomat. In the spring of 1863, and again in early 1864, Seward dispatched Evarts to Great Britain as a special envoy to deal with the legal and diplomatic implications of that government's recognition of the Confederacy as a "belligerent" under international law—rather than as a "domestic insurgency"—sufficient to trigger the provisions of the Neutrality Act that existed between the United States and Great Britain.[80] Seward's concerns were two-fold: first, he wanted to prevent Great Britain from recognizing the Confederacy as a state under international law and, second, he wanted to halt the use of British ports in Great Britain and the Caribbean by Confederate vessels and the construction of Confederate warships in British shipyards.[81]

Evarts was a wise choice to undertake this mission, which required a combination of lawyerly expertise (particularly in international law), diplomatic skills, and social acceptance at the highest levels of British government and society.[82] Advocating now outside the courtroom, Evarts presented with calm and amiable assurance the United States' position to all who mattered in Britain's upper echelons. He persuasively made the Union's case to important figures in British business, law and government, including the Liberal Prime Minister William Gladstone and Tory leader Benjamin Disraeli.[83]

The results, on the whole, were favorable: Great Britain never formally recognized the Confederacy as a state and, after considerable prodding by Evarts, blocked deals that would have greatly aided the Confederacy, including a pending sale of ironclad ships under construction in Liverpool and in the Clyde. Evarts contributed significantly to reducing friction between the United States and Great Britain.[84] During Evarts's missions Richard Cobden, an English correspondent to Massachusetts Senator

Charles Sumner, wrote Sumner that Evarts was the "right man in the right place."[85] The Englishman reported, "He is an able international lawyer. Quite a match for anyone here in his own special walk. His manners are quiet and impressive. He is mixing very much in our best society, and I hear him spoken of with great respect."[86]

## VI. DEFENSE OF PRESIDENT JOHNSON

While Evarts's work on behalf of the Union cause was considerable, it did not capture much public attention. His national prominence was elevated after the war, however, when in 1868 he eloquently and persuasively defended President Andrew Johnson at his impeachment trial in the Senate. Johnson was a Tennessee Democrat who in 1864 had been placed on the Lincoln ticket in part as a symbol of Northern unity in a time of war. At war's end, the Republican Party was in control of both houses of Congress but was split between conciliatory Reconstructionists, who sided with Lincoln, and the Radicals, who sought retribution against the former Confederate states. This latter faction at first believed that Johnson was an ally but was soon angered by his adoption of Lincoln's conciliatory agenda.[87] With fourteen months remaining in President Johnson's term, the House filed impeachment charges based upon Johnson's removal of Secretary of War Edwin Stanton who had been collaborating with the Radicals. The President had removed Stanton despite the Senate's refusal to concur in the removal and had therefore violated the recently passed—and constitutionally suspect—Tenure in Office Act that proscribed removal of a cabinet officer without Senate approval.[88] Congress specifically targeted President Johnson in the Act by using language from the Constitution's impeachment provision in stating that such a removal of an officer would be punishable as a "high misdemeanor."[89]

President Johnson's retention of Evarts was a testament to Evarts's reputation for independence and zealous advocacy. Evarts was neither a friend nor supporter of Johnson, whom he had sharply criticized at a Republican rally at Cooper Union the previous year.[90] Although Johnson had concerns about Evarts's political sentiments, he also knew that Evarts was a lawyer of surpassing ability.[91] Seward greatly influenced Johnson's decision to hire Evarts, assuring the President, "[Y]ou cannot do better."[92] Evarts allayed any lingering concerns by pledging to Johnson the zealous advocacy due to every client.[93]

Despite the best efforts of Chief Justice Samuel Chase, Johnson's trial was largely a political circus.[94] The defense argued, and the chief justice agreed, that the Senate should be regarded as a court of law.[95] The House managers, in their customary role as prosecutors during impeachment proceedings, derided this notion and took the position that the trial was political and that the Senate, which was 42-12 Republican, could do anything it wanted. Early in the trial, this sentiment prevailed as the Senate repeatedly overturned the chief justice's evidentiary rulings whenever they favored the defense.

Evarts's summation lasted fourteen hours spanning four days and was a masterpiece.[96] He ridiculed the House managers' politically driven prosecution, methodically detailed the lack of evidence of any official act warranting impeachment, and decried the institutional damage to government if a President could simply be removed by two-thirds of the Senate for political reasons.[97] The House managers had overreached by throwing in charges that the President had made intemperate speeches. Evarts skillfully countered them by citing the managers' own highly intemperate speeches during the trial.[98]

Evarts argued that Johnson's conviction would amount to no less than a revolutionary coup under a legal veneer.[99] On the last day, he made the point that the Tenure in Office Act was ambiguous as to whether it applied to pre-enactment appointees like Stanton, that some senators had themselves sought the removal of certain members from Lincoln's cabinet, and that, in any event, the Act was unconstitutional.

During the Senate deliberations, the Radicals tried unsuccessfully to pressure the Republicans holdouts.[100] The vote to convict was 35-19—a single vote shy of the two-thirds majority needed.[101] The trial brought Evarts national recognition as a great constitutional lawyer and scholar of the law, a man of civility and integrity, and one of the nation's foremost orators.[102]

## VII. ATTORNEY GENERALSHIP

As Johnson's term drew to a close, Evarts's success at the impeachment trial led the President to appoint Evarts as attorney general (again on the advice of Seward).[103] Evarts was confirmed by a vote of 27-7, over Radical opposition.[104] He took office as attorney general in July 20, 1868, and was honored at a gala dinner in New York with 400 present, including Ulysses S. Grant, who later that year would be elected President.[105]

Evarts served as attorney general of the United States from July 1868 to March 1869,[106] and was the last attorney general to leave office before the creation of the Justice Department in 1870.[107] During his short time in office, Evarts dealt with a few matters of great importance. One of them was the fate of Jefferson Davis, the first and only president of the Confederacy.[108] In 1865, following the end of the war, Davis had been captured and clapped in irons.[109] Indicted for treason in Richmond in 1866, Davis had been released on bail in 1867 as the case dragged on.[110] Evarts doubted the possibility of a conviction and requested that his aide and former classmate Richard Dana prepare a letter outlining the reasons for closing the case.[111]

In the letter that Evarts forwarded to the President, Dana explained that because "the only question of fact submitted to the jury [would] be whether Jefferson Davis took any part in the war," and because "it is one of the great facts of history that he was its head, civil and military," there was no reason to "make a question of it and refer its decision to a jury, with power to find in the negative or affirmative, or to disagree."[112] Dana cautioned,

> It gives that jury [drawn from the region of the rebellion] [an] opportunity to ignore the fact that Jefferson Davis took any part in the late civil war. And one man upon the jury can secure these results. The risks of such absurd and discreditable issues of a great State trial are assumed for the sake of a verdict which, if obtained, will settle nothing in law or national practice not now settled. . . .[113]

Evarts agreed with Dana that despite the overwhelming evidence of treason, the great political risk of a trial was not worth the effort. The rest of the cabinet, as well as President Johnson, concurred.[114] Evarts agreed to enter a *nolle prosequi* in exchange for Davis dropping his motion to quash the indictment, and on Christmas Day 1868 Johnson granted a complete amnesty to the Confederates and the case against Davis ended.[115]

The other matter of enduring significance that Evarts addressed as attorney general was the *Legal Tender Cases.*[116] During the war, Congress had for the first time authorized paper currency as legal tender.[117] This was challenged on constitutional grounds. In December 1968, Evarts argued in the Supreme Court in support of the act, relying on the doctrine of implied powers articulated by Chief Justice Marshall in *McCulloch v. Maryland.*[118] Evarts eloquently pointed out that Congress had authorized paper money at a time of war. Why, asked Evarts, would the government have the power to draft men to fight and die, and yet not have the power to pay soldiers in the field and the suppliers of provisions to the army?[119]

Several months later, the Court issued a 4-3 decision, reaffirming the implied-powers doctrine but rejecting the constitutionality of paper money.[120] Within a few weeks, however, two new justices joined the Court, which then issued a decision reversing the earlier ruling and upholding the validity of paper money.[121] The reversal was controversial, and Evarts later said that his "thorough regret was that the just result was not reached by less uncertain steps."[122]

## VIII. EVARTS AND THE CITY BAR

The origins of the Association of the Bar of the City of New York, of which Evarts would be a founder and its first president, lay in the ashes of the dismal reputation of the legal profession in New York in the years following the Civil War.

This decline in reputation started with the New York Constitutional Convention of 1846, which lowered the standards of bar admission in furtherance of the anti-rent movement. The anti-rent movement pitted tenant farmers against heretofore legally protected land-owning gentry, who in land disputes had monopolized the best legal talent in what was seen as a highly exclusive and difficult to enter legal profession.[123] After the 1846 Constitution, the standards for bar admission were lowered such that the doors to the profession were wide open.[124] At the same time, the Convention substituted the election of judges for appointment to the bench by the governor.

These two changes provided the fertile soil in which corruption could take root. The seeds were planted by the notorious ring of "Boss" Tweed, which in the decades before 1870 had gained control of the machinery of government at the City and then the State levels.[125] By 1868, lawyer George Templeton Story could write in his diary that, "Bench and Bar settle deeper in the mud every year and every month. They must be near bottom now."[126] Yet scandals continued to multiply such that, nine months later, he wrote: "To be a citizen of New York is a disgrace . . . . The New Yorker belongs to a community worse governed by lower and baser blackguard scum than any citizen in Western Christendom, or in the world."[127]

The scandalous situation was epitomized by the corrupt legal machinations surrounding the spectacular fight over the ownership of the Erie Railroad Company – a fight that pitted Cornelius Vanderbilt against David Drew, Jay Gould, and Jim Fisk.[128] As Vanderbilt acquired Erie stock, the Gould faction kept issuing more of it. Each side conscripted judges to issue *ex parte* injunctions against the other (which was possible because under New York law, each judge in New York's 33 judicial districts could enjoin activities statewide).[129] Many judges, whose offices were filled by "Boss" Tweed, were seen as corrupt and corruptible, bringing the legal profession into corresponding disrepute. At the same time, the Drew, Gould and Fisk faction attempted to purchase votes in the Legislature.[130]

Throughout 1869, Evarts had a series of meetings with bar leaders in New York City with the objective of forming a new association that many hoped could be at the forefront of the reform of the profession. Two years earlier, at the Constitutional Convention of 1867, Evarts had lost an amendment to replace elected judges with judges who would hold office during good behavior.[131] It was his view that the election of judges for short terms, when coupled with the corrupting influence of lawyers, had led to the absolute downfall of the New York judiciary. Now he would lead the effort to elevate the Bar.[132]

The "call for organization" for the new City Bar Association was not extended to all lawyers. Rather it went out, not as a general notice, but as an invitation to selected lawyers. The new association might seek reform (and the extent to which that should occur was the subject of debate among the subscribers), but it certainly would be an association of worthies – those who saw themselves as the best, brightest, and best connected leaders of the Bar. In that sense, it had some of the characteristics of a private men's club, albeit one bound by professional ties.[133] The difference between those who would press for reform of bench and bar and those who primarily valued the virtues of professional association were evident at the first organizational meeting, and this uneasy dichotomy of purpose has continued into modern times.

In any event, that Evarts's signature was at the top of the "call to organization" leaves little doubt that it had been privately settled that he would be the Association's first president.[134] He was now at the pinnacle of the legal profession in New York City. He was widely known among his peers for his political and legal achievements and, at age fifty-one, following the Johnson impeachment trial and his stint as attorney general, had become a national figure.

While it is not possible to measure the effect of the Association on cleansing the bench and bar, the very creation of the Association plainly stood as a strong anti-corruption statement from the profession.[135] The press started to champion corruption reform, and in July 1871 *The New York Times* began its successful exposure of the Tweed "Ring."[136] In the election of November 1871, most of the "Ring" leaders were expelled from office and prosecutions against them, including Tweed, began.[137] With the purification of the legislature and its freedom from the "Ring," a similar purification of the courts could begin and the most notorious of the corrupt judges were impeached or reassigned.[138]

## IX. EVARTS AND U.S. DISPUTES WITH BRITAIN

In 1871, the United Kingdom and the United States signed the Treaty of Washington,[139] which was intended to resolve all outstanding disputes between the two countries.[140] Among these disputes were the *Alabama* claims, which the countries agreed would be resolved through arbitration.[141] The treaty required the arbitrators to decide whether Great Britain had violated the principle of neutrality by permitting five warships, the *Alabama* among them, to be constructed or outfitted in its shipyards, with the knowledge that the Confederacy would use these ships against the Union.[142] President Grant and Hamilton Fish, his secretary of state, appointed Bancroft Davis to be the agent in charge of the American case and chose Evarts as one of three attorneys for the United States on the basis of his "legal ability and charming social manner."[143]

Great Britain and the United States initially disagreed about the scope of claims covered by the treaty—a difference that threatened to torpedo the arbitration—but after extensive negotiations, in which Evarts played a leading role, the parties agreed to adopt the narrower British position of what was covered by the treaty.[144] Evarts's British counterpart described him as "a good lawyer and a skilful advocate [who] also had the qualities of a statesman . . . . [H]e was a man of whom any country might be proud."[145]

With this dispute resolved, the arbitrators began to consider each side's arguments.[146] Evarts drafted one-fourth of the United States' argument.[147] In his first two sections, Evarts defined the contours of the countries' dispute and described the origin of the arbitration agreement and the claims contained within it.[148] In his later sections, Evarts applied the relevant law to the facts to analyze the questions of what was required of Great Britain as a neutral party and whether it had met these requirements.[149]

In the Treaty of Washington, the parties had agreed that a neutral government must use "due diligence" both to prevent ships in its jurisdiction from being equipped for use against a country with which it is at peace and to prevent such ships from departing its jurisdiction.[150] The treaty, however, did not define "due diligence."[151] In the arbitration, the parties disagreed about what that term meant, with Britain taking the position that "due diligence" should be measured against the level of diligence a nation uses in its own affairs.[152] Evarts argued for a higher standard: "due" meant that the diligence must be "seasonable, appropriate, and adequate to the exigencies which call for its exercise."[153] Evarts argued that Britain had not exercised the requisite level of diligence when it failed to take legal and practical steps against British citizens who aided the Confederacy by constructing or outfitting the Confederate ships.[154]

The British submission was very short, and after internal discussion and urging by the British representatives, the tribunal agreed to ask them for another written statement.[155] The United States responded in writing and orally, with Evarts presenting the only oral argument in the proceedings.[156] Although Evarts was interrupted repeatedly by the British arbitrator and by the British representatives, he remained poised.[157] The tribunal easily concluded that Britain was liable for the losses produced by three ships, the *Alabama*, the *Florida*, and the *Shenandoah*,[158] but deliberated at length before finally determining that the United State should receive $15.5 million in damages.[159] Joseph Choate, Evarts's junior partner and later American ambassador to the United Kingdom, described Evarts's success at the arbitration as his "finest laurel" and "the most notable professional achievement that ever fell to the lot of an American advocate."[160]

After Evarts returned to private practice in the United States, he was not officially involved in determining how the money should be distributed.[161] However, as the attorney for several insurance companies that had insured ships whose property had been destroyed, he argued to Congress that these companies should receive a portion of the damages.[162] He was almost entirely unsuccessful.[163]

In the cases of the *Meteor* and the *Springbok*, Evarts next considered the question of neutrality in the context of a nation attempting to enforce its own neutrality obligations.[164] The *Meteor* was a steamship built in the United States during the Civil War for the use of the Union government in pursuing Confederate ships.[165] The government did not buy it, however, and its owners then negotiated with agents of the Chilean government, who wished to use it in its war with Spain.[166] After the two sides failed to reach an agreement, the owners prepared to sail the ship to Panama with the intention of finding another buyer. Before they left port, the U.S. marshal seized the *Meteor* and declared that its owners had violated the Neutrality Act of 1818 through its negotiations with Chile.[167] Evarts defended the owners in the ensuing court proceedings, working to narrow the scope of the Act, which decades earlier he had worked to enforce as an Assistant United States Attorney.[168]

Evarts lost in the district court but won on appeal.[169] He argued that, to violate the Neutrality Act, it is not enough for a party to intend only to sell an armed ship abroad. Instead, the violator must intend, at the time the ship departs from the United States, that the ship will take part in hostilities on behalf of a party that is forbidden from using American ports.[170] This difference of intent distinguished the *Meteor* case from the case of the *Alabama* and similar ships built in Britain for the Confederacy.[171] The appellate court adopted Evarts's reasoning.[172]

More significant was the case of the *Springbok*, a British ship seized by the United States in the belief that it was intended to breach a blockade.[173] During the Civil War, the United States made illegal all trade with Confederate ports.[174] Because of the volume of blockade runners, the United States relied on the doctrine of continuous voyage to seize neutral vessels ostensibly bound for neutral ports if the final destination of the contraband was a blockaded port. (The practice of many blockade runners was to dock at a neutral port in the Caribbean where they would transfer the contraband to a small, fast boat for delivery to a Confederate port.[175]) Pursuant to this doctrine, the United States seized the *Springbok* en route from London to Nassau.[176] The district court condemned both the vessel and its cargo; the Supreme Court, however, released the vessel but not the cargo.[177]

A court had never released a vessel while holding its cargo, so the owners of the cargo, represented by Evarts, filed a claim for damages against the United States with a commission established pursuant to the Treaty of Washington.[178] Evarts marshaled significant evidence in support of his argument that the cargo was intended for sale at Nassau rather than for delivery to a Confederate port, attacked the government's evidence, and argued that the government had not proven that the *Springbok* itself would make any journey beyond Nassau.[179] Although Evarts did not prevail, his brief received commendation from authorities on international law.[180] One authority described it as containing "an argument which is one of the ablest expositions of international law in this relation which has ever appeared, and is recognized as such by the highest foreign authority."[181]

## X. Evarts Considered for the Supreme Court

With the death of Roger Taney in 1864, there were two leading candidates to fill the vacancy for chief justice of the Supreme Court: Salmon P. Chase and Evarts. Evarts was not a reluctant suitor. He wrote to his friend Richard Dana:

> The Ch[ief]-Justiceship is, it seems to me, for the next ten years a place of great political importance over and above its simple judicial authority. I am sure no man at all fit for it would wish to take it at the cost to the country of keeping out a better man.[182]

Evarts had no reservations about who would be the "better man." He continued:

> I am willing to take the office and willing to be presented as the candidate of the profession and of public opinion for the place even if I should not get it.
>
> I do not feel any public duty that requires me to wish for, or aid in, the appointment of Gov[ernor] Chase. On the contrary, if I were the appointing power, I should think many reasons dissuaded from it.[183]

He had considerable support: The New York Court of Appeals urged Lincoln to appoint him; friends E.R. Hoar and Richard Dana went to Washington to do the same and to present letters from the Massachusetts Judiciary; and Massachusetts Governor John Albion Andrew supported him.[184]

Chase, who was ultimately appointed by President Lincoln, had a high regard for Evarts's abilities as a lawyer but held reservations about his judgment. Chase wrote at the time of their consideration:

> Evarts is a man of sterling abilities and excellent learning and a much greater lawyer than I ever presented to be. The truth is I always thought myself much overestimated.

> And yet I think I have more judgment than Evarts, and that tried by the Marshall standard should make a better judge; while he might, tried by the Story standard.[185]

When Chase died in 1873, Evarts's name was again put forward to replace him.[186] Evarts, less enthusiastic about taking the job than he had been a decade earlier, still viewed the position as "the ark of the covenant of all our tribes of lawyers."[187] He was passed over by President Grant, who selected Morrison R. Waite (after putting forth several nominees rejected by the Senate).[188] When Waite left office in 1888, Evarts was 70 years old and was not considered for the job.

## XI. Centennial Celebration Oration

The centennial of the Declaration of Independence on July 4, 1876, was celebrated across the country, but the celebration's epicenter was naturally Philadelphia, where a century earlier the Continental Congress had formally adopted the Declaration that separated the United States from Great Britain. The executive committee of the United States Centennial Commission, without dissent, chose Evarts to be the orator of the day. Before a crowd of thousands, including international leaders and political luminaries such as Governor and Republican presidential nominee Rutherford Hayes, Evarts—whose own grandfather Roger Sherman was a member of the committee of five appointed to draft the Declaration—delivered his oration. His speech of little more than an hour was brief by any contemporary standard.

Evarts thoughtfully recalled the virtues of the founding fathers whose foresight had avoided the post-revolution pitfalls that befell France and Great Britain. He summarized the economic, social and political progress of the country over the century and attributed the qualities that characterized the nation—unity, liberty, power and prosperity—to the foundation laid in 1776 and the years soon after. His speech envisioned a bright future for the nation and was animated and suffused throughout by his deeply felt appreciation and pride, not only for the work of the founders but for the nation that work had wrought.[189]

## XII. CAMPAIGN OF 1876

In the election of 1876, Evarts was the subject of a "draft movement" by reformist Republicans who sought to recruit him to run for governor of New York as a rival to Alonzo B. Cornell, the candidate of Senator Roscoe Conkling's Republican political machine.[190] Evarts did not desire the nomination and was not openly a candidate.[191] He allowed his friends, however, to put his name forward under the rationale that an Evarts nomination would help Republican presidential candidate Rutherford B. Hayes of Ohio carry New York over the state's own governor, Samuel J. Tilden, a reformer.[192]

At the state Republican convention, the uproar against the Conkling machine persuaded Cornell to withdraw, and the delegates chose between Evarts and former Governor Edward D. Morgan.[193] The Conkling faction, fearing that the nomination of Evarts eventually would make him a rival to Conkling himself, preferred Morgan as "the lesser of two evils."[194] Evarts was not disappointed—in truth he had asked his friends to withdraw his name from the delegates' consideration even before the convention met.[195]

Evarts was politically inactive through the summer of 1876, and even some Democrats in New York—in an awkward move—had suggested nominating Evarts as their own candidate for governor.[196] But as the fall election approached and chances in New York for Morgan and Hayes grew dimmer, Chief Justice Waite privately—and many others publicly—urged Evarts to campaign in support of the national Republican ticket.[197] A group of some 200 "merchants, bankers, and lawyers" of New York City wrote:

> The independency of your political position, your professional and public career, and your wide experience and acquaintanceship both in Europe and America will give high authority to your views, and make them of gravest consequence to the country in this hour of peril.[198]

Evarts agreed to campaign and gave a two-hour oration to a packed crowd at the Cooper Institute.[199] Nevertheless, Tilden carried New York by 30,000 votes and Morgan lost to State Comptroller Lucius Robinson.[200]

## XIII. Disputed Election of 1876: Evarts Before the Electoral Commission

After the presidential electoral vote count, Tilden had 184 undisputed electoral votes—one short of that required for victory.[201] The results were contested, however, in four states—Oregon, South Carolina, Louisiana, and Florida.[202] These four states each submitted two different returns—one for Tilden, and one for Hayes.[203] There was no rule or precedent for recounting these disputed returns.

The Constitution states that, "The President of the Senate shall, in the presence of the Senate and House of Representatives, open all the certificates and the votes shall then be counted."[204] But the Constitution does not specify *by whom.* Is it the president of the Senate? The Senate? Or the House?[205] The Senate and its president were Republican, while the House was Democratic.[206] The nation teetered on the edge of a constitutional crisis unparalleled since the end of the Civil War. The Republicans, naturally, took the position that the president of the Senate should count the votes, while the Democrats said that the House, or the House and Senate jointly, should count the votes.[207]

Evarts wrote a brief supporting the Republican position that the president of the Senate should make the count.[208] At the end of January,[209] to resolve the crisis, Congress created the first-ever "Electoral Commission"—a fifteen-member body of five senators, five representatives, and five Supreme Court justices—to determine which returns from the disputed states would be counted.[210] Of the fifteen seats, eight were to be held by Democrats and eight by Republicans. Four Supreme Court justices, two Democratic and two Republican, were specifically named in the act. These four were to select a fifth justice, expected to be an independent, as the tiebreaking vote.[211] The independent justice was elected to the Senate by the Illinois Legislature shortly afterward, however, and a Republican fifth justice was selected instead—giving the Republicans an 8-7 majority.[212]

Prior to the passage of the bill creating the Commission, the Republicans secured Evarts's services as chief counsel to represent Hayes before the Commission.[213] The Democrats were also represented by distinguished counsel, including Charles O'Conor (Evarts's admiring adversary in the *Lemmon* case).[214]

Evarts argued the four disputed elections before the Commission. While his performance was greatly praised,[215] all of the decisions of the Commission favored Hayes by party-line votes of 8-7, placing in some doubt how much Evarts had actually influenced the outcome.[216] Nevertheless, Evarts made the Republican case powerfully and consistently.[217] His three-hour oration against the admissibility of evidence of irregularities and fraud in Louisiana was particularly well received; future President James A. Garfield, a member of the Commission, declared it "very masterly" and "most admirable."[218] Hayes was sworn in as President, averting a renewed constitutional crisis and marking another key achievement for Evarts.[219]

## XIV. SECRETARY OF STATE

When Hayes nominated Evarts to be his secretary of state, some of Tilden's friends derided the nomination as simply a payment for Evarts's arguments before the Electoral Commission.[220] In truth, Hayes had considered Evarts for the position long before the Electoral Commission met.[221] Hayes had long admired Evarts's ability and his knowledge of foreign affairs.[222] Carl Schurz, who advised Hayes on many cabinet appointments and was later named secretary of the interior, had written to Hayes of Evarts's high qualifications and had opined that Evarts did not "belong to that class . . . who would intrigue for the promotion of personal ends, or permit their ambition to affect their sense of duty."[223]

The Republican Senate confirmed Evarts over the determined opposition by Conkling and others who objected to Evarts's political independence and his consistent refusal to "participate in the intrigues of political bosses."[224] Public sentiment favored Evarts's confirmation, and his skills and experience plainly qualified him for the office.[225] Whitelaw Reid, a prominent newspaper editor and politician, wrote glowingly of Evarts upon his appointment,

> He has an intimate knowledge . . . of the subjects with which the department must be chiefly concerned. He is already known and esteemed in the countries with which we chiefly desire to stand well . . . [and] his personal intercourse with foreign representatives could not fail to increase the respect of foreigners.[226]

Evarts himself expressed some trepidation at assuming the cabinet position, doubting whether he would be able to "make official life comport with [his] habits and life of independence and with the essential interests of [his] family."[227] He wrote to a colleague that he "would gladly have seen some one else take the place but there seemed to be no one obvious for it and it might have been critical . . . to decline it."[228]

Hayes's cabinet members enjoyed a collegial spirit despite some of their political differences, and biweekly cabinet meetings were "marked by free discussion and good fellowship."[229] Evarts became not only a trusted advisor to Hayes but also his close personal friend.[230] He accompanied the president on several tours throughout the country, and he displayed his unique sense of humor during these expeditions. In Vermont, he delivered an address that consisted of a single sentence: "It is only fair that I should warn you that although I am very slow to begin a speech, I am much slower to end it, and I know your only safety is in my retiring before I commence."[231] In the capital of Virginia, Evarts mused to a crowd of 10,000 people who had waited to greet the presidential party in inclement weather, "I should have regarded the people of Richmond as the most intelligent in Virginia, had I not discovered that they do not know enough to go inside when it rains."[232] During a later speaking event in Virginia, after President Hayes attempted to introduce Evarts and could not locate him, the secretary of state eventually emerged shouting, "The lost is found." [233] When the crowd of 30,000 burst into applause, Evarts—speaking with what one historian describes as "biblical solemnity"—pronounced, "There is more joy over the finding of one Cabinet minister who was absent than over the three that had not gone astray."[234]

Upon assuming his cabinet position, Evarts quickly distinguished himself as a zealous protector of American life and property abroad.[235] When Spanish naval vessels interfered with the operations of American whaling ships, Evarts secured $10,000 in damages and Spain's promise to take steps to prevent future interference.[236] After an American missionary in Turkey was murdered, Evarts insisted that Turkey promptly punish his killers and take measures to protect other missionaries.[237] A firm believer in religious tolerance, Evarts repeatedly spoke out against the persecution of Jews in foreign countries, citing a "deep[] interest[] in the welfare of . . . [this] much-injured people."[238] In 1880, amidst increasing persecution of Jews in Russia, Evarts announced publicly that the United States "impartially seeks to protect all its citizens of whatever origin or faith."[239]

Although as secretary of state Evarts had the portfolio for foreign affairs, he also assisted Hayes in resolving a number of complex domestic problems, including the carrying out of Hayes' "Southern policy."[240] During reconstruction following the Civil War, state government power was frequently contested. Both Evarts and Hayes believed that the military should not be used "to sustain one government against another in case of contested elections."[241] They remained wary, however, of causing disorder and violence by completely ending the use of military power in the South before the establishment of a single legal government in several southern states in which dual governments persisted.[242] In South Carolina, where a Democratic government had the support of the citizens of the state and a Republican legislature continued to exist only due to the presence of federal troops, Evarts helped to quietly remove the Republican legislature and return control of the government to the citizens.[243] In Louisiana, Evarts helped to persuade members of the Republican legislature to join the Democratic legislature and then collapsed the remainder of the Republican government.[244] These unification efforts facilitated the withdrawal of federal troops.[245] Yet the efforts also engendered resentment in a large section of the Republican Party that objected to the abandonment of the Republican governments in the two states.[246]

On the foreign-policy front, Evarts devoted considerable attention to relations between the United States and Mexico.[247] After a revolutionary movement led by Porfirio Díaz ousted the Mexican president, Evarts initially refused to recognize Díaz's de facto presidency.[248] Although up until that point the United States had promptly recognized newly established governments, Evarts withheld recognition in the absence of assurances that Díaz would respect Mexico's foreign obligations.[249] Evarts demanded that Díaz work to abolish a "free zone" on the Mexican side of the border where smuggling flourished, suppress cattle stealing on the Rio Grande border, and respond appropriately to other crimes that Mexican citizens allegedly committed on American land.[250] When Díaz failed to meet these demands, the United States government implemented a "hot pursuit" policy, which authorized American troops to pursue raiders across the Mexican border when "either in sight of them or upon a fresh trail."[251]

Evarts's policies fueled anti-American sentiment in Mexico, and the Mexican government sent troops to the border to repel any American troops that crossed.[252] The policies were also controversial in the United States where many were concerned that they would lead to a dangerous increase in hostilities. Eventually Evarts reversed his original stance and the United States recognized Díaz's presidency unconditionally.[253] Mexico and the United States continued to clash over conditions along the border throughout the remainder of the Hayes administration.[254]

Although Evarts's strategy with Mexico had proved largely unsuccessful, Díaz made some efforts to suppress disorder and raiding and some of Evarts's contemporaries attributed improved conditions to Evarts's initial hardline positions. In 1878, the United States minister to Mexico wrote of Evarts that nothing but his "firm attitude would ever have brought about the condition of peace which for a year past has existed on the lower Rio Grande."[255]

The remainder of Evarts's time as secretary of state was similarly marked with stumbles as well as successes. His attempts to bring an end to Chile's violent conflict with Bolivia and Peru proved ineffective,[256] as did his attempts to secure a new canal treaty with Columbia.[257] Yet he succeeded in his tireless efforts to expand American foreign commerce, and he managed to keep America at peace with all other nations throughout a turbulent period in world history.[258] Historians would later note of Evarts's time in office that, like most secretaries of state, Evarts "could look back upon his work with a measure of satisfaction and a measure of regret."[259]

## XV. Return to Law Practice

After Evarts stepped down as secretary of state in March of 1881, he returned to his New York law practice, but his public engagements continued. Later that year, at the request of President Garfield, he led an American delegation to the International Monetary Conference in Paris.[260] From his office in New York his civic activities included leading the fundraising for the pedestal for the Statute of Liberty,[261] serving as president of the Union League Club, and chairing a committee for the reform of the municipal government.[262] In the summer of 1883, he traveled west by train to celebrate the opening of the Northern Pacific Railroad in Montana, sharing a private car with former President Grant, whom Evarts found to be "in all respects a most agreeable companion."[263]

## XVI. Evarts in the Senate and the Evarts Act

After James G. Blaine of Maine, whom Evarts supported, lost the presidency to New York Governor Grover Cleveland in 1884, Evarts's name once again surfaced as a candidate for senator from New York.[264] The Republican caucus in the Legislature would control the outcome. Evarts's opponent, financier Levi Morton, echoed Conkling's earlier complaint that Evarts was not partisan enough, citing a string of acts of claimed disloyalty to the party that to others evidenced his independence.[265] *The New York Times* opposed them both, favoring some third person. The paper preferred Evarts over Morton, but was critical of Evarts's uneven support of reform and progressive change.[266] In the caucus where it mattered, however, Evarts's support was deep: he won on the first ballot with 61 votes to 28 for Morton and three for a third candidate.[267]

While in the Senate, Evarts was engaged with bills involving Chinese immigration,[268] presidential succession,[269] electoral-vote counting,[270] the repeal of the Tenure in Office Act,[271] the regulation of interstate commerce,[272] antitrust law,[273] and the purchase of silver by the Treasury.[274]

Among his committee assignments were two for which he was superbly qualified: Foreign Relations and Judiciary.[275] The Foreign Relations Committee was faced with the important question of fishing rights between the United States and British Canada. The issue was whether the three-mile territorial-waters limit would conform to the coastline or to a line drawn from headland to headland as Great Britain wanted.[276] In February 1888, the Bayard-Chamberlain Treaty adopted the latter approach and was submitted to the Senate for ratification.[277] In this political year, Republican opposition was strong and Evarts joined in by accusing the Democrats of favoring foreign interests over those of the nation.[278] Ratification failed to gain a simple majority, much less the two-thirds vote required.[279]

His labors on behalf of the Judiciary Committee resulted in an act to restructure the courts of appeals that has come to be known as the Evarts Act.[280] This Act was the crowning achievement of his Senate term.[281]

At the time of the Evarts Act's inception and passage, the Supreme Court faced an acute and persistent backlog problem. By 1890, the Court's docket had reached 1,800 and years of delay before argument were commonplace.[282] The trend was a product of the rapid growth of the nation following the war and the passage of the Reconstruction Amendments to the Constitution, in particular the Fourteenth Amendment.[283] The critical need for action to deal with the backlog was plain, but Congress—as it frequently did in matters pertaining to judicial administration—had left the need unaddressed in favor of more pressing concerns.[284]

In finally attending to the matter, Congress had several broad policy options. It could restrict the Court's direct appeal subject matter jurisdiction (for example, by raising the amount in controversy required), it could divide an enlarged Supreme Court into panels, or it could create regional courts of appeals. Years prior to the Evarts Act's passage, Evarts had expressed a preference for creating divisions within the Court because he feared that the creation of regional courts of appeals would endanger the consistency of common law development.[285] A minority of senators favored this approach, but Evarts believed that it would be politically impossible to pass such a reform through Congress. He therefore shaped his bill to be broadly acceptable to a majority of senators.[286]

The result was the creation of nine regional courts of appeals to which appeal from the lower trial courts would be as of right.[287] At the same time, direct appeals to the Supreme Court would be constrained, but not eliminated, and a Supreme Court writ of certification of appeals from final court of appeals decision would be recognized.[288] The Evarts bill passed the Senate by a vote of 44 to 6 on September 24, 1890 and a less enthusiastic House on February 28, 1891.[289]

## XVII. Retirement Years and Legacy

Evarts served only a single term in the Senate.[290] At age 73, he was losing his eyesight and his remarkable public career was coming to a close.[291] On March 4, 1891, days after the House passed the Evarts Act, he retired from both public life and private practice of law.[292] He died ten years later, on February 28, 1901.[293]

Evarts's legacy lives on in the federal courts of appeals, but the Act that created them—the Act for which he is best remembered—represents only one of many significant public contributions made over the course of his remarkable career.

He was, foremost, a very good lawyer. He possessed considerable skills and an exceptional power to persuade others through oratory, and he brought distinction to the legal profession and to high public office as he met the diplomatic and legal challenges that inevitably came his way.[294] The strength of his personal character and integrity matched that of his mental acumen. Henry Adams once wrote that Evarts was "[g]enerous by nature," and that "[h]e laughed where he could; he joked if a joke was possible; he was true to his friends[;] and [he] never lost his temper or became ill-natured."[295] His great strength lay in his ability to "accept[] the world without fearing or abusing it."[296]

Had he been elected earlier to the Senate as he had hoped in 1861, Evarts might have launched a political career that would have fully utilized his extraordinary qualities of mind and character.[297] Yet for a person who did not hold elected office except at the end of his career, his significant activities in New York and on the national and international stage put him on the same level as many of the great leaders of his time.[298] As the Court of Appeals for the Second Circuit celebrates its 125th anniversary, it is entirely fitting to also celebrate the life of William Maxwell Evarts, the lawyer-statesman whose labors brought it into being.[299]

* Senior Circuit Judge, Court of Appeals for the Second Circuit. The assistance of Ariela C. Anhalt, Benjamin L. Cavataro, and Katherine V. Mackey in the preparation of this essay is gratefully acknowledged.

1. BRAINERD DYER, THE PUBLIC CAREER OF WILLIAM M. EVARTS 258-59 (Wallace D. Farnham ed., Da Capo Press 1969) (1933).
2. *Id.* at 261.
3. *Id.* at 261-62.
4. *Id.* at 1.
5. *Id.* at 1-2.
6. James F. Nagle, *Robert Morris: Financier of the American Revolution by Charles Rappleye*, 40 PUB. CONT. L.J. 891, 891 (2011) (book review). The other man was Robert Morris. *Id.*
7. DYER, *supra* note 1, at 4.
8. *Id.* at 8-9.
9. *Id.*
10. *Id.* at 9.
11. *Id.* at 9-10.
12. *Id.* at 265-66; CHESTER L. BARROWS, WILLIAM M. EVARTS: LAWYER, DIPLOMAT, STATESMAN 493-94 (1941).
13. *See generally* DYER, *supra* note 1, at 25-27, 35-38, 40-41.
14. *Id.*
15. *Id.*
16. *Id.* at 10.
17. *Id.* at 10-12.
18. *Id.* at 11-13. The name of this firm changed repeatedly over the years as partners joined and retired. *Id.*
19. *Id.* at 12-13.
20. *Id.* at 12.
21. *Id.* at 13.
22. *Id.*
23. *Id.*
24. *Id.* at 14.

25. *Id.* at 14-17.
26. *Id.* at 17.
27. *Id.*
28. *Id.* at 17-18.
29. *Id.* at 18.
30. *Id.*
31. *Id.*
32. *Id.* at 20.
33. *Id.*
34. *Id.*
35. *Id.* at 21.
36. *Id.*
37. *Id.* at 22.
38. *Id.* at 21.
39. *Id.* at 23-25.
40. *Id.* at 25-27.
41. *Id.* at 35.
42. *Id.* at 34.
43. *Id.*
44. *Id.* at 35.
45. *Id.*
46. *Id.*
47. *Id.* at 35-37.
48. *Id.* at 38-39.
49. *Id.* at 38.
50. *Id.*
51. *Id.* at 39.
52. *Id.* at 39-40.
53. *Id.*
54. *Id.* at 40.
55. *Id.*
56. *Id.* at 40-41.
57. *Id.* at 41.
58. *Id.* at 42-43.
59. *Id.* at 44.
60. *Id.* at 43.
61. *Id.* at 45.
62. *Id.*
63. *Id.*
64. *Id.*
65. *Id.* at 50-51.
66. *Id.* at 50.
67. *Id.*
68. *Id.* at 55.
69. *Id.* at 54.
70. *Id.* at 56-57.
71. *Id.*
72. *Id.* at 57.
73. *Id.*

74. *Id.* at 56-57.

75. *Id.* at 58.

76. *Id.*

77. *Id.*

78. *Id.* at 59.

79. *Id.*; BARROWS, *supra* note 12, at 112.

80. DYER, *supra* note 1, at 62-64.

81. *Id.* at 62.

82. *See* BARROWS, *supra* note 12, at 114.

83. *Id.* at 114-17; DYER, *supra* note 1, at 67-68.

84. BARROWS, *supra* note 12, at 119-22; DYER, *supra* note 1, at 68-69.

85. BARROWS, *supra* note 12, at 115; DYER, *supra* note 1, at 68 (both quoting Richard Cobden to Charles Sumner)).

86. BARROWS, *supra* note 12, at 115; DYER, *supra* note 1, at 68 (both quoting Richard Cobden to Charles Sumner)).

87. DYER, *supra* note 1, at 79; *see also* STEPHEN M. KRASON, THE TRANSFORMATION OF THE AMERICAN DEMOCRATIC REPUBLIC 124-25 (2012).

88. BARROWS, *supra* note 12, at 139-40; DYER, *supra* note 1, at 84-85.

89. Tenure in Office Act, ch. 154, § 9, 14 Stat. 430 (1867).

90. DYER, *supra* note 1, at 82.

91. BARROWS, *supra* note 12, at 142; DYER, *supra* note 1, at 81-82.

92. DYER, *supra* note 1, at 82.

93. BARROWS, *supra* note 12, at 142.

94. *Id.* at 139-41 ("The framers [of the articles of impeachment] had no thought of justice. . . . the whole procedure of the House in bringing the indictment was defective: there was no preliminary hearing and the resolution to impeach did not go, as it should have done, to the Committee on the Judiciary, but to the Committee on Reconstruction, led by Thaddeus Stevens, [who was] bitterly hostile toward Johnson."); William B. Perkins, *The Political Nature of Presidential Impeachment in the United States*, *in* CHECKING EXECUTIVE POWER: PRESIDENTIAL IMPEACHMENT IN COMPARATIVE PERSPECTIVE 27 (eds. Jody C. Baumgartner & Naoko Kada, 203) (noting that articles of impeachment against Johnson were "rambling and exceedingly political" and trial was "highly politicized").

95. BARROWS, *supra* note 12, at 141.

96. *Id.* at 152-61; DYER, *supra* note 1, at 92-96.

97. DYER, *supra* note 1, at 93-94; *see also* BARROWS, *supra* note 12, at 154-55.

98. BARROWS, *supra* note 12, at 154-58.

99. *See, e.g.*, BARROWS, *supra* note 12, at 154-55.

100. DYER, *supra* note 1, at 97.

101. BARROWS, *supra* note 12, at 162; DYER, *supra* note 1, at 98.

102. BARROWS, *supra* note 12, at 160-61 ("[E]ven the hostile press did not conceal its admiration for Evarts' argument. . . . Encomiums poured in upon Evarts from many sources.").

103. DYER, *supra* note 1, at 101.

104. BARROWS, *supra* note 12, at 164.

105. *Id.* at 165.

106. *Id.* at 178; DYER, *supra* note 1, at 101-02.

107. BARROWS, *supra* note 12, at 169.

108. *Id.* at 171.

109. WILLIAM J. COOPER, JR., JEFFERSON DAVIS, AMERICAN 572-79 (2000).

110. BARROWS, *supra* note 12, at 172-73; DYER, *supra* note 1, at 105-06.

111. DYER, *supra* note 1, at 106.

112. *Id.* at 107 (quoting Letter from Dana to Evarts (Aug. 24, 1868)).

113. *Id.*

114. BARROWS, *supra* note 12, at 174.

115. *Id.*; DYER, *supra* note 1, at 108.

116. BARROWS, *supra* note 12, at 175; DYER, *supra* note 1, at 108.

117. Legal Tender Act of 1862, ch. 33, 12 Stat. 345 (1862).

118. 17 U.S. 316 (1819).

119. DYER, *supra* note 1, at 109; *see also* BARROWS, *supra* note 12, at 176-77.

120. BARROWS, *supra* note 12, at 177-78; DYER, *supra* note 1, at 110.

121. *Legal Tender Cases*, 79 U.S. 457 (1870); *see also* BARROWS, *supra* note 12, at 178; DYER, *supra* note 1, at 110.

122. DYER, *supra* note 1, at 110.

123. Renee Lettow Lerner, *From Popular Control to Independence: Reform of the Elected Judiciary in Boss Tweed's New York*, 15 GEO. MASON L. REV. 109, 114-16 (2007) (discussing the populist 1846 convention and its effect on the judiciary); DYER, *supra* note 1, at 152 ("The state constitution of 1846 had made it ridiculously easy for persons to gain admission to the bar, and as a result the standard of the profession had been decidedly lowered. There was no dearth of unprincipled lawyers to tempt the judges to misconduct . . . .").

124. DYER, *supra* note 1, at 152.

125. *See generally* KENNETH D. ACKERMAN, BOSS TWEED: THE RISE AND FALL OF THE CORRUPT POL WHO CONCEIVED THE SOUL OF MODERN NEW YORK 9-60 (2005).

126. GEORGE MARTIN, CAUSES AND CONFLICTS: THE CENTENNIAL HISTORY OF THE ASSOCIATION OF THE BAR OF THE CITY OF NEW YORK 1870-1970 3 (1997).

127. *Id.*

128. *Id.* at 3-4.

129. *Id.* at 4-5.

130. *Id.* at 6-7.

131. BARROWS, *supra* note 12, at 182; DYER, *supra* note 1, at 151.

132. BARROWS, *supra* note 12, at 182-83; DYER, *supra* note 1, at 152-53.

133. MARTIN, *supra* note 126, at 15 (quoting the call for organization of the City Bar: "The undersigned Members of the Bar of the City of New York, believing that the organized action and influence of the Legal Profession, properly exerted, would lead to the creation of more intimate relations between its members than now exist, and would, at the same time, sustain the profession in its proper position in the community, and thereby enable it . . . to promote the interests of the public, do hereby mutually agree to unite in forming an Association . . ."); *see also id.* at 43-45 (noting new Association's high fees and "[t]he ease with which the Association established itself as an institution with its own house, furniture, and librarian, as well as pleasant atmosphere, reflect[ing] the wealth of the men who founded it").

134. *Id.* at 23; *see also* BARROWS, *supra* note 12, at 183.

135. BARROWS, *supra* note 12, at 190 ("Evarts played a secondary role in the smashing of the Ring, for at the critical period he was absent on an important mission in Europe; but his speeches; his legal advice, and his moral support as president of the Bar Association were valuable factors in the outcome."); *see also* Lerner, *supra* note 123, at 147-52 (discussing the instrumental role of the City Bar in ending the Ring).

136. BARROWS, *supra* note 12, at 187; DYER, *supra* note 1, at 154.

137. BARROWS, *supra* note 12, at 189; MARTIN, *supra* note 126, at 110-23 (describing Tweed's three trials and his death in jail in 1878).

138. DYER, *supra* note 1, at 155.

139. Claims, Fisheries, Navigation of the St. Lawrence, American Lumber on the River St. John, Boundary, U.S.-Gr. Brit., May 8, 1871, 17 Stat. 863.

140. DYER, *supra* note 1, at 113.

141. *Id.* at 114.
142. *Id.*
143. DYER, *supra* note 1, at 114-15.
144. *Id.* at 116-28.
145. *Id.* at 128.
146. *Id.* at 129.
147. *Id.*
148. *Id.* at 129-30.
149. *Id.* at 130.
150. *Id.* at 131.
151. *Id.*
152. *Id.*
153. *Id.* (emphasis omitted).
154. *Id.* at 131-32.
155. *Id.* at 132-33.
156. *Id.* at 134.
157. BARROWS, *supra* note 12, at 212.
158. *Id.*
159. DYER, *supra* note 1, at 135.
160. BARROWS, *supra* note 12, at 213.
161. DYER, *supra* note 1, at 136.
162. *Id.* at 138.
163. *Id.* at 139-41.
164. *Id.* at 142.
165. *Id.*
166. *Id.*
167. *Id.*
168. *Id.* at 142-43.
169. *Id.* at 143.
170. *Id.*
171. *Id.*
172. *Id.* at 144.
173. *Id.*
174. *Id.*
175. *Id.* at 145.
176. *Id.*
177. *Id.*
178. *Id.* at 146.
179. *Id.* at 147-48.
180. *Id.*
181. *Id.* at 147.
182. *Id.* at 156 (quoting Letter from Evarts to Dana (Oct. 15, 1864)).
183. *Id.*
184. *Id.*
185. *Id.* at 157 (quoting ALBERT BUSHNELL HART, SALMON PORTLAND CHASE 320-21 (1899)).
186. BARROWS, *supra* note 12, at 225; DYER, *supra* note 1, at 158.
187. DYER, *supra* note 1, at 158.
188. BARROWS, *supra* note 12, at 226.
189. DYER, *supra* note 1, at 164-67.

190. *Id.* at 167-68; BARROWS, *supra* note 12, at 297.

191. DYER, *supra* note 1, at 167; BARROWS, *supra* note 12, at 297-98.

192. DYER, *supra* note 1, at 167-68; BARROWS, *supra* note 12, at 297-98.

193. DYER, *supra* note 1, at 168.

194. *Id.*

195. *Id.* "If nominated, [Evarts] would doubtless have accepted out of duty to the party, but certainly he had no desire for the office." *Id.*

196. *Id.* at 169. That such a suggestion could be publicly made (in the *New York World*) shows the depth of Evart's political independence. *Id.*

197. *Id.*

198. *Id.* at 169-70.

199. *Id.* at 170.

200. *Id.* at 171.

201. *Id.*

202. *Id.*

203. *Id.* at 172-73.

204. U.S. CONST. amend. XII. The text of the original Constitution provides identical text to that of the Twelfth Amendment, differing only in punctuation and capitalization. U.S. CONST. art. II, § 1, cl. 3.

205. DYER, *supra* note 1, at 173.

206. *Id.* Ordinarily, of course, the President of the Senate is the Vice President of the United States. U.S. Const. art. I, § 3, cl. 4. "However, President Grant's Vice President had died during his term in office, and the role of President of the Senate had shifted to the president pro tempore, a Republican." Nathan L. Colvin & Edward B. Foley, *The Twelfth Amendment: A Constitutional Ticking Time Bomb*, 64 U. MIAMI L. REV. 475, 505 (2010).

207. DYER, *supra* note 1, at 174.

208. *Id.* at 173-74; BARROWS, *supra* note 12, at 300.

209. At the time, of course, the president assumed office in March. The inauguration date was moved to January only after a constitutional amendment was adopted in 1933, shortening the lame-duck period. U.S. CONST. amend. XX.

210. Act of Jan. 29, 1877, 19 Stat. 227; *see also* DYER, *supra* note 1, at 174.

211. DYER, *supra* note 1, at 174.

211. *Id.*

212. *Id.*

213. *Id.*; BARROWS, *supra* note 12, at 300-01. Three other lawyers were selected by the Republican Party to act as counsel for Hayes before the Commission. *Id.*

214. DYER, *supra* note 1, at 175; BARROWS, *supra* note 12, at 301.

215. DYER, *supra* note 1, at 176-81.

216. DYER, *supra* note 1, at 181; *accord* BARROWS, *supra* note 12, at 307-09 ("The proceedings and result were governed by political, not judicial, considerations").

217. DYER, *supra* note 1, at 181-82.

218. DYER, *supra* note 1, at 179.

219. DYER, *supra* note 1, at 184.

220. DYER, *supra* note 1, at 185-86.

221. *Id.*

222. BARROWS, *supra* note 13, at 311.

223. DYER, *supra* note 1, at 185.

224. *Id.* at 186; BARROWS, *supra* note 12, at 21.

225. DYER, *supra* note 2, at 186-87.

226. BARROWS, *supra* note 12, at 313.

227. *Id.* at 313.

228. *Id.*

229. *Id.* at 314.

230. *Id.*

231. *Id.* at 317.

232. *Id.* at 318.

233. *Id.*

234. *Id.*

235. *Id.* at 216.

236. *Id.* These steps were not entirely sufficient: during Evarts' last year in office, four American vessels faced interference from Spanish gunboats, and Evarts was not able to secure reparations by the time his service ended. *Id.*

237. *Id.* at 217.

238. DYER, *supra* note 1, at 218 (quoting Letter from Evarts, Sec. of State, to Kasson, Min. to Austria-Hungary (Nov. 28, 1879)).

239. *See id.* (quoting letter from Evarts to Foster (June 28, 1880)).

240. DYER, *supra* note 1, at 188-190.

241. *Id.* at 188.

242. *Id.* at 188-89.

243. *Id.* at 189.

244. *Id.* at 189-90.

245. *Id.* at 189-90.

246. *Id.* at 190.

247. *Id.* at 193.

248. *Id.* at 193-94.

249. *Id.* at 194.

250. *Id.* at 194-95.

251. *Id.* at 195 (quoting H.R. REP NO. 45-701, at 241).

252. *Id.* at 196.

253. *Id.* at 199-200.

254. *Id.* at 201-03.

255. *Id.* at 203.

256. *Id.* at 228-33, 238.

257. *Id.* at 238.

258. *Id.* at 235-38.

259. *Id.* at 238; see BARROWS, *supra* note 12, at 405-06.

260. DYER, *supra* note 1, at 243-45.

261. BARROWS, *supra* note 12, at 472-89.

262. DYER, *supra* note 1, at 245-46; BARROWS, *supra* note 12, at 413.

263. DYER, *supra* note 1, at 246 (quoting letter from Evarts to E. R. Hoar (Oct. 3, 1883)); BARROWS, *supra* note 12, at 421.

264. DYER, *supra* note 1, at 247; BARROWS, *supra* note 12, at 436-37.

265. DYER, *supra* note 1, at 248-49; BARROWS, *supra* note 12, at 437.

266. DYER, *supra* note 1, at 249-50; BARROWS, *supra* note 12, at 437.

267. DYER, *supra* note 1, at 250; BARROWS, *supra* note 12, at 437-38.

268. DYER, *supra* note 1, at 253-54; BARROWS, *supra* note 12, at 476.

269. DYER, *supra* note 1, at 254-55.

270. *Id.* at 255.

271. *Id.*

272. *Id.* at 255-56.

273. *Id.* at 257.

274. *Id.* at 255-57; BARROWS, *supra* note 12, at 457-58.

275. DYER, *supra* note 1, at 251; BARROWS, *supra* note 12, at 443, 449-50.

276. DYER, *supra* note 1, at 251-52; BARROWS, *supra* note 12, at 451.

277. DYER, *supra* note 1, at 252.

278. *Id.* at 252-53; BARROWS, *supra* note 12, at 452-53.

279. DYER, *supra* note 1, at 253.

280. Act of Mar. 3, 1981, ch. 517, 26 Stat. 826.

281. DYER, *supra* note 1, at 257-58.

282. *Id.* at 258; BARROWS, *supra* note 12, at 480 (both discussing the urgent need for relief of the Supreme Court at the time); *see also* Kathryn A. Watts, *Constraining Certiorari Using Administrative Law Principles*, 160 U. PA. L. REV. 1, 10 (2011) (noting that the number of cases pending before the Supreme Court skyrocketed from 253 in 1850 to 1,816 cases in 1890, that the Court was at the time obligated to hear all these cases, and that as a result, by 1890 "it took three and a half years between the time a case was first docketed in the Supreme Court and the time it was orally argued before the justices" (quoting WILLIAM H. REHNQUIST, THE SUPREME COURT 236 (2001)).

283. DYER, *supra* note 1, at 258 (noting that "[t]he new problems created by the war, the rapid development of business and commerce throughout the country, and the broad interpretation given by the Court to the Fourteenth Amendment" contributed to the growth in the Court's docket); Watts, *supra* note 282, at 10 (noting that growth in caseload corresponded with country's growth "in scale and complexity in the wake of the Civil War").

284. DYER, *supra* note 1, at 258 (noting that "bills for the relief of the Supreme Court were persistently sidetracked" for years before the Evarts Act's enactment in 1890, with Congress only passing "some minor measures of relief" before that time, rather than the dramatic overhaul required).

285. *Id.* at 259-60; BARROWS, *supra* note 12, at 480.

286. DYER, *supra* note 1 at 259-60; BARROWS, *supra* note 12, at 480-81.

287. DYER, *supra* note 1, at 259.

288. *Id.* The Evarts Act had the additional benefit of ameliorating a problem at the circuit level. The Judiciary Act of 1789 required Justices of the Supreme Court to "ride circuit" (i.e. travel around the country to serve as judges of the circuit courts). David R. Stras, *Why Supreme Court Justices Should Ride Circuit Again*, 91 MINN. L. REV. 1710, 1715 (2007). As judicial dockets grew with the nation's expansion, the burdens placed on the Supreme Court led Justices "'either to slight their Supreme Court work with an undue delay in the disposition of appeals or to slight their circuit work by insufficient attendance on circuit, or both.'" *Id.* at 1722 (quoting FELIX FRANKFURTER & JAMES M. LANDIS, THE BUSINESS OF THE SUPREME COURT: A STUDY IN THE FEDERAL JUDICIAL SYSTEM 34 (1928)). District judges began to preside alone over circuit court proceedings, sometimes reviewing their own prior rulings. *Id.* The Evarts Act followed a series of unsuccessful congressional attempts to end or limit circuit-riding. An outgoing Congress temporarily abolished circuit-riding with the Judiciary Act of 1801, but the incoming Congress repealed the entirety of that Act within a year. *Id.* at 1720. Congress limited circuit-riding requirements in 1844, but burdens on the Court remained overwhelming. *Id.* at 1723-25. The Judiciary Act of 1869 further diminished circuit-riding obligations and created a full-time circuit judge for each of the nine then-existent circuits, but the need for reform remained. *Id.* at 1725. The Evarts Act placed the penultimate nail in the coffin of circuit-riding by permitting but no longer requiring the Justices to ride circuit. *Id.* at 1726. Only a few Justices continued to ride circuit from the time of the Evarts Act until the formal abolition of circuit-riding in 1911. *Id.*

289. DYER, *supra* note 1, at 260; BARROWS, *supra* note 12, at 482.

290. BARROWS, *supra* note 12, at 480.

291. DYER, *supra* note 1, at 261-62; BARROWS, *supra* note 12, at 442, 480, 484.

292. DYER, *supra* note 1, at 261-63; BARROWS, *supra* note 12, at 486-90.

293. DYER, *supra* note 1, at 267; BARROWS, *supra* note 12, at 492.
294. DYER, *supra* note 1, at 263-64.
295. *Id.* at 267-68 (quoting HENRY ADAMS, THE EDUCATION OF HENRY ADAMS 244-45 (1907)).
296. *Id.*
297. *Id.* at 265.
298. *Id.* at 264.
299. *See* BARROWS, *supra* note 12, at 482 ("His reform . . . still endures").

# INTRODUCTION

*Jon O. Newman,*[*] *with Jason Lebowitz*

The following pages detail the lives of the judges who have sat on the Court of Appeals for the Second Circuit during its 125-year history. Although the modern court as we know it came into existence in 1891 with the passage of the Evarts Act, its geographical configuration and appellate jurisdiction derive from a series of congressional acts starting in the late eighteenth century.

## THE CIRCUIT COURTS AND DISTRICT COURTS

The Judiciary Act of 1789 divided the nation into 13 districts, each with one district judge.[1] The district courts had jurisdiction over minor crimes, maritime and admiralty cases, and certain categories of civil cases.[2] The 1789 act further established three circuits: the eastern, middle, and southern.[3] There were no circuit judges. Rather, three judges (two Supreme Court justices and a district court judge) conducted the proceedings in the circuit court; two constituted a quorum.[4] A circuit court had appellate jurisdiction over the district courts' proceedings involving amounts in controversy exceeding specific values,[5] and original jurisdiction over civil disputes with an amount in controversy greater than $500 initiated by the United States or between citizens of different states, and most federal crimes.[6] Under the Judiciary Act of 1789, Supreme Court justices traveled to the circuits twice a year,[7] a practice known as "circuit riding."[8] The system of circuit riding would remain fundamentally unchanged until the passage of the Evarts Act in 1891.[9]

The Midnight Judges Act of 1801 temporarily altered the federal judiciary. According to Justice Felix Frankfurter, the act "combined thoughtful concern for the federal judiciary with selfish concern for the Federalist party."[10] The presidential election of 1800 guaranteed the Democratic-Republicans' control of the White House when it ended in a tie between the party's two candidates, Thomas Jefferson and Aaron Burr.[11] In addition to losing the presidency, the Federalists also lost control of both houses of Congress[12] and viewed the Democratic-Republicans' victory as "the triumph of the mob."[13] In order to "entrench Federalist policy interests within the incoming Jeffersonian regime," the Federalists set out to create 16 new judgeships.[14] While the House was voting to break the tied presidential election, President John Adams signed the Midnight Judges Act into law,[15] "less than a month before the expiration of his administration. Adams appointed most of the judges to the circuit courts on February 20, 1801,"[16] and Jefferson was inaugurated just two weeks later, on March 4, 1801.[17]

In addition to establishing the new judgeships, the Midnight Judges Act "reorganized [the] judicial districts into six circuits, reduced the size of the Supreme Court (from six to five justices, including the chief justice), granted federal question jurisdiction to lower courts," and expanded removal jurisdiction.[18] The Midnight Judges Act assigned three judges to most of the newly constituted circuits, which were then numbered.[19] One of these was called the "Second Circuit," the first time that name was used. It covered the four districts of Connecticut, Vermont, Albany, and New York.[20] Though the Midnight Judges Act represented the Federalists' attempt to pack the judiciary, several of these provisions, including the appointment of circuit judges and expanding the federal courts' jurisdiction, had been debated in Congress over the previous decade.[21]

On March 8, 1802, the Jeffersonian Congress repealed the Midnight Judges Act,[22] abolished the 16 circuit judgeships, and returned to the former three circuits, thereby temporarily eliminating the name Second Circuit. Recognizing the need to restructure the judiciary because of the nation's population growth and westward expansion, Congress passed the Act of April 29, 1802, which restored the six numbered circuits of the Midnight Judges Act, including what was again called the Second Circuit. The districts of Connecticut, Vermont, and New York continued to be grouped together in the Second Circuit.[23] The former district of Albany was absorbed into the district of New York. The Act of April 29, 1802 provided that a justice of the Supreme Court and a district judge could sit together as circuit judges but also allowed the circuit court to convene with only one judge.[24] In 1814, the district of New York was divided into the Southern and Northern Districts of New York.[25]

Through most of the nineteenth century, Supreme Court justices continued to ride circuit. In addition to fulfilling their duties on the circuit courts (duties that included both trial and appellate work), circuit riding had a civic function: to educate the public about new national laws,[26] and to ensure that the justices remained connected to the local laws, ideas, and people of the nation.[27] For example, the Supreme Court justices "utilized charges to the grand juries as opportunities for popular education."[28] In 1837, Congress expanded the Supreme Court to nine justices, and increased their travel duties by creating two new circuits, for a total of nine nationwide.[29]

As the country's population grew, so too did the federal courts' dockets. The Southern District of New York was particularly pressed. Around 1840, the Circuit Court for the Southern District of New York alone had "decided almost three times as many cases as the courts of the Northern District of New York and the District of Vermont combined," and was disposing of 130 matters yearly, all without a single full-time judge.[30] By 1850, the Circuit Court for the Southern District of New York was responsible for more cases than all of the district courts in the southern states.[31] In 1870, the Second Circuit's district and circuit courts' caseload amounted to almost half of all cases in the lower federal courts.[32] District judges were stretched particularly thin by their circuit court duties when the Supreme Court justices were preoccupied in Washington with their Supreme Court docket.[33] District judges from throughout the Second Circuit often traveled to New York to assist the Southern District with its caseload.[34]

In 1869, a bill authored by Senator Lyman Trumbull of Illinois, then chairman of the Judiciary Committee, was enacted with an eye toward easing this pressure. It created nine new circuit judgeships.[35] Each circuit judge handled both trials and appeals in all of the districts within his respective circuit. The Supreme Court justices' circuit-riding duties were reduced to once every two years.[36] Lewis Bartholomew Woodruff was the first judge appointed to a circuit court judgeship for the Circuit Courts for the Second Circuit,[37] serving from 1869 to 1875.[38]

As some members of Congress predicted,[39] the new circuit judgeships did not eliminate the docket pressure, in large part because Congress had subsequently expanded the jurisdiction of the federal courts with the Jurisdiction and Removal Act of 1875.[40] The act opened a new stream of litigation in the federal courts:

> Congress gave the federal courts the vast range of power which had lain dormant in the Constitution since 1789. These courts ceased to be restricted tribunals of fair dealing between citizens of different states and became the primary and powerful reliances for vindicating every right given by the Constitution, the laws, and treaties of the United States.[41]

The federal courts could hear "all cases involving the Constitution, federal law, treaty, and by removal, cases originally brought before state courts."[42] The Jurisdiction and Removal Act permitted the same district court judge both to try a case, and, sitting as a one-judge appellate court, hear the appeal.[43] The act disposed of many cases because of the disparity in the amount in controversy required for the circuit court to hear a case and for a case to be appealed to the Supreme Court.[44] These aspects triggered an increase in forum shopping.[45] Additionally, "in a series of cases spanning the late 1870s and early '80s, the [Supreme] Court not only affirmed the broad nationalizing intent behind the judicial reforms of the Reconstruction Congresses but also began to develop a doctrine of 'corporate citizenship' that facilitated removal to federal courts."[46]

The Jurisdiction and Removal Act flooded the Second Circuit with cases. The first circuit judge affected by the Jurisdiction and Removal Act was Alexander Smith Johnson.[47] "It was commonly accepted that Johnson's death after three years as a circuit judge 'was hastened by the undue pressure of judicial labors and responsibilities against which he struggled with self-sacrificing toil.'"[48] Following Johnson's death, Samuel Blatchford was appointed as circuit judge; four years later, he was elevated to the Supreme Court.[49] Circuit Judge William James Wallace, who succeeded Blatchford, described his workload as "too onerous to be properly disposed of by any single judge," explaining that "corporations, and citizens from different states, doing business [in the Second Circuit], habitually brought their controversies to the Federal Courts, that from this source alone these courts were burdened beyond their capacity with common law and equity litigations of every kind."[50]

To handle the new stream of litigation and the continued growth of the docket, Congress created an additional circuit judgeship for the Second Circuit.[51] Emile Henry Lacombe was appointed to this new judgeship in 1887, joining Judge Wallace.[52] Judgeships were added to other circuits, but the swell of cases reaching the federal courts became unmanageable.

## THE EVARTS ACT OF 1891

Congress debated restructuring the federal judiciary for many years, but rarely passed legislation. Because it had become ingrained in the judiciary, circuit riding continued to cause the most tension:

> The 1789 requirement that the Supreme Court justices ride circuit . . . often featured in debates over how Congress could relieve the Court's congested docket . . . [C]ircuit riding had become both an important link between citizens and government and a cherished feature of regional representation in the federal government. As a result, almost any comprehensive reform plan that suggested either serious alterations to it or abolition of it stood little chance of success.[53]

The 1891 Evarts Act, named for its sponsor, Senator William M. Evarts of New York, represented a compromise: It comprehensively restructured the judiciary while still permitting (although not realistically expecting) Supreme Court justices to ride circuit.[54] It established a court of appeals in each of the nation's nine circuits. Although it preserved the circuit courts, it shifted (and expanded) their appellate jurisdiction to the newly established courts of appeals.[55] The act authorized the President to appoint an additional circuit judge in each circuit,[56] "who, together with the present circuit judge, the district judge, and the

Supreme Court justices" could convene as a court of appeals in three-judge panels.[57] Additionally, the Evarts Act narrowed the scope of direct appeals that could be taken to the Supreme Court,[58] so that many of the courts of appeals' decisions were final, subject to certiorari by the Supreme Court.[59] After the Evarts Act, a circuit judge served concurrently on the circuit court (where he tried cases) and the court of appeals (where he heard appeals).[60] He received a single commission stating that he was appointed a "United States Circuit Judge for the Second Judicial Circuit."[61] The act prohibited a judge from hearing an appeal for which he had been the trial judge.[62]

The Evarts Act eased the federal courts' docket pressure. In its initial years, the Court of Appeals for the Second Circuit, heard roughly 120 to 160 cases per year, which allowed the judges to engage in eight to ten weeks of trials for the circuit court.[63] However, by the start of the twentieth century, the docket of the Court of Appeals for the Second Circuit was more than three judges could handle. In 1902, Congress provided a fourth judge for the Second Circuit,[64] but the judges rarely conducted trials in their capacity as circuit judges,[65] and many of their appellate decisions were per curiam, brief, and made in open court.[66]

## ESTABLISHING THE MODERN THREE-COURT SYSTEM

Shortly after the passage of the Evarts Act, commentators questioned the need for the essentially vestigial circuit courts. In 1897, the American Bar Association appointed a special committee to propose revisions to "the federal court system in order to consolidate the district and circuit courts, since the circuit courts had no appellate function and often duplicated the functions of the district courts."[67]

Fourteen years later, in 1911, Congress abolished the circuit courts, leaving the district courts with exclusive trial jurisdiction.[68] The sitting circuit judges were assigned to the courts of appeals for their given circuit.[69] The Judicial Code of 1911 thus established the modern structure of the district courts and the courts of appeals.[70]

However, it was not until 1925, with the passage of the Judges' Bill, that the court of appeals became the final arbiter for the cases it heard. "All cases disposed of in the [courts of appeals] were by the [Judges' Bill] made reviewable only by discretionary writ of *certiorari*."[71] The Judges' Bill largely eliminated direct appeals from the district courts to the Supreme Court.[72] This was a significant step beyond the Evarts Act, which had eliminated only some categories of direct appeals.[73]

The courts of appeals continued to grow. Like many of the courts of appeals around the country, the Second Circuit's growth can be tied to Congress' actions. As Congress expanded the federal government's regulatory power and expanded the jurisdiction of the federal courts, Congress expanded the number of judges to ease the increased pressure.[74] From 1902 until 1984, the Court of Appeals for the Second Circuit expanded to four judges,[75] to five,[76] to six,[77] to nine,[78] to eleven,[79] and finally to the 13 judges it has today.[80]

* Senior Judge, Court of Appeals for the Second Circuit.

1. Act of Sept. 24, 1789, ch. 20, §§ 2–3, 1 Stat. 73, 73–74 (1789).

2. *Id.* §§ 9, 11, 21–22, 1 Stat. at 76–79, 83–85. The Judiciary Act of 1789 granted the district courts jurisdiction over alien tort cases, suits brought by the United States with amounts in controversy exceeding $100, and suits against consuls or vice-consuls. *Id.* § 9, at 77.

3. *Id.* § 4, 1 Stat. at 74.

4. *Id.* § 4, 1 Stat. at 74–75.

5. For civil cases, the district court case must have had an amount in controversy greater than $50, and for maritime and admiralty, $300. *Id.* §§ 21–22, 1 Stat. at 76–77, 83–84.

6. *Id.* §§ 9, 11, 21–22, 1 Stat. at 76–79, 83–85.

7. The justices were required to hold the proceedings of the circuit courts twice annually in each district. *Id.* § 4, 1 Stat. at 74. In some districts, such as New York, the location of the circuit courts alternated between cities (New York and Albany). *Id.* § 5, 1 Stat. at 75.

8. FELIX FRANKFURTER & JAMES M. LANDIS, A STUDY IN THE FEDERAL JUDICIAL SYSTEM 14 (1972).

9. *See id.* at 69–70.

10. *Id.* at 25; *see also* JUSTIN CROWE, BUILDING THE JUDICIARY: LAW, COURTS, AND THE POLITICS OF INSTITUTIONAL DEVELOPMENT 65 (2012) ("Even though the Judiciary Act of 1801, in addition to advancing [the] Federalist policy interests, exhibited some 'thoughtful concern for the federal judiciary,' it did so at a moment when Democrat[ic]-Republicans could hardly see it as anything other than a partisan power grab." (internal citations omitted)).

11. CROWE, *supra* note 10, at 66. The President and Vice President were elected by electoral votes. The candidate who received the most votes became President and the candidate receiving the second most became Vice President regardless of whether they represented the same party. *See id.*

12. *Id.* at 61, 66.

13. FRANKFURTER & LANDIS, *supra* note 8, at 26.

14. CROWE, *supra* note 10, at 61.

15. *Id.* at 66.

16. Erwin C. Surrency, *The Judiciary Act of 1801*, 2 AM. J. LEGAL HIST. 53, 61–62 (1958).

17. *See Swearing-In Ceremony for President Thomas Jefferson*, JOINT CONG. COMM. ON INAUGURAL CEREMONIES, http://www.inaugural.senate.gov/swearing-in/event/thomas-jefferson-1801.

18. CROWE, *supra* note 10, at 66–67.

19. *Id.* at 66.

20. Act of Feb. 13, 1801, ch. 4, § 6, 2 Stat. 89, 90 (1801).

21. CROWE, *supra* note 10, at 66.

22. Act of Mar. 8, 1802, ch. 8, 2 Stat. 132 (1802).

23. Act of April 29, 1802, ch. 31, § 4, 2 Stat. 156, 157 (1802).

24. *Id.*

25. JEFFREY B. MORRIS, FEDERAL JUSTICE IN THE SECOND CIRCUIT 37 (1987).

26. FRANKFURTER & LANDIS, *supra* note 8, at 20.

27. *See id.* at 100.

28. *Id.* at 20.

29. Act of March 3, 1837, ch. 34, 5 Stat. 176 (1837). The Supreme Court was briefly expanded to ten justices to serve the newly created Tenth Circuit, encompassing California and Oregon; however, it was then reduced to seven justices, Act of July 23, 1866, ch. 202, 14 Stat. 209 (1866), and then back to nine justices, Act of April 10, 1869, 16 Stat. 44 (1869).

30. MORRIS, *supra* note 25, at 37.

31. *Id.*

32. *Id.*

33. *Id.* at 37–38.

34. *Id.*

35. Act of Apr. 10, 1869, ch. 22, § 2, 16 Stat. 44, 44 (1869); FRANKFURTER & LANDIS, *supra* note 8, at 70–71, 73–74, 76.

36. ERWIN C. SURRENCY, HISTORY OF THE FEDERAL COURTS 53 (2002).

37. The plural "circuit courts" was the nomenclature used. The Judiciary Act of 1802, building on the original Judiciary Act of 1789, provided for circuit courts to be held twice annually in each district (which had been established previously) and grouped those districts by numbered circuit. The 1802 Act further provided that the circuit court for each district would be held by the associate justice of the Supreme Court assigned to that circuit and by the district judge of the district for which the circuit court was being held. This structure imposed a heavy burden on the Supreme Court justices, who were not always available for circuit duties. To alleviate this burden, by the Judiciary Act of 1869 Congress created a new office, that of circuit judge, whose function was to hold the circuit court for each district in his numbered circuit, sitting with the associate justice of the Supreme Court or, in his absence, with the district judge, or in his absence, alone. Under the 1869 Act, the commissions of the circuit judges appointed them to all the circuit courts within their numbered circuit. In the Second Circuit, there were five circuit courts, in the districts of Vermont and Connecticut, and the Southern, Northern and Eastern Districts of New York.

38. MORRIS, *supra* note 25, at 74. This seat was later filled by Alexander Smith Johnson (1875–1878), Samuel M. Blatchford (1878–1882), William James Wallace (1882–1907), and Walter Chadwick Noyes, (1907–1913). STAFF OF S. COMM. ON THE JUDICIARY, 85TH CONG., LEGISLATIVE HISTORY OF THE UNITED STATES CIRCUIT COURT OF APPEALS AND THE JUDGES WHO SERVED DURING THE PERIOD THROUGH MARCH 1958, 53–55 (Comm. Print 1958).

39. FRANKFURTER & LANDIS, *supra* note 8, at 76. An article in the *Central Law Journal* also criticized the ineffectiveness of adding circuit judges by stating that "[t]he dockets of all the courts are crowded. The available judicial force is everywhere inadequate to the demands upon it." A.I., *Our Federal Judiciary*, 2 CENT. L.J. 551, 553 (1875).

40. Act of March 3, 1875, ch. 37, 18 Stat. 470 (1875); *see also* CROWE, *supra* note 10, at 173–74.

41. FRANKFURTER & LANDIS, *supra* note 8, at 65.

42. RICHARDSON & VINES, THE POLITICS OF THE FEDERAL COURTS 29 (1970); *see also* CROWE, *supra* note 10, at 167 (Congress decided "to allow virtually any case involving a federal right or claim to begin in federal court and virtually any case involving a federal right or claim that began in state court to finish in federal court.").

43. *See* FRANKFURTER & LANDIS, *supra* note 8, at 77–78, 87.

44. *Id.*; A.I., *supra* note 39, at 551–53 (stating that some cases terminated at the circuit court level because the circuit court heard cases with amounts in controversy exceeding $500, while for the Supreme Court heard appeals with amounts in controversy exceeding $2,000).

45. CROWE, *supra* note 10, at 173–74.

46. *Id.* at 174–75.

47. Alexander Smith Johnson was a circuit judge for the Second Circuit from 1875 until his death in 1878.

48. MARVIN SCHICK, LEARNED HAND'S COURT 48–49 (1970) (internal citation omitted).

49. *Id.* at 50.

50. *Id.* at 51 (quoting WILLIAM JAMES WALLACE, ADDRESS AT DINNER IN HONOR OF JUDGE WILLIAM J WALLACE ON HIS RETIREMENT FROM THE BENCH GIVEN BY MEMBERS OF THE BAR OF THE STATE OF NEW YORK, May 29, 1907, 18–19 (1907)).

51. *See* Act of Mar. 3, 1887, ch. 347, 24 Stat. 492 (1887).

52. MORRIS, *supra* note 25, at 74; STAFF OF S. COMM. ON THE JUDICIARY, 85TH CONG., *supra* note 38, at 53–55.

53. CROWE, *supra* note 10, at 169.

54. FRANKFURTER & LANDIS, *supra* note 8, at 99–100.

55. Act of Mar. 3, 1891, ch. 517, § 4, 26 Stat. 826, 827 (1891); FRANKFURTER & LANDIS, *supra* note 8, at 99.

56. Act of Mar. 3, 1891, ch. 517, § 1, 26 Stat. 826, 826 (1891). Already having two circuit judges, the Second Circuit gained a third judge. *Id.* Nathaniel Shipman was appointed to this judgeship. STAFF OF S. COMM. ON THE JUDICIARY, 85TH CONG., *supra* note 38, at 54.

57. RICHARDSON & VINES, *supra* note 42, at 30; *see also* Act of March 3, 1891, ch. 517, § 3, 26 Stat. 826, 827 (1891) ("That the Chief-Justice and the associate justices of the Supreme Court assigned to each circuit, and the circuit judges within each circuit, and the several district judges within each circuit, shall be competent to sit as judges of the circuit court of appeals within their respective circuits in the manner hereinafter provided."). Although the circuit court consisted of three judges, two constituted a quorum. *Id.* at § 2, 26 Stat. at 826.

58. Litigants in the circuit or district courts were permitted direct appeals to the Supreme Court in certain circumstances, which included "conviction of a capital or otherwise infamous crime," and cases involving application, interpretation, construction of the Constitution, treaty, or law of the United States. *Id.* § 5, 26 Stat. at 827–28.

59. FRANKFURTER & LANDIS, *supra* note 8, at 99. The courts of appeals were responsible for all appeals of the district and circuit court not listed in section 5 of the Act of March 3, 1891.

60. Act of March 3, 1891, ch. 517, § 1, 3, 26 Stat. 826, 826–27 (1891) (creating an additional circuit judgeship in each circuit "who shall have the same power and jurisdiction therein that the circuit judges of the United States . . . now have under existing laws" and establishing a court of appeals in each circuit, where the circuit judges were assigned appellate duties); *see also* SURRENCY, *supra* note 36, at 88 ("It was definitely the intent of Congress . . . that the circuit judges continue to hold sessions of the Circuit Courts within their circuits [after the enactment of the Evarts Act] which many of them did.").

61. Copies of the commissions are on file with the United States Courts Library for the Second Circuit.

62. Act of March 3, 1891, ch. 517, § 3, 26 Stat. 826, 827 (1891).

63. SCHICK, *supra* note 48, at 55.

64. Act of Apr. 17, 1902, ch. 530, 32 Stat. 106 (1902). Alfred Conkling Coxe, Sr., was the first to fill this judgeship (1902–1911). STAFF OF S. COMM. ON THE JUDICIARY, 85TH CONG., *supra* note 38, at 54.

65. SCHICK, *supra* note 48, at 56.

66. *Id.* at 57.

67. RICHARDSON & VINES, *supra* note 42, at 31.

68. *See id.* at 31–32.

69. Act of Mar. 3, 1911, ch. 231, §§ 24–27, 36 Stat. 1087, 1091–94 (1911); SURRENCY, *supra* note 36, at 88.

70. *See* RICHARDSON & VINES, *supra* note 42, at 31–32.

71. FRANKFURTER & LANDIS, *supra* note 8, at 262–63 (internal citations omitted).

72. *See* RICHARDSON & VINES, *supra* note 42, at 32–33.

73. FRANKFURTER & LANDIS, *supra* note 8, at 262–63. The Evarts Act permitted cases involving "the 'construction or application of the Constitution of the United States,' the constitutionality of any law of the United States or the validity or construction of any treaty made under its authority,' or the jurisdiction of the district court as a federal court, and cases in which a state constitution or law was 'claimed to be in contravention of the Constitution of the United States,' [and] prize cases" to be appealed as of right to the Supreme Court. *Id.* (internal citations omitted). All appeals as of right were eliminated with four exceptions: "(1) suits under the anti-trust and interstate commerce laws; (2) wits of error by the United States in criminal cases; (3) suits to enjoin the enforcement of state statutes or action by administrative officers of the states; (4) suits to enjoin orders of the Interstate Commerce Commission." *Id.*

74. MORRIS, *supra* note 25, at 128, 168–69 (citing the Securities Act of 1933, the Securities and Exchange Act of 1934, the Clayton Act, the Freedom of Information Act of 1974 as well as additional legislation for the increased Federal docket).

75. Act of April 17, 1902, ch. 530, 32 Stat. 106 (1902).

76. Act of Jan. 17, 1929, ch. 73, 45 Stat. 1081 (1929). The Second Circuit temporarily had five judges when, in 1910, Congress created the Commerce Court and with it, five circuit judgeships. Act of June 18, 1910, ch. 309, 36 Stat. 539, 540 (1910). One Commerce Court judge, Martin Augustine Knapp, was assigned to the Second Circuit. After the Commerce Court was abolished in 1913, its judges were assigned by the Chief Justice of the Supreme Court to serve as "relief" judges on the courts of appeals. *See* STAFF OF S. COMM. ON THE JUDICIARY, 85TH CONG., *supra* note 38, at 55; *see, e.g.*, HARRY BARNARD, THE FORGING OF AN AMERICAN JEW: THE LIFE AND TIMES OF JUDGE JULIAN W. MACK 119 (1974). This is how Judge Julian Mack came to serve on the Second Circuit. *See* BARNARD, *supra.*

77. Act of May 31, 1938, ch. 290, 52 Stat. 584 (1938).

78. Act of May 19, 1961, Pub. L. No. 87-36, 75 Stat. 80 (1961).

79. Act of Oct. 20 1978, Pub. L. No. 95-486, 92 Stat. 1629 (1978).

80. Act of July 10, 1984, Pub. L. No. 98-353, 98 Stat. 333 (1984).

# THE HISTORICAL COURT

# LEWIS BARTHOLOMEW WOODRUFF
## 1809-1875

Circuit Courts for the Second Circuit: 1869-1875*

A man of firsts. Lewis Bartholomew Woodruff was born in Litchfield, Connecticut on June 19, 1809.[1] Woodruff came from an established Connecticut family. He descended from early settlers of Litchfield and Farmington on his father's side, and early settlers of Hartford on his mother's side.[2] His father, General Morris Woodruff, "had been a County Court judge, a state legislator, and 'a gentleman of some prominence.'"[3] In 1835, Woodruff married Harriette Burnet Hornblower, the daughter of New Jersey Chief Justice Joseph Coerten Hornblower of Newark. Harriette's sister married Supreme Court Justice Joseph P. Bradley.[4] Woodruff and Harriette had three children, Charles Hornblower Woodruff, Morris Woodruff, and Mary Burnet Woodruff, and fourteen grandchildren.[5] Both Charles and Morris carried on the family tradition and became lawyers.[6]

Woodruff attended Yale College, graduating in 1830. Unlike most lawyers of his day, Woodruff did not merely "read" law; he completed a course in law at the Litchfield Law School in 1832.[7] The law school—the first in the United States[8]—was founded in 1774, when Tapping Reeve (then a lawyer and later chief justice of the Connecticut Supreme Court) began instructing a handful of students in the law; his first student was his wife's brother, Aaron Burr.[9] The "school" moved from Reeve's home to a one-room schoolhouse in 1784, and grew into a course of lectures spanning more than a year.[10] Before the school closed in 1833,[11] it educated two future vice presidents (Burr and John C. Calhoun), dozens of U.S. congressmen and senators, as well as cabinet members, governors, and Supreme Court justices (Henry Baldwin, Levi Woodbury, and Ward Hunt).[12] In 1860, Woodruff received an honorary doctor of laws degree from Columbia University.[13] In remarks on the reorganization of New York University Law School in 1870, Woodruff posited that lawyers "must be educated up to a higher standard" to provide "more real, hearty, earnest, honest, truth-loving men at the New York Bar."[14]

After completing his course at Litchfield, Woodruff embarked for New York City, engaging in private practice from 1832 to 1849.[15] He practiced with Willis Hall until 1836, when Hall became attorney general of New York.[16] In a letter to his brother, Woodruff described Hall as doing "very little of the business of the office" and predicted that Hall would "sooner or later destroy the confidence of his clients in him."[17] Woodruff indicated that he would not mind setting up his own practice, but felt beholden to Charles F. Sanford, who had recently been induced to relocate to New York and join the practice "upon an understanding that the present arrangement would continue for two years."[18] Woodruff left in 1836; he had a solo practice until 1840, when he joined forces with George Wood and Richard Goodman, in the firm of Woodruff and Goodman.[19]

In 1849, he was elected to the Court of Common Pleas of the City of New York, and served until his term expired in 1855, at which time he was elected as a justice of the New York City Superior Court.[20] When his term ended in 1861, he left the bench to practice with his son Charles and Sanford, his former colleague. They worked together until Governor Ruben E. Fenton appointed Woodruff to the New York State Court of Appeals in 1868.[21]

One of Woodruff's notable decisions while on that court was *King v. Talbot*, "a case that developed the prudent investor rule for trusts and remains important precedent."[22] In the decision, Woodruff wrote that trustees must employ the same "fidelity, diligence and prudence" that they "employ in their own like affairs."[23]

Woodruff served on the New York State Court of Appeals for only one year. President Ulysses S. Grant appointed Woodruff to the Circuit Courts for the Second Circuit in 1869.[24] Announcing Woodruff's confirmation, *The New York Times* reported that Judge Woodruff had "earned universal confidence" while serving on the New York courts and would fill his new position "with usefulness and distinction."[25]

Woodruff was the first judge appointed to serve exclusively on the Circuit Courts for the Second Circuit pursuant to the 1869 act that created nine new circuit judgeships.[26] These judges handled both trials and appeals within the circuit. The Circuit Courts had original jurisdiction over civil disputes with amounts in controversy greater than $500 initiated by the United States or between citizens of different states, and most federal crimes, and appellate jurisdiction over district court proceedings exceeding specific values.[27] Woodruff's oath of office ceremony "attracted an immense crowd of spectators"; "the Court was filled to excess, and so great was the concourse of persons who lined the corridors and halls . . . that it was with difficulty the professional gentlemen and others who had business in Court could effect an entrance."[28] The salary for the position was $6,000.[29]

The period from Judge Woodruff's appointment in 1869 until 1891 witnessed great activity in the federal courts located within the circuit, particularly in New York. "The great economic expansion following the Civil War unloosed a flood of litigation which swamped the federal courts," compounded by Congress's expansion of federal jurisdiction through the Bankruptcy Act of 1867 and the Removal Act of 1875.[30] During Judge Woodruff's service "the Second Circuit was easily the busiest circuit in the number of United States government civil suits terminated" and "it is probable that the private litigation disposed of by the Second Circuit was of a more difficult type than that terminated elsewhere in the country."[31]

In this newly created role, Judge Woodruff interpreted the 1869 act under which he was appointed. A habeas corpus petition challenged a conviction imposed by a district judge on the ground that the creation of circuit judgeships precluded a district judge from sitting outside his designated district. Judge Woodruff disagreed, holding that the new act did not contain any express prohibition on judges sitting in districts other than their own.[32]

Court decisions of the day were reported extensively in *The New York Times*, including transcript excerpts, and provided insight into Judge Woodruff's views on the legal system.[33] In sentencing a defendant convicted of setting fire to a ship, Judge Woodruff pointed out the seriousness of the offense: "You were heretofore charged with a most heinous crime, the burning of a ship on the high seas, unmindful of the horrors of such a scene, regardless of the destruction of property you were bound to protect and preserve, reckless of human lives brought into fearful peril."[34] He followed by observing that the conviction arose from the decisions of the grand jury, "selected with care from among citizens of high character—intelligent, impartial, just men," and the trial jury, "twelve fair and impartial men, having no motive and no purpose but to learn and declare the truth."[35] Judge Woodruff then reminded the defendant that he had been provided the opportunity to exclude or reject unsatisfactory jurors.[36] After the defendant declined to address the court, Judge Woodruff described the crime, emphasizing that the fire was set to "terminate a voyage which did not . . . bid fair to yield the hoped-for profits."[37] But for the ships that happened to be passing, the crew would have had "only the alternative of death by fire or death by water."[38] Before imposing the sentence required by law—that the defendant "be hanged by the neck until [he] shall be dead"—Judge Woodruff, at some length, implored the defendant to pray for forgiveness and make his peace with God.[39]

Some of the language in Judge Woodruff's opinions sounds foreign to the modern ear. In the *Penniman* case, Judge Woodruff was confronted with the legal question of "whether a citizen of the United States whose daughter marries in France, [may be] prosecuted here upon a decree of a French court requiring him and his wife to pay an annuity for the support of their son-in-law," whom *The New York Times* described as "a penniless adventurer."[40] Judge Woodruff concluded that the father could not be required to pay such an annuity, declining to hold that such a "rash or unfortunate marriage," on a temporary visit to France, could "put upon the parents the perpetual burden of an annuity for the support of the wife or the husband."[41]

Other opinions, however, dealt with jurisdictional and procedural issues similar to those that arise today. In *Pond v. Vermont Valley Railroad Company*, Judge Woodruff addressed the intersection of the court's power to adjudicate a case based on diversity jurisdiction and its power to exercise personal jurisdiction over a defendant. Judge Woodruff held that a suit brought under the court's diversity jurisdiction could include necessary defendants from multiple states. However, the court would acquire personal jurisdiction over the out-of-state defendants only if they appeared voluntarily.[42]

Judge Woodruff also presided over admiralty cases, and *The Albany Law Journal* commented that he had "gain[ed] the title of the ablest Admiralty Judge in the United States."[43] His admiralty decisions similarly reflected timeless procedural and jurisdictional concepts. In one case he explained that the defendant's failure to raise an issue or objection precluded the raising of it on appeal; to allow it would be "unfair to the appellee, who, if the objection were earlier taken, might, in very many cases, obviate the objection or supply other proof to sustain his claim."[44] Although he was considered an admiralty expert, the Supreme Court did not always agree with his interpretations. In one case about admiralty jurisdiction, he addressed whether the appearance of an individual residing outside the district could be compelled by the attachment of property within the district.[45] Judge Woodruff said admiralty jurisdiction did not extend that far, concluding that if a defendant was an inhabitant of the United States and could be found in his home district, then he should not be made to appear in a different district simply because the suit was one in admiralty as opposed to equity or law.[46] The Supreme Court reversed, holding that jurisdiction could be obtained by attachment in admiralty cases.[47]

Judge Woodruff construed the tax laws in a case addressing "the condemnation of 36 barrels of high wines and 7 barrels of grape brandy," which the United States deemed forfeited for violation of the Internal Revenue Act of June 30, 1864. The issue was whether the goods were in the defendants' possession while stored in a warehouse controlled by a government inspector.[48] Judge Woodruff interpreted possession broadly and concluded that the spirits remained in sufficient control of the defendants, who had been surreptitiously removing them from the warehouse. Judge Woodruff explained that he was interpreting the law "in a manner adapted to effect the purpose of its enactment."[49]

> The statute should be construed reasonably and fairly, and not be made a trap, to deceive or catch the innocent and well-intentioned party, who endeavors to render full obedience to the law. But, I deny that the statute is to be construed strictly, in the sense that if, by any possible construction, it may furnish a chance of escape, and a means of evasion, to the guilty party, who is engaged in endeavors to defraud.[50]

In addition to their decision-making authority, circuit judges of the era were responsible for commissioning "Supervisors of Election, under the recent law of Congress."[51] This responsibility carried the risk of controversy. In 1870, *The New York Times* defended Judge Woodruff against *The Sun*, which had accused him of striking "nearly a hundred of the Tammany men" in collusion with a political opponent of Tammany Hall.[52] The *Times* reported that a Tammany representative had been present and agreed to the removal of the individuals, the majority of whom "had been charged with or indicted for crimes of greater or less heinousness; some were notorious repeaters."[53] One year later, *The New York Times* reported that no action had been taken against Judge Woodruff by the state legislature, explaining that the Democrats had printed a document (at "Boss" William Marcy Tweed's New York Printing Company and at taxpayer expense) asking for Judge

Woodruff's indictment, but then failed to raise the issue before the legislature, thereby proving that the document had been nothing more than a campaign tool.[54] And in 1872, Judge Woodruff presided over a dispute between the Tammany Hall Democrats and the Apollo Hall Reformers, also Democrats, over which organization had the right to choose the Democratic supervisors in the election districts.[55] The law required one Democrat and one Republican from each district, but did not dictate how to choose between competing interests within a party. Judge Woodruff held that the court could not "be expected to inquire of every applicant for supervisorship for whom he intends to vote," and concluded that "[t]he law is satisfied . . . by a selection from either" Tammany Hall or Apollo Hall.[56]

Judge Woodruff died on September 10, 1875, in Litchfield, Connecticut of kidney disease.[57] "Most of the State courts adjourned . . . as a mark of respect . . . and the flags on the new Post Office and other public buildings were placed at half mast. None of the United States courts were in session,"[58] but when they resumed on September 15, the courtroom was "draped in mourning" and Judge Samuel Blatchford of the Southern District of New York presided over a meeting of the bench and bar to eulogize Judge Woodruff.[59] Joseph H. Choate, an attorney, expressed the bar's regard for Judge Woodruff:

> [He] pursued the practice of the law as a science and not as a trade, and did his part always to maintain and uphold it as a dignified and liberal profession. He scouted the low arts that would debase it, and abhorred and denounced every attempt or tendency to prostitute it to unworthy purposes. He had a conscience that never slept, and he followed its light through all the mazes of the law. His laborious and absorbing devotion to the cause of his client was proverbial, and, with his ample learning and honest and manly character, made him always a leading figure among his brethren, an ornament of the profession, and a most valuable member of society. . . . His idea of what constituted a Judge was that old-fashioned standard which exacted of him the richest learning, the deepest study, the liveliest conscience, and

> absolute honesty. And he did his best to live up to it as nearly as human infirmity would permit.[60]

Joseph S. Bosworth, a former New York State judge and a personal friend of Judge Woodruff's, stated that Judge Woodruff "died loved and respected by all who knew him on account of his good qualities as a neighbor, citizen, lawyer, Judge, and Christian."[61] Judge Nathaniel Shipman of the District of Connecticut wrote that Judge Woodruff "fully appreciated his position, and well understood the functions of a Judge to be to administer justice according to settled rules." He had "a high sense of equity. . . . But he would never weaken established rules nor unsettle the foundation of principles in order to relieve the exceptional hardship of an isolated cause. He knew too well that both law and equity, to be of any value to an enlightened community, must be administered with steady uniformity."[62] On a more personal level, Judge Shipman wrote:

> Judge Woodruff was a man of massive and hearty nature. He was not one to reverence overmuch the higher graces and ornamental accomplishments of a fine gentleman. But no man ever gave a higher regard or a heartier recognition to the solid virtues which constitute the essential riches of character. Within his strong and rugged frame beat a warm, gentle, and manly heart, whose sympathies were limited by no partisan or sectarian lines. He was open, frank, and generous.[63]

Judge Woodruff's funeral service was held at the Collegiate Church at Fifth Avenue and Twenty-Ninth Street where he had been a member. He was buried in Woodlawn Cemetery.[64] The Reverend Doctor Ormiston, officiating at the funeral, described Judge Woodruff as "a man of great natural ability and high mental gifts, distinguished for untiring devotion to the duties of the exalted office which he filled and justly esteemed for his well-known probity, dignity, and impartiality."[65]

Elizabeth Duwe

* The reason for the plural "circuit courts" is explained in the Introduction at page lxii, note 37.

1. FEDERAL JUDICIAL CENTER, Biographical Directory of Federal Judges, Lewis Bartholomew Woodruff, http://www.fjc.gov/servlet/nGetInfo?jid=2645&cid=999&ctype=na&instate=na.

2. THE NEW YORK COURT OF APPEALS, THE JUDGES OF THE NEW YORK COURT OF APPEALS 117 (Albert M. Rosenblatt, ed. 2007).

3. *Id.* (quoting Yale College, Memorial of the Class of 1830, Case, Lockwood & Brainard (1871), p. 108.).

4. THE NEW YORK COURT OF APPEALS, *supra* note 2, at 118-19.

5. *Id.* at 119.

6. *Id.* at 118.

7. *Id.*

8. Hon. John Hamilton King, *Influence of Litchfield Law School on American Law*, 40 CONN. BUS.J. 440 (1966) (address delivered June 23, 1966 by Chief Justice of the Supreme Court of Connecticut "on the occasion of recognition of the Litchfield Law School by the U.S. Department of Interior as the first law school in the nation"). The Department of Interior, which oversees the national register of historic places program, later clarified that Litchfield was the first law school "in the United States not associated with a college or university" to avoid a dispute with the College of William and Mary, which three years earlier the Department had recognized as the first law school. *The Best That Is in the Old*, 55 A.B.A. J. 842, 843 (1969) (editorial).

9. King, *Influence of Litchfield Law School*, *supra* note 8, at 443 (explaining that in 1774, Tapping Reeve began teaching students in his home); *The Best That Is in the Old*, *supra* note 8, at 843.

10. King, *Influence of Litchfield Law School*, *supra* note 8, at 443. *Samuel H. Fisher*, 1 SAMUEL HERBERT FISHER THE LITCHFIELD LAW SCHOOL 1, 5 (1933).

11. Although the school closed in 1833, Tapping Reeve's involvement ended around 1820 when, after he lost his teeth, the students complained that his speech was too indistinct and threatened to enroll with a competitor. Litchfield Historical Society, Ingraham Memorial Library, Woodruff family Collection 1779-1966, Series 1, Subseries 6, Folder 17 (Letters of June 1873 between Henry Guy Gould and his brother W.T. Gould).

12. King, *Influence of Litchfield Law School*, *supra* note 8, at 444; *Fisher*, *supra* note 10, at 27-29.

13. THE NEW YORK COURT OF APPEALS, *supra* note 2, at 118.

14. *A School For Lawyers*, N.Y. TIMES, Dec. 20, 1870, at 8.

15. FEDERAL JUDICIAL CENTER, *supra* note 1.

16. THE NEW YORK COURT OF APPEALS, *supra* note 2, at 118.

17. Litchfield Historical Society, Woodruff Family Collection, Series 1: Subseries 6: Folder 93 (Letter dated February 7, 1836 from Lewis Bartholomew Woodruff to his brother George C. Woodruff) (transcript on file with the United States Courts Library for the Second Circuit).

18. *Id.* (Letter dated February 18, 1836 from Lewis Bartholomew Woodruff to his brother George C. Woodruff).

19. THE NEW YORK COURT OF APPEALS, *supra* note 2, at 118; *see also* http://www.litchfieldhistoricalsociety.org/ledger/students/2867.

20. THE NEW YORK COURT OF APPEALS, *supra* note 2, at 118. The Court of Common Pleas existed from 1686 to 1895. It was a civil court with "unlimited jurisdiction in law and equity." ALDEN CHESTER, E. MELVIN WILLIAMS, COURTS AND LAWYERS OF NEW YORK: A HISTORY 1609-1925, VOL. II 896 (1925). The court initially was limited to New York City, but later expanded throughout the state, before once again being restricted to New York City. *Id.* at 894-95. Upon its abolition, its jurisdiction was transferred to the New York Supreme Court. *Id.* at 896-97, 902; http://www.nycourts.gov/history/legal-history-new-york/other-courts/court-of-common-pleas.html. The New York City Superior Court, 1828 to 1894, was created to alleviate congestion in the New York Supreme Court and the Court of Common Pleas. It was a civil court with "the same jurisdiction as the Supreme Court possessed in all civil cases." CHESTER, COURTS AND LAWYERS at 900.

21. THE NEW YORK COURT OF APPEALS, *supra* note 2, at 118.

22. *Id.*

23. King v. Talbot, 1 Hand. 76 (N.Y. 1869).

24. THE NEW YORK COURT OF APPEALS, *supra* note 2, at 118.

25. N.Y. TIMES, Dec. 24, 1869.

26. FELIX FRANKFURTER & JAMES M. LANDIS, THE BUSINESS OF THE SUPREME COURT, 70, 73-74 (1972). A history of the evolution of the federal courts can be found in the Introduction at page lv.

27. Act of Sept. 24, 1789, §§ 9, 11, 21-22, 1 Stat. at 76–77, 83-84 (1789).

28. *The New Circuit Judge*, N.Y. TIMES, Jan. 13, 1870, at 2.

29. *The Late Judge Woodruff*, N.Y. TIMES, Sept. 12, 1875, at 12.

30. MARVIN SCHICK, LEARNED HAND'S COURT 46 (1970).

31. *Id.* at 47-48.

32. *Judge Benedict's Right to Sit as Circuit Judge—Affirmative Decision by Judge Woodruff*, N.Y. TIMES, Dec. 31, 1870, at 2.

33. *Purdue To Be Hanged*, N.Y. TIMES, Mar. 16, 1871, at 3.

34. *Id.*

35. *Id.*

36. *Id.*

37. *Id.*

38. *Id.*

39. *Id.*

40. *A Righteous Judgment*, N.Y. TIMES, Feb. 25, 1873.

41. *Id.*

42. Pond v. Vermont Valley Railroad Co, 12 Blatchf. 280 (C.C. Vt. 1874).

43. *Obituary*, 12 ALB. L.J. 191 (1875-1876).

44. Harris v. Wheeler, 8 Blatchf. 1 (C.C.N.Y. 1870).

45. Atkins v. Fibre Disintegrating Co, 7 Blatchf. 555 (C.C.N.Y. 1870).

46. *Id.*

47. Atkins v. Fibre Disintegrating Co., 85 U.S. 272 (1873).

48. United States v. Thirty-Six Barrels of High Wines, 28 F. Case 67 (C.C.N.Y. 1870).

49. *Id.* at 68.

50. *Id.* at 69.

51. *Board of Supervisors, The List Complete—Names of Republicans and Democrats Appointed by Judge Woodruff*, N.Y. TIMES, Oct. 20, 1870.

52. *Judge Woodruff's Action in Respect to the Inspectors of Election*, N.Y. TIMES, Oct. 4, 1872, at 1.

53. *Id.*

54. *The Supply and Charity Bills—Total Appropriated by the Latter, $800,000—Dennis Burns' Document Against Judge Woodruff—Closing Scenes and Final Adjournment*, N.Y. TIMES, Apr. 22, 1871, at 5.

55. *Tammany vs. Apollo Hall*, N.Y. TIMES, Oct. 2, 1872, at 2.

56. *Id.*

57. *Obituary, Judge Lewis B. Woodruff*, N.Y. TIMES, Sept. 11, 1875, at 4.

58. *Id.*

59. *A Mourned Judge, The Later Lewis B. Woodruff*, N.Y. TIMES, Sept. 16, 1875, at 8.

60. *Id.* Choate was a prominent New York attorney. He was a partner at Evarts, Choate & Beaman, and served as president of the American Bar Association, the New York State Bar Association, and the Bar Association of the City of New York. In 1871, he joined the "'Committee of Seventy,' which brought the reign of Boss Tweed to an end." In 1899, President William McKinley appointed him U.S. ambassador to the Court of St. James. *See Joseph Hodges Choate Dies Suddenly; Famous Lawyer and Statesman Was 85; Last Week's Activities Weakened Him*, N.Y. TIMES, May 15, 1917, at 1.

61. *A Mourned Judge*, *supra* note 60, at 8.

62. *Id.*

63. *Id.*
64. *Judge Woodruff's Funeral*, N.Y. TIMES, Sept. 15, 1875.
65. *Id.*

# ALEXANDER SMITH JOHNSON
## 1817-1878

New York State Court of Appeals:
1851-1859, 1874-1875
Circuit Courts for the Second Circuit: 1875-1878*

Alexander Smith Johnson was known for his intellect, impartiality, and scientific mind. He was born in Utica, New York on July 30, 1817.[1] His mother, Abigail Louisa Smith, was a granddaughter of John Adams, and his father was Alexander Bryan Johnson, a native of Gosport, England,[2] who immigrated to the United States in 1801.[3] A successful banker, Alexander Bryan Johnson was an influential philosopher and semanticist.[4] His most famous work was a *Treatise on Language; or, The Relation Which Words Bear to Things*, in which he asserted "that language is 'subordinate' to nature because there are not enough words to describe limitless experiences."[5] Expounding on this assertion, he developed a method for studying the different components of language, and how they function.[6] Alexander Bryan Johnson's intellectual writings were not limited to language and philosophy, but also included topics such as economics, morality, politics, and the nature of knowledge.[7]

Alexander Smith Johnson attended a private school in Utica and entered Yale College in 1831, at age fourteen.[8] He graduated in 1835 and attended Yale Law School for one year.[9] Johnson then returned to Utica and continued to study law under Charles P. Kirklan[10] and Samuel Beardsley,[11] a well-known lawyer and politician who eventually became chief justice of the New York Supreme Court of Judicature.[12] Following his admission to the bar in 1838, at age 21, Johnson formed a partnership with Beardsley in Utica.[13] Johnson soon discovered, to his frustration, that those who had known him as a child were unwilling to trust him as an attorney. So, he moved to New York City in 1839 and formed a partnership with E.P. Hubert,[14] who later became a justice of the New York Supreme Court.[15]

In 1851, at age 34, Johnson was elected to an eight-year term as a judge of the New York State Court of Appeals.[16] At the time, he was the youngest judge ever to serve on the Court of Appeals.[17] In 1852, he married 19-year-old Catherine Maria Crysler of Niagara Village, Ontario, Canada, because, as he jocularly complained, he was being "berated" for "the disgrace . . . [he was] bringing on the Court by being a bachelor."[18] During his courtship of Catherine, Judge Johnson rued the "necessary journeyings" of the five hundred miles between New York City and Niagara Village to visit his "fair lady," which made it difficult to focus on his work as a judge.[19] Johnson and Catherine had four children: Catherine, Abigail, Alice, and Alexander.[20]

While on the Court of Appeals, Judge Johnson's decisions were "simple and precise expressions of a mind quick in the appreciation of the facts and equipped with a varied and extensive knowledge of the law, and were absolutely impartial."[21] Fellow Court of Appeals Judge George F. Comstock once remarked of Judge Johnson that "his was the most absolutely impartial mind that I ever knew."[22] Judge Johnson authored an opinion in

*Wynehamer v. People*,[23] striking down a law that prohibited the sale of alcohol as a violation of the Due Process Clause of the New York State Constitution.[24] *Wynehamer* has since been regarded as "a seminal decision in substantive due process law."[25] Judge Johnson served as chief judge of the New York State Court of Appeals in 1858 and 1859.

Following Judge Johnson's term on the Court of Appeals, "the fortunes of politics retired him to private life," and he returned to practice.[26] Meanwhile, Judge Johnson developed a number of other interests, spanning from philosophy to art to literature.[27] He was particularly engrossed, however, with scientific subjects that were far removed from the practice of law.[28] An avid student of chemistry,[29] he was "an enthusiastic microscopist."[30] Judge Johnson also enjoyed both hunting and fishing; these hobbies were a reflection of his "quiet and unostentatious" private life.[31] Off the bench, Judge Johnson was often sought out to settle private disputes because of his "modest and unassuming manner" as well as his "integrity and ability."[32]

In 1863, Johnson became a regent of the University of the State of New York,[33] and, in that capacity, built up the state library and "cabinet of natural history"—in keeping with his private intellectual pursuits.[34] The following year, President Abraham Lincoln appointed him U.S. commissioner to settle claims between the Hudson Bay Company and the Puget Sound Agricultural Company, arising from the Oregon Treaty of 1846 (which settled the Oregon boundary dispute between Great Britain and the United States).[35] The claims totaled about $6 million, and Johnson and his Canadian associate[36] spent three years resolving them.[37] Johnson's settlement of these claims was finally completed in 1867, and was widely celebrated by both the American and British parties.[38]

Over the next few years, Johnson continued to practice law while also serving as a manager of the "[s]tate [l]unatic [a]sylum," and then as a trustee of the Utica Savings Bank.[39] In 1873, New York Governor John Adams Dix appointed Johnson to become commissioner of appeals, where he served for one year.[40]

In 1874, Judge Johnson was again appointed to serve as an associate judge on the New York State Court of Appeals,[41] after his predecessor, Judge Rufus W. Peckham, Sr., was "lost at sea" in a steamer crash.[42] During his second term on the court, Judge Johnson authored a notable opinion in *People ex rel. Pac. Mail S.S. Co. v. Comm'rs of Taxes & Assessments of New York*, which dealt with state taxation of a vessel.[43] The owner had registered the vessel's "home port" as New York; however, the vessel was employed in the Pacific Ocean and had not returned to New York since it was first sent out.[44] Judge Johnson held, in accordance with relevant Supreme Court precedent, that the *situs* of a vessel for purposes of taxation was the vessel's registered "home port," regardless of whether the vessel was employed elsewhere; accordingly, the tax was valid.[45] Judge Johnson's term as an associate judge ended in 1874; he sought reelection on the Republican ticket, but lost.[46]

In March 1875, New York Governor Samuel J. Tilden appointed Johnson to serve on a commission to revise New York state statutes.[47] His time on the commission was cut off within the year by his appointment to the Circuits Court for the Second Circuit by President Ulysses S. Grant.

Judge Johnson served on the federal court for only a little over two years.[48] During that time, he put his methodical, scientific mind to use, authoring a number of opinions in patent and trademark cases.[49] "Patent cases were a staple of the Second Circuit during this period" because New York and Connecticut were "centers of invention."[50] Furthermore, trademark litigation had become "frequent and acrimonious" after the Civil War, and Congress had just passed the first law for the registration of trademarks in 1870.[51] In *Fairbanks v. Jacobus*, Judge Johnson examined Fairbanks's attempt to restrain Jacobus from using the words "Fairbanks Patent" on platform scales, and from making and selling an imitation of a Fairbanks scale.[52] Johnson declined to issue a preliminary injunction because Fairbanks's patent had expired; accordingly, even the words "Fairbanks Patent" were fair game.[53] He explained that apart from patents and designs, "any one may make anything in any form, and may copy with exactness that which another has produced, without inflicting any legal injury, unless he attributes to that which he has made a false origin, by claiming it to be the manufacture of another person . . . What is not free is to pretend that a scale is made by one person, which is, in fact, made by another."[54] In *Harrington v. Libby*, Judge Johnson held that "the exclusive use of a tin pail with a bail or handle to it, the tin ornamented with a geometrical pattern, and used to contain paper collars for sale and sold with the collars" could not be claimed as a trademark, pursuant to either common or statutory law—even if the plaintiff was the first to have used a pail in this way.[55]

In 1877, Judge Johnson's health waned.[56] In early January 1878, he went to the Bahamas, hoping to regain his health in a more favorable climate.[57] He passed away there at age 60.[58] Judge Johnson was buried in Utica, and the New York legal community mourned his passing.[59] Chief Judge Sanford E. Church of the New York State Court of Appeals, in offering a tribute to Judge Johnson, remarked:

> [H]e manifested the qualities of a great Judge. His mind was not only judicial, but scientific. He was patient and laborious. He had a firm grasp of legal principles, a sound judgment guided by strong common sense, and broad culture; and his opinions will always be regarded as among the best to be found in our reports. His was a robust nature. He was high-toned and chivalrous in his feelings, a sincere friend, and a genial and interesting associate.[60]

Emily Seiderman

* The reason for the plural "circuit courts" is explained in the Introduction at page lxii, note 37.

1. Clifton R. Branch, Jr., *Alexander Smith Johnson*, HIST. SOC'Y N.Y. CTS., http://www.nycourts.gov/history/legal-history-new-york/history-legal-bench-court-appeals.html.

2. *Id.*

3. *Overview: Alexander Bryan Johnson*, OXFORD REFERENCE, http://www.oxfordreference.com/view/10.1093/oi/authority.20110803100022417.

4. THE EDITORS OF THE ENCYCLOPÆDIA BRITTANICA, *Alexander Bryan Johnson: American Philosopher and Semanticist*, ENCYCLOPÆDIA BRITANNICA, http://www.britannica.com/biography/Alexander-Bryan-Johnson.

5. *Id.*

6. *Id.*

7. *Id.* (citing influential works, including *The Philosophy of Human Knowledge; or, A Treatise on Language* (1828), and *Religion in Its Relation to the Present Life* (1841; 2d ed. retitled *Morality and Manners*, 1862)).

8. Branch, *supra* note 1.

9. *Id.*

10. *Judge Woodruff's Successor*, N.Y. TIMES, Oct. 21, 1875, at 1.

11. Branch, *supra* note 1.

12. *Samuel Beardsley*, HIST. SOC'Y N.Y. CTS., http://www.nycourts.gov/history/legal-history-new-york/luminaries-supreme-court/beardsley-samuel.html.

13. Branch, *supra* note 1.

14. *Id.*

15. *Judge Johnson: Sketch of the Republican Candidate for Associate Justice of the Court of Appeals*, N.Y. TIMES, Sept. 26, 1874, at 4.

16. *Id.*

17. 5 AM. COUNCIL OF LEARNED SOC'YS, DICTIONARY OF AMERICAN BIOGRAPHY 79 (Dumas Malone ed. 1961).

18. Branch, *supra* note 1.

19. *Id.*

20. *Id.*

21. 5 AM. COUNCIL OF LEARNED SOC'YS, *supra* note 17.

22. Branch, *supra* note 1 (internal quotation marks and citation omitted).

23. 13 N.Y. 378 (1856); *see also* JEFFREY B. MORRIS, FEDERAL JUSTICE IN THE SECOND CIRCUIT 74 (1987).

24. *Wynehamer*, 13 N.Y. at 422-23.

25. MORRIS, *supra* note 23, at 74.

26. 5 AM. COUNCIL OF LEARNED SOC'YS, *supra* note 17.

27. *Judge Johnson*, *supra* note 15.

28. 5 AM. COUNCIL OF LEARNED SOC'YS, *supra* note 17.

29. Branch, *supra* note 1.

30. 5 AM. COUNCIL OF LEARNED SOC'YS, *supra* note 17.

31. *Id.*

32. *Id.*

33. Branch, *supra* note 1.

34. 5 AM. COUNCIL OF LEARNED SOC'YS, *supra* note 17.

35. *Id.*

36. *Judge Johnson*, *supra* note 15.

37. 5 AM. COUNCIL OF LEARNED SOC'YS, *supra* note 17.

38. *Judge Johnson*, *supra* note 15.

39. Branch, *supra* note 1.

40. *Id.*; *see also Judge Johnson*, *supra* note 15.

41. Branch, *supra* note 1; *see Judge Woodruff's Successor*, *supra* note 10.

42. *See* Megan W. Bennett, *Rufus W. Peckham, Sr.*, HIST. SOC'Y N.Y. CTS., http://www.nycourts.gov/history/legal-history-new-york/history-legal-bench-court-appeals.html.

43. 58 N.Y. 242 (1874).

44. *Id.* at 245.

45. *Id.* at 246.

46. Branch, *supra* note 1.

47. *Id.*; *see also* 5 AM. COUNCIL OF LEARNED SOC'YS, *supra* note 17.

48. FEDERAL JUDICIAL CENTER, Biographical Directory of Federal Judges, Alexander Smith Johnson, http://www.fjc.gov/servlet/nGetInfo?jid=1177.

49. *See, e.g.*, Fairbanks v. Jacobus, 8 Fed. Cas. 951 (S.D.N.Y. 1877) (No. 4608); Harrington v. Libby, 11 Fed. Cas. 605 (S.D.N.Y. 1877) (No. 6107).

50. MORRIS, *supra* note 23, at 79.

51. *Id.* at 81.

52. *Fairbanks*, 8 Fed. Cas. at 952.
53. *Id.*
54. *Id.* at 952-53.
55. *Harrington*, 11 Fed. Cas. at 605.
56. Branch, *supra* note 1.
57. *Id.*
58. *Id.*
59. *Id.*
60. *Id.*

# SAMUEL M. BLATCHFORD
# 1820-1893

District Court for the Southern District of
New York: 1867-1878
Circuit Courts for the Second Circuit: 1878-1882*
Supreme Court: 1882-1893

Samuel M. Blatchford was an industrious judge, "most noteworthy for his businesslike approach and his orderly, prosperous, and placid career."[1] He was born on March 3, 1820, to a distinguished and affluent family.[2] His grandfather, the Reverend Samuel Blatchford, emigrated from England and became the first president of Rensselaer Polytechnic Institute.[3] His father, Richard Milford Blatchford, graduated from Union College.[4] Richard later studied law and established a practice in New York City focusing on mercantile law and finance, served as counsel for the Bank of England and the Bank of the United States, and was a Whig member of the New York State legislature.[5] Blatchford's mother, Julia Ann Mumford Blatchford, the daughter of publicist John R. Mumford,[6] was "a noted belle in Knickerbocker society."[7] Blatchford was the eldest of five children and the only son of the family.[8]

Blatchford attended boarding school in Pittsfield, Massachusetts, followed by Columbia Grammar School in New York City, where he was the student of Dr. Charles Anthon, an expert in classical studies.[9] In 1833, at age 13, Blatchford enrolled at Columbia College. There, he was a member of Alpha Delta Phi and graduated at the top of his class.[10] Blatchford then studied law in his father's office.[11] Soon after, William H. Seward, the governor of New York and a close friend of Blatchford's father, recruited Blatchford to serve as his private secretary.[12] Thus began a close relationship between Blatchford and Seward.[13] Blatchford worked for Seward in Albany for two years[14] before being admitted to the bar in 1842 and joining the firm of his father and uncle, R. M. & E. H. Blatchford.[15]

Blatchford married Caroline Frances Appleton in Boston in 1844.[16] She was the daughter of a prominent New York City merchant.[17] Their only child, Samuel Appleton Blatchford (known as Appleton),[18] became, like his father and grandfather, a lawyer and joined the family firm in 1868.[19]

In the 1840s and 50s, Blatchford's legal career flourished. In 1845, he joined Seward, whose governorship had ended, as a partner in Seward's law firm in Auburn, New York. "There is no doubt that those nine years of quiet practice, of opportunity for study, and especially of close association with so great, so active, and so ambitious a spirit as Governor Seward did vastly contribute to [Blatchford's] subsequent success . . . ."[20] After the firm dissolved in 1854, Blatchford returned to New York City and formed a new firm, Blatchford, Seward, and Griswold, with Clarence A. Seward, nephew and adopted son of the former governor, and Burr W. Griswold.[21] That firm was a predecessor to Cravath, Swaine & Moore.[22] Blatchford's practice focused on admiralty and international law.[23]

Blatchford contributed to the profession by reporting federal cases. That work began in 1852, when Justice Samuel Nelson appointed him to serve as the reporter of the Circuit Courts for the Second Judicial Circuit.[24] *Blatchford's Reports* ultimately filled 24 volumes and was published through 1888.[25] He also published admiralty decisions of the District Court for the Southern District of New York from 1827 to 1837 in *Blatchford's and Howland's Reports*, and other circuit and district court decisions in *Blatchford's Prize Cases*.[26] In addition to these reports, Blatchford published *New York Civil and Criminal Justice* in 1850 and *General Statutes of New York* in 1852.[27]

In 1867, President Andrew Johnson gave Blatchford a recess appointment to a seat on the Southern District of New York.[28] Blatchford's appointment was well-received by the legal community because Judge Betts, whom he replaced, "had really fallen into a superannuated condition," and had come to rely on Blatchford for assistance with significant legal questions arising out of the Civil War and Reconstruction.[29]

In 1878, President Rutherford Hayes appointed Blatchford to the Circuit Courts for the Second Circuit.[30] Blatchford wrote several opinions on admiralty, equity, and patent law.[31] His work in patent law was especially noteworthy; one lawyer said, "In the law of patents especially he found the field that was worthy of his greatest mental efforts, and on this branch of jurisprudence . . . Blatchford has left a broad and deep mark."[32] An example is *American Cotton Tie Supply Company v. McCready*, which held that the court had the power to enjoin infringement of a patent by a steamship company responsible for transporting an infringing device.[33] The steamship company aided the infringers by refusing to disclose their identity and by transporting the devices for sale and use elsewhere.[34] Because an injunction is available to prevent the violation of any right secured by a patent, independent of the award of any other relief in the lawsuit, the steamship company was prevented from carrying the infringing devices.[35]

Blatchford's opinion in *United States v. Bennett* upheld D.M. Bennett's conviction for knowingly mailing an obscene book.[36] Bennett was the "leader of the most militantly antireligious and socially radical wing of the freethought movement."[37] Although most of Blatchford's opinion analyzed the sufficiency of the indictment, it also considered the test for obscenity and adopted the standard set forth in an English case, *Regina v. Hicklin*.[38] Under the *Hicklin* standard, material was obscene if it tended to "deprave and corrupt those whose minds are open to such immoral influences."[39] The Supreme Court followed suit,[40] and the *Hicklin* standard remained the test for obscenity until the mid-twentieth century.[41] Bennett's conviction was controversial. Although President Hayes's attorney general believed that the book was not obscene and Bennett's supporters vigorously campaigned for his release, Hayes refused to grant a pardon.[42] One historian suspected that Hayes succumbed to pressure from the public and, in particular, religious groups.[43]

In 1882, President Chester A. Arthur, a New Yorker, appointed Judge Blatchford to the Supreme Court.[44] Blatchford was President Arthur's third choice after two others declined.[45] The Senate easily confirmed Blatchford's appointment, thus carrying on the tradition of the so-called "New York seat," occupied by natives of the state since 1806.[46]

Blatchford was a workhorse and consensus builder: in eleven years on the Supreme Court, he wrote over 400 majority opinions, but only two dissenting opinions.[47] Blatchford is one of only three jurists to have served as district judge, circuit judge, and Supreme Court justice. The others are Justices Charles E. Whittaker and Sonia Sotomayor.[48]

Justice Blatchford was wealthy; he amassed a four million dollar fortune due to his years in private practice, inheritance, and real estate.[49] In his spare time, he vacationed at his Newport, Rhode Island home.[50] He was an avid collector of calendars and almanacs.[51] He owned an impressively large and varied collection: "'From the stateliest nautical almanac down to the humblest patent medicine annual, nothing with the signs of the zodiac and the phases of the moon is foreign to his tastes.'"[52] He also enjoyed playing a card game called whist, and exercising, as evidenced by his daily habit of walking from his home on K Street to the Supreme Court, over a mile each way.[53]

Blatchford died in his Newport home on July 7, 1893, at age seventy-three. Although he was still an active member of the Supreme Court at his death, he had suffered a series of slight paralysis attacks before a more significant attack that ended his life. He was buried in the Greenwood Cemetery in Brooklyn.[54] At his memorial service, Blatchford was described this way: "Faithfulness, conscientiousness, purity, intelligence, learning, industry must combine to mark one worthy of a place in this great Court. Samuel M. Blatchford possessed all these requirements. Absolutely without stint, he poured into his life work all he had to give."[55]

Emer M. Stack

* The reason for the plural "circuit courts" is explained in the Introduction at page lxii, note 37.

1. THE OXFORD COMPANION TO THE SUPREME COURT OF THE UNITED STATES 92 (Kermit L. Hall et al. eds. 2005).

2. TIMOTHY L. HALL, A BIOGRAPHICAL DICTIONARY: SUPREME COURT JUSTICES 191 (2001).

3. SAMUEL BLATCHFORD, THE BLATCHFORD MEMORIAL 1, 38 (1871).

4. CLARE CUSHMAN, THE SUPREME COURT JUSTICES: ILLUSTRATED BIOGRAPHIES 211 (3d ed. 2013).

5. *Id.*

6. *Id.*

7. ROBERT T. SWAINE, THE CRAVATH FIRM AND ITS PREDECESSORS, 1819-1947, Vol. 1, 10 (2012).

8. *Id.*

9. CUSHMAN, *supra* note 4.

10. SWAINE, *supra* note 7, at 235.

11. CUSHMAN, *supra* note 4.

12. *Id.*

13. A. Oakey Hall, *Justice Samuel Blatchford*, 5 GREEN BAG 489 (1893).

14. *Id.*; SWAINE, *supra* note 7, at 31.

15. HALL, *supra* note 2; *The President's Selections.: Sketches of the Careers of Judge Blatchford*, N.Y. TIMES, Mar. 14, 1882, at 1.

16. *Justice Blatchford Dead*, N.Y. TIMES, Jul. 8, 1893, at 1; ELIPHALET WILKES BLATCHFORD, BLATCHFORD MEMORIAL II: A GENEALOGICAL RECORD OF THE FAMILY OF REV. SAMUEL BLATCHFORD, D.D. 69 (1912).

17. *Justice Blatchford Dead*, *supra* note 16.

18. ELIPHALET WILKES BLATCHFORD, *supra* note 16, at 76.

19. SWAINE, *supra* note 7, at 235.

20. *See* Joseph H. Choate, Remarks at the Proceedings of the Bar and Bench of the Supreme Court of the United States, In Memoriam, Samuel Blatchford 8 (Oct. 13, 1893) *in* IN MEMORIAM: SAMUEL BLATCHFORD (1893). Choate served as chairman of the Bar of the Supreme Court of the United States.

21. HALL, *supra* note 2; *see also Current Topics*, 48 ALB. L. J. 41 (1893).

22. JEFFREY B. MORRIS, FEDERAL JUSTICE IN THE SECOND CIRCUIT 38 (1987); *see* SWAINE, *supra* note 7, at 1-2.

23. HALL, *supra* note 2.

24. SWAINE, *supra* note 7, at 123.

25. SWAINE, *supra* note 7, at 123; MORRIS, *supra* note 22, at 38.

26. MORRIS, *supra* note 22, at 73.

27. SWAINE, *supra* note 7, at 123.

28. FEDERAL JUDICIAL CENTER, Biographical Directory of Federal Judges, Samuel M. Blatchford, http://www.fjc.gov/servlet/nGetInfo?jid=192&cid=999&ctype=na&instate=na.

29. Joseph H. Choate, Remarks, *supra* note 20, at 9-10; *see also* CUSHMAN, *supra* note 4, at 212.

30. 14 Blatchf. iii (1878), *in* SAMUEL BLATCHFORD, REPORTS OF CASES ARGUED AND DETERMINED IN THE CIRCUIT COURT OF THE UNITED STATES FOR THE SECOND CIRCUIT (1878); *Law Reports, The New Federal Judges*, N.Y. TIMES, Apr. 16, 1878, at 2; CUSHMAN, *supra* note 4, at 212.

31. MORRIS, *supra* note 22, at 73.

32. Julien T. Davies, Remarks at the Proceedings of the Bar and Bench of the Supreme Court of the United States, In Memoriam, Samuel Blatchford 20-21 (Oct. 13, 1893) *in* IN MEMORIAM: SAMUEL BLATCHFORD (1893). Davies was a prominent lawyer and leader of the American Bar.

33. 17 Blatchf. 291 (C.C.S.D.N.Y. 1879) *in* SAMUEL BLATCHFORD, REPORTS OF CASES ARGUED AND DETERMINED IN THE CIRCUIT COURT OF THE UNITED STATES FOR THE SECOND CIRCUIT (1881).

34. *Id.* at 298-99.

35. *Id.* at 301-02.

36. 16 Blatchf. 338, 339 (C.C.S.D.N.Y. 1879) *in* SAMUEL BLATCHFORD, REPORTS OF CASES ARGUED AND DETERMINED IN THE CIRCUIT COURT OF THE UNITED STATES FOR THE SECOND CIRCUIT (1880).

37. DAVID M. RABBAN, FREE SPEECH IN ITS FORGOTTEN YEARS 36 (1999).

38. 16 Blatchf. at 366-67.

39. *Id.* at 367.

40. *See* Rosen v. United States, 161 U.S. 29, 43 (1896).

41. It was not until 1957 that the Supreme Court supplied a new formulation: "whether to the average person, applying contemporary community standards, the dominant theme of the material taken as a whole appeals to prurient interest." Roth v. United States, 354 U.S. 476 (1957).

42. RABBAN, *supra* note 37, at 40-41.

43. *Id.*

44. SWAINE, *supra* note 7, at 221-22; *The Vacant Judgeship*, N.Y. TIMES, Mar. 14, 1882, at 1.

45. *The Vacant Judgeship*, *supra* note 44; CUSHMAN, *supra* note 4, at 239.

46. CUSHMAN, *supra* note 4, at 213.

47. MELVIN I. UROFSKY, THE SUPREME COURT: A BIOGRAPHICAL DIRECTORY 31 (1994).

48. MORRIS, *supra* note 22, at 73; Michael J. Gerhardt, *Constitutional Branding*, 40 HOFSTRA L. REV. 655, 681 (2012).

49. *Current Topics*, *supra* note 21, at 42.

50. *Justice Blatchford Dead*, *supra* note 16; SWAINE, *supra* note 7, at 207.

51. *Justice Blatchford Dead*, *supra* note 16.

52. *Current Topics*, *supra* note 21, at 42.

53. *Id.*

54. *Will Rest To-Day in Greenwood*, N.Y. TIMES, Jul. 12 1893, at 8.

55. Julien T. Davies, Remarks, *supra* note 32, at 22.

# WILLIAM JAMES WALLACE
# 1837-1917

District Court for the Northern District of New York: 1874-1882
Circuit Courts for the Second Circuit: 1882-1907[*]
Court of Appeals for the Second Circuit: 1891-1907

William James Wallace took political detours, both as a candidate and a friend to great politicians of his time.

The son of a prominent New England family, he considered Syracuse, New York his home. He was born there on April 14, 1837, to Elisha Fuller Wallace and Lydia Wheelwright Wallace.[1] The Wallace Family hailed from Argyllshire, Scotland, and immigrated to Northern Ireland in the mid-seventeenth century.[2] Wallace's great-grandfather, William Wallace, was born in Ireland. The family immigrated to Londonderry, New Hampshire, when the future judge was six years old. Wallace's father, Elisha Fuller Wallace, grew up in Amherst, Massachusetts, with eight siblings and graduated from Dartmouth College.[3] Wallace's mother, Lydia Wheelwright, was born in Boston in 1801.

Elisha and Lydia married in 1820 before moving to Syracuse in 1825, among the first settlers of the area (the village of Syracuse was incorporated in 1825).[4] Elisha was said to have started a legal career, but found it unappealing. He found his career path eventually, becoming the U.S. consul in Cuba from 1861 to 1869.[5] Elisha was a prominent member of the Syracuse community and had a particular passion for children's issues, playing an integral role in the establishment of the Syracuse Orphan's Home.[6]

Wallace grew up in Syracuse, with his only sibling, Caroline, ten years his senior. He planned to attend Dartmouth College, in keeping with his father's example, but instead pursued a "course of general preparatory studies" under Thomas Barlow, of Canastota, New York, a small town on the Erie Canal twenty-five miles east of Syracuse.[7] He lived with Barlow's family and studied law under him for three years before enrolling in the law department at Hamilton College.[8] Wallace graduated from Hamilton in 1858 and was examined for admission to the bar the next year.[9] The examining committee consisted of the mayor of Syracuse, Roscoe Conkling, in addition to Ward Hunt and J. Wyman Jones.[10] Conkling, later a U.S. senator and representative, became a close friend.[11] Conkling was the uncle of Alfred Coxe, Sr., Wallace's future colleague on the bench.[12]

Wallace was admitted to the bar in 1858 and began practicing law when he turned twenty-one. While in private practice in Syracuse, he partnered with Levi W. Hall, William C. Ruger, and Edwin S. Jenney.[13] In November 1867, Wallace married Josephine Robbins, the daughter of a Brooklyn shipowner.[14] They had three children, Malcolm, Kennick, and Josephine, all of whom died in childhood.[15] Wallace's wife died in 1874 at age 32, likely during the birth of their third child.[16]

While Wallace experienced tragedy in his personal life, his career continued to accelerate. According to a local newspaper article cited by *The New York Times*, Judge Wallace "embraced the profession of the law, to which he . . . devoted himself with untiring energy, and achieved a very high degree of success."[17] He was in private practice until 1873, when he "was elected by a very flattering majority" as the Republican mayor of Syracuse.[18] A Syracuse newspaper remembered him as "[meeting] every responsibility with firmness, decision and integrity, and to Mayor Wallace's official acts does our city owe the first checking of the sway of corrupting influences," which had prevailed prior to his term.[19]

In 1874, after Wallace had served only one year as mayor, President Ulysses S. Grant appointed him to the District Court for the Northern District of New York.[20] When he was nominated, an article cited by *The New York Times* observed that Judge Wallace was only 36 years old and credited "[h]is brilliant talents and close application to his profession" for his success at such a young age.[21] Wallace was described as "an earnest and devoted Republican in politics" who did not seek "political station," but nonetheless embraced his role as a public servant. He resigned as mayor for his new position "with the increased confidence and esteem of the community" and received a resounding endorsement from his hometown.[22]

In 1878 Judge Wallace married Alice Heyward Wheelwright.[23] They had one child, Jesse, born in 1879.[24]

Three years later, President Chester A. Arthur appointed Wallace to serve as a circuit judge on the Circuit Courts for the Second Circuit in 1882.[25] The circuit courts had limited appellate jurisdiction over district court proceedings and original jurisdiction over certain civil disputes and most federal crimes. Judge Wallace remained a Syracuse resident, traveling from Syracuse to Albany and New York City when required.

In 1891, the Evarts Act established in each of the nation's nine circuits a court of appeals and abolished the appellate jurisdiction of the circuit courts.[26] Thereafter, Judge Wallace, Emile Lacombe, and Nathaniel Shipman served concurrently on the Circuit Courts and the Court of Appeals for the Second Circuit.[27] Because of its large caseload, only the Court of Appeals for the Second Circuit, covering New York, Connecticut, and Vermont, was authorized to have three judges.[28] Judge Wallace served as the court's "senior judge," the precursor of the position of "chief judge,"[29] from June 16, 1891, when the court first convened, until he resigned in 1907.[30]

Wallace's son, Jesse, died at the age of 13 in May of 1892.[31] Soon thereafter, Wallace and his wife moved to Albany and lived at 148 State Street, a ten-minute walk from the governor's mansion.[32] Judge Wallace traveled often to New York City for both work and social occasions. In his early years, he stayed at the New York Hotel.[33] During the 1890s, Judge Wallace stayed at the Hoffman House, near Madison Square Park, on his frequent trips to the city, at least two or three times a year.[34]

Judge Wallace garnered great respect in the legal community for the way he executed his official duties at the court. Occasionally, Judge Wallace presided over trials in his capacity as a circuit judge. One was a patent dispute between Thomas Edison and the U.S. Electric Lighting Company.[35] Edison owned a patent on "an improvement in electric lamps." Judge Wallace issued an injunction in favor of Edison, ruling that Edison's inventions were "of great value, and the perfected commercial lamp of today is far superior."[36] On appeal, Judge Lacombe, with Judge Shipman, upheld the validity of Edison's patent.[37]

Judge Wallace was involved in one procedurally unusual case. He stopped the extradition of a prisoner to Cuba to face trial for fraud, rejecting the ruling of his colleague, Judge Lacombe, who had upheld the constitutionality of the extradition.[38] After Judge Lacombe's ruling, counsel for the prisoner petitioned Judge Wallace directly at his vacation home in Cazenovia, outside Syracuse, for a writ of habeas corpus.[39] Judge Wallace denied the petition, but issued an order stopping the extradition pending an appeal to the Supreme Court. Judge Lacombe, later appearing in court to execute Judge Wallace's decision, stated that the move was unprecedented and that he "[didn't] know upon what information Judge Wallace acted," but could not "see what else [could] happen to the appeal" other than dismissal.[40]

His judicial duties carried weighty tasks of administration: Judge Wallace wrote a letter to the first comptroller of the U.S. Treasury asking that the court's supply of "water-closet paper" (six packages of toilet paper costing ninety cents) be paid for by the government, instead of from the judges' own pockets.[41] In making his case, he quipped:

> Whether [water-closet] paper should be treated as for official use is a mixed question of law and fact. . . . Water-closet paper is undoubtedly applied to private use, and is not ordinarily used officially. In former times . . . the judges were accustomed to urinate in the court rooms, turning their backs to the spectators, and using a vessel provided for the purpose. Such a vessel would seem to be officially used when used in that way. By analogy, water-closet paper, although not used in the Court room, may be used *sub modo* in the discharge of a judicial duty. . . . The Government of the United States seem[s] to have recognized the theory that its judicial officers should keep themselves clean. . . . Does it make any material difference whether the article is used to clean the judge's hands or his backsides?[42]

Judge Wallace was no stranger to controversy. In 1889, an unnamed government lawyer in Buffalo sent a letter to a U.S. congressman in Missouri offering money for improper assistance in recovering a sum of money owed to the lawyer by the federal government. The congressman, offended by the letter, sent it to Judge Wallace, who, recognizing the lawyer's handwriting from personal experience, had the lawyer fired from his job.[43]

Judge Wallace became embroiled in a legal battle of his own when he sued his stock brokers in New York City and Syracuse to recover $6,000, allegedly owed to him as a result of stock transactions.[44] One of the brokers publicly responded that "it [was] not unusual for Judges and other public men to speculate in stocks."[45]

Judge Wallace was a witness in an accident case in the New York State Common Pleas Court. The plaintiff was a newsboy who sued to recover $5,000 in damages from a coach company after he was run over by the coach in which Judge Wallace and his wife were traveling.[46] Judge Wallace testified that the coach was not being driven furiously, as alleged, but that it was simply going fast. He said he "felt a jolt," and when he looked out he thought he saw the boy lying on the sidewalk. The resolution of the case was not reported.

In 1897, Judge Wallace ran on the Republican ticket for chief judge of the New York State Court of Appeals, seeking to succeed Judge Charles Andrews.[47] Judge Wallace received the endorsement of former Senator Francis Hendricks, who wished to see more Syracusans on New York's highest court. Judge Wallace lost, in a "hotly contested fight," to Judge Alton B. Parker, a justice of the New York State Supreme Court.[48] Parker's campaign was sponsored by former New York Governor and U.S. Senator David B. Hill.[49] It was speculated that Judge Wallace's record as a Republican supporter of President Grover Cleveland cost him votes.[50] After his loss, Wallace remained on the federal bench. Judge Wallace was the only sitting Second Circuit judge to have run for a state judgeship. Later, Judge Learned Hand and Judge Jack Weinstein would also run (unsuccessfully) for the same chief judgeship while sitting as district judges.[51]

Judge Wallace and his wife, Alice, were prominent members of Albany and New York City society. In 1899, Alice assisted Edith Roosevelt in receiving her first guests at the governor's mansion, two weeks after Governor Roosevelt took office in Albany.[52] Alice performed a similar role to the next First Lady of New York, Linda Odell.[53] Judge Wallace regularly socialized with high society in New York City, often including foreign dignitaries. In the fall of 1889, Judge Wallace attended "a very elaborate entertainment" dinner at the Hotel Brunswick in New York City, which honored the delegates to the International Marine Conference, particularly those who were lawyers in their own countries, including Germany, England, and Uruguay.[54]

Judge Wallace was an honorary member of the New York Yacht Club. While ordinary members were numerous, only twelve honorary members had been selected to join the New York Yacht Club in its first 58 years of existence. Judge Wallace's name was thus in the company of the Prince of Wales, the Marquis of Dufferin, and the Grand Duke Alexis of Russia. President Theodore Roosevelt was an "ex-officio" member, along with the secretary of the Treasury and the secretary of the Navy.[55]

Judge Wallace retired from the judiciary in the spring of 1907. A dinner was given in his honor at the Waldorf-Astoria, attended by 500 lawyers and judges.[56] Alton B. Parker, former chief judge of the New York State Court of Appeals and Judge Wallace's campaign opponent ten years earlier (and unsuccessful Democratic candidate for President in 1904), presided. Judge Parker paid tribute to Judge Wallace, describing him as "faithful to that most exalted cause in which men can engage—the cause of justice." Reflecting on his own career, Judge Wallace said that all who came before him were "gentlemen as well as lawyers" and that "[n]o impatient word of mine has ever met with a discourteous retort, no disappointing ruling with a harsh complaint, no error of mine with a rude criticism." Wallace remarked, "I look back upon those long years as one who in the twilight glow looks upon a placid lake and forgets that it was ever ruffled."[57]

Wallace's farewell speech continued into a more controversial terrain: at the time, there was talk of removing life tenure from the federal judiciary and replacing it with seven-year elected terms. Judge Wallace said, "Now, as no longer a Federal Judge, I may speak freely of the National judiciary." He believed that

> selection by appointment and the life tenure have contributed more than all else to secure an independent, efficient, and honored judiciary; and I believe with these features moderate salaries will secure as fit men as any who can be tempted by larger pay. Many of the Federal Judges have accepted their places at large pecuniary sacrifice, and few of them would have accepted them if it had not been for the life tenure.

He declared that "[n]o blow more fatal than this could be aimed at all that is valuable in this existing system."[58]

In Judge Wallace's opinion, the proposal existed only because of the federal courts' recent decisions "restraining the lawless acts of trades unions" and urged that the federal courts remain "the sanctuary of that justice which consists in administering the law of the land according to the ordained principles of our present form of government."[59] He emphasized that the "will of the majority is not law when it transcends the constitutional limitations upon its exertion of power." Judge Wallace expounded on the recent decisions of state legislatures to "arbitrarily interfere with private businesses" under the guise of protecting public interest and instead imposing "unusual and unnecessary restrictions upon lawful occupation." Judge Wallace hoped that life tenure for federal judges would help protect the individual businessman against the "unwarranted Governmental domination" so that he could "enjoy the fruits of his enterprise . . . without the risk of Governmental confiscation." Wallace's speech was later described by *The New York Times* as "[w]ise and timely words, to which the whole country may well give heed."[60]

After leaving the court in 1907, Judge Wallace reentered private practice and lived in New York City until he died in 1917. He joined the Wall Street firm of Wallace, Butler and Brown.[61] His practice remained prominent; he litigated cases in the Second Circuit and in the Supreme Court.[62] He also maintained a healthy criminal defense practice, including the successful defense of Fritz Augustus Heinze, president of the Mercantile National Bank and controlling interest holder in the United Copper Company, against criminal charges of misappropriating $2.25 million in a fraudulent copper scheme.[63] In his later years, Judge Wallace kept a vacation home in Winter Park, Florida, a "golfer's paradise."[64] Winter Park, halfway between Jacksonville and Tampa, about sixty miles from the gulf coast, was described as "a jewel in the midst of ten beautiful lakes."[65]

Judge Wallace died on March 11, 1917, just three weeks shy of his eightieth birthday. He left $160,000 and two parcels of New York City real estate "for the benefit and assistance of indigent children."[66] He is buried alongside his two wives, four children, parents, and sister, in Oakwood Cemetery in Syracuse, New York.[67]

Abigail Dwyer Maltz

* The reason for the plural "circuit courts" is explained in the Introduction at page lxii, note 37.

1. *See* MEMORIAL HISTORY OF SYRACUSE, NY: FROM ITS SETTLEMENT TO THE PRESENT TIME 436 (Dwight H. Bruce ed., vol. 2, H.P. Smith & Co.) (1834-1908).

2. GENEALOGICAL AND FAMILY HISTORY OF THE STATE OF NEW HAMPSHIRE: A RECORD OF THE ACHIEVEMENTS OF HER PEOPLE IN THE MAKING OF A COMMONWEALTH AND THE FOUNDING OF A NATION 253 (Ezra S. Stearns, William Frederick Whitcher, & Edward Everett Parker, eds., vol. 1, 1908).

3. REV. GEORGE T. CHAPMAN, SKETCHES OF THE ALUMNI OF DARTMOUTH COLLEGE, FROM THE FIRST GRADUATION IN 1771 TO THE PRESENT TIME, WITH A BRIEF HISTORY OF THE INSTITUTION 158 (Riverside Press) (1867).

4. MEMORIAL HISTORY OF SYRACUSE, *supra* note 1, at 436.
5. CHAPMAN, *supra* note 3, at 158.
6. *Fourth from Left, East Side: Wallace*, May Memorial Unitarian Universalist Society, http://history.mmuus.org/wallace.html.
7. MEMORIAL HISTORY OF SYRACUSE, *supra* note 1, at 436.
8. *Id.*
9. *Id.*
10. *Id.*
11. *Id.*
12. District Judge Roger J. Miner, Annual Lecture, The United States District Court for the Northern District of New York – Its History and Antecedents, Federal Bar Council and the Second Circuit Historical Committee 24–25 (April 10, 1984) (transcript on file with the United States Courts Library for the Second Circuit).
13. MEMORIAL HISTORY OF SYRACUSE, *supra* note 1, at 436-37.
14. FIND A GRAVE, William James Wallace, http://www.findagrave.com/cgi-bin/fg.cgi?page=gr&GRid=81970094.
15. *Id.*
16. MEMORIAL HISTORY OF SYRACUSE, *supra* note 1, at 437.
17. *Hon. William J. Wallace,* N.Y. TIMES, Apr. 5, 1874, at 10.
18. *Id.*
19. *Id.*
20. Special Supplement, *Colleagues for Justice: One Hundred Years of the United States Court of Appeals for the Second Circuit*, 65 ST. JOHN'S L. REV. 937, 941 (1991).
21. *Hon. William J. Wallace, supra* note 17.
22. *Id.*
23. MEMORIAL HISTORY OF SYRACUSE, *supra* note 1, at 437.
24. *See Wallace,* N.Y. TIMES, May 28, 1892.
25. *Colleagues for Justice*, *supra* note 20, at 941-42.
26. Act of Mar. 3, 1891, ch. 517, § 2, 26 Stat. 826 (1891).
27. *Id.* § 1, 3, 26 Stat. at 826–27 (creating an additional circuit judgeship in each circuit "who shall have the same . . . power and jurisdiction therein that the circuit judges of the United States . . . now have under existing laws" and establishing a court of appeals in each circuit, where the circuit judges were assigned appellate duties.); *see also* ERWIN SURRENCY, HISTORY OF THE FEDERAL COURTS 88 (2002) ( "It was definitely the intent of Congress . . . that the circuit judges continue to hold sessions of the Circuit Courts within their circuits [after the enactment of the Evarts Act] which many of them did.").
28. Sonia Sotomayor, *Another Historical Moment: Motion by the Federal Bar Association and Others to Admit New Members on Nov. 15, 2005*, 53 Fed. Law 29, 30 (2006).
29. The senior-most active judge was known as the "senior circuit judge" until 1948, when the term "chief judge" was established under 28 U.S.C. § 45. The term was adopted "in recognition of the great increase in administrative duties of such judge." REPORT FROM THE HOUSE COMM. ON THE JUDICIARY, TO ACCOMPANY H.R. 3214, H.R. 308, 80th CONG., 1st Sess., A6 (1947); *see also* Act of June 25, 1948, ch. 646, § 45(a) 62 Stat. 869, 871 ("The circuit judge senior in commission shall be the chief judge of the circuit.").
30. *Wallace, supra* note 24.
31. *Id.*
32. *Candidates Nominated by the Republican Party*, SUPPLEMENT TO EASTERN STATE JOURNAL, Oct. 30, 1897.
33. *Personal Intelligence*, N.Y. TIMES, Jan. 24, 1885, Dec. 7, 1887, January 3, 1889.
34. *Personal Intelligence*, N.Y. TIMES, Mar. 10, 1890, Apr. 29, 1890, Oct. 20, 1890, Jan. 5, 1891, Jan. 24, 1885, Dec. 7, 1887, Jan. 3, 1889.
35. Edison Elec. Light Co. v. U.S. Elec. Lighting Co., 47 F. 454, 454 (S.D.N.Y. 1891).
36. *Id.* at 463.
37. Edison Elec. Light Co. v. United States Elec. Lighting Co., 52 F. 300 (2d Cir. 1892).
38. *Neely Not Extradited,* N.Y. TIMES, Aug. 14, 1900, at 12.
39. *Id.*
40. *Id.*
41. Letter from Judge William J. Wallace to the First Comptroller of the Treasury (on file with the United States Courts Library for the Second Circuit).

42. *Id.*
43. *Removed by Judge Wallace*, N.Y. TIMES, Feb. 7, 1889, at 2.
44. *He Wants His Money Back*, N.Y. TIMES, Jun. 5, 1885, at 1.
45. *The Judge Was Speculating*, N.Y. TIMES, Jun. 6, 1885, at 8.
46. *Judge Wallace A Witness*, N.Y. TIMES, Dec. 12, 1895, at 14.
47. *Judge Wallace A Candidate*, N.Y. TIMES, Jul. 7, 1897, at 3.
48. Robert M. Mandelbaum, Alton Brooks Parker, *Legal History of the New York Court of Appeals*, https://www.nycourts.gov/history/legal-history-new-york/luminaries-court-appeals/parker-alton.html.
49. *Id.*
50. *Republicans to Meet*, N.Y. TIMES, Sep. 18, 1897, at 2.
51. GERALD GUNTHER, LEARNED HAND: THE MAN AND THE JUDGE 233–236 (2d ed. 2010). *See also* JEFFREY B. MORRIS, LEADERSHIP ON THE BENCH: THE CRAFT AND ACTIVISM OF JACK WEINSTEIN 155–60 (2011) (discussing Judge Weinstein's unsuccessful election campaign).
52. *Mrs. Roosevelt's First Reception*, N.Y. TIMES, Jan. 18, 1899, at 6.
53. *Mrs. Odell's Second At Home*, N. Y. TIMES, Jan. 22, 1903, at 7.
54. *Lawyers Among Flowers*, N.Y. TIMES, Nov. 24, 1889, at 2.
55. *Herreshoff Not Yet Elected*, N.Y. TIMES, Feb. 15, 1902, at 6.
56. *Wallace Speaks for the Judiciary*, N.Y. TIMES, May 30, 1907, at 7.
57. *Id.*
58. *Id.*
59. *The Rock of Safety*, N.Y. TIMES, May 31, 1907, at 7.
60. *Id.*
61. *Wallace Speaks for the Judiciary*, *supra* note 56, at 7.
62. *See Brief of American Tobacco Co. Filed in U.S. Supreme Court*, N.Y. TIMES, Oct. 14, 1909, at 7.
63. *Indict Heinze for Copper Pool Loans*, N.Y. TIMES, May 15, 1909, at 18.
64. *Golfers' Paradise At Winter Park, Fla.*, N.Y. Times, Dec. 17, 1916 at 3.
65. *Id.*
66. *Colleagues for Justice*, *supra* note 20, at 942.
67. FIND A GRAVE, *supra* note 14.

# EMILE HENRY LACOMBE
# 1846-1924

Circuit Courts for the Second Circuit: 1887-1911[*]
Court of Appeals for the Second Circuit: 1891-1916

Emile Henry Lacombe was a New York City man. Lacombe was born January 29, 1846,[1] on Prince Street,[2] the son of a prominent New York merchant.[3] He attended Columbia Grammar[4] and graduated from Columbia College in 1863 as "fourth honor man" at the age of 17.[5] He later graduated from Columbia Law School and won a $200 prize in the Political Science Department[6] for excellence in constitutional law.[7] Too young to be admitted to the bar, he had to wait two years to begin practice.[8]

Lacombe preserved his ties to Columbia. The class of 1863 held its first reunion in April 1899 at the Reform Club, and "[t]he occasion was so agreeable that, on motion of Judge Lacombe, it was voted to have an annual reunion."[9] A May 1913 account reports "Columbia Graduates of '63 to Reassemble" and described

Lacombe, then a judge, as a "prominent member of the class."[10] Columbia conferred an honorary LLD degree upon Judge Lacombe in 1894.[11]

During the Civil War he served as a private with the Seventh Regiment[12] K Company,[13] and was present with the Regiment at Baltimore and Frederick City.[14]

After a period of private practice, Lacombe worked for the New York City Law Department, assigned "to straighten out the civil suit complications that sprang out of the Tweed contracts,"[15] and played an "inconspicuous but useful part in sending that gang to stripes."[16] He also represented the City in condemnation proceedings intended to increase the City's control over the water supply and drafted the 1883 Aqueduct Act.[17] He ultimately became corporation counsel. He was, at the time, living at 81 Clinton Place,[18] now 8th Street in Greenwich Village.[19] While at the Law Department, he compiled tables of cases involving questions of law peculiar to the City and County of New York.[20] Appointment as corporation counsel was highly political. At one point, when his incumbency was challenged by the president of the Board of Aldermen, who wanted to install his own candidate, Lacombe reportedly "barricaded the entry of the Law Department's offices and obtained a fire hose to turn [away] potential invaders."[21] Lacombe organized the department into substantive divisions, hired a clerical staff (mainly women), embraced new technology such as telephones and typewriters, and cleared a backlog.[22]

In 1887, President Grover Cleveland appointed Lacombe to serve as a circuit judge on the Circuit Courts for the Second Circuit.[23] The circuit courts had limited appellate jurisdiction over district court proceedings and original jurisdiction over certain civil disputes and most federal crimes.[24] One paper commented: "Mr. Lacombe's salary as Circuit Judge will be only half his salary as Counsel to the Corporation. But his appointment will be for life, and the duties probably less onerous."[25] On the other hand, *The New York Times* observed that "[t]he office will bring with it an immense amount of hard work, but Mr. Lacombe, by training and temperament, is qualified to undertake it."[26]

In 1891, the Evarts Act established in each of the nation's nine circuits a court of appeals and abolished the appellate jurisdiction of the circuit courts.[27] Thereafter, Judge Lacombe, William Wallace, and Nathaniel Shipman served concurrently on the Circuit Courts and the Court of Appeals for the Second Circuit.[28] When the three judges of the new court of appeals assembled, they wore robes, at the request of the bar: reportedly, "Judge Lacombe tried on his new robe yesterday, and was well pleased with it."[29]

Many cases about government regulation of business came before him. A contemporary account describes Judge Lacombe as "partial to corporations," and an opponent of "the modern school of radicalism."[30] Several newspapers reported his presence on a panel directed by the Supreme Court to "decide how [the] tobacco trust may rearrange and keep within the law."[31] The panel was to be "arbiters of what is business and what is crookedness," and had to "decide that this thing is and that thing is not straight and square business."[32] The Supreme Court had ruled the American Tobacco Company in violation of the Sherman Act. On remand, in what was known as the "Tobacco Trust" case, the Lacombe panel approved a reorganization.[33] In another antitrust case, concerning Cream of Wheat cereal (technically known as "purified middlings"), he opined: "We have not yet reached the stage where the selection of a trader's customers is made for him by the government."[34]

In his time, Judge Lacombe was perhaps best known for the Tobacco Trust case, and two cases whose fame has diminished: "the traction case," and "the eighty-cent gas litigation."[35] The traction case concerned the dissolution of two traction companies (street railways). The gas case was a challenge to a 1906 state statute that limited the price of gas (then commonly a source of lighting) in Manhattan to 80 cents per 1,000 feet.

Other cases received newspaper attention and gave a taste of Judge Lacombe's personality. Presiding in his capacity as a circuit judge, he discharged a hung jury in the trial of the former director of finances of the Cuban post office. After an obstreperous juror asked, "[I]s the opinion of this court any better than that of any other citizen?" Lacombe responded, "If you fail to conduct yourself properly as a juror, you will see the importance of the court's opinion."[36] He denied habeas corpus to prevent the deportation of an avowed anarchist, rejecting the argument that an alien anarchist was practicing a religion protected by the First Amendment: "It is difficult to understand upon what theory the exclusion of an alien, who is an anarchist can be held to be a prohibition of the free exercise of religion."[37]

Important patent cases came before the court. Together, Judge Lacombe and Judge Shipman upheld the validity of Thomas Edison's patent on an incandescent electric lamp, affirming an injunction issued by their Second Circuit colleague, Judge Wallace, who handled the case in his capacity as a circuit judge.[38]

One of Judge Lacombe's rulings was predicted to "have a most important effect on the moving picture business all over the country."[39] He decided that "moving picture shows come within the copyright law."[40] Previously, "moving pictures concerns have never troubled themselves with royalties."[41] But the copyright owners of the book *Ben-Hur* sought to enjoin the *Ben-Hur* "moving picture."[42] Judge Lacombe concluded that showing filmed scenes of copyrighted books or plays violated those copyrights, likening them to pantomimes, and accordingly, theatrical productions.[43]

Judge Lacombe's career was not without controversy. In January 1905, a Philadelphia law firm wrote every member of the House of Representatives listing twelve charges of misconduct against Lacombe.[44] According to *The New York Times*, which headlined "Demand Impeachment of Judge Lacombe," the case arose from a patent infringement action concerning a cofferdam used in building the Brooklyn Bridge piers.[45] Lacombe was accused of delaying the case.[46] This impeachment effort failed: "It made a nine days' wonder in the newspapers, but the Judiciary Committee refused to take it seriously and seemed rather astonished that Lacombe should do so."[47]

Lacombe retired from the court in 1916.[48] Upon his retirement, *The New York Times* described him as "noted for his capacity for hard work," and "famed for his industry."[49] He had "vigor and enthusiasm" for complex cases and also did "hard work on the general business of the court, which has long been heavy in this circuit."[50] Judge Lacombe was by then the only circuit judge to also do "first instance work," hearing a general motion calendar each month and handling most of "the trials growing out of the Metropolitan Street Railway Company situation."[51]

From 1916 until his death in 1924 he was associated with the law firm of Masten & Nichols, with a stint as a master in chancery.[52] In that role he passed on "claims against the [Brooklyn Rapid Transit Company] arising out of the [subway] wreck in the Malbone Street tunnel."[53] His office was at 49 Wall Street.[54]

Lacombe was an inveterate writer of letters to the editor, particularly *The New York Times.* From 1915 to 1918, he wrote numerous letters, later collected, to New York and Boston newspapers about the sinking of the Lusitania, the conduct of the war, and America's role in it.[55] Expressing the view that the war should be fought to an end and the loser (Germany, he assumed) forced to accept the winners' terms, he remarked: "[I]t was in precisely this way that our civil war ended; and that the generation that fought it out—except those who anticipated defeat—would have deemed unfriendly and insidious any effort by the nations of Europe to put a stop to it before the fight was finished."[56]

Lacombe's wife, Elizabeth, with whom he had two children, died the year before he became a judge.[57] Lacombe died on November 28, 1924.[58] His funeral was held at the First Presbyterian Church in Greenwich Village.[59] He is buried in Evergreen Cemetery in Morristown, New Jersey.[60]

Catherine J. Minuse

* The reason for the plural "circuit courts" is explained in the Introduction at page lxii, n. 37.

1. FEDERAL JUDICIAL CENTER, Biographical Directory of Federal Judges, Emile Henry Lacombe, http://www.fjc.gov/servlet/nGetInfo?jid=1326.
2. *The New Corporation Counsel: Mayor Edson Confers the Appointment on E. Henry Lacombe*, N.Y. TIMES, June 1, 1884, at 3.
3. *Fate of Trusts in Hands of Four New York Judges*, N.Y. TIMES, June 4, 1911.
4. WHO'S WHO IN NEW YORK CITY AND STATE 640 (Herman W. Knox ed., 1918).
5. *The New Corporation Counsel*, *supra* note 2, at 3.
6. *Columbia College Law School Sixth Annual Commencement*, N.Y. TIMES, May 18, 1865, at 8.
7. *The New Corporation Counsel*, *supra* note 2, at 3.
8. *Ex-Judge Lacombe, Federal Jurist, Dies*, N.Y. TIMES, Nov. 29, 1924, at 13.
9. *Alumni Notes*, 1 COLUM. U. Q. 397, 397 (1899).

10. *Columbia Graduates of '63 to Reassemble*, N.Y. SUN, May 30, 1913, at 7.

11. *Received Their Degrees*, N.Y. HERALD, June 14, 1894, at 10.

12. *Emile Henry Lacombe*, BROOKLYN DAILY EAGLE, Nov. 30, 1924 at 4B; *Ex-Judge Lacombe, Federal Jurist, Dies*, *supra* note 8.

13. *Death Notices*, N.Y. TIMES, Nov. 30, 1924, at E7.

14. WHO'S WHO, *supra* note 4.

15. *Emile Henry Lacombe*, *supra* note 12, at 4B.

16. *Fate of Trusts in Hands of Four New York Judges*, *supra* note 3.

17. *Id.*; *Ex-Judge Lacombe, Federal Jurist, Dies*, *supra* note 8, at 13.

18. *The New Corporation Counsel*, *supra* note 2, at 3.

19. *Eighth Street History*, VILLAGE ALLIANCE, http://villagealliance.org/eighthstreet-history/.

20. E. HENRY LACOMBE & A.H. MASTEN, TABLE OF CASES, INVOLVING QUESTIONS OF LAW PECULIAR TO THE CITY AND COUNTY OF NEW YORK (1882).

21. WILLIAM E. NELSON, FIGHTING FOR THE CITY: A HISTORY OF THE NEW YORK CITY CORPORATION COUNSEL 76 (2008).

22. *Id.* at 77-78.

23. *Judge Lacombe in Office*, N.Y. TIMES, July 2, 1887, at 8.

24. Act of March 3, 1875, ch. 137, 18 Stat. 470, 470 (1875); Act of Sept. 24, 1789, §§ 9, 11, 21–22, 1 Stat. 73, 76–77, 83–84 (1789).

25. *Emile Henry Lacombe, 1846-1924*, NYPL DIGITAL GALLERY, http://digitalgallery.nypl.org/nypldigital/id?1551617.

26. *A New Circuit Judge*, N.Y. TIMES, May 27, 1887, at 1.

27. Act of Mar. 3, 1891, ch. 517, § 2, 26 Stat. 826 (1891).

28. *Id.* § 1, 3, 26 Stat. at 826–27 (creating an additional circuit judgeship in each circuit "who shall have the same power and jurisdiction therein that the circuit judges of the United States . . . now have under existing laws" and establishing a Court of Appeals in each circuit, where the circuit judges were assigned appellate duties.); *see also* ERWIN SURRENCY, HISTORY OF THE FEDERAL COURTS 88 (2002) (stating "[i]t was definitely the intent of Congress . . . that the circuit judges continue to hold sessions of the Circuit Courts within their circuits [after the enactment of the Evarts Act] which many of them did").

29. *They Will Wear Gowns*, N.Y. TIMES, June 9, 1891, at 8.

30. *Fate of Trusts in Hands of Four New York Judges*, *supra* note 3.

31. *These Judges Will Decide How Tobacco Trust May Rearrange and Keep Within the Law*, UTICA HERALD DISPATCH, May 31, 1911, at 1.

32. *Fate of Trusts in Hands of Four New York Judges*, *supra* note 3.

33. United States v. American Tobacco Co., 191 F. 371 (C.C.S.D.N.Y. 1911).

34. Great Atlantic & Pacific Tea Co. v. Cream of Wheat Co., 227 F. 46, 49 (2d Cir. 1915).

35. *See Lacombe, Retiring, Ends Traction Suit*, N.Y. TIMES, Feb. 16, 1916, at 6; *see* Consolidated Gas v. Mayer, 146 F. 150 (C.C.S.D.N.Y. 1906); *see Judge Lacombe Dead*, N.Y. L.J., Dec. 1, 1924, at 1.

36. *Neely Jury Disagrees*, BUFFALO COURIER, Apr. 13, 1904, at 3.

37. United States ex rel. Turner v. Williams, 126 F. 253 (C.C.S.D.N.Y. 1903); *Anarchist Must Go*, N.Y. DAILY TRIBUNE, Nov. 8, 1903, at 7.

38. Edison Elec. Light Co. v. United States Elec. Lighting Co., 52 F. 300 (2d Cir. 1892).

39. *Must Pay Royalties on Moving Pictures*, N.Y. TIMES, May 6, 1908, at 5.

40. *Id.*

41. *Id.*

42. *See id.*

43. Harper & Bros. v. Kalem Co., 169 F. 61 (2d Cir. 1909) (appeal from injunction); *see Must Pay Royalties on Moving Pictures*, *supra* note 39, at 5.

44. *Demand Impeachment of Judge Lacombe*, N.Y. TIMES, Jan. 25, 1905, at 1.

45. *Id.*

46. *See Case Comes Up Today*, N.Y. TIMES, Jan. 25, 1905, at 1.

47. *Fate of Trusts in Hands of Four New York Judges*, *supra* note 3; *Judge Lacombe Fails to Obtain a Hearing*, N.Y. TIMES, Jan. 28, 1905, at 5.

48. *Lacombe Leaves Bench Tomorrow*, N.Y. TIMES, Feb. 14, 1916, at 5.

49. *Id.*

50. *Id.*

51. *Id.*; *see New York Railways*, WALL. ST. J., Jan. 19, 1915, at 5.

52. *Ex-Judge Lacombe, Federal Jurist, Dies*, *supra* note 8.

53. *Id.*

54. *Financial Notices*, N.Y. TIMES, Oct. 11, 1921, at 34.

55. E. HENRY LACOMBE, A FILE OF LETTERS 1915-1918.

56. *Id.* at 65; *see* Emile Henry Lacombe, *Letter to the Editor*, N.Y. TIMES, Nov. 25, 1916.

57. WHO'S WHO, *supra* note 4; FIND A GRAVE, Henry Lacombe, http://www.findagrave.com/cgi-bin/fg.cgi? page=gr&GSvpid=48253989&GRid=6712503&.

58. *Ex-Judge Lacombe, Federal Jurist, Dies*, *supra* note 8.

59. *Death Notices*, *supra* note 13.

60. *Henry Lacombe*, *supra* note 57.

# NATHANIEL SHIPMAN
# 1828-1906

District Court for the District of Connecticut:
1873-1892
Circuit Courts for the Second Circuit: 1892-1902*
Court of Appeals for the Second Circuit: 1892-1902

Nathaniel Shipman was throughout his life a deeply religious man. He was perhaps most satisfied when serving as a philanthropist for charities that promoted education, agriculture, art, and Christian missionary work. Born on August 22, 1828 in Southbury, Connecticut, a small town twenty miles northwest of New Haven, Shipman was the only son of a well-known and successful minister, the Reverend Thomas Leffingwell Shipman, and his first wife, Mary Thompson Deming.[1] His father had two more children with a second wife.[2] Nathaniel's Connecticut heritage dated back to 1639, when his ancestor, Edward Shipman, sailed from Hull, England, and settled in Saybrook, Connecticut.[3]

The Shipmans were stalwarts of Connecticut society: his great-grandfather, also Nathaniel Shipman, was one of the founding members of the Second Congregational Church in Norwich, Connecticut. He served congregations from South Carolina to Brooklyn and Ohio, always returning home to Connecticut for years at a time.[4] Shipman's grandfather became a prominent probate and county judge in Norwich.[5] The historian of Norwich and New London wrote the following about the grandfather in 1911: "Judge Shipman was a man of great simplicity of habits, of vigorous common sense, upright, honorable and independent . . . [His] affability and a taste for social enjoyment made him a delightful companion."[6]

Nathaniel Shipman attended public school and Plainfield Academy before following in his father's footsteps, attending Yale College and Yale Law School.[7] He did not graduate, however, opting to study the law with Thomas B. Osborne, in Fairfield.[8] He was later admitted to the bar in Hartford in 1850, where he began his career and became a prominent lawyer in private practice at the firm of Welch & Shipman, until his partner passed away in 1870.[9]

Shipman served as a member of the Connecticut House of Representatives from Hartford in 1857, when he was not yet 30 years old, and as the executive secretary to Governor William Alfred Buckingham during the start of the Civil War, from 1858 to 1862.[10] Shipman also served as the head of the state Republican Party. While serving in these political positions, he continued to practice law in Hartford.[11]

In 1873, President Ulysses S. Grant appointed Shipman to the District Court for the District of Connecticut, filling the seat vacated by Shipman's cousin, William D. Shipman.[12] Had Judge Shipman not been appointed to the federal judiciary, he would have attempted to fulfill a longtime dream of obtaining a state judicial appointment.[13] In 1889, Governor Morgan Gardner Bulkeley of Connecticut offered Judge Shipman the nomination for the chief justiceship of the Connecticut Supreme Court of Errors, but Judge Shipman, "after careful consideration of the matter . . . declined the honor," citing his lifetime appointment as a federal district judge.[14]

While on the district court, Judge Shipman regularly lectured at Yale Law School on jurisdiction and procedure.[15] In 1884, he received an honorary LLD degree from Yale.[16]

The judiciary landscape changed in 1891, when the Evarts Act established nine courts of appeals.[17] The following year, President Benjamin Harrison appointed Judge Shipman to serve as a circuit judge on the Circuit Courts and the Court of Appeals for the Second Circuit.[18] He, William Wallace, and Emile Lacombe were the first three judges appointed to the Court of Appeals for the Second Circuit.[19] With Shipman's appointment, "geographic balance" was achieved: Judge Wallace was from upstate New York, Judge Lacombe from New York City, and Judge Shipman from Connecticut.[20] When Judge Shipman retired, the "Connecticut Seat" went to his successor in the district court, William Townsend.[21]

The early years of the newly minted Court of Appeals for the Second Circuit were dominated by admiralty cases.[22] Judge Shipman opposed Judge Wallace's proposal to render most decisions *per curiam*, although many decisions were either affirmances *per curiam* or oral affirmances in open court.[23] Signed opinions tended to be very short (fewer than two pages); dissents were uncommon and concurring opinions extraordinarily rare.[24] For example, in 1893, Judge Shipman's first full year on the bench, the court issued 70 signed opinions, 52 opinions *per curiam*, three dissents, and no concurring opinions.[25]

Over the course of his career, Judge Shipman authored more than 240 reported opinions. He attained "leadership in his profession" and became "an authority on the law of patents."[26] Most of his opinions were brief, although he wrote opinions of more than 200 pages on various patents that came before him.[27] As a circuit judge, he tried a variety of patent cases, ranging from "designs to machinery and from chemical processes to electricity."[28] He also dealt with patent cases on the Court of Appeals. In his most famous patent decision, he and Judge Lacombe upheld the validity of Thomas Edison's patent on the incandescent electric lamp in 1892, affirming their colleague,

Judge Wallace, who handled the case at the trial level in his capacity as a circuit judge.[29]

In *Westinghouse Electric Manufacturing Company v. New England Granite Company*, Judge Shipman ruled that a method of transmitting electricity to distant points by utilizing alternating currents was a patentable invention and held that an inventor should not be prevented from obtaining a patent for creating a method of electrical transmission where others had previously failed.[30] In *Le Republique Francaise v. Saratoga Vichy Springs Company*, Judge Shipman held that the Saratoga sparkling water company could no longer label their bottles "Vichy," which falsely implied that the water originated in Vichy, France, as opposed to Saratoga, New York.[31]

A contemporary account of Judge Shipman described him as "noticeable for an uncompromising honesty, bluntly spoken, which is tempered by great kindliness of nature."[32] It went on to state: "As a private citizen, lawyer and judge, he is universally respected and esteemed in Hartford, and wherever he goes, his name is a synonym for uprightness, fair-mindedness and wisdom."[33] His professional career was recounted as "increasingly useful and honorable, making his name known far beyond the boundaries of his residential city and native state."[34]

On a personal note, Judge Shipman was described as "actively and deeply interested in the religious life of his community, and [was] a prominent and much valued member of the Congregational Church."[35] As a member of a socially prominent Connecticut family, his family was said to be "peculiarly blessed and happy."[36]

Judge Shipman married Mary C. Robinson, of another socially distinguished Hartford family, on May 25, 1859 in the Robinsons' Hartford home.[37] They had five children: Frank Robinson, Arthur Leffingwell, Mary Deming, Thomas Leffingwell, and Henry Robinson. Frank attended Yale and became a minister and pastor of the South Church in Andover, Massachusetts; Arthur, after graduating from Yale Law School, was a founding member of Shipman & Goodwin, LLP; Mary became president of the Young Women's Christian Association and married Dr. Stephen B.L. Penrose, president of Whitman

College; and Henry became a professor of history at Princeton University.[38] In Hartford, Judge Shipman and his family lived on Charter Oak Place, a fashionable neighborhood, and his home still stands today.[39]

Judge Shipman served as a director of the Phoenix Mutual Life Insurance Company, the Aetna Insurance Company, the Travelers Insurance Company of Hartford, the Collins Company of Collinsville, and the Hartford City Gas Light Company.[40] Additionally, he was involved in a variety of philanthropic efforts in his community. He was president of the American College and Education Society, vice president and member of the executive committee of the Wadsworth Athenaeum, and a trustee of the Watkinson Library, the Hartford Grammar School, and the Watkinson Juvenile Asylum and Farm School.[41]

In 1901, Judge Shipman participated in Yale's celebration of "John Marshall Day," marking the one hundredth anniversary of Marshall's elevation to chief justice of the Supreme Court.[42] In his speech, Judge Shipman explained that "[t]he present working, efficient capacity of the Constitution, the strength of the power and dignity with which the Federal government now possesses, are due to Marshall's wisdom and foresight."[43] Judge Shipman invoked *Cohen v. Virginia*, which authorized the Supreme Court to review state supreme court criminal decisions when the defendant claimed a constitutional violation: "If a man of narrow theories, or of weak courage, had been Chief Justice when *Cohen v. Virginia* was decided, the country would have been a petty, third-rate power, with not much more vigor and capability of expansion than it had under the Articles of Confederation."[44]

Yale preserved correspondence between Judge Shipman and James Wesley Cooper, a prominent Congregational minister and fellow of Yale University. Judge Shipman wrote to Dr. Cooper from his chambers in Hartford and New York about their work together on the Prudential Committee at the American Board of Commissioners for Foreign Missions.[45] The board was the first organized missionary society in the United States, and by 1910, it had established 102 mission stations and a missionary staff of more than 600 in India, Ceylon, West Central Africa (Angola), South Africa and Rhodesia (Zimbabwe), Asiatic and European

Turkey, China, Japan, Micronesia, the Philippines, the "Papal Lands" of Mexico, Spain, and Austria.[46]

Judge Shipman served on the Second Circuit for ten years, before retiring in 1902, on account of ill health. On January 14, 1902, President Theodore Roosevelt accepted Judge Shipman's resignation, writing:

> I desire to express my very real regret that your impaired health has demanded this notion. Throughout your able and honorable judicial services for nearly thirty years as District Judge and Circuit Judge, you have borne an unblemished reputation, and your high personal worth and great professional capacity have redounded to the honor of your State and Circuit and of the whole country.[47]

Judge Shipman died in Hartford in 1906. He is buried at Cedar Hill Cemetery in Hartford, with his wife and children.[48]

Abigail Dwyer Maltz

* The reason for the plural "circuit courts" is explained in the Introduction at page lxii, note 37.

1. WILLIAM RICHARD CUTTER, GENEALOGICAL AND FAMILY HISTORY OF THE STATE OF CONNECTICUT (Vol. II, New York Lewis Historical Publishing Company) (1911).
2. *Id.*
3. *Id.* at 601.
4. *Id.*
5. *Id.* at 602.
6. *Id.*
7. *Id.* at 603.
8. *Id.*
9. MEN OF PROGRESS: BIOGRAPHICAL SKETCHES AND PORTRAITS OF LEADERS IN BUSINESS AND PROFESSIONAL LIFE IN AND OF THE STATE OF CONNECTICUT 159 (1898), https://archive.org/details/menofprogress00hern.
10. *Id.*
11. *Id.*
12. *See* José A. Cabranes, *Notes on the History of the Federal Court of Connecticut*, 57 CONN. B.J. 351, 364–65 (1983).
13. *See Judge Nathaniel Shipman of Connecticut*, N.Y. TIMES, Apr. 18, 1873 at 1.
14. *See A Judge Satisfied As He Is*, N.Y. TIMES, Mar. 3, 1889 at 14.
15. REPORT OF THE PRESIDENT OF YALE UNIVERSITY 43 (1887).
16. CUTTER, *supra* note 1, at 603.
17. Act of Mar. 3, 1891, ch. 517, § 2, 26 Stat. 826 (1891).

18. Pursuant to the Evarts Act, a "circuit judge" served on both the circuit courts (which had trial jurisdiction) and the court of appeals (which had appellate jurisdiction). That practice ended in 1911, when the circuit courts were abolished and the modern district courts were created. *See* Act of Mar. 3, 1891, ch. 517, 26 Stat. 826 (1891); Act of Mar. 3, 1911, ch. 231, §§ 24–115, 36 Stat. 1087, 1091–1130 (1911); ERWIN C. SURRENCY, HISTORY OF THE FEDERAL COURTS 88 (2002); *see also* Cabranes, *supra* note 12, at 364–65.

19. *See* JEFFREY B. MORRIS, FEDERAL JUSTICE IN THE SECOND CIRCUIT 94 (1987).

20. *Id.* at 96.

21. Cabranes, *Notes on the History of the Federal Court of Connecticut, supra* note 12, at 364–65.

22. MORRIS, *supra* note 19, at 94.

23. *Id.*

24. *Id.*

25. *Id.*

26. *Nathaniel Shipman,* CASE AND COMMENT, (vol. 5) May 1899, at 133.

27. *Id.*

28. *Id.*

29. Edison Elec. Light Co. v. United States Elec. Lighting Co., 52 F. 300 (2d Cir. 1892).

30. Special Supplement, *Colleagues for Justice: One Hundred Years of the United States Court of Appeals for the Second Circuit,* 65 ST. JOHN'S L. REV. 937, 943–44 (1991).

31. *Id.*

32. MEN OF PROGRESS, *supra* note 9, at 159.

33. *Id.*

34. *Id.*

35. *Id.*

36. *Id.*

37. CUTTER, *supra* note 1, at 603.

38. *Id.*

39. *Charter Oak Place*, Connecticut Historical Society: Museum & Library, http://emuseum.chs.org/emuseum/view/objects/asitem/Objects$004018418/0;jsessionid=E12CB8831CBFC1CE318C295D65301193?t:state:flow=bf15e725-eac2-40af-a434-48d13dfed2a9.

40. 19 THE NATIONAL CYCLOPAEDIA OF AMERICAN BIOGRAPHY, SHIPMAN, NATHANIEL 234–35 (1924) http://babel.hathitrust.org/cgi/pt?id=mdp.39015078229070;view=1up;seq=559.

41. *Id.*

42. *Celebration of John Marshall Day in Connecticut*, 10 Yale L. J. 5, 184 (1901).

43. *Id.*

44. *Id.*

45. Letters from Nathaniel Shipman to Dr. James Wesley Cooper (Sep. 30, 1893 and Apr. 25, 1898) (on file with the United States Courts Library for the Second Circuit).

46. *American Board of Commissioners for Foreign Missions Guide* (Harvard University Library, 2004). http://oasis.lib.harvard.edu/oasis/deliver/~hou01467.

47. Letter from President Theodore Roosevelt to Nathaniel Shipman (January 14, 1902).

48. FIND A GRAVE, Nathaniel Shipman, http://www.findagrave.com/cgi-bin/fg.cgi?page=gr&GRid=7372465.

## WILLIAM KNEELAND TOWNSEND
## 1848-1907

District Court for the District of Connecticut: 1892-1902
Circuit Courts for the Second Circuit: 1902-1907[*]
Court of Appeals for the Second Circuit: 1902-1907

He was "one of Yale's most brilliant sons."[1] William Kneeland Townsend was born in New Haven, Connecticut on June 12, 1848 to James Mulford Townsend and Maria Theresa Clark.[2] Townsend's "Connecticut roots were deep."[3] The Townsend family became a fixture in New Haven life; it "occupied a prominent place in the business, intellectual, political and professional life of the city."[4] Townsend continued that tradition. He attended Yale College, graduating with high honors in 1871, and then Yale Law School, where he won the Jewell and

Civil Law Composition prizes and, in 1874, graduated second in his class.[5] He was one of the first to enter Yale's graduate course in law, created in 1875, and became a doctor of civil law in 1880.[6]

Townsend had an active career in private practice, public service, and education in New Haven. He was associated with Simeon E. Baldwin, future governor and chief justice of the Supreme Court of Errors of Connecticut.[7] Townsend was a member of the New Haven Court of Common Council in 1880, and an alderman in 1881 and 1882.[8] In 1885, he and George Dutton Watrous started the firm of Townsend & Watrous, where Townsend practiced until his appointment to the federal bench.[9]

While in private practice, Townsend continued to serve the public and the students of Yale Law School. "[A]fter much excited campaigning," he was elected corporation counsel for the City of New Haven in 1889.[10] And beginning in 1881, he taught at Yale Law School, first as professor of pleading, and then in 1887 as the Edward J. Phelps Professor of Contracts and Commercial Law, and also taught admiralty.[11] His law partner described admiralty cases as Townsend's "chief delight."[12] Townsend imparted the humorous side of the law to his students: "'There is a branch of the law where there are no attorneys, no complaints, and no rules of evidence, but where all that a prudent ship owner has to do in order to make a profitable venture is to insure his ship heavily, and then negligently collide with and sink another vessel.'"[13] A contemporaneous article describing Townsend's teaching stated that he took "great pains to emphasize the more practical points and to develop each topic fully by the citation and discussion of leading and recent cases, and succeed[ed] to a remarkable degree, not only in guiding his classes to the knowledge of the facts, but also in arousing among all the students a hearty enthusiasm for their professional work."[14]

In addition to teaching, Townsend rewrote the Connecticut practice manual in 1881, which aided practitioners for decades. He also contributed to a volume celebrating Yale's bicentennial in 1901, penning "chapters on patents, copyrights, trademarks, and admiralty," which Judge José A. Cabranes has described as "keen synopses of case law and legal theory enlivened with literary gleanings and shrewd comments on practical matters."[15]

While Townsend's career thrived, he and his family were not immune to tragedy. Townsend married Mary Leavenworth Trowbridge in 1874 and they had three children, only one of whom outlived him.[16] His son, Winston Trowbridge Townsend, died in 1898 at the age of 19 while a freshman at Yale when his bicycle collided with a team of horses.[17] His daughter, Mary Leavenworth Townsend Day, died in Colorado in 1902, where she and her family had relocated for her health.[18] Judge Townsend's friend and mentor Chief Justice Baldwin stated that "Judge Townsend had his happy days. He had his sad days, too, and he had occasion for them. Only those who knew him best were aware how often his pleasant smile . . . marked an endeavor to hide from others a heavy heart."[19]

Judge Townsend's third child, George H. Townsend, graduated from Yale College in 1908 and was a successful businessman and sportsman; he was an "internationally known" speed boat racer in the 1930s,[20] an interest he apparently shared with his father. Judge Townsend, as a member of the St. Regis Yacht Club in the Adirondacks, had the "ambition to possess the fastest launch afloat on St. Regis waters" despite the fact that he was "already credited with having the fastest launch."[21] Judge Townsend did not restrict his outdoor activities to the east but went on big game hunting trips to the west and on his death was remembered as a "keen sportsman" who was "extremely fond of outdoor life."[22] One colleague remarked on Judge Townsend: "There never was a man who had a bigger power of enjoyment of men and things, of work and play, than he."[23]

In 1892, President Benjamin Harrison appointed Townsend to the District Court for the District of Connecticut, where he served until 1902.[24] There was some concern prior to his nomination that health problems would prevent him from serving, as he had recently departed for Florida "on account of unfavorable developments in his physical condition."[25] President Theodore Roosevelt appointed him to serve as a circuit judge on the Circuit Courts and the Court of Appeals for the Second Circuit in 1902, in which capacity Townsend served until his death in 1907.[26] A contemporary remarked that Judge Townsend's "judicial work was very congenial to him and he often spoke with keen pleasure of his close and cordial relationship with his brethren on the bench."[27] The elevation was not without its drawbacks; Judge Townsend "reluctantly" left teaching in 1902 when this new appointment demanded his presence in New York.[28]

On the bench, Judge Townsend became known as an expert in patents,[29] an area in which he had been "most distrustful of himself."[30] And he "was himself a student of mechanics, spending much time in designing and constructing motors."[31] Edmund Wetmore, a well-known New York attorney, commented that Judge Townsend "delighted to apply the laws of statutory interpretation and evidence to the profound questions of fact arising over disputed inventions and he brought to the solution of the problems presented, the keen insight of the man of science and the clear judgment of the man of law."[32] His patent decisions ran the gamut from women's clothing to cash register parts to electrical sockets to the duplication of sound records. In 1904, he described the progress of women's fashion, ultimately upholding a patent (held by a woman) for garment fasteners:

> But when, at the close of the nineteenth century, the decrees of fashion transformed the circular waist of nature, characteristic of that period, into the conventional downwardly curved slope in front, in the similitude of a girdle, or the pointed waist of the Elizabethan period, a new problem was presented to the designers of garment clasps. They must no longer fasten and support the garments at the waist line of nature, and in a natural position. They must now force the meeting edges of skirt band and belt, and incidentally of the skirt waist, down below the true waist, and 'draw and hold the front of the skirt downward' by an attachment so firmly fastened as to be adapted to the anatomy of a woman having a prominent abdomen, and to prevent the skirt and belt from rising above it.[33]

Judge Townsend concluded that in creating a new steel fastener, the patent holder had "exercised in a humble way . . . the faculty of invention . . . producing a practical fastener, superior to all the devices of the prior art."[34]

In another patent case, *Victor Talking Machine Company v. American Graphophone Company,*[35] Judge Townsend addressed a patent for use of hard rubber in the duplication of sound records, explaining that once an applicant for a patent accepts a more narrow patent than originally applied for, he is bound by that decision:

> [I]f, upon notice from the Patent Office that some portion of said territory is the property of another or is held in common by the public, he acquiesces in such statement and alters his boundaries accordingly, he is concluded by such abandonment, and cannot afterward undertake to define his territory by rolling stones, which he may move about across the lines of his original boundaries so as to appropriate property previously conceded to belong to others.[36]

In reaching that conclusion Judge Townsend noted the public interest "in securing due limitations upon the claim of an exclusive monopoly."[37]

Judge Townsend published two books: *The History of the American Law of Patents* and *Trademarks, Copyrights, and Admiralty.*[38] His expertise is further memorialized in *Two Centuries' Growth of American Law* (the volume prepared for Yale's bicentennial). Judge Townsend remarked on "'the inventive genius of the Yankee'" and, quite ahead of his time, called attention to the nearly six thousand patents held by female inventors.[39] In memorial proceedings held in the Second Circuit on his death, his patent decisions were described as "characterized by a luminous insight into the perplexities of these litigations, and a felicity of reasoning and expression which have rarely been equalled and never excelled by the decisions of any other judge."[40]

Judge Townsend died in 1907 and was buried in the Grove Street Cemetery near Yale Law School.[41] At Yale, Judge Townsend's death was marked by a series of commemorative addresses, which opened with the reading of a telegram in which Supreme Court Justice David Brewer said the following about Judge Townsend:

> Clear-headed, studious, faithful, he filled every place in life to which he was called. The light of every gathering, the pride of countless friends, he was of the noblest type of Yale graduates. A Yale commencement without him will seem like a rose bush without a bloom.[42]

Those sentiments were reiterated by all who spoke and throughout the legal community in New York and Connecticut. Chief Justice Simeon E. Baldwin of Connecticut remarked that "Billy Townsend was welcome everywhere" and "was a universal favorite" and "the life of every circle into which he entered."[43] Judge Townsend's former law partner, George Dutton Watrous, emphasized Townsend's "light-heartedness, his love for a joke or a good story, his fondness for all honest pleasures," while he was also "painstaking and industrious" in his work and "brilliant" at cross-examination.[44] He was described as a "successful teacher" and as a "popular teacher in the best sense."[45] An article about Yale law professors marked him as "the professor who comes nearest to the heart of the student" and described him as "eminently fitted" to the teaching of law.[46] Yale Law School created the William K. Townsend Professorship, later filled by Second Circuit Judge Ralph K. Winter.[47]

The bench and bar memorialized Judge Townsend with an equally fitting tribute, recalling the high regard for him in the legal community, his commitment to justice, and "his joyous spirit" and dedication in the face of adversity. Judge Lacombe closed the proceedings by noting Judge Townsend's "noble" choice to continue to work through his illness:

> And so he made his choice and we cannot say his choice was not the better, the wiser, and the happier one; yes, the happier one, for his was a happy life despite the pain and suffering and the burden of many heavy sorrows; because he had an absolutely dauntless courage that could shake off all adversities, because he had a supreme sunniness of temperament which was able to irradiate and illuminate the darkest surroundings; to win love as he

gave it and thus make his life so full of what is best and noblest that there seemed no space left in it for aught beside.[48]

Elizabeth Duwe

* The reason for the plural "circuit courts" is explained in the Introduction at page lxii.

1. *Notes*, THE NATION, June 6, 1907, at 521.

2. STILLMAN FOSTER KNEELAND, SEVEN CENTURIES OF THE KNEELAND FAMILY 77–79 (1897), https://archive.org/stream/sevencenturiesin1897knee#page/78/mode/2up.; MEN OF MARK IN CONNECTICUT, IDEALS OF AMERICAN LIFE TOLD IN BIOGRAPHIES AND AUTOBIOGRAPHIES OF EMINENT LIVING AMERICANS, VOL. II, 9–10 (Colonel N.G. Osborn, ed. 1904).

3. Special Supplement, *Colleagues For Justice: One Hundred Years of the United States Court of Appeals for the Second Circuit*, 65 ST. JOHN'S L. REV. 937, 944 (1991).

4. *Drake Sent to Oil Creek By Townsend*, THE TITUSVILLE (PA) HERALD, Aug. 22 1934, at 45.

5. KNEELAND, *supra* note 2, at 77–79.

6. Chief Justice Baldwin, Remarks at the Commemorative Addresses at the Yale Law School (June 18, 1907) *in* WILLIAM KNEELAND TOWNSEND, COMMEMORATIVE ADDRESSES 7 (1907).

7. MEN OF MARK IN CONNECTICUT, *supra* note 2, at 9. Baldwin was in private practice and a professor at Yale Law School before being appointed to the Connecticut Supreme Court of Errors in 1893. He became chief justice in 1907, serving until 1911, when at 70 he reached mandatory retirement age. Although deemed too old for the court, Baldwin ran for, and was elected governor of Connecticut. He was reelected to a second term in 1913. *See Many Tributes Paid*, N.Y. TIMES, Jan. 31, 1927, at 17.

8. MEN OF MARK IN CONNECTICUT, *supra* note 2, at 9.

9. Professor Watrous, Remarks at the Commemorative Addresses at the Yale Law School (June 18, 1907) *in* WILLIAM KNEELAND TOWNSEND, COMMEMORATIVE ADDRESSES 15-19 (1907).
at 15–19; *Watrous, George Dutton*, http://libguides.ctstatelibrary.org/c.php?g=281136&p=2000142#s-lg-box-6140380.

10. Professor Watrous, Remarks, *supra* note 9, at 18.

11. Chief Justice Baldwin, Remarks, *supra* note 6, at 8.

12. Professor Watrous, Remarks, *supra* note 9, at 17.

13. José A. Cabranes, *Notes on the History of the Federal Court of Connecticut*, 57 CONN. B.J. 351, 365 (1983) (quoting "Hotchpotch," The Yale Shingle (1893)).

14. Leonard M. Daggett, *The Yale Law School*, 1 GREEN BAG 239, 245 (1889).

15. Cabranes, *supra* note 13, at 366 (quoting "Hotchpotch," The Yale Shingle (1893)).

16. MEN OF MARK IN CONNECTICUT, *supra* note 2, at 10.

17. *Winston T. Townsend Killed: Son of the United States Judge in New Haven Run Down on His Wheel*, N.Y. TIMES, May 3, 1898, at 12.

18. *Obituary, Mrs. Mary Townsend Day*, NEW YORK HERALD, July 29, 1902, at 14.

19. Chief Justice Baldwin, Remarks, *supra* note 6, at 10.

20. Lincoln McCabe, *G.H. Townsend, Speedboat Racer: Ex-Manufacturer of Power Craft Dies—Put up Capital for Auto Gauge Concern*, N.Y. TIMES, Feb 20, 1957, at 33.

21. *With Adirondack Campers*, N.Y. TIMES, July 26, 1903, at 23.

22. *Death of Judge W. K. Townsend*, Forest and Stream, Vol. LXVIII. No. 23, June 8, 1907, at 897.

23. Thomas Thacher, Remarks at the Commemorative Addresses at the Yale Law School (June 18, 1907) *in* WILLIAM KNEELAND TOWNSEND, COMMEMORATIVE ADDRESSES 13 (1907).

24. FEDERAL JUDICIAL CENTER, Biographical Directory of Federal Judges, William Kneeland Townsend, http://www.fjc.gov/servlet/nGetInfo?jid=2402&cid=999&ctype=na&instate=na.

25. *Vacant District Judgeship: There Are Two Candidates for Justice Shipman's Seat*, N.Y. TIMES, Jan 5, 1892, at 8.

26. FEDERAL JUDICIAL CENTER, *supra* note 24. Pursuant to the Evarts Act of 1891, a "circuit judge" served on both the circuit court (which had trial jurisdiction) and the court of appeals (which had appellate jurisdiction). That practice ended in 1911, when the circuit courts were abolished and the modern district courts were created. *See* Act of Mar. 3, 1891, ch. 517, 26 Stat. 826 (1891); Act of Mar. 3, 1911, ch. 231, §§ 24–27, 36 Stat. 1087, 1091–94 (1911); ERWIN C. SURRENCY, HISTORY OF THE FEDERAL COURTS 88 (2002).

27. Professor Watrous, Remarks, *supra* note 9, at 20.

28. Chief Justice Baldwin, Remarks, *supra* note 6, at 9.

29. *Colleagues for Justice*, *supra* note 3, at 944–45.

30. Professor Watrous, Remarks, *supra* note 9, at 17.

31. *Mourn Judge Townsend*, N.Y. TIMES, June 4, 1907, at 7.

32. Edmund Whetmore, Remarks at a Special Session of the United States Court of Appeals for the Second Circuit, In Memoriam, Honorable William Kneeland Townsend 8 (June 7, 1907) (transcript on file with the United States Courts Library for the Second Circuit).

33. Lowrie v. H. A. Meldrim Co., 130 F. 886, 887 (2d Cir. 1904).

34. *Id.*

35. 151 F. 601 (2d Cir. 1907).

36. *Id.* at 605.

37. *Id.*

38. *Death of Judge W. K. Townsend*, *supra* note 22; 1 WHO WAS WHO IN AMERICA, 1897–1942, at 1249 (1943).

39. Cabranes, *supra* note 13, at 366–67 (quoting TWO CENTURIES' GROWTH OF AMERICAN LAW (1701–1901) (1901), 419–20).

40. Judge William J. Wallace, Remarks at a Special Session of the United States Court of Appeals for the Second Circuit, In Memoriam, Honorable William Kneeland Townsend 8 (June 7, 1907) (transcript on file with the United States Courts Library for the Second Circuit).

41. *Colleagues for Justice*, *supra* note 3, at 944.

42. Justice Brewer, telegram, read at the Commemorative Addresses at the Yale Law School (June 18, 1907) *in* WILLIAM KNEELAND TOWNSEND, COMMEMORATIVE ADDRESSES 4 (1907).

43. Chief Justice Baldwin, Remarks, *supra* note 6, at 6–7.

44. Professor Watrous, Remarks, *supra* note 9, at 16–17.

45. Chief Justice Baldwin, Remarks, *supra* note 6, at 8.

46. George E. Beers, Yale Law School, THE INTERCOLLEGIATE LAW JOURNAL, Vol. II, No. 3, Feb. 1893 (reprinted in Yale Law School Legal Scholarship repository).

47. Cabranes, *supra* note 13, at 367.

48. Judge Emile Lacombe, Remarks at a Special Session of the United States Court of Appeals for the Second Circuit, In Memoriam, Honorable William Kneeland Townsend 8 (June 7, 1907) (transcript on file with the United States Courts Library for the Second Circuit).

# ALFRED CONKLING COXE, SR.
# 1847-1923

District Court for the Northern District of New York:
1882-1902
Circuit Courts for the Second Circuit: 1902-1911*
Court of Appeals for the Second Circuit: 1902-1917

The reputation of a great jurist, like that of a great author, must be looked for in his published works. The lives of such men are eventless and common place from the point of view of the historian and biographer, but their beneficent influence upon the country fortunate to possess them is more lasting than that of the soldier or statesman whose life scintillates with political and martial electricity.

— Alfred Conkling Coxe, Sr.[1]

Born in Auburn, New York, on May 20, 1847, Alfred Conkling Coxe, Sr., was a product of two prominent New York families. His father, the Reverend Dr. Samuel Hansen Coxe, came from a line of Protestant clergymen (Alfred's uncle was an Episcopal bishop for western New York), and his paternal grandmother, Abiah Hyde (Cleveland) Cox,[2] was a distant cousin of the future Governor and President Grover Cleveland. His mother, Eliza (Conkling) Coxe, came from a family of politically connected lawyers and politicians. When Coxe was born, her father, Alfred Conkling, who had previously served in the U.S. House of Representatives, was entering his twenty-second year of service as the district judge for the Northern District of New York (the seat his grandson would later occupy). Her brother, Roscoe Conkling, was a U.S. senator from 1867 to 1881.[3]

Coxe graduated from Hamilton College in 1868, and was admitted to the New York bar that year. He was in private practice from 1868 to 1870 in Utica. In 1870, he joined the law firm Conkling, Holmes & Coxe, whose three partners were Coxe, his uncle Senator Roscoe Conkling, and a former New York state judge and U.S. congressman, Judge Sidney T. Holmes. Holmes left the firm in 1872 to travel, and was succeeded by former New York State Supreme Court Justice Scott Lord. Lord was elected to Congress in 1875, and the partnership dissolved. Coxe was a solo practitioner (retaining the firm's clients) until 1882. In 1880, Governor Alonzo B. Cornell appointed him manager of the Utica State Hospital.[4]

In 1878, he married Maryette Doolittle, the daughter of former New York State Supreme Court Justice Charles H. Doolittle, who had died after being swept out to sea off an ocean liner in 1874. Coxe and Doolittle had five children: three daughters, and two sons, one of whom, Alfred Conkling Coxe, Jr., would later become a district judge for the Southern District of New York.[5]

President Chester A. Arthur had a long history with Coxe's uncle, Senator Roscoe Conkling. Conkling headed New York's Republican political machine, and it was at Conkling's insistence that Arthur (a loyal supporter of the machine) was appointed collector of the New York Custom House. While Arthur was collector, there was a good deal of corruption.[6] It is unknown how much was with Arthur's knowledge, but it is known that he required employees to donate a portion of their salaries to the Republican Party.[7] When Arthur became Vice President in 1881, President James A. Garfield was engaged in a brutal battle with Senator Conkling and other senators over the degree of influence they would have over party patronage. During this confrontation, Conkling resigned his seat, with the plan of having the New York State legislature reelect him to show his political clout.[8] However, in the interim, Garfield was shot by a Republican who supported the Conkling-Arthur faction, the Stalwarts, over Garfield's faction, the Half-Breeds, and Arthur became President on September 19, 1881.[9] Despite his reputation as a machine politician and a Conkling creature, Arthur endorsed civil service reform in December 1881, something anathema to political machines.[10] When Conkling was not reelected to the Senate by the New York State legislature, Arthur nominated him to serve as an associate justice of the Supreme Court. Conkling was confirmed by the Senate, but he declined the position.[11] Conkling and Arthur's split over civil service reform had resulted in a mutual hatred, which was not thawed by the Supreme Court nomination.[12]

Nonetheless, on April 24, 1882, President Arthur nominated Conkling's nephew, Coxe, to become the district judge for the Northern District of New York, the position previously held by Coxe's grandfather.[13] Newspaper reactions to Coxe's nomination varied. The *Brooklyn Eagle* surmised that his appointment "is not only a compliment to his abilities, but a delicate recognition of the magic of his middle name."[14] By contrast, *The Saratoga Sentinel* wrote that "[n]o lawyer in the interior of the state is better known as an advocate and an orator."[15]

Coxe served for 20 years as a district judge. During that time, he lectured on admiralty and shipping law at Cornell Law School, and became an expert on patent law. In 1902, President Theodore Roosevelt nominated Coxe for a newly created judgeship on the Court of Appeals for the Second Circuit.16

Coxe's most famous decision was his dissent in a tort case. In *Cadillac Motor Car Company v. Johnson*, he wrote that a privity-of-contract requirement between an automaker and a car owner was archaic, and that if "the law be insufficient to provide a remedy for such negligence [as the manufacturer using a shoddy wheel] it is time that the law should be changed."17 He wrote that, under the majority's decision, there can be "an injury [which] may be occasioned by the grossest negligence and no one be legally responsible. Such a situation would, it seems to me, be a reproach to our jurisprudence."[18] One year later, Judge Benjamin N. Cardozo of the New York State Court of Appeals agreed, in *McPherson v. Buick Motor Company.* Cardozo's opinion noted Judge Coxe's "vigorous dissent."[19]

One of Coxe's final opinions involved a dispute between Thomas Edison's phonograph company and a popular singer of the day. Mary Carson Kidd, a soprano better known by her stage name, Mary Carson, sued Thomas A. Edison, Inc., for breach of contract.[20] Edison's company engaged in so-called "tone tests," where a singer would perform in front of an audience, and a phonograph would then play the same song so the audience could compare the two.[21] Kidd entered into a contract with Edison's agent, in which Edison would book her performances and pay her; she was forbidden from working for anybody other than Edison during the term of the contract. The principal issue on appeal was whether, under the contract, Kidd was to be paid her weekly salary in weeks when Edison did not book her services.[22] Coxe's opinion noted that, under Edison's interpretation of the contract, "[u]nless [Edison] chose to give her employment she was, so far as appears from this record, without the means of livelihood. Such a contract might be made, it is true, but the presumptions, conceding the sanity of the singer, are overwhelmingly against it."[23]

During his time on the bench, Judge Coxe wrote six law review articles. His writing style was straightforward and featured a caustic brand of humor. In comparing United States and United Kingdom law, he noted some striking similarities: discussing a British negligence case, he noted that a horse's "kick had produced all the familiar symptoms of permanent and progressive mental and physical disintegration, which happily, on both sides of the Atlantic, disappear soon after the verdict is affirmed on appeal."[24] In that same paper, he described the United States jury empaneling system: "Then begins a series of questions which proceed upon the basal assumption that though there may be honest and competent men in the box, the competent men are not honest, and the honest men are not competent."[25]

He wrote that law reporters "come with amazing rapidity and relentless regularity."[26] However, his prophesies failed him when analyzing one potential cure to the glut of law reports: when discussing the possibility that judges might render unpublished opinions, he claimed that it "is hardly to be expected that they will, [sua sponte], deprive the profession of the priceless fruits of their judicial labors."[27]

He wrote articles about procedure, history, and admiralty. However, his magnum opus was an article published in the *Yale Law Journal* entitled *Is Brief-Making a Lost Art?*[28] In it, he traced the inexorable decline of well-written briefs to two well-known scourges: the law's evolution from a science to a business, and that all-too-familiar technological innovation that dulls the lawyer's mind and destroys any tendencies toward clarity and concision, the human stenographer. In Coxe's estimation, the "brief of fifty years ago contained little that was counterfeit, it was the product of hard, intellectual labor, labor freely and enthusiastically bestowed, it was honest thought distilled and crystallized."[29] In discussing the evils of stenographers, he noted that the "dictated brief saves the time of the bar at the expense of the bench. The dictated opinion saves the time of the bench at the expense of the bar."[30] He wrote that the long, rambling briefs, all too common in his day, occasionally produced judicial opinions of similar characteristics, though he had the humility to admit he could be incorrect: "It is freely conceded that the foregoing has been written from the view point of the bench. It is altogether probable that a member of the bar would trace the true cause of the difficulty to long and rambling opinions so prevalent of late."[31]

As a jurist, Coxe was known for his work in patent and admiralty law. His expertise in patent law was such that, while he was sitting on the Court of Appeals for the Second Circuit, President William Howard Taft nominated him to be the presiding judge of the Court of Customs Appeals. President Taft withdrew the nomination a month and a half later.[32]

While serving on the Second Circuit, Judge Coxe gave Columbia Law School's 1904 commencement address and received an honorary LLD degree.[33] He retired in 1917 and died on April 22, 1923, in Hartford, Connecticut. His colleagues on the federal bench served as honorary pallbearers at his funeral on April 23.[34]

David Byowitz

* The reason for the plural "circuit courts" is explained in the Introduction at page lxii, note 37.

1. Alfred C. Coxe, *In Marshall's Day and Ours*, 3 COLUM. L. REV. 88, 88–89 (1903).

2. Dr. Samuel Hansen Coxe, Judge Coxe's father, changed the spelling of the family name from "Cox" to "Coxe."

3. 2 NEW YORK STATE MEN: BIOGRAPHIC STUDIES AND CHARACTER PORTRAITS 138 (Frederick S. Hills ed., 1910); BIOGRAPHICAL DICTIONARY OF THE FEDERAL JUDICIARY 59 (Gale Research Co. 1976).

4. *In Judge Wallace's Place* (Utica newspaper article from the Family Scrapbook, courtesy of Mayor Alfred C. Coxe)(copy on file with the United States Courts Library for the Second Circuit); NEW YORK STATE MEN, *supra* note 3, at 138; JUDGES OF THE UNITED STATES 87 (1978).

5. NEW YORK STATE MEN, *supra* note 3, at 138; 3 THE TWENTIETH CENTURY BIOGRAPHICAL DICTIONARY OF NOTABLE AMERICANS (R. Johnson ed., 1904).

6. THOMAS C. REEVES, GENTLEMAN BOSS: THE LIFE AND TIMES OF CHESTER ALAN ARTHUR 62–63 (1975).

7. *Id.* at 76–77.

8. NEIL MACNEIL & RICHARD A. BAKER, THE AMERICAN SENATE: AN INSIDER'S HISTORY 76 (Oxford Univ. Press 2013). The Seventeenth Amendment, providing for popular election of senators, had not yet been proposed; senators were elected by their state legislatures. U.S. CONST. art. I, § 3.

9. MACNEIL & BAKER, *supra* note 8, at 76.

10. *Id.*

11. *Id.* at 73–76; *see also* THE MILLER CTR, UNIV. OF VA., *American President: Chester A. Arthur (1829–1886)*, http://millercenter.org/president/arthur.

12. REEVES, *supra* note 6, at 244, 260–61.

13. FEDERAL JUDICIAL CENTER, Biographical Directory of Federal Judges, Alfred Conkling Coxe, Sr., http://www.fjc.gov/servlet/nGetInfo?jid=527&cid=999&ctype=na&instate=na.

14. *Political Comment*, ALBANY EVENING JOURNAL, May 4, 1882 (quoting the *Brooklyn Eagle*).

15. *Personals*, THE SARATOGA SENTINEL, Apr. 26, 1882.

16. FEDERAL JUDICIAL CENTER, *supra* note 13. For a history honoring Judge Coxe during his lifetime, see P.C.J. De Angelis, *Hon. Alfred C. Coxe*, 1 CORNELL L. J. 88, 88–90 (1894). Pursuant to the Evarts Act of 1891, a "circuit judge" served on both the circuit courts (which had trial jurisdiction) and the court of appeals (which had appellate jurisdiction). That practice ended in 1911, when the circuit courts were abolished and the modern district courts were created. *See* Act of Mar.

3, 1891, ch. 517, 26 Stat. 826 (1891); Act of Mar. 3, 1911, ch. 231, §§ 24–115, 36 Stat. 1087, 1091–130 (1911); ERWIN C. SURRENCY, HISTORY OF THE FEDERAL COURTS 88 (2002).

17. 221 F. 801, 805 (2d Cir. 1915).

18. *Id.*

19. 111 N.E. 1050, 1054 (N.Y. 1916).

20. Thomas A. Edison, Inc. v. Kidd, 242 F. 923, 923 (2d Cir. 1917).

21. *Id.*

22. The principal issue on appeal was different from the main issue raised before the district court. The district court, in a motion to set aside the jury's verdict in Kidd's favor, dealt exclusively with the subject of whether Fuller had the implied authority to bind Edison to pay Kidd. *See* Kidd v. Thomas A. Edison, Inc., 239 F. 405, 406 (S.D.N.Y. 1917) (L. Hand, J.).

23. *Thomas A. Edison, Inc.*, 242 F. at 924.

24. Alfred C. Coxe, *The Trials of Jury Trials*, 1 COLUM. L. REV. 286, 286 (1901).

25. *Id.* at 287.

26. *In Marshall's Day and Ours*, *supra* note 1, at 105.

27. *Id.*; ADMIN. OFFICE OF THE U.S. COURTS, REPORT OF THE PROCEEDINGS OF THE JUDICIAL CONFERENCE OF THE UNITED STATES MARCH 16-17, 1964, 11 (1964) ("Resolved: That the judges of the courts of appeals and the district courts authorize the publication of only those opinions which are of general precedential value and that opinions authorized to be published be succinct.").

28. Alfred C. Coxe, *Is Brief-Making a Lost Art?*, 17 YALE L. J. 413, 414–15 (1908).

29. *Id.* at 415.

30. *Id.* at 420.

31. *Id.* at 421.

32. FEDERAL JUDICIAL CENTER, *supra* note 13; *Taft Chooses Men for Customs Court*, N.Y. TIMES, Jan. 5, 1910, at 18.

33. Alfred C. Coxe, *Overproduction of Law*, 6 COLUM. L. REV. 102, 102 (1906); JUDGES OF THE UNITED STATES, *supra* note 4, at 87.

34. *Judge Coxe's Funeral Today*, N.Y. TIMES, Apr. 18, 1923, at 2.

# HENRY GALBRAITH WARD
## 1851-1933

Circuit Courts for the Second Circuit: 1907-1911[*]
Court of Appeals for the Second Circuit: 1907-1924

Henry Galbraith Ward was "handsome in appearance, graceful in bearing, gracious in manner, magnanimous always and a man who held the highest ideals and lived up to them," according to a lawyer who knew him.[1] Ward was born on April 19, 1851, in New York City to the Reverend Henry Dana and Charlotte Galbraith Ward.[2] Ward's great-grandfather was Artemas Ward, President George Washington's first major general, known for commanding the continental forces at the Battle of Bunker Hill and later serving in the Continental Congress.[3]

Ward studied at the Anthon School and an Episcopal academy in Philadelphia before attending the University of Pennsylvania.[4] As a student, he was awarded the junior philosophical prize and shared the senior Greek prize.[5] He was also the moderator of the Philomathean Society, one of the oldest collegiate literary societies in the United States.[6] He graduated with high honors and BA and MA degrees in 1870.[7] The University of Pennsylvania later awarded him an honorary LLD degree in 1917.[8]

Following his study of law in the Philadelphia office of Richard C. McMurtrie, Ward was admitted to the Pennsylvania bar in 1873.[9] He then worked in private practice in Philadelphia for several years and became a partner of the firm Biddle & Ward.[10] His practice focused primarily on admiralty law; his peers described him as the "Bayard of the Admiralty Bar."[11] He was also counsel for the Pennsylvania Railroad.[12] In addition to his practice, Ward served as vice president and then president of the Philadelphia Law Academy.[13]

In 1883, Ward moved to Biddle & Ward's New York City office, where he continued to specialize in corporate, railroad, and maritime law.[14] Charles Merrill Hough was also a partner in the firm's New York City office and would later serve on the bench alongside Ward.[15] Ward and Hough maintained a close relationship; one lawyer recalled that Hough, who first met Ward in Philadelphia, had "said that there had been one attraction only which had brought him to New York and that attraction was Henry Galbraith Ward."[16]

On August 13, 1891, Ward married Mabel Marquand at Linden Gate, her father's Newport, Rhode Island mansion.[17] *The New York Times* reported the details of their wedding, "the first society event of the season," including the bride's attire, the many varieties of flowers used in the décor, and notable attendees.[18] After the wedding, the couple took a honeymoon in Europe.[19] Their first son, Galbraith Ward, was born on August 9, 1892, followed by a second son, Marquand Ward, born on December 9, 1894. Less than two years after Marquand's birth, Mabel passed away suddenly at age 36 on November 23, 1896.[20] Both of Ward's sons served in World War I and passed away within two months of each other in France: Marquand was killed in action on October 18, 1918; Galbraith died of pneumonia on December 17.[21]

Ward left private practice when, on May 18, 1907, President Theodore Roosevelt gave him a recess appointment to serve as a circuit judge on the Circuit Courts and the Court of Appeals for the Second Circuit.[22] It was reported that Ward "had the practically unanimous [e]ndorsement of the bench and bar" and of Senators Thomas C. Platt and Chauncey M. Depew of New York.[23] Later in 1907, President Roosevelt permanently appointed Judge Ward to the court.[24]

While on the bench, Judge Ward authored the opinion in one of the first cases to construe the Food and Drug Act of 1906.[25] The defendants were convicted of misbranding, in violation of the act, for selling cans of sesame oil labeled as "Imported Salad Oil Morel Brand."[26] According to the indictment, "salad oil" meant olive oil and so the defendants' label deceived consumers.[27] The court reversed their convictions.[28] It ruled that a defendant's intent was immaterial to a finding of criminal liability under the act; however, the defendants in this case were entitled to a directed verdict in their favor because the evidence did not justify the conclusion that the cans were misbranded.[29] The lower court erred by not permitting dealers of "salad oil" not made from olives to testify as to the meaning of "salad oil" and to whether their customers had complained of being misled.[30]

Judge Ward also wrote an opinion holding that a person of Indian Parsee origin was a "free white person" within the meaning of the naturalization laws and thus eligible to become a United States citizen.[31] He determined that the plain meaning of "free white persons" would allow any member of the Caucasian race to naturalize.[32] The Second Circuit reversed course two decades later after intervening decisions of the Supreme Court took the view that the phrase "free white person" should be interpreted according to its popular meaning.[33]

Judge Ward was the "senior circuit judge,"[34] the equivalent of chief judge, from 1917 until he assumed senior status on June 30, 1921.[35] He retired on October 31, 1924.[36] Off the bench, Judge Ward was active in the Sons of the Revolution, Phi Beta Kappa, the University and Century Clubs of New York, and the University Club of Philadelphia.[37]

Judge Ward died on the night of August 23, 1933 in his nephew's Shelter Island summer home.[38] His body was found in a partially full bathtub; the coroner determined that his death was accidental.[39] Eerily, when court began the next day at the federal post office and courthouse building, its superintendent reported that an oil portrait of Judge Ward had fallen in the night and was found on the floor of the courtroom where it had been hung.[40] Circuit and district judges and former associates from his time in private practice attended the funeral at St. James Episcopal Church on the upper east side.[41] Judge Ward was buried in Greenwood Cemetery in Brooklyn.[42]

Emer M. Stack

* The reason for the plural "circuit courts" is explained in the Introduction at page lxii, note 37.

1. Charles S. Haight, *Memorial of Honorable Henry Galbraith Ward*, *in* MAR. LAW ASS'N OF THE UNITED STATES, at 1976 (Doc. No. 192) (Mar. 1934).

2. *H.G. Ward Dead; Once Jurist Here*, N.Y. TIMES, Aug. 25, 1933, at 15.

3. *General Ward*, GEN. ARTEMAS WARD HOUSE MUSEUM, HARVARD UNIV., http://wardhouse.harvard.edu/general-ward.

4. *Henry G. Ward, Former Circuit Judge, Is Dead*, N.Y. HERALD TRIB., Aug. 25, 1933, at 15.

5. *H.G. Ward for Judge*, N.Y. TIMES, May 24, 1907, at 9.

6. *Id.*; THE PHILOMATHEAN SOC'Y, http://www.philomathean.org/about/.

7. Haight, *supra* note 1, at 1975.

8. *Henry G. Ward, Former Circuit Judge, Is Dead*, *supra* note 4.

9. Haight, *supra* note 1, at 1975.

10. *Id.*

11. *Id.* at 1976.

12. *A Wedding in Newport*, N.Y. HERALD TRIB., Aug. 14, 1891, at 6.

13. *H.G. Ward for Judge*, *supra* note 5.

14. Haight, *supra* note 1, at 1975; *see* Special Supplement, *Colleagues for Justice: One Hundred Years of the United States Court of Appeals for the Second Circuit,* 65 ST. JOHN'S L. REV. 937, 946 (1991).

15. George Wharton Pepper, *Transitional Years in the University of Pennsylvania Law School*, 101 U. PA. L. REV. 169, 170 (1952).

16. Haight, *supra* note 1, at 1978.

17. *Married Amid Flowers*, N.Y. TIMES, Aug. 14, 1891, at 1.

18. *Id.*

19. *See id.*

20. *Died*, N.Y. TIMES, Nov. 25, 1896, at 5.

21. *Galbraith Ward '15, Marquand Ward '17*, THE PRINCETON ALUMNI WKLY., Apr. 2, 1919, at 511–12.

22. *H.G. Ward for Judge. supra* note 5; FEDERAL JUDICIAL CENTER, Biographical Directory of Federal Judges, Henry Galbraith Ward, http://www.fjc.gov/servlet/nGetInfo?jid=2497&cid=999&ctype=na&instate=na. Pursuant to the Evarts Act of 1891, a "circuit judge" served on both the circuit courts (which had trial jurisdiction) and the court of appeals (which had appellate jurisdiction).

*See* Act of Mar. 3, 1891, ch. 517, §§ 2, 4, 7, 26 Stat. 826, 826, 827, 828. That practice ended in 1911, when the circuit courts were abolished and the modern district courts were created. Act of Mar. 3, 1911, ch. 231, §§ 24–115, 36 Stat. 1087, 1091–30; ERWIN C. SURRENCY, HISTORY OF THE FEDERAL COURTS 88 (2002).

23. *H.G. Ward for Judge*, *supra* note 5.

24. FEDERAL JUDICIAL CENTER, *supra* note 22.

25. Von Bremen v. United States, 192 F. 904 (2d Cir. 1912); *Colleagues for Justice*, *supra* note 14, at 946.

26. *Von Bremen*, 192 F. at 905.

27. *Id.*

28. *Id.* at 906.

29. *Id.*

30. *Id.*

31. United States v. Balsara, 180 F. 694, 696 (2d Cir. 1910).

32. *See id.*

33. Wadia v. United States, 101 F.2d 7, 8–9 (2d Cir. 1939) (citing Ozawa v. United States, 260 U.S. 178 (1922)).

34. The presiding judge was known as the "senior circuit judge" until 1948, when the term "chief judge" was established under 28 U.S.C. § 45. The term was adopted "in recognition of the great increase in administrative duties of such judge." REPORT FROM THE HOUSE COMM. ON THE JUDICIARY, TO ACCOMPANY H.R. 3214, H.R. 308, 80th CONG., 1st Sess., A6 (1947); *see also* Act of June 25, 1948, ch. 646, § 45(a) 62 Stat. 869, 871 ("The circuit judge senior in commission shall be the chief judge of the circuit.").

35. *Colleagues for Justice*, *supra* note 14, at 939, 946; FEDERAL JUDICIAL CENTER, *supra* note 22.

36. FEDERAL JUDICIAL CENTER, *supra* note 22.

37. *Sons of Revolution Pick Olyphant as President,* N.Y. HERALD TRIB., Dec. 5, 1923, at 24; *Henry G. Ward, Former Circuit Judge, Is Dead*, *supra* note 4.

38. *Tributes are Paid to Henry G. Ward*, N.Y. TIMES, Aug. 27, 1933, at 30.

39. *H.G. Ward Dead; Once Jurist Here*, *supra* note 2.

40. *Id.*

41. *Tributes are Paid to Henry G. Ward*, *supra* note 38.

42. *Id.*

# WALTER CHADWICK NOYES
# 1865-1926

Circuit Courts for the Second Circuit: 1907-1913*
Court of Appeals for the Second Circuit: 1907-1913

Judge Walter Chadwick Noyes, "a natural leader of men but with no inclination towards assertions of leadership," led a life "of steady and unobtrusive usefulness."[1] He was born in Lyme, Connecticut, on August 8, 1865,[2] the only child of Richard Noyes and Catherine DeWolf Chadwick.[3] Richard Noyes was a farmer who lived all of his life in the town now known as Old Lyme.[4]

The Noyes family was one of the oldest and most prominent families in Connecticut, and remains so today.[5] Another of Noyes's ancestors, the Reverend Moses Noyes, was the minister of the church established by Lyme's first settlers in 1666.[6] Moses Noyes's wife, Ruth Pickett, was the great-granddaughter of Elder

William Brewster, one of the original Mayflower passengers and a Plymouth colony preacher.[7] In lieu of a salary, the town of Old Lyme granted Moses Noyes a tract of land as compensation for his ministerial services.[8] The Noyes family passed down this land for generations,[9] and Noyes grew up in a home built by his great-grandfather on part of Moses Noyes's original land grant.[10] The house passed to Noyes after his mother died in 1904, and it is still intact today.[11] Although Noyes moved his family to New York after his federal judicial appointment, he continued to maintain the ancestral home as a country residence.[12] It was known as "Indian Rock Farms."[13]

Noyes's mother, Catherine DeWolf Chadwick, also belonged to a well-known and established New England family. The Chadwicks had lived in Lyme since at least 1767,[14] and Catherine's father was Daniel Chadwick, a prominent ship captain.[15]

Noyes traced his lineage back to England.[16] The Reverend Moses Noyes himself, though born in Massachusetts, was educated at Oxford and known as a "man of mark" and "extensive learning."[17] Moses Noyes's father was also a minister and emigrated from England in 1634.[18] Noyes's ancestors also included doctors, judges, and Army officers.[19] He was the grand-nephew of Morrison R. Waite, the seventh chief justice of the Supreme Court from 1874 to 1888.[20]

For his early education, Walter Chadwick Noyes attended private schools in Connecticut and a preparatory school in Gouverner, New York.[21] He attended Cornell University for one year, from 1884 to 1885.[22] Noyes read law with Judge Daniel Chadwick and at the law office of Samuel Parks, both located in New London, Connecticut.[23] He studied under Judge Augustus Brandegee as well, who was a leading Connecticut politician and lawyer.[24]

After his admission to the New London County bar in 1886,[25] Noyes embarked on an illustrious legal and judicial career. For several years, he worked at Judge Brandegee's New London firm, renamed Brandegee, Noyes & Brandegee.[26] In 1895, Noyes was elected to the Court of Common Pleas of New London County, where he served for twelve years.[27] That same year he married Luella Shapely Armstrong. They had three daughters, Marian Armstrong, Catherine Chadwick, and Ruth Brewster.[28]

While serving as a state court judge, Judge Noyes developed an expertise in both corporate and railroad law. In 1902, he published *A Treatise on the Law of Intercorporate Relations.*[29] The treatise thoroughly covered a broad range of topics in corporate law, including corporate sales, leases, consolidations, and stockholding and control.[30] It also analyzed the leading cases and statutes in corporate law, focusing on public policy.[31] The publication was very successful: its first edition sold out within ten days after publication,[32] and by 1905 it had gone through three editions and received high praise from judges, lawyers, and the press. Several law journals reviewed the treatise and uniformly praised it as a welcome addition to a previously undeveloped, but rapidly growing, area of the law.[33]

In 1904, Noyes became president of the New London Northern Railroad Company.[34] The following year Noyes published a book entitled *American Railroad Rates*, addressing the legal and economic aspects of railroad transportation.[35] The work compared American and foreign railroad rates, discussing government regulation of those rates.[36] Noyes asserted that there was a need for more government railroad regulation and that the Interstate Commerce Commission should make the rates[37]—an interesting position, given that he was president of a major railroad company. *American Railroad Rates* was also met with great success, although praise for the book was more tempered than for *A Treatise on the Law of Intercorporate Relations.* One law review asserted that "[n]o book ever appeared at a more opportune time" and that it addressed a question of "burning importance,"[38] while another stated that the book addressed the topic fairly, although it was "easy to see that the author's views [were] colored by his railroad interests."[39]

In 1907, President Theodore Roosevelt appointed Judge Noyes to serve as a circuit judge on the Circuit Courts and the Court of Appeals for the Second Circuit.[40]

During his tenure on the federal bench, Judge Noyes authored 166 appellate opinions[41] and participated in several important cases, including proceedings against the American Tobacco Company and the Standard Oil Company, and several patent law cases.[42] He also participated in the "Patten cotton corner case," which addressed whether members of a cotton syndicate violated antitrust laws by "running a corner" on the stock exchange.[43] Specifically, the defendants were accused of conspiring to monopolize the cotton trade across several states.[44] Judge Noyes found no violation (with certain exceptions), but the Supreme Court reversed.[45] While serving as a federal judge, Noyes also represented the United States at the third international conference on maritime law in Brussels, where two treaties were negotiated.[46]

Judge Noyes resigned from the bench in 1913, at the age of 47, announcing that his judicial salary of $7,000 was insufficient to support his family and educate his children.[47] His resignation drew nationwide attention,[48] and a flurry of commentary followed discussing the low federal judicial salaries.[49] One article vilified the high salaries of U.S. ambassadors to other nations who, "with large private fortunes, have set a bad example of living like princes," while federal judges were not paid a living wage.[50] The author also commented that the elected state judges in New York were paid more than twice what Judge Noyes was paid, and that "very few, if any, of them [were] his equals in capacity and learning."[51]

Judge Noyes's legal career did not wane with his resignation from the bench. He opened a law firm in New York City focusing on corporate law.[52] While in private practice, Judge Noyes was also general counsel of the Delaware & Hudson Company, where he used his expertise in corporate and railroad law.[53] He also administered several important receiverships, including those for the South American Securities Company, the American Real Estate Company, and the Chicago, Rock Island, & Pacific Railroad Company.[54]

Judge Noyes's private law practice was lucrative and brought him before the Supreme Court several times.[55] His most famous Supreme Court case was *North German Lloyd v. Guaranty Trust Company of New York*, more commonly known as *The Kronprinzessin Cecilie*, in which he represented the German owners of a vessel that failed to complete a voyage on the eve of World War I.[56]

The German steamship had left New York on July 28, 1914, to transport kegs of gold to Plymouth, England, and Cherbourg, France, with an eventual destination of Bremerhaven, Germany.[57] On July 31, when the steamship was about 1,070 miles from England, the ship's captain knew, based on several wireless messages, "that war had been declared by Austria against Servia [*sic*], that Germany had declined a proposal by Sir Edward Grey for a conference of ambassadors in London," that the countries were militarizing, and "that business was practically suspended on the London Stock Exchange."[58] At that point, the captain promptly turned the steamship around and returned to the United States, fearing that the German-owned vessel would be seized as a prize of war once it reached England.[59] The German Emperor declared a state of war the same day.[60] The Second Circuit found that the German defendants were liable, but Judge Noyes successfully persuaded the Supreme Court to reverse.[61] Justice Holmes delivered the opinion of the Court, finding that the captain's actions fell within an implied exception to the vessel's bill of lading, which allowed the captain to prudently judge that war would soon break out and that he should turn around to avoid seizure by the English government.[62] Judge Noyes argued the case only ten days after the United States had declared war on Germany.[63]

Judge Noyes died at age sixty-one, after a three-month-long illness, on Saturday, June 12, 1926, in his home on Fifth Avenue in Manhattan.[64] His family arranged simple funeral services in both his New York and Connecticut residences.[65] Several judges attended, including Judge Learned Hand.[66] He was buried in a family plot at Old Lyme,[67] in what is now known as Duck River Cemetery.[68]

Emily Seiderman

* The reason for the plural "circuit courts" is explained in the Introduction at page lxii, note 37.

1. H.T. Newcomb, *Memorial of Walter C. Noyes*, *in* THE ASSOCIATION OF THE BAR OF THE CITY OF NEW YORK YEARBOOK 1928, at 413, 416 (1928).

2. 2 HENRY E. NOYES & HARRIETTE E. NOYES, GENEALOGICAL RECORD OF SOME OF THE NOYES DESCENDANTS OF JAMES, NICHOLAS AND PETER NOYES 169 (1904).

3. *Id.*

4. GENEALOGICAL AND BIOGRAPHICAL RECORD OF NEW LONDON COUNTY CONTAINING BIOGRAPHICAL SKETCHES OF PROMINENT AND REPRESENTATIVE CITIZENS AND GENEALOGICAL RECORDS OF MANY OF THE EARLY SETTLED FAMILIES 718 (1905).

5. *See Local History: Collections*, OLD LYME PHOEBE GRIFFIN NOYES LIBRARY, http://www.oldlyme.lioninc.org/local-history/collections/ (listing the Noyes family as one of the Old Lyme and Connecticut "families of note").

6. GENEALOGICAL AND BIOGRAPHICAL RECORD OF NEW LONDON COUNTY, *supra* note 4, at 718 (noting that Judge Walter Chadwick Noyes was the "sixth lineal descendant" of the Reverend Moses Noyes).

7. *Id.* at 719.

8. 13 AM. COUNCIL OF LEARNED SOC'YS, DICTIONARY OF AMERICAN BIOGRAPHY 591 (Dumas Malone ed., 1984).

9. GENEALOGICAL AND BIOGRAPHICAL RECORD OF NEW LONDON COUNTY, *supra* note 4, at 719.

10. Record History of 105 Lyme Street, http://www.oldlymehistoricalsociety.org (transcript on file with the United States Courts Library for the Second Circuit). *See also* GENEALOGICAL AND BIOGRAPHICAL RECORD OF NEW LONDON COUNTY, *supra* note 3, at 719.

11. GENEALOGICAL AND BIOGRAPHICAL RECORD OF NEW LONDON COUNTY, *supra* note 4, at 719; *see also* Record History of 105 Lyme Street, *supra* note 10.

12. *See Ex-Federal Judge Walter Noyes Dies*, N.Y. TIMES, June 14, 1926, at 19; *see also* AM. COUNCIL OF LEARNED SOC'YS, *supra* note 8, at 592.

13. AM. COUNCIL OF LEARNED SOC'YS, *supra* note 8, at 592.

14. *History of Goberis Chadwick Preserve*, OLD LYME LAND TRUST, http://oldlymelandtrust.org/03i_goberis.html.

15. *Id.*

16. GENEALOGICAL AND BIOGRAPHICAL RECORD OF NEW LONDON COUNTY, *supra* note 4, at 719.

17. *Id.*

18. *Id.*

19. *Id.*; *see also* NOYES & NOYES, *supra* note 2, at 158–71 (listing the descendants of Reverend Moses Noyes).

20. *See* AM. COUNCIL OF LEARNED SOC'YS, *supra* note 8, at 591; FEDERAL JUDICIAL CENTER, Biographical Directory of Federal Judges, Morrison Remick Waite, http://www.fjc.gov/servlet/nGetInfo?jid=2474&cid=0&ctype=sc&instate=na&highlight=null.

21. AM. COUNCIL OF LEARNED SOC'YS, *supra* note 8, at 591; GENEALOGICAL AND BIOGRAPHICAL RECORD OF NEW LONDON COUNTY, *supra* note 4, at 719.

22. AM. COUNCIL OF LEARNED SOC'YS, *supra* note 8, at 591.

23. *Id.*; *see also* GENEALOGICAL AND BIOGRAPHICAL RECORD OF NEW LONDON COUNTY, *supra* note 4, at 719.

24. *Id.*

25. 1 A MODERN HISTORY OF NEW LONDON COUNTY, CONNECTICUT 337 (Benjamin Tinkham Marshall ed., 1922).

26. AM. COUNCIL OF LEARNED SOC'YS, *supra* note 8, at 591.

27. *Id.*

28. GENEALOGICAL AND BIOGRAPHICAL RECORD OF NEW LONDON COUNTY, *supra* note 4, at 719; *Rites Are Held for Noyes: Former Associates on Bench Attend Simple Services Here*, N.Y. TIMES, June 16, 1926, at 25.

29. GENEALOGICAL AND BIOGRAPHICAL RECORD OF NEW LONDON COUNTY, *supra* note 4, at 719.

30. *Review: A Treatise on the Law of Intercorporate Relations by Walter Chadwick Noyes*, 16 HARV. L. REV. 314, 315 (1903).

31. *Id.*

32. *Review: A Treatise on the Law of Intercorporate Relations by Walter Chadwick Noyes*, 12 YALE L.J. 255, 255 (1903).

33. *See, e.g.*, *Review: A Treatise on the Law of Intercorporate Relations by Walter Chadwick Noyes*, *supra* note 30, at 314–15; *Review: A Treatise on the Law of Intercorporate Relations by Walter Chadwick Noyes*, *supra* note 32, at 255–56; H. L. Wilgus, *Review: A Treatise on the Law of Intercorporate Relations by Walter Chadwick Noyes*, 1 MICH. L. REV. 243, 243–48 (1903).

34. GENEALOGICAL AND BIOGRAPHICAL RECORD OF NEW LONDON COUNTY, *supra* note 4, at 719.

35. WALTER CHADWICK NOYES, AMERICAN RAILROAD RATES (1905).

36. *Review: American Railroad Rates by Walter Chadwick Noyes*, 11 VA. L. REG. 703, 703 (1905).

37. *Id.*

38. *Id.*

39. *Review: American Railroad Rates by Walter Chadwick Noyes*, 4 MICH. L. REV. 322 (1906).

40. FEDERAL JUDICIAL CENTER, Biographical Directory of Federal Judges, Walter Chadwick Noyes, http://www.fjc.gov/servlet/nGetInfo?jid=1788&cid=999&ctype=na&instate=na. Pursuant to the Evarts Act of 1891, a "circuit judge" served on both the circuit courts (which had trial jurisdiction) and the court of appeals (which had appellate jurisdiction). That practice ended in 1911, when the circuit courts were abolished and the modern district courts were created. *See* Act of Mar. 3, 1891, ch. 517, 26 Stat. 826; Act of Mar. 3, 1911, ch. 231, §§ 24–115, 36 Stat. 1087, 1091–30; ERWIN C. SURRENCY, HISTORY OF THE FEDERAL COURTS 88 (2002).

41. Special Supplement: *Colleagues for Justice: One Hundred Years of the United States Court of Appeals for the Second Circuit*, 65 ST. JOHN'S L. REV. 937, 946–47 (1991).

42. AM. COUNCIL OF LEARNED SOC'YS, *supra* note 8, at 591; *Noyes Quits Bench: Salary Too Small*, N.Y. TIMES, June 6, 1913, at 1; *Supreme Court's Decision in Tobacco Case Makes Circuit Court Jurists and the Arbiters of That Corporation's Destiny—for the First Time a Court is to Decide What a Company Must Do in Order to Become a "Good Trust,"* N.Y. TIMES, June 4, 1911.

43. *Cotton Corner Case: Judge Noyes Allows Exceptions, But Denies Motion to Quash Indictment*, N.Y. TIMES, Apr. 13, 1911, at 6.

44. *Patten Cotton Corner is Held To be Clearly Against the Law*, WALL ST. J., Jan. 7, 1913, at 2.

45. *Id.*

46. AM. COUNCIL OF LEARNED SOC'YS, *supra* note 8, at 591.

47. *Noyes Quits Bench: Salary Too Small*, *supra* note 42.

48. AM. COUNCIL OF LEARNED SOC'YS, *supra* note 8, at 591.

49. *Id.*; *see also The Loss of a Good Judge*, N.Y. TIMES, June 7, 1913, at 10.

50. *The Loss of a Good Judge*, *supra* note 49.

51. *Id.*

52. AM. COUNCIL OF LEARNED SOC'YS, *supra* note 8, at 591.

53. *Id.*

54. *Ex-Federal Judge Walter Noyes Dies*, *supra* note 12.

55. *Id.*

56. 244 U.S. 12 (1917).

57. *Id.* at 20; *see also Kronprinzessin Cecilie Returns with $10,600,000 Gold*, N.Y. TIMES, Aug, 5, 1914, at 1.

58. *N. German Lloyd*, 244 U.S. at 21.

59. *Id.*

60. *Id.*

61. *Colleagues for Justice*, *supra* note 41, at 947.

62. *N. German Lloyd*, 244 U.S. at 21.

63. *Colleagues for Justice*, *supra* note 41, at 947.

64. *Ex-Federal Judge Walter Noyes Dies*, *supra* note 12; *Biographical Directory of Federal Judges: Noyes, Walter Chadwick*, *supra* note 40.

65. *Rites Are Held for Noyes: Former Associates on Bench Attend Simple Services Here*, *supra* note 28.

66. *Id.*

67. *Id.*

68. FIND A GRAVE, Walter Chadwick Noyes, http://www.findagrave.com/cgi-bin/fg.cgi?page=gsr&GSfn=Walter&GSmn=Chadwick&GSln=Noyes&GSbyrel=in&GSby=1865&GSdyrel=in&GSdy=1926&GScntry=4&GSst=8&GSgrid=&df=all&GSob=n.

# MARTIN AUGUSTINE KNAPP
# 1843-1923

Commerce Court: 1910-1913
Court of Appeals for the Second Circuit: 1910[1]-1916
Court of Appeals for the Fourth Circuit: 1916-1923

"[I]ntegrity, tolerance, and persistent effort for others."[2] Such were the attributes identified by Judge Martin A. Knapp as necessary for those who wished to attain the "highest success."[3] By all accounts, Knapp embodied these attributes himself, especially the last. And it certainly brought him success. His efforts on behalf of others led him from his family farm in upstate New York to chairmanship of the powerful Interstate Commerce Commission and then to appointment as an Article III judge, in which capacity he would serve on the (now defunct) Commerce Court before being assigned by the chief justice to serve on the Court of Appeals for the Second Circuit and, finally, the Court of Appeals for the Fourth Circuit.

Born on November 6, 1843 in the Village of Spafford in Onondaga County, New York, Knapp spent his early years working the family farm.[4] His father, Justus Norton Knapp, was a descendent of one of the first pioneer families to settle in the region and a man "who served his community in various positions of trust."[5] Knapp's mother, Polly McKay Knapp, was instrumental in fostering his education.[6] At her urging, Knapp attended the public school as often as his farm work would permit and, due to her efforts, eventually left home to prepare for college at the Homer Academy and, later, the Cazenovia Seminary, a Methodist secondary school.[7]

After graduating with distinction from both institutions, Knapp completed his undergraduate degree at Wesleyan University in Middletown, Connecticut.[8] There, he met and engaged in a "college romance" with Marian Hotchkiss, the daughter of a local family.[9] Knapp graduated from Wesleyan with the highest honors in 1868 and returned to Onondaga County, where he taught at the Homer Academy while studying law in the office of a local attorney.[10] Knapp completed his legal studies and gained admission to the New York bar in November 1869.[11] One month later, he returned to Middletown, where he and Hotchkiss married.[12] The newlyweds returned to New York in early 1870 and settled in Syracuse, where Knapp began his law practice.[13]

Over the next 20 years, Knapp became a pillar of the Syracuse community, becoming fast friends with James J. Belden, the future Republican mayor of Syracuse and representative to the U.S. Congress.[14] One of Knapp's first endeavors was to establish, with two partners, the law firm of Knapp, Nottingham & Andrews.[15] His partners described Knapp as an "industrious lawyer" who "lived up to the highest ideal of the profession" and "stood in the front ranks in Syracuse, both as a trial lawyer and in the Appellate Court."[16] During this time, Knapp also became active in the "local councils" of the Republican Party.[17] In 1877, when Belden was elected mayor, he appointed Knapp as the city attorney.[18] Knapp held that position until 1883, when he ran for mayor of Syracuse on the Republican ticket, losing the election by only 85 votes.[19]

Knapp's career took him to the national stage in 1891, when President Benjamin Harrison, at Belden's urging, nominated him as a commissioner on the fledgling Interstate Commerce Commission.[20] Established by the Interstate Commerce Act of 1887, the ICC was the first truly national regulatory agency.[21] The impetus behind the ICC was the railroad companies' excesses during the latter half of the nineteenth century, which included competitive "rate wars," bribery of public officials, discriminatory pricing that favored certain shippers over others, and repressive labor practices.[22] The ICC's primary purposes were to curb these excesses by ensuring that the carriers' rates were "just and reasonable," and to eliminate rate discrimination between different areas of the country and between types of shipments.[23]

Following his initial appointment, Knapp served as an ICC commissioner for nearly 20 years, reappointed by Presidents Grover Cleveland and Theodore Roosevelt.[24] For the last 13 of those years, he was the Commission's chairman.[25] This period saw reforms passed by the progressive era Congress that increased the Commission's control over the railroads and broadened its jurisdiction to include the regulation of other forms of interstate commerce, such as oil pipelines.[26] Through it all, Knapp struggled to strike a balance between the necessary regulation of the industries to prevent abuses and his commitment to private ownership. Thus, while he favored criminal charges against railroads that engaged in discriminatory or inflated pricing,[27] he vehemently opposed any suggestion of a government takeover of the rail carriers.[28] As he saw it, the essential task was "to devise a system of regulating laws which, while preserving the benefits of private ownership, shall furnish sufficient control over railway carriers to ensure transportation charges which are reasonable and relatively just."[29]

Knapp's years at the ICC were also marked by personal upheaval. His wife, Marian, died in December 1904 and was buried in her hometown of Middletown, Connecticut.[30] Three years later, Knapp married Nellie Maynard Gardner, the daughter of George Maynard, who had served as postmaster of Syracuse under President Abraham Lincoln.[31]

In 1910, Knapp resigned from the ICC after being nominated by President William Howard Taft to serve as the presiding judge of the newly formed and short-lived United States Commerce Court, in Washington, DC.[32] The Commerce Court, created by the Mann-Elkins Act of 1910, replaced the federal district and circuit courts in reviewing decisions made by the ICC.[33] It was made up of five Article III circuit judges who served on the Commerce Court for designated terms.[34] Congress authorized President Taft to nominate the five initial judges, who would serve on the Commerce Court for no longer than five years.[35] Upon their confirmation, the chief justice of the Supreme Court simultaneously assigned these five initial judges to an existing federal circuit, "where they would go with life tenure once their special court terms expired."[36] If the business of the Commerce Court did not "require the services of all the judges," the Mann-Elkins Act authorized the chief justice to temporarily assign its judges to any other circuit.[37] Attorney General George W. Wickersham praised this provision, observing that it effectively created a "body of five circuit judges at large" who could be "sent to places where there [wa]s a congestion of business or a shortage of judges."[38]

Knapp was confirmed for his five-year term as presiding judge of the Commerce Court in December 1910; Chief Justice Edward Douglass White simultaneously assigned him to be an additional circuit judge on the Court of Appeals for the Second Circuit.[39] Although the Commerce Court opened its doors in February 1911, Judge Knapp did not serve out his five-year term there because Congress abolished the court less than three years later.[40] The reasons for the court's demise are manifold. First, it appears that toward the end of his tenure at the ICC, Knapp was viewed with suspicion by many progressives, who resented remarks he delivered to the Railway Business Association in November 1910 that appeared to side with railway interests.[41] This suspicion deepened when it was perceived by many that the newly constituted Commerce Court used its authority to overturn many decisions of the ICC that disfavored railroad interests.[42]

Indeed, one of the Commerce Court judges, Judge Robert Archbald, was impeached and removed from office on charges of judicial corruption for using his office to promote his private interests in the railroads.[43] Finally, the Supreme Court took a harsh view of the Commerce Court, sharply overturning many of its decisions and narrowly interpreting the scope of its jurisdiction.[44]

Confidence in the Commerce Court reached its nadir in 1913 and, in October of that year, Congress voted to abolish the court and return jurisdiction to review ICC decisions to the federal district and circuit courts.[45] In so doing, Congress was sharply divided as to what should be done with the court's judges.[46] The House voted to abolish the judgeships entirely but the Senate, by a two-vote margin, voted to retain them as additional judgeships on the courts of appeals.[47] Much of the debate centered on the constitutionality of eliminating the judges' Article III life tenure by legislating away the court on which they sat.[48] In the end, the Senate's view prevailed, and the remaining Commerce Court judges retained their life tenure.[49] The provision of the Mann-Elkins Act authorizing the chief justice to assign the former Commerce Court judges to sit on other federal courts also survived the abolition of the court.[50] Congress specified, however, that the five seats created for the Commerce Court judges would expire upon their retirement or death and no successors would be appointed.[51]

When the Commerce Court was shuttered in December 1913, Judge Knapp continued in his capacity as an additional circuit judge on the Second Circuit.[52] One of his former Commerce Court colleagues, Julian W. Mack, would follow Judge Knapp to the Second Circuit in 1929.[53] During his time on the Second Circuit, Judge Knapp was designated by President Woodrow Wilson to serve on the newly formed Board of Mediation and Conciliation, which was created to mediate wage disputes between the railways and labor unions.[54] Research discloses no opinions written by Knapp or panels on which he sat during his tenure at the Second Circuit.

In January 1916, Chief Justice White transferred Judge Knapp to the Court of Appeals for the Fourth Circuit, where he would serve as an additional circuit judge until his death.[55] At the time, the Fourth Circuit had only two judges, meaning that, until Judge Knapp's arrival, a visiting judge always had to be called upon to form a three-judge panel.[56] Judge Knapp was respected by his Fourth Circuit colleagues but had some difficulty with the circuit's law, which was unfamiliar to him.[57] According to one of his colleagues, Judge Knapp confided that "he often felt lost in many cases; especially in land cases."[58] Although he contemplated retirement, he decided against it because, "having no successor, he stood in no one's way."[59]

Judge Knapp died in Washington on February 10, 1923 after undergoing two unsuccessful operations for an "intestinal disorder."[60] He was remembered as having "possessed in the highest degree those Socratic characteristics which become a Judge[:] to listen patiently, to answer courteously, to reason wisely and to decide impartially."[61] His body was returned to Middletown, Connecticut, to join that of his first wife, Marian.[62] He was 79.

Lucas C. Buzzard

1. Although appointed to the Court of Appeals in 1910, Knapp served only on the Commerce Court until 1913.

2. MEN OF MARK IN AMERICA, VOLUME II 95 (Merrill E. Gates ed., 1906).

3. *Id.*

4. *Judge Martin A. Knapp, 79, Distinguished Jurist, Former Syracusan, Dies in Washington*, SYRACUSE JOURNAL, Feb. 10, 1923, at 2.

5. MEN OF MARK, *supra* note 2, at 94; *see also Judge Martin A. Knapp, 79, Distinguished Jurist, supra* note 4, at 2.

6. *Judge Martin A. Knapp, 79, Distinguished Jurist, supra* note 4, at 2.

7. *Id.*; *Belden's Man Appointed*, N.Y. TIMES, Feb. 22, 1891, at 5.

8. *Judge Martin A. Knapp Dies in Washington*, N.Y. TIMES, Feb. 11, 1923, at S6.

9. *Judge Martin A. Knapp, 79, Distinguished Jurist, supra* note 4, at 2; *Mrs. Martin A. Knapp*, COURTLAND N.Y. STANDARD, Dec. 5, 1904, at 8.

10. *Belden's Man Appointed, supra* note 7, at 5.

11. *Id.*

12. *Judge Martin A. Knapp, 79, Distinguished Jurist, supra* note 4, at 2; *Mrs. Martin A. Knapp, supra* note 9, at 8.

13. *Belden's Man Appointed, supra* note 7, at 5.

14. *Id.*

15. *Id.*

16. *Former Associates Join in Tributes to Late Judge Knapp*, SYRACUSE JOURNAL, Feb. 10, 1923, at 2.

17. *Belden's Man Appointed, supra* note 7, at 5.

18. *Id.*

19. *Id.*

20. *Id.*

21. Thomas W. Merrill, *Article III, Agency Adjudication, and the Origins of the Appellate Review Model of Admin. Law*, 111 COLUM. L. REV. 939, 950 (2011); *see also* Paul Stephen Dempsey, *The Rise and Fall of the Interstate Commerce Commission: The Tortuous Path from Regulation to Deregulation of America's Infrastructure*, 95 MARQ. L. REV. 1151, 1162–63 (2012).

22. *See* Dempsey, *supra* note 21, at 1154–60.

23. *See id.* at 1160–61.

24. *Judge Martin A. Knapp Dies in Washington*, *supra* note 8, at S6.

25. *Judge Martin A. Knapp, 79, Distinguished Jurist*, *supra* note 4, at 2.

26. *See* Dempsey, *supra* note 21, at 1163–64.

27. *Knapp Says Look Out for Graft*, BINGHAMTON N.Y. PRESS, Oct. 14, 1906, at 1.

28. *Knapp Flouts Our Railroad Laws*, N.Y. TIMES, Nov. 23, 1910, at 4.

29. Martin A. Knapp, *National Regulation of Railroads*, 26 ANNALS OF THE AM. ACAD. OF POL. & SOC. SCI. 613, 166 (1905).

30. *Mrs. Martin A. Knapp*, *supra* note 9, at 8.

31. *Martin A. Knapp Marries Widow*, SYRACUSE HERALD, Aug. 16, 1097, at 4.

32. *Judge Martin A. Knapp, 79, Distinguished Jurist*, *supra* note 4, at 2; *see also* George E. Dix, *The Death of the Commerce Court: A Study in Institutional Weakness*, 8 AM. J. LEGAL HIST. 238, 239 (1964).

33. Mann-Elkins Act ch.309 § 1, 36 STAT. 539, 539 (1910); Dix, *supra* note 32, at 239.

34. Mann-Elkins Act § 1 at 540; *Staff of S. Comm. on the Judiciary, 85th Cong.*, LEGIS. HISTORY OF THE UNITED STATES CIRCUIT COURTS OF APPEALS AND THE JUDGES WHO SERVED DURING THE PERIOD 1801 THROUGH MARCH 1958, at 23 (1958); J. Newton Baker, *The Commerce Court—Its Origin, its Powers and its Judges*, 20 YALE L.J. 555, 560 (1911).

35. Mann-Elkins Act § 1, at 540; *see* Theodore W. Ruger, *The Judicial Appointment Power of the Chief Justice*, 7 U. PA. J. CONST. L. 341, 360 (2004).

36. Ruger, *supra* note 35, at 360 n.79; *see also* Mann-Elkins Act § 1, at 540; *Staff of S. Comm. on the Judiciary, 85th Cong.*, *supra* note 34, at 23.

37. Mann-Elkins Act § 1, at 540-41.

38. 48 Cong. Rec. 7972 (1912) (letter from Attorney General George W. Wickersham to Senator Francis E. Warren).

39. *Staff of S. Comm. on the Judiciary, 85th Cong.*, *supra* note 34, at 23.

40. *Id.*

41. Dix, *supra* note 31, at 244; *see also Opposition to Knapp*, WALL ST. J., Dec. 16, 1910, at 2.

42. Merrill, *supra* note 21, at 966–67; Dix, *Death of the Commerce Court*, *supra* note 32,at 243–44.

43. Merrill, *supra* note 21, at 967; Dix, *Death of the Commerce Court*, *supra* note 32, at 256; *see also Staff of S. Comm. on the Judiciary, 85th Cong.*,, *supra* note 34, at 25.

44. Merrill, *supra* note 21, at 967; Dix, *Death of the Commerce Court*, *supra* note 32, at 246–47.

45. *See* Felix Frankfurter, *The Business of the Supreme Court of the United States – A Study in the Federal Judicial System*, 39 HARV. L. REV. 587, 613–14 (1926); *see also Staff of S. Comm. on the Judiciary, 85th Cong.*,, *supra* note 34, at 25; Merrill , *supra* note 21, at 966.

46. *See* Frankfurter, *supra* note 45, at 609–10, 613–14.

47. *Id.* at 613–14.

48. *See, e.g.*, 50 Cong. Rec. 5590–96 (1913).

49. *See* Frankfurter, *supra* note 45, at 614.

50. Donegan v. Dyson, 269 U.S. 49, 53–55 (1925); Frankfurter, *supra* note 45, at 614 & n.134.

51. Law of Oct. 22, 1913, ch. 32, 38 STAT. 208, 219 (1913).

52. *Staff of S. Comm. on the Judiciary, 85th Cong.*, *supra* note 34, at 24; *see also* Frankfurter, *supra* note 44, at 609 n.112.

53. *Staff of S. Comm. on the Judiciary, 85th Cong.*, *supra* note 34, at 23.

54. *Names Mediation Board*, N.Y. TIMES, July 18, 1913, at 2; *Mediation Board is Ready*, WALL ST. J., July 19, 1913, at 1.

55. *Staff of S. Comm. on the Judiciary, 85th Cong.*, *supra* note 34, at 24.

56. District Judge George W. McClintic, Address at the Judicial Conference for the Fourth Circuit: Fifty Years of the Circuit Court of Appeals for the Fourth Circuit 4 (June 20, 1941) (transcript on file with the United States Courts Library for the Second Circuit).

57. *Id.* at 18–19.

58. *Id.* at 18.

59. *Id.*

60. *Judge Martin A. Knapp, 79, Distinguished Jurist, supra* note 4, at 2.

61. District Judge George W. McClintic, Address, *supra* note 55, at 19.

62. *Id.*

# HENRY WADE ROGERS
# 1853-1926

Court of Appeals for the Second Circuit: 1913-1926

Even as a judge, Henry Wade Rogers was an educator. The dean of two law schools and the president of a university, Rogers felt more comfortable in a classroom than a law office. And he brought his academic bearing to the bench. According to Judge Charles M. Hough, Rogers "regarded his judgeship as an honorable opportunity of teaching a larger and more mature body of pupils than can be found in any collegiate institution, and he did it the better because he never thought of himself as an attorney."[1] Prior to taking the bench, Rogers helped professionalize the American legal academy. As a judge, his scholarly and workmanlike opinions reflected his devout idealism and preference for judicial restraint.

Rogers was born in 1853, in Holland Patent, a speck of a village in Oneida County, New York. He pursued his education at the University of Michigan, earning a BA degree in 1874 and an MA degree in 1877. In 1876, Rogers attended lectures at Michigan's law department, where he was a student of the renowned Thomas M. Cooley.[2]

Rogers's legal education lacked the trappings that have since become familiar: textbooks, the Socratic method, class sections, and final exams. Professors taught through lectures. At the time, attorneys disfavored academic training, and office apprenticeship was the norm. But Michigan was a fast-growing law school that provided something a law office could not: Thomas Cooley, its founder and the leading constitutional scholar of his generation.[3] Cooley gave formidable lectures, but paid little heed to pedagogy.[4] He was effective because he was brilliant, but that quality is notably difficult to reproduce. When Cooley left Michigan, the law school needed new teaching methods to retain its relevance.

Rogers would bring those new methods to Michigan. Following a brief interregnum in Minnesota, where he practiced law with Democratic Party leader Eugene M. Wilson, and New Jersey, where he relocated with his ailing wife, Rogers returned to his alma mater.[5] In 1883, Rogers joined Michigan's faculty as its first full-time law professor.[6] In 1885, he succeeded Cooley as dean.[7]

Rogers transformed Michigan's law department. He introduced textbooks, written examinations, and student recitations.[8] He extended the curriculum to cover two years, separated the students into junior and senior classes, and divided each class into sections.[9] As a teacher, he introduced Socratic teaching methods and textbooks and began to modernize Michigan's approach to classroom education.[10] These reforms brought Michigan into the modern legal academy, which was eclipsing the office apprenticeship. By 1894, Rogers could declare that "we are no longer obliged to debate the question whether a Law School is a better place than a law office in which to study law."[11]

One reform that Rogers refused to introduce was the case method. Rogers concluded that "life was too short and the time that a student could spend in a law school was altogether too limited to permit one's acquiring a knowledge of the law simply through a study of cases, and that while such a system might be advantageously used with students whose intellectual powers had been thoroughly developed and whose mental grip was strong, it was quite unsuited to the average student."[12] Still, he made sure his students were familiar with the "leading cases."[13]

In 1890, Rogers left Michigan to accept the presidency of Northwestern University, where he continued his record of modernization.[14] He reformed Northwestern's curriculum by introducing new fields of study such as political science and economics.[15] He united Northwestern's diverse professional schools under the aegis of a single board of trustees.[16] Rogers transformed "a loosely joined federation of schools" into "an organized whole."[17]

During his time at Northwestern, Rogers took an active role in law and politics. He chaired the World's Congress on Jurisprudence and Law Reform at the Chicago Exposition in 1893 and the Saratoga Conference on the Foreign Policy of the United States in 1898.[18] Throughout this period, he chaired the American Bar Association's Section for Legal Education.[19] Faced with unaccredited diploma mills that were devaluing the universities, Rogers advocated state supervision of higher education.[20]

Rogers also took controversial political stands. He was an early advocate of university coeducation.[21] In the wake of the Spanish-American War, he joined the Anti-Imperialist League and opposed the annexation of the Philippines.[22] Rogers wrestled publicly with territorial expansion, concerned that the rush to establish an American empire had subordinated the Constitution.[23] He argued that imperial expansion violated the intent of the nation's founders.[24] Rogers's anti-imperialism led to him to endorse William Jennings Bryan in the 1900 presidential race, despite differences with him on monetary policy.[25]

In 1900, under pressure, Rogers resigned from presidency of Northwestern. His public opposition to the annexation of the Philippines and continued support for coeducation had not endeared him to the Board of Trustees.[26] Perhaps more fundamentally, Rogers was "a scholarly educator but not a hustler, and he [lacked] the power to charm money out of the pockets of the rich."[27] The University of Chicago had simply raised more funds.

Northwestern's Board of Trustees wanted a president who could compete.[28]

Ousted from Northwestern, Rogers moved to Yale. He joined the law faculty in 1900 and became dean in 1903. While at Yale, he would radically transform the law school's admission standards, pedagogy, and professoriate, and chart its course to preeminence.

Rogers believed in academic rigor, and had a reputation as a demanding professor. In one well-publicized fracas, he denied a Yale diploma to Cornelius Vanderbilt's scion Reginald, who failed to complete Rogers's course.[29] As dean, Rogers institutionalized his high standards. He required, for the first time, an undergraduate degree for admission to the law school.[30] He wrote, "A university law school must determine whether it is willing to confer professional degrees on persons of limited general culture, and whether it can do so without prejudice to its prestige as a university."[31]

As dean of Yale Law School, Rogers "revivified" what *The New York Times* called "a backward and decaying institution."[32] Over vigorous opposition, he undid the faculty's conservatism.[33] Rogers reluctantly introduced the case method, by then ascendant, even as he regretted using it in his own classes.[34] He altered the composition of the faculty by replacing judges and practicing lawyers with academic specialists who viewed legal education as an independent profession.[35]

Rogers served as dean from 1903 until 1916, retaining the post even after his 1913 appointment to the Court of Appeals for the Second Circuit. Despite his efforts to professionalize the faculty, Rogers had no compunction about being a part-time dean.[36] In response, younger scholars, led by Arthur Corbin, formed a "faculty cabal" to oust Rogers from the deanship.[37] The insurgents sought a more engaged dean, who would embark upon even more radical reforms. They found their candidate in Thomas Swan, who replaced Rogers and accelerated his efforts to modernize the law school, and who would later inherit Rogers's seat on the Second Circuit.[38]

As a scholar, Rogers was a traditionalist and a generalist. His writings started with Roman law, wove through the English Year

Books, early French law, and still more recent English common law, and ended with a survey of contemporary American authorities. He wrote about municipal corporations, insurance law, the insanity defense, and international law.[39] He tackled the controversial question of whether photographs could be protected by copyright.[40] (He thought they could be.) He burnished the legacy of his mentor, Thomas Cooley, by penning Cooley's entry in *Distinguished American Lawyers*, citing his work extensively, and writing a full-length, albeit unpublished, biography.[41] But Rogers's most significant accomplishment was a treatise on expert evidence, which traced the use of experts to ancient times, examined its problems, and surveyed the growing number of legal fields where expert evidence was required.[42]

Rogers was an active and devout Methodist. He held numerous positions of lay authority within the Methodist Episcopal Church, ultimately overseeing the Committee on the Judiciary, which set policies for the congregation.[43] As a Methodist, "Rogers belonged to the broad school. He had little interest in the narrow, the limited, the merely sectarian. His interest was always in the broad outlines and the underlying principles."[44]

Rogers married Emma Winner, a minister's daughter from New Jersey. Her civic participation matched Rogers's own. In Evanston, Emma founded the Northwestern University Settlement, an urban outpost where social reformers assisted the urban poor.[45] She published a brief pamphlet describing the moral decay found in America's cities. She was a committed suffragist, a cause that her husband shared, and she served as an officer in the National American Woman Suffrage Association.[46] After moving to a country residence in the New Jersey Palisades following Judge Rogers's appointment to the bench, Emma published a diary celebrating the virtues of country life. As she wrote, "While the world revolves we can never escape toil and trouble, cares and fears, but we can get strong and free and joyful in the country, ready to bear our burdens with smiling faces and steady nerves."[47] Judge Rogers commuted to work from the country house, and, while on vacation, Emma would assign him to the wood lot, where, "for three or four hours daily," she made him chop wood.[48] Emma Winner Rogers predeceased her husband in 1922.[49]

Even while dean at Yale, Rogers's political involvement never waned. He was an early leader of the American peace movement, which had its origins in the anti-imperialism of Rogers and other like-minded progressives.[50] He penned an essay supporting a constitutional amendment granting women the right to vote.[51] And he was an active Democrat in Republican Connecticut. Although the party courted him for political office, he never ran.[52]

Rogers's Yale colleague, the Democratic power broker Simeon E. Baldwin, shared his progressive politics. Rogers gave the nominating speeches when Baldwin ran successfully for governor of Connecticut, in 1910, and sought the nomination for president, in 1912.[53] In 1912, Baldwin stood little chance against Woodrow Wilson, but Rogers's speech drew national attention.[54] The next year, Baldwin convinced President Wilson to nominate Rogers to the Court of Appeals for the Second Circuit.[55]

Rogers was 60 when he took the bench, an advanced age for the time. Despite his lack of experience, Judge Rogers joined the Second Circuit as "a fellow worker of untiring assiduity."[56] But Judge Rogers's career had left him innocent. He "frankly sought help in matters of procedure, and needed to be told what tricks of the trade were only half concealed in some fairly printed pages of motions and supporting affidavits."[57] Nevertheless, Judge Rogers's untiring commitment to the court yielded a productive 13 years on the bench.

Judge Rogers's "opinions show his fondness for searching and accumulating the authorities."[58] A Rogers opinion besieged the battlements of a legal problem with precedent—Popham and Coke as the footmen, Justices Marshall and Story as the cavalry, Judge Cooley as the siege engine. Yet despite his array of legal armaments, Judge Rogers had a restrained view of judicial power.

For example, in *Masses Publishing Company v Patten*,[59] Judge Rogers reversed District Judge Learned Hand, who had enjoined the postmaster of New York City from enforcing the Espionage Act against an anarchist magazine. *The Masses* magazine had criticized the United States' entry into World War I and praised draft resisters like Emma Goldman and Alexander Berkman. The postmaster general decided that the publication violated the Espionage Act and instructed the postmaster of New York City to exclude it from the mail. The magazine brought suit under the First Amendment to enjoin the enforcement of the Espionage Act.

Without mentioning the First Amendment, Judge Hand gave the statute a narrow interpretation that would avoid ascribing political censorship to Congress.[60] Judge Hand reasoned that the statute prohibited explicit incitement to resist the draft, but that it did not prohibit all criticism of the draft laws. Concluding that the magazine had engaged in criticism, not outright incitement, Judge Hand enjoined the postmaster.

Writing for the Second Circuit, Judge Rogers reversed. His lengthy opinion dismissed the magazine's constitutional challenges, rejected Judge Hand's statutory construction, and chided his lack of judicial restraint. Judge Rogers accused Judge Hand of ignoring "the principle that the head of a department of the government in a doubtful case will not be overruled by the courts in a matter which involves his judgment and discretion, and which is within his jurisdiction."[61] The case was not reviewed by the Supreme Court. Judge Hand believed that this reversal and the adverse reaction to his opinion contributed to his being passed over in 1918 for appointment to the Second Circuit.[62] That appointment went to Martin Manton.[63] Hand was appointed six years later.[64]

Judge Rogers also wrote *United States v. Reisenweber*,[65] a major Prohibition opinion. Reisenweber's Café was a roomy cabaret on Columbus Circle that hosted New York's elite. When the Original Dixieland Jazz Band cut the world's first jazz recordings, they were playing a residency at Reisenweber's.[66] Naturally, during the age of Prohibition, Reisenweber's was a notorious speakeasy.[67] After a series of raids, the government sought to close the cabaret, which, under the Volstead Act, required a district court injunction.[68] In an opinion that recounted the history of public nuisance law, Judge Rogers held that the statute did not violate due process, and affirmed the district court's injunction.[69] An important Prohibition precedent, *Reisenweber* also confirmed the government's power to snare criminal defendants through ruses and subterfuge.[70]

Judge Rogers's other significant opinions included *Bens v. United States*,[71] which held that a person could be charged with both conspiracy and the completed crime without violating double jeopardy, and *Yaselli v. Goff*,[72] which reaffirmed prosecutorial immunity. In 1924, Judge Rogers raised eyebrows when he invalidated a devise from the famous tomb raider Theodore M. Davis to the Metropolitan Museum of Art.[73] The gift, valued at $300,000, included irreplaceable Egyptian artifacts. Judge Rogers held that the collection belonged to the residual estate, and awarded it to the heirs of Davis's widow.[74]

Judge Rogers served as senior circuit judge from 1921 until 1926,[75] when he died unexpectedly at his summer home near Trenton, New Jersey.[76]

Rick Sawyer

1. Charles M. Hough, Address *in* IN MEMORY OF HENRY WADE ROGERS: JUDGE ROGERS THE JURIST 10, 15 (1926).

2. *See* ELIZABETH GASPAR BROWN, LEGAL EDUCATION AT MICHIGAN 1859-1959 at 41 (1959).

3. *See* H.B. Hutchins, *Thomas McIntyre Cooley*, MICHIGAN ALUMNUS, Oct. 1, 1906, at 23-29, http://um2017.org/faculty-history/faculty/thomas-mcintyre-cooley/article.

4. *See id.* at 24.

5. *Henry W. Rogers, Noted Jurist, Dead*, N.Y. TIMES, Aug. 17, 1926, at 21.

6. Paul D. Carrington, *Legal Education for the People: Populism and Civic Virtue*, 43 U. KAN. L. REV. 1, 17 (1994).

7. *Henry W. Rogers, Noted Jurist, Dead*, *supra* note 5, at 21.

8. BROWN, *supra* note 2, at 41.

9. *Id.*

10. *See id.* at 42.

11. Henry Wade Rogers, Chairman of the Section of Legal Education, Address Delivered Before the Section of Legal Education, Faculty Scholarship Series (1894), http://digitalcommons.law.yale.edu/fss_papers/4084.

12. Henry Wade Rogers, *Law School of the University of Michigan*, 1 GREEN BAG 189, 194 (1889).

13. *Id.*

14. *Henry W. Rogers, Noted Jurist, Dead*, *supra* note 5.

15. *Henry Wade Rogers*, THE PRESIDENTS OF NORTHWESTERN, http://exhibits.library.northwestern.edu/archives/exhibits/presidents/rogers.html.

16. *Id.*

17. *Id.*

18. *Memorial: Henry Wade Rogers*, THE MICHIGAN ALUMNUS, Oct. 23, 1926, at 61, http://um2017.org/faculty-history/faculty/henry-wade-rogers/memorial.

19. *Id.*

20. *See* Henry Wade Rogers, *Fraudulent Diplomas: A Necessity for State Supervision*, Address at the Illinois State Teachers' Association at Springfield, at 9-11 (Dec. 28, 1898).

21. THE PRESIDENTS OF NORTHWESTERN, *supra* note 15.

22. *See The Anti-Imperialist League*, N.Y. TIMES, May 24, 1899, at 3; *see Ownership of the Islands*, N.Y. TIMES, May 9, 1898, at 2.

23. *See* Henry Wade Rogers, *The Treaty-Making Power*, 16 ANN. REPORT AM. BAR ASSOC. 243 (1893); *see* Henry Wade Rogers, *The Acquisition and Government of Territory*, 38 J. SOC. SCI. 173 (1900).

24. *See The National Policy: Discussion of the Doctrine of Colonial Extension at the Saratoga Convention in All Phases*, N.Y. TIMES, Aug. 20, 1898, at 4.

25. *Dr. Rogers for Bryan: Educator Declares Gold Democrats are Anti-Imperialists*, N.Y. TIMES, Aug. 19, 1900, at 3.

26. THE PRESIDENTS OF NORTHWESTERN, *supra* note 15.

27. *President Rogers Resigns*, N.Y. TIMES, June 13, 1900, at 1.

28. *Id.*

29. *Young Vanderbilt's Diploma*, N.Y. TIMES, June 24, 1902, at 1.

30. *See* Comment, *Henry Wade Rogers*, 36 YALE L. J. 112, 113 (1926) (attributed to Arthur L. Corbin, see *Bibliography of the Published Writings of Arthur Linton Corbin*, 74 YALE L. J. 311, 318 (1964)).

31. Report to the Fellows of Yale University 115 (1902), *quoted in* Mark Bartholomew, *Legal Separation: The Relationship Between the Law School and the Central University in the Late Nineteenth Century*, 53 J. LEGAL EDUC. 368, 390 (2003).

32. *Dean Rogers*, N.Y. TIMES, Aug. 18, 1926, at 20.

33. *See* Bartholomew, *supra* note 31, at 389.

34. Comment, *supra* note 30, at 113.

35. *Id.*

36. *See* Eugene V. Rostow, *Myres S. Mcdougal*, 84 YALE L.J. 704, 706 (1975).

37. Eugene V. Rostow, *Thomas W. Swan*, 85 YALE L.J. 159, 160 (1975).

38. *Id.*

39. *See* Henry Wade Rogers, *Corporations*, 11 YALE L.J. 223 (1902); *see* Henry Wade Rogers, *Insurance, Life: Intemperate Habits of Assured*, 20 F. 490 (1884); *see* Henry Wade Rogers, *Insanity Proved by Evidence Fairly Preponderating*, 31 AM. L. REG. 191 (1883); *see* Henry Wade Rogers, *International Extradition*, 6 FORUM 612 (1884); *see* Henry Wade Rogers, *The Essentials of a Law Establishing an International Court*, 22 YALE L.J. 277 (1913).

40. *See* Henry Wade Rogers, *Protection by Copyright of Photographs*, 17 F. 596 (1883).

41. *See* Henry Wade Rogers, *Thomas McIntyre Cooley*, *in* DISTINGUISHED AMERICAN LAWYERS, WITH THEIR STRUGGLES AND TRIUMPHS IN THE FORUM 205 (Henry W. Scott ed., 1891).

42. *See* HENRY WADE ROGERS, THE LAW OF EXPERT TESTIMONY (2d ed. reprint 1991) (1891).

43. David G. Downey, Reverend, Address in In Memory of Henry Wade Rogers: Henry Wade Rogers the Churchman 20, 20 (1926).

44. *Id.*

45. *Our History*, NORTHWESTERN SETTLEMENT, http://www.nush.org/item/show/7.

46. *Suffragists Stop Attacks on Parties*, N.Y. TIMES, Nov. 17, 1914, at 13.

47. EMMA WINNER ROGERS, THE JOURNAL OF A COUNTRY WOMAN 5 (1912).

48. *Id.* at 39, 76.

49. *See* THE PRESIDENTS OF NORTHWESTERN, *supra* note 15.

50. *See* James L. Tryon, *The Rise of the Peace Movement*, 20 YALE L.J. 358, 368 (1911).

51. *See* Henry Wade Rogers, *Federal Action and State Rights*, *in* WOMAN SUFFRAGE BY FEDERAL CONSTITUTIONAL AMENDMENT 55 (Carrie Chapman Catt ed., 1917).

52. Hartford Daily Courant, *Tribute in* IN MEMORY OF HENRY WADE ROGERS: HARTFORD DAILY COURANT 44, 44–45.

53. *Rogers, Henry Wade*, *in* DICTIONARY OF AMERICAN BIOGRAPHY 97, 97 (Dumas Malone ed., 1935).

54. Hartford Daily Courant, *supra* note 52, at 45.

55. *Rogers, Henry Wade*, *supra* note 53, at 97.

56. Hough, *supra* note 1, at 12.

57. *Id.*

58. Comment, *supra* note 30, at 114.

59. 246 F. 24, 39 (2d Cir. 1917).

60. Masses Pub. Co. v. Patten, 244 F. 535 (S.D.N.Y. 1917).

61. *Masses Pub. Co.*, 246 F. at 39.

62. GERALD GUNTHER, LEARNED HAND THE MAN AND THE JUDGE 152, 161, 259 (1994).

63. *Id.* at 161.

64. *Id.* at 235.

65. 288 F. 520 (2d Cir. 1923).

66. John S. Wilson, *Jazz*, N.Y. TIMES, June 28, 1987, at G2.

67. *"Close Reisenweber's," Dry Officials Demand*, N.Y. TIMES, Sept. 13, 1922, at 20.

68. *U.S. Sues to Close Reisenweber Cafe*, N.Y. TIMES, Mar. 31, 1922, at 18; *Reisenweber*, 288 F. at 524.

69. *Reisenweber*, 288 F. at 523–25.

70. *Order Closing Cafe for Year Sustained*, N.Y. TIMES, Jan. 19, 1923, at 3 (*Reisenweber* first decision in United States to uphold an injunction under the Volstead Act); *Reisenweber*, 288 F. at 526 ("If the officers of the government act in good faith and in the honest belief that the defendant is engaged in an unlawful business, of which the offense charged in the indictment is a part, and the purpose of the entrapment is not to induce an innocent man to commit a crime, but to secure evidence upon which a guilty man can be brought to justice, the defense of entrapment is without merit."); Sorrells v. United States, 287 U.S. 435, 441 (1932) (citing *Reisenweber* approvingly for the proposition that "[a]rtifice and stratagem may be employed to catch those engaged in criminal enterprise").

71. 266 F. 152 (2d Cir. 1920).

72. 12 F.2d 396 (2d Cir. 1926).

73. *Museum Loses Suit and Davis Art Gifts*, N.Y. TIMES, Mar. 18, 1924, at 26.

74. Boal v. Metro. Museum of Art of the City of New York, 298 F. 894 (2d Cir. 1924).

75. The presiding judge was known as the "senior circuit judge" until 1948, when the term "chief judge" was established under 28 U.S.C. § 45. The term was adopted "in recognition of the great increase in administrative duties of such judge." Report from the House Comm. on the Judiciary, to Accompany H.R. 3214, H.R. 308, 80th Cong., 1st Sess., A6 (1947); *see also* Act of June 25, 1948, ch. 646, § 45(a) 62 Stat. 869, 871 ("The circuit judge senior in commission shall be the chief judge of the circuit.").

76. *Henry W. Rogers, Noted Jurist, Dead*, *supra* note 5.

# CHARLES M. HOUGH
## 1858-1927

District Court for the Southern District of New York: 1906-1916
Court of Appeals for the Second Circuit: 1916-1927

"He is a judge, every inch of him," said Chief Justice William Howard Taft of Charles Merrill Hough.[1]

Hough was born on May 18, 1858 in Philadelphia to Alfred Lacey Hough, a brigadier general in the Army, and Mary Hough.[2] Hough spent much of his early life in the South. His father was stationed in Tennessee and Kentucky during and following the Civil War.[3] Although he was considered a "Yankee," Hough rejected that label.[4] Hough aspired to follow in his father's footsteps. He "looked on a uniform as the only wear, the Infantry the only corps, the West as the place for work, and the East pleasant to visit."[5] Hough, however, was prevented from joining the Army due to poor eyesight.[6] Hough's parents dismissed his nearsightedness, believing that he would outgrow it.[7] They would prove wrong. Hough ultimately "resigned himself to attending Dartmouth rather than West Point."[8]

Before leaving for college, Hough visited New York. He later observed, "Downtown New York singularly enough impressed me not at all."[9] The only building that Hough admired was the federal post office and courthouse building, home to the federal courts in New York. But he stated: "if anyone had told me that I would spend most of my life working in it as a lawyer and judge I would have shrunk back in horror—for the whole region was dreadful to the country-boy side of me, and utterly rowdy and undisciplined to the Army lad."[10]

Unaccustomed to Hanover's harsh winters, Hough spent his entire first year at Dartmouth in a spring overcoat.[11] During winter breaks, Hough remained on campus and read books. He could not "read 30,000 books in four years," but "could and did find and read books of every kind."[12] In his final year, Hough brought "modern" football to Dartmouth, with rules learned from books. He "claim[ed] the honor . . . of carrying into play the first oval leather football ever seen in Hanover."[13] Hough graduated in 1879 and remained an active alumnus for life.[14]

Hough did not attend law school. He believed that "legal studies were not only unattractive but also a mere continuance of dependence."[15] Instead, he read law and was admitted to the Pennsylvania bar in 1883.[16] He joined the firm of Biddle & Ward and, when the firm opened a new office, moved to New York City.[17] In both offices, he worked with Henry Ward, who would later be his colleague on the bench. Ward was, in fact, the reason that the man who refused to be called a "Yankee" moved to New York. A lawyer recalled that Hough "said that there had been one attraction only which had brought him to New York and that that attraction was Henry Galbraith Ward."[18] Hough soon became known as an expert in admiralty law.[19] Early in his career, he was able to attract many large steamship companies as clients.[20] Later in his career, Hough developed a reputation as an authority in bankruptcy law.[21] He was often appointed receiver by bankruptcy judges.[22]

Law was not Hough's only concern. Never abandoning his bent toward military service, Hough enlisted in the Naval Militia of New York, Fourth Division, and served from 1892 to 1899.[23] He served in the Spanish-American War as a member of the militia crew of the Monitor Nahant.[24] Hough achieved the rank of boatswain's mate.[25] He was also a member of the local school board for two years, and was chairman of the Institute for the Improved Instruction of Deaf Mutes.[26]

After Hough had been in private practice for 20 years,[27] President Theodore Roosevelt appointed him to the District Court for the Southern District of New York in 1906.[28] The newly established district court seat was created during an ongoing factional fight within the Republican Party.[29] As a result, each potential candidate put forward met heavy criticism.[30]

More than 50 prominent lawyers were considered for the vacant seat.[31] The United States Attorney for the Southern District of New York recommended those best suited for appointment.[32] Attorney General William Henry Moody requested "not only the names of those who had offered themselves, or who had been offered by others as candidates, but also the names of any men who, without formally becoming candidates, would accept the position if it were tendered to them."[33] The United States Attorney narrowed the field to three potential candidates.[34]

It was initially thought that Hough was too closely aligned with the Pennsylvania Railroad, his firm's client, and other large businesses.[35] After thorough investigation, however, Attorney General Moody wrote, "It was stated that of the three, Mr. Hough, in the opinion of the district attorney and the Judges with whom he conferred, would make the most satisfactory judge. I was informed that it was the belief that Hough would be a remarkably good appointment, and in a marked degree was the best candidate."[36] Word of Hough's potential appointment generated "[a] large number of letters of endorsement of Mr. Hough, which seem to have been voluntarily offered."[37] The attorney general concluded that Hough's "reputation is unassailable, and he is in the prime of life, with the prospect of many years of judicial usefulness before him."[38] He continued, "I think that his appointment would be a most admirable one."[39] Hough was sworn in on July 6, 1906 at the age of 48.[40]

Hough was "'at his best as a trial judge,' where 'the high initial velocity of his mind was conspicuously effective in mastering facts, analyzing evidence, and applying general principles to concrete cases.'"[41] In the courtroom, Hough was "impatient of irrelevance, incompetence and prolixity."[42] Reflecting on his earlier years at the bar, Judge J. Edward Lumbard, Jr. asserted: "Men like Charles M. Hough did not merely preside. They literally scared you to death."[43] Despite Hough's constant struggle with illness, he was an industrious trial judge. He conducted 1,200 trials and wrote 1,809 opinions.[44]

Hough acquired new areas of expertise on the bench. He soon became an authority in patent law.[45] Hough's expertise as a litigator in admiralty and bankruptcy also carried over to the bench. Judge Learned Hand said that Hough's "authority in admiralty [was] unequalled anywhere" and that Hough "probably understood the actual administration of the bankruptcy law better than any judge alive."[46]

President Woodrow Wilson appointed Hough to the Court of Appeals for the Second Circuit in 1916.[47] Hough was nominated after many of the leading lawyers in New York signed a petition advocating his appointment.[48]

As an appellate judge, Hough heard 2,047 cases and wrote 675 opinions.[49] Attorneys and judges alike believed that Hough's decisions were well reasoned.[50] Judge Augustus Hand commented of his own time as a district judge, "When he reversed me, his skill in presentation and the weight of his opinions nearly always persuaded me that the right thing had been done and I must have been wrong."[51] Hough's power of persuasion could partly be attributed to his thoroughness. One attorney recalled a complex patent case in which Hough read the record three times before casting his vote.[52]

Hough wrote the opinion in a newsworthy copyright case that was upheld by the Supreme Court and is still studied in law schools today. In *Associated Press v. International News Service*, Hough's opinion recognized a common law cause of action for misappropriation through the tort of unfair competition.[53] The

AP published stories covering World War I in its New York newspapers, after which the International News Service would wire the contents of those stories to its west coast affiliates. The AP and International News Service newspapers on the west coast—sold approximately three hours later than those on the east coast—competed for the same morning customers, nullifying the AP's advantage of otherwise being first-to-market. Hough's opinion overturned the district court's denial of an injunction against the International News Service, concluding that the International News Service had infringed upon the AP's "reasonable reward of industry."[54]

In *The Saturnus*, an admiralty case, Hough refused to expand the traditional category of maritime liens to cover the execution of a contract.[55] The Midland Company sued *The Saturnus*, a steamship, in rem after its captain had breached a contract to ship cakes. Per the custom, Midland ordered *The Saturnus* to a particular pier to pick up the cakes. The captain, however, wrongfully refused and went to a distant pier, causing Midland to incur an expense of $1,287. Midland asserted that their contract had created a lien against *The Saturnus* upon which it could recover. Hough rejected this proposition, concluding: "This litigation exemplifies a common tendency to regard any floating property used in the performance of contract, as in some sort a pledge or surety for satisfactory performance; such security to be enforced by asserted maritime lien. No such principle is known to the admiralty."[56]

Opinions were not all that Hough wrote. Upon discovering the old records of the Court of Vice Admiralty in the attic of the federal post office and courthouse building, Hough compiled the court's decisions between 1715 and the American Revolution.[57] He published a history of the Southern District and the judges who served on it.[58] And he wrote his own memoirs. Never published, the memoirs describe Hough's family, childhood in the South, college years, legal career, and thoughts on the state of the legal profession and the United States. One passage was prescient. Observing World War I, he wrote: "The World War taught me how little I knew; why it did not teach everyone to walk humbly before God and man I cannot see; but I believe that the next generation will probably do the same kind of thing, and even more thoroughly make fools of themselves."[59]

While on the bench, Hough continued to be a leader in admiralty law. In addition to publishing the reports of the Vice Admiralty Court, Hough served as the president of the Maritime Law Association for eight years.[60] He also represented the United States at the fifth international conference on maritime law in Brussels, making recommendations that would affect shipping across the world.[61]

As Hough's career progressed, he compiled accolades. Charles Wyzanski, an eminent district judge in Massachusetts and law clerk of both Learned and Augustus Hand, considered Hough to be "one of the nine great commercial judges of the English speaking world."[62] On several occasions, Hough was considered for the Supreme Court.[63] Chief Justice Taft was among those who wished to see Hough elevated. Taft described him as "a burly, hard hitting, industrious, independent and very able lawyer whom the bar and the community greatly respect," and concluded that Hough "would give great strength" to the Supreme Court.[64]

Hough died on April 22, 1927, at his home in New York, at age 68.[65] He had been resting due to illness, which was initially not considered serious.[66] Hough's associates, unaware of the extent of his illness, were surprised to learn of Hough's death.[67] After a short eulogy was delivered from the bench, the Second Circuit adjourned for several days.[68] Hough had served on the Court of Appeals bench for ten years.[69] His wife, Ethel, daughter, E. Baldwin Smith, and son, John, survived him.[70] He was buried at a family plot in Burlington County, New Jersey.[71]

Daniel Principato

1. Letter from Chief Justice William Howard Taft to President Warren Harding, (Dec. 4, 1922) *quoted in* William J. Cibes, *Extra-Judicial Activities of Justices of the United States Supreme Court 1790-1960*, at 1214 (unpublished Ph.D. dissertation, Princeton University, 1975), *reprinted in* JEFFREY B. MORRIS, FEDERAL JUSTICE IN THE SECOND CIRCUIT 97 (1987).

2. MORRIS, *supra* note 1, at 249.

3. Charles M. Hough, *Memoirs*, 69–73 (unpublished) (on file with the United States Courts Library for the Second Circuit).

4. *Id.* at 73.

5. *Id.* at 114.

6. AMERICAN COUNCIL OF LEARNED SOCIETIES, 9 DICTIONARY OF AMERICAN BIOGRAPHY 249 (Dumas Malone ed., 1943).

7. *Memoirs*, *supra* note 3, at 90–91.

8. GERALD GUNTHER, LEARNED HAND: THE MAN AND THE JUDGE 279 (1994).

9. *Memoirs*, *supra* note 3, at 138.

10. *Id.*

11. *Id.* at 144.

12. *Id.* at 167–68.

13. *Id.* at 162.

14. AMERICAN COUNCIL OF LEARNED SOCIETIES, *supra* note 6, at 249.

15. *Memoirs*, *supra* note 3, at 181. In his later years, Hough asserted: "I have often said of late that I am the youngest 'articled clerk' in the United States, certainly north of Mason and Dixon's line; for quite unwittingly I embarked on a style of legal education fast passing away. The law schools . . . were proving that learning the law was something that most men would better acquire academically, under the guidance of scholars, than empirically by watching busy legal artisans, or by grinding privately over textbooks that were either worthless compilations or couched in language of which only a finished lawyer could grasp the implications." *Id.* at 194.

16. *Id.*

17. *Id.*

18. Charles S. Haight, *Memorial of Honorable Henry Galbraith Ward*, MAR. LAW ASS'N OF THE UNITED STATES, Mar. 1934, at 1978, http://www.mlaus.org/archives/library/1288.pdf.

19. *See Hough for District Judge*, N.Y. TIMES, June 21, 1906, at 7.

20. *Charles M. Hough, Noted Jurist, Dead*, N.Y. TIMES, April 23, 1927, at 17.

21. *See Hough for District Judge*, *supra* note 19.

22. *Id.*

23. *Charles M. Hough, Noted Jurist, Dead*, *supra* note 20.

24. *Id.*

25. *Id.*

26. *Id.*

27. MORRIS, *supra* note 1, at 97.

28. *See Judge Hough to be Sworn in Friday*, N.Y. TIMES, July 3, 1906, at 16; *Hough for District Judge*, *supra* note 19.

29. *Charles M. Hough, Noted Jurist, Dead*, *supra* note 20.

30. *See id.*

31. *"Judge" Young it May Be*, NEW ROCHELLE PRESS, June 9, 1906, at 1.

32. *Hough for District Judge*, *supra* note 21.

33. *Id.*

34. *Id.*

35. *See id.*

36. *Id.*

37. *Id.*

38. *Id.*

39. *Id.*

40. *See Judge Hough to be Sworn in Friday*, *supra* note 27.

41. MORRIS, *supra* note 1, at 97.

42. *Id.*

43. *Id.*

44. *Id.*

45. *Wilson Names Hough to Succeed Lacombe*, N.Y. TIMES, Aug. 16, 1916, at 4.

46. MORRIS, *supra* note 1, at 98 (citations omitted).

47. *See Judge Hough's Promotion*, N.Y. TIMES, Aug. 17, 1916, at 10.

48. *Wilson Names Hough to Succeed Lacombe*, *supra* note 43.

49. AMERICAN COUNCIL OF LEARNED SOCIETIES, *supra* note 6, at 249.

50. Charles Evans Hughes and Drury W. Cooper, Remarks at a Memorial From the Bench and Bar to Charles M. Hough, Minutes of the United States Circuit Court of Appeals for the Second Circuit and of the United States District Court for the District Court for the Southern District of New York 4, 10 (May 2, 1927) (transcript on file with the United States Courts Library for the Second Circuit). Hughes served as judge on the Court of International Justice and later served as chief justice of the United States. Cooper was a leading patent attorney and served as trustee of the New York Patent Law Association.

51. MORRIS, *supra* note 1, at 98 (citations omitted).

52. Cooper, Remarks, *supra* note 50, at 8-9.

53. 245 F. 244 (2d Cir. 1917), *aff'd* 248 U.S. 215 (1918).

54. *Id.* at 253.

55. 250 F. 407 (2d Cir. 1918).

56. *Id.* at 414.

57. *Id.*; *see also* Charles Merrill Hough, *Report of Cases in the Vice Admiralty of the Province of New York and in the Court of Admiralty of the State of New York 1715-1788*, YALE UNIVERSITY PRESS, 1925.

58. Charles Merrill Hough, *The United States District Court of the Southern District of New York—Its Growth, and the Men Who Have Done Its Work*, 1789-1919, NEW YORK MARITIME LAW ASSOCIATION, June 1934.

59. *Memoirs*, *supra* note 3, at 241.

60. The Maritime Law Association of the United States—the first hundred years, http://www.maritimeadvocate.com/law_cases/the_maritime_law_association_of_the_united_states_the_first_hundred_years.htm.

61. *24 Nations Make New Marine Rules*, N.Y. TIMES, Nov. 19, 1922, at 33.

62. MORRIS, *supra* note, 1 at 97.

63. *Charles M. Hough, Noted Jurist, Dead*, *supra* note 20.

64. MORRIS, *supra* note, 1 at 97.

65. *Charles M. Hough, Noted Jurist, Dead*, *supra* note 20.

66. *Id.*

67. *Id.*

68. *Id.*

69. *Id.*

70. *Id.*

71. FIND A GRAVE, Charles Merrill Hough, http://www.findagrave.com/cgi-bin/fg.cgi?page=gr&GRid=80909248.

# MARTIN MANTON
## 1880-1946

District Court for the Southern District of New York: 1916-1918
Court of Appeals for the Second Circuit: 1918-1939

The verdict of history has not been kind to Martin Manton, and rightly so: he betrayed the court. Instructing the jury, the judge at Manton's criminal trial observed, "The charge of conspiracy on the part of a judge of a Federal appellate court to sell justice is hitherto unprecedented in the history of 150 years of this nation."[1]

The son of Irish immigrants,[2] Manton was born in New York City in August 1880 and attended public schools in Sayville, Long Island.[3] He worked his way through Columbia Law School, graduating in 1901.[4] Manton practiced negligence law in Brooklyn.[5]

Supreme Court Chief Justice William Howard Taft later described him as "an ambulance chaser."[6] He became the protégé and eventually the partner of Democratic Party-Tammany Hall leader W. Bourke Cochran.[7] In 1914, Manton defended Police Lieutenant Charles Becker in his trial for the murder of gambler Herman Rosenthal.[8]

Manton was appointed to the District Court for the Southern District of New York by President Woodrow Wilson in 1916.[9] The appointment was largely brought about by Cochran and Brooklyn Democratic "Czar" John McCooey.[10] Manton was also popular with the hierarchy of the Roman Catholic Church.[11] At 36, Manton was the youngest federal judge in the country.[12] Eighteen months later, he was elevated to the Court of Appeals for the Second Circuit.[13] In 1927, Manton became the senior circuit judge.[14]

Manton was not well regarded by his colleagues. While a district judge, Learned Hand opposed Manton's elevation to the Second Circuit. In 1918 Hand wrote to Felix Frankfurter, hoping "a better man than Manton" would be picked.[15] Later, on the Court of Appeals, Judge Learned Hand told his law clerk "to be wary of fraternizing with Manton's law clerk" and opined that Manton did not have "the judicial temperament."[16] Learned Hand's biographer described Manton as "a loner" at the court, "preoccupied with his political cronies."[17] Manton developed a reputation as a "scissors and paste-pot" judge for his "lifting" of portions of parties' briefs.[18] Judge Augustus Hand thought Manton was lazy.[19] He once took a draft Manton opinion to Manton's secretary to point out that she had missed a line when copying from a party's brief.[20] Judge Hand, a classics major at Harvard, versed in Greek and Latin, took a dim view of behavior he regarded as akin to a student's using a "pony to translate Virgil."[21]

Contributing to Manton's unpopularity was his "high-handed manner of exercising the limited administrative functions of the senior judge."[22] He clashed with other judges over scheduling.[23] *Time* magazine described him as the court's "irascible domineering senior judge."[24]

In 1922, Manton was in the running for a seat on the Supreme Court. Judge Learned Hand was astonished that Manton had backing for the vacancy: he marveled at Manton's "most amazing astuteness."[25] Chief Justice Taft wrote a friend that he thought Manton was a "shrewd, cunning, political [j]udge," who was "unethical and never should have been appointed to the bench in the first place."[26] Nonetheless, Manton had strong support in some influential quarters for what was then regarded as "the Catholic seat" on the Supreme Court. The New York Roman Catholic Archbishop wanted him to be appointed.[27] Governor Al Smith backed him.[28] Taft's former attorney general, George Wickersham, said "I understand Manton is pulling every wire he can."[29] Wickersham was appalled by the English in one of Manton's opinions and brought it to Taft's attention.[30] The Judiciary Committee of the Association of the Bar of the City of New York voted to do everything it could to stop Manton.[31] Taft wrote to another candidate, Pierce Butler of Minnesota, explaining why he thought Manton's appointment would be a disaster, declaring Manton "utterly unfit," and observing that Manton lacked "moral qualities" essential to a judge.[32] Ultimately Manton's church support was "neutralized": Butler too was a Roman Catholic.[33] Butler got the appointment.[34] Over time, Manton still campaigned for a Supreme Court spot.[35] The leading commentator on the 1922 contest mused: if Manton had risen to the Supreme Court would he have reformed or would he have been corrupt "only on a grander scale?"[36]

Chief Justice Taft did see the value of a judge who was a "politician down to the ground" and appointed Manton to a Judicial Conference committee "to secure legislative authorization for law clerks."[37] Manton was instrumental in establishing the Administrative Office, the federal judiciary's "housekeeping agency."[38] He also worked to get the new Foley Square courthouse built.[39]

Manton was a tireless self-promoter.[40] He was a "[p]olitician, publicity-seeker, and lover of luxury."[41] Manton had an apartment at the Hotel Madison, at 15 E. 58th Street, and a country home in Bayport, Long Island.[42] He made himself available for speeches.[43] In 1929, he spoke at the cornerstone laying for the New York County Lawyers' Association building, extolling the "independence and integrity of the American Bar."[44] In 1933, before the Vermont Bar Association, he opined that "nothing can take the place of that commodity called an honest lawyer."[45] He garnered honorary degrees and bar association awards, "exaggerating his distinction as a jurist."[46] He wrote articles such as "Building Up a Law Practice," (counseling how to do so "honorably and ethically"), and "A 'New Deal' for Lawyers."[47] In the "New Deal" article, Manton encouraged lawyers to become business men and advised, "[T]he opportunities are measureless for integrity and effort. As natural as day follows night, come the rewards of honor."[48] He also wrote the foreword to the first edition of *Moore's Federal Practice*.[49]

Meanwhile, his chambers swarmed with his "political cronies."[50] He kept large amounts of cash in a safe in chambers.[51] One commentator observed that "knowing Knickerbockers" nicknamed him "the preying Manton."[52] "Lawyers disliked his air of domineering omniscience which seemed seldom justified by his understanding of their cases, and some lawyers worried about his off-bench business affairs which were known to be extensive and intricate."[53]

Manton was a millionaire when he joined the Southern District bench, mostly through real estate holdings.[54] He owned a laundry, hotels, and a paper products company.[55] The Depression "was the basic cause of his undoing."[56] *The New York Times* first brought his financial troubles to light in February 1931, reporting on a bank failure and on Manton's substantial borrowing.[57] According to the *Times,* Manton was said to be one of the wealthiest federal judges.[58] In 1937, the *Times* reported an SEC investigation into big loans "made to men prominent in New York," right before the 1929 crash: "A series of loans made to [Manton] was a high-light of the transactions."[59]

Manton seemed to see dispensing patronage as his natural right. He inserted himself into the designation of receivers in the district court, assigning himself to the district court so he could bestow lucrative appointments, despite district court opposition.[60] This struggle wound up before the Supreme Court in a case about the insolvency of the Interborough Rapid Transit Company.[61] The Supreme Court began its opinion: "These cases exhibit an acute controversy between the Senior Circuit Judge of the Second

Circuit and the District Judges of the Southern District of New York. . . ."[62] The Supreme Court found "no jurisdictional infirmity" in Manton's orders.[63] But, it observed, "The possession of power is one thing; the propriety of its exercise in particular circumstances is quite a different thing," and concluded that Manton had "acted hastily and evidently with questionable wisdom."[64] Manton continued to resist but eventually bowed out of the proceeding.[65]

The *Times* later reported that "rumors began to be circulated among lawyers regarding Manton's conduct."[66] In early January 1939, Judge Learned Hand wrote his wife that Manton was under a "cloud," but Hand thought the trouble would blow over.[67] In January 1939, the *New York World Telegram* printed an exposé of Manton's business dealings.[68] New York County District Attorney Thomas E. Dewey, who had been investigating Manton's activities,[69] wrote the chairman of the House Judiciary Committee naming cases in which Manton had received payments from litigants in exchange for judicial favors.[70] Dewey said his office initially had been looking into possible violation of state income tax laws.[71] Asked if the investigation was "in connection with State or Federal income taxes," Manton answered, "In connection with Mr. Dewey's ambitions."[72] A federal investigation and prosecution followed.[73] Meeting with reporters in his twenty-fourth floor chambers, Manton said, "What charges? Hasn't a judge the right to buy stocks and bonds?"[74] Manton resigned on January 30. He asked that his resignation not take effect until March, but President Franklin Delano Roosevelt gave him a week and directed that he no longer sit on cases.[75]

"The government packed together . . . its entire trial case against . . . Manton" in a superseding indictment dated April 26, 1939.[76] The charge was conspiracy to obstruct the administration of justice and to defraud the United States.[77] One theory holds that prosecutors were deterred from charging bribery by one of Manton's own opinions, where he wrote that there could not be a conspiracy to bribe.[78] The indictment listed six cases in which Manton took gifts: five patent cases and one criminal. Manton had four co-defendants, including John L. Lotsch and William J.

Fallon, both of whom pled guilty.[79] Certain officers of companies with patent suits were named as unindicted co-conspirators.[80]

District Judge W. Calvin Chestnut was brought in from Maryland to preside.[81] The trial lasted from May 22 to June 3, 1939.[82] The weather was "scorching."[83] Mid-trial, one of Manton's lawyers was seized by a painful recurrence of a stomach ulcer.[84]

Trial evidence revealed that Fallon acted as the go-between (the "bagman"), matching up people interested in certain cases and passing money from them to Manton "to buy [his] favorable offices."[85] Fallon professed intimacy with Manton, on one occasion saying to a litigant: "I gave the judge the dickens about the decision last night."[86] In one instance a company with a patent case on appeal entered a $10,000 payment to Fallon in its books as "Prepaid Royalties," and later changed it to "litigation expense."[87] Manton importuned the company's president to destroy records reflecting that Fallon was on the company's payroll, and the company complied.[88] In another instance, Manton manipulated sitting schedules in order to preside over a case where he had been paid to "fix things up."[89]

The *Times* said that Manton's methods "were almost incredibly brazen."[90] Another example is illustrative. Co-defendant Lotsch was a patent lawyer enmeshed in three of the six cases in the indictment. Two were patent appeals in which Lotsch was an advocate; the third was a criminal case in which he was the defendant. Lotsch was charged with extortion in his role as a special master in the district court. When he appealed from the denial of habeas corpus relief, Manton presided over the appeal and advised Lotsch about what to argue in his reply brief. Manton arranged to meet Lotsch on a Long Island Railroad train. In a parlor car on the Patchogue Express, Manton showed Lotsch the panel's draft opinion, which Lotsch critiqued. While Manton accepted some edits, he demurred at one, "because his colleagues would not stand for it." The panel ruled in Lotsch's favor.[91] Lotsch testified against Manton, relating this and other incidents.[92]

Manton called eight reputation witnesses, including former Governor Al Smith.[93] But the bulk of his defense was his own testimony (flat denials) and that of his secretary, Marie Schmalz.[94]

On cross-examination, Manton admitted that despite earning a judge's salary of $12,500, he went from $500,000 in debt in 1934 to $750,000 in assets in 1935.[95] The defense subpoenaed Judges Augustus and Learned Hand, Thomas Swan, and Harrie Chase. Each judge testified that he had observed, while sitting on cases with Manton, nothing that made him think Manton was "acting otherwise than according to his oath of office and the dictates of his conscience."[96] Commentators have observed that this showed Manton was a good actor.[97]

The jury was out for four hours, including over an hour for dinner, and brought in a guilty verdict at 11:15 Saturday night.[98] At sentencing, Manton argued, "A judge can no more be guilty of obstructing justice in his own court than he can be guilty of contempt of his own court," but nonetheless he was sentenced to two years' imprisonment and a $10,000 fine.[99] The appeal was heard by a special panel of newly appointed Second Circuit Judge Charles E. Clark, retired Supreme Court Justice George Sutherland, and Supreme Court Justice Harlan Fiske Stone.[100] Going to hear the oral argument of his appeal, Manton used the judges' private elevator, angering the two Hands.[101]

Justice Sutherland summarized the most damning evidence:[102]

- Manton's relationship with Fallon
- Fallon's role in getting loans for Manton's companies
- Fallon's introducing Manton to litigants
- Lotsch's testimony that he paid money and got favors
- Manton's calls to the company's president about destroying evidence of payments to Fallon
- Manton's altering the calendar so he could sit on a given case
- Loans Manton requested from interested parties

The panel conceded that the evidence against Manton "came from the lips of convicted co-conspirators and other witnesses of bad or dubious character. Indeed, in a case like this, it is unlikely that it would be otherwise."[103] But the jury had weighed their credibility and the "mass of documentary evidence."[104]

One of Manton's arguments on appeal was that the trial judge erred in declining to charge the jurors "that they might consider the question whether the decisions here involved were correct." The logic was that if the decisions were correct there could be no obstruction of justice.[105] The appeals court rejected this notion on the ground that "judicial action *taken for a price*" bears the "stain of corruption" and, no matter that the decision is correct, this does not exonerate the bought judge.[106] The appeals court even suggested that Manton, seeking to avoid discovery, only took payments in cases where the outcome appeared clear.[107] The Supreme Court declined to review the case.[108] Manton had audaciously argued, "[I]t serves no public policy for a high judicial officer to be convicted of a judicial crime. It tends to destroy the confidence of the people in the courts."[109]

Manton surrendered with tears in his eyes.[110] He served his time (ultimately, one year and seven months) at the federal correctional facility in Lewisburg, Pennsylvania beginning in March, 1940.[111] He was released on October 13, 1941, having worked in the prison greenhouse when "his health permit[ted]."[112] Manton died in Fayetteville, in upstate New York, in 1946.[113]

In the year of Manton's trial and conviction, the American Bar Association editorialized that judges should refrain from "[a]ctive conduct of business affairs." The ABA reasoned, "This does not mean that the judge who happens to have resources must sell all he has and give it to the poor. But it does mean that, in discharge of his duty, he should act as though he has done just that." The ABA went on: "This is exactly how the overwhelming number of Federal judges have always acted and may be expected to act."[114]

The court Manton betrayed prevailed. In the end, Martin Manton disgraced only himself.

Catherine J. Minuse

1. *Spector Guilty, Too*, N.Y. TIMES, June 4, 1939, at 1.

2. MILTON S. GOULD, THE WITNESS WHO SPOKE WITH GOD 189 (1979).

3. *Text of Manton's Testimony Given in His Own Defense at His Trial Yesterday*, N.Y. TIMES, June 2, 1939, at 19.

4. JOSEPH BORKIN, THE CORRUPT JUDGE 28-29 (1962).

5. *Id.* at 29.

6. DAVID J. DANELSKI, A SUPREME COURT JUSTICE IS APPOINTED 59 (1964).

7. MARVIN SCHICK, LEARNED HAND'S COURT 62 (1970); GOULD, *supra* note 2, at 189.

8. *Becker's Lawyers Plan Final Move*, N.Y. TIMES, July 13, 1915, at 20; *Body is Brought Here for Funeral*, N.Y. TIMES, July 31, 1915, at 3; *First-Degree Conviction for Directing Slaying of Rosenthal*, N.Y. TIMES, May 23, 1914, at 1.

9. *Manton Appointed by Wilson in 1916*, N.Y. TIMES, Jan. 30, 1939, at 3.

10. GOULD, *supra* note 2, at 190; GERALD GUNTHER, LEARNED HAND THE MAN AND THE JUDGE 431 (2d ed. 2011).

11. GUNTHER, *supra* note 10, at 431.

12. SCHICK, *supra* note 7, at 62.

13. BORKIN, *supra* note 4, at 30; GOULD, *supra* note 2, at 190; GUNTHER, *supra* note 10, at 221, 231; *Judge Manton Promoted*, N.Y. TIMES, March 13, 1918, at 4.

14. *Associates Honor Late Judge Hough*, N.Y. TIMES, May 7, 1927, at 17. The senior-most active judge was known as the "senior circuit judge" until 1948, when the term "chief judge" was established under 28 U.S.C. § 45. The term was adopted "in recognition of the great increase in administrative duties of such judge." REPORT FROM THE HOUSE COMM. ON THE JUDICIARY, TO ACCOMPANY H.R. 3214, H.R. 308, 80th Cong., 1st Sess., A6 (1947); *see also* Act of June 25, 1948, ch. 646, § 45(a) 62 Stat. 869, 871 ("The circuit judge senior in commission shall be the chief judge of the circuit.").

15. CONSTANCE JORDAN, REASON AND IMAGINATION: THE SELECTED CORRESPONDENCE OF LEARNED HAND: 1897-1961, at 66, 67 (2013); *see also* GUNTHER, *supra* note 10, at 221.

16. MARCIA NELSON, THE REMARKABLE HANDS 59 (1983).

17. GUNTHER, *supra* note 10, at 237.

18. GUNTHER, *supra* note 10, at 434.

19. NELSON, *supra* note 16, at 59.

20. *Id.* at 60.

21. *Id.*; *see also* GUNTHER, *supra* note 10, at 26.

22. GUNTHER, *supra* note 10, at 242.

23. *Id.* at 437.

24. Warren T. Jessup, *The Judge and the Cigar Lighter*, 5 ANTITRUST BULL. 633, 634 (1960) (quoting TIME, June 5, 1939).

25. GUNTHER, *supra* note 10, at 234.

26. DANELSKI, *supra* note 6, at 45.

27. *Id.* at 43-45, 48.

28. *Id.* at 87.

29. *Id.* at 11, 47.

30. *Id.*

31. *Id.* at 74.

32. *Id.* at 58-60.

33. *Id.* at 63.

34. *Id.* at 1.

35. *Id.* at 195-97.

36. *Id.* at 197.

37. PETER GRAHAM FISH, THE POLITICS OF FEDERAL JUDICIAL ADMINISTRATION 45 (1973); *see also* JEFFREY B. MORRIS, FEDERAL JUSTICE IN THE SECOND CIRCUIT 134 (1987).

38. FISH, *supra* note 37, at 125, 138, 143, 166.

39. MORRIS, *supra* note 37, at 134; *Drive on to Speed Federal Building*, N.Y. TIMES, Dec. 1, 1927, at 29.

40. GUNTHER, *supra* note 10, at 221.

41. MORRIS, *supra* note 37, at 131.

42. JESSUP, *supra* note 24, at 640; *Dewey Says Judge Manton Got $400,000 from Litigants; Sends Charges to Congress*, N.Y. TIMES, Jan. 30, 1939, at 1; *Text of Manton's Testimony*, *supra* note 3, at 19.

43. JESSUP, *supra* note 24, at 634; MORRIS, *supra* note 37, at 134.

44. Allan D. Vestal, *A Study in Perfidy*, 35 IND. L.J. 17, 18 (1959).

45. *Id.* at 30.

46. MORRIS, *supra* note 37, at 134.

47. Martin T. Manton, *Building Up a Law Practice*, 63 U.S. L. REV. 566, 566 (1929); Martin T. Manton, *A "New Deal" for Lawyers*, 19 A.B.A. J. 596 (1933).

48. Manton, "*New Deal*," *supra* note 47, at 599, 600.

49. 1 JAMES WM. MOORE & JOSEPH FRIEDMAN, MOORE'S FEDERAL PRACTICE (1st ed. 1938).

50. GUNTHER, *supra* note 10, at 221, 237, 244, 431.

51. Vestal, *supra* note 44, at 33; *Manton Is Accused of Letting Litigant Help with Opinion*, N.Y. TIMES, May 25, 1939, at 1; *Manton Testifies to Big Cash Loans from Litigants*, June 3, 1939, at 1.

52. JESSUP, *supra* note 24, at 634.

53. *Id.* at 634 (quoting TIME, Feb. 6, 1939); *see also* GOULD, *supra* note 2, at 182-83.

54. GOULD, *supra* note 2, at 190; SCHICK, *supra* note 7, at 62; *Text of Manton's Testimony*, N.Y. TIMES, June 2, 1939, at 20.

55. BORKIN, *supra* note 4, at 49.

56. *Ex-Judge Manton of U.S. Bench Here*, N.Y. TIMES, Nov. 18, 1946, at 21; GOULD, *supra* note 2, at 190; SCHICK, *supra* note 7, at 62-63; Vestal, *supra* note 45, at 20-21 (quotes jury charge); *Judge Manton's Statement*, N.Y. TIMES, Jan. 31, 1939, at 8 ("[T]he depression and the fall in real estate values entailed heavy losses on me . . . .").

57. *Inventory of Bank of U.S. Shows Condition the Day Before It Was Closed by* State, N.Y. TIMES, Feb. 2, 1931, at 10; *see also* BORKIN, *supra* note 4, at 39.

58. *Inventory of Bank*, *supra* note 57; *see also* BORKIN, *supra* note 4, at 40.

59. *Heavy Loss Taken by Trust on Loans*, N.Y. TIMES, May 5, 1937, at 37.

60. GUNTHER, *supra* note 10, at 438-39; Vestal, *supra* note 44, at 24.

61. Johnson v. Manhattan Ry. Co., 289 U.S. 479 (1933).

62. *Id.* at 483.

63. *Id.* at 502.

64. *Id.* at 504-05.

65. BORKIN, *supra* note 4, at 37; *Manton Retires from I.R.T. Case*, N.Y. TIMES, Oct. 1, 1933, at N7.

66. *Ex-Judge Manton of U.S. Bench Here*, *supra* note 56.

67. GUNTHER, *supra* note 10, at 432. Judge Learned Hand later told Murray Gurfein, once on Thomas Dewey's staff and eventually a Second Circuit Judge: "We suspected that Manton did political favors from time to time, although we could not prove it, but that he took money, *money*, this we never suspected." THOMAS E. DEWEY, TWENTY AGAINST THE UNDERWORLD 454 (1974).

68. GUNTHER, *supra* note 10, at 431; JESSUP, *supra* note 24, at 634-35. S. Burton Heath later won the Pulitzer Prize for his reporting on the scandal. DEWEY, *supra* note 68, at 454.

69. BORKIN, *supra* note 4, at 44-55; GOULD, *supra* note 2, at 198-99; GUNTHER, *supra* note 10, at 431-32.

70. *Dewey Letter on Manton*, N.Y. TIMES, Jan. 30, 1939, at 1; *see also* BORKIN, *supra* note 4, at 44; GOULD, *supra* note 2, at 199; GUNTHER, *supra* note 10, at 431-32.

71. *Dewey Letter on Manton*, *supra* note 70. Over two years earlier, a racketeering investigation had brought to light a large loan to Manton that aroused Dewey's suspicions. RICHARD NORTON SMITH, THOMAS E. DEWEY AND HIS TIMES 281(1982).

72. JESSUP, *supra* note 24, at 635.

73. GOULD, *supra* note 2, at 201-02.

74. JESSUP *supra* note 24, at 635; *Manton's Conduct Under U.S. Inquiry; He Defers Defense*, N.Y. TIMES, Jan. 29, 1939, at 1, 10.

75. *Roosevelt Orders Manton Out Feb. 7; U.S. Inquiry On Here*, N.Y.TIMES, Feb. 1, 1939, at 1.

76. *Manton Case Told in New Indictment*, N.Y. TIMES, Apr. 27, 1939, at 32; *see also* BORKIN, *supra* note 4, at 45; GUNTHER *supra* note 10, at 432-34; GOULD, *supra* note 2, at 204.

77. United States v. Manton, 107 F.2d 834, 836 (2d Cir. 1939), *cert. denied*, 309 U.S. 664 (1940). Marvin V. Ausubel, *The Rise and Fall of Martin Thomas Manton*, 82 N.Y. ST. B.A. J. 28, 31 (2010) ("It has been theorized that the government elected to proceed under the conspiracy statute because of the greater latitude of permissible evidence.").

78. United States v. Sager, 49 F.2d 725, 727 (2d Cir. 1931); *.3,000 Manton Cases Facing a Reopening on His Conviction*, N.Y. TIMES, June 5, 1939, at 1.

79. 107 F.2d at 836-37; BORKIN, *supra* note 4, at 45-48.

80. 107 F.2d at 836-37; BORKIN, *supra* note 4, at 45-48.

81. *Maryland Judge To Sit at Trial of Manton*, N.Y. TIMES, Apr. 20, 1939, at 12.

82. BORKIN, *supra* note 4, at 79; *Ex-Judge Manton Faces Trial Today*, N.Y. TIMES, May 22, 1939, at 17.

83. JESSUP, *supra* note 24, at 636.

84. *Manton Is Accused of Letting Litigant Help with Opinion*, *supra* note 51.

85. 107 F.2d at 840; *see also* GUNTHER, *supra* note 10, at 434.

86. JESSUP, *supra* note 24, at 637; *Manton Litigant Tells of Payments*, N.Y. TIMES, May 24, 1939, at 21.

87. 107 F.2d at 840.

88. *Id.*

89. *Id.* at 842-43.

90. *Justice for Sale*, N.Y. TIMES, June 5, 1939, at 14; BORKIN, *supra* note 4, at 80.

91. 107 F.2d at 842; *Manton is Accused of Letting Litigant Help with Opinion*, *supra* note 51.

92. 107 F.2d at 844.

93. *Smith and Davis Give Aid to Manton*, N.Y. TIMES, June 1, 1939, at 1.

94. Vestal, *supra* note 44, at 41.

95. JESSUP, *supra* note 24 at 641; *Manton On Stand Denies All Charges, Admits Gain of $1,250,000 in a Year*, N.Y. TIMES, June 2, 1939, at 1.

96. GUNTHER, *supra* note 10, at 433; *Manton Testifies to Big Cash Loans from Litigants*, N.Y. TIMES June 3, 1939, at 1.

97. GOULD, *supra* note 2, at 227; BORKIN, *supra* note 4, at 49.

98. *Judge Manton Is Convicted by Jury of Selling Justice; Judge Martin is Acquitted*, N.Y. TIMES, June 4, 1939, at 1; *Spector Guilty, Too*, *supra* note 1.

99. *Manton Sentenced to Two-Year Term After Futile Plea*, N.Y. TIMES, June 21, 1939, at 1, 2.

100. 107 F.2d 834; BORKIN, *supra* note 4, at 80-81; *Manton Pays Fine, Surrenders Today*, N.Y. TIMES Mar. 7, 1940, at 25.

101. Bennett Boskey, *Seymour J. Rubin-Some of the Origins*, 10 AM. U. J. INT'L L. & POL'Y 1245, 1247-48 n.2 (1995).

102. 107 F.2d at 844.

103. *Id.* at 843.
104. *Id.*
105. *Id.* at 845.
106. *Id.* at 846.
107. *Id.*; GUNTHER, *supra* note 10, at 434.
108. *High Court Backs Manton Conviction*, N.Y. TIMES, Feb. 27, 1940, at 1.
109. *Id.*
110. *Manton, Tearful, Lodged in Prison*, N.Y.TIMES, Mar. 8, 1940, at 10.
111. *Id.; Ex-Judge Manton of U.S. Bench Here, supra* note 56.
112. *Manton To Leave Prison Cell Today*, N.Y. TIMES, Oct. 13, 1941, at 19.
113. *Ex-Judge Manton of U.S. Bench Here, supra* note 56.
114. Vestal, *supra* note 44, at 44.

# JULIUS MARSHUETZ MAYER
## 1865-1925

District Court for the Southern District of New York: 1912-1921
Court of Appeals for the Second Circuit: 1921-1924

The formation of New York City, the rise of federal regulation of the economy, and World War I: Julius Marshuetz Mayer, lawyer and statesman, the first Jewish judge on the Second Circuit, confronted some of the most important events of his time. He was born in New York City on September 6, 1865.[1] As a boy, he attended Hebrew Grammar School No. 68.[2] After graduating from City College, he received his law degree from Columbia Law School and went into private practice for several years.[3]

Mayer then entered New York City politics. In 1892, he was elected president of the Republican Party in the Twenty-Eighth Assembly District,[4] which then covered a section of the upper east side.[5] He was involved in helping the party reorganize under the auspices of the Committee of Thirty, giving speeches at Cooper Union in support of the reorganization, which was a hotly contested issue among members of New York City's minority party.[6] Republicans had a notoriously weak presence in Tammany Hall-controlled New York City, but Mayer began his political career just as this dynamic broke down under pressure for reform. Mayer organized the party's 1894 campaign for seats on the Board of Aldermen, the last election before the city's 1898 consolidation.[7]

Mayer soon advanced in the city's political class, but not before a setback. He ran for a judgeship in the Ninth Judicial District, but lost.[8] He rebounded, however, with an appointment to the city's excise board, where he gained expertise in taxation that led to his later, successful defense of the city's franchise tax before the Supreme Court.[9] At the time, Thomas C. Platt–a member of the House and Senate at the turn of the century–was the "boss" of New York's Republicans, and Mayer was one of his strongest supporters.[10] Unfortunately for Mayer, William L. Strong, a reformist Republican opposed by Platt, was elected mayor of New York in 1896.[11] Strong refused to swear Mayer into his position on the Constable Building Commission.[12] Mayer was forced to bide his time.

In 1902, however, under a new administration, Mayer was appointed justice of Special Sessions.[13] After serving for two years, he obtained Platt's backing and ran successfully for New York attorney general.[14] There, Mayer's career intersected with a major change in American law and society. Mayer represented the State of New York in *Lochner v. New York*,[15] one of the most important constitutional cases in American history. Mayer, however, didn't know that *Lochner* would inaugurate a revolution in constitutional law. To him, the case was less important than the *Franchise Tax Cases*, to be argued shortly after *Lochner*.[16] And, at that time, it *was* innocuous–few thought *Lochner* was an important case, even after it was decided.[17] Unsurprisingly, with more pressing cases to attend to, Mayer gave *Lochner* less than his full attention. His brief has been criticized for its brevity and lack of legal argument.[18] This criticism, however, is grounded on hindsight; better to say that Mayer–like everyone else at the time–could not have anticipated *Lochner*'s impact.

Mayer's tenure as attorney general was short, but it was not without political controversy. His time in office coincided with the 1905 governor's race between incumbent George McClellan, a Tammany Hall Democrat, and William Randolph Hearst, who decided to mount a third-party challenge shortly before the election.[19] The race was extremely close, and McClellan won by only a few thousand votes.[20]

Hearst would not go down easily. He claimed the election was corrupted by Tammany Hall fraud and demanded a recount.[21] Hearst lost in the courts and then turned to the state legislature, where he lobbied for a bill retroactively authorizing a recount.[22] He was again thwarted. This left Hearst with one option: an appeal to Attorney General Mayer to institute a suit on behalf of voters challenging McClellan's right to the office.[23] Mayer denied Hearst's application, which led to a predictable outburst of ire from Hearst's army of journalists.[24] In considering Hearst's appeal, however, Mayer remained neutral, fair, and level-headed, a rare feat when one considers the power Hearst wielded in the press.[25]

Mayer paid for his neutrality. He was defeated for reelection as attorney general by Hearst's running mate, William Jackson, in 1906.[26] Jackson of course immediately filed the suit instituting a recount in the 1905 governor's race.[27] Three years later, McClellan was again declared the winner, thereby vindicating Mayer's decision.[28] By this point, Mayer had returned to private practice.

In 1912, President William Howard Taft nominated Mayer to the District Court for the Southern District of New York. Women's and children's rights advocates protested based on Mayer's record on labor rights as attorney general.[29] Otherwise, he received significant support from his fellow Republicans in New York. His nomination provided President Taft a chance to please the New York Republicans whose support he needed for the state's Republican presidential primary against Teddy Roosevelt.[30]

Judge Mayer's time on the federal bench was eventful. As a district judge, he presided over the trial of anarchist Emma Goldman. He imposed the maximum sentence (two years imprisonment and a $10,000 fine), which led Goldman to pillory Judge Mayer in the courtroom.[31] He also presided over proceedings concerning the Lusitania.[32] The Lusitania, a British passenger ship, was torpedoed and sunk by a German submarine on a trip from New York to Liverpool in 1915, killing 1,195, including 128 Americans, and launching numerous suits against the ship's owner. Judge Mayer, in an exhaustive opinion, found that the ship's owner was not liable for any losses.[33]

By far the most important case of Judge Mayer's career concerned the bankruptcy and restructuring of the Brooklyn Rapid Transit Company (BRT). By the turn of the century, the BRT controlled most of the rapid transit in New York City, and after 1913, the BRT gained control of many of the subway lines in use today.[34] However, labor unrest and flawed contracts for building new lines led to the BRT's bankruptcy, which Judge Mayer oversaw.[35] At the end of these proceedings, which determined the future of New York City's subway system, the BRT reemerged as the Brooklyn-Manhattan Transit Corporation (BMT). There are still numerous BMT lines in New York,[36] a testament to the importance of Judge Mayer's work in saving the BRT from dissolution.

In 1921, Judge Mayer was appointed by President Warren G. Harding to the Court of Appeals for the Second Circuit.[37] His time on the Second Circuit was brief; he retired in 1924 after only two and a half years of service.[38]

Judge Mayer was involved with very few opinions, but one case, *Luckenbach S.S. Company & United States v. Thekla*,[39] provides an interesting example of a practice that has disappeared from American law: certifying questions to the Supreme Court. In *Luckenbach*, owners of the *Luckenbach* and the *Thekla*, two steamships, sued one another after a collision.[40] The United States intervened, declaring its ownership of the *Luckenbach* pursuant to a charter.[41] At the time of the collision, the *Luckenbach* was under the control of the War Department, which used the ship to deliver army stores to France.[42] The district court found for the owners of the *Thekla* and awarded $156,622.41 in damages, to be paid by the United States.[43] On appeal, the United States argued that the district court erred in ordering affirmative relief against the United States.[44] Instead of resolving the question, the Court of Appeals certified two questions to the Supreme Court: first, whether the district court had the power to order affirmative relief against the United States; and second, whether the United States was required to pay the damages.[45] The Supreme Court ruled that the district court could order the relief and that the United States had to pay the damages.[46]

*Luckenbach*, with its quaintly named ships and turn of the century circumlocution, is a relic, particularly because of its use of the certified question. The Supreme Court retains this jurisdiction: it is codified at 28 U.S.C. § 1254, immediately after the section providing for the writ of certiorari.[47] But the Supreme Court has answered certified questions only four times since 1946,[48] and the practice has not been mentioned in a Supreme Court opinion since 1996.[49] Its pedigree is long, however: the practice dates from 1802, and, until 1889, was the only method by which criminal cases could reach the Supreme Court.[50] It was used in two high-profile national security cases, *Ex Parte Milligan* and *Korematsu v. United States.*[51] By 1930, however, the practice had begun to decline.[52]

Judge Mayer's personality was businesslike and stern, and he had a reputation as a taskmaster in the courtroom.[53] However, Judge Mayer's office attendant, Abram Adler, was apparently something of a character, meriting two *New York Times* pieces on his activities at the court. He gave Judge Mayer a beautiful model yacht named Edith, but Judge Mayer sold it to a "rich Republican" with a daughter named Edith to sail on the Atlantic off Long Island.[54] Later, the *Times* wrote a story on Adler's interactions with the family of pigeons that clustered on the window outside Judge Mayer's chambers.[55] Two of the older pigeons, apparently in some kind of relationship, became cross with one another and separated, but Adler steadfastly refused to disclose the nature of the pigeon's quarrel.[56] The story gives some sense of the solemn eccentricity of Judge Mayer's attendant.

Judge Mayer's retirement was indicative of the state of the judiciary at the time. He was admittedly dissatisfied with the job.[57] He felt his role on the bench prohibited him from engaging in "the many useful activities which may be participated in by private citizens."[58] He was also troubled by the low salary of federal judges,[59] a concern that animated several resignations during this period,[60] and even led to a *New York Times* piece reacting to Judge Mayer's resignation with a call for higher salaries.[61]

After leaving the bench, Judge Mayer joined a firm that would be renamed Mayer, Warfield & Watson, which specialized in patent litigation, a subject to which Judge Mayer had devoted years of thought and an article during his judicial career.[62] Judge Mayer suffered a heart attack and passed away shortly after retiring. His health had been good, and his death was unexpected.[63] He never married and had no children. He was survived by a brother, a sister, her husband, and his nieces and nephews, all of whom lived with him at his home at 11 East 9th Street in Greenwich Village.[64]

Stephen Strother

1. *Judge Mayer Dies of Heart Attack*, N.Y. TIMES, Dec. 1, 1925, at 1.
2. *Id.*
3. *Id.*
4. *Id.*
5. APPLETON'S DICTIONARY OF GREATER NEW YORK AND ITS VICINITY 218 (1898).
6. *Judge Mayer Dies of Heart Attack*, *supra* note 1, at 1.
7. *Id.*; *From Royal Rule to Public Finance*, GOTHAM GAZETTE, http://www.gothamgazette.com/index.php/archives/1944-a-brief-history-of-election-law-in-new-york.
8. *From Royal Rule*, *supra* note 7.
9. *See* New York Central R. Co. v. Miller, 202 U.S. 584 (1906).
10. *Judge Mayer Dies of Heart Attack*, *supra* note 1; APPLETON'S DICTIONARY, *supra* note 5, at 217.
11. RALPH J. CALIENDO, NEW YORK CITY MAYORS, VOLUME I: THE MAYORS OF NEW YORK BEFORE 1898 392–93 (2010).
12. *Judge Mayer Dies of Heart Attack*, *supra* note 1, at 2.
13. *Id.*
14. *Id.*
15. 198 U.S. 45 (1905).

16. PAUL KENS, JUDICIAL POWER AND REFORM POLITICS: THE ANATOMY OF *LOCHNER V. NEW YORK* 113–14 (1990).

17. Stephen E. Hessler, *The Story of Benjamin Cardozo, Learned Hand & The Southern District of New York*, 47 N.Y.L. SCH. L. REV. 191, 203 (2003).

18. KENS, *supra* note 16, at 112–13.

19. Hessler, *supra* note 17, at 203–04.

20. *Id.* at 204.

21. *Id.*

22. *Id.*

23. *Id.*

24. *Id.*

25. *Mr. Hearst's Application*, N.Y. TIMES, Jul. 17, 1906, at 6.

26. Hessler, *supra* note 17, at 204–05.

27. *Id.*

28. *Id.*

29. *Id.* at 205.

30. *Id.* at 205, 228–31, 245–52. The 1912 Republican primaries were the first closely contested primaries in the United States. They were held in only a few states. Roosevelt won all the primaries save Massachusetts, New York, and Wisconsin. However, Taft claimed most of the delegates from states that didn't hold primaries. Thus, at the end of voting, neither Roosevelt nor Taft had the delegates necessary to claim the nomination. Taft won at the Republic Convention through the support of the Republican National Committee. Lewis L. Gould, *1912 Republican Convention: Return of the Rough Rider*, SMITHSONIAN MAG., Aug. 2008, http://www.smithsonianmag.com/history/1912-republican-convention-855607/?all.

31. *Convict Berkman and Miss Goldman; Both Off to Prison*, N.Y. TIMES, July 10, 1917, at 1.

32. *The Lusitania*, 251 F. 715 (S.D.N.Y. 1918).

33. *Id.* at 735–36.

34. Mark S. Feinman, *Early Rapid Transit in Brooklyn, 1878-1913*, NYCSUBWAY.ORG, http://www.nycsubway.org/wiki/Early_Rapid_Transit_in_Brooklyn,_1878-1913.

35. James Poulos, *History*, BMT LINES, www.bmt-lines.com/history/.

36. Specifically, the B, D, J, L, M, N, Q, R, and Z trains run on BMT lines set up during the late nineteenth and early twentieth century. *See Line by Line Guide*, NYSUBWAY.ORG, www.nycsubway.org/wiki/Line_By_Line_Guide.

37. *Judge Mayer Quits to Enter Law Firm*, N.Y. TIMES, July 17, 1924, at 2.

38. *Id.* at 1.

39. 295 F. 1020 (2d Cir. 1924).

40. *Id.* at 1020.

41. *Id.* at 1020–21.

42. *Id.* at 1022.

43. *Id.*

44. *Id.*

45. *Id.*

46. U.S. v. The Thekla, 266 U.S. 328, 329 (1924).

47. Aaron Nielson, *The Death of the Supreme Court's Certified Question Jurisdiction*, 59 CATH. U. L. REV. 483, 484–85 (2010).

48. *Id.* at 484.

49. Felker v. Turpin, 518 U.S. 651, 667 (1996) (Souter, J., concurring); *see also* United States v. Penaranda, 375 F.3d 238 (2004) (*en banc*) (certifying questions to the Supreme Court pursuant to 28

U.S.C. § 1254(2)), certified questions dismissed, 543 U.S. 1117 (2005) (dismissing the Second Circuit's certified questions without opinion).

50. Nielson, *supra* note 47, at 486.

51. *Id.* at 484.

52. *Id.* at 486–87.

53. *Judge Mayer Dies of Heart Attack*, *supra* note 1, at 2.

54. *Judge Mayer's Yacht to Sail the Sea Again*, N.Y. TIMES, Apr. 16, 1922, at 1–2.

55. *Bird Romance Nearly Blasted*, N.Y. TIMES, May 25, 1924, at 1–2.

56. *Id.*

57. *Judge Mayer Quits to Enter Law Firm*, *supra* note 31, at 1–2.

58. *Id.*

59. *Id.*

60. Emily Field Van Tassel, *Resignations and Removals: A History of Federal Judicial Service—And Disservice—1789-1992*, 142 U. PA. L. REV. 333 (1993).

61. *Judge Mayer*, N.Y. TIMES, Dec. 2, 1925, at 1–2.

62. *Judge Mayer Quits to Enter Law Firm*, *supra* note 31, at 1–2; Julius M. Mayer, *The Judge and the Patent Case*, 8 A.B.A.J. 709 (1922).

63. *Judge Mayer Dies of Heart Attack*, *supra* note 1.

64. *Id.*

# BILLINGS LEARNED HAND
# 1872-1961

District Court for the Southern District of New York: 1909-1924
Court of Appeals for the Second Circuit: 1924-1961

Learned Hand, widely regarded as one of the greatest judges in American history, was as imaginative and courageous as he was intellectually gifted and accomplished in the law. His opinions achieved literary dimensions and are still taught in law schools today. Yet his brilliance was not unalloyed: he was plagued by self-doubt. Judge Jerome Frank once cautioned: "To write a competent biography of Learned Hand would be singularly perplexing. For he is an exquisitely complex person, or, rather, a complex multitude of persons."[1]

Hand was born in Albany, New York on January 27, 1872.[2] He deemed his given name, Billings, too "pompous," and was often called "B," but preferred Learned—his mother's maiden name.[3]

Hand's grandfather, Augustus Cincinnatus, born in 1803, was a justice of the New York Supreme Court,[4] a member of State Congress, a State senator, and a leader at the bar.[5] Hand's father, Samuel, was regarded as one of the best lawyers in the state, argued more cases in the New York State Court of Appeals than any attorney of his time,[6] and was (briefly) an associate judge on the New York State Court of Appeals.[7] Samuel died in 1886, when Hand was only 14 years old.[8] Hand's mother was said to have passed on to her son a strong sense of duty and guilt, consistent with her Calvinist upbringing.[9]

Hand's uncle and Samuel's brother, Richard Hand, was also a prominent attorney,[10] and was father to Hand's cousin, Augustus Noble Hand, who followed Hand on the district court and the court of appeals. The cousins were friends from boyhood, often hunting and sledding together in the Adirondack countryside near Gus's home.[11] When they were boys, the Hand family viewed Gus as the one with better judgment.[12]

At Albany Academy, Hand was the "hunting and trapping" editor of his school newspaper.[13] At Harvard, he was a member of Phi Beta Kappa, graduated *summa cum laude*, and was the class orator.[14] He graduated from Harvard College with AB and AM degrees in 1893 and 1894, respectively,[15] and from Harvard Law School with honors in 1896.[16]

In 1902, Hand married Bryn Mawr College graduate Frances Amelia Fincke of Utica, New York.[17] The couple had three daughters: Mary Deshon, Frances Lydia, and Constance.[18] Their marriage was loving, though complicated, and strained by long separations.[19]

The Hand family lived in a brownstone at 142 East 65th Street.[20] Summers were spent in the artistic community of Cornish, New Hampshire, which Hand referred to as "Low Court."[21] During the summer of 1908, in Cornish, Hand befriended the political commentator Herbert Croly, and helped him to form *The New Republic* magazine.[22] It was also in Cornish that Judge Hand later developed a close friendship with the reclusive J.D. Salinger.[23]

Hand began his legal career in 1897 as a law clerk in the Albany law office of Marcus T. Hun and later was a member of the firm of Hun, Johnson and Hand.[24] He moved his legal practice to New York City in 1902, where he was a managing clerk for the firm of Zabriskie, Burrill and Murray.[25] Hand then joined the firm of Gould & Wilkie; he remained there until 1909.[26] He had mixed success as a lawyer, and did not find the work intellectually stimulating.[27]

On the recommendations of Attorney General George Wickersham and New York lawyer Charles C. Burlingham, President William Howard Taft appointed Hand to a newly created fourth judgeship in the District Court for the Southern District of New York in 1909.[28] Augustus Hand joined the court in 1914.[29]

During his 15 years on the district court, Hand wrote 637 opinions in all areas of the law.[30] Perhaps his best known decision on that court was *Masses Publishing Company v. Patten*,[31] which considered the protections to be afforded in wartime to an antiwar publication. The postmaster of New York City claimed that the August issue of *The Masses* violated the recently enacted Espionage Act that criminalized interference with the war effort and refused to deliver the issue. Hand enjoined the enforcement of the Act with an opinion that interpreted the statute without mentioning the First Amendment. Judge Hand read the statute narrowly to prohibit explicit incitement to resist the draft, but not general criticism of the draft law, and concluded that *The Masses* did not urge its readers to violate the law and thus could not be banned.[32]

The Second Circuit reversed the judgment in a lengthy opinion by Judge Henry Wade Rogers that rejected Judge Hand's narrow construction and chided his lack of judicial restraint.[33] This reversal and the public's adverse reaction to Hand's opinion caused him to be passed over for elevation to the court of appeals in 1918.[34] (That appointment went to Martin Manton.)[35]

In the years after Judge Hand took the bench, he became a quick but enthusiastic convert to progressive politics.[36] (It is widely believed that President Taft viewed this shift as a betrayal.)[37] Hand supported Theodore Roosevelt's Progressive (Bull Moose) party and, under the influence of Herbert Croly, embraced an agenda of federal control over corporations and social legislation to assist factory workers, women, and children.[38] In a series of letters, Judge Hand and Roosevelt deplored the impact of *Lochner v. New York*[39] on legislative efforts to address social problems.[40] Judge Hand wrote to Roosevelt: "[E]ither the courts must give up their constitutional prerogative, a by no means unthinkable alternative, or they must change, or we shall have our constitutions codes of general administrative and substantive legislation, which seems a cumbersome form of making law. . ."[41]

By the eve of the 1912 presidential election, Judge Hand was giddy with the prospect of a Bull Moose victory, writing to Roosevelt: "Nearly all of us are with you heart and soul. The greater part of the conscience and brains—under forty—of the country that I see are fine Bull Moose."[42] Roosevelt lost, but Judge Hand saw the campaign as the beginning of a meaningful national progressive political movement.[43]

In 1913, the Bull Moose Party courted Judge Hand to run for chief judge of the New York State Court of Appeals.[44] Judge Hand agreed—a bold move—but only on the condition that he not be required to campaign, which he considered unseemly for a sitting judge.[45] Still, his decision to run for office as a sitting federal judge earned the disapproval of Louis Brandeis.[46] When Judge Hand lost the election to Democrat Willard Bartlett, a friend wrote: "Your vote is practically a vote of protest, as everyone understood you would not be elected."[47] It was Judge Hand's only political campaign.[48]

While on the district court, Judge Hand worked with a group of lawyers and teachers to found the American Law Institute, later serving on the ALI's executive committee and as its vice president.[49] The ALI promotes the clarification and simplification of United States common law by publishing *Restatements of the Law*, *Principles of the Law*, model codes, and other proposals for law reform.[50]

On December 2, 1924, President Calvin Coolidge nominated Judge Hand to the Court of Appeals for the Second Circuit. The *New York Law Journal* confidently predicted that Hand would be confirmed quickly[51] and he was, on December 20, 1924.[52] He was delighted when his cousin Augustus followed, in 1927.[53] Charles C. Burlingham observed of the cousins: "They [were] a remarkable pair, both open-minded and fearless—Learned brilliant and speculative—Augustus wise and unwavering."[54] Justice Robert H. Jackson later agreed, famously advising the bench and bar to quote Learned; but follow Gus.[55]

Although Judge Hand's view of the judicial role was robust, particularly in developing common law doctrine, he felt strongly about the limited role judges should play in curbing legislative choices.[56] He emphasized adherence to precedent, but also felt free in statutory cases to imagine what a hypothetical legislator would have determined to be the appropriate interpretation in a particular case.[57] Judge Charles E. Wyzanski, Jr., who clerked for both Learned and Augustus Hand, referred to the cousins and Judge Thomas Swan as the Second Circuit's "first team."[58] According to Judge Henry Friendly, "no court possessed greater moral or professional authority."[59]

Judge Hand's meticulous approach to judging is evident in hundreds of pre-conference memoranda, which reflect the "sheer joyful thoroughness with which he tackled each case."[60] Judge Hand was especially masterful in the Second Circuit's "historic specialties" of antitrust, admiralty, patent, copyright, trademark, and unfair competition.[61] He issued significant opinions in many of these areas, while always doubting the value of his own work.[62]

Perhaps Judge Hand's most notable contribution to constitutional law was his decision in *United States v. Dennis*, in which he was again called upon to balance the values of free speech against the state's interest in national unity in stressful times.[63] In *Dennis*, the Second Circuit affirmed the subversion convictions of eleven Communist Party leaders under the 1940 Smith Act. Writing for the panel, Judge Hand expressed his view that their calls for the violent overthrow of the American government posed a "probable danger" that justified curtailing their right to free speech:

> Their only plausible complaint is that freedom of speech which they would be the first to destroy, has been denied them. We acknowledge that that freedom is not always easy to protect; and that there is no sharp line which marks its scope. We have tried to show that what these men taught and advocated is outside the zone. . . .[64] In contrast to the "clear and present danger" standard set out by the Supreme Court in *Schenck v. United States*,[65] Judge Hand's opinions in *Masses Publishing Company* and, to a lesser extent, *Dennis,* advocated for an "incitement approach" to First Amendment law.[66] Later, in *Brandenburg v. Ohio*,[67] the Supreme Court would combine Judge Hand's incitement test with Justice Holmes's clear and present danger test to create the modern standard for the application of the First Amendment to anti-government speech.[68]

Judge Hand was close to his law clerks. During the 1927-1928 term, he shared with Judge Swan the services (and salary) of his first law clerk.[69] Judge Hand preferred to discuss cases orally, rather than receive written memoranda from his clerks.[70] It was common knowledge that Judge Hand's law clerks did not write his opinions."[71] Gerald Gunther, Judge Hand's law clerk from 1953-1954, would later publish Hand's definitive biography, the product of decades of scholarship.[72] Hand shared warm relationships with his colleagues' law clerks as well.[73]

District Judge Miriam Goldman Cedarbaum recalled that, when she was a law clerk for District Judge Edward Dimock, Hand sat in her office one evening, waiting for a ride home with Judge Dimock. Cedarbaum mentioned favorably an opinion by Justice Frank Murphy, and said of Murphy: "He has a lot of heart." Hand, who was less impressed with the decision, replied, "Yes, one must use the organs he has."[74]

Judge Hand adopted a rule that he would not hire a woman to be his law clerk because he could not swear in front of a woman. He thus rejected Ruth Bader Ginsburg, who instead clerked for District Judge Edmund L. Palmieri.[75] Palmieri also drove Hand home from work in the evening. With young Ginsburg sitting in the back, Hand would sit in the front, singing sea shanties and swearing up a storm. One day, Ginsburg mustered the courage to ask Hand why he would not hire her as a law clerk if he was willing to say "whatever came into his head" in the car. Hand responded, "Young lady, I am not *looking* at you."[76]

Judge Hand was subpoenaed by the defense to answer one question during Martin Manton's criminal trial for conspiracy to obstruct the administration of justice: whether he observed anything that led him to believe "he was acting otherwise than according to his oath of office and the dictates of his conscience."[77] Like his colleagues, Hand said no. Judge Hand had long held Manton in low esteem.[78] To start, Manton had a reputation as a "scissors and paste-pot" judge, who drafted his opinions by cutting useful passages from the brief of the prevailing party.[79] Judge Hand was also deeply troubled that he had sat with Manton in two cases (both involving patent litigation) in which Manton had accepted bribes.[80] The first, *General Motors Corporation v. Preferred Electric & Wire Corporation*, was unanimous;[81] but in the second case, *Art Metal Works v. Abraham & Straus*, Judge Hand disagreed with Manton and Judge Harrie Chase.[82] A fresh panel of Judges Learned and Augustus Hand and Robert P. Patterson reheard the appeal and unanimously fell in line with Judge Hand's earlier dissent.[83]

Judge Hand became senior circuit judge on Manton's resignation in 1939.[84] He despised the post, largely ignored developments in federal judicial administration, opposed the relatively new *en banc* process, and opposed the creation of judicial councils.[85] When Charles E. Clark assumed the position of chief judge in 1954, he inherited a court with a record of remarkable productivity, yet severely neglected administration.[86]

Biographer Ken Gormley commented that Judge Hand's "craggy face, stern features, and huge, quizzical eyebrows made him immediately recognizable as a judge's judge."[87] Widely known by his colleagues across the country, he was for a long time little known to the American people. That changed following his speech in Central Park in May 1944 at the "I Am an American Day" celebration. Mayor Fiorello LaGuardia presided over the event, which drew a crowd of more than a million and a half Americans,[88] including 150,000 newly naturalized citizens.[89] Judge Hand spoke about liberty:

> The spirit of liberty is the spirit which is not too sure that it is right; the spirit of liberty is the spirit which seeks to understand the minds of other men and women; the spirit of liberty is the spirit which weighs their interests alongside its own without bias; the spirit of liberty remembers that not even a sparrow falls to earth unheeded; the spirit of liberty is the spirit of Him who, near two thousand years ago, taught mankind that lesson it has never learned, but has never quite forgotten: that there may be a kingdom where the least shall be heard and considered side by side with the greatest.[90]

The crowd was captivated; but not one newspaper quoted the speech until it was mentioned on a radio talk show.[91] Once the speech was reprinted in papers nationally, Judge Hand became an "unlikely American folk hero."[92]

In honor of his seventy-fifth birthday, the *Harvard Law Review* dedicated its February, 1947 issue to Judge Hand.[93] A few years later, in 1951, Judge Hand took senior status.[94] In 1959, the Second Circuit held a special session in honor of Judge Hand's 50 years of federal judicial service, then the longest in American history.[95] Chief Judge Clark presided over the ceremony.[96] The principal speaker was Chief Justice Earl Warren:

> Because Judge Hand is a man to whom vanity is wholly foreign, our swelling chorus of praise must be something of a trial for him. He nonetheless cheerfully permits us to make him the center of our attentions because, I think, he recognizes that we are doing it for our own good, more than for his. In according this recognition to Judge Hand we express our pride and reaffirm our faith in our country, our courts, and our profession.[97]

Other speakers included Supreme Court Justices Felix Frankfurter and John Marshall Harlan, Judge Carroll C. Hincks, and Judge Hand himself.[98] Justice Frankfurter—a lifelong friend—described Judge Hand by using five adjectives: daring, romantic, antediluvian, sophisticated, and, most important, lucky.[99] He continued: "But luckier have we been that he was endowed with these gifts and has put them to the uses to which he has put them. After every one of us in this room will no longer be here, long after that, Learned Hand will still be serving society so long as law will continue to exercise its indispensable role in helping to unravel the tangled skein of the human situation."[100]

Irving Dilliard collected and edited Hand's occasional speeches and essays in *The Spirit of Liberty: Papers and Addresses of Learned Hand.*[101] It was first published in 1952; later editions followed in 1953 and 1960.[102] Judge Hand wrote to Dilliard after the first publication: "*The Spirit of Liberty*—i.e., ten copies—came yesterday, and I was delighted at its make-up and appearance; it seems to me that the publisher could not have done better. I do hope that his loss will not be great."[103]

Throughout his life, Judge Hand corresponded with Justices Oliver Wendell Holmes and Felix Frankfurter, Walter Lippman, Bernard Berenson, and Theodore Roosevelt, among others. The exchanges with philosophers, politicians, lawyers, and judges covered current events: both World Wars, the Great Depression, the New Deal, and McCarthyism. They also discussed pressing legal issues: segregation, and the First, Fifth, and Fourteenth Amendments.[104]

Judge Hand's correspondence with Justice Frankfurter spanned nearly 50 years.[105] Among many other things, the two men discussed Hand's disappointment that, despite being considered on multiple occasions, he was passed over for the Supreme Court. Each time, the political stars were aligned against him.[106] President Warren Harding considered appointing him in 1922, but Chief Justice Taft, whom Hand had abandoned a decade earlier, warned that Judge Hand had "turned out to be a wild Roosevelt man."[107] Twenty years later, President Franklin Delano Roosevelt considered nominating him, and even asked Frankfurter to draft a statement announcing the nomination. But Roosevelt changed his mind, likely hesitant about Judge Hand's age (70), and possibly put off by Frankfurter's relentless advocacy.[108]

In a January 1943 letter, Judge Hand acknowledged Frankfurter's unwavering support on Hand's behalf:

> Just a word to say that out of all this effort to get me into the Court has come what has been especially gratifying to me: a sense of your regard and affection, which I suppose I ought not to have needed this to demonstrate to me. I shall never forget the warmth and the persistence with which you pressed me for the place, long after it was in the least probable that I could be appointed.[109]

Frankfurter responded that same month: "You may or may not know that one of the real ambitions of my own public concerns for now 25 years has been the yearning to see you on this court; that's where you have belonged as have only less than a handful of men during that period."[110] Frankfurter also reflected on the issue at the special session, saying that Hand "was lucky in not having drawn a successful ticket in that odd lottery by which men are picked for the Supreme Court . . . his views would have been diluted eight-ninths and here only two-thirds."[111]

Judge Hand served as a federal judge for nearly 53 years, including 37 on the Court of Appeals for the Second Circuit.[112] He wrote some 4,000 opinions.[113] While only a few of them attained national notoriety, his entire body of work reflected his careful craftsmanship. Of Hand's work, Judge Henry Friendly remembered the "great way in which [Hand] dealt with a multitude of little cases, covering almost every subject in the legal lexicon. Repeatedly he would make the tiniest glow-worm illuminate whole field."[114]

His friend Jerome Frank remarked: "Now and then, one comes on a man who has made of his life a work of art, like a novel written by himself. Such a man is Learned Hand."[115]

Judge Hand died in New York City on August 18, 1961.[116]

Eva Saltzman

1. Jerome N. Frank, *Some Reflections on Judge Learned Hand*, 24 U. CHI. L. REV. 666, 668 (1956).

2. Ernest H. Breuer, *Learned Hand, January 27, 1872-August 18, 1961: Bibliography*, 59 L. LIBR. J. 284, 286 (1966).

3. *Id.*; Leonard P. Moore, *Learned Hand: An Appreciation*, 29 BROOK. L. REV. 2, 2 (1962).

4. Charles C. Burlingham, *Judge Learned Hand*, 60 HARV. L. REV. 330, 330 (1947).

5. Thomas D. Thacher, *Judge Learned Hand*, 2 REC. ASS'N B. CITY N.Y. 189, 190 (1947).

6. Burlingham, *supra* note 4, at 330.

7. *Id.*

8. Breuer, *supra* note 2, at 287.

9. GERALD GUNTHER, LEARNED HAND: THE MAN AND THE JUDGE xvi, 7-8, 13-14, 18, 26-28 (2d ed. 2011).

10. Burlingham, *supra* note 4, at 330.

11. Moore, *supra* note 3, at 2.

12. Charles E. Wyzanski, Jr., *Learned Hand*, ATLANTIC MONTHLY, Dec. 1961, at 54, 55.

13. Breuer, *supra* note 2, at 287.

14. Moore, *supra* note 3, at 2.

15. *See* Harvard Law School Library, *Hand, Learned, 1872-1961. Papers, 1840-1961: Finding Aid*, http://oasis.lib.harvard.edu/oasis/deliver/~law00059.

16. Moore, *supra* note 3, at 2-3.

17. Breuer, *supra* note 2, at 287.

18. Harvard Law School Library, *supra* note 15.

19. GUNTHER, *supra* note 9, at 145-160; *see also* 1 JOHN R. VILE, GREAT AMERICAN JUDGES: AN ENCYCLOPEDIA 319, 319 (2003).

20. Telephone Interview with Constance Jordan, granddaughter of Learned Hand (May 29, 2015) (on file with the United States Courts Library for the Second Circuit).

21. 1 VILE, *supra* note 19, at 324.

22. GUNTHER, *supra* note 9, at 161.

23. *Id.* at 554-55.

24. Breuer, *supra* note 2, at 287.

25. *Id.*

26. *Id.*

27. GUNTHER, *supra* note 9, at 88-90.

28. Breuer, *supra* note 2, at 287.

29. Burlingham, *supra* note 4, at 331.

30. Breuer, *supra* note 2, at 288.

31. 244 F. 535 (S.D.N.Y. 1917).

32. *Id.* at 541-42.

33. *Masses Pub. Co. v Patten*, 246 F. 24, 39 (2d Cir. 1917).

34. GUNTHER, *supra* note 9, at 231.

35. *Id.*

36. GUNTHER, *supra* note 9, at 161-62.

37. Burlingham, *supra* note 4, at 330.

38. GUNTHER, *supra* note 9, at 162-65, 171.

39. 198 U.S. 45 (1905).

40. *See* REASON AND IMAGINATION: THE SELECTED CORRESPONDENCE OF LEARNED HAND: 1897-1961, 20 (Constance Jordan ed. 2013) (Letter from Learned Hand to Theodore Roosevelt (May 8, 1911)).

41. *Id.* at 21.

42. REASON AND IMAGINATION, *supra* note 40, at 34 (Letter from Learned Hand to Theodore Roosevelt (Aug. 11, 1912)).

43. GUNTHER, *supra* note 9, at 196-98.

44. *Id.* at 198-99.

45. *Id.*

46. REASON AND IMAGINATION, *supra* note 40, at 41 (Letter from Learned Hand to Herbert Croly (Oct. 14, 1913)).

47. REASON AND IMAGINATION, *supra* note 40, at 42 (Letter from Gilbert E. Roe to Learned Hand (Nov. 6, 1913)).

48. Breuer, *supra* note 2, at 287-88.

49. American Law Institute, *ALI Overview: Creation*, http://www.ali.org/index.cfm?fuseaction=about.creation; *see also* GUNTHER, *supra* note 9, at 350-57; Herbert F. Goodrich, *Judge Learned Hand and the Work of the American Law Institute*, 60 HARV. L. REV. 345, 346 (1947).

50. *Id.*

51. *Promotion of Judge Learned Hand*, N.Y. L.J., Dec. 4, 1924.

52. GUNTHER, *supra* note 9, at 236.

53. *Id.* at 242.

54. Burlingham, *supra* note 4, at 331.

55. Wyzanski, Jr., *supra* note 12, at 55.

56. GUNTHER, *supra* note 9, at xv.

57. REASON AND IMAGINATION, *supra* note 40, at xxii.

58. Wyzanski, Jr., *supra* note 12, at 55.

59. Henry J. Friendly, *Learned Hand: An Expression from the Second Circuit*, 29 BROOK. L. REV. 6, 7 (1962).

60. GUNTHER, *supra* note 9, at 248.

61. JEFFREY B. MORRIS, FEDERAL JUSTICE IN THE SECOND CIRCUIT 160 (1987); *see also* Stephen H. Philbin, *Judge Learned Hand and the Law of Patents and Copyright*, 60 HARV. L. REV. 394, 394-97 (1947).

62. *See, e.g.*, Helvering v. Gregory, 69 F.2d 809 (2d Cir. 1934), *aff'd.* 293 U.S. 465 (1935). Judge Friendly described this decision as "perhaps the most fundamental decision in the whole field of income tax law"; Henry J. Friendly, *Book Review*, 86 POL. SCI. Q. 470, 472 (1971); United States v. Aluminum Company of America, 148 F.2d 416 (2d Cir. 1945). The ALCOA decision has been described as having "a direct and great influence on the development of antitrust"; Friendly, *supra*, at 471 (quoting MARVIN SCHICK, LEARNED HAND'S COURT 170-71 (1970); The T.J. Hooper, 60 F.2d 737 (2d Cir. 1932) (admiralty).

63. 183 F.2d 201 (2d Cir. 1950); *see also* MORRIS, *supra* note 61, at 119-120.

64. *Dennis*, 183 F.2d at 234.

65. 249 U.S. 47 (1919).

66. *See* GUNTHER, *supra* note 9, at 515-16.

67. 395 U.S. 444 (1969).

68. MORRIS, *supra* note 61, at 120.

69. GUNTHER, *supra* note 9, at 246.

70. *Id.*

71. *Id.* at 247.

72. *See generally* GUNTHER, *supra* note 9.

73. Interview with Raymond Troubh, former law clerk to Judge Thomas W. Swan (1952-53 term) (Apr. 30, 2015) (on file with the United States Courts Library for the Second Circuit).

74. Judge Miriam Goldman Cedarbaum, Southern District of New York, Remarks at the Federal Bar Council Program, Judge Learned Hand: 15 Years on the District Court & Beyond (Apr. 30, 2015) (on file with the United States Courts Library for the Second Circuit).

75. SCOTT DODSON, THE LEGACY OF RUTH BADER GINSBURG 5 (2015).

76. *Id.*

77. GUNTHER, *supra* note 9, at 433.

78. *Id.* at 431-33.

79. *Id.* at 434.

80. *Id.*

81. 79 F.2d 621 (2d Cir. 1935); GUNTHER, *supra* note 9, at 434.

82. 70 F.2d 641 (2d Cir. 1934); GUNTHER, *supra* note 9, at 434-436.

83. *Id.* at 436.

84. The senior-most active judge was known as the "senior circuit judge" until 1948, when the term "chief judge" was established under 28 U.S.C. § 45. The term was adopted "in recognition of the great increase in administrative duties of such judge." REPORT FROM THE HOUSE COMM. ON THE JUDICIARY, TO ACCOMPANY H.R. 3214, H.R. 308, 80th CONG., 1st Sess., A6 (1947); *see also* Act of June 25, 1948, ch. 646, § 45(a) 62 Stat. 869, 871 ("The circuit judge senior in commission shall be the chief judge of the circuit."); *see also* GUNTHER, *supra* note 9, at 431.

85. MORRIS, *supra* note 61, at 135.

86. GUNTHER, *supra* note 9, at 442-43; MORRIS, *supra* note 61, at 135.

87. 1 VILE, *supra* note 19, at 325.

88. *American-Day Fete in Park Attracts Record City Crowd*, N.Y. TIMES, May 22, 1944, at 1. The *Times* covered the event, but, with regard to Judge Hand, simply stated that he had led the pledge of faith. *Id.*

89. 1 VILE, *supra* note 19, at 325.

90. LEARNED HAND, THE SPIRIT OF LIBERTY (1944).

91. Philip Hamburger, *Notes on Freedom*, NEW YORKER, June 10, 1944, at 15-16.

92. 1 VILE, *supra* note 19, at 325.

93. *See* Felix Frankfurter, *Judge Learned Hand*, 60 HARV. L. REV. 325, 325 (1947). Judge Hand received numerous other awards: a Distinguished Service Medal from the Theodore Roosevelt Memorial Foundation in 1947; the American Civil Liberties Medallion in 1955; an award from the Freedom Foundation in 1956; a gold medal for distinguished service from the New York State Bar Association in 1960; and a Distinguished Service Award from the Council of Harvard Law School Association, also in 1960. The United States Chamber of Commerce presented him with the Great Living American award in 1960.

94. When Judge Hand left active service, the term "senior judge" was not yet used to describe a federal judge who left active service but continued to perform some judicial duties. *See* Act of Feb. 25, 1919, ch. 29, § 6, 40 Stat. 1156, 1157-58. A judge who took this option was considered to have "retired." Under a statute enacted in 1948, such a "retired" judge received the same salary increases and cost-of-living adjustments as an active judge. Act of June 25, 1948, ch. 646, §§ 294, 371, 372, 62 Stat. 901, 903-04. *See* Stephen B. Burbank, et al., *Leaving the Bench, 1970-2009: The Choices Federal Judges Make, What Influences Those Choices, and Their Consequences*, 161 U. PA. L. REV. 1, 8-10 (2012).

95. *See United States Court of Appeals for the Second Circuit Special Session in Honor of Judge Learned Hand*, N.Y. L.J. Apr. 17, 1959.

96. *Id.*

97. *Id.*

98. *See Id.*

99. *Id.*

100. *Id.*

101. REASON AND IMAGINATION, *supra* note 40, at 313 (Letter from Learned Hand to Irving Dilliard (Apr. 3, 1952)).

102. IRVING DILLARD, THE SPIRIT OF LIBERTY: PAPERS AND ADDRESSES OF LEARNED HAND (1st ed. 1952); IRVING DILLARD, THE SPIRIT OF LIBERTY: PAPERS AND ADDRESSES OF LEARNED HAND (2d ed. 1953); IRVING DILLARD, THE SPIRIT OF LIBERTY: PAPERS AND ADDRESSES OF LEARNED HAND (3d ed. 1960).

103. *United States Court of Appeals for the Second Circuit Special Session in Honor of Judge Learned Hand*, *supra* note 95.

104. *See generally* REASON AND IMAGINATION, *supra* note 40.

105. REASON AND IMAGINATION, *supra* note 40, at xvi.

106. 1 VILE, *supra* note 19, at 324.

107. MORRIS, *supra* note 61, at 138.

108. *Id.*

109. REASON AND IMAGINATION, *supra* note 40, at 233 (Letter from Learned Hand to Felix Frankfurter (Jan. 11, 1943)).

110. REASON AND IMAGINATION, *supra* note 40, at 234 (Letter from Felix Frankfurter to Learned Hand (Jan. 11, 1943)).

111. *United States Court of Appeals for the Second Circuit Special Session in Honor of Judge Learned Hand*, *supra* note 95.

112. *Id.*

113. GUNTHER, *supra* note 9, at xv.

114. Friendly, *supra* note 59, at 13.

115. Jerome N. Frank, *Some Reflections on Judge Learned Hand*, 24 U. CHI. L. REV. 666, 668 (1956).

116. 1 VILE, *supra* note 19, at 329; J. Edward Lumbard, *Remarks at the Opening of the Term of the Court of Appeals*, 33 N.Y. ST. B.J. 410, 410 (1961).

# THOMAS WALTER SWAN
## 1877-1975

Court of Appeals for the Second Circuit: 1927-1965

Judge Thomas Swan "represented the best of what a New England Yankee would produce."[1] Born in Norwich, Connecticut in 1877 to Thomas W. and Jane Maynard Swan, he was educated at the Williston Academy in Northampton, Massachusetts.[2] Like his father before him, Swan attended Yale College, graduating in 1900. He went on to study law at Harvard, where he was president of the *Harvard Law Review*. After graduating in 1903 with distinction and serving as marshal of his class, he practiced in Chicago at the firm of Bentley, Burling & Swan and helped a fellow Harvard Law School alumnus, Professor J. H. Beale, establish the law department at the University of Chicago.[3] He also lectured there, teaching classes on suretyship and mortgages.[4]

In 1916, Swan was lured away from Chicago to the deanship at Yale Law School. According to Dean Eugene V. Rostow, his selection "was the only dramatic event in his career, although the drama was not of his making."[5] A "faculty cabal" headed by Swan's "great friend and stalwart partner in many good deeds, Arthur Corbin," tried to persuade Judge Henry Wade Rogers to step down as dean. Rogers had been appointed to the Court of Appeals for the Second Circuit in 1913; Corbin and Wesley Hohfield, another member of the "cabal," thought that Yale Law School "needed and deserved a full-time Dean, and a Dean far more vigorous and imaginative than Dean Rogers."[6] In their view, "the Deanship should not be a somnabulent sinecure to be handled in the Judge's spare time."[7] Corbin and Hohfield also believed that to attract a top-flight faculty, the dean had to be a graduate of Yale College and to have studied the case method, which was, at the time, considered progressive and associated with Harvard.[8] Swan fit the bill, and Corbin traveled to Chicago to recruit him. "After a number of moves and countermoves," Dean Swan was installed, but only after holding the position for six months without pay.[9] He was dean for eleven years.[10]

During his tenure as dean, Swan married Mabel Eleanor Dick, a native of Lake Forest, Illinois. The heiress to the Dictaphone fortune, she was "quietly elegant."[11] The couple never had children.[12]

In the words of Dean Rostow, Swan had that "striking inner gift" that permits certain people to lead: "modest and self-deprecating as he was—it was a quality of character as well as judgment which made his warmth and his wisdom so manifest an influence on those with whom he worked."[13] Similarly, Arthur Corbin wrote that Swan's "modesty was such that he appeared to defer to the opinions of Hoh[field] and me. In fact, he was the wisest of advisers and the best of administrators. His opinion often prevailed, without appearing to be overruling us."[14]

Swan was also generous. When the *Yale Law Journal* was in financial straits, he loaned it $6,000 from his own pocket.[15] When the law school accepted students who could not pay full freight, "Dean Swan found ways and means from resources that many suspected came from him and Mrs. Swan."[16] Douglas Arant, who graduated from Yale Law School in 1923, recalled that without Swan's "understanding and generosity I would never have been able to stay through because I reached the place two or three times when I did not have enough money to spend another week there."[17] Dean Swan paid Arant $25 a month to bring his mail from Yale Station to Hendrie Hall, and occasionally paid him $5 to drive Mabel to "some place nearby, such as Hartford."[18] When Arant told Dean Swan that he "simply did not have the money to stay," Swan "took out his check book and said he was advancing me my salary," writing a check for $100 that permitted Arant to finish law school.[19]

Under Dean Swan's leadership, Yale Law School began to admit women. He was also a talent scout for academics. With him at the helm, Yale Law School recruited Edmund Morgan, William Vance, and Karl Llewellyn to its faculty.[20] Swan also hired Charles E. Clark, who succeeded him as dean and later joined him on the Second Circuit.[21] Some say that Swan's deanship transformed Yale into a competitive national law school.[22] The school's mock trial organization still bears his name: the Thomas Swan Barristers' Union.[23]

Swan was also influential as an academic and as a proponent of legal realism. He and his fellow realists "rejected what they saw as the empty formalism of the nineteenth century; they saw law not as a search for abstract rules but rather as a study of what decision-makers actually do, and why."[24]

After he joined the bench, Swan maintained his strong connection to Yale. Dean Rostow recalls that Swan continued to be "a familiar figure in the library, working on his opinions as we worked on our student projects—without his jacket, going to the shelves himself for a book he needed, a simple and direct symbol of our fraternity."[25] While on the Second Circuit, Judge Swan served as a Fellow (trustee) of the Yale Corporation. Dean Rostow tells the following story about deliberations over a controversial appointment to the law school faculty:

> A committee of the Corporation met with us in the Dean's office. After a long discussion, Judge Swan spoke for the first time. "I should like to ask what some of you may feel is an old-fashioned question," he said. "Is the

> candidate a gentleman?" In a most disarming and personal way, Swan's question put the responsibilities of the faculty and of the Corporation with regard to faculty appointments into a perspective acceptable to both. What could have been a dangerous confrontation disappeared. On our assurance that the man was indeed a gentleman, the debate was over, and the appointment was made.[26]

In the 1950s, Judge Swan influenced the academy's response to McCarthyism—specifically, what a university should do when a faculty member "took the Fifth" in a congressional investigation. Yale President A. Whitney Griswold, Professor Corbin, and Judge Swan caucused and reached a conclusion of "high principle—that the universities should do nothing at all."[27] Other universities followed suit.[28]

As he did at Yale, Swan replaced Judge Henry Wade Rogers on the bench. In 1927, President Calvin Coolidge appointed Swan to the Court of Appeals for the Second Circuit. (Two years earlier, rumors had circulated that the President was considering nominating Swan to serve as his attorney general.)[29] Judge Swan's new colleagues welcomed him to the bench at a luncheon at the Lawyers' Club in lower Manhattan.[30]

For his first sitting in New York, Judge Swan brought Herman Finkelstein, a recent graduate of Yale Law School, to serve as a law clerk to him and Judge Learned Hand.[31] The two judges split Finkelstein's $1,800 salary.[32] They continued to share law clerks for the next six years, until the Conference of Senior Circuit Judges (the predecessor of the Judicial Conference of the United States) persuaded Congress to fund a law clerk's salary for each circuit judge.[33] Judge Swan remained loyal to Yale, selecting one of its graduates each year to serve as his law clerk.[34]

He treated his law clerks to more than a salary. He and his wife had no children, but "each new law clerk became a member of the family, welcomed at the New York apartment the Swans maintained until 1953, and at their home in Guilford."[35] By tradition, the law clerks would begin their tenure by spending a week in July at the Swans' Guilford beach house. The law clerks would discuss the court's upcoming docket with Judge Swan.[36]

Many of the judge's afternoons passed, however, with his playing a round of golf with friends, followed by a martini and a long bath.[37] At night, the Swans and his law clerks would gather for formal dinners.[38] To a young law graduate, the scene could be intimidating.[39]

Judge Swan has been described as an "aristocrat" of the bench, with "self-effacing modesty," and a "kindly, contained courtesy."[40] One observer compared his mien on the bench to that of the "Lord speaking to His retainers."[41] Dean Rostow described Judge Swan as "an old-fashioned Yankee" who was "staunch rather than ebullient; disciplined and reliable, rather than spectacular; a child of duty, not of ambition; a leader by quiet example and force of character, never by panache or charisma."[42] Judge J. Edward Lumbard wrote that as "a colleague, Judge Swan was all that one could want: considerate, helpful, sagacious in counsel, even tempered, modest and excellent company."[43] Judge Robert P. Anderson is reported to have said, "Judge Swan's mother called Judge Swan 'Walter' while his contemporaries called him 'Tom.' 'Walter' never smoked, drank or swore. 'Tom' did."[44]

In 1939, Judge Swan's colleague, Martin Manton, resigned from the court, and shortly thereafter was indicted in the Southern District of New York for conspiracy to obstruct the administration of justice. Manton subpoenaed his former colleagues as witnesses. At trial, Manton's counsel asked Judge Swan, and his colleagues, one question: "whether, in any of the cases in which they sat with Manton, they *observed* anything that led them to believe '[Manton] was acting otherwise than according to his oath of office and the dictates of his conscience.'"[45] Judge Swan and his colleagues answered that they had observed nothing to indicate that Manton was deciding on anything other than the merits of each case.[46]

Following the Manton conviction, Charles Clark, who had succeeded Judge Swan as dean of Yale Law School, was appointed to the Second Circuit by President Franklin Delano Roosevelt. In 1941, Judge Jerome Frank joined the court, and its membership remained stable for ten years. In Judge Lumbard's view, "during that decade, the Second Circuit won a position with the bar and the public which has probably not been equaled by any other court, State or federal, since the founding of the Republic."[47] Its docket was weighted toward commercial disputes, patent, copyright, tax, bankruptcy, admiralty, personal injury litigation, and administrative law decisions. Judge Swan was regarded as one of the greatest commercial law judges; in the area of tax, Judge Learned Hand viewed him as a sage. Hand wrote: "Again and again I have found myself utterly bewildered by the involution of phrase with phrase and term with term, until this kindly light showed the turn which I had missed, and led me out of what appeared to be a cul-de-sac."[48]

Judge Swan was a "logician"; his opinions were not "flashy" and did not "put the spotlight on him" as judge.[49] Two of his high-profile written decisions were *G. Ricordi & Company v. Paramount Pictures, Inc.*,[50] dealing with who had the right to make a motion picture based on the story of *Madame Butterfly*, and *NLRB v. American Laundry Machinery Company*,[51] in which Judge Swan affirmed an order of the NLRB requiring an employer to notify employees by mail that it would not retaliate against them. The employer had intimated that employees who voted to unionize would be subject to unfavorable employment action.

Three major Cold War prosecutions took place in the Southern District of New York: "that of Alger Hiss for perjury; that of eleven leaders of the American Communist Party for conspiracy to advocate the overthrow of the government by force and violence; and that of the Rosenbergs and Morton Sobell for espionage."[52] Judge Swan was on the appellate panels reviewing all three.[53] One of the eleven defendants in what was known as the Communist Conspiracy case, *Daily Worker* editor John Gates, was jailed for contempt after he refused to answer a question about a pamphlet on the underground Communist movement that he had introduced into evidence.[54] Judge Swan authored the decision that declined to free Gates. Gates argued that his refusal was protected by his Fifth Amendment right against self-incrimination. But Gates "voluntarily took the stand, introduced the exhibit, and testified on cross-examination that it was prepared by three persons acting under his direction."[55] Judge Swan doubted that the pamphlet itself incriminated Gates; but even if it did, Gates had "waived his privilege by voluntarily bringing the pamphlet before the court and testifying to his part in its preparation."[56]

Swan voted to affirm the conviction of Alger Hiss.[57] And he was on the panel that affirmed the convictions and death sentences of Ethel and Julius Rosenberg for having funneled secrets on the atomic bomb to the Soviet Union.[58] With Judges Augustus Hand and Frank, Judge Swan affirmed the denial of the Rosenbergs' bid for a new trial and motions for a stay of execution.[59] Together with Judge Frank, he heard the Rosenbergs' last-minute motion for a stay on the ground that their execution would violate the Jewish Sabbath. According to *The New York Times*, the Rosenbergs' attorney "conferred first with Judge Swan, the court's senior judge, who accompanied him to Judge Frank's home."[60] The judges denied the motion, reasoning that "further proceedings to litigate were unwarranted."[61]

In 1951, at the age of 74, Judge Swan succeeded Judge Learned Hand as chief judge. After holding the post for two years, he and Augustus Hand both took senior status.[62] When they did, *The New York Times* declared: "The nation is the poorer because it has lost the services, through retirement, of two eminent jurists."[63] When pressed for an explanation, Judge Swan, then 75 years old, said, "I'm old enough to retire."[64]

Although he called it retirement, Judge Swan continued to take cases as a senior judge and was "as alert as ever through his last sitting in the court of appeals in May 1965, when he was eighty-seven."[65] The clerk offered to carry his briefcase; Judge Swan replied, "When I can't carry this, I won't come in anymore."[66]

Judge Swan died in New Haven in 1975 at the age of 97.

Sally Pritchard

1. Interview with Raymond Troubh, former law clerk, in New York, N.Y. (Apr. 30, 2015) at 3:50—3:56 (recording on file with the United States Courts Library for the Second Circuit).

2. FEDERAL JUDICIAL CENTER, Biographical Directory of Federal Judges, Thomas Walter Swan, http://www.fjc.gov/servlet/nGetInfo?jid=2320&cid=999&ctype=na&instate=na.

3. *Alumni Notes*, HARVARD BULLETIN, Sept. 29, 1915, at 339 .

4. *Judge Thomas W. Swan Dies; Led U.S. Appeals Court Here*, N.Y. TIMES, July 15, 1975, at 36; 3 CHARLES WARREN, HISTORY OF THE HARVARD LAW SCHOOL AND OF EARLY LEGAL CONDITIONS IN AMERICA 317 (1908).

5. Eugene V. Rostow, *Thomas W. Swan, 1877-1975*, 85 YALE L.J.159, 160 (1975).

6. *Id.*

7. *Id.*

8. *Nascent Realism, 1916-1927*, YALE LAW SCHOOL, http://www.law.yale.edu/cbl/3083.htm.

9. Rostow, *supra* note 5, at 160.

10. *Id.* at 160–61.

11. Interview with Raymond Troubh, *supra* note 1, at 0:13–40, 1:49–1:55.

12. *Id.*

13. Rostow, *supra* note 5, at 161.

14. Letter from Arthur Corbin to Eugene V. Rostow (Sept. 13, 1957) (on file with the United States Courts Library for the Second Circuit). Corbin was a professor at Yale Law School; Rostow was dean.

15. Rostow, *supra* note 5, at 161.

16. J. Edward Lumbard, *Thomas Walter Swan, 1877—1975*, 42 BROOK. L. REV. xv, xvi (1976).

17. Letter from Douglas Arant to Eugene V. Rostow (Mar. 25, 1976) (on file with the United States Courts Library for the Second Circuit).

18. *Id.*

19. *Id.*

20. Rostow, *supra* note 5 at 160.

21. JEFFREY B. MORRIS, FEDERAL JUSTICE IN THE SECOND CIRCUIT 143 (1987).

22. *Nascent Realism, 1916-1927, supra* note 8; *see also* Letter from Arthur Corbin to Eugene Rostow, *supra* note 14 ("During Swan's administration, the prestige of YLS improved.").

23. *Thomas Swan Barrister's Union*, YALE LAW SCHOOL, http://www.law.yale.edu/stuorgs/barristers.htm.

24. Special Supplement, Colleagues for Justice: One Hundred Years of the United States Court of Appeals *for the Second Circuit*, 65 ST. JOHN'S L. REV. 937, 951 (1991).

25. Rostow, *supra* note 5, at 161.

26. *Id.* at 161–62.

27. *Id.* at 162.

28. *Id.*

29. *Coolidge Conferring on Next Step with Warren, Who Is Expected to Reject Recess Appointment*, N.Y. TIMES, Mar. 17, 1925, at 1.

30. *Welcome to Judge Swan: Colleagues on Federal Bench His Hosts at a Luncheon*, N.Y. TIMES, Jan. 25, 1927, at 25.

31. *See* GERALD GUNTHER, LEARNED HAND: THE MAN AND THE JUDGE 505 (2d ed. 1994); MARCIA NELSON, THE REMARKABLE HANDS: AN AFFECTIONATE PORTRAIT 37 (1983).

32. Lumbard, *supra* note 16, at xvi.

33. *Id.* at xvi–xvii.

34. *Id.* at xvii.

35. *Id.*

36. Interview with Raymond Troubh, *supra* note 1, at 1:24–1:37, 2:22-2:25.

37. *Id.* at 2:30–3:05.

38. *Id.* at 3:10–3:33.

39. *Id.* 3:37–3:40.

40. John P. Frank, *The Top U.S. Commercial Court*, FORTUNE MAG., Jan. 1951, at 110.

41. *Id.*

42. Rostow, *supra* note 5, at 159.

43. Lumbard, *supra* note 16, at xxi.

44. Judge J. Joseph Smith, Remarks at a Joint Session United States Court of Appeals for the Second Circuit and the United States District Court for the District of Connecticut, In Memory of the Honorable Robert P. Anderson 1, 21 (June 19, 1978) (transcript on file with the United States Courts Library for the Second Circuit).

45. GUNTHER, *supra* note 31, at 433.

46. *Id.*

47. *Id.*

48. Frank, *supra* note 40, at 108.

49. Interview with Raymond Troubh, *supra* note 1, at 5:10–5:30.

50. 189 F.2d 469 (2d Cir. 1951).

51. 152 F.2d 400 (2d Cir. 1945).

52. MORRIS, *supra* note 21, at 156.

53. United States v. Hiss, 185 F.2d 822 (2d Cir. 1950); United States v. Dennis, 183 F.2d 201 (2d Cir. 1950); United States v. Rosenberg, 195 F.2d 583 (2d Cir. 1952).

54. Russell Porter, *Contempt Jailing of Gates Upheld*, N.Y. TIMES, July 2, 1949, at 2.

55. United States v. Gates, 176 F.2d 78, 80 (2d Cir. 1949).

56. *Id.*

57. *Hiss*, 185 F.2d 822.

58. *Rosenberg*, 195 F.2d 583.

59. United States v. Rosenberg, 204 F.2d 688 (2d Cir. 1953).

60. *Swan and Frank Say No*, N.Y. TIMES, June 20, 1953, at 6.

61. *Id.*

62. When Judge Swan left active service, the term "senior judge" was not yet used to describe a federal judge who left active service but continued to perform some judicial duties. *See* Act of Feb. 25, 1919, ch. 29, § 6, 40 Stat. 1156, 1157-58. A judge who took this option was considered to have "retired." Under a statute enacted in 1948, such a "retired" judge received the same salary increases and cost-of-living adjustments as an active judge. Act of June 25, 1948, ch. 646, §§ 294, 371, 372, 62 Stat. 901, 903-04. *See* Stephen B. Burbank, et al., *Leaving the Bench, 1970-2009: The Choices Federal Judges Make, What Influences Those Choices, and Their Consequences*, 161 U. PA. L. REV. 1, 8-10 (2012).

63. *Two Fine Judges*, N.Y. TIMES, July 3, 1953, at 18.

64. *Two Judges Ending U.S. Court Career*, N.Y. TIMES, July 1, 1953, at 21.

65. Lumbard, *supra* note 16, at xix.

66. *Id.*

# AUGUSTUS NOBLE HAND
# 1869-1954

District Court for the Southern District of New York:
1914-1927
Court of Appeals for the Second Circuit: 1927-1954

A remarkable man and a distinguished jurist, Augustus Noble Hand is often remembered together with his more famous cousin, Learned Hand. Born in 1869 in Elizabethtown, New York, the seat of Essex County,[1] Hand's rural upstate boyhood was something out of *The Adventures of Tom Sawyer*, at least as seen through the eyes of that cousin. Learned Hand lived in Albany but spent summers and winter vacations in the country with Gus (two and one-half years older), enjoying camping and sledding, singing, and forging a lifetime bond.[2] A letter from nine-year-old Learned to "Dear Gussy" related the misadventure of trying to ride a bicycle in the snow.[3] Twelve-year-old Learned wrote of the fun they would have with Gus's new dog. Learned went on: "You don't know how much I would like to be with you in the country, and how often I think of the good times we used to have together in Elizabethtown."[4] One summer Gus wrote to his mother, reporting that he and Learned camped ("I killed one of my chickens for the occasion."), hiked, and drank homemade root beer.[5]

Lawyering was in Augustus's blood: his father, grandfather and uncles were lawyers. Seven-year-old Gus attended a trial at the Elizabethtown courthouse in which a farmer complained that a traveling circus had negligently frightened his horse; in reaction, Gus was inspired to write and declaim "a speech and a charge."[6]

Augustus graduated from the local Elizabethtown schools at 14 and then devoted two years to "'resting, trapping, shooting, studying French,' and learning songs."[7] He attended Philips Exeter Academy, where new boys had to run a race; he didn't do well because he didn't think to remove his overcoat and galoshes.[8] Then came Harvard College, from which he graduated in 1890, having studied classics.[9] At Harvard, he was less conscious of the social scene than was his cousin. At one point, Learned Hand confided in Augustus his interest in joining the Porcellian Club; Augustus responded that he had never heard of the club and that it probably no longer existed.[10]

Augustus worked for a year in his father's law office before starting Harvard Law School. He later said that law school, although difficult, was made easier by his apprenticeship with his father, which exposed him to legal terms and how things were done in a law office and in court.[11] His overall average was 83 (75 was an A) and he was on the Law Review.[12] He graduated in 1894 and was admitted to the New York bar the same year.[13]

He went to New York City and practiced law with the firm of Curtis, Mallet-Prevost & Colt.[14] When his Uncle Clifford died in 1901, he joined his uncle's former firm, Hand, Bonney & Jones.[15] In a letter, Augustus Hand's father, Richard Hand, admonished him not to labor long hours (acknowledging that "a young man who is so fond of his work as you are will find this difficult") and to cultivate other interests rather than be "narrow and incomplete."[16] Augustus found time to write an article about the developing law of the right to privacy.[17] In a letter to his cousin Learned (who was also practicing law), Augustus offered comfort after Learned had a rough time arguing a case before an impatient judge, dismissing "the idiots who are on the bench."[18]

Augustus Hand married Susan Train in 1899. Her father was a Navy captain and they were wed on his ship, the U.S.S. Massachusetts, at Bar Harbor, Maine.[19] They had one daughter, Serena.[20]

In 1914 President Woodrow Wilson appointed Augustus Hand to the District Court for the Southern District of New York.[21] About his tenure there, *The New York Times* later observed that he "was always lenient in his attitude toward aliens seeking to remain in this country" and that "he once warned the public against race prejudice that might mar the assimilation of the newcomers."[22] His "ways and means of getting judicial business done" included "evening or night sessions of the court," resulting in "stripping away of nonessentials."[23] He also counseled that a trial judge should "accept proffered evidence if the matter was at all doubtful either way."[24] During World War I, he presided over one of the criminal trials of the editors of *The Masses* under the Espionage Act and one defendant, Max Eastman, described him as "a judge who could have upheld in a hurricane the dignity of the law."[25]

In 1924, both Hands were under consideration for the Second Circuit. Learned wrote to Augustus, "you old rooster," admitting he hoped he would get the job himself and acknowledging that his cousin was "more selfless" than he.[26] Learned was elevated.[27]

Three years later, President Calvin Coolidge appointed Augustus Hand to the Second Circuit.[28] Augustus wrote that he was flattered and "looked forward to the pleasure of being in the same Appellate Court as Learned," because they "have been like brothers."[29] He described himself as "almost abnormally without ambition" and wondered if "I am not better [fitted] to administer an important trial court, full of interest to me, than to sit in appeals."[30] He later confided to friends that he preferred the work of the district court.[31]

Judge Augustus Hand heard many important cases while on the Court of Appeals. Some concerned public morals. He wrote the opinion declaring that James Joyce's *Ulysses* was not obscene and therefore could be brought into the country for sale. Judge Hand found that *Ulysses* was "a book of originality and sincerity of treatment and that it has not the effect of promoting lust . . . even though it justly may offend many."[32] Judge Manton vigorously dissented: "Masterpieces have never been produced by men given to obscenity or lustful thoughts—men who have no Master."[33] In another case, Judge Hand wrote that a package of vaginal pessaries could enter the country despite a statute barring import of an article "to prevent conception."[34] Doctors were excepted from the literal terms of the statute when use was for patient health.[35]

Judge Augustus Hand wrote an opinion affirming a conviction for failing to report for induction into the army during World War II. The would-be conscientious objector did not qualify because his opposition to war was not based on "religious training and belief," but on "philosophical and political considerations."[36] Judge Hand explained, "Religious belief arises from a sense of the inadequacy of reason as a means of relating the individual to his fellow-men and to his universe."[37] Opposition to all war grew out of such religious impulse, while opposition to a particular war was political.[38]

In another World War II draft case, Judge Augustus Hand was on a panel that affirmed the dismissal of a habeas petition seeking a soldier's release from the Army. The petitioner argued that his induction "as a member of a 'Negro quota'" violated the Selective Training and Service Act of 1940, which prohibited discrimination on the basis of race or color.[39] Judge Thomas Swan wrote that "[t]he induction routine that has been established is calculated to supply men in conformity with the contemplated military organization which permits separate colored regiments" and "separate quotas in the requisitions based on relative racial proportions of the men subject to call do not constitute the prohibited 'discrimination.'"[40] Judge Charles Clark dissented.

In a securities case, Judge Augustus Hand interpreted the Securities Exchange Act of 1934, writing that Rule 10b-5 protects only a defrauded buyer or seller and that section 10(b) was not directed at "fraudulent mismanagement of corporate affairs."[41]

The Court confronted cases growing out of the trial of Communist Party leaders under the Smith Act for advocating government overthrow by force and violence. One opinion by Judge Augustus Hand sustained the convictions of the defense lawyers for contempt of court: "[W]hen counsel differ as to the rulings of a judge, they acquire no privilege to charge him with bad faith and misconduct, and to obstruct the trial. Their only remedy is by an appeal."[42] Another upheld disbarment for that behavior.[43]

Judge Augustus Hand was a member of the panel that upheld denial of new trials to Julius and Ethel Rosenberg and denial of their motions for relief under 28 U.S.C. § 2255. The panel also declined to stay their executions.[44] In reporting the decision, *The New York Times* related that the couple were scheduled to die in the electric chair at Sing Sing a few days later and that demonstrators were protesting in Union Square.[45] The panel was "besieged in the last few days before the Rosenbergs went to the chair on June 19 by defense moves to get the court to grant a stay of execution."[46] Judge Hand was also on panels that upheld the perjury conviction of Alger Hiss.[47]

The Supreme Court's expansion of habeas corpus and the rights of the accused did not always meet with Judge Hand's approval. In one pre-conference memorandum he griped about some of the Supreme Court justices: "If we sanction writs like this we might as well give up, and inaugurate a school to correspond with jail birds and employ a staff of Murphys and Rutledges with proper psychiatrists to attend to all their wants."[48]

When Chief Judge Martin Manton was tried for corruption, Judge Augustus Hand was subpoenaed by the defense, as were Judges Learned Hand, Swan, and Chase. Each was asked whether, while sitting on cases with Manton, he observed anything that made him think Manton was "acting otherwise than according to his oath of office and the dictates of his conscience."[49] Each judge answered no.[50]

Judge Augustus Hand sat on the committee that approved Cass Gilbert's design for a new courthouse at Foley Square to replace the old post office and federal courthouse building at City Hall Park.[51] Gilbert's design was "intended to accommodate ten circuit and fifteen district judges, the clerks' offices of both courts, as well as offices for the U.S. Attorney, the FBI and other federal personnel."[52]

Judge Augustus Hand's role on the court has been described as that of "team player," and "center of gravity," and his personality as "well suited to reconciling intellectual differences."[53] Judge Swan said that Hand was "without vanity" and his opinions demonstrated he had no "desire to shine."[54] He rarely dissented.[55] In the Smith Act case, he convinced Judge Frank to vote with him.[56] He had an "ability to swing the court to an unforeseen result."[57] He tried to reduce conflict, mediate between colleagues, and (at least once, in the Smith Act case) was caught in the middle of a "bitter exchange" between Judges Clark and Frank.[58] One law clerk observed that Judge Hand "avoids petty squabbles with his brethren; he does not fuss about their foibles or try to restrain their exuberance."[59] Of his writing, Judge Clark said "the dignity and restraint of his opinions did not permit of the levity to which his gay and humorous outlook on life continually brought him."[60]

Although they shared many childhood experiences, the Hand cousins were "temperamentally . . . poles apart."[61] One commentator described Augustus as "by far the more gentle of the two."[62] And they differed as lawyers: Learned "cultivated exotic language in his opinions and Gus emphasized the pedestrian."[63] Judge Learned Hand's biographer observed that "Gus was never given to moody introspection."[64] When they were young men, Learned pronounced Augustus to be of "stouter timber" than himself, and Augustus criticized Learned for his "nerves," and "brooding."[65] In later years, Judge Augustus Hand referred to himself and his cousin as "the Hand boys" and described himself as "the balance wheel in the Hand combination."[66] Both had chambers on the twenty-fourth floor of the Foley Square courthouse.[67] Judge Clark said they were "perfect foils to each other."[68] He related battles in the middle of Foley Square about where the judges would eat lunch, ending with one Hand going to one restaurant while the other decamped for his own choice, while the rest of the jurists sorted themselves out.[69] Justice Robert H. Jackson is generally credited with the maxim: quote Learned but follow Gus.[70]

Felix Frankfurter picked many of Judge Augustus Hand's law clerks, as he did for several leading jurists.[71] One law clerk recalled that Judge Augustus Hand would sometimes say that the "invention of the typewriter was the root of all evil" and it would be better if lawyers had to write out briefs by hand.[72] Another related that he "decried pompousness," and strove for a "deft and workmanlike approach."[73] When the cousins sat together, Judge Augustus Hand might say to his clerk, "I wonder what Learned will come up with this time," while Judge Learned Hand's clerk said that Judge Augustus Hand wrote slowly and "was often months behind."[74] In addition, Judge Augustus Hand enjoyed talking about Judge Learned Hand's "foibles and eccentricities."[75] On occasion, they both talked about their colleagues' foibles. According to one law clerk, the cousins sarcastically called Judge Clark "GLAPP" for "Greatest Living Authority on Practice and Procedure."[76] Asked about judges who complained of low judicial pay, Judge Augustus Hand replied: "[T]o Hell with them. Let them retire to opulence or obscurity as the case may be."[77] One clerk reported that the law clerks sometimes attended conferences among the judges. On one such occasion, asked his opinion, the clerk began by expressing his "limitations," but Judge Augustus Hand cut him off, saying, "quit being so damned humble and tell us what you think."[78]

In the summer, Judge Augustus Hand would visit Elizabethtown, where he was born.[79] But he would bring his law clerk and plenty of work.[80] One law clerk reported that there was little leisure, even when counting in that category "an execrable game of golf."[81] Judge Hand's grandchildren would visit. One summer, he was shocked to learn that his high-school-age granddaughter had studied Latin but not been exposed to Virgil. They spent evenings translating portions of the *Aeneid*.[82]

As his words in the conscientious objector case may suggest, religion was an important part of Judge Augustus Hand's life. He was elected to the vestry of Grace Church in 1917 when his family was living nearby on 9th Street in Greenwich Village.[83] Later he became senior warden at Grace.[84] In the *Ulysses* case, Judge

Learned Hand asked his cousin to write the opinion; "no one would criticize his morals" because he was a vestryman of an Episcopal church.[85]

On his eightieth birthday *The New York Times* observed that Judge Augustus Hand "graced" the bench and wished him "many more years of fruitful service."[86] He retired from the Second Circuit in 1953, but was to remain "available for special assignments."[87] *The New York Times* observed: "Of strong character, sound in fundamental principles and possessed of a keen sense of humor, Judge Hand has a wide knowledge of the law and a natural liking for it."[88]

Judge Augustus Hand died in 1954 while vacationing in Vermont and was buried in Elizabethtown.[89] *The New York Times* said: "For some forty years as a jurist his was the clear voice of common sense, of humanism, of traditional wisdom tempered by experience. He was never sentimental, but he was always just."[90] Justice Frankfurter wrote Susan Train Hand in "gratitude" not "commiseration" after her husband's death, saying he was "one of those very rare persons who make virtue attractive and nobility convincing."[91]

Catherine J. Minuse

1. MARCIA NELSON, THE REMARKABLE HANDS 3 (1983).

2. GERALD GUNTHER, LEARNED HAND: THE MAN AND THE JUDGE 16-17 (2D ED. 2011); NELSON, *supra* note 1, at 95.

3. NELSON, *supra* note 1, at 90.

4. SUSAN TRAIN HAND, LETTERS OF THE HAND FAMILY 1796-1912, at 311 (1923).

5. *Id.* at 310.

6. Judge Charles E. Wyzanski Jr., Remarks at a Special Meeting of the New York County Lawyers' Association and The Association of the Bar of the City of New York for the Memorial for Augustus Noble Hand 12 (May 4, 1955) (transcript on file with the United States Courts Library for the Second Circuit).

7. *Id.*

8. Telephone Interview with Susan Speers, granddaughter of Judge Augustus Noble Hand (May 27, 2015) (on file with the United States Courts Library for the Second Circuit).

9. NELSON, *supra* note 1, at 1, 96; GUNTHER, *supra* note 2, at 26.

10. GUNTHER, *supra* note 2, at 21-22.

11. NELSON, *supra* note 1, at 121.

12. *Id.* at 125, 130; Letter from Henry Hudson, Secretary of Harvard Law Review, to A.N. Hand (Jan. 27, 1893) Hand Family Papers, Division of Rare and Manuscript Collections, Cornell University Library, No. 3624, box 8, Scrapbook of A. N. Hand.

13. Letter from Henry Hudson, *supra* note 12.

14. *Augustus N. Hand, Jurist, Dies at 85*, N.Y. TIMES, Oct. 29, 1954.

15. *Id.*; GUNTHER, *supra* note 2, at 57.

16. SUSAN TRAIN HAND, *supra* note 4, at 322-23.

17. Augustus N. Hand, *Schuyler Against Curtis and the Right to Privacy*, 45 AM. L. REG. & REV. 745 (1897).

18. GUNTHER, *supra* note 2, at 48-49.

19. NELSON, *supra* note 1, at 132, Charles E. Wyzanski Jr., *Augustus Noble Hand*, 61 HARV. L. REV. 573 (1948).

20. NELSON, *supra* note 1, at 132.

21. *Augustus N. Hand Named*, N.Y. TIMES, Sept. 29, 1914.

22. *Judge Hand Raised to Circuit Bench*, N.Y. TIMES, May 21, 1927.

23. Judge Charles E. Clark, Remarks at a Special Meeting of the New York County Lawyers' Association and The Association of the Bar of the City of New York for the Memorial for Augustus Noble Hand 4, 5 (May 4, 1955) (transcript on file with the United States Courts Library for the Second Circuit).

24. *Id.* at 5.

25. MARVIN SCHICK, LEARNED HAND'S COURT 24 (1970); JEFFREY B. MORRIS, FEDERAL JUSTICE IN THE SECOND CIRCUIT 118 (1987); John Sayer, *Art and Politics, Dissent and Repression: The Masses Magazine Versus the Government, 1917-1918*, 32 AM. J. LEGAL HIST. 42 (1988).

26. CONSTANCE JORDAN, REASON AND IMAGINATION:THE SELECTED CORRESPONDENCE OF LEARNED HAND 130-31 (2013).

27. *Id.* at 131 n.54.

28. *Judge Hand Raised to Circuit Bench*, *supra* note 22; *Judge Hand Is Approved*, N.Y. TIMES, Jan. 17, 1928, at 22.

29. Judge Charles E. Wyzanski Jr., Remarks, *supra* note 6, at 15.

30. *Id.*

31. NELSON, *supra* note 1, at 8; SCHICK, *supra* note 25, at 24-25.

32. United States v. One Book Entitled Ulysses, 72 F.2d 705, 708-09 (2d Cir. 1934); *'Ulysses' is Upheld by Appeals Court*, N.Y. TIMES, Aug. 8, 1934, at 15.

33. 72 F.2d at 711.

34. United States v. One Package, 86 F.2d 737 (2d Cir. 1936).

35. *Id.*

36. United States v. Kauten, 133 F.2d 703, 707 (2d Cir. 1943).

37. *Id.* at 708.

38. *Id.*

39. United States ex rel. Lynn v. Downer, 140 F.2d 397 (2d Cir. 1944).

40. *Id.* at 400, 401.

41. Birnbaum v. Newport Steel Corp., 193 F.2d 461, 464 (2d Cir. 1952).

42. United States v. Sacher, 182 F.2d 416, 430 (2d Cir. 1950), *aff'd*, 343 U.S. 1 (1952).

43. In re Sacher, 206 F.2d 358 (2d Cir. 1953), *rev'd*, 347 U.S. 388 (1954).

44. United States v. Rosenberg, 204 F.2d 688 (2d Cir. 1953).

45. *2 Rosenbergs Lose in Appeals Court*, N.Y. TIMES, June 12, 1953.

46. *Two Judges Ending U.S. Court Careers*, N.Y.TIMES, July 1, 1953.

47. United States v. Hiss, 185 F.2d 822 (2d Cir. 1950); United States v. Hiss, 201 F.2d 372 (2d Cir. 1953).

48. SCHICK, *supra* note 25, at 146, n.60.

49. GUNTHER, *supra* note 2, at 433; *Manton Testifies to Big Cash Loans from Litigants*, N.Y. TIMES, June 3, 1939.

50. *Id.*

51. MORRIS, *supra* note 25, at 131.

52. *Id.*
53. *Id.* at 142, 195.
54. SCHICK, *supra* note 25, at 315.
55. *Id.* at 26, 317.
56. *Id.* at 290-92.
57. *Id.* at 198.
58. *Id.* at 200.
59. Wyzanski Jr., *supra* note 19, at 583.
60. Judge Charles E. Clark, Remarks, *supra* note 23, at 8.
61. NELSON, *supra* note 1, at 54.
62. SCHICK, *supra* note 25 at 139, n.41.
63. NELSON, *supra* note 1, at 54.
64. GUNTHER, *supra* note 2, at 22.
65. *Id.* at 44, 71.
66. *Id.* at 558, 679 n.43.
67. *Id.* at 556.
68. Charles E. Clark, *Augustus Noble Hand*, 68 HARV. L. REV. 1113, 1114 (1955).
69. *Id.*
70. Robert H. Jackson, *Why Learned and Augustus Hand Became Great*, Address Before the New York County Lawyers' Association (December 13, 1951), http://www.roberthjackson.org/documents.
71. Augustus Noble Hand, *Felix Frankfurter*, 62 HARV. L. REV. 353, 354 (1949).
72. NELSON, *supra* note 1, at 27.
73. *Id.* at 30.
74. *Id.* at 31-32.
75. *Id.* at 42.
76. *Id.* at 42; GUNTHER, *supra* note 2, at 447.
77. *Id.* at 47.
78. *Id.* at 61.
79. *To Observe Dicker Day*, N.Y. TIMES, Jul. 17, 1938.
80. SCHICK, *supra* note 25, at 70.
81. Charles A. Horsky, *Augustus Noble Hand*, 68 HARV. L. REV. 1118, 1120 (1955).
82. Telephone Interview with Susan Speers, *supra* note 8.
83. Letter from Augustus N. Hand to "Mr. Stewart"(Dec. 16, 1917) (on file with Grace Church archives).
84. GUNTHER, *supra* note 2, at 287; *Dr. Pitt Inducted at Grace Church*, N.Y. TIMES, Feb. 5, 1940, at 12; THE BULLETIN OF GRACE CHURCH IN NEW YORK, Vol. 1, no. 5, p. 3, Hand Family Papers, Division of Rare and Manuscript Collections, Cornell University Library, No. 3624, box 54.
85. NELSON, *supra* note 1, at 57-58.
86. *Augustus Hand at 80*, N.Y. TIMES, Jul. 26, 1949.
87. *Two Judges Ending U.S. Court Careers*, *supra* note 46; *Two Fine Judges*, N.Y. TIMES, Jul. 3, 1953 at 18; *Eisenhower Hails "Inspiration" in A.N. Hand's Career as a Judge*, N.Y. TIMES, Jul. 24, 1953, at 11. When Judge Hand left active service, the term "senior judge" was not yet used to describe a federal judge who left active service but continued to perform some judicial duties. *See* Act of Feb. 25, 1919, ch. 29, § 6, 40 Stat. 1156, 1157-58. A judge who took this option was considered to have "retired." Under a statute enacted in 1948, such a "retired" judge received the same salary increases and cost-of-living adjustments as an active judge. Act of June 25, 1948, ch. 646, §§ 294, 371, 372, 62 Stat. 901, 903-04. See Stephen B. Burbank, et al., *Leaving the Bench, 1970-2009: The Choices Federal Judges Make, What Influences Those Choices, and Their Consequences*, 161 U. PA. L. REV. 1, 8-10 (2012).
88. *Two Fine Judges*, *supra* note 87.

89. *Augustus N. Hand, Jurist, Dies at 85*, *supra* note 14.
90. *A Great Jurist Passes*, N.Y. TIMES, Oct. 29, 1954.
91. NELSON, *supra* note 1, at 182-83.

# HARRIE BRIGHAM CHASE
## 1889-1969

Court of Appeals for the Second Circuit: 1929-1969

Harrie Brigham Chase was the first judge from Vermont to serve on the Court of Appeals for the Second Circuit.[1] Appointed by his fellow Vermonter, President Calvin Coolidge, in 1929, Chase was on the court for 40 years: the first 25 in active service (with a stint as chief judge), and the 15 years before his death as a senior judge.[2]

Chase was born in Whitingham, Vermont in 1889 to Charles Sumner and Carrie Emily Chase.[3] His father was a lawyer and served as a justice of the peace.[4] At Phillips Exeter Academy, he received the Kingman and Phillips prizes for scholarship each year he was there.[5] At Dartmouth College, he was a member of the Chi Phi fraternity.[6] He followed in his father's profession, and attended the Boston University School of Law. Having earned his degree in 1911,[7] he married Mina A. Gilman. They had three children: Madeline, Alice, and Dana.

In the autumn following his law school graduation, Chase was one of nine candidates to take the Vermont bar examination.[8] He entered private practice with his father in Brattleboro, Vermont, and worked for seven years at Chase & Chase.[9] During this time, he also served as town grand juror of Brattleboro for Windham County,[10] a position later obviated by the modern practice of the Vermont attorney general, but at the time, one that gave Chase "the authority to enforce criminal misdemeanor laws, including ordinance violations in the town."[11]

He left Chase & Chase upon his 1919 election as the state's attorney of Windham County, getting "the largest vote of any candidate for any office named on the ticket."[12] His three-month tenure ended when his judicial career began. It started locally, when Governor Percival W. Clement appointed him to the Vermont Superior Court. Chase was 29 years old, making him one of the youngest judges in the state.[13] He began with a bang: in one of his first cases he signed the "final decree" between two parties that had been suing each other for 20 years over a dispute that began around the turn of the nineteenth century.[14] Because the parties mutually agreed to the settlement terms, Chase did not "have any objection to winding up this famous case."[15]

He served on that court for nine years—the last two as chief judge—before appointment as an associate judge on the Supreme Court of Vermont. At 38, he was the youngest judge ever nominated.[16] He served for two years before his appointment to the federal judiciary.

Judge Chase's seat on the Second Circuit was created by Congress[17] to better manage the busiest docket in the nation,[18] and as part of a failed attempt to "re-circuit" the country to more evenly distribute cases.[19] President Coolidge, then a lame duck, selected Chase to fill the new seat. Chase had been passed over once by Coolidge, who instead selected Augustus Noble Hand for an open seat.[20] This time, Coolidge and his attorney general, John G. Sargent (also a Vermonter),[21] "immediately agreed that the new seat would belong to Vermont."[22] Coolidge and Chase were "old friends,"[23] and Sargent was very close to the Chase family.[24]

The nomination of a young and relatively unknown jurist from Vermont did not sit well with Judge Learned Hand, who reportedly said, "[M]y heart sinks a little at a man who carries the name 'Harrie.'"[25] Judge Hand preferred District Judge Thomas D. Thacher, who had been appointed by Coolidge years earlier to the bench of the Southern District of New York, succeeding Hand. Judge Hand and his New York allies thought that Thacher was an excellent trial judge and unsuccessfully pushed for his appointment. Judge Hand did, however, consider that the Chase nomination presented "all sorts of possibilities" and wrote Chase a letter of welcome. Others were less optimistic: Justice Louis D. Brandeis recounted that prominent New York attorney Charles C. Burlingham once said that Chase's appointment to the court "was the worst yet."[26]

Judge Hand's biographer described Judge Chase as one who never "claimed to be an intellectual or a penetrating student of the law, but [one who] did possess integrity and competence."[27] Judge Chase was modest. In response to Judge Hand's letter after the nomination, he said that he did "not dare hope that you will find me all that you have the right to expect."[28] He did not stand out on the court and was "ordinarily restrained and taciturn."[29] Some who later practiced before Judge Chase remarked how he would have been more recognizably outstanding as a judge had it not been for his more colorful colleagues on the bench.[30] His "reputation suffered because he sat alongside such illustrious judges."[31] But even without the stature of his colleagues, one student of the court's history observed that his opinions were "remarkable for their clarity in outlining difficult situations and legal principles."[32] He added: "It is difficult to conceive of a judicial career of comparable length and importance cloaked in a greater degree of anonymity."[33]

Judge Chase maintained chambers in Brattleboro,[34] generally handled the cases that arose in Vermont, and wrote nearly all of his opinions at home.[35] As a result, he never became a part of the central core of the circuit—either socially or intellectually.[36] To outsiders, he was "the least known member of the Court."[37]

However, because the composition of the court had remained stable for the decade following his appointment, Judge Chase and his colleagues nonetheless had "formed a tightly knit group."[38] Newcomers were a different matter: he sarcastically referred to Judge Charles E. Clark as "the great dissenter" and bristled at Clark's habit of writing separate opinions.[39] Judge Chase once wrote to Judge Learned Hand, wondering "how many times should a certain so-and-so be allowed to get stubborn about nothing and get away with it?"[40]

Judge Chase was well respected for his tax opinions.[41] One important decision was *Farid-Es-Sultaneh v. Commissioner*, where he wrote for Judge Clark and Judge Thomas Swan to clarify the definition of "gift" for estate, gift, and income tax purposes.[42] His decision set the cost basis of a stock gift at the fair market value at the time of transfer, not the original cost basis.

He had a conservative approach to free speech and was "perhaps the least sympathetic of Learned Hand's seven principal colleagues to civil liberties claims."[43] In *United States v. Dennis*,[44] (which reconsidered Justice Holmes's "clear and present danger" test for speech), Judge Chase only concurred in the judgment, arguing that the majority approach was too liberal.[45] Years earlier, he had written the majority opinion in *Sweeney v. Schenectady Union Publishing Company*,[46] reversing the dismissal of a libel suit and concluding that "freedom of speech is, as it always has been, freedom to tell the truth and comment fairly upon facts and not a license to spread damaging falsehoods. . ."[47] In a 1940 speech, he remarked that in the "freedom of speech which we cherish is found one of the most effective ways to spread the foreign doctrines and the false notions of security which may destroy us."[48]

Judge Chase also wrote the 6,000-word decision affirming the perjury conviction of the former State Department official Alger Hiss.[49] (According to the FBI, Hiss was not indicted for espionage because the statute of limitations had run.)[50] Chase wrote for a panel that included Judges Augustus Hand and Swan, concluding that the testimony of Hiss's principal accuser was "of such breadth and scope that if it was adequately substantiated by other evidence, as the law required, there was enough to support the verdict."[51]

When Supreme Court Chief Justice Harlan Fiske Stone died in 1946, Judge Chase was on the short list to replace him.[52] However, President Harry S. Truman selected Judge Fred M. Vinson, a former colleague in Congress and secretary of the Treasury, and Judge Chase remained at the Second Circuit.[53] Judge Chase was not often the subject of rumors and speculation: during his 25 years on the court, "his name never appeared in the newspapers except in connection with court opinions; he was not the subject of a critical study in any law journal; and there is no record of any address or article of his on a judicial topic or a statement of his philosophy."[54]

Judge Chase became chief judge in 1953, but assumed senior status in 1954.[55] In ill health at age 65, Judge Chase chose to take "advantage of a liberalized retirement statute and retire at full pay" instead of continuing active service.[56] Fellow Vermonter Sterry R. Waterman was appointed to fill his seat.[57] Chase continued to live in Vermont; he traveled less frequently to New York and heard fewer cases.[58] In the late 1950s he came to New York for a sitting and the "experience convinced him that he no longer had any desire to sit as a judge or undergo the rigors of regular travel."[59]

Judge James L. Oakes, who would himself become chief judge, served two separate terms as law clerk for Judge Chase, from 1947 to 1948 and again from 1949 to 1950.[60]

Judge Chase enjoyed playing golf at the Brattleboro Country Club.[61] Golf was his chief sporting diversion,[62] and he preferred it to writing opinions.[63] He was involved in local organizations and community groups: as a trustee of the Brattleboro Retreat, the first facility dedicated for the care of the mentally ill in Vermont,[64] and as a member of the All Souls Church in Brattleboro.[65]

Judge Chase died in Vernon, Vermont in 1969. He was 80 years old.[66]

Greg Capobianco

1. JEFFERY B. MORRIS, FEDERAL JUSTICE IN THE SECOND CIRCUIT 143 (1987).
2. *Id.*
3. MARVIN SCHICK, LEARNED HAND'S COURT 27 (1970).
4. JOURNAL OF THE SENATE OF THE STATE OF VERMONT: BIENNIAL SESSION, 1906, at 567 (1907).
5. *Two New Lawyers in Brattleboro*, VERMONT PHOENIX, Oct. 4, 1912 at 6.
6. *Famous Chi Phi Members*, CHI PHI FRATERNITY, https://www.chiphi.org/alumni/famous-members.
7. *Two New Lawyers in Brattleboro*, *supra* note 5.
8. *Id.*
9. *Id.*
10. ARTHUR F. STONE, THE VERMONT OF TODAY 19-20 (1929).
11. VERMONT LEAGUE OF CITIES AND TOWNS, HANDBOOK FOR VERMONT TOWN OFFICERS ch. 17 (2014).
12. *Young Judge; Short Court Term*, MIDDLEBURY REGISTER, May 23, 1919 at 1 (describing Chase as the "newest and youngest" judge in the state).
13. *Id.*
14. *See* Cloyes v. Middlebury Elec. Co., 66 A. 1039 (1907); *The Flashboard Obituary Written*, MIDDLEBURY REGISTER, June 6, 1919 at 1.
15. *The Flashboard Obituary Written*, *supra* note 14.
16. Special Supplement, *Colleagues for Justice: One Hundred Years of The United States Court of Appeals for the Second Circuit*, 65 ST. JOHNS L. REV. 937, 952 (1991).
17. 45 Stat. 1081 (1929).
18. GEORGE MARTIN, CCB: THE LIFE AND CENTURY OF CHARLES C. BURLINGHAM 258 (2005).
19. *Id.*
20. SCHICK, *supra* note 3, at 28.
21. *Id.*
22. *Id.*
23. *Coolidge Appoints Chase as New Judge*, N.Y. TIMES, Jan. 20, 1929 at 3.
24. John P. Frank, *The Top U.S. Commercial Court*, FORTUNE MAG., January 1951, at 110.
25. GERALD GUNTHER, LEARNED HAND: THE MAN AND THE JUDGE 244 (2011).
26. LETTERS OF LOUIS D. BRANDEIS, VOLUME V 368-69 (1978).
27. GUNTHER, *supra* note 25, at 244.
28. *Id.*
29. *Id.* at 444.
30. Frank, *supra* note 24, at 110.
31. SCHICK, *supra* note 3, at 28.
32. *Id.* at 29.
33. SCHICK, *supra* note 3, at 27.
34. Frank, *supra* note 24, at 110.
35. MARTIN, *supra* note 18, at 258.
36. *Id.*
37. Frank, *supra* note 24, at 110.
38. GUNTHER, *supra* note 25, at 443.
39. *Id.* at 447-48.
40. *Id.* at 448.
41. Special Supplement, *supra* note 16, at 952.
42. 160 F.2d 812, 813 (2d Cir. 1947).
43. MORRIS, *supra* note 1, at 143.

44. 183 F.2d 201 (2d Cir. 1950).

45. SCHICK, *supra* note 3, at 204.

46. 122 F.2d 288 (2d Cir. 1941).

47. *Id.* at 206 (quoting *Sweeney*, 122 F.2d at 291).

48. *Id.* at 205.

49. United States v. Hiss, 185 F.2d 822 (2d Cir. 1950); Edward Ranzal, *3 Judges Uphold Hiss Conviction; He Plans Appeals to Supreme Court*, N.Y. TIMES, Dec. 8, 1950 at 1.

50. *A Byte Out of History*, FEDERAL BUREAU OF INVESTIGATION, http://www.fbi.gov/news/stories/2013/january/a-byte-out-of-history-the-alger-hiss-story/a-byte-out-of-history-the-alger-hiss-story.

51. Ranzal, *supra* note 46, at 17.

52. CHRISTINE L. NEMACHECK , STRATEGIC SELECTION: PRESIDENTIAL NOMINATION OF SUPREME COURT JUSTICES FROM HERBERT HOOVER THROUGH GEORGE W. BUSH 149 (2007).

53. *Id.*

54. SCHICK, *supra* note 3, at 27.

55. When Judge Chase left active service, the term "senior judge" was not yet used to describe a federal judge who left active service but continued to perform some judicial duties. *See* Act of Feb. 25, 1919, ch. 29, § 6, 40 Stat. 1156, 1157-58. A judge who took this option was considered to have "retired." Under a statute enacted in 1948, such a "retired" judge received the same salary increases and cost-of-living adjustments as an active judge. Act of June 25, 1948, ch. 646, §§ 294, 371, 372, 62 Stat. 901, 903-04. *See* Stephen B. Burbank, et al., *Leaving the Bench, 1970-2009: The Choices Federal Judges Make, What Influences Those Choices, and Their Consequences*, 161 U. PA. L. REV. 1, 8-10 (2012).

56. SCHICK, *supra* note 3, at 28.

57. *Sterry Waterman Nominated as Federal Judge*, BENNINGTON EVENING BANNER, May 13, 1955 at 1.

58. MORRIS, *supra* note 1, at 143.

59. SCHICK, *supra* note 3, at 28.

60. *James L. Oakes Obituary*, BRATTLEBORO REFORMER, http://www.legacy.com/obituaries/brattleboro/obituary-print.aspx?n=james-l-oakes&pid=96179420.

61. STONE, *supra* note 10, at 20.

62. *Id.*

63. GUNTHER, *supra* note 25.

64. STONE, *supra* note 10, at 20.

65. *Id.*

66. *Harrie Chase, 80, of Appeals Court*, N.Y. TIMES, Nov. 18, 1969 at 47.

# JULIAN W. MACK
## 1866-1943

Commerce Court: 1911-1913
Court of Appeals for the Seventh Circuit: 1911-1929
Court of Appeals for the Sixth Circuit 1929-1930
Court of Appeals for the Second Circuit 1929-1940

Judge Mack arrived in the Court of Appeals for Second Circuit by a route that was circuitous and open only for a brief time. Appointed as an Article III judge on the (now defunct) Commerce Court, the chief justice assigned him to the Second Circuit in 1929. Mack's illustrious judicial career spanned over 40 years.[1] He also distinguished himself outside the courtroom as a preeminent Zionist spokesperson and leader in the Jewish community.

Julian William Mack was born on July 19, 1866 into a German Jewish family.[2] Along with his four brothers, Mack took his middle name from his father, William Jacob Mack.[3] Growing up, Julian lacked interest in commercial pursuits,[4] perhaps as "a reaction against the gloom he noticed in the family at times when business was bad."[5] On "Black Friday" in 1869, William Mack's gold mine stocks collapsed and never recovered.[6] Within a month, William Mack decided to move to Cincinnati, and the family set out for their new home in July 1869.[7]

Julian Mack decided on a career early. As he recalled, "I knew from the time I was four that I would go into the law."[8] Mack completed high school in three years, and delivered a speech as salutatorian, emphasizing the need for municipal reform—a topic thought particularly "audacious," given the grip of Boss Cox's political machine on the city.[9] His first public notice was the award of a special medal, given at graduation, recognizing that he "had made such extraordinary progress in his studies and won so much esteem by his good behavior and consideration for others."[10] The *American Israelite* and *Cincinnati Enquirer* both ran the story.[11]

Mack's uncle Max insisted that he attend Harvard, and cinched the deal by offering to pay tuition.[12] Mack enrolled directly in the law school, where he formed a study group called the Langdell Society.[13] Unlike the typical study group, the Langdell Society conducted more serious discussions of law.[14] During one session, the members observed that Columbia Law School was publishing its own journal, the *Columbia Jurist*, and decided that Harvard should have a publication as well.[15] The discussions of the Langdell Society helped Mack become the essential founder of the *Harvard Law Review*.[16] Mack graduated in 1887 and was the class orator.[17] A coveted Parker Fellowship—a three-year $750 annual scholarship—underwrote Mack's study of comparative law at the Universities of Berlin and Leipzig.[18]

On his return to the United States in 1890, he moved to Chicago,[19] and was admitted to the bars of Chicago and Cincinnati.[20] That same year, he met his future wife, Jessie Fox, at his brother's wedding.[21] They had one child, named Ruth.[22] Mack began his legal career as a law clerk in the firm of Julius Rosenthal.[23] Mack later co-founded the firm of Hofheimer, Zeisler & Mack.[24] He gained prominence as the sole attorney representing a leading Chicago investment firm in a "sensational" bankruptcy.[25] However, after being "practically ignored" in the fee apportionment, Mack pulled out of the partnership and began solo practice,[26] eventually becoming a law professor at Northwestern University.[27] Mack later joined the original faculty at the University of Chicago Law School.[28]

During this time, Mack was active in many Jewish charities. The United States was experiencing a wave of Jewish migration from Russia.[29] Mack helped found the Young Men's Russian Relief Association to assist those arriving in Chicago.[30] At one meeting, Mack gave a speech that drew attention in the Jewish community. Many were fearful of a large influx of immigrants, but Mack explained that "[a]mong their number you will find hundreds of honest, able and industrious workmen," and concluded that they were "a people worthy and fit to take their place as citizens of this great republic."[31] A few weeks later, the United Jewish Charities of Chicago elected Mack secretary.[32] He thus "became, in effect, the directing official of Jewish charities in Chicago."[33]

Mack's charitable role led to his first judgeship. Mayor Carter Harrison, seeking to "do something for" Jews, appointed Mack civil service commissioner on a rabbi's recommendation.[34] Three months later, the mayor nominated Mack as a candidate for judge of the Circuit Court of Cook County.[35] Although Mack failed to win the recommendation of the Bar Association because he was too young (still in his thirties) he ultimately won election.[36] Despite his youth, Judge Mack had a comprehensive knowledge of the law, often citing statutes and case law that experienced attorneys had neglected.[37] He also preferred to get to the point. When a lawyer would spew a string cite of case law, Mack would ask the classic judge's question: "Well, what is your *best* case?"[38]

Initially assigned to the chancery division, Judge Mack was soon transferred to a court where he could make a difference in the lives of the underprivileged: the new Juvenile Court of Chicago.[39] Mack was a pioneer in the juvenile court movement,[40] and "championed the notion of the Juvenile Court as guardian of the youth who came before it, rather than as arbiter in a conflict where the youth was pitted against the state."[41] Judge Mack often held court at his desk and eschewed traditional judicial robes.[42] He advocated for staffing the court with social workers, and visited the reformatories to which youths were sent.[43] His article in the *Harvard Law Review* stressed the advantages of the Juvenile Court, and explained its underlying moral and policy foundations.[44]

When the Illinois State Supreme Court entered an order promoting Mack to the appellate court, he fought it. Pleading with the justices to withdraw the order, Mack wrote, "I feel that my work in the Juvenile Court is unfinished."[45] They acquiesced only after social reform groups "bombarded" the justices with letters protesting the order.[46] The agreement to withdraw the order would prove fortunate for generations of children. Mack helped establish, and served as the chairman of, the Juvenile Protective Association, as well as the first president of the Juvenile Protective League, a forerunner of the Child Welfare League of America, the oldest and largest child welfare organization in the United States.[47] Nevertheless, one year after withdrawing its previous order, the Illinois Supreme Court again entered an order assigning Mack to the appellate court. This time the promotion stuck.[48]

During his time as a state judge, Mack met the mother of Henry Friendly.[49] Friendly had planned to spend a year in Europe and return to seek a Ph.D. in medieval English history, rather than attend Harvard Law School.[50] Friendly's mother was crushed. She wrote to Mack "about this dreadful thing that was about to occur."[51] Mack put young Friendly in touch with Felix Frankfurter, then a law professor at Harvard, who persuaded Friendly to attend law school when he returned from Europe.[52] Mack would later preside over one of Friendly's first cases as a lawyer.[53]

Mack continued to be active in various causes. He was the first president of the Immigrants' Protective League, an organization dedicated to combating anti-immigrant propaganda.[54] He participated in meetings that led to the National Association for the Advancement of Colored People, and joined other activists as a "sponsor" of the American Civil Liberties Union.[55] Mack's colleagues on the appellate court thought that he was spending too much time on "outside activities," and Mack was unhappy there.[56] But he would not stay long.

In 1910, Congress created the United States Commerce Court,[57] to replace the federal district and circuit courts in reviewing decisions made by the Interstate Commerce Commission, the agency charged with regulating railroads.[58] The ill-fated court was created due to a split between the progressive and conservative wings of the Republican Party. The progressives believed the court would stem the tide of federal court reversals of the Interstate Commerce Commission, and the conservatives believed the court would curb the commission's perceived overregulation.[59]

The Commerce Court had five judges.[60] Each judge was appointed to serve on that court for a term of one to five years, after which he would be permanently reassigned to a court of appeals and replaced on the Commerce Court by a sitting circuit judge.[61] So, though a judge's term on the Commerce Court was limited, his appointment to the court of appeals was for life. Congress authorized President William Howard Taft to nominate the five judges who would serve on the Commerce Court for no longer than five years.[62] Upon their confirmation, the chief justice assigned the five Commerce Court judges to the courts of appeals, "where they would go with life tenure once their special court terms expired."[63] Seeking to fill the court with judges who were above politics, President Taft nominated Mack. The Senate confirmed Mack's nomination in January 1911.[64] Mack served on the Commerce Court with a future colleague on the Court of Appeals for the Second Circuit, Martin A. Knapp.[65]

The Commerce Court came with an added benefit—Mack could serve as a relief judge in other federal courts if the Commerce Court did not "require the services of all the judges."[66] United States Attorney General George W. Wickersham observed that this provision created "a body of five circuit judges at large" who could be "sent to places where there [wa]s a congestion of business or a shortage of judges."[67] Judge Mack served primarily on two other courts: the Court of Appeals for the Seventh Circuit in Chicago, and the Second Circuit in New York.[68] The chronically overburdened Second Circuit availed itself of Mack's relief services so frequently that he bought a New York apartment.[69]

The Commerce Court was abolished after one of its judges was impeached and convicted for accepting bribes.[70] Congress initially intended to abolish the judgeships along with the court, but later decided that the judges would serve as "additional Circuit Court judges for assignment to crowded dockets."[71] Mack was thus an "ambulatory" federal judge, beholden for assignment only to the chief justice.[72]

By 1914, Mack was sitting almost exclusively in New York,[73] serving on the Second Circuit as well as the District Court for the Southern District of New York. In the district court, he presided over many noteworthy trials, including the prosecutions of: former United States Attorney General Harry M. Daugherty; the founder of the United States Black Nationalist Movement, Marcus Garvey;[74] and "Big Bill" Dwyer, "king of the bootleggers."[75] Judge Mack also jailed Albany Democratic boss Daniel P. O'Connor for contempt in refusing to answer grand jury questions investigating a baseball gambling ring.[76] Among his civil trials, Judge Mack presided over the Sugar Institute antitrust case, the reorganization of Fox Metropolitan Theaters, and a securities case against Insull Utility Investment Corporation.[77] Mack was reassigned as a permanent judge on the Second Circuit in 1929.[78]

Mack remained involved in Jewish causes. In one curious episode, he became active in the orange business. Aaron Aaronsohn, one of the first Jewish settlers in Palestine, pleaded with Mack for assistance in selling the year's orange crop.[79] Oranges were an important source of income for the early settlers, but the outbreak of World War I prevented the export of the crop to Europe.[80] Mack persuaded prominent businessmen to underwrite the import of the oranges to the United States.[81] And Mack arranged for the financing, import licenses, packaging, and sale of the oranges as well.[82] The orange crop was saved.[83]

Mack, initially ambivalent to whether there should be a permanent Jewish state in Palestine, was inching closer to becoming a committed Zionist. Louis D. Brandeis, then the unchallenged leader of American Zionism, a minor movement among American Jews, recruited Mack to the cause.[84] Reluctant at first, Mack ultimately accepted Brandeis's invitation to serve on an advisory council with Felix Frankfurter to the Provisional Executive Committee for General Zionist Affairs.[85] Mack's early ambivalence to Zionism was not uncommon at the time, but he and Brandeis together recruited many prominent Jews to the movement.[86] Mack's standing in the Jewish community reached its pinnacle when he was elected president of the first American Jewish Congress.[87]

Mack was also elected president of the Zionist Organization of America, and became the de facto leader of the "Mack-Brandeis" group.[88] Brandeis might have been elected president had he not been appointed to the Supreme Court.[89] This alliance would end painfully for Mack. An ideological schism that involved "both principles and personalities" split the Zionist Organization of America in two.[90] In short, Brandeis "wanted to go forward to build a Jewish state at once, practically, ideally" through settlement, while the opposition, led by Chaim Weizmann, prioritized political recognition of the right to such a state.[91] Following a failed attempt at compromise, Mack was ousted with a vote of "no confidence."[92]

Mack continued to support Zionism in other roles. He served as a director of the Palestine Cooperative Company, which was later succeeded by the Palestine Economic Corporation.[93] Its purpose was to carry out many of the policies advocated by the Mack-Brandeis group.[94] Mack was also elected as an overseer at Harvard.[95] In a noteworthy victory, he was able to help defeat a "Jewish quota" sought by Harvard President A. Lawrence Lowell.[96] Mack would ultimately return to the Zionist Organization of America in a show of unity. He rejected pleas to return as president, but accepted an "honorary" presidency.[97]

Jessie Fox Mack, Judge Mack's wife, died in November 1938 after several months of illness.[98] Two years later, Mack suffered a stroke.[99] Increasingly poor eyesight and memory lapses made it impossible for him to continue as a judge.[100] He resigned from the bench in September 1940.[101] Mack married his daughter Ruth's mother-in-law, Cecile Brunswick,[102] "Cec," in his final years.[103] On September 5, 1943, Mack died sitting in a chair in his apartment at the age of 77,[104] survived by Cec and Ruth.[105] Ruth had one daughter, Mathilda Juliana Brunswick, and died in 1946.[106]

Daniel Principato

1. *Julian Mack Dies: 40 Years on the Bench*, N.Y. TIMES, Sept. 6, 1943, at 17.
2. HARRY BARNARD, THE FORGING OF AN AMERICAN JEW: THE LIFE AND TIMES OF JUDGE JULIAN W. MACK 3 (1974).
3. *See id.* at 14.
4. *See id.* at 16.
5. *Id.* (internal quotations omitted).
6. *Id.*
7. *Id.* at 16–17.
8. *Id.* at 21.
9. *Id.*
10. *Id.*
11. *Id.*
12. *Id.* at 22.
13. *Id.* at 23–25.
14. *Id.*
15. *See id.*
16. *Id.* at 25; *Julian W. Mack—A Tribute*, 24 ISR. L. REV. 1, 1 (1990).
17. BARNARD, *supra* note 2, at 26.
18. *Id.* at 27.
19. *See Julian W. Mack—A Tribute*, *supra* note 16, at 1.
20. *Mack a Jurist 25 Years*, N.Y. TIMES, Feb. 1, 1936, at 17.
21. BARNARD, *supra* note 2, at 40.
22. *Mrs. Julian Mack, Wife of U.S. Judge*, N.Y. TIMES, Dec. 1, 1938, at 23.
23. *See* BARNARD, *supra* note 2, at 36.
24. *See Id.* at 37-39.
25. *Id.* at 37–38.
26. *Id.* at 39–40.
27. *Julian W. Mack—A Tribute*, *supra* note 16, at 1.
28. *Id.*
29. *See* BARNARD, *supra* note 2, at 49.
30. *Id.*
31. *Id.* at 49–50.
32. *Id.* at 51.
33. *Id.*
34. *Id.* at 56–57.
35. *Id.* at 57.
36. *Id.* at 58.
37. *Id.* at 61–62.
38. *See id.*
39. *See Julian W. Mack—A Tribute*, *supra* note 16, at 1.
40. *Id.* at 1–2
41. *Id.* at 1.

42. BARNARD, *supra* note 2, at 67.

43. *Julian W. Mack—A Tribute*, *supra* note 16, at 1.

44. Julian W. Mack, *The Juvenile Court*, 23 HARV. L. REV. 104 (1909).

45. Barnard, *supra* note 2, at 72.

46. *Id.*

47. *Id.* at 72, 88; *see* THE CHILD WELFARE LEAGUE OF AMERICA, *OUR STORY*, http://www.cwla.org/about-us/history.

48. BARNARD, *supra* note 2, at 73.

49. DAVID M. DORSEN, HENRY FRIENDLY: GREATEST JUDGE OF HIS ERA 20 (2012).

50. *Id.*

51. *Id.*

52. *Id.*

53. *See* Stansbury v. Koss, 10 F. Supp. 477 (S.D.N.Y. 1931).

54. BARNARD, *supra* note 2, at 87–88.

55. *Id.* at 113.

56. *Id.*

57. Mann-Elkins Act, ch.309, § 1, 36 Stat. 539, 539 (1910); George E. Dix, *The Death of the Commerce Court: A Study In Institutional Weakness*, 8 AM. J. LEGAL HIST. 238, 239 (1964).

58. BARNARD, *supra* note 2, at 114.

59. *Id.*

60. Mann-Elkins Act, § 1, 36 Stat. at 540; STAFF OF S. COMM. ON THE JUDICIARY, 85th CONG., LEGIS. HISTORY OF THE UNITED STATES CIRCUIT COURTS OF APPEALS AND THE JUDGES WHO SERVED DURING THE PERIOD 1801 THROUGH MARCH 1958 23 (Comm. Print 1958); J. Newton Baker, *The Commerce Court—Its Origin, its Powers and its Judges*, 20 YALE L. J. 555, 560 (1911).

61. *See* Baker, *supra* note 60, at 560

62. Mann-Elkins Act, § 1, 36 Stat. at 540; *see* Theodore W. Ruger, *The Judicial Appointment Power of the Chief Justice*, 7 U. PA. J. CONST. L. 341, 360 (2004).

63. Ruger, *supra* note 61, at 360 n.79; *see also* Mann-Elkins Act, § 1, 36 Stat. at 540; LEGIS. HISTORY OF THE UNITED STATES CIRCUIT COURTS OF APPEALS, *supra* note 60, at 23.

64. BARNARD, *supra* note 2, at 116-18 (describing the political atmosphere and debates leading to Macks confirmation).

65. *See* LEGIS. HISTORY OF THE UNITED STATES CIRCUIT COURTS OF APPEALS, *supra* note 60, at 23, 26.

66. Mann-Elkins Act, § 1, 36 Stat. at 541.

67. 48 Cong. Rec. 7972 (1912) (reading of a letter from Attorney General George W. Wickersham to Senator Francis E. Warren (June 4, 1912) by Senator Warren during a congressional session).

68. *See* BARNARD, *supra* note 2, at 119.

69. *See id.*

70. *Id.* at 137–39.

71. *Id.* at 139.

72. *Id.* at 143.

73. *Id.* at 150.

74. *See* THE MARCUS GARVEY AND UNIVERSAL NEGRO IMPROVEMENT ASSOCIATION PAPERS 14, 208 (Robert A. Hill, ed., vol. VI, 1989).

75. *Julian Mack Dies: 40 Years on the Bench*, *supra* note 1 (describing the Daugherty and Big Bill trials); JEFFREY B. MORRIS, FEDERAL JUSTICE IN THE SECOND CIRCUIT 104 n.* (1987).

76. *Julian Mack Dies: 40 Years on the Bench*, *supra* note 1.

77. *Id.*

78. FEDERAL JUDICIAL CENTER, Biographical Directory of Federal Judges, Julian William Mack, http://www.fjc.gov/servlet/nGetInfo?jid=1453&cid=999&ctype=na&instate=na. Mack was simultaneously assigned to serve for one year on the Court Appeals for the Sixth Circuit.

79. BARNARD, *supra* note 2, at 163.

80. *Id.*

81. *Id.*

82. *Id.*

83. *Id.*

84. *See id.* at 174.

85. *Id.* at 188–89.

86. *Id.* at 197–98.

87. *Id.* at 212.

88. *Julian W. Mack—A Tribute*, *supra* note 16, at 4. The Mack-Brandeis group was a faction within the Zionist Organization of America. Opponents charged that "Judge Mack was merely a stand-in for Brandeis" as president of the organization. Mack "did not object to that view," as long as "standing-in" meant "representing Brandeis'[s] views." BARNARD, *supra* note 2, at 213.

89. *Id.* at 213–14.

90. *Id.* at 261-77.

91. *Id.*

92. *Id.*

93. *Id.* at 287-88.

94. *See id.* at 288.

95. *Id.* at 291.

96. *Id.* at 292-99.

97. *Id.* at 290.

98. *See Mrs. Julian Mack, Wife of U.S. Judge*, *supra* note 22.

99. *See* BARNARD, *supra* note 2, at 313.

100. *See id.* at 313-14.

101. *Id.* at 321.

102. *Id.* at 320–21

103. *Id.* at 321.

104. *Id.* at 322.

105. *See Notables at Rites for Julian Mack*, N.Y. TIMES, Sept. 8, 1943, at 23.

106. *See Ruth Brunswick, Freud Associate: Instructor at Psychoanalytic Institute Here Dies at 47—Daughter of Julian Mack*, N.Y. TIMES, Jan. 26, 1946, at 13.

# CHARLES EDWARD CLARK
## 1889-1963

Court of Appeals for the Second Circuit: 1939-1963

Judge Charles Edward Clark was a man of rules. He wrote them. He taught them. He lived by them.

Yale Law School Dean Eugene V. Rostow described Judge Clark as "an authentic child of New England Puritanism, part of that extraordinary band to whom the nation owes so much: its sense of mission and of guilt; its zeal in pious causes; and many features of its ideal of right behavior."[1] He was a Puritan by both work ethic and ancestry: "His ancestors fled from the Massachusetts Bay Colony because they thought it was becoming too fond of money and power, and devoting too little effort to the pursuit of salvation through good works."[2] Clark was warm but serious, "with broad shoulders, blue eyes, a shock of iron-gray hair and a pleasant, almost cherubic countenance that could, however, become stern when occasion demanded."[3]

At his core, however, Clark was a "staunch and creative son of Yale."[4] Born in 1889 in Woodbridge, Connecticut, the son of a farmer,[5] he graduated from Yale College in 1911 and Yale Law School in 1913.[6]

In 1915, Clark married Dorothy Gregory, a fellow Connecticut native. They had two children, Sarah and Elias. Clark practiced law in New Haven for six years and was a member of the Connecticut House of Representatives for a year. In 1919, Dean Thomas Swan recruited Clark back to Yale to teach property, civil procedure, and constitutional law. Ten years later, when Swan was appointed to the Second Circuit, Clark became dean. Clark recruited academic heavyweights to the Yale faculty, including William O. Douglas and Eugene V. Rostow.[7]

Clark remained on the Yale Law School faculty for 44 years. All who knew Clark described him as a consummate teacher. Judge J. Edward Lumbard remarked that his colleague "took great pride in all the young men who studied under him at Yale Law School. They were ever after 'his boys.'"[8] Judge Harold Medina described seeing Clark "with all the finest attributes of humanity, taking these erstwhile tyros to his bosom and basking in the sunshine of their affection and esteem. He was always ready with a word of advice, sharing their problems and their set-backs, always delighted to hear of their successes and their triumphs."[9] One of Clark's "boys" was Supreme Court Justice Potter Stewart, who reflected that as a teacher Clark "was able to impart to even the dullest of his students at least a flash of understanding of his own abiding convictions about the whole meaning and purpose of seemingly technical procedural rules, and ultimately of the whole meaning and purpose of the law itself."[10]

Clark imparted passion for procedural rules in part, no doubt, because he wrote them. In 1934, President Franklin Delano Roosevelt signed a law that empowered the Supreme Court to promulgate rules that would govern federal civil procedure and unite law and equity. Clark immediately recognized the statute as "an unusual opportunity for introducing effective measures of reform in law administration into our most extended court system and of developing a procedure which may properly be a model to all the states."[11]

This was no simple task. In the nineteenth century, "pleading in the courts of common law had become unduly formalized, following what was technically known as 'special' pleading; while practice in the quite separate courts of chancery was hopelessly bogged down in details presented not through the testimony of live witnesses, but through depositions, affidavits, and other written materials."[12] The result: formalized, superfluous pleadings. David Dudley Field, a New York lawyer, wrote what became known as the Field Code of 1848, which merged courts of law and chancery and streamlined pleading standards.[13] States across the country copied the Field Code.[14]

Federal courts, however, continued to divide law and equity when it came to procedure. The procedure "at law" was to conform "'as near as may be' to the local practice where the federal court was held."[15] But "the equity practice was governed by the court's uniform rules," which were based on English chancery.[16] In Clark's words, "The confusion and conflicts resulting from this system were so great that federal practice became an activity only for specialists and an abomination for the profession generally."[17] A state practitioner "accustomed to a local system of merged law and equity" would find in federal court "not only the ancient separation," but also a system that was itself "a confusing mixture of local and general law."[18]

Recognizing the need for reform, Clark led a group known as the New York Law Society, which included a future colleague on the bench, Harold Medina.[19] Together, they "probed the efficacy of a variety of experiments in new procedural devices, had field workers accumulating data for statistics," and held conferences to discuss the results, which Judge Medina would later recall as "some of the most stimulating and exciting conferences" he ever attended.[20]

Many of the New York Law Society's advocates for reform gathered at the American Bar Association's annual meetings. Clark was viewed as "Chief" of this set; other members included Whitney North Seymour, Sr., and Eli Whitney Debevoise.[21] Judge Medina looked back with fondness on his memories of

Clark "presiding, sitting there in the chair in the middle of the group and holding forth. Sometimes we used to call that pontificating."[22]

After Congress empowered the Supreme Court to make rules, the Supreme Court appointed fifteen attorneys to serve on its Advisory Committee on the Rules of Civil Procedure, with Clark as their reporter.[23] (Some say that it was a law review article by Clark that spurred the Supreme Court to create the very committee that Clark would lead for 20 years.)[24]

The committee revolutionized federal practice: their rules merged law and equity; created a pleading standard that avoided the details of "special" pleading and the vagueness of notice pleading; and crafted pretrial procedures aimed at unearthing the merits early in a case. The committee's work triggered near-jubilation among members of the bar. "Federal practice permitted the advancement of cases to decision on the merits with a minimum of procedural encumbrances. Lawyers were less likely to make irreversible mistakes in pleading."[25] In the words of Yale University President Kingman Brewster, Clark, as an "[a]rchitect of court reform," had "helped to free the judicial process from obstructive and useless technicalities."[26] Clark's philosophy on the law was enshrined in Federal Rule of Civil Procedure 1: "the just, speedy, and inexpensive determination of every action." In rapid succession, 18 states, the District of Columbia, and Puerto Rico adopted the federal rules.[27]

Clark not only wrote the rules: he wrote the standard text on how to use the rules, *Code Pleading* (1928, West). He was a prolific author: he wrote 14 books, 88 book reviews, and 90 other articles.[28]

Although he was a Republican early in his career, Clark supported the New Deal. As dean of Yale Law School, he testified publicly in support of President Franklin Delano Roosevelt's court-packing plan.[29] Presidents Herbert Hoover and Roosevelt offered him judgeships on the Court of Appeals for the DC Circuit; Clark declined both offers. In 1939, Roosevelt nominated Clark to the Second Circuit to fill a newly created seat. Judge Clark accepted and served for the next 24 years, including five years as chief judge from 1954 to 1959.[30]

Judge Clark's years on the bench were marked by his "continuing disagreements with Jerome Frank"[31]—what political scientist Marvin Schick compared to "a marriage gone wrong."[32] The two served together on the court for 16 years. "Hardly anything relating to their activities in the 1940's was off limits to the combatants."[33] According to Schick,

> Frank's course on fact-finding at the Yale Law School, Clark's work on the Supreme Court's Advisory Committee on the Federal Rules of Civil Procedure, relations with Supreme Court justices and with colleagues on the Second Circuit, the extrajudicial writings of both judges, their law clerks, and their writing styles—all these, and many other matters, figured at one time or another in their disagreements.[34]

Historian Gerald Gunther posits that the rift may not have been "an ideological clash but, rather, personality conflicts."[35] There is some evidence to support that theory: both taught at Yale in the 1940s; they "shared associates and friends"; and each joined the Second Circuit as "a vigorous (and courageous) champion of the underdog and each had rejected the old mechanical jurisprudence."[36] Nonetheless, they diverged on an array of legal issues: partial judgments under Federal Rule of Civil Procedure 54(b),[37] the harmless error doctrine in criminal law, the use of special verdict forms in jury trials,[38] and whether a court could decide a patent's validity absent a dispute about infringement.[39] Judge Learned Hand often took Judge Frank's side in these battles.[40]

Clark and Frank's most "fundamental disagreement" was "on questions of judicial procedure."[41] As one of the chief draftsmen of the Federal Rules of Civil Procedure, Judge Clark viewed himself as their defender "against attack by carping critics and the refusal of judges," including his own colleagues, "to properly abide by them."[42] Judge Clark recognized that this put him in an uncomfortable position; at one point, he asked Judge Learned Hand whether he should resign from the Federal Rules Advisory Committee, confessing to finding it "hard to know where to draw the lines" between his dual roles of judge and reporter.[43]

One particularly colorful disagreement between Clark and Frank arose from Federal Rule of Civil Procedure 56, which governs summary judgment. Judge Clark "strongly favored enhancing the power of judges to award a summary judgment rather than submitting the case to a jury."[44] Judge Frank was a critic: he "was no lover of juries, but distrusted judges even more."[45] Their disagreement was on full display in a copyright infringement action brought by a pro se plaintiff against Cole Porter. At issue was whether Porter had access to the plaintiff's musical composition (and might therefore have copied it). At his deposition, Porter denied access or copying; according to the district judge, the plaintiff's deposition testimony was nothing short of "fantastic."[46] The district court entered summary judgment in favor of Porter. Writing for the panel, Judge Frank reversed on the ground that "as credibility is unavoidably involved, a genuine issue of material fact presents itself. With credibility a vital factor, plaintiff is entitled to a trial where the jury can observe the witnesses while testifying."[47] Judge Clark wrote a spirited dissent. He described the majority decision as "anti-intellectual and book-burning," and rooted in "dislike of the summary-judgment rule."[48] He closed with a dire prediction: "If, however, we are going to the other extreme of having all decisions of musical plagiarism made by ear, the more unsophisticated and musically naive the better, then it seems to me we are reversing our own precedents to substitute chaos, judicial as well as musical."[49]

Judge Clark differed openly with Judge Learned Hand over the Warren Court's expansion of constitutional civil rights. Judge Clark took "issue with Hand's judicial passivity where the Bill of Rights was concerned,"[50] writing: "For my part I do not fear to be governed by 'Plato's wise men,' or even replicas of them; I do fear to be left to the tender mercies of judges who shiver to take the responsibility of forthright decision along lines never before attempted."[51] Justice Potter Stewart echoed this sentiment: "Where there is no remedy, there is no right, Charlie Clark kept reminding us; and those plowed under by the status quo remain helpless."[52] To that end, Judge Clark praised the Warren Court in his remarks at a Law Day ceremony on May 1, 1958, when he said: "I truly believe we owe the Court a debt of high gratitude for restoring us to the vigor which youthful democracy should show its foes as well as its friends."[53] Judge Clark particularly admired the Warren Court's decision in *Gideon v. Wainwright*:

> What greater and indeed more gallant experiment can we conceive of than the Court's recent concern to see that the indigent accused receive exactly the same treatment at bar, even down to the assistance of counsel, as do any of the wealthiest of the land? Can this be achieved? I do not know, but I find it an ideal truly inspiring. . . . I am proud and shall remain proud to be a part of a system and an institution which treats individual man, no matter how lowly and unworthy, as an entity entitled to respect and which endeavors to give a truly practical content to that faith.[54]

Judge Clark's concern for the rights of the individual was on display in what was commonly known as the *Communist Conspiracy* case, a prosecution under the Smith Act. Eleven leaders of the Communist Party were charged with knowingly conspiring to overthrow the U.S. government and propagating Marxist-Leninist doctrines of violent revolution.[55] Judge Medina entered a post-trial judgment of summary contempt against the defendants' lawyers for having disrupted the criminal trial with theatrics.[56] The Second Circuit affirmed, with Judge Clark in dissent. He agreed that "[t]o one schooled in [A]nglo-[S]axon traditions of legal decorum, the resistance pressed by these appellants on various occasions to the rulings of the trial judge necessarily appears abominable."[57] But that did not justify resort to summary contempt. Federal Rule of Criminal Procedure 42 "indicate[d] the extraordinary character of that remedy and prescribe[d] elaborate safeguards of notice and hearing before punishment for the usual contempt."[58] To Clark, summary contempt at the end of trial made no sense: either the disruption was an emergency to be punished immediately, or it was not, and could be punished after a hearing. In Judge Clark's words, summary contempt "is an extraordinary exception to due process of law, justified only by the urgent needs of the moment. When the need for this drastic action passes, the power so to act also passes."[59] Despite their shameful conduct, the defendants and their lawyers were entitled to due process. This was a bold and unpopular statement. One commentator has remarked that Judge Clark "probably kissed all his Supreme Court chances goodby[e]" when he published his dissenting opinion.[60]

Judge Clark's appetite for reform remained voracious on the bench. He immediately identified ways to streamline appellate practice in the Second Circuit. Parties routinely engaged in lengthy disputes over the contents of the record on appeal. Judge Clark would have none of it: he spearheaded an amendment to the local rules that permitted the appellant to file the appendix and the clerk of court to accept it. Judge Medina reflected: "The net result was a very great saving of expense to the litigants and what is believed to be an unprecedented simplification of the whole procedure to be followed in taking appeals to our Court—and a perfect triumph for Judge Clark."[61]

Meanwhile, Judge Clark's son, Charles Elias ("Eli") Clark, followed in his father's footsteps. After graduating from Yale College and Yale Law School, Eli Clark joined the law school faculty in 1949 to teach estates. He remained on the faculty for the next 55 years. For nearly 20, the younger Clark was the master of Silliman College. Like his father before him, he reveled in administration: as chairman of the Council of Masters from 1967 to 1970, he oversaw the integration of women into Yale's residential colleges.[62]

In 1954, Clark became chief judge and focused on improving administration throughout the Second Circuit. Clark "used an assortment of techniques to induce three chief district judges then in their mid-80s to step down from their administrative posts," which included pressuring a judge's secretary and threatening that "'"the Bar Association was going to take the matter to the newspapers."'"[63] Judge Clark himself called the latter tactic "a sort of high-grade blackmail."[64] In 1958, the Judicial Conference successfully persuaded Congress to pass a law capping the age of chief judges at 70, which led to the retirement of the octogenarian chief of the Eastern District of New York (and, ironically, to Judge Clark's own retirement in 1959).[65] That move helped Chief Judge Clark tackle severe congestion in one of the nation's busiest district courts: the Eastern District posted a median disposition time of 49.9 months—nearly four times the national average.[66] Additionally, the Judicial Conference deployed 15 visiting judges on three-month tours of duty to the Eastern District. The visitors cleared 681 civil cases and reduced the average disposition time to 30 months.[67]

Judge Clark also revamped the Second Circuit's judicial conference. For years, he had longed for a conference that lasted days, not hours, "with substantial representation from the lawyers and the law schools in the circuit. He wanted the judges to become better acquainted with one another, and this was to be accomplished by just the right combination of profit and pleasure."[68] Judge Clark turned to Whitney North Seymour, Sr., who served as chair of the first bench-and-bar conference. According to Judge Medina, Clark "presided over the Conference with graciousness and wit; and the presence of the wives made everyone happy."[69] Judge Clark also used the conference to encourage young lawyers to work in the public interest—the same goal he had voiced after the Great Depression when he was dean of Yale Law School.[70] To that end, "he went out of his way to see that young men were assigned to legal aid cases," and that they "were then rewarded in many cases by being invited to the Conference."[71]

Even while carrying duties as a judge and administrator, Judge Clark never stopped teaching. In a speech at Syracuse Law School in 1955, he said this:

> Teaching, I find, is a disease of the most insidious character; once exposed to it, recovery is virtually impossible. Although time is fast working its corrective, I have actually spent more of my adult life in this occupation than in any other; that is my choicest memory and my proudest boast. Even now, I succumb regularly to the virus, and, like an old fire-horse, return for periods of law teaching in vacation time or other judicial breathing spells.[72]

Judge Clark remained on the bench until his death in 1963, at the age of 74, in his Hamden, Connecticut, home.

Sally Pritchard

1. Eugene V. Rostow, Remarks at a Special Session of the United States Court of Appeals for the Second Circuit, In Memoriam, Honorable Charles E. Clark 6 (April 14, 1964) (transcript on file with the United States Courts Library for the Second Circuit). Rostow was dean of Yale Law School.

2. *Id.* at 7.

3. *Charles Clark, Ex-Chief Judge of U.S. Appeals Court, Is Dead*, N.Y. TIMES, Dec. 14, 1963, at 27.

4. Rostow, Remarks, *supra* note 1, at 9.

5. JEFFREY B. MORRIS, FEDERAL JUSTICE IN THE SECOND CIRCUIT 143 (1987).

6. FEDERAL JUDICIAL CENTER, Biographical Directory of Federal Judges, Charles Edward Clark, http://www.fjc.gov/servlet/nGetInfo?jid=439&cid=999&ctype=na&instate=na.

7. MORRIS, *supra* note 5, at 143–44.

8. Chief Judge J. Edward Lumbard, Remarks at a Special Session of the United States Court of Appeals for the Second Circuit, In Memoriam, Honorable Charles E. Clark 13 (April 14, 1964) (transcript on file with the United States Courts Library for the Second Circuit).

9. Judge Harold R. Medina, Remarks at a Special Session of the United States Court of Appeals for the Second Circuit, In Memoriam, Honorable Charles E. Clark 11 (April 14, 1964) (transcript on file with the United States Courts Library for the Second Circuit).

10. Justice Potter Stewart, Remarks at a Special Session of the United States Court of Appeals for the Second Circuit, In Memoriam, Honorable Charles E. Clark 14 (April 14, 1964) (transcript on file with the United States Courts Library for the Second Circuit).

11. Charles E. Clark and James William Moore, *A New Federal Civil Procedure*, 44 YALE L.J. 387, 387 (1935).

12. Charles E. Clark, *Practice and Procedure*, 328 ANNALS AM. ACAD. POL. & SOC. SCI. 61, 63 (1960).

13. *Id.* at 62.

14. *Id.* at 63.

15. *Id.*

16. *Id.*

17. *Id.* at 64.

18. *Id.*

19. Judge Harold R. Medina, Remarks, *supra* note 9, at 10.

20. *Id.*

21. *Id.*

22. *Id.*

23. *Practice and Procedure*, *supra* note 12, at 64.

24. MORRIS, *supra* note 5, at 144 (citing Clark and Moore, *A New Federal Civil Procedure*, 44 YALE L.J. 387 (1935)).

25. MORRIS, *supra* note 5, at 129.

26. Rostow, Remarks, *supra* note 1, at 8.

27. *Practice and Procedure*, *supra* note 12, at 66.

28. MORRIS, *supra* note 5, at 144.

29. *Id.*

30. FEDERAL JUDICIAL CENTER, *supra* note 6.

31. MORRIS, *supra* note 5, at 144.

32. MARVIN SCHICK, LEARNED HAND'S COURT 222 (1970).

33. *Id.* at 221.

34. *Id.*

35. GERALD GUNTHER, LEARNED HAND: THE MAN AND THE JUDGE 446 (2d ed. 2011).

36. SCHICK, *supra* note 32, at 222.

37. GUNTHER, *supra* note 35, at 454–456.

38. SCHICK, *supra* note 32, at 227.

39. SCHICK, *supra* note 32, at 227–28 (citing Cover v. Schwartz, 133 F.2d 541, 549 (2d Cir. 1942) (Clark, J., concurring) (saying, of the majority decision of Judge Learned Hand and Judge Frank, "my brethren should be allowed to draw such sustenance as they can for their admittedly technical ruling")).

40. Pabellon v. Grace Line, 191 F.2d 169, 176 (2d Cir. 1951) (Frank, J., concurring) (labeling Judge Clark's discussion of Rule 54(b) "dictum"); Flegenheimer v. General Mills, 191 F.2d 237, 241 (2d Cir. 1951) (L. Hand, J.) (explaining that because Clark's discussion was not "necessary to the decision" in *Pabellon*, the panel need not "yield to it"); Lopinsky v. Hertz Drive-Ur-Self Systems, 194 F.2d 422, 429 (2d Cir. 1951) (Clark, J., concurring) (citing Judge Hand's decision in *Flegenheimer* and positing that "[s]uch freedom from the confines of precedent is confusing not only to the public, but also to colleagues who have no notice of the impending doom before it appears in print").

41. SCHICK, *supra* note 32, at 223.

42. *Id.* at 224.

43. In the same letter to Judge Learned Hand, Judge Clark observed that "the greater the judges, the less patience they will have with procedural matters." *Id.* at 246. Gerald Gunther writes: "It was not that Clark's colleagues were dismissive of procedural problems, but they frequently grew impatient with Clark's insistence on his own interpretation of a particular rule." GUNTHER, *supra* note 35, at 447.

44. *Id.* at 456, n.*.

45. *Id.*

46. Arnstein v. Porter, 154 F.2d 464, 469 (2d Cir. 1946).

47. *Id.*

48. *Id.* at 478–79.

49. *Id.* at 480.

50. MORRIS, *supra* note 5, at 144.

51. Charles E. Clark, *A Plea for the Unprincipled Decision*, 49 VA. L. REV. 660 (1963), *reprinted in* PROCEDURES, THE HANDMAID OF JUSTICE 237, 241 (C.A. Wright & H.M. Reasoner ed. 1965).

52. Justice William O. Douglas, Remarks at a Special Session of the United States Court of Appeals for the Second Circuit, In Memoriam, Honorable Charles E. Clark 22 (April 14, 1964) (transcript on file with the United States Courts Library for the Second Circuit).

53. Charles E. Clark, *Law Day U.S.A.*, 13 THE RECORD OF THE ASSOCIATION OF THE BAR OF THE CITY OF NEW YORK, 346, 348 (1958).

54. *Id.*

55. 2 GREAT AMERICAN JUDGES: AN ENCYCLOPEDIA 522 (John R. Vile ed., 2003).

56. For example, the defense attorneys challenged the jury system as administered by the Southern District of New York. They called a member of an earlier petit jury panel to testify and asked about the value of the juror's home. After Judge Medina precluded inquiry into "details as to the juror's economic status," the defense lawyers "continued to interrogate the witness as to details of his property holdings, his income, other information such as had been excluded by the court in previous rulings, and many quite irrelevant matters." The questions "continued over many pages of the record," despite having been precluded by Judge Medina. United States v. Sacher, 182 F.2d 416, 421–22 (2d Cir. 1950). The defense attorneys also launched personal attacks on Judge Medina, repeatedly charging him with "bias, prejudice, corruption, and partiality." *Id.* at 431. Twice each day, just before the morning and afternoon newspapers went to print, the defense lawyers accused Medina of lying. *Harold Medina, U.S. Judge, Dies at 102*, N.Y. TIMES, Mar. 16, 1990, at B7.

57. *Sacher*, 182 F.2d at 463.

58. *Id.* at 464.

59. *Id.* at 465.

60. John P. Frank, *The Top U.S. Commercial Court*, FORTUNE MAG., Jan. 1951, at 108.

61. Judge Harold R. Medina, Remarks, *supra* note 9, at 12–13.

62. *Professor Emeritus Charles Elias Clark '47*, YALE LAW REPORT, Winter 2012, at 14–15.

63. PETER GRAHAM FISH, THE POLITICS OF FEDERAL JUDICIAL ADMINISTRATION 416 (1973).

64. Charles E. Clark, *The Role of United States Courts of Appeals in Law Administration*, *in* UNIVERSITY OF CHICAGO LAW SCHOOL, CONFERENCE ON JUDICIAL ADMINISTRATION 87, 96 (1957).

65. Act of Aug. 6, 1958, Pub. L. No. 85-593, 72 Stat. 497 (1958).

66. MORRIS, *supra* note 5, at 136.

67. *Id.*

68. Judge Harold R. Medina, Remarks, *supra* note 9, at 10.

69. *Id.* at 11.

70. To Clark, the meaning and purpose of the law included a "devotion to the public interest." In his 1934 Dean's Report to Yale University President James Rowland Angell, Clark wrote that in the post-depression era, "the lawyer should be willing by virtue of his training and civic obligations to assume leadership; but in any event his very function of serving clients in time of need will in natural course present to him the opportunity to play a major role which will be accentuated by his traditional share in all the activities of government." *Lawyers of Vision Needed, Clark Says*, N.Y. TIMES, Dec. 23, 1934, at N3.

71. Whitney North Seymour, Jr., Remarks at a Special Session of the United States Court of Appeals for the Second Circuit, In Memoriam, Honorable Charles E. Clark 19 (April 14, 1964) (transcript on file with the United States Courts Library for the Second Circuit). Seymour was the United States attorney for the Southern District of New York, president of the American Bar Association, and a partner at Simpson, Thatcher & Bartlett, LLP.

72. *Remarks of Judge Charles E. Clark*, 6 SYRACUSE LAW REVIEW 233, 233 (1955).

# ROBERT PORTER PATTERSON
## 1891-1952

District Court for the Southern District of New York: 1930-1939
Court of Appeals for the Second Circuit: 1939-1940

The Arlington gravestone of Robert Porter Patterson bears the words: "Soldier-Jurist Statesman."[1] He served on the Second Circuit for less than two years (his service on the Southern District court was substantially longer) and the more significant portion of his public life was in the role of soldier-statesman for which he left the bench. Such was his career that the list of posts he refused would rival in distinction the posts he held.

Patterson was born in 1891 and grew up in Glens Falls, New York.[2] His father was a lawyer who served two terms as district attorney of Warren County.[3] Patterson was elected to Phi Beta Kappa at Union College.[4] At Harvard Law School, he was president of the law review.[5] He commenced law practice in New York City with Root, Clark, Buckner & Howland.[6] He joined the National Guard and saw service at the Mexican border in 1916. He recalled that his Mexican border experience taught him "a fair knowledge of infantry close-order drill," "a feeling of sympathy for the ordinary private who marches all day with a pack on his back," and "a realization that in the army it is useless to be a kicker."[7] This third lesson he summed up as "cheerful and willing obedience costs no more than sullen and halting obedience," and concluded that upon acquiring this perspective, a man "begins to be a soldier."[8] When America entered World War I he secured a commission and fought in France, earning the Distinguished Service Cross for heroism for a "daring daylight reconnaissance into the enemy lines."[9] He was awarded a Silver Star for service during the Argonne offensive; the citation praised his "efficiency, coolness and courage, and utter disregard to personal danger."[10]

Returning to the United States, he returned to Root Clark. In 1930, President Herbert Hoover nominated him to the Southern District bench.[11] Felix Frankfurter wrote to him that, "I feel about the Southern District of New York as though it were my very family, and I rejoice that so high-minded, courageous, and able an addition has come to that court." Judge Learned Hand welcomed the appointment, saying, "[I]t is almost too good to be true that a man of your capacities and character can be got. Nothing has pleased me more since my cousin [Augustus] came to join me here. . . "[12]

President Franklin Delano Roosevelt elevated Judge Patterson to the Second Circuit in 1939.[13] Judge Patterson quickly gained the friendship of his colleagues, particularly Learned Hand, who shared his upstate New York origins; Hand became an intimate friend and tireless supporter.[14] In a pre-conference memorandum in a deportation case, Judge Patterson teased his friend, explaining that his observations were "[f]or the benefit of the senior circuit judge." He went on: "I realize that this is a sentence of perpetual banishment, that the case is one that wrings my heart, that the realtor was born too soon and in the wrong place, and so on and so on, but nevertheless I vote to affirm."[15]

During Judge Patterson's service on the Second Circuit from March 1939 until July 1940, he wrote 58 opinions, many of them in tax cases.[16] In one, with a Learned Hand dissent, the court held that certain payments from a mother to her son were subject to the gift tax and were not contractual nor the result of a trust.[17] Another opinion ruled that a case against New York City for damage to a deck scow used for fireworks displays was properly brought in admiralty.[18] He wrote an affirmance of a conviction of communist leader Earl Browder for passport fraud.[19] Another opinion upheld a conviction for possession of unregistered stills, making mash, carrying on a distillery business, and conspiracy.[20] A motion picture about life in a reform school was held not to have infringed copyrights for a novel and plays about the same general subject.[21] A panel on which he sat refused to restrain radio broadcast of recordings of the Paul Whiteman orchestra.[22] In one of his last acts on the bench, Judge Patterson served on a panel that reversed an early securities law conviction for trial error.[23]

Learned Hand was later to observe: "[J]udging is not his *métier.* He must be in the world of will."[24] Hand added, "[N]or was he interested in the ordering of words so that they should fit a variant mass of human relations with the minimum violence. That kind of thing annoyed him."[25] Patterson became intensely concerned that the country was not ready to cope with international threats. A law clerk, who had worked in turn for both Hands, reported hearing, in spring 1940, "Patterson bluster loudly in chambers, in the presence of the Hands, venting his concerns for the nation's security and his frustrations with the mundane work of appellate judging at a time when the world was aflame."[26]

Anticipating a new war, Judge Patterson undertook refresher army training designed for business and professional men at a privately organized camp in Plattsburg, New York.[27] There, he received a summons to the War Department. *The New York Times* reported that Judge Patterson "is ready to terminate a brilliant ten-year career on the Federal Bench to go to a post where, in this time of crisis and defense building, more effective use can be made of his talents."[28] First appointed as assistant secretary of war, he became under-secretary of war and was expected to "continue to concentrate on the rearmament program."[29] That was rearmament in every sense: he set to rousing the nation. On a radio broadcast just before Pearl Harbor, he said, "We have no time to lose. . . . We have no strength to waste. . . . The fate of America hangs in the balance."[30] Post-war, Patterson said of this period: "To some Americans, Europe still seemed far away in the spring of 1940, and Japan appeared almost as remote as the moon."[31] He pointed to "the failure of the American people to recognize promptly and fully the magnitude of the emergency which faced us."[32]

In the War Department, he set right to work. Touring an army installation, he was described as having "an undisguised liking for military life."[33] Judge Patterson played an essential role in mobilizing the country for the war. He was responsible for "logistics," defined as "the equipping, supplying, and transporting of armed forces."[34] At war's end, he was given a Distinguished Service Medal; the citation read: "The entire immediate responsibility for the greatest procurement program ever undertaken by any nation rested upon him . . . His contribution to victory cannot be overestimated."[35]

Judge Patterson's uncompromising style was celebrated in a *Saturday Evening Post* article called "The Toughest Man in Washington."[36] Patterson had a Spartan attitude toward the home front, believing citizens should sacrifice as the soldiers were sacrificing. He decried complaints of a whiskey shortage caused when distilleries were diverted to producing industrial alcohol.[37] He was appalled by civilians' greedy consumption of rubber and gasoline, both needed for the war effort. He criticized "joy-riding"[38] and motorized "petting parties."[39] He was dismayed that trucks were ferrying around soft drinks to be drunk by "bobby soxers."[40] At a "somber war conference," he was assured the soda was headed for Army post exchanges.[41] Journalists dubbed the episode the "Battle of Seven-Up"[42] and he earned the nickname "Judge Seven-Up."[43]

President Harry Truman offered Judge Patterson his choice of posts: secretary of war or United States Supreme Court justice. Patterson said he would serve where the President thought he was "best fitted."[44] President Truman appointed him secretary in 1945, and in that capacity, Judge Patterson led the fight to unify the country's armed services.[45]

Patterson returned to practicing law and formed the firm of Patterson, Belknap and Webb.[46] An associate reported that he "was in much demand as a trial and appellate lawyer," but had "an aversion to tax cases. He ardently believed that taxes were the price we paid for civilization. . ."[47] He became president of the City Bar, Freedom House, and the Council on Foreign Relations.[48] He resisted attempts to lure him back to the bench, turning down appointment to the New York State Court of Appeals in 1948 and re-appointment to the Second Circuit in 1951, when Learned Hand retired.[49] He twice declined the post of dean of Harvard Law School because he did not consider himself a scholar.[50]

Patterson was married to Margaret Tarleton Winchester.[51] The couple had three daughters and a son,[52] Robert Patterson, Jr., who became a long-serving judge on the Southern District of New York.[53]

Judge Patterson died at age 60 in a plane crash returning from an upstate federal court appearance.[54] Mourners filed past his bier at the Park Avenue Armory, home of his old National Guard regiment. The funeral was at the National Cathedral in Washington, DC and the burial in Arlington National Cemetery.[55] Judge Charles Clark remembered him as "a judge's judge or a lawyer's judge," whose "judicial work was marked by the simple, direct and effective way he did things."[56] Judge Learned Hand delivered a memorial remembrance at the City Bar. Judge Hand spoke of Patterson's "sense of the comic," recalling that Patterson could never find *The New Yorker* funny but enjoyed repeating parts of *The Adventures of Huckleberry Finn.* According to Judge Hand, Judge Patterson's district court opinions were "clear, penetrating, short, crisp, thorough, unostentatious, and unobtrusive, without a trace of vanity or of any desire to shine." Judge Patterson had "an unconcealed scorn for that temper, then and still orthodox in many quarters, which transfigures a judge into a crusader for righteousness as righteousness may appear to his incandescent conscience." Judge Patterson, his friend said, "was incorruptible in a sense that few men are."[57]

Looking back on his public life, one newspaper described him as having "combined the work of a jurist with that of a soldier," while avoiding the limitations of the law ("sharpen[ing] the mind only to narrow it") and the military ("preoccupation with force to the exclusion of ideals").[58] His biographer called him "lawyer by profession . . . soldier at heart."[59]

Catherine J. Minuse

1. *Robert Porter Patterson*, ARLINGTON NATIONAL CEMETERY WEBSITE (Mar. 10, 2007), http://www.arlingtoncemetery.net/robertpo.htm.

2. KEITH E. EILER, MOBILIZING AMERICA: ROBERT P. PATTERSON AND THE WAR EFFORT 1940-1945 12 (1997).

3. *Id.* at 13.

4. MANFRED JONAS & LOUIS MORTON, UNION WORTHIES NO. 21, ROBERT PORTER PATTERSON: CLASS OF 1912, at 5 (1966); EILER, *supra* note 2, at 16.

5. EILER, *supra* note 2, at 17.

6. *Id.* at 18.

7. ROBERT PORTER PATTERSON, THE WORLD WAR I MEMOIRS OF ROBERT P. PATTERSON 5 (J. Garry Clifford ed., 2012).

8. *Id.*

9. *Id.* at 9, 87.

10. EILER, *supra* note 2, at 22 n.*.

11. *Id.* at 24; *Patterson Nomination to Senate*, WALL ST. J., Apr. 25, 1930, at 20.

12. Letter from Keith E. Eiler to Robert P. Patterson, Jr. (Dec. 8, 1988) (attaching extracts from letters to Robert P. Patterson) (on file with the United States Courts Library for the Second Circuit).

13. *Patterson in Line for Manton Post*, N.Y. TIMES, Feb. 9, 1939, at 11; *Patterson Nomination Confirmed*, N.Y. TIMES, Mar. 21, 1939, at 13.

14. GERALD GUNTHER, LEARNED HAND: THE MAN AND THE JUDGE 443-46 (2d ed. 2011).

15. Keith Edward Eiler, The Constant Service: A Biography of Robert P. Patterson 259-60 (May 1974) (unpublished Ph.D. thesis, Harvard University) (on file with the United States Courts Library for the Second Circuit).

16. EILER, *supra* note 2, at 11-12, 29; *Patterson Nomination Confirmed*, *supra* note 13.

17. Housman v. Commissioner, 105 F.2d 973 (2d Cir. 1939).

18. Kenny v. City of New York, 108 F.2d 958 (2d Cir. 1940).

19. United States v. Browder, 113 F.2d 97 (2d Cir. 1940); *Browder Sentence Upheld on Appeal*, N.Y. TIMES, June 25, 1940, at 25.

20. United States v. Jackskion, 102 F.2d 683 (2d Cir. 1939).

21. Bein v. Warner Bros. Pictures, 105 F.2d 969 (2d Cir. 1939).

22. RCA Mfg. Co. v. Whiteman, 114 F.2d 86 (2d Cir. 1940).

23. United States v. Minuse, 114 F.2d 36 (2d Cir. 1940); *Brokers' Conviction Reversed on Appeal*, N.Y. TIMES, Aug. 8, 1940, at 21.

24. EILER, *supra* note 2, at 29-30.

25. *Id.* at 30.

26. *Id.* at 28-29 n.*.

27. *Id.* at 11-12, 29; ROBERT P. PATTERSON, ARMING THE NATION FOR WAR xxix, 240 n.11 (Brian Waddell ed., 2014).p

28. *Judge Patterson, Plattsburg Buck Private, Considered for Post as Stimson Assistant*, N.Y. TIMES, July 23, 1940, at 1.

29. *Patterson Slated for New War Post*, N.Y. TIMES, Dec. 7, 1940, at 6.

30. EILER, *supra* note 2, at 216.

31. PATTERSON, *supra* note 27, at 1.

32. *Id.* at 217.

33. *Patterson Praises Progress of 27th*, N.Y. TIMES, Nov. 8, 1940, at 9.

34. PATTERSON, *supra* note 27, at 143.

35. EILER, *supra* note 2, at 444-45.

36. Forrest Davis, *The Toughest Man in Washington*, SATURDAY EVENING POST, Sept. 5, 1942, at 12.

37. PATTERSON, *supra* note 27, at 174.

38. *Id.* at 82.

39. *Id.* at 258 n.22 (quoting Davis, *supra* note 36, at 59).

40. JONAS & MORTON, *supra* note 4, at 11.

41. Arthur Krock, *The Epitaph of a Simple and Extraordinary Man*, N.Y. TIMES, Jan. 24, 1952, at 26.

42. *Fighting Judge*, TIME, Feb. 4, 1952, at 14.

43. EILER, *supra* note 2, at 265.

44. *Patterson Held Key Post in War*, N.Y. TIMES, Jan. 23, 1952, at 20.

45. EILER, *supra* note 2, at 466.

46. PATTERSON BELKNAP WEBB & TYLER LLP, ROBERT PORTER PATTERSON, https://www.pbwt.com/content/uploads/2015/07/RobertPorterPatterson_book.pdf.

47. PATTERSON, *supra* note 27, at xiv-xv.

48. *Patterson Held Key Post in War*, *supra* note 44.

49. JEFFREY B. MORRIS, FEDERAL JUSTICE IN THE SECOND CIRCUIT 143 n.* (1987); *Patterson Says No to Bench Offer*, N.Y. TIMES, Dec. 29, 1948, at 15.

50. *Patterson Held Key Post in War*, *supra* note 44.

51. EILER, *supra* note 2, at 24.

52. *Id.* at 26.

53. Richard Pérez-Peña, *Judge Was a New York Fixture Before His Federal Appointment*, N.Y. TIMES, Nov. 9, 1995, at B8.

54. *Patterson, Booked on Trains, Decided at Last Minute to Fly*, N.Y. TIMES, Jan, 23, 1952, at 1.

55. *Truman to Attend Patterson Service*, N.Y. TIMES, Jan. 25, 1952, at 9.

56. *Law Institute Unveils Patterson Portrait and Sets Up Memorial Fund to Secretary*, N.Y. TIMES, June 6, 1952, at 21.

57. Learned Hand, *Robert P. Patterson*, *in* THE SPIRIT OF LIBERTY: PAPERS AND ADDRESSES OF LEARNED HAND 263, 254-65, 269, 271-72 (Irving Dilliard ed., 3d ed. 1974).

58. JONAS & MORTON, *supra* note 4 (quoting *On Continuing Service*, N.Y. HERALD TRIBUNE, Dec. 8, 1948, at 32); PATTERSON, *supra* note 27, at xvi (same).

59. EILER, *supra* note 2, at 472.

## JERONE NEW FRANK
## 1889-1957

Court of Appeals for the Second Circuit: 1941-1957

Being married to Jerome is like being tied to the tail of a comet.

— Florence Kiper Frank[1]

Jerome New Frank was born on September 10, 1889, in New York City. His parents, Herman and Clara, relocated to Chicago when Frank was seven years old. Frank attended high school, college, and law school in Chicago, attaining a PhB degree from the University of Chicago in 1909 and a JD degree in 1912. He would also receive an honorary LLD from the University of Chicago in 1953.[2]

Frank initially wanted to be a fiction writer, and in college took an interest in political science after meeting the political scientist Charles E. Merriam. (Frank took a year's leave from law school to serve as Merriam's secretary when Merriam became an alderman on Chicago's city council.) In 1914, Frank married Florence Kiper; their daughter, Barbara, suffered from a psychosomatic paralysis of her legs as a child, which led Frank to become interested in psychoanalysis and psychiatry. Frank's diverse non-legal interests would become relevant to his future work in legal theory.[3]

Following law school, Frank joined the Chicago corporate law firm Levinson, Becker, Cleveland & Schwartz; he became a partner in 1919. In 1928, he left that firm, joining Chadbourne, Stanchfield & Levy in New York City, known today as Chadbourne & Parker.[4]

Frank was a lively and gregarious man, full of energy and vitality. Felix Frankfurter described him as "warm-hearted and generous. . . . a devoted, uncritical friend and a compassionate observer of the human scene."[5] William O. Douglas described him as a "warmhearted, generous, witty, lovable, brilliant man."[6] His Yale Law School colleague Professor Fred Rodell described him as a "warm and witty and gay and generous and kindly man."[7] Judge Charles E. Clark wrote that he was "a blithe and gay comrade of infinite charm,"[8] and a man of "vast kindliness and good humor."[9]

In 1930, Frank published one of the seminal works of the legal realism movement, *Law and the Modern Mind.*[10] In it, he drew upon his interests in psychology, political science, and literature, among other fields. He argued that legal decisions were influenced by more than the mechanical application of principles to facts, as advanced by the then-prevalent legal positivism school. In particular, he argued that legal rules are influenced strongly by judges' prejudices and personalities.[11]

By 1932, his book had brought him academic success, and he had become a lecturer at the New School for Social Research in New York and a research associate at Yale Law School. The affiliation with Yale, which would last the rest of Frank's life, began with an appointment to the faculty by Charles E. Clark, later Frank's colleague on the Second Circuit.[12] His appointment to the Yale faculty also connected him with Felix Frankfurter, then a professor at Harvard Law School. Frankfurter was only a casual acquaintance, but Frank wrote to him in early 1933, asking Frankfurter's assistance in finding employment with the federal government. He wrote that he "want[ed] to get out of this Wall Street racket," and join the government "for the duration" of the crisis (the Great Depression) the government faced.[13]

Although Frank knew nothing about farm policy, Frankfurter recommended that Rexford G. Tugwell, the director of the Agricultural Adjustment Administration, hire Frank as his general counsel. In this capacity, Frank brought his reformist views and liberal politics to the AAA, and filled the agency's ranks with brilliant, like-minded lawyers, upsetting the "administrative domination of the AAA by agri-business interests."[14] The lawyers who worked for him at the AAA included Adlai Stevenson, Abe Fortas, Thurman Arnold, Telford Taylor, and Alger Hiss.[15]

Frank's time at the AAA was tinged with controversy. In 1933, he led an administrative revolt against George Peek, the conservative, pro-business administrator of the AAA. The Peek faction clashed with Frank and his allies over whether federal regulation should cut prices for consumers or keep profits in the hands of agricultural processors. While Frank lost this battle, he won the war: Peek was fired after Secretary of Agriculture Henry A. Wallace sided with Frank regarding marketing agreements in the dairy industry.[16] In 1935, Frank himself was fired from the AAA as a result of a second "purge" within the agency, ostensibly motivated by Frank's stance in favor of sharecroppers. Some historians attribute Frank's firing to Peek's conservative successor, Chester Davis, seeking revenge for Frank's victory in the dairy industry fight.[17]

After Frank's dismissal from the AAA, President Franklin Delano Roosevelt appointed him to the Reconstruction Finance Corporation, where he served as a special counsel dealing primarily with railroad reorganizations. However, the domination of the agency by Jesse Jones, the "czar" of the RFC, led Frank to return to private practice in New York, at the firm of Greenbaum, Wolff & Ernst.[18] But he continued working part-time for the federal government. His greatest litigation victory came when he represented Secretary of the Interior Harold Ickes in his attempt to allow the Public Works Administration to make loans to public power projects, over the opposition of private power companies.[19] During his time in New York, Frank founded the National Lawyers Guild, then an organization of liberal, reform-minded (and some radical) lawyers disenchanted with the regular organized bar.[20]

In December 1937, the chairman of the Securities and Exchange Commission, William O. Douglas, recommended to Roosevelt that Frank become one of the five SEC commissioners. Frank returned to Washington in that capacity. In 1939, Roosevelt appointed Douglas to the Supreme Court, and Frank took Douglas's place as chairman.[21] During his time as chairman, he reorganized the New York Stock Exchange, to the general appreciation of investors, and persuaded utility leaders to downsize and rationalize holding companies, leading to increased gains and investor confidence.[22] He gave a speech in 1938 that demonstrated his erudition and ability to synthesize a dizzying variety of sources (a prose style he took to the bench). As *Time* magazine wrote, Frank "denounced fixed charges in favor of equity dividends. To make his point, he invoked the following authorities: Aristotle, Lactantius, St. Luke, St. Basil, St. Chrysostom, St. Ambrose, St. Thomas Aquinas, Dante, Calvin, Cotton Mather, Andrew D. White, Chesterton, [and] Will Rogers."[23]

In February 1941, President Roosevelt nominated Frank to the Court of Appeals for the Second Circuit.[24] Both before and during his judicial career, Judge Frank continued writing. He wrote five books (three of which were published after he became a judge); co-wrote a sixth book with his daughter; and his selected writings were compiled into a seventh.[25] He continued his association with Yale Law School, teaching there as a visiting lecturer from 1946 until his death in 1957; he also taught at the New School and Brandeis University.[26] His teaching activities were described as "pioneer[ing] in modern times" for a sitting judge.[27] He also managed to write more than 20 articles in legal periodicals.[28]

As a judge, he was equally prolific, penning 597 concurrences and 128 dissents.[29] Many of them foreshadowed or informed later Supreme Court decisions. He knew two Supreme Court Justices from his New Deal years (Justices Frankfurter and Douglas), and was close to Justices Hugo Black and Robert H. Jackson. In all, at least eleven justices referred to him by name in 39 opinions, and the Supreme Court agreed with his position in over 70 percent of his cases.[30] He occasionally found himself the target of good-natured ribbing from friends and colleagues for his loquaciousness; Justice Frankfurter and Judge Learned Hand wrote particularly memorable passages about his tendency to expound.[31]

Despite his penchant for lengthy exegesis, or perhaps because of it, he was one of the more influential appellate judges of his day. His experience as chairman of the SEC made him a particularly important voice in securities cases; he wrote one of the early decisions finding a private cause of action under the Securities Exchange Act's Rule 10b-5 for a purchaser of securities to sue the issuer.[32] He also espoused Congress's ability to confer standing to sue on individuals: an opinion of his contains the first known use by a United States Court of the term "private Attorney Generals [sic]."[33]

A defining feature of the Second Circuit in Judge Frank's day was his warfare with Judge Clark. "It would take a volume to detail the various quarrels these judges had over rules and procedure," among other issues.[34] It is ironic that they disagreed so often and so vehemently given the similarities in their backgrounds: both "were New Dealers, certainly in the economic sense, and they were appointed by President Roosevelt . . . [e]ach was a vigorous (and courageous) champion of the underdog and each had rejected the old mechanical jurisprudence."[35] Both also taught at Yale Law School, during their time on the bench as well as before.[36]

One of their most bitter areas of disagreement, where Frank found himself in a minority of one on the Second Circuit, was on the "harmless error" doctrine in criminal cases. The doctrine provides that, in Frank's words, not "every technical slipup . . . will be automatically held to be fatal," but rather "only the seriously prejudicial defects will be dignified by appellate attention."[37]

Frank believed that the Second Circuit's application of the harmless error doctrine in criminal cases was, in effect, "that the upper court judges would review the trial record and, if they concluded that the convicted man was guilty, they would rule that the defect in the proceedings was harmless."[38] He felt that this was an absurd proposition: he could not "subscribe to a rule that what is substantial reversible error depends not on whether it probably affected the jury to the substantial prejudice of the defendant but on whether we appellate judges think the defendant guilty or innocent."[39] Rather, as he wrote, courts should affirm only where, "if there had been no error, no reasonably sane jury could have acquitted, or there is no reasonable ground for thinking that the jury was misled by error."[40]

One harmless error case triggered several months of bitter clashes between Clark and Frank.[41] In *United States v. Antonelli Fireworks Company*,[42] the Italian-American owners of a munitions company were charged with conspiracy to defraud the government by producing defective munitions. Two days after the Allied landing at Normandy, the prosecutor, in his closing argument, appealed to the patriotism of the jurors, asking them to "render a verdict of which you can always be proudly justified in the presence of your fellowmen . . . [including] those of us beyond the seas who look to us for the things they need to sustain them in their hour of extreme sacrifice."[43] Judge Clark, writing for the majority with Judge Learned Hand, affirmed the conviction.

Judge Frank would have reversed, in part because reversal "might well serve as a deterrent" for over-aggressive prosecutors who otherwise failed to "live up to professional standards of courtroom decency."[44] He wrote:

> This court has several times used vigorous language in denouncing government counsel for such conduct as that of the United States attorney here. But, each time, it has said that, nevertheless, it would not reverse. Such an attitude of helpless piety is, I think, undesirable. It means actual condonation of counsel's alleged offense, coupled with verbal disapprobation. If we continue to do nothing practical to prevent such conduct, we should cease to disapprove it.[45]

Judge Clark responded that "it is comparatively easy" to reverse a criminal conviction under these circumstances; "[s]uch an opinion writes itself, chances of reversal and reinstatement of the verdict are remote, and academic acclaim is assured."[46]

On other topics related to criminal law, many of Judge Frank's dissents later became Supreme Court precedent. He preceded the Supreme Court (and his colleagues on the Second Circuit) in finding that the Due Process clause guaranteed a right to counsel to indigent criminal defendants; and his opinions helped to liberalize judicial interpretations of the *in forma pauperis* statute.[47] One of his last criminal opinions well emphasizes his commitment to the procedural guarantees of the Bill of Rights:

> We are committed to the principle that any method of pursuing suspected criminals must give way when it clashes with these constitutional guarantees. . . . Considered solely in terms of procedure, those constitutional safeguards seem logically indefensible. Considered, however, as conferring substantive rights, they assume a different significance: They express the high value our democracy puts on the individual's right of privacy.[48]

At the intersection of criminal and immigration law, a Judge Frank dissent in 1954 foreshadowed the Supreme Court's 2010 decision in *Padilla v. Kentucky*.[49]

Also noteworthy was Judge Frank's concurring opinion in an obscenity case urging the Supreme Court to narrow the definition of "obscenity."[50] The concurrence has been described as drawing "on a host of historical, literary, and social science studies to point to the dangers and contradiction of all forms of government censorship of ideas and images."[51]

Judge Frank criticized the criminal justice system and jury trials over the course of his legal career. He wrote in his first book that "[t]he jury makes the orderly administration of justice virtually impossible."[52] He later wrote that the "jury system, praised because, in its origins, it was apparently a bulwark against an arbitrary tyrannical executive, is today the quintessence of governmental arbitrariness."[53] His final book, co-written with his daughter, was a collection of 36 histories of cases resulting in wrongful convictions. They finished the final edits on the book two days before his death in 1957.[54]

During his last years, Judge Frank suffered from leukemia, which he kept secret from his family and all but his two or three closest friends.[55] On January 13, 1957, he had a sudden heart attack at his home in New Haven and died that evening.[56] Following his death, his friends raised $25,000 to acquire his personal papers and literary effects for Yale Law School, for the use of future scholars.[57] He was eulogized by, among many others, Justice Frankfurter,[58] Justice Douglas,[59] and Chief Judge Clark.[60] He was also eulogized by an inmate at the Stormville, New York penitentiary, who secured pro bono counsel through Frank's efforts. The inmate wrote that Frank was "[o]ne of the Great Judges of the Federal Judge's [sic] for the poor man and for a man's constitutional rights . . . He was our friend."[61]

David Byowitz

1. Letter from Florence Kiper Frank to Walter Volkomer, (Feb. 12, 1961), *quoted in* ROBERT JEROME GLENNON, THE ICONOCLAST AS REFORMER: JEROME FRANK'S IMPACT ON AMERICAN LAW 9 (1985).

2. *See* JOHN R. VILE, GREAT AMERICAN JUDGES: AN ENCYCLOPEDIA, Vol. 1, 257–62 (2003).

3. *Id.* at 258–59.

4. JEFFREY B. MORRIS, FEDERAL JUSTICE IN THE SECOND CIRCUIT 145 (1987).

5. Felix Frankfurter, *Jerome N. Frank*, 24 U. CHI. L. REV. 625, 625 (1957).

6. Justice William O. Douglas, Remarks at a Special Meeting of the New York County Lawyers' Association and The Association of the Bar of the City of New York, Memorial of Jerome N. Frank, 1889-1957 (May 23, 1957) (transcript on file with the United States Courts Library for the Second Circuit).

7. Fred Rodell, *Jerome N. Frank: A Remembrance*, 3 YALE L. REP. 3, 3 (1957).

8. Judge Charles E. Clark, Remarks at a Special Meeting of the New York County Lawyers' Association and The Association of the Bar of the City of New York, Memorial of Jerome N. Frank, 1889-1957 (May 23, 1957) (transcript on file with the United States Courts Library for the Second Circuit).

9. Clarkes E. Clark, *Jerome N. Frank*, 66 YALE L.J. 817, 818 (1957).

10. JEROME N. FRANK, LAW AND THE MODERN MIND (1930).

11. *See* VILE, *supra* note 2, at 259.

12. *See* MORRIS, *supra* note 4, at 145.

13. *Id.* at 145; *see* VILE, *supra* note 2, at 259-60; *see also* PETER H. IRONS, THE NEW DEAL LAWYERS, 121 (1993) (citing Feb. 26, 1933, letter from Frank to Frankfurter, Frank Papers, Yale University Library).

14. IRONS, *supra* note 13, at 123.

15. VILE, *supra* note 2, at 260.

16. *See SEC's Jerome Frank*, 35 TIME MAG., Mar. 11, 1940, at 73; *see generally* IRONS, *supra* note 13, at 128-32 (discussing Wallace's engineering of the first purge in the AAA).

17. On the purge, *see generally* IRONS, *supra* note 13, at 173–80. On historians' (and some observers') contention that the purge was motivated by the fight over the AAA's power to inspect dairy processors' books and records, *see id.* at 179–80, especially n. 90 (citing Richard Lowe, "Fallen Warrior of Reform: Jerome N. Frank as General Counsel of the Agricultural Adjustment Administration").

18. *See* VILE, *supra* note 2, at 260; *see* Fred Rodell, *Jerome N. Frank: A Remembrance*, 3 YALE L. REP. 3, 8 (1957).

19. *See* VILE, *supra* note 2, at 260; *see SEC's Jerome Frank*, *supra* note 16, at 73; *see* Ala. Power Co. v. Ickes, 302 U.S. 464 (1938).

20. VILE, *supra* note 2, at 260.

21. *SEC's Jerome Frank*, *supra* note 16, at 72.

22. ROBERT JEROME GLENNON, THE ICONOCLAST AS REFORMER: JEROME FRANK'S IMPACT ON AMERICAN LAW 28–29 (1985).

23. *See SEC's Jerome Frank*, *supra* note 16, at 74; *quoted in* Rodell, *Jerome Frank: A Remembrance*, 3 YALE L. REP. at 8.

24. FEDERAL JUDICIAL CENTER, Biographical Directory of Federal Judges, Jerome New Frank, http://www.fjc.gov/servlet/nGetInfo?jid=789&cid=999&ctype=na&instate=na.

25. *See* Library of Congress Catalog. The books are: LAW AND THE MODERN MIND (1930); SAVE AMERICA FIRST (1938); IF MEN WERE ANGELS (1942); FATE AND FREEDOM: A PHILOSOPHY FOR FREE AMERICANS (1945); and COURTS ON TRIAL: MYTH AND REALITY IN AMERICAN JUSTICE (1949); JEROME FRANK & BARBARA FRANK KRISTEIN, NOT GUILTY (1957); and THE SELECTED WRITINGS OF JEROME FRANK: A MAN'S REACH (Barbara Frank Kristein ed., 1965).

26. Jerome New Frank Papers (MS 222), Yale Univ. Library, "Biographical History," http://drs.library.yale.edu/HLTransformer/HLTransServlet?stylename=yul.ead2002.xhtml.xsl&pid=mssa:ms.0222&clear-stylesheet-cache=yes.

27. Edward McWhinney, *Judge Jerome Frank and Legal Realism: An Appraisal*, 3 N.Y. L. FORUM, 113, 114 (1957).

28. Hein Law Journal Library, http://heinonline.org/HOL/AuthorProfile?action=edit&search name=Frank, Jerome&collection=journals.

29. VILE, *supra* note 2, at 262.

30. *Id.* at 262.

31. *See, e.g.*, MORRIS, *supra* note 4, at 145 (quoting a letter from Justice Frankfurter remarking that "You are teeming with ideas and the world needs their expression. But there is no reason why you should take a simple case which Holmes would have disposed of in a page and a half and use it as a peg for an essay on mercantilism."); *id.* at 148 (quoting a memorandum from Judge Hand, in response to a stream of memoranda between Judge Frank and his Yale colleague Judge Clark, which stated: "I like to dance in the moonlight as well as any man, but my wind is not as good as it once was, and I cannot keep time with the antiphonal strophe and antistrophe of my youthful colleagues. When, as, and if between you – and supposing that happy time shall ever arrive – you come to the point of exhaustion, I shall play upon the harp and timbrel and lift up my voice in praise to God. BUT, while all this agitating cerebration remains in parturition, I shall merely sit on the side lines, contemplate my navel, and repeat the syllable, OM.").

32. Fischman v. Raytheon Mfg. Co., 188 F.2d 783 (2d Cir. 1951).

33. Assoc. Indus. of N.Y. State, Inc. v. Ickes, 134 F.2d 694, 704 (2d Cir. 1943) ("[T]here is nothing constitutionally prohibiting Congress from empowering any person, official or not, to institute a proceeding involving such a controversy, even if the sole purpose is to vindicate the public interest. Such persons, so authorized are, so to speak, private Attorney Generals.").

34. MARVIN SCHICK, LEARNED HAND'S COURT 227 (1970).

35. *Id.* at 221-22.

36. *See id.* at 221.

37. Perkins v. Endicott Johnson Corp., 128 F.2d 208, 211–212 (2d Cir. 1942).

38. SCHICK, *supra* note 35, at 269.

39. United States v. Liss, 137 F.2d 995, 1002 (2d Cir. 1943) (Frank, J., dissenting). His criticism was not entirely unjustified: in the majority opinion, Learned Hand wrote that "[p]erhaps all that a court should ever say is that the remote chance of prejudice should not balance the extreme probability that the jury came to the right result." *Id.* at 999.

40. United States v. Rubenstein, 151 F.2d 915, 924 (2d Cir. 1945) (Frank, J., dissenting).

41. *See* SCHICK, *supra* note 5, at 271–76. Clark accused Frank of propagandizing Supreme Court clerks in favor of overturning Second Circuit harmless error cases; a dispute arose as to whether Frank's Yale Law School class on judicial process was a forum for attacks on Clark's harmless error jurisprudence; and Clark accused Frank of leveling "violent, unrestrained personal attacks upon the individual members of this court which are not sustained on the record of our conduct."

42. 155 F.2d 631 (2d Cir. 1946).

43. 155 F.2d at 637.

44. *Id.* at 661–62 (Frank, J., dissenting).

45. *Id.* at 661.

46. *Id.* at 641.

47. *See* United States v. Johnson, 238 F.2d 565, 567, 571 (2d Cir. 1956) (Frank, J., dissenting) ("I think the Griffin doctrine [that a state providing a right to appeal a criminal conviction may not discriminate in the practical availability of such a right to appeal on grounds of poverty, Griffin v. Illinois, 351 U.S. 12 (1956)] requires that an indigent defendant have such legal assistance; I think the spirit of the Sixth Amendment, taken together with Criminal Rules 39(a) and 44, reinforces that requirement."); *see also id.* at 568-69 ("[T]he trial judge's certificate of 'bad faith' [of an appeal] enjoys no unqualified finality . . . . [I]f it is made to appear to the appeal court that there is merit in a poor man's claims of errors at the trial, an appeal in forma pauperis will be allowed, notwithstanding the trial judge's adverse certificate.").

48. United States v. Gordon, 236 F.2d 916, 920 (2d Cir. 1956).

49. Compare United States v. Parrino, 212 F.2d 919, 922 (2d Cir. 1954) (Frank, J., dissenting) (finding that a criminal defendant, advised by his counsel that a guilty plea could not result in deportation, was entitled to vacatur of his plea), *with* Padilla v. Kentucky, 559 U.S. 356 (2010) (holding that a criminal defense lawyer who failed to advise his client of the immigration consequences of a guilty plea had rendered ineffective assistance).

50. United States v. Roth, 237 F.2d 796, 802 (2d Cir. 1957) (Frank, J., concurring), at 806 (Appendix). The Supreme Court did so less than twenty years later. *See* Miller v. California, 413 U.S. 15 (1973).

51. Walter E. Volkomer, *Jerome N. Frank*, in Roger K. Newman, ed., THE YALE BIOGRAPHICAL DICTIONARY OF AMERICAN LAW, 201–02 (2009).

52. FRANK, LAW AND THE MODERN MIND, *supra* note 10, at 181.

53. FRANK, COURTS ON TRIAL, *supra* note 25, at 133.

54. JEROME FRANK & BARBARA FRANK KRISTEN, *supra* note 25; Francis A. Allen, *Review: Not Guilty*, 24 U. CHI. L. REV. 779 (1957).

55. GLENNON, *supra* note 22, at 37.

56. *Jerome N. Frank, U.S. Judge, Dead*, N.Y. TIMES, Jan. 14, 1957, at 20.

57. Judge Charles E. Clark, Remarks, *supra* note 8; *see* Jerome New Frank Papers, *supra* note 26.

58. Felix Frankfurter, *Jerome N. Frank*, 24 U. CHI. L. REV. 625 (1957).

59. Justice William O. Douglas, Remarks, *supra* note 6.

60. Charles E. Clark, *Jerome N. Frank*, 66 YALE L.J. 817 (1957). Florence Frank, Jerome's wife, recalled Clark being "singularly kind" to her after Frank's death. GLENNON, *supra* note 22, at 37.

61. Rodell, *Jerome N. Frank: A Remembrance*, *supra* note 7, at 12 (quoting an excerpt of a letter).

# HAROLD RAYMOND MEDINA
## 1888-1990

District Court for the Southern District of New York: 1947-1953
Court of Appeals for the Second Circuit: 1953-1980

"Strong enough to disdain desires and to despise distinctions. A whole man in himself, polished and wellrounded." This is the text inscribed on the Fiorello LaGuardia Medal awarded to Harold Raymond Medina.[1]

Medina was born in Brooklyn, in 1888, to Joaquin Adolfo Medina and Elizabeth Fash.[2] Medina's father came from an affluent family in Merida, Yucatan, and was educated at Seton Hall Academy in New Jersey.[3] Medina's mother, described as a "New York Episcopalian of Dutch ancestry," is reported to have forbidden Spanish and Catholicism in the home.[4] Medina was raised in Brooklyn and attended Public School 44 during the Spanish-American War. His schoolmates called him the epithet "greaser," based on his Mexican heritage.[5]

Medina attended the Holbrook Military Academy, a private high school in Ossining, New York.[6] From there, he went on to Princeton University, where he met scholastic success but disappointment in his pursuit of extracurricular activities. He joined the freshman football team, but when, in his own words, a "big hyena jumped on me," he was left with a misplaced vertebra that kept him off the field permanently.[7] He tried water polo, fencing, and writing for Princeton's *Tiger* magazine, but despite all of his efforts, he never felt he was "a great social success."[8] Medina graduated in 1909 *summa cum laude* and Phi Beta Kappa.[9]

Medina was torn as to what vocation to pursue. He was passionate about the study of languages and wanted to become a teacher, focusing on modern languages.[10] However, he had become engaged to Ethel Forde Hillyer, a native of East Orange, New Jersey.[11] In his words, "I didn't see how I could get married and bring up a family on an instructor's salary; so I went back to my first love, the law."[12] Medina attended Columbia Law School, graduating in 1912. He won the Ordronaux Prize, given to the third-year student with the most distinguished scholastic standing.[13] In fact, Medina earned straight A's, until he took a one-credit course in his last semester, in which he earned a B.[14] While at Columbia, Medina married Hillyer.[15]

After graduating, Medina adopted an ambitious schedule. He joined the law office of Davies, Auerbach & Cornell, where he worked as a clerk for the next six years, starting at a salary of eight dollars a week.[16] Medina also started a bar review course, helping students "cram" for the New York State bar examination.[17] By the time he retired from teaching the course in 1940, he had coached 39,788 students.[18] Meanwhile, his law practice blossomed. When Medina left Davies, Auerbach & Cornell, he opened his own law office, Medina and Sherpick, in the Mutual Life Building at 34 Nassau Street.[19] Over the course of his practice, he argued approximately 1,400 cases before the New York State Appellate Division and was reported to have achieved an impressive record of not losing a single case from 1931 to

1945.[20] During this time, Medina became a vice president of the Association of the Bar of the City of New York, then a club-like group of lawyers; a director of the American Judicature Society; and president of the Manhattan Lawyer's Club.[21] Medina was known for his incredible memory and ability to speak without notes. For "big" cases, Medina practiced his arguments "before two witnesses that never lied: his mirror and his wife."[22] In addition to building his law practice and teaching his bar review course, Medina taught at Columbia Law School from 1915 to 1940 and wrote several law books.[23]

One of Medina's best-known cases from his years in private practice was *United States v. Cramer.*[24] Medina was assigned to represent Anthony Cramer, who was charged with treason for harboring Nazi saboteurs during World War II.[25] Medina unsuccessfully appealed Cramer's conviction to the Court of Appeals for the Second Circuit.[26] Undeterred, he petitioned for a writ of certiorari, which the Supreme Court granted.[27] Medina had two oral arguments before the Supreme Court and ultimately persuaded a majority of justices to reverse the conviction based on the Constitution's two-witness requirement for treason.[28]

Despite his thriving bar review, flourishing legal practice, and demanding teaching schedule, Medina's most cherished role was being a husband and father. He and Ethel had two sons, Standish and Harold, Jr., both of whom followed their father to Princeton University and Columbia Law School.[29] Harold, Jr., spent his career at Cravath, Swaine & Moore, where he was a partner from 1949 to 1974.[30] Standish worked in trusts and estates law, and he was a joint partner in his firm, Medina & Miller. In 1972, he became a solo practitioner until his death in 2002.[31]

The Medina family divided their time between an apartment at 14 East 75th Street in Manhattan and a 55-acre estate in Westhampton, Long Island, which accommodated a spacious home, a library that housed Medina's 15,000 volumes of Greek, Latin, and French literature, and later, two homes for their sons.[32] Ethel Medina was a longtime member of the Westhampton Garden Club; she was renowned for her gardening skills (Medina also loved gardening).[33]

By the mid-1940s, Medina had made a small fortune. When he was offered a job on July 1, 1947 that would cut his annual income by 85 percent and foist him into the national spotlight, exposing him to intense scrutiny and criticism, Medina took it. President Harry S. Truman nominated Medina to the District Court for the Southern District of New York.[34] Medina explained that the decision to take the job was simple: "I've made plenty of money," he said. "Now I'd like to do something for my country. I guess the best thing I have to contribute is law."[35] Medina was sworn in as a district judge at the age of 59.[36] Moments before his swearing-in ceremony, Medina frantically searched for the sleeves of his black robe. Unable to locate them, he instead "wore it like a cape" for the ceremony.[37]

Within 18 months of his appointment, Medina was assigned to what was known as the Communist Conspiracy case, which thrust him into sensational media coverage in the early years of the Cold War. Eleven leaders of the Communist Party were charged under the Smith Act with knowingly conspiring to overthrow the government and to "organize and be members of a political party that propagated Marxist-Leninist doctrines of violent revolution."[38] The trial was later described as "one of the longest, bitterest, most controversial criminal jury trials in the history of the Federal Court."[39] For nine months, picketers displayed nasty signs and hollered mean-spirited messages at Medina. "How do you spell Medina? RAT," read one sign. Another urged Medina to commit suicide from his 40 Foley chambers: "Jump, jump. You've got to jump."[40] Abuse came not only from picketers. Defense attorneys levied charges of bias and race prejudice against Medina, and argued he was unfit to try the case.[41] While he usually kept a steady calm despite the inflammatory tactics of the attorneys in the courtroom, there were times when, red-faced, he called a recess to allow himself to regain his composure.[42]

Of all the verbal attacks and hurtful rumors, Medina admitted that the ones that "annoyed [him] most" were the allegations of race discrimination (defense counsel argued that Jews and African-Americans were systematically excluded from the jury).[43] In light of the race-based taunts he withstood in grade school,

Medina felt certain that, "If there ever was in this world a man who never had a particle of [race discrimination] in his make-up, I'm that man."[44]

The trial ended in a guilty verdict for all of the defendants.[45] So egregious was the conduct of the defense attorneys that, after trial, Medina entered summary contempt orders against several and sentenced them to terms of imprisonment ranging from 30 days to six months.[46] The Second Circuit affirmed the contempt convictions and sentences.[47] The Supreme Court granted certiorari on a discrete procedural question, and a divided Court upheld Medina's actions.[48] The case made Medina a national hero. He received over 15,000 letters of congratulations, and he was even approached to run for governor of New York, an offer that he declined.[49] As Medina once explained, "I would be impeached inside of a month or two. . . . I'd shoot off my mouth about something or other and get in wrong with everybody and I don't want to do it."[50] In 1953, President Truman appointed Medina to the Court of Appeals for the Second Circuit.[51]

Medina classified his opinions into three groups.[52] The first were institutional cases that had a significant influence on public law. One example was *Robert Lawrence Company, Inc. v. Devonshire Fabrics, Inc.*, in which a fabric buyer claimed that fraudulent misrepresentations induced him to enter into a contract for defective merchandise.[53] The contract had an arbitration clause, and the seller moved to stay federal district court proceedings for arbitration; the buyer argued that because the contract was fraudulent, the arbitration clause had no effect. The district court agreed with the buyer, holding that state law provided that if the contract was fraudulent at its creation the buyer could void the contract, including the arbitration provision.[54] On appeal, Medina wrote an opinion reversing the district court.[55] Determining that federal law controlled, Medina considered the case under the Federal Arbitration Act and held that the parties had agreed to arbitrate any disagreements related to the contract, which included any disagreement over whether fraudulent misrepresentations were made at the contract's inception.[56] He reasoned that, because:

> [A]rbitration agreements are 'valid, irrevocable, and enforceable' we know of no principle of law that stands as an obstacle to a determination by the parties to the effect that arbitration should not be denied or postponed upon the mere cry of fraud in the inducement, as this would permit the frustration of the very purposes sought to be achieved by the agreement to arbitrate, i.e. a speedy and relatively inexpensive trial before commercial specialists.[57]

The second category contained "stinkers," Medina's term for terribly complex cases. While he occasionally volunteered to take a "stinker," Medina was known for then jocularly complaining to his colleagues about how the other panel members had "stuck him" with the most complicated opinions.[58] When Medina offered to write an opinion in a particularly complex admiralty case, Judge Irving R. Kaufman responded, "Well, you can write the opinion provided you promise you won't go around the building telling everyone that we stuck you with a 'stinker.'" Medina replied that he would write the opinion, but would make no other promises.[59] Of the many "stinkers" he was assigned, one particularly colorful example was *United States v. Ortega,* a drug smuggling case involving over 93 kilograms of heroin hidden in secret compartments in the chassis of a car, discovered through the help of an undercover agent.[60] The case involved such rich facts that it was made into the hit movie *The French Connection.*[61]

The third category was made up of cases that revealed the humanity underlying the law. One example was *Wolff v. Selective Service Local Board*, in which student protesters of the Vietnam War challenged the Selective Service Board's policy of reclassifying them as "delinquents," which eliminated their student draft deferments.[62] The district court dismissed the action for lack of a "justiciable controversy."[63] Medina wrote an opinion finding that attempts to administratively exhaust claims through the Selective Service System would be futile when the threat to the students' First Amendment rights required "prompt action by the courts to avoid an erosion of these precious constitutional rights."[64] While the court was reluctant to bring the operation of the Selective Service System under judicial scrutiny, Medina explained that it was "imperative that the public debate be full and that each segment of our society be permitted freely to express its views."[65] The opinion concluded that "the allegations of the complaint in this case that the draft boards have unlawfully suppressed criticism must take precedence over the policy of non-intervention in the affairs of the Selective Service."[66] Medina felt a great sense of pride in this outcome.[67]

In 1958, Medina took senior status, but he continued hearing cases until 1980.[68] He was known for being perhaps the most prepared judge on every panel, even reading trial transcripts before a sitting.[69] He would pepper the parties with questions, and "he would always attempt to bring out the best of the arguments for the pro se appellant."[70]

Time did not lessen his love of the law or the quality of his work. Medina planned to follow the example of his mentor, Judge Learned Hand: "He sat on the court until the day he died. He was in his 90th year. I love the work, and as long as I'm able to do it, I'm going to keep it up," Medina said in 1966.[71] Even a heart attack in 1976 did not stop him.[72] "I damn near died," he recalled, and he was forced to give up his habit of smoking cigars.[73] However, to his great delight, Medina's doctor saw no harm in allowing him to work and maintain his habit of drinking two martinis per day—one before lunch and the other before dinner.[74] His other activities included playing golf and billiards, buying fine books at auction, cruising in his boat, and driving his 1942 Lincoln Continental.[75]

Over the years, Medina showed his unconventional side. In one memorable episode in the district court, Medina was presiding over a trial known as the Investment Bankers case, a complicated action made worse because, in Medina's words, "I didn't know anything about the anti-trust laws and I was having a hell of a time." Meanwhile, the "lawyers were fighting right and left and after about a year we weren't getting anywhere," and "the personalities, the way they were cussing one another . . . was just terrible." One day, when proceedings were particularly heated, Medina said, "Now look fellows, what we need is to go to a ball game." The next day, on May 28, 1952, Medina adjourned court so that the lawyers and "court attendants"—over 50 people—

could attend the baseball game between the Brooklyn Dodgers and the New York Giants at Ebbets Field; the group was considered special guests of Walter O'Malley, whom *The New York Times* identified as "president of the Brooklyn Dodgers, and former law student of Judge Medina."[76] A photo of the group made the front page of *The Herald Tribune*, which Medina found humorous because all of the "government lawyers were looking glum," fearful they would "get cussed out for going to the game." The rest of the lawyers, however, "were hi-dee-hi-ing and laughing around and I was doing my regular stuff."[77] After the ballgame, a sense of civility prevailed in court. "You just can't imagine what that did for the trial," Medina recalled. "All the troubles we had were over, the case began to move, progress was made, no more of these recriminations and everything was fine."[78]

Even as he advanced in age, Medina insisted on doing his share of each panel's work. In 1980, at age 92, Medina retired after 33 years of service as a federal judge.[79] It was a difficult decision for him. "I had a fine time," he said, "I just hated to say goodbye."[80] Reflecting on his legal career, the case he believed the public would most remember him by was the 1947 Communist Conspiracy case.[81] But he insisted that his most important day was June 6, 1911, when he married his "sweetie," as he referred to his beloved wife, Ethel.[82] Medina lived to be 102 years old and was survived by his sons, six grandchildren, and ten great-grandchildren.[83]

Medina made a lasting impression on the court and his colleagues. In the words of Judge James L. Oakes, Medina was remembered for his "enthusiasm, his laughter, his colorful expressions—'He tried to give me a lot of that ballyhoo and razzle-dazzle'—his zest for everything, for every day, for everybody, his passion for justice, his joy, his approach to age, his concern for others."[84]

Molly Guptill Manning

1. James L. Oakes, *Memorial to Harold R. Medina*, 90 COLUM. L. REV. 1459, 1461–62 (1990).
2. 2 JOHN R. VILE, GREAT AMERICAN JUDGES: AN ENCYCLOPEDIA 520 (2003).
3. *Id.*
4. *Id.*

5. *Id.*

6. *Id.*

7. *Communists: The Presence of Evil*, TIME MAGAZINE (Oct. 24, 1949), http://www.time.com/time/magazine/article/0,9171,805104-1,00.html.

8. *Id.*

9. *Id.*; *see also Harold Medina, U.S. Judge, Dies at 102*, N.Y. TIMES, Mar. 16, 1990, at B7.

10. Stacey Okun, *Judge Medina's 100th Birthday: Time for Tributes*, N.Y. TIMES, Feb. 16, 1988, at B3.

11. *Mrs. Harold Medina; Judge's Wife was 83*, N.Y. TIMES, Sept. 21, 1971, at 40.

12. *Id.*

13. *Harold Medina, U.S. Judge, Dies at 102*, *supra* note 9; *see also Academic Recognition and Prizes*, COLUMBIA LAW SCHOOL, http://web.law.columbia.edu/prizes-awards (discussing Ordronaux Prize).

14. Chief Judge Irving R. Kaufman, Remarks at the Proceedings in Honor of U.S. Senior Circuit Judge Harold R. Medina 1 (Sept. 11, 1975) (transcript on file with the United States Courts Library for the Second Circuit).

15. *Miss Ethel Hillyer Weds*, N.Y. TIMES, Jun. 7, 1911, at 9; *Communists: The Presence of Evil*, *supra* note 7.

16. Judge Harold R. Medina, *Introduction* to ARTHUR TRAIN, MR. TUTT AT HIS BEST vii (1961).

17. *Harold Medina, U.S. Judge, Dies at 102*, *supra* note 9, at B7.

18. *Id.*

19. Judge Harold R. Medina, *supra* note 16, at vii; VILE, *supra* note 2, at 520.

20. *Communists: The Presence of Evil*, *supra* note 7.

21. VILE, *supra* note 2, at 521.

22. *Id.*

23. *Harold Medina, U.S. Judge, Dies at 102*, *supra* note 9, at B7.

24. 137 F.2d 888 (2d Cir. 1943).

25. VILE, *supra* note 2, at 521; *see also Cramer*, 137 F.2d at 890.

26. *Cramer*, 137 F.2d at 898.

27. Cramer v. United States, 320 U.S. 730 (1943).

28. VILE, *supra* note 2, at 521; *see also* Cramer v. United States, 325 U.S. 1 (1945).

29. *Harold Medina, U.S. Judge, Dies at 102*, *supra* note 9, at B7.

30. Glenn Fowler, *H.R. Medina Jr., 78, Lawyer and Expert in Libel and Privacy*, N.Y. TIMES, Feb. 20, 1991, at D23.

31. *Id.*

32. *Id.*; *Mrs. Harold Medina; Judge's Wife was 83*, *supra* note 11, at 40.

33. *Mrs. Harold Medina; Judge's Wife was 83*, *supra* note 11, at 40; Oakes, *supra* note 1, at 1459.

34. VILE, *supra* note 2, at 521.

35. *Harold Medina, U.S. Judge, Dies at 102*, *supra* note 9, at B7.

36. VILE, *supra* note 2, at 522.

37. J. Woodford Howard, Jr., *Judge Harold R. Medina: The 'Freshman' Years*, 69 JUDICATURE 127, 127 (1985).

38. VILE, *supra* note 2, at 522.

39. Gregory Jaynes, *Harold Medina, at 89, Still Loves Law, Columbia and Telling Stories*, N.Y. TIMES, Jan. 20, 1978, at B4.

40. Alpheus Mason, *The Triumph Is Spiritual*, N.Y. TIMES, Sept. 20, 1959, at 3.

41. *Harold Medina, U.S. Judge, Dies at 102*, *supra* note 9, at B7.

42. VILE, *supra* note 2, 523.

43. Russell Porter, *Challenge to Jury in Red Trial Ended*, N.Y. TIMES, Mar. 2, 1949, at 17.

44. *Medina Recalls Trial's Bad Day*, N.Y. TIMES, Oct. 15, 1949, at 2.

45. *Id.*

46. Oakes, *supra* note 1, at 1460; Sacher v. United States, 343 U.S. 1, 3 (1952).

47. United States v. Sacher, 182 F.2d 416, 429–30 (2d Cir. 1950).pa

48. *Sacher*, 343 U.S. at 4–5, 14.

49. Oakes, *supra* note 1, at 1460.

50. Judge Harold R. Medina, Remarks at the Proceedings in Honor of U.S. Senior Circuit Judge Harold R. Medina 11 (Sept. 11, 1975) (transcript on file with the United States Courts Library for the Second Circuit).

51. Oakes, *supra* note 1, at 1460.

52. VILE, *supra* note 2, at 527.

53. 271 F.2d 402, 404 (2d Cir. 1959).

54. *Id.* at 409.

55. *Id.* at 402.

56. *Id.* at 410.

57. *Id.*.

58. Judge Harold R. Medina, Remarks, *supra* note 50, at 19.

59. *Id.*

60. 471 F.2d 1350, 1352 (2d Cir. 1972).

61. VILE, *supra* note 2, at 527.

62. 372 F.2d 817, 820 (2d Cir. 1967).

63. *Id.*

64. *Id.*

65. *Id.* at 822.

66. *Id.*

67. VILE, *supra* note 2, at 527.

68. *At 92, Judge Medina Ends Long Career on Full Day*, N.Y. TIMES, Feb. 23, 1980, at 23.

69. Oakes, *supra* note 1, at 1461.

70. *Id.*

71. *Vigorous Senior Judge Harold Raymond Medina*, N.Y. TIMES, Oct. 7, 1966, at 31.

72. *At 92, Judge Medina Ends Long Career on Full Day*, *supra* note 68, at 23.

73. Jaynes, *supra* note 39, at B4.

74. *Id.*

75. Edward N. Costikyan, Remarks at a Special Session of the United States Court of Appeals for the Second Circuit, Memorial Service for Judge Harold R. Medina (May 21, 1990), *in* 917 F.2d at XCVI. Costikyan was a law clerk to Judge Harrie B. Chase, and a partner at Paul Weiss.

76. *Stuart Envisages Banker as Adviser*, N.Y. TIMES, May 28, 1952, at 47.

77. Judge Harold R. Medina, Remarks, *supra* note 50, at 12–13.

78. *Id.* at 13.

79. *At 92, Judge Medina Ends Long Career on Full Duty*, *supra* note 68, at 23.

80. *Id.*

81. *Id.*

82. *Harold Medina, Federal Judge, 102, Dies*, *supra* note 9, at B7; Judge Harold R. Medina, Remarks, *supra* note 50, at 21-23.

83. *Harold Medina, Federal Judge, 102, Dies*, *supra* note 9, at B7.

84. Oakes, *supra* note 1, at 1462.

# CARROLL C. HINCKS
# 1889-1964

District Court for the District of Connecticut:
1931-1953
Court of Appeals for the Second Circuit: 1953-1959

Judge Carroll Clark Hincks was a true son of New England. Born on November 30, 1889, in Andover, Massachusetts, to a clergyman and a homemaker, he graduated from Phillips Academy Andover before attending Yale College and Yale Law School, receiving a law degree in 1917.[1] Aside from service in the military, Hincks never moved out of Connecticut and dedicated his life to the law, Yale, and the New Haven community.

Hincks's time at Yale was eventful. He was the manager of the football team and a member of the debate team.[2] He was also a participant in a piquant piece of Yale lore, the Fence Oration.

The Yale Fence was a rail fence on Old Campus where students congregated.[3] Freshmen were allowed to sit on the fence only after the Fence Oration.[4] At the end of each year, the sophomore fence orator gave a speech yielding the fence, and the freshman fence orator accepted the oration and occupied the fence.[5] Hincks was his freshman class's elected orator—a distinguished honor.[6]

After graduating from Yale, Hincks served in the Army from 1914 to 1918, attaining the rank of captain.[7] In 1916, he was stationed along the Texas-Mexico border as part of the Punitive Expedition, also known as the Pancho Villa Expedition, an unsuccessful attempt to capture a Mexican revolutionary after he attacked the town of Columbus, New Mexico, and killed 16 American citizens.[8]

When he returned from service, Hincks entered private practice in Waterbury, Connecticut, at the firm of Meyer, Hincks & Traurig.[9] He practiced there until President Herbert Hoover appointed him to the District Court for the District of Connecticut in 1931.[10] The task that defined Judge Hincks's time on the district court was reorganizing the New Haven Railroad after its bankruptcy in 1935. The bankruptcy proceedings lasted 12 years, but were ultimately unsuccessful: the railroad encountered difficulties immediately after restructuring.[11] Judge Hincks's diagnosis of the problem that led to years of protracted negotiations reveals his salty humor:

> Now, I think the trouble in reorganization proceedings is that the Bar is too . . . gentlemanly. If only they'd insult each other more, maybe we could get something settled. Why, gentlemen, as I review your conduct in these proceedings you are as coy and skittish in approaching any possible compromise as a Victorian bride when finally faced with the facts of life.[12]

Despite Judge Hincks's efforts, the railroad went back into bankruptcy receivership in 1961 and was absorbed by Penn Central in 1969.[13] District Judge Robert Palmer Anderson oversaw the second bankruptcy receivership proceedings, which did not end until 1978.[14]

Judge Hincks's time on the district court was busy. For the first two years of his appointment, he was the only judge in the district, and he shouldered a heavy workload as Connecticut's population expanded.[15] He handled the New Haven Railroad's bankruptcy while maintaining a full, diverse caseload, and yet he found time to preside over complicated trials in other districts and serve on several committees.[16] He participated in the first study of the business of the federal courts, which was produced by President Hoover's National Commission on Law Observance and Enforcement in 1935.[17] The study tracked the caseloads of 13 federal districts, providing important data on the types of civil and criminal cases coming through the federal courts, including procedural postures, use of motions, duration, and results.[18]

Some would have complained about the district court's workload, but Judge Hincks seemed to enjoy the challenge, asking his clerk at the start of the day, "[A]nd what have counsel arranged for our entertainment today?"[19]

Judge Hincks's compassion influenced his approach to sentencing in criminal cases, where he viewed existing practices as deficient. He thought that defense lawyers and prosecutors did a poor job of providing judges with information about the defendant, so he tried to gather that information himself.[20] As a member of the U.S. Judicial Conference's Committee on the Punishment for Crime, he recommended legislation that would treat youthful offenders separately in sentencing, impose indeterminate sentences, reduce pretrial detention, and increase the use of minimum security facilities and probation as an alternative to incarceration.[21] He used probation liberally in his own sentencing practice, hoping to provide defendants with a chance at rehabilitation, and arranged for psychiatric treatment of serious offenders through his connections at Yale.[22]

The bench and bar viewed Judge Hincks as an exceptional district judge. Judge Thomas Swan recommended Judge Hincks for appointment to the Court of Appeals, stating, "Judge Hincks is the outstanding District Judge in the Second Circuit and no other appointment could possibly add so much to the strength and reputation of the Court of Appeals."[23] Judge Learned Hand followed with another glowing recommendation, writing to the attorney general that, "[I]n balance, penetration and in that craftsmanship that only long experience can give, he stands without an equal. I should feel deep chagrin to have him passed over."[24] Judge Hand respected Judge Hincks so much that, though he ignored editing advice from every other judge, he was said to have made any changes Judge Hincks suggested.[25] Judge Hand's admiration was complete: "I cannot think of any judge whom I value more than Carroll Hincks."[26] The recommendations of Swan and Hand were followed by a five-point memo from 23 judges and members of the bar to the attorney general outlining Judge Hincks's qualifications.[27] All of this support came after Judge Hincks specifically requested that no one make any effort to get him elevated to the Second Circuit.[28] President Dwight D. Eisenhower appointed Judge Hincks to the Second Circuit in 1953.[29]

His character, just as much as his legal ability, explains the esteem of his contemporaries. He was described as quiet but not reserved, filled with good cheer and a wry sense of humor, and always generous with his time and advice.[30] He was independently minded, advising Judge Herbert S. MacDonald of the Connecticut Superior Court that he was right to risk reversal to do what he felt was right, rather than write an opinion that was certain to be affirmed.[31] He was an important mentor to another judge of the District of Connecticut, William H. Timbers, helping usher a young and inexperienced judge through his first difficult years on the federal bench.[32] College classmates described him as "the most articulate and least talkative among them," a person who measured his words and made them count.[33] This quiet, authoritative character gave him a natural authority. As Judge José A. Cabranes noted, he was "the only person who could instruct a jury to disregard testimony and have it disregarded."[34]

Judge Hincks authored several important opinions during his brief time on the Second Circuit. Certainly the most controversial was *Winston v. United States*, which held that federal prisoners may maintain an action for negligence against the United States under the Federal Tort Claims Act.[35] The government contended that allowing prisoner suits would so disrupt prison discipline that Congress could not have intended to waive the government's sovereign immunity with respect to that class of plaintiffs.[36] Judge Hincks, over a vigorous dissent by Judge Irving R. Kaufman, disagreed and held that the effects on prison discipline would be no worse than those already presented by suits against individual prison officials, which had been allowed for some time.[37] The court agreed to rehear this case *en banc*, and in a five-to-four decision adopted Judge Hincks's opinion as its own.[38]

An unusual situation was presented in *Cox v. Commissioner of Internal Revenue.*[39] In 1941, May Cox executed a will dividing her property among her four sons.[40] One of her sons, Lewis, was a Jesuit priest.[41] In 1950, he took his final vows, one of which included perpetual poverty.[42] To that end, he executed a contract agreeing that any property he inherited would devolve to the Society of Jesus.[43] May Cox died in 1954, and Lewis's share of her estate thus became the property of the Jesuit order.[44] Ms. Cox's executor, however, took a tax exemption on the theory that the bequest was "to or for the use of" a religious institution.[45] A deficiency of $3,800 was levied on Cox's estate, which it contested in the Tax Court.[46] Judge Hincks held that the bequest was not "to or for the use of" the Society of Jesus because it was intended for Lewis, not the order, even though Ms. Cox knew by the time of her death that Lewis could not inherit the property.[47] The only intent that mattered, Judge Hincks held, was Ms. Cox's intent when she executed the will.[48]

In his life away from the court, Judge Hincks was devoted to Yale and its community. He was a fellow of Branford College and a member of the Alumni Advisory Board, which approved the university's plan to pursue construction of the Yale Bowl. When it opened in 1914, the bowl was the world's largest stadium.[49] It is now a national historic landmark.[50] A lifelong lover of music, Judge Hincks was the president of the New Haven Symphony Orchestra.[51] In 1945, he arranged to use the Yale Bowl for a summer Pops concert that raised money for the orchestra shell. It was ultimately named the Carroll C. Hincks Shell.[52] On a lighter note, Judge Hincks had a long connection with the Mory's Association, a private social club for Yale students that began in a pub on Wooster Street in 1849.[53] The club, according to its 1909 constitution, is devoted to eating, drinking, and good fellowship.[54]

He even won the Mory's Cup for "conspicuous service to Yale and life at Mory's."[55]

Judge Hincks's time on the Second Circuit was brief; he served for five years and retired in 1959, after which he continued to assist both the District of Connecticut and the Second Circuit until his death in 1964.[56] He had no children, and his retirement was spent doing what he had always done: tending his garden, listening to music, reading poetry, and spending time with his wife, Edith Walker Hincks.[57]

Ultimately, Judge Hincks was a true son of New England—devoted to the region and its culture, he made his entire life there and strove to improve it for more than 70 years. According to Judge MacDonald, "Carroll Hincks was . . . the living personification of his beloved New England—in which he was born and in which he lived his full life."[58] Judge MacDonald identified him with the world of Nathaniel Hawthorne, comparing him to the "Old Man of the Mountain," a series of cliff ledges resembling a jagged, jutting face that protruded from Cannon Mountain in New Hampshire's White Mountains. To Judge MacDonald, Hawthorne, writing of the Old Man of the Mountain, could have been describing Judge Hincks: "All the features were noble and the expression was at once grand and sweet as if it were the glow of a vast warm heart that embraced all mankind in its affection—and had room for more."[59]

Stephen Strother

1. Carroll Hincks, *U.S. Judge, Dead: Retired Member of Court of Appeals Here Was 74*, N.Y. TIMES, Oct. 1, 1964, at 35.

2. ROBERT A. GIBNEY & HARRY S. IRONS, HISTORY OF THE CLASS OF 1911: YALE COLLEGE 23 (James Dwight Dana ed. 1911).

3. Judith Ann Schiff, *Tales of the True Fence*, YALE ALUMNI MAGAZINE (Summer 1998), http://archives.yalealumnimagazine.com/issues/98_07/old_yale.html.

4. *Id.*

5. *Id.*

6. GIBNEY & IRONS, *supra* note 2 at 19.

7. *Carroll Hincks, U.S. Judge, Dead*, *supra* note 1, at 35.

8. *Punitive Expedition in Mexico, 1916-1917*, U.S. DEPARTMENT OF STATE, http://2001-2009.state.gov/r/pa/ho/time/wwi/108653.htm.

9. *Carroll Hincks, U.S. Judge, Dead*, *supra* note 1, at 35.

10. FEDERAL JUDICIAL CENTER, Biographical Directory of Federal Judges, Carroll Clark Hincks, http://www.fjc.gov/servlet/nGetInfo?jid=1052.

11. *A Brief History of the New Haven Railroad*, NEW HAVEN RAILROAD HISTORICAL AND TECHNICAL ASSOCIATION, INC., http://www.nhrhta.org.

12. Oscar Landon, *Investment and Finance*, 81 BANKING L.J. 84, 84 (1964).

13. *A Brief History of the New Haven Railroad*, *supra* note 11.

14. *The New Haven Railroad Reorganization Proceedings, or the Little Railroad that Couldn't*, 78 Harv. L. Rev. 861, 861-80 (Feb. 1965); Judge J. Joseph Smith, Remarks at a Joint Session of the United States Court of Appeals for the Second Circuit and the United States District Court for the District of Connecticut, In Memory of Honorable Robert P. Anderson (June 19, 1978), *in* 581 F.2d 1, 19.

15. Judge J. Joseph Smith, Remarks at a Joint Session of the United States Court of Appeals for the Second Circuit and the United States District Court for the District of Connecticut, In Memory of Honorable Carroll C. Hincks (Dec. 21, 1964), *in* 342 F.2d 1, 16; District Court Chief Judge William H. Timbers, Remarks at a Joint Session of the United States Court of Appeals for the Second Circuit and the United States District Court for the District of Connecticut, In Memory of Honorable Carroll C. Hincks (Dec. 21, 1964), *in* 342 F.2d 1, 11.

16. Judge J. Joseph Smith, Remarks, *supra* note 15, at 17; District Court Chief Judge William H. Timbers, Remarks, *supra* note 15, at 11.

17. Carroll C. Hincks, *Study of the Business of the Federal Courts. American Law Institute, 1934. 2 Vols. in One. PP. 370, with Appendices*, 45 YALE L.J. 189 (1935) (book review).

18. *Id.*

19. Judge J. Joseph Smith, Remarks, *supra* note 15, at 17.

20. *Id.* at 18.

21. JUDICIAL CONFERENCE OF THE UNITED STATES, REPORT OF THE JUDICIAL CONFERENCE, SEPTEMBER SESSIONS, 1942 7-8 (1942).

22. Judge J. Joseph Smith, Remarks, *supra* note 15, at 18.

23. District Court Chief Judge William H. Timbers, Remarks, *supra* note 15, at 12-13.

24. *Id.* at 13.

25. Judge Harold R. Medina, Remarks at a Joint Session of the United States Court of Appeals for the Second Circuit and the United States District Court for the District of Connecticut, In Memory of Honorable Carroll C. Hincks (Dec. 21, 1964), *in* 342 F.2d 1, 25-26.

26. Judge J. Joseph Smith, Remarks, *supra* note 15, at 17.

27. District Court Chief Judge William H. Timbers, Remarks, *supra* note 15, at 14.

28. *Id.* at 11-12.

29. *Carroll Hincks, U.S. Judge, Dead*, *supra* note 1, at 35.

30. Connecticut Superior Court Judge Herbert S. MacDonald, Remarks at a Joint Session of the United States Court of Appeals for the Second Circuit and the United States District Court for the District of Connecticut, In Memory of Honorable Carroll C. Hincks (Dec. 21, 1964), *in* 342 F.2d 1, 9; Judge J. Joseph Smith, Remarks, *supra* note 15, at 17, 19; District Court Chief Judge William H. Timbers, Remarks, *supra* note 15, at 14.

31. Connecticut Superior Court Judge Herbert S. MacDonald, *supra* note 30, at 9.

32. District Court Chief Judge William H. Timbers, Remarks, *supra* note 15, at 14.

33. Judge J. Joseph Smith, Remarks, *supra* note 15, at 19.

34. Jose A. Cabranes, *Notes on the History of the Federal Courts of Connecticut*, SECOND CIRCUIT HISTORY LECTURES, Apr. 21, 1983.

35. 305 F.2d 253 (2d Cir. 1962).

36. *Id.* at 255.

37. *Id.* at 255-56.

38. *Id.* at 264.

39. 297 F.2d 36 (2d Cir. 1961).

40. *Id.* at 37.

41. *Id.*

42. *Id.*

43. *Id.*

44. *Id.*

45. *Id.* at 37-38.

46. *Id.* at 37.

47. *Id.* at 38.

48. *Id.*

49. REPORT OF THE PRESIDENT OF YALE UNIVERITY AND OF THE DEANS AND DIRECTORS OF ITS SEVERAL DEPARTMENTS FOR THE ACADEMIC YEAR 1911-12 52 (1912); Connecticut Superior Court Judge Herbert S. MacDonald, supra note 30, at 9; David McCullough, *The Yale Bowl: A Storied Century*, YALE DAILY NEWS (Sept. 26, 2014), http://yaledailynews.com/weekend/2014/09/26/the-yale-bowl-a-storied-century/.

50. McCullough, *supra* note 49.

51. Connecticut Superior Court Judge Herbert S. MacDonald, supra note 30, at 9.

52. *Id.*; *see also History*, NEW HAVEN SYMPHONY ORCHESTRA, http://newhavensymphony.org/about-nhso/history/.

53. THE STORY OF MORY'S: A YALE TRADITION C. 1849 (on file with the United States Courts Library for the Second Circuit).

54. *Id.*

55. Connecticut Superior Court Judge Herbert S. MacDonald, supra note 30, at 9.

56. When Judge Hincks left active service, the term "senior judge" was not yet used to describe a federal judge who left active service but continued to perform some judicial duties. *See* Act of Feb. 25, 1919, ch. 29, § 6, 40 Stat. 1156, 1157-58. A judge who took this option was considered to have "retired." Under a statute enacted in 1948, such a "retired" judge received the same salary increases and cost-of-living adjustments as an active judge. Act of June 25, 1948, ch. 646, §§ 294, 371, 372, 62 Stat. 901, 903-04. *See* Stephen B. Burbank, et al., *Leaving the Bench, 1970-2009: The Choices Federal Judges Make, What Influences Those Choices, and Their Consequences*, 161 U. PA. L. REV. 1, 8-10 (2012).

57. District Court Chief Judge William H. Timbers, Remarks, *supra* note 15, at 14.

58. Connecticut Superior Court Judge Herbert S. MacDonald, *supra* note 30, at 10.

59. *Id.*

# JOHN MARSHALL HARLAN
# 1899-1971

Court of Appeals for the Second Circuit: 1954-1955
Supreme Court: 1955-1971

John Marshall Harlan had "a thoroughgoing, elegant grace that put you at ease because he was at ease."[1] Though he was born to a wealthy family and a jurisprudential legacy, he "did not condescend because it would never occur to him to claim some special, higher status."[2] A capable private litigator and a jurist who believed in judicial restraint, Harlan stopped at the Second Circuit on his way to the Supreme Court.

The grandson of Supreme Court Justice John Marshall Harlan, Harlan grew up in a three-story house in a fashionable Chicago neighborhood.[3] He attended preparatory schools in Chicago, Toronto, and Lake Placid, New York.[4] At Princeton, he rubbed elbows with Adlai Stevenson and briefly dated Stevenson's sister.[5] Following Princeton, Harlan was awarded a Rhodes scholarship and studied law at Oxford's Balliol College.[6]

In 1923, Harlan returned from Oxford to a job at the storied firm of Root, Clark, Buckner & Howland (later Dewey, Ballantine).[7] Partner Emory Buckner's mentorship would shape Harlan's early legal career. Buckner worried that Harlan's Oxford education had not prepared him for New York practice and sent the young lawyer to afternoon classes at New York Law School.[8]

Harlan's first assignment was to brief an appeal that Buckner would argue before the Second Circuit. As Buckner began his argument, Judge Learned Hand asked him who wrote the brief. Before Buckner could answer, Judge Hand "threw the brief across the courtroom, remarking, 'well you can just take it back because it is too long and I won't read it.'"[9] Judge Hand later apologized to Harlan and allowed that the brief was excellent.[10]

When Buckner became the United States Attorney for the Southern District of New York in 1925, he brought his most promising associates with him. Harlan headed Buckner's Prohibition unit.[11] He prosecuted crooked breweries, druggists, physicians, and other providers of illicit alcohol.[12] Using the Volstead Act's civil forfeiture power, Harlan's unit seized hundreds of cafes, restaurants, and social clubs in what became known as the "padlock campaign."[13] Harlan prosecuted small-time operators and New York's most elite clubs with equal fervor. He worried:

> Shall the criminal law, and particularly the Prohibition law, be enforced against saloons, cabarets, places of amusement where any one may go, and ordinary individuals generally, and yet be restrained from enforcement when it comes to private clubs, fraternal organizations, or secret societies?[14]

Harlan's most colorful Prohibition case began with an "all-night bacchanalian orgy" at a Manhattan theater that featured a nude dancer in a bathtub filled with wine.[15] The event drew press attention, and Harlan charged the theater's eponym and host, Earl Carroll, with violating the Volstead Act. Before the grand jury, Carroll falsely denied serving alcohol at the party, and Harlan added a perjury charge to the indictment.[16] At trial, Carroll admitted the perjury, but explained in defense that he had "lied like a gentleman" to protect his dancer's reputation.[17] The jury acquitted on the Volstead Act charges, but, notwithstanding Carroll's gallantry, convicted him of perjury. Harlan viewed the verdict as "a triumph" in anti-Prohibition New York.[18]

In 1927, Harlan followed Buckner from the United States Attorney's office back to Root, Clark.[19] By the mid-thirties, he led the firm's litigation practice. As a litigator, Harlan would "fill his mind totally with the facts of a case," and when it was over, he would "pull the plug" to make room in his mind for the facts of the next case.[20] He recorded a remarkable string of successes.[21]

Harlan displayed his deftness when he defended the estate of Ella Wendel, a Fifth Avenue eccentric who left behind a large estate.[22] In life, her dearest companions had been a series of 18 Maltese poodles, each named Tobey.[23] Her will failed to provide for the final Tobey's upkeep, and the omission was one of the factors that drew its authenticity into question.[24] Wendel's death brought a host of putative heirs, represented by renowned lawyers like Arthur Garfield Hays and Samuel Untermyer.[25] In all, 2,303 claimants came forward.[26] But Harlan had an army of able associates, including a young Henry Friendly, who routed the pretenders.[27]

The strongest challenge came from Thomas Patrick Morris, who claimed to be Wendel's illegitimate nephew. Morris specified several occasions when he had allegedly spent time with Wendel, but Harlan's associates uncovered hard evidence that proved he was lying, and Harlan demolished Morris on the witness stand.[28] According to Friendly, Harlan's "questions were put in such a sympathetic manner that Morris got the impression he was being afforded an opportunity to strengthen his case and furnished supporting detail in abundance—most of which afforded further opportunities for us to prove his inability to tell the truth."[29]

Among other famous clients, Harlan represented the boxer Gene Tunney in a contract dispute against his manager;[30] he was counsel to the DuPont family and their business interests; and he joined forces with the ACLU to defend the philosopher Bertrand Russell, whose unpopular views and unconventional lifestyle had lost him a teaching position at City College.[31] The Russell matter was a rare loss.[32]

When the United States entered World War II, Harlan returned to public service. As chief of the Army Air Force's Operations Analysis Division, Harlan analyzed U.S. bombing patterns and proposed ways to improve their efficiency.[33] His team also developed radar countermeasures and wrote the Army's textbook for destroying infrastructure.[34] Perhaps most influentially, the group wrote a secret report advocating an independent U.S. Air Force.[35] To get the flavor of combat, Harlan once sat in the gunner's seat during a bombing run.[36] He earned the U.S. Legion of Merit and the Croix de Guerre of Belgium and France.[37]

After the war, Harlan again returned to Root, Clark and his slate of corporate work. His most consuming matter was the defense of DuPont against a decade-long antitrust suit.[38] The government alleged that DuPont used its General Motors investments to build a vertical monopoly over automotive finishes and fabrics.[39] Harlan argued that DuPont was the innocent owner of GM stock, and asserted that there had been no collusion. In 1954, Harlan won the case,[40] only to have the result overturned three years later—by his Supreme Court brethren.[41]

In 1951, Harlan agreed to serve without pay on Governor Thomas E. Dewey's state crime commission.[42] The commission investigated New York's organized crime in the wake of U.S. Senator Estes Kefauver's Crime Committee report.[43] Dewey, a Republican like Harlan, made the committee strictly bipartisan.[44] Nevertheless, politics asserted itself. Harlan had uncovered evidence that Herman Methfessel, the Staten Island Democratic district attorney, had been involved in illegal gambling.[45] Methfessel promptly jailed Harlan's lead witness on perjury charges.[46] Through the offices of Governor Dewey, Harlan freed the witness and stripped Methfessel of his authority to investigate organized crime and gambling.[47] Methfessel claimed he was the victim of a political witch hunt, a charge which both Harlan and the Democratic committee head, Joseph M. Proskauer, publicly denied.[48]

Harlan's connection with Governor Dewey would help him rise to the bench. At the 1952 Republican convention, Dewey supported Dwight D. Eisenhower over Robert Taft and had the new President's ear when Eisenhower assumed office.[49] Dewey and other prominent New York attorneys pushed Harlan's name as a candidate for the Supreme Court, but Eisenhower concluded that Harlan needed some judicial experience.[50] In June 1953, Eisenhower nominated Harlan to serve on the Second Circuit.[51] *The New York Times* predicted that the public would "rejoice" in Harlan's nomination.[52] Ever scrupulous, Harlan cleared the decision with his law partners and the DuPont family, whose antitrust suit was still in the courts.[53] With their permission, he accepted, and the Senate approved the nomination.

Judge Harlan served on the Second Circuit for little more than a year, authoring nearly two dozen opinions.[54] Few were noteworthy, but the legal issues varied, including admiralty, tax, bankruptcy, tort, and contract.

One case that captured popular attention was *United States v. Flynn*,[55] which considered the convictions of "thirteen secondary Communist leaders" for advocating the overthrow of the U.S. government.[56] The defendants, admitted Communists, had argued that they could not receive a fair trial in the anti-Communist climate of the early 1950s. Harlan's opinion rejected the claim:

> In essence what the appellants are asking us to do is hold that there can be no proper trial of Communist Party members until the world situation quiets down and public opinion about Communism changes. We think there is nothing in our concepts of Constitutional due process which leads us to any such weird result.[57]

He also dismissed the argument that the jury should have been more demographically representative:

> To hold otherwise would involve the assumption that Negroes can expect justice only at the hands of Negroes or that the poor cannot be judged except by others equally poor. We are unwilling to make an assumption which is so obnoxious to the traditions of a nation whose

> free institutions have flourished under a mixture of racial and economic interests unparalleled in history.[58]

Centrally, *Flynn* concerned whether a conspiracy to advocate overthrowing the government could meet the "clear and present danger" test that had convicted the defendants' comrades.[59] Harlan's interpretation favored the government; he concluded that the test required no more than a reasonable conclusion that the subversive speech "may result in an attempt" to overthrow the government.[60] The convictions were affirmed.

In October 1954, Justice Robert H. Jackson died unexpectedly, and Eisenhower appointed Judge Harlan to Jackson's seat on the Supreme Court.[61] Judge Learned Hand, among others, expressed enthusiastic support, noting Harlan's "wide experience," "clear and penetrating mind," and sense of judicial detachment and public duty.[62] *The New York Times* was no less effusive: "Felicitously named for his grandfather, who was one of the great justices of the Supreme Court and who in turn bore the name of perhaps the greatest of them all, Judge Harlan will carry with him to Washington the good wishes and highest esteem of his fellow New Yorkers."[63]

But in Washington, the nomination encountered a punishing Senate confirmation campaign lasting four months. *Brown v. Board of Education* had just been decided, and Southern Democrats wanted to delay its implementation by any means at their disposal, including sitting on a Supreme Court nomination.[64] The Senate's most conservative Republicans also opposed the nomination. One, William Langer, stood on regional grounds; Langer refused to accept any Supreme Court nominee until a North Dakotan joined the bench.[65]

Judge Harlan's opponents battered him with an array of accusations. They trotted out Herman Methfessel and his stale allegations that Harlan had misused the State Crime Commission for political advantage.[66] They questioned his defense of the "well-known leftist" Bertrand Russell.[67] And they accused him of supporting an unconstitutional "One World" government, an allegation based on his membership in former Justice Owen Roberts's Atlantic Union Committee.[68]

The nomination battle took its toll on Harlan. Although he testified with aplomb and his nomination was never truly in doubt, he briefly considered withdrawing his name.[69] Nevertheless, the Senate confirmed Harlan by a vote of 71-11.[70] Following the vote, President Eisenhower consoled Harlan on his rough nomination: "[A]s I have grown wiser, I hope, in the ways of political life, such things tend to bother me less—or perhaps I merely become inured to them."[71]

"The first Justice Harlan was known as a great dissenter," according to Chief Justice Earl Warren, "and John Harlan followed in his footsteps."[72] Though Justice Harlan dissented often, he did so without malice. According to law clerk Norman Dorsen, "he never personally criticized another Justice or anyone else."[73] An ally of Justice Felix Frankfurter, Justice Harlan urged judicial restraint on an activist court.[74] He chided judges who believed "that all deficiencies in our society which have failed of correction by other means should find a cure in the courts."[75] He believed "this cosmic view of the place of the judiciary" endangered the very integrity of the judicial system.[76] Justice Harlan had a great respect for the Bill of Rights; he authored the seminal First Amendment case *NAACP v. Alabama*.[77] But he did not agree with the Court that the Fourteenth Amendment had incorporated the Bill of Rights—and decades of Supreme Court jurisprudence—against the states. He dissented, "[N]either history, nor sense, supports using the Fourteenth Amendment to put the States in a constitutional straightjacket."[78] Ironically, it was Justice Harlan's grandfather who first argued for incorporation—in a dissent.[79]

Justice Harlan retired from the bench on September 23, 1971, and died of cancer three months later.[80] He left behind his wife, Ethel, and daughter, Eve.[81]

Rick Sawyer

1. JUSTICE JOHN MARSHALL HARLAN II: REMEMBRANCES BY HIS LAW CLERKS (Norman Dorsen & Amelia Ames Newcomb eds., 2001) (remembrance of Charles Fried).

2. *Id.*

3. TINSLEY E. YARBOROUGH, JOHN MARSHALL HARLAN: GREAT DISSENTER OF THE WARREN COURT 9 (1992).

4. *Id.* at 9-12.

5. *Id.* at 12, 79.
6. *Id.* at 13.
7. *Id.*
8. *Id.* at 15.
9. REMEMBRANCES BY HIS LAW CLERKS, *supra* note 1 (remembrance of Martin D. Minsker).
10. *Id.*
11. *Buckner to Resign Within Two Months*, N.Y. TIMES, Feb. 26, 1927, at 17.
12. *Would Put Padlock on Mayer Brewery*, N.Y. TIMES, Nov. 3, 1925, at 27; *Liquor Fraud Laid to 27 Physicians*, N.Y. TIMES, Mar. 18, 1926, at 1.
13. *Locks Go on 6 Cafes, Last of 14 on List*, N.Y. TIMES, May 1, 1925, at 3; *Buckner to Drop 297 Padlock Cases*, N.Y. TIMES, Mar. 19, 1927, at 19.
14. *Elks Lose Fight to Stop Inquiry*, N.Y. TIMES, Nov. 14, 1925, at 17.
15. *Police Investigate Tale of Stage Orgy*, N.Y. TIMES, Feb. 25, 1926, at 3.
16. *Id.* at 25.
17. *Harlan Dies at 72; On Court 16 Years*, N.Y. TIMES, Dec. 30, 1971, at 1, 29.
18. YARBOROUGH, *supra* note 3, at 28.
19. *Buckner to Resign Within Two Months*, *supra* note 11.
20. REMEMBRANCES BY HIS LAW CLERKS, *supra* note 1 (remembrance of William T. Lifland).
21. *Id.*
22. YARBOROUGH, *supra* note 3, at 43-44.
23. *Id.* at 43.
24. *Id.* at 44.
25. *Id.* at 45.
26. DAVID M. DORSEN, HENRY FRIENDLY: GREATEST JUDGE OF HIS ERA 39 (2012).
27. *Id.*
28. YARBOROUGH, *supra* note 3, at 46-49.
29. *Id.* at 49.
30. *Harlan Dies at 72*, *supra* note 17, at 29.
31. YARBOROUGH, *supra* note 3, at 52-57.
32. *Id.* at 57.
33. *Id.* at 58.
34. *Id.* at 59.
35. *Id.*
36. *Id.*
37. TIMOTHY L. HALL, SUPREME COURT JUSTICES: A BIOGRAPHICAL DICTIONARY 355 (2001).
38. YARBOROUGH, *supra* note 3, at 63-69.
39. *Id.* at 65.
40. *Harlan Dies at 72*, *supra* note 17, at 29.
41. United States v. E.I. du Pont de Nemours & Co., 353 U.S. 586 (1957).
42. *Harlan Dies at 72, supra* note 17, at 29; *Harlan is Named to Federal Bench*, N.Y. TIMES, Jan. 14, 1954, at 8.
43. YARBOROUGH, *supra* note 3, at 74.
44. *Id.*
45. *Id.* at 76.
46. *Id.*
47. *Id.* at 77.
48. *Id.*
49. *Id.* at 79.
50. *Id.* at 80.

51. *Id.* at 79-80, 82.

52. *Another Judge Harlan?*, N.Y. TIMES, Jan. 15, 1954, at 18.

53. YARBOROUGH, *supra* note 3, at 80-81.

54. *Id.* at 82.

55. 216 F.2d 354 (2d Cir. 1954).

56. *Court Kills Plea of 13 Lesser Reds*, N.Y. TIMES, Oct. 15, 1954, at 14.

57. *Flynn*, 216 F.2d at 376.

58. *Id.* at 389.

59. Dennis v. United States, 341 U.S. 494, 509-11 (1951).

60. *Flynn*, 216 F.2d at 366.

61. YARBOROUGH, *supra* note 3, at 87.

62. *Id.*

63. *Again Mr. Justice Harlan*, N.Y. TIMES, Nov. 10, 1954, at 32.

64. YARBOROUGH, *supra* note 3, at 92.

65. *Id.* at 90-91.

66. *Id.* at 104.

67. *Id.* at 100.

68. *Id.* at 92-94.

69. *Id.* at 112.

70. *Supreme Court Nominations, present-1789*, UNITED STATES SENATE, http://www.senate.gov/pagelayout/reference/nominations/Nominations.htm.

71. YARBOROUGH, *supra* note 3, at 113.

72. Earl Warren, *Mr. Justice Harlan, As Seen by a Colleague*, 85 HARV. L. REV. 369, 370 (1971).

73. REMEMBRANCES BY HIS LAW CLERKS, *supra* note 1 (remembrance of Norman Dorsen).

74. YARBOROUGH, *supra* note 3, at 120.

75. John M. Harlan, *Thoughts at a Dedication: Keeping the Judicial Function in Balance*, 49 A.B.A. J. 943, 943 (1963).

76. *Id.*

77. 357 U.S. 449 (1958).

78. Duncan v. Louisiana, 391 U.S. 145, 175 (1968) (Harlan, J., dissenting).

79. Hurtado v. California, 4 S.Ct. 292 (1884) (Harlan, J., dissenting); *see also* Plessy v. Ferguson, 163 U.S. 537, 552 (1896) (Harlan, J., dissenting).

80. *Harlan Dies at 72*, *supra* note 17, at 29.

81. *Id.*

# J. EDWARD LUMBARD, JR.
# 1901-1999

Court of Appeals for the Second Circuit: 1955-1997

Joseph Edward Lumbard, Jr., "was an admirable jurist, and a remarkable individual, in every respect."[1] He was born on August 18, 1901 in New York City, and grew up at 116th Street and Seventh Avenue.[2] Lumbard's father, Joseph Edward Lumbard, Sr., was a physician from Acushnet, Massachusetts, who worked his way through medical school at the University of Vermont and moved to New York City after graduation.[3]

Lumbard attended public schools.[4] He was a bright student: he skipped grades and finished DeWitt Clinton High School in three and a half years.[5] Lumbard was heavily involved in the Harlem YMCA.[6] He spent most summers at the YMCA boys' camp in Cold Spring, New York, from age 13 until he finished law school.[7] The YMCA gave Lumbard a taste of debate and public speaking: he gave his first public speech at the age of 12, announcing a future event in the Harlem YMCA auditorium.[8] Lumbard continued to pursue his interests in public speaking and debate throughout high school, where he was elected class representative and won medals in various oratorical contests.[9]

Lumbard graduated from high school in 1918.[10] He received a New York State Regents scholarship to attend college. Although few high school students went on to attend college at the time, his father, whom Lumbard described as "a New Englander and a Unitarian," was "anxious" for him to go to college, and Harvard in particular.[11]

Lumbard enrolled at Harvard College in 1918, at the age of 17.[12] Then known as Joseph, he focused on American history, studying under Frederick Jackson Turner, Samuel Eliot Morison, and Edward Channing.[13] Lumbard's education was interrupted when Harvard's Secret Court of 1920 expelled him. The Secret Court was formed to investigate charges of homosexual activity among students.[14] The Secret Court did not find that Lumbard engaged in homosexual relations, but expelled him nonetheless because of his friendship with his roommate, Edward Say, an active member of Harvard's gay scene.[15] Lumbard had accompanied Say to parties hosted by members of Say's social circle, which the Secret Court deemed a sufficient reason to expel him.[16] Years later, one of Lumbard's law clerks would comment that this incident reflected his "solidarity for friends in the face of discrimination . . . [his] humanity, independence, and support for the underdog."[17]

Showing immeasurable "'grit' in coming back from the setback to later excel,"[18] Lumbard was readmitted to Harvard College a year later, and graduated with his classmates in 1922.[19] During his year away, Lumbard worked as a messenger for a New York City law firm and attended Fordham Law School at night.[20] In spite of the Secret Court's actions, Judge Lumbard went on to have an illustrious legal career that spanned eight decades and fittingly, was elected to Harvard's Board of Overseers from 1959 to 1969.[21]

After he graduated from Harvard College, Judge Lumbard entered Harvard Law School, graduating in 1925.[22] Following law school, he accepted an offer from Emory R. Buckner to become an Assistant United States Attorney for the Southern District of New York.[23] At the time, future Supreme Court Justice John Harlan was chief of the Prohibition division, to which Lumbard was assigned.[24] It was the beginning of a close, lifelong friendship between Lumbard and Harlan. While at the United States Attorney's Office, Lumbard and Harlan would play golf on the weekends in Englewood, New Jersey.[25]

Lumbard continued to work in the Prohibition division until 1928, when a scandal erupted in Queens over the cost of sewer construction.[26] In response to allegations of kickbacks, New York Governor Alfred E. Smith appointed Buckner as a special prosecutor.[27] Buckner named Harlan as his chief assistant, and Lumbard worked as Harlan's assistant.[28] The investigation resulted in several indictments, including that of Queens Borough President Maurice E. Connolly.[29] After Connolly was convicted, Lumbard worked on the appeal.[30]

In the summer of 1929, Lumbard married Polly Poindexter, a graduate of Smith College from Connecticut who went on to study architecture at both Columbia University and the Massachusetts Institute of Technology.[31] The couple married in Fontainebleau, France, where Polly was spending the summer at Fontainebleau's architectural school.[32] Lumbard and Polly had two children, Abigail and Thomas.[33]

After the kickbacks case in Queens, Lumbard made a name for himself as a tough prosecutor.[34] He moved between the United States Attorney's Office and the private sector several times. In 1929, Lumbard left the office to form a partnership with a friend from Harvard and a fellow assistant in the Prohibition division.[35] Lumbard returned to the United States Attorney's Office in 1931 to serve as the chief of its criminal division, working under George Z. Medalie and Thomas E. Dewey.[36]

In 1933, Lumbard left the United States Attorney's Office again to help found Donovan, Leisure, Newton & Lumbard.[37] One of the law firm's leading partners was General William J.

Donovan, also known as "Wild Bill."[38] Donovan was a well-known World War I hero and recipient of the Congressional Medal of Honor;[39] his contacts throughout the United States helped the firm grow quickly.[40] Donovan Leisure would represent a wide variety of clients over the years, including oil companies and trade associations, and tackled issues ranging from corporate to antitrust to criminal law.[41]

At Donovan Leisure, Lumbard also worked on important pro bono matters. In 1935, the American Civil Liberties Union enlisted the firm to defend ten copper miners in New Mexico who were charged with murder arising from labor unrest.[42] After the miners went on strike, the mining company evicted them from their company-owned homes, sparking a riot during which a sheriff was killed.[43] Lumbard traveled to New Mexico to organize the miners' defense and secured acquittals for many of them.[44]

Lumbard worked at Donovan Leisure until the 1950s, but left the firm several times for public service. In 1935, he served as a special assistant attorney general of New York in the investigation of the murder of a Brooklyn garage worker widely known as the "Drukman Murder" case.[45] In the early days of World War II, Lumbard helped Donovan form the Office of Strategic Services, the precursor to the CIA.[46] (Two of his future colleagues on the bench, Walter Mansfield and Murray Gurfein, also worked for Donovan at the OSS.) Lumbard served another stint as a New York special assistant attorney general in 1943, overseeing a newly formed elections fraud bureau.[47] Although the Attorney General's Office had investigated election law violations and fraud in the past, this was the first time a "large permanent bureau" was established to handle the problem throughout New York.[48]

In 1947, Lumbard accepted a six-month appointment to the New York State Supreme Court in New York County, filling the vacancy created by the death of Justice Francis Martin.[49] Lumbard subsequently ran as a Republican for a full term on the court, but lost the election in the overwhelmingly Democratic county.[50] Years later, he commented that although serving on the court was a good experience, he was "very glad to return to private practice."[51] Back at Donovan Leisure, he tried several important cases, including an antitrust case against Imperial

Chemical Industries, the DuPont Company, and Remington Arms.[52]

Through his membership in the Young Republicans and work in the Republican Party, Lumbard became close to Thomas E. Dewey, a future governor of New York, and Herbert Brownell, who would serve as attorney general under President Dwight D. Eisenhower.[53] Lumbard served as Dewey's assistant campaign manager, under Brownell, in Dewey's second unsuccessful run for president.[54] In 1953, due in part to the influence of Governor Dewey and Attorney General Brownell, Lumbard was appointed United States Attorney for the Southern District of New York, where he served for two and a half years.[55]

As United States Attorney, Lumbard handled several high-profile cases, including the prosecution of Gerhard Puff, who was charged with murdering an FBI agent; post-conviction motions in the Julius and Ethel Rosenberg capital espionage case; the prosecution of Puerto Rican nationalists who fired shots at members of the U.S. House of Representatives on the floor of the House in 1954; and the income tax prosecution of Frank Costello, a prominent underworld figure.[56] Lumbard also had considerable influence over the appointment of district judges, including Lloyd F. MacMahon, Harold R. Tyler, Arnold D. Bauman, Gerard L. Goettel, Richard Owen, Robert W. Sweet, and Leonard B. Sand.[57] Overall, Lumbard helped to appoint about 70 Assistant United States Attorneys to the state and federal benches.[58] Lumbard initiated programs for training law students in the United States Attorney's Office and improved the standards for hiring new attorneys.[59] Lumbard later said that he took care to ensure that there was "a good cross section" of ethnic, religious, and racial backgrounds among both assistants and judges.[60]

In 1955, President Dwight D. Eisenhower appointed Lumbard to the Court of Appeals for the Second Circuit.[61] Four years later, Judge Lumbard became chief judge.[62] His colleagues included Learned Hand, Henry Friendly, Charles Clark, and Harold Medina.[63] Judge Friendly became a close friend.[64] As chief judge, Judge Lumbard instituted several changes to the court's administration and management. He began scheduling appellate arguments for specific dates to ensure that the judges hearing each case were familiar with it.[65] Previously, the court's calendar for a particular week would list twenty or more cases; every Monday, the attorneys in those cases had to appear in court to schedule their arguments.[66] Judge Lumbard stopped that practice, commenting, "Lawyers should have better things to do with their time."[67] Judge Lumbard also began encouraging his fellow judges to read the parties' briefs prior to oral argument.[68]

Judge Lumbard expedited the process for deciding easy cases. In 1961, he and other judges and lawyers visited England to confer with appellate judges there.[69] Judge Lumbard noticed that his English counterparts would decide cases immediately following oral argument, and instituted a similar process in the Second Circuit for cases that did not warrant an opinion.[70] By the time Judge Lumbard assumed senior status, the court was deciding approximately 40 percent of its cases in this way.[71] (Summary orders would later replace this practice.)[72] Judge Lumbard also expedited the process for deciding the increasing number of pro se appeals by creating the Pro Se Clerk's Office.[73]

Judge Lumbard remained committed to improving the criminal justice system and pushed for court system reforms.[74] In 1964, he gave a keynote speech at a summer convention for the National District Attorneys Association in which he expressed his concern about law enforcement's abilities to adapt to the changing times and the courts' increasing tendency to specify a criminal defendant's legal rights.[75] He commented, "Surely there has never been a time when our bar and our bench were better trained and more expert in civil matters—yet never a time when the level of professional effort in the criminal courts was at lower ebb."[76] Improvements, he said, were needed in the systems of setting bail, depoliticizing the process for appointing prosecutors, providing annual reports to the public, and encouraging a system for providing competent counsel for the indigent.[77]

Judge Lumbard frequently wrote articles, participated in panel discussions, and commented on criminal justice.[78] These issues were at the fore of public discussion,[79] particularly after the Supreme Court's decision in *Gideon v. Wainwright*,[80] which extended the right to counsel to felony cases in state courts. From 1963 to 1968, Judge Lumbard served as chairman of the

American Bar Association's Committee to Develop Minimum Standards for Criminal Justice.[81] He worked with law professors, judges, and other members of the bar to produce about 18 separate reports, which proposed improvements to the administration of criminal justice.[82]

In 1971, Judge Lumbard assumed senior status. He persuaded four of his colleagues to join him, which allowed for the appointment of five new judges to the circuit.[83] These appointments were sorely needed to handle the court's increasing caseload.[84]

After taking senior status, Judge Lumbard continued to mentor his law clerks. Referring to them as "Assistant Judges," Judge Lumbard instructed his clerks to approach each case on the merits, and frequently warned that they should "never assume a God-damn thing!"[85] On one occasion, Judge Lumbard received a petition to declare the Vietnam War unconstitutional. Two of his clerks spent hours poring over the petition and writing a long bench memo explaining why the war was unconstitutional. After reading the memo, Judge Lumbard responded, "Boys, I can't enjoin the war!"[86]

The writing of his law clerks mattered to Judge Lumbard: he would occasionally bring a short story to chambers to highlight what he viewed as good writing,[87] and "[t]wo things were banned from his work—showy big words and split infinitives."[88] Legal writing, in his eyes, should be "simple, direct, and complete," particularly in a statement of facts.[89] He was never satisfied with a draft that referred "antiseptically" to the parties as "plaintiff" or "defendant"; as he once remarked to a clerk, "these are real people. Give their names and backgrounds."[90] Furthering his role as a mentor, Judge Lumbard even took on trials as a district court judge (an unusual practice for a circuit judge) so that his law clerks could observe and work on both trials and appeals.[91]

Judge Lumbard also had a "remarkable memory for cases and case citations. He could literally recall a case, and go straight to the volume where the decision appeared, without referring to any notes."[92] This memory extended to personal details about his friends and colleagues. Judge Kevin Thomas Duffy, a Lumbard law clerk, remarked that Judge Lumbard not only remembered

Duffy's wedding anniversary (and once reminded him to buy his wife a present), but knew the birthdays of the judge's friends, his former colleagues from the United States Attorney's Office, and all of his law clerks.[93]

Together with Judges Learned Hand and Henry Friendly, Judge Lumbard considered whether to reverse a conviction in which a judge rendered an inconsistent verdict.[94] A grand jury had indicted the defendant, Joseph Maybury, on two counts that related to a $68 U.S. Treasury check: the first charged Maybury with forging another person's name on the back of the check, and the second charged him with "uttering," or "publishing," the check with the knowledge that it had been forged.[95] The judge acquitted Maybury of forgery, but found him guilty of uttering—an inconsistent verdict.[96] Judge Friendly, who would eventually write for the majority, favored a new trial on both counts, drawing a distinction between verdicts reached by judges versus juries.[97] Judge Lumbard, who wrote a partial dissent, voted to dismiss the indictment in its entirety, relying on precedent relating to inconsistent jury verdicts. His view was that retrial on the first count would be foreclosed by double jeopardy (a point supported by one of the Supreme Court cases Judge Friendly cited)[98] and retrial on the second count would be foreclosed by collateral estoppel—"determination of the fact of Maybury's knowledge of his lack of authority favorable to him in the first trial precludes a new determination of the same fact in a second suit."[99] Judge Hand resolved the impasse by voting in favor of sustaining the acquittal on the first count and reversing only the uttering conviction and remanding for a new trial on that count.[100] The decision touched on many complicated aspects of criminal and constitutional law, and carefully analyzed Supreme Court precedent.

Judge Lumbard was on the panel that heard the landmark case of *Bivens v. Six Unknown Named Agents of the Federal Bureau of Narcotics*.[101] Walter Bivens sued federal agents for damages on the grounds that they searched his home and arrested him without a warrant, in violation of his Fourth Amendment rights.[102] The district court dismissed Bivens's complaint for lack of subject matter jurisdiction, reasoning that there is no private right of action under the Fourth Amendment; in the alternative, it concluded that even if there were such a right, the federal agents were immune from suit.[103] Judge Lumbard's opinion for the court affirmed, concluding that the Fourth Amendment did not authorize private suits for damages caused by unreasonable searches and seizures, without reaching the immunity issue.[104] The Supreme Court reversed and remanded, holding that federal courts could infer a private right of action for monetary damages against federal officials if no other federal remedy existed for the violation of constitutional rights.[105]

On remand, the Second Circuit, in an opinion by Judge Medina, held that federal agents did not have immunity from damages suits alleging violations of constitutional rights; however, establishing that the agent acted in good faith and with reasonable belief in the validity of the arrest and search warrant, as here, was a valid defense.[106] Judge Lumbard concurred, emphasizing that in evaluating the reasonableness defense, "there are two standards to be considered": first, "what constitutes reasonableness for purposes of defining probable cause under the [F]ourth [A]mendment for the protection of citizens against governmental overreaching"; second, and "less stringent," was "the reasonable man standard of the tort action against government agents."[107] This second standard, Judge Lumbard suggested, was more appropriate, because it is difficult for federal agents to predict "what federal judges frequently have considerable difficulty in deciding and about which they frequently differ among themselves."[108]

Other opinions by Lumbard ran the gamut from arcane distinctions between summary and plenary jurisdiction under the Bankruptcy Act,[109] to whether a prior conviction on predicate acts was necessary to bring a civil RICO suit.[110] He initiated the creation of the Second Circuit's Speedy Trial Rules when, to his dismay, he learned during an oral argument that the appellant had been detained for more than a year before trial.[111]

Judge Lumbard once remarked that "[j]udicial temperament means to be a good listener, to be patient, to be considerate."[112] He criticized judges who were "arbitrary . . . and unreasonable,"[113] and believed that the most important way to strengthen the federal judiciary was to support those who have "the essential qualifications of judicial temperament and experience and ability and good health and [who are] generally . . . decent human being[s]."[114] Second Circuit Judge Debra Ann Livingston, a Lumbard law clerk, remarked in a letter that he taught by his own example on the bench, "what it means to have a good character, and to act in accordance with that character, both at momentous points in one's life, and in the daily goings on around a law office."[115]

When it came to deciding difficult cases, Judge Lumbard was known as practical, thoughtful, and restrained.[116] He was not an ideologue,[117] nor did he "try to change the world" with each opinion.[118] With difficult issues he focused on the facts of each individual case, one at a time. He once commented to a law clerk who had asked about the implications of a decision, "I am not deciding the next case. I have to decide this case."[119] If he was wrong, he said, "there are nine people in Washington who can tell me so."[120] Although he had once been a prosecutor and would direct his law clerks to read the briefs from the United States Attorney's Office first, Judge Lumbard "held [that] office to the highest standards and would be merciless on the government if it slipped up."[121]

As Judge Lumbard once remarked to Judge Duffy, "All any of us can do is try to do what is fair and just under the circumstances."[122] Judge Lumbard retired in 1997, two years before his death on June 7, 1999, at his home in Fairfield, Connecticut.[123] He was 97 years old.[124]

Emily Seiderman

1. E-mail from Allan J. Arffa, former law clerk, to Guy Miller Struve (Mar. 13, 2015, 3:47 EST) (on file with the United States Courts Library for the Second Circuit). Arffa is a partner at Paul Weiss. Struve is senior counsel at Davis, Polk & Wardwell, LLP.

2. A CONVERSATION WITH J. EDWARD LUMBARD: AN ORAL HISTORY PROJECT OF COLUMBIA UNIVERSITY AND THE NEW YORK BAR FOUNDATION 1 (1980).

3. *Id.*

4. *Id.*

5. *Id.* at 1–2.

6. *See id.* at 1.

7. *Id.* at 1–2.

8. *Id.* at 2.

9. *Id.*

10. Nick Ravo, *J. Edward Lumbard, Jr., 97, Judge and Prosecutor, is Dead*, N.Y. TIMES, June 7, 1999, at B9.

11. A CONVERSATION WITH J. EDWARD LUMBARD, *supra* note 2, at 3.

12. *Id.*

13. JEFFREY B. MORRIS, FEDERAL JUSTICE IN THE SECOND CIRCUIT 173 (1987).

14. *See* Amit R. Paley, *The Secret Court of 1920: Part I*, THE HARV. CRIMSON (Nov. 21, 2002), http://www.thecrimson.com/article/2002/11/21/the-secret-court-of-1920-at/?page=single.

15. *See id.*

16. WILLIAM WRIGHT, HARVARD'S SECRET COURT: THE SAVAGE 1920 PURGE OF CAMPUS HOMOSEXUALS 88–91, 176–77 (2005).

17. E-mail from Lyndon M. Tretter, former law clerk, to Guy Miller Struve (Mar. 9, 2015, 11:24 EST) (on file with the United States Courts Library for the Second Circuit). Tretter is a partner at Schlam, Stone & Dolan.

18. E-mail from Ira Rubinfeld, former law clerk, to Guy Miller Struve (Mar. 9, 2015, 1:44 EST) (on file with the United States Courts Library for the Second Circuit). Rubinfeld is a member of Ray, Quinney & Newbeker.

19. WRIGHT, *supra* note 16, at 178.

20. A CONVERSATION WITH J. EDWARD LUMBARD, *supra* note 2, at 4.

21. Ravo, *supra* note 10.

22. *Obituary: J. Edward Lumbard, Jr.*, N.Y. L.J., June 7, 1999, at 32.

23. A CONVERSATION WITH J. EDWARD LUMBARD, *supra* note 2, at 8–9.

24. *Id.*

25. *Id.* at 12.

26. *See id.*

27. Ravo, *supra* note 10.

28. *Id.*

29. *Id.*; A CONVERSATION WITH J. EDWARD LUMBARD, *supra* note 2, at 14.

30. A CONVERSATION WITH J. EDWARD LUMBARD, *supra* note 2, at 14.

31. *Polly Poindexter Married in France: Student in Architecture is Wed to J. Edward Lumbard, Jr., New York Lawyer*, N.Y. TIMES, Sept. 6, 1929, at 33.

32. *Id.*

33. *Obituary: J. Edward Lumbard, Jr.*, *supra* note 22.

34. Nathan Lewin, *Memories of Judge J. Edward Lumbard, Jr.: A Remembrance*, N.Y. L.J., June 24, 1999, at 27.

35. A CONVERSATION WITH J. EDWARD LUMBARD, *supra* note 2, at 14.

36. MORRIS, *supra* note 13, at 173; Ravo, *supra* note 10.

37. MORRIS, *supra* note 13, at 173.

38. *Id.*

39. A CONVERSATION WITH J. EDWARD LUMBARD, *supra* note 2, at 18.

40. *Id.*

41. *Id.* at 18–19, 24–25; WRIGHT, *supra* note 16, at 179.

42. A CONVERSATION WITH J. EDWARD LUMBARD, *supra* note 2, at 23–24; Ravo, *supra* note 10. For more information about the labor unrest, see LOUIS COLMAN, NIGHT RIDERS IN GALLUP (1935).

43. A CONVERSATION WITH J. EDWARD LUMBARD, *supra* note 2, at 24–25; State v. Ochoa, 72 P.2d 609, 611 (1937).

44. A CONVERSATION WITH J. EDWARD LUMBARD, *supra* note 2, at 24–25.

45. *Id.* at 25; Ravo, *supra* note 10.

46. WRIGHT, *supra* note 16, at 180.

47. *Id.*; Ravo, *supra* note 10.

48. *Vote Fraud Board Created by State: Goldstein Sets Up New Bureau for Election Inquiries Under J. E. Lumbard, Jr.*, N.Y. TIMES, Oct. 7, 1943, at 11.

49. A CONVERSATION WITH J. EDWARD LUMBARD, *supra* note 2, at 32.

50. *Id.* at 32-34; *see also Vote for Lumbard Urged by City Bar*, N.Y. TIMES, Oct. 22, 1947, at 33.

51. *Id.* at 34.

52. *Id.* at 37.

53. *Id.* at 29–31, 39; MORRIS, *supra* note 13, at 173.

54. *Obituary: J. Edward Lumbard, Jr.*, *supra* note 22.

55. A CONVERSATION WITH J. EDWARD LUMBARD, *supra* note 2, at 39; Rayo, *supra* note 12.

56. A CONVERSATION WITH J. EDWARD LUMBARD, *supra* note 2, at 44-47; *see also* Edward Ranzal, *Anti-U.S. Plot Is Laid to 17 Puerto Ricans*, N.Y. TIMES, May 27, 1954, at 1.

57. MORRIS, *supra* note 13, at 173–74.

58. A CONVERSATION WITH J. EDWARD LUMBARD, *supra* note 2, at 41.

59. *Id.* at 40–44.

60. *Id.* at 41.

61. *Obituary: J. Edward Lumbard, Jr.*, *supra* note 22.

62. Lewin, *supra* note 39.

63. *Id.*

64. *See* E-mail from Lyndon M. Tretter, *supra* note 17.

65. Ravo, *supra* note 10.

66. A CONVERSATION WITH J. EDWARD LUMBARD, *supra* note 2, at 63; District Judge Kevin Thomas Duffy, Remarks at a Special Session of the United States Court of Appeals for the Second Circuit, In Memoriam, Honorable J. Edward Lumbard 22 (Sept. 22, 1999) (transcript on file with the United States Courts Library for the Second Circuit).

67. District Judge Kevin Thomas Duffy, Remarks, *supra* note 67, at 22.

68. A CONVERSATION WITH J. EDWARD LUMBARD, *supra* note 2, at 64.

69. *Id.* at 65.

70. *Id.*

71. *Id.* at 66.

72. MORRIS, *supra* note 13, at 174.

73. District Judge Kevin Thomas Duffy, Remarks, *supra* note 67, at 21.

74. *See* WRIGHT, *supra* note 16, at 179–80.

75. Francis X. Clines, *Judge Says Professional Level in Criminal Courts is "at Ebb,"* N.Y. TIMES, Aug. 19, 1964, at 14.

76. *Id.*

77. *Id.*

78. *See, e.g.*, J. Edward Lumbard, Remarks before the Richmond County Bar Association: The Criminal Justice Revolution and the Grand Jury (May 16, 1967); Address to the Annual Judicial Conference, Second Judicial Circuit of the United States (June 25, 1964), *in* 37 F.R.D. 365 (1964); J. Edward Lumbard, *Trial by Jury and Speedy Justice*, 28 WASH. & LEE L. REV. 309 (1971); J. Edward Lumbard, *The Citizen's Role in Law Enforcement*, 56 J. CRIM. L., CRIMINOLOGY, & POLICE SCI. 67 (1965); Arnold H. Lubasch, *Project for National Standards of Criminal Justice Wins Funds*, N.Y. TIMES, Dec. 30, 1964.

79. A CONVERSATION WITH J. EDWARD LUMBARD, *supra* note 2, at 79.

[80] 372 U.S. 335 (1963).

81. A CONVERSATION WITH J. EDWARD LUMBARD, *supra* note 2, at 79; *see also Obituary: J. Edward Lumbard, Jr.*, *supra* note 22.

82. A CONVERSATION WITH J. EDWARD LUMBARD, *supra* note 2, at 79.

83. MORRIS, *supra* note 13, at 174.

84. *Id.*

85. *See* e-mail from Lyndon M. Tretter, *supra* note 17.

86. E-mail from James Bieke, former law clerk, to Guy Miller Struve (Mar. 16, 2015, 3:29 EST) (on file with the United States Courts Library for the Second Circuit). Bieke is a partner at Sidley Austin.

87. E-mail from Ira Rubinfeld, *supra* note 18.

88. District Judge Kevin Thomas Duffy, Remarks, *supra* note 67, at 21.

89. *Id.*

90. E-mail from Lyndon M. Tretter, *supra* note 17.

91. E-mail from Allan J. Arffa, *supra* note 1.

92. E-mail from Ira Rubinfeld, *supra* note 18; *see also* e-mail from Thomas Moers Mayer, former law clerk, to Guy Miller Struve (Mar. 15, 2015, 11:03 EST) (on file with the U.S. Courts Library for the Second Circuit). Mayer is a partner at Kramer, Levin, Naftalis & Frankel.

93. District Judge Kevin Thomas Duffy, Remarks, *supra* note 67, at 23.

94. *See* DAVID M. DORSEN, HENRY FRIENDLY: GREATEST JUDGE OF HIS ERA 177 (2012); United States v. Maybury, 274 F.2d 899 (2d Cir. 1960).

95. DORSEN, *supra* note 95, at 177–78.

96. *Id.*; *Maybury*, 274 F.2d at 901.

97. DORSEN *supra* note 95, at 178–79.

98. *Maybury*, 274 F.2d at 904 (citing United States v. Ball, 163 U.S. 662 (1896)).

99. *Id.* at 907 (Lumbard, C.J., dissenting in part).

100. *Id.* at 908 (Hand, J., dissenting in part and concurring in part).

101. 409 F.2d 718 (2d Cir. 1969), *rev'd*, 403 U.S. 388 (1971), *remanded to* 456 F.2d 1339 (2d Cir. 1972).

102. *Bivens*, 409 F.2d at 719.

103. *Id.* at 719–20

104. *Id.* at 720–21.

105. Bivens v. Six Unknown Named Agents of the Fed. Bureau of Narcotics, 403 U.S. 388, 389 (1971).

106. Bivens v. Six Unknown Named Agents of the Fed. Bureau of Narcotics, 456 F.2d 1339, 1341 (2d Cir. 1972).

107. *Id.* at 1348–49 (Lumbard, J., concurring).

108. *Id.* at 1349.

109. Redington v. Touche Ross & Co., 612 F.2d 68 (2d Cir. 1979).

110. Sedima, S.P.R.L. v. Imrex Co., 741 F.2d 482 (2d Cir. 1984) *rev'd*, 473 U.S. 479 (1985).

111. E-mail from Guy Miller Struve, former law clerk, to Sally Pritchard (Mar. 24, 2015, 3:02 EST) (on file with the United States Courts Library for the Second Circuit).

112. A CONVERSATION WITH J. EDWARD LUMBARD, *supra* note 2, at 94.

113. *Id.* at 93–94.

114. *Id.* at 99.

115. Email from Judge Debra Ann Livingston, former law clerk, to Sally Pritchard (May 6, 2015, 3:01 EST) (on file with the United States Courts Library for the Second Circuit).

116. Judge Thomas J. Meskill, Remarks at a Special Session of the United States Court of Appeals for the Second Circuit, In Memoriam, Honorable J. Edward Lumbard 15 (Sept. 22, 1999) (transcript on file with the United States Courts Library for the Second Circuit).

117. E-mail from Allan J. Arffa, *supra* note 1.

118. Judge Thomas V. Meskill, Remarks, *supra* note 116, at 15.

119. E-mail from Ira Rubinfeld, *supra* note 18.

120. *Id.*

121. E-mail from Lyndon M. Tretter, *supra* note 17.

122. District Judge Kevin Thomas Duffy, Remarks, *supra* note 67, at 20.

123. *Obituary: J. Edward Lumbard, Jr.*, *supra* note 22.

124. *Id.*

# STERRY ROBINSON WATERMAN
# 1901-1984

Court of Appeals for the Second Circuit: 1955-1984

"He looked the part of a great judge, white haired, tall, handsome and full of personality—just as you might imagine from central casting."[1] The appearance was not deceiving.

Waterman was born in Taunton, Massachusetts on June 12, 1901, the son of a dry goods merchant; the family later moved to St. Johnsbury, Vermont, where Waterman lived most of his life.[2] Waterman became an integral part of the Vermont legal community, but his entry into the practice of law, to use the words of another celebrated Vermonter, followed the road "less traveled."[3] After graduating from Dartmouth in 1922, Waterman studied law at Harvard, but left in 1923 to work for Commissioner-General of Immigration William Walter Husband, a fellow Vermonter, in Washington, DC.[4] There, Waterman worked on efforts to amend the Quota Act.[5] Late in life, Judge Waterman described the quotas as "working out very cruelly" and having "unfair results."[6]

Waterman continued his legal education at night at the George Washington University Law School.[7] After he failed to attend his evidence class, the professor refused to allow him to sit for the final examination and prevented him from graduating.[8] But Waterman had already passed the bar exam before graduation; his wife's understanding was that, once he did, he "simply stopped studying."[9]

Waterman would make up for it. Dartmouth awarded him an honorary law degree in 1963 (after Waterman had been on the Second Circuit for eight years).[10] Honorary degrees followed from New York University and the University of Vermont.[11] In 1977, the Vermont Law School, which Waterman had helped to develop (he is "credited with greatly improving [its] chances of gaining ABA accreditation")[12] awarded him a JD degree for his "experiential learning," concluding that "his writings in F.2d over a period of 22 years were the equivalent of one course in Evidence."[13]

Waterman married Frances Chadbourne Knight (whom he had met on a blind date) in 1932.[14] Waterman's best man described Frances as able to "buil[d] up" Waterman on the rare times that was necessary and "[w]ith banter and teasing, she kept his ego within normal restraint and proper parameters."[15] The Watermans had two sons, Robert and Thomas, whom they raised in St. Johnsbury.[16]

Waterman was active in his Vermont community. He served as president of the Board of Trustees of St. Johnsbury Academy (which he and his sons attended), and he and Frances worked with the Congregational Church, the St. Johnsbury Athenaeum, and the Fairbanks Museum.[17] Waterman served as president of the Vermont Bar Association, the American Academy of Judicial Education, and the American Judicature Society.[18] He helped establish the Vermont Law School and served as president of its Board of Trustees; the school continues to hold an annual lecture series named in his honor.[19] In 1983, he received "citizen of the year" awards from both St. Johnsbury and the State of Vermont.[20]

Waterman was a visible figure in Republican politics in Vermont: he founded the Vermont Young Republicans and was a "prominent member of the progressive wing of Vermont's Republican party,"[21] managing the successful gubernatorial campaign of George D. Aiken, but losing his own primary campaign for U.S. Senate in 1946 to Ralph Flanders.[22] (Senator Flanders would later recommend Waterman to President Dwight D. Eisenhower for appointment to the Second Circuit, noting that Waterman's "Republicanism [was] beyond reproach.")[23] He "ventured into presidential politics, managing the Vermont campaign of Republican Alf Landon in 1936."[24] Vermont was one of only two states that Landon won in the landslide for Franklin Delano Roosevelt.[25]

Waterman's legal career in Vermont was varied. He returned home in 1926, after finishing (but not graduating from) law school, and spent a brief time in private practice with the firm of Searles and Graves (subsequently Searles, Graves, and Waterman).[26] As the junior attorney at the firm during Prohibition, he defended bootleggers and rumrunners, and lost a suit against customs officers for wrecking a bootlegger's car: "The bootlegger was going a little too fast, and the bullets were flying, and that was that."[27]

When the Great Depression hit, Waterman started his own practice. His work in that era reflects the struggle to make a living.[28] While practicing law, he also served as assistant secretary of the Vermont Senate from 1933 to 1940, and as the Caledonia County state's attorney from 1933 to 1937.[29] As assistant secretary he earned $7.00 a day,[30] which also had to cover his expenses in Montpelier.[31] For ten years starting in 1936, Waterman was the executive director of the Vermont Unemployment Compensation Commission. He was tasked with building the commission to comply with a federal law that would have otherwise required Vermont to pay "three percent to the United States government . . . that would disappear into Franklin D. Roosevelt's coffers."[32] Waterman enjoyed the work; he remarked in an interview: "We had to build the agency. I'm very fond of building. After I got them built sometimes I lost a little interest in them."[33]

In 1946, Waterman returned to private practice. He ran the Northern Farms Cooperative (an organization for independent milk producers that battled the New England Milk Producers Association),[34] represented the "St. Johnsbury Trucking Company, St. Johnsbury and Lake Champlain Railroad, often called the St. Jeezlebury and Late Coming," as well as small-town clients, and did lobbying work.[35] At Judge Waterman's memorial in the Second Circuit, his law partner John H. Downs noted that Waterman carried scars from the Great Depression: he hesitated to bill clients or request large retainers. The St. Johnsbury Trucking Company paid him $100 per week, even when that week consisted of six or seven days working ten to 12 hours.[36] Downs said of Waterman's time in private practice: "Perhaps in a sense he was marking time, doing well what a fine lawyer has to do, but without much sense of purpose or personal satisfaction." Downs believed that appointment to the bench "literally saved [Judge Waterman's] life."[37]

While in private practice, Waterman was "instrumental in obtaining passage of the Uniform Commercial Code, the law that regulates commercial activity in all 50 states."[38] He did so despite an accident in 1952 that left him with both his arms and legs in traction. "But typical of his courage and stamina and optimism, he recovered . . . fully."[39]

In 1955, President Eisenhower appointed Waterman to the United States Court of Appeals for the Second Circuit. The appointment had the strong backing of Senators Flanders and Aiken. To ensure that one seat on the court would be designated for a Vermonter, they negotiated an agreement whereby J. Edward Lumbard would be appointed—i.e., receive his commission—one day ahead of Waterman, ensuring that Lumbard would become chief judge.[40] Judge Waterman considered preserving the Vermont seat to be his "greatest political accomplishment."[41] Waterman was the second Vermonter on the court; he replaced the first, Judge Harrie Brigham Chase. As he remembered it, he faced a physical difficulty in taking over Judge Chase's place at the bench. In

Judge Waterman's first sitting, he took his seat only to "disappear[] behind the bench" when his chair fell apart. To Judge Frank's query as to whether he was hurt, Judge Waterman replied, "No, I wasn't, but the chair was." A telegram from Judge Chase and Judge Gibson of the District of Vermont "arrived suspiciously soon after the event. . . Either they got the news of the accident very quickly or expected it!"[42]

Judge Waterman kept chambers in St. Johnsbury, first in a maple sugar factory and later, when space opened up, in the local post office.[43] (At least one law clerk remembered fielding requests for syrup in five-gallon cans.)[44] Waterman had a rigorous schedule: a ten-hour work day, a drive home for dinner and an hour of cribbage with Frances, followed by a review of the documents he had brought home. He kept up a similar schedule in New York, staying in a hotel in Murray Hill and taking the subway down to the courthouse at Foley Square.[45]

Judge Waterman participated in more than 600 decisions in his 28 years on the bench.[46] Of particular note is his opinion in *SEC v. Texas Gulf Sulphur Company*,[47] a landmark decision on insider trading. Texas Gulf's officers and employees had traded shares based on an ore strike that had "turn[ed] out to be one of the wealthiest bodies of copper, zinc and silver ever discovered."[48] At the same time, Texas Gulf downplayed the discovery in the press, so that the public was unaware of the possible value of the discovery.[49] Judge Waterman, describing the Securities Exchange Act of 1934 as intended "to prevent inequitable and unfair practices and to insure fairness in securities transactions generally,"[50] held "that company insiders—such as Texas Gulf's officers and directors—may not legally trade in their own company's shares if they are privy to inside information not disclosed publicly."[51] Within days, the decision sold 2,000 copies, resulting in unexpected profits for Record Press, the printing company then responsible for reprinting Second Circuit rulings. The manager of Record Press declared: "This thing is hot as hell. Almost everybody and his uncle who knows anything about law or the stock market wants it. It's the biggest thing we've ever gotten."[52] Judge Waterman wrote the opinion over 18 months;

when it was done, he turned it over to the publisher and left for Vermont.[53]

Another landmark Waterman opinion, *Flood v. Kuhn*,[54] upheld the dismissal of baseball player Curt Flood's challenge to the reserve clause (which precludes players from negotiating with any but the team they initially sign with or to which they are traded). Judge Waterman explained that the court was bound by the Supreme Court's ruling in *Federal Baseball Club v. National League*,[55] that baseball was exempt from antitrust laws: "We freely acknowledge our belief that *Federal Baseball* was not one of Mr. Justice Holmes' happiest days, that the rationale of *Toolson* [that of leaving it to Congress to remove the exemption] is extremely dubious and that, to use the Supreme Court's own adjectives, the distinction between baseball and other professional sports is 'unrealistic,' 'inconsistent' and 'illogical.'"[56] Although Judge Waterman wrote that "we should not fall out of our chairs with surprise at the news that *Federal Baseball* and *Toolson* had been overruled," he considered it unclear that the Supreme Court was "ready to give them a happy despatch."[57] He was right. The Supreme Court affirmed,[58] and *Federal Baseball* remains the law today.[59]

A member of the bar commented that Judge Waterman's opinions had an urgency and immediacy, going out to the bar "like bulletins from a combat zone."

> While he never pretended to be an elegant stylist, his opinions were invested with a simple beauty and deep insight. His literary gifts were those of economy and clarity and a certain willful discipline. He pared language to the bone and wrote in a simple style that was democratic. The grain of his sentences was stark and austere. Few judges revealed so much with so few words.
>
> Among his many strengths none was more dazzling than his ability to reduce the issues in a case to so few lucid lines. In an age of murky prose, this quality won him an enthusiastic readership. Uniquely free of cant, his straightforward decisions were unencumbered by the superfluous scholarly apparatus that burdens so many

> other appellate judgments. We were never in doubt about what Judge Waterman had to say.[60]

Judge Waterman's writing "involved a conscious intent to eschew the making of value judgments," but he believed in a "'function of accommodation' between the rights and duties of the individual on the one hand and the public on the other."[61] A law clerk remembers Judge Waterman remarking on the "difference between being technically right and being morally right, especially when a government agent is the actor."[62] He taught his law clerks that "it was the responsibility of the judiciary to monitor" the interaction between the individual and society "in a way that would ensure, on the one hand, that the workings of the social order are fair and reasonable and hence worthy of respect . . . and, on the other hand, to hold those individuals accountable for their breaches of the social contract."[63]

In 1970, Chief Judge Lumbard convinced Judge Waterman and three others to join him in taking senior status, so that five new judges could be appointed to tackle a rising caseload.[64] Judge Waterman continued to hear cases until just months before his death in February 1984. He died of cancer in St. Johnsbury, Vermont.[65]

In the words of his successor, Judge James L. Oakes: "[I]t is as a human being that he will be best remembered. He cared about other people. From the lowliest to the mighty he was genuinely concerned with their well-being, their progress, their problems."[66] And although he was "not hesitant about letting his views of people, principles, or practicalities be known[,] . . . he did so in a way not to offend, because he was inherently fairminded."[67] Another observer wrote: "He was an open and decent man who always had a smile for everyone."[68] When asked towards the end of his career what he thought was the most important quality in a judge, Judge Waterman replied simply: "To be fair."[69]

Elizabeth Duwe

1. E-mail from James Morse, former law clerk, to Judge Peter W. Hall, (May 26, 2015, 6:50 EST) (transcript on file with the United States Courts Library for the Second Circuit). James Morse clerked for Judge Waterman and went on to a distinguished career as the defender general in Vermont, a superior court judge and associate justice of the Vermont Supreme Court, and commissioner of Vermont's Department of Children and Families.

2. Joseph B. Treaster, *Sterry R. Waterman; U.S. Appeals Judge Served for 28 Years*, N.Y. TIMES, Feb. 9, 1984, at D22.

3. ROBERT FROST, THE ROAD NOT TAKEN (1920).

4. Special Supplement, *Colleagues for Justice: One Hundred Years of the United States Court of Appeals for the Second Circuit,* 65 ST. JOHN'S L. REV. 937, 957-58 (1991); Interview by Gregory Sanford with Judge Waterman, in St. Johnsbury Vt. (July 13, 1981) (transcript on file with the United States Courts Library of the Second Circuit); UNITED STATES CITIZENSHIP AND IMMIGRATION SERVICES, *William Walter Husband*, http://www.uscis.gov/unassigned/william-walter-husband.

5. The Quota Act of 1921 set limits on the number of immigrants on the basis of nationality; the intent was to cut down on immigrants from southern and eastern Europe in favor of those from northern and western Europe. The distinctions in large part were based on race or religion, or in some cases on a perception that immigrants from certain countries were radicals. *See* John M. Lund, *Boundaries of Restriction: The Dillingham Commission*, 6 UNIV. VT. HIST. REV. Dec. 1994 (1994).

6. Interview with Judge Waterman, *supra* note 4.

7. *Colleagues for Justice, supra* note 4, at 957.

8. Granville Brumbaugh, Remarks at a Special Session of the United States Court of Appeals for the Second Circuit, In Memoriam for The Honorable Sterry R. Waterman (Oct. 17, 1984) *in* 751 F.2d XCV. Brumbaugh was a longtime friend of Judge Waterman and was senior partner of Brumbaugh, Graves, Donohue & Raymond.

9. Treaster, *supra* note 2.

10. *Id.*

11. Sally Johnson, *Judge Sterry Waterman Dies at 82*, RUTLAND HERALD, Feb. 8, 1984.

12. E-mail from James Morse, *supra* note 1.

13. Thomas M. Debevoise, Remarks at a Special Session of the United States Court of Appeals for the Second Circuit, In Memoriam for The Honorable Sterry R. Waterman (Oct. 17, 1984) *in* 751 F.2d XCV. Debevoise was a former dean of Vermont Law School. "The Vermont Law School was established in 1972 and held its first classes in the summer of 1973." The first class graduated in 1976 and the school received ABA accreditation in 1978. VERMONT LAW SCHOOL, *History and Mission*, http://www.vermontlaw.edu/community/about-vls/history-mission. Judge Waterman was the president of the Vermont Law School Board of Trustees, and the Sterry R. Waterman Lecture has been given annually since 1975. *See Waterman Lecture*, HERALD RANDOLPH, http://www.ourherald.com/news/2005-04-14/Community_News/com03.html.

14. *Districting Case Judge Sterry Robinson Waterman*, N.Y. TIMES, May 11, 1965, at 28.

15. Brumbaugh, Remarks, *supra* note 8, at C.

16. Treaster, *supra* note 2.

17. Christopher E. Ryan, Letter to the Editor, *Remembering the Legacy of Late Judge Sterry R. Waterman*, LITTLETON RECORD, Jan. 23, 2014.

18. *1983 Vermont Citizen Award Presented to Judge Sterry R. Waterman*, 9 VT. B. J. VT. B. ASS'N 31 (1983).

19. Stephen Dycus, *Introduction to the Sterry R. Waterman Lectures*, 25 VT. L. REV. 449 (2000-2001).

20. Johnson, *supra* note 11.

21. FIND A GRAVE, Sterry Robinson Waterman, http://www.findagrave.com/cgi-bin/fg.cgi?page=gr&GSln=waterman&GSfn=sterry+&GSmn=robinson&GSby=1901&GSbyrel=in&GSdy=1984&GSdyrel=in&GSob=n&GRid=33429328&df=all&.

22. D. Gregory Sanford, *You Can't Get There From Here: The Presidential Boomlet for Governor George D. Aiken, 1937-1939*, 49 VT. HIST. 197, 198 (1981), http://catalog.vermonthistory.org/vhsweb2/tramp2.exe/see_record/A1pj1avp.004?server=1home&item=12&item_source=1home.

23. SHELDON GOLDMAN, PICKING FEDERAL JUDGES: LOWER COURT SELECTION FROM ROOSEVELT THROUGH REAGAN 124 (1997).

24. Johnson, *supra* note 11.

25. *Id.*

26. Virginia C. Downs, *Sterry Robinson Waterman-From Small Town Lawyer to Big City Judge*, 28 Vt. B.J. 19, 19 (2002).

27. *Id.*

28. Interview with Judge Waterman, *supra* note 4. Judge Waterman noted that he initially wanted to run for state's attorney in 1930, in part because the salary was $1,000. *Id.*

29. FIND A GRAVE, *supra* note 21.

30. Interview with Judge Waterman, *supra* note 4.

31. Downs, *supra* note 26, at 19.

32. Interview with Judge Waterman, *supra* note 4.

33. *Id.*

34. Interview with Judge Waterman, *supra* note 4. The firm, which started out as Waterman and Downs, is now Downs, Rachlin, and Martin, the largest law firm in Vermont, with offices in Vermont, New Hampshire, and New York. *See* DOWNS RACHLIN MATRIN PLLC, *About Us*, http://www.drm.com/about-us/history.

35. John H. Downs, Remarks at a Special Session of the United States Court of Appeals for the Second Circuit, In Memoriam for The Honorable Sterry R. Waterman (Oct. 17, 1984) *in* 751 F.2d XCV. Downs founded a firm with Judge Waterman in 1950 named Waterman and Downs and was partner at Downs, Rachlin, and Martin.

36. *Id.*

37. *Id.*

38. Johnson, *supra* note 11.

39. Brumbaugh, Remarks, *supra* note 8.

40. JEFFREY B. MORRIS, FEDERAL JUSTICE IN THE SECOND CIRCUIT 174 (1987); E-mail from James Morse, *supra* note 1.

41. Interview with Judge Waterman, *supra* note 4. The Vermont seat, first held by Judge Chase, then by Judge Waterman, was later filled in turn by Judges James Lowell Oakes, Fred I. Parker, and (currently) Peter W. Hall. *See* UNITED STATES COURT OF APPEALS FOR THE SECOND CIRCUIT, *Judges*, *Peter W. Hall*, http://www.ca2.uscourts.gov/judges/bios/pwh.html.

42. Downs, *supra* note 26, at 19.

43. *Remembering the Legacy*, *supra* note 17.

44. Frederick A. Terry, Jr., former law clerk, Remarks at a Special Session of the United States Court of Appeals for the Second Circuit, In Memoriam for The Honorable Sterry R. Waterman (Oct. 17, 1984) *in* 751 F.2d XCV. Terry serves as senior counsel of Sullivan & Cromwell and as honorary trustee of the Natural Resources Defense Council.

45. *Districting Case Judge Sterry Robison Waterman*, *supra* note 14.

46. Herald Price Fahringer, *Sterry R. Waterman—An Uncommon Man*, N.Y. L.J., Feb. 21, 1984.

47. 401 F.2d 833 (2d Cir. 1968); *see also* Christopher E. Ryan, Letter to the Editor, *Remembering a Great Man from St. Johnsbury*, CALEDONIAN RECORD, Jan. 7, 2010.

48. Terry Robards, *Texas Gulf Drama Is a Tragedy for Key Actors*, N.Y. TIMES, Aug. 18, 1968.

49. SEC v. Texas Gulf Sulphur Co., 401 F.2d 833, 843-47 (2d Cir. 1968) (*en banc*).

50. *Texas Gulf Sulphur*, 401 F.2d at 848.

51. Robards, *supra* note 48, at F1.

52. Alan Adelson, *Texas Gulf Decision Brings a Tidy Profit to Printing Concern*, WALL ST. J., Aug. 19, 1968, at 5.

53. *Id.*

54. 443 F.2d 264, 266 (2d Cir. 1971).

55. 259 U.S. 200 (1922).

56. *Kuhn*, 443 F.2d at 266. Judge Waterman's law clerk at the time, Carl Lisman, initially drafted an opinion ruling in Flood's favor. The draft was returned to him unedited with the following notation from Judge Waterman: "You may think that you have the power to overturn the Supreme Court. I do not have that power. Please revise." E-mail from Carl Lisman to Judge Peter W. Hall (May 27, 2015, 8:40 EST) (on file with the United States Courts Library for the Second Circuit). Lisman is a senior partner in Lisman, Webster, Kirkpatrick & Leckerling in Burlington, VT.

57. *Id.*

58. *Kuhn*, 407 U.S. at 258.

59. For a thorough history of Flood's fight against the reserve clause, see BRAD SNYDER, A WELL-PAID SLAVE, CURT FLOOD'S FIGHT FOR FREE AGENCY IN PROFESSIONAL SPORTS (2006).

60. Fahringer, *supra* note 46. Fahringer was a well-known member of the bar with an infamous roster of clients that included Larry Flynt, Claus von Bulow, and Lynne Stewart. He died in February 2015. *See* Sam Roberts, *Herald Price Fahringer, a Defender of Free Speech, Dies at 87*, N.Y. TIMES, Feb. 19, 2015, http://nyti.ms/1DtGRfk.

61. James L. Oakes, *Judge Sterry R. Waterman: A Dedication*, 50 BROOK L. REV. XVII 1983-1984.

62. E-mail from Carl Lisman, *supra* note 56 (discussing a search and seizure case in which a local sheriff raided a defendant's home, with a warrant, in the early morning while the defendant's family was asleep).

63. Terry, Jr., Remarks, *supra* note 44.

64. MORRIS, *supra* note 40, at 174.

65. Treaster, *supra* note 2.

66. Oakes, *supra* note 61.

67. *Id.*

68. Johnson, *supra* note 11 (quoting Judge Oakes).

69. Fahringer, *supra* note 46.

# LEONARD PAGE MOORE
## 1898-1982

Court of Appeals for the Second Circuit: 1957-1982

Judge Leonard Page Moore described his modest approach to judging this way: "I still have the notion that cases are to decide what's right and wrong between the particular litigants in specific cases, and therefore I try to shy away from speaking in generalities. I have no desire to write for posterity."[1]

Born on July 2, 1898 in Evanston, Illinois, a Chicago suburb,[2] Moore majored in classics at Amherst College, where he was class president and elected to Phi Beta Kappa, and served in the Naval Reserve.[3] He earned tuition money by playing the banjo in a dance band with his roommate, George W. Cornell, who played the piano.[4] In the year following his 1919 graduation,[5] Moore remained at Amherst, teaching Latin, while Cornell went on to

Columbia Law School.[6] But for Cornell, Moore might have remained a teacher; however, Cornell persuaded Moore to join him,[7] and, Moore graduated from Columbia with an LLB degree in 1922.[8]

At Columbia, Moore and Cornell were reunited as bandmates.[9] Performing with Cornell at a Smith College Club dance, Moore met Patricia Brown, who would become his wife.[10] Patricia Brown was the daughter of a prominent New London, Connecticut family that owned and operated the Brown Cotton Gin Company.[11] Moore and Brown announced their engagement in November 1925 and were married on March 8, 1927, in El Paso.[12] They had two sons, Leonard and Dion, and two daughters, Sarah and Margot.[13]

Moore began a career in private practice at the New York firm of Zabriskie, Sage, Gray & Todd.[14] In 1929, he joined the law firm of Chadbourne, Parke, Whiteside & Wolff, now known as Chadbourne & Parke. He was a civil litigator representing significant clients in state and federal courts and before administrative agencies during the litigation boom that followed the 1929 stock market crash.[15] He became a senior litigation partner of the firm in 1934.[16]

District Judge Edward R. Neaher, who, prior to becoming the United States Attorney for the Eastern District of New York, was hired by Moore at Chadbourne. He said of Moore, "Above all, he was a kind and patient teacher, whose door was always open to an associate in need of advice."[17] Moore shared with others his particular expertise in the areas of trial technique and motion practice, lecturing on trial preparation at the Practising Law Institute,[18] and publishing "Motion Practice and Strategy," a booklet that was part of the Trial Practice series published by the Practising Law Institute.[19]

In 1953, Moore left Chadbourne to succeed Frank J. Parker as the United States Attorney for the Eastern District of New York. His fellow New York Republicans Herbert Brownell, Jr., the attorney general, and John R. Crews, the Brooklyn Republican leader, recommended him for the position,[20] and President Dwight D. Eisenhower appointed him. Moore had supported Eisenhower in the 1952 election as treasurer of the Brooklyn

Citizens Committee for Eisenhower.[21] Moore was sworn in by the chief judge of the Eastern District of New York, Robert A. Inch.[22] With his new position came a significant pay cut: the United States Attorney's salary was then only $10,800 per year.[23]

When he became the United States Attorney, Moore had a reputation as one of the city's best litigators, but he had not tried a criminal case.[24] He won the respect of the criminal bar and his staff by personally trying a number of sensitive and complex cases,[25] including the successful prosecution of Internal Revenue Commissioner Joseph D. Nunan, Jr., for tax evasion.[26] Under his leadership, the United States Attorney's office tackled a rash of bank robberies, undertook the first prosecutions involving securities fraud, and focused on the growing problem of drug trafficking.[27] Moore set high professional standards for the United States Attorney's office, emphasizing preparation, fairness, and efficiency, as he believed that the office not only represented the United States but was an outgrowth of it as well.[28] Service as the United States Attorney was a natural fit for Moore, who had a strong commitment to public service. The position led to a judgeship.[29] When Moore was sworn in as United States Attorney, Manhattan Supreme Court Justice Henry Clay Greenberg was quoted as saying that he hoped Moore would take to the bench within two years.[30] In September 1957, President Eisenhower appointed Moore to the Second Circuit.[31] A recess appointee, Judge Moore was formally nominated in January 1958 and received Senate confirmation the following month.[32]

Judge Moore authored over 600 majority opinions and 200 concurring or dissenting opinions.[33] His range was broad, but he is perhaps best remembered for his role in a series of cases on the issues of freedom of speech and obscenity during the 1960s and 1970s.[34] For example, Judge Moore wrote the majority opinion in *United States v. 35 MM. Motion Picture Film "Language of Love."*[35] A New York customs agent had seized the Swedish-made, pseudo-educational film, and shortly after, the United States Attorney sought to have it banned for obscenity.[36] The court ruled that the film was protected under the First Amendment.[37]

Judge Moore was "quite dignified, but he had a wry sense of humor,"[38] which he employed in opinions "to puncture exaggerations and irrelevant argument."[39] For example, when dissenting from the majority's opinion that a Florida restaurant could successfully maintain an unfair competition claim against a Brooklyn restaurant of the same name, Judge Moore wrote,

> I cannot but believe that unfair competition should mean (1) competition and (2) that it is unfair. Obviously, there is no competition between Wolfies (Miami) and Wolfies (Brooklyn). If the Brooklyn College student who seeks physical rehabilitation from his mental debilitation caused by a two-hour examination believes that he is walking across the street into Wolfies of Miami, he would truly be in a state of post-examination shock. Nor is it possible that a family from the midwest, anxious to visit Wolfies, would find itself in Brooklyn instead of Miami. Everyone gets lost in Brooklyn—but not that lost.[40]

Judge Moore took senior status in March 1971, but he continued to sit on the Second Circuit and sat as a visiting judge in all but two of its sister circuit courts.[41][42]

Throughout his career, Judge Moore was recognized with many professional awards and honors. He received honorary degrees from Brooklyn Law School in 1957 and Amherst College in 1959.[43] The Federal Bar Council awarded him the Emory Buckner Medal for Excellence in Jurisprudence in 1965.[44] The Columbia Law School Alumni Association awarded him the Medal for Excellence in 1978.[45]

Those who knew Judge Moore well described him as "the embodiment of the word 'gentleman.'"[46] He was neither arrogant nor demanding of reverence.[47] District Judge John S. Martin, a Moore law clerk who also served as the United States Attorney for the Southern District of New York, said of him: "From our first meeting he was courteous and kind and I never heard him raise his voice. While he had strong views on many of the issues that came before him, he was open to any opposing argument and did not hesitate to change his mind where appropriate."[48] Another clerk recalled that Judge Moore "treat[ed] us clerks as if we were intellectual partners regardless of the vast gaps in our knowledge and experience . . . Judge Moore never gave the impression of having to work at being so unfailingly courteous; it was simply his nature."[49] Moore's graciousness towards his clerks extended beyond chambers; he took genuine interest in their personal lives and often welcomed them to his family home.[50] Another law clerk fondly remembered those gatherings: "Judge [Moore] and Mrs. Moore, called Patty by those who knew her well, were low-key, informal and gracious hosts, ensuring that everyone felt comfortable. The Judge adored being surrounded by younger lawyers with whom he shared a fond attachment."[51]

Judge Moore lived with his family at 118 Willow Street in Brooklyn Heights.[52] As a longtime Brooklyn Heights resident, Judge Moore was active in the affairs of his borough and devoted his time to various community organizations.[53] He was a trustee of the Brooklyn YMCA, a trustee of the Brooklyn Institute of Arts and Sciences, chairman of the Brooklyn Botanic Garden, and member of the Board of Regents of the Long Island College Hospital.[54] In 1967, he was elected president of the Board of Trustees of Brooklyn Law School.[55]

Judge Moore was also a fixture of the community in Mystic, Connecticut. He purchased several acres at 100 Stanton Lane there in 1930 and was only the third owner of the property since the area was settled in the 1600s.[56] The Moore family spent weekends and summers in Mystic,[57] where they kept a turkey farm.[58] The turkey farm was at one point producing as many as 2,000 turkeys per year.[59] Mrs. Moore, in particular, was passionate about the birds: she was involved in all stages of their lives, from incubation to their arrival at market, and turkey shows in between; Judge Moore helped, as deliveryman.[60]

Judge Moore also served as a trustee emeritus of the Mystic Seaport, the popular maritime museum.[61] The Moore family left its mark on Mystic through land donations.[62] In the 1970s, they donated a 35-acre parcel to the town.[63] In 1981, they donated an adjoining 24 acres to the Mashantucket Land Trust.[64] These two parcels of land, along with another parcel donated by a neighbor, make up Beebe Pond Park.[65]

Judge Moore died of pneumonia at the age of 84 on December 7, 1982, at home in Mystic.[66] He had been sitting with the Second Circuit regularly up until a few months before his death.[67] He was survived by his wife, children, and several grandchildren and great grandchildren.[68]

Emer M. Stack

1. District Judge John S. Martin, Jr., Remarks at the Extraordinary Session of the United States Court of Appeals for the Second Circuit, In Memoriam, Honorable Leonard P. Moore 12 (May 10, 1983) (internal quotation marks omitted), *reprinted in* 710 F.2d LXXI.

2. FEDERAL JUDICIAL CENTER, Biographical Directory of Federal Judges, Leonard Page Moore, http://www.fjc.gov/servlet/nGetInfo?jid=1679&cid=999&ctype=na&instate=na.

3. Edward R. Neaher, *Leonard Page Moore*, 49 BROOK. L. REV. xv (1983); District Judge Edward R. Neaher, Remarks at the Extraordinary Session of the United States Court of Appeals for the Second Circuit, In Memoriam, Honorable Leonard P. Moore 6 (May 10, 1983), *reprinted in* 710 F.2d LXXI; FEDERAL JUDICIAL CENTER, *supra* note 2.

4. Wendell Hanmer, *Brooklyn's Man of the Week: Preparation is His Key to Success*, BROOK. DAILY EAGLE, May 31, 1953, at 21.

5. Special Supplement, *Colleagues for Justice: One Hundred Years of the United States Court of Appeals for the Second Circuit*, 65 ST. JOHN'S L. REV. 937, 958 (1991).

6. Hanmer, *supra* note 4, at 21.

7. *Id.*

8. *Colleagues for Justice*, *supra* note 5, at 958.

9. Hanmer, *supra* note 4, at 21.

10. *Id.*; District Judge Edward R. Neaher, Remarks, *supra* note 3, at 6.

11. John Foley, *Patricia Brown Moore*, THE DAY, Apr. 21, 1998, at B4.

12. *Id.*; *Society in the Suburbs*, NEW YORK EVENING POST, Nov. 19, 1925, at 15.

13. Foley, *supra* note 11, at B4.

14. District Judge Edward R. Neaher, Remarks, *supra* note 3, at 6.

15. Neaher, *Leonard Page Moore*, *supra* note 3, at xii.

16. *Colleagues for Justice*, *supra* note 5, at 958.

17. District Judge Edward R. Neaher, Remarks, *supra* note 3, at 6.

18. Hanmer, *supra* note 4, at 21.

19. Neaher, *Leonard Page Moore*, *supra* note 3, at xiv; LEONARD P. MOORE, MOTION PRACTICE AND STRATEGY (Practising Law Inst. 1946).

20. *L.P. Moore Named U.S. Attorney Here*, N.Y. TIMES, May 14, 1953, at 32.

21. Arnold H. Lubasch, *Judge Leonard Moore, 84, Dies; Served on U.S. Court of Appeals*, N.Y. TIMES, Dec. 9, 1982, at B20.

22. *L.P. Moore Named U.S. Attorney Here*, *supra* note 20, at 32.

23. *Id.*

24. *See* United States v. Nunan, 236 F.2d 576 (2d Cir. 1956) (affirming judgment of conviction); Paul Windels, Jr., *Leonard Page Moore—A Splendid Lawyer*, 49 BROOK L. REV. xvii (1983); Paul Windels, Jr., Remarks at the Extraordinary Session of the United States Court of Appeals for the Second Circuit, In Memoriam, Honorable Leonard P. Moore 8 (May 10, 1983), *in* 710 F.2d LXXI. Windels, Jr., was founder of Windels, Marx, Lane & Mittendorf and former President of Brooklyn Law School.

25. Windels, Jr., *Leonard Page Moore*, *supra* note 24.

26. Windels, Jr., Remarks, *supra* note 24.

27. *Id.*

28. *Id.*

29. Hanmer, *supra* note 4, at 21.

30. *Moore Begins Duties as New U.S. Attorney*, BROOK. DAILY EAGLE, Jun. 19, 1953, at 4.

31. Lubasch, *supra* note 21, at B20; *Colleagues for Justice*, *supra* note 5, at 955.

32. FEDERAL JUDICIAL CENTER, *supra* note 2.

33. Judge Neaher, *Leonard Page Moore*, *supra* note 3, at xiv.

34. United States v. Various Articles of Obscene Merchandise, 562 F.2d 185 (2d Cir. 1977); United States v. One Reel of 35MM Color Motion Picture Film Entitled "Sinderella," Sherpix, Inc., 491 F.2d 956 (2d Cir. 1974); United States v. One Carton Positive Motion Picture Film Entitled "491," 367 F.2d 889 (2d Cir. 1966).

35. 432 F.2d 705 (2d Cir. 1970).

36. *Language of Love,* 432 F.2d at 706-07.

37. *Id.* at 715.

38. Letter from Caren Deane Thomas, former law clerk, to Sally Pritchard (July 6, 2015) (on file with the United States Courts Library for the Second Circuit). Thomas practiced at Sidley Austin.

39. Judge J. Edward Lumbard, Remarks at the Extraordinary Session of the United States Court of Appeals for the Second Circuit, In Memoriam, Honorable Leonard P. Moore 16 (May 10, 1983), *reprinted in* 710 F.2d LXXI.

40. Lincoln Rest. Corp. v. Wolfies Rest. Inc., 291 F.2d 302, 305 (2d Cir. 1961).

41. FEDERAL JUDICIAL CENTER, *supra* note 2.

42. Judge J. Edward Lumbard, Remarks, *supra* note 39.

43. District Judge Edward R. Neaher, Remarks, *supra* note 3; *see also* Honorary Degree Recipients by Class Year, AMHERST COLLEGE, https://www.amherst.edu/aboutamherst/news/specialevents/commencement/awards/classyear.

44. Neaher, *Leonard Page Moore*, *supra* note 3, at xvi; *Judge Moore Gets Award from Federal Bar Group*, N.Y. TIMES, Nov. 25, 1965, at 50.

45. Neaher, *Leonard Page Moore*, *supra* note 3, at xvi.

46. District Judge John S. Martin, Jr., Remarks, *supra* note 1.

47. *Id.*

48. Letter from District Judge John S. Martin, former law clerk, to Sally Pritchard (May 26, 2015) (on file with the United States Courts Library for the Second Circuit).

49. Letter from David S. Versfelt, former law clerk, to Sally Pritchard (May 13, 2015) (on file with the United States Courts Library for the Second Circuit). Versfelt is a partner at K&L Gates.

50. District Judge John S. Martin, Jr., Remarks, *supra* note 1.

51. Thomas, *supra* note 38.

52. *L.P. Moore Named U.S. Attorney Here*, *supra* note 20, at 32.

53. *Id.*

54. *Id.*

55. Lubasch, *supra* note 21, at B20.

56. *Land Trust Receives Donation of 24 Prime Acres*, THE DAY, Nov. 12, 1981, at 11.

57. John Foley, *Leonard Brown Moore, 71*, THE DAY, Sept. 1, 1999, at C3.

58. Alice Cogan, *British War Relief or Turkeys, Mrs. Moore Delivers the Goods*, BROOK. DAILY EAGLE, Dec. 18, 1940, at 11; *Land Trust Receives Donation of 24 Prime Acres*, *supra* note 56, at 11.

59. Cogan, *supra* note 58, at 11; *Land Trust Receives Donation of 24 Prime Acres*, *supra* note 56, at 11.

60. Cogan, *supra* note 58, at 11.

61. Lubasch, *supra* note 21, at B20.

62. *Land Trust Receives Donation of 24 Prime Acres*, *supra* note 56, at 11.

63. *Gift Benefits Trust*, THE DAY, Nov. 16, 1981, at 11.

64. *Id.*

65. *Id.*

66. Lubasch, *supra* note 21, at B20.

67. Chief Judge Wilfred Feinberg, Remarks at the Extraordinary Session of the United States Court of Appeals for the Second Circuit, In Memoriam, Honorable Leonard P. Moore 5 (May 10, 1983), *reprinted in* 710 F.2d LXXI.

68. Lubasch, *supra* note 21, at B20.

## HENRY JACOB FRIENDLY
## 1903-1986

Court of Appeals for the Second Circuit: 1959-1986

Judge Henry Friendly was a judge's judge whose luminous opinions set a standard for judicial erudition. During his lifetime, Friendly was generally recognized as the great intellect and scholar not only of the Second Circuit but of the federal judiciary. Justice Felix Frankfurter described him as "the best judge . . . on the American scene."[1] Professor Herbert Wechsler, long-time director of the American Law Institute, observed: "Only the genius that Henry Friendly was could produce scholarly material of [such] quality and volume."[2] For Seventh Circuit Judge Richard Posner, he was "the most powerful legal reasoner in American legal history."[3] Judge Jon O. Newman described him as "quite simply the preeminent appellate judge of his era."[4] And Justice Thurgood Marshall, commenting on the conventional Second

Circuit wisdom that one should "Quote Learned, but follow Gus," said that for him the rule will always be: "Quote Friendly, and follow Friendly."[5] What particularly distinguished him was his encyclopedic knowledge and profound understanding of law. In virtually every area that he touched, his writings clarified the meaning and limits of doctrine and furnished valuable guidelines for future adjudication. And his scholarly writings profoundly changed prevailing perceptions of law and the proper role of federal courts.

Friendly was born on July 3, 1903, in Elmira, a small town in New York's Southern Tier.[6] His grandfather and namesake, born Heinrich Freundlich, had emigrated there from Bavaria in 1852.[7] Growing up Jewish in a town without many Jews, Friendly was bar mitzvahed but also celebrated Christmas as a child.[8] He excelled in school, graduating from the Elmira Free Academy with the highest score yet recorded on the New York State Regents examinations.[9]

In 1919, Friendly enrolled at Harvard College; he was two years younger than most of his classmates.[10] Due to his youth, temperament, and scholarly ambition, as well as to religious divisions at the university in that time, Friendly spent little time socializing.[11] He studied, and immersed himself in Boston's cultural institutions—the Boston Symphony Orchestra, the Museum of Fine Arts, and the opera.[12] He excelled in his classes, earning A's in every subject (with the exception of physical training).[13] He taught himself French so as to read Proust as written. His great love was history. His undergraduate papers showed an early command of such diverse topics as the Risorgimento, the life of Columbus, and the relationship between church and state under William the Conquerer.[14] Friendly's history professors steered him toward a Harvard professorship, a path that did not coincide with his parents' hopes for his financial security.[15] Through a family friend, Friendly's mother contacted Judge Julian Mack, who arranged for Friendly to meet Professor Felix Frankfurter, who coaxed Friendly toward law.[16]

After a year in Europe, Friendly enrolled in Harvard Law School.[17] On his legendary first day of torts class, Professor Manley O. Hudson began by asking in what language the well-known fourteenth century English assault decision, *I.D.S et Wife. v. W.D.S.*, was written.[18] Friendly answered that it was written in Law French and offered to translate.[19] He became president of the *Harvard Law Review* and earned an almost inconceivable grade point average of 86.[20] (An average of 80 was usually sufficient to earn *summa cum laude* and top rank in a class.)[21] While comparisons are somewhat difficult because of occasional tinkering in the school's scoring standards, Friendly is generally credited to have achieved, in a tie with his later mentor Louis Brandeis, the highest average in the school's history. Professor T. R. Powell called Friendly a "highly unrewarding student" because "[w]hen called on to state a case and comment on it, Friendly's response left nothing for the professor to say except, 'The next case is . . .'"[22]

While at Harvard Law School, Friendly cemented his relationship with Frankfurter, who stoked Friendly's early interest in administrative law and federal jurisdiction.[23] (Friendly practiced administrative law for 30 years representing Pan American Airlines, and federal jurisdiction became a deep interest after he took the bench.) Friendly credited Frankfurter with an invaluable "threefold imperative" on statutory interpretation: "(1) Read the statute; (2) read the statute; (3) read the statute!"[24] Frankfurter connected Friendly to legal luminaries, including Emory Buckner, United States Attorney for the Southern District of New York, who employed Friendly during his second summer of law school and influenced his career decisions.[25]

Upon Friendly's graduation, Frankfurter recommended him for a clerkship with Justice Brandeis, but then suggested that Friendly do a fourth year at the law school before the clerkship.[26] Buckner disagreed.[27] Friendly, who was eager to move on from school, followed Buckner's advice and went directly to the Brandeis clerkship.[28]

As Friendly himself would later do, Justice Brandeis drafted his opinions himself, rather than rely on clerks for the first draft.[29] Friendly's brilliance and industriousness nonetheless made a major mark with the justice, who jokingly complained to Frankfurter, "Don't you ever send me another such man as Friendly. . . . I would not have to do a lick of work myself."[30]

In Friendly's assessment, Justice Brandeis "had Frankfurter's relish for statutes, but he was their valiant defender against constitutional attack and niggling construction, rather than their sensitive interpreter."[31] Brandeis's judicial restraint was a product of his liberalism—he sat during the *Lochner* era when the Constitution was used to undo progressive social legislation. Friendly, more conservative, would later internalize the Brandeis approach and use it in his own jurisprudence, resisting the liberal activism of the Warren Court.

Justice Brandeis was a frequent dissenter. His famed dissent in *Olmstead v. United States*, written during Friendly's clerkship, set forth Brandeis's argument that a wiretap constituted a search and seizure under the Fourth Amendment[32]—a position that would eventually become law.[33] Friendly saved the justice from making the embarrassing blunder of claiming that the government could spy on people through their televisions.[34] Justice Brandeis was convinced only when Friendly produced articles from the Library of Congress showing that television signals moved in only one direction.[35]

In 1928, rejecting Brandeis's advice, Friendly turned down an offer to teach at Harvard Law School and instead joined the Manhattan firm Root, Clark, Buckner, Howland & Ballantine.[36] Buckner, who had returned to Root, Clark the previous year as a name partner, assigned Friendly to work with Grenville Clark. Although Clark had an aversion to young associates, Buckner believed that Clark would change upon encountering Friendly's brilliance.[37] Buckner was wrong, and the arrangement soon ended.[38] Nonetheless, Friendly's time with Clark sparked his interest in railroad reorganization, which would occupy a significant part of his time on the bench.[39] During the 1970s, Friendly was appointed chief judge of the special court established by Congress to reorganize the nation's railroads.[40] After a decade of litigation, in which Friendly was heavily involved, and after he had drafted an elaborate opinion to resolve the dispute, the parties reached a settlement.[41] Rather than waste the work, Judge Friendly published the opinion as a ratification of the settlement agreement.[42]

One of Friendly's earliest cases in law practice was a memorable one. It involved the will of Ella Wendell, a Park Avenue eccentric who died without leaving any relatives.[43] Her will doled out her sizeable fortune primarily to charities, but a sizable bequest also went to her lawyer and his daughter. A group of persons claiming to be Wendell's relatives challenged the will, and they brought the firepower of New York's premiere litigators, including Arthur Garfield Hays and Samuel Untermyer. The executor hired Root, Clark to defend the will.[44] Future Second Circuit Judge and Supreme Court Justice John Marshall Harlan led the defense and enlisted Friendly's crucial support.[45]

Hays had filed a petition in federal court seeking to circumvent a pending state court probate proceeding, and Friendly's first task was to challenge federal jurisdiction.[46] Friendly argued that the pendency of the probate action deprived the federal court of jurisdiction over parallel proceedings. Judge Mack, sitting in district court, disagreed, but nevertheless concluded that it would be inappropriate to continue proceedings until the state court action was resolved.[47] According to Friendly, "It must have been one of the earliest applications of the doctrine of abstention."[48]

In the probate proceeding, Friendly helped dismantle the story of Scotsman Thomas Patrick Morris, "the most charming and potentially dangerous" claimant to the Wendell fortune.[49] Friendly's research uncovered 21 lies in Morris's testimony[50] and enabled Harlan to demolish Morris on the stand.[51] Reflecting on the matter decades later, Friendly observed that his pleasure in the case had not come from "public interest considerations" but "from the *gaudium certaminis*, the joy of battle, and from pride in a task well done."[52]

While at Root, Clark, Friendly earned the trust of Juan T. Trippe, the eccentric president of Pan American Airlines, and their relationship would last decades.[53] Representing Pan Am in preparation for a hearing in the United States Senate, where Senator Hugo Black was eager to investigate Pan Am's contracts with the U.S. Post Office,[54] Friendly developed the point that the statute gave the airline, not the government, the right to a hearing.[55] Friendly waived the hearing before it began, thwarting Black's ambitions and effectively ending the investigation.[56] Over time, Pan Am sent Friendly before the Civil Aeronautics Board dozens of times to defend its interest in international and domestic routes.[57] During World War II, he represented Pan Am in connection with the War Department's commissioning of the airline to build bases in Brazil, to ferry equipment to North Africa, and to repel any attempted air invasion of the Western Hemisphere.[58] Pan Am undertook the job, but at such high cost that Senator Harry Truman launched an investigation into the negotiations.[59] He found nothing incriminating.[60]

Friendly's work at Root, Clark included the Paramount Pictures bankruptcy and important rate cases for AT&T and the New York Telephone Company.[61] He also argued two cases before the Supreme Court. In the first, a pro bono case, Friendly argued that his client, a petitioner for habeas corpus, was eligible for *in forma pauperis* relief on appeal, notwithstanding the district court's unchallenged certification that any appeal would not be taken "in good faith."[62] The second was a telephone rate case, which hinged on the propriety of the New York Telephone Company's accounting methods used in its rate applications.[63] He lost both cases.

Friendly became a partner at Root, Clark in 1937, but changes in the firm's structure soon distressed him.[64] Buckner was in declining health, and his absence from the firm led to a crisis in leadership.[65] This allowed Wilkie Bushby, whom Friendly considered an anti-Semite, to play an increasingly influential role in the firm's affairs—to the widespread dissatisfaction of younger partners.[66] Friendly and his colleagues bided their time during World War II, but by late 1945 were ready to open their own shop.[67]

Cleary, Gottlieb, Friendly & Cox opened for business in January 1946 with seven lawyers in New York and Hugh Cox, who later migrated to Covington & Burling, in Washington, DC.[68] Friendly also became general counsel of Pan Am, and so he held what was essentially two full-time jobs.[69] Cleary, Gottlieb was immediately successful, more than doubling its revenue in its first five years.[70] By 1949, it had landed the French government as a client and opened an office in Paris—the first American firm to do so since World War II.[71] In 1954, Elihu Root, Jr., and Grenville Clark, the eponyms of Root, Clark, defected from that firm to Cleary, Gottlieb, cementing the impression that the newer firm had largely succeeded to the mantle of the older.[72]

By the 1950s, Friendly was ready to leave private practice, but only if he could win an appointment to the appellate bench.[73] In January 1958, when Judge Harold Medina took senior status, the road seemed clear for President Dwight D. Eisenhower to appoint Friendly, a Republican, to the Second Circuit.[74] Justice Frankfurter, who actively campaigned on Friendly's behalf for 56 months,[75] acted quickly to place Friendly's name in the right hands, but politics got in the way of a speedy nomination.[76] District Judge Irving R. Kaufman wanted Medina's seat, and he had secured the support of New York's powerful senior Republican Senator Jacob Javits.[77]

Eisenhower delayed, and, by 1959, he still had not nominated Medina's successor.[78] In February, Judge Learned Hand took the extraordinary step of publicly endorsing Friendly in an open letter to Eisenhower.[79] It worked. In March, Eisenhower sent Friendly's name to the Senate.[80] Friendly thanked Judge Hand, writing, "The amateurs can't win this kind of victory over the professionals without a *deus ex machina*—and I've always regarded you as a kind of *deus*."[81]

Notwithstanding the enthusiastic support of Justice Frankfurter, Judge Hand, and the press,[82] the Senate sat on Friendly's nomination for six months.[83] During this interim, Friendly took the opportunity to "refresh" his knowledge of federal jurisdiction—by reading Hart and Wechsler's *The Federal Courts and the Federal System* cover to cover.[84] He said that it "proved to be the most stimulating and exciting law book I had encountered since Wigmore's *Evidence*."[85] Eventually, a call from Justice Frankfurter to Senate Majority Leader Lyndon B. Johnson put the Senate into motion.[86] On September 9, 1959, Friendly's appointment was confirmed.[87]

Friendly became "a teacher to the profession at large."[88] His opinions uniquely combined a comprehensive familiarity with law, legal history, and other disciplines.[89] In the words of his clerk, Second Circuit Judge Pierre Leval, "He carried virtually all of law in his head. . . . What is more, in his head he saw clearly the junctions, overlaps, disputed territories, and uneasy interactions among the snakes' nests of rules that make up the not-so-seamless web. And his mind worked with the speed of computer circuitry, that is, the speed of computer circuitry on a computer's good day."[90]

Given his prodigious intelligence and comprehensive knowledge of the law, Judge Friendly had little need for law clerks.[91] When assigned the case, with astonishing rapidity, he learned the record and wrote the opinion.[92] He wrote longhand, writing at approximately the same speed as if he were copying an existing text, which in fact was almost true, as in most cases the entire opinion was already organized and spelled out in his head as he embarked on the task.[93] The drafting was often completed in less than a day.[94] These were not rough drafts, but complete, perfect opinions, including string citations and favored quotations from the trenchant opinions of Judge Learned Hand.[95] As his clerk First Circuit Judge Michael Boudin described Judge Friendly's writing, "[H]is sometimes cryptic sentences mirror the train of his actual thinking as words flowed from his mind through his pen."[96] Despite doing his own drafting, Judge Friendly wrote 20 percent more opinions than the average Second Circuit judge.[97] With most of these opinions, there was little remaining for the clerk to do beyond adding *certs denied*.[98] The principal benefit Friendly derived from his clerks was occasional disagreement with his analysis. In such cases, it took him only seconds to understand the implications of the disagreement and to decide whether to accept or reject it. He was never more joyous than when he received what he considered a cogent and correct criticism from his clerk.[99]

While sustaining this level of judicial output, Judge Friendly also published dozens of articles. Judge Friendly's extrajudicial writing was dense, and bold. His pen could turn an abstract legal problem into a landscape. Administrative law was either a "widening pasture" or John Milton's "Serbonian bog . . . where armies whole have sunk."[100] In discussing Congress's failure to fix faulty statutes, Judge Friendly lamented "that the legislature has diminished the role of the judge by occupying vast fields and then has failed to keep them plowed."[101]

Friendly did not hesitate to criticize Supreme Court decisions openly. He was particularly critical of *Miranda v. Arizona*,[102] expressing wonderment as to where lurking in the Constitution the

Supreme Court had found the opinion's highly detailed procedural specifications.[103] He sarcastically lampooned what he saw as naiveté of the opinion's views of the arrest process and its self-satisfied assurance that the new requirements would not seriously affect the detection or prosecution of crime.[104] The five-man *Miranda* majority, in Friendly's harsh appraisal, realized the vision of Shakespeare's Miranda of a world that was "indeed brave and new, and peopled with 'many goodly creatures.'"[105] He expressed the view that *Miranda*, if read as an inflexible rule, would inappropriately impair real world policing. Eventually, the Supreme Court came around to Judge Friendly's way of thinking by limiting *Miranda*'s seemingly inflexible mandate.[106]

Another aspect of Judge Friendly's scholarly writings that has received significant attention is his conception that habeas corpus relief was granted far too liberally and should be limited to those who could show actual innocence.[107] While his suggested actual-innocence requirement has never been fully adopted, both Congress and the Supreme Court have substantially curtailed the availability of habeas to overturn criminal convictions.[108]

Notwithstanding his reservations about overturning the convictions of guilty offenders, Friendly did occasionally make such rulings. For example, he concluded with some reluctance that the conviction of a drug smuggler, which had been upheld on appeal, should be overturned because the government had failed to advise the defense that the star witness's identification of the defendant had been extracted through hypnosis. Friendly concluded that this bit of withheld evidence, while not establishing the defendant's innocence, was enough to require a new trial.[109]

In chambers, Judge Friendly kept a regular routine. He would take lunch alone in his office, eating the same thing every day: "a glass of College Inn tomato juice, cottage cheese, a slice of pumpernickel, and herring from a jar."[110] To summon his staff, he would press a buzzer—the number of buzzes would indicate which of his staff he wanted.[111] Although his clerks did not draft his opinions, he demanded a high level of commitment to the job. When future Chief Justice John Roberts was stuck between floors in the unreliable courthouse elevator, the judge sent down briefs so that Roberts could make use of his time.[112] Judge Friendly enjoyed ranking the intellects of those he worked with. He ranked Michael Boudin first among his law clerks.[113] In an essay about Roger Traynor entitled "Ablest Judge of His Generation," Friendly fastidiously noted that the ablest-of-his-generation ranking did not encompass Learned Hand, as Hand was not part of Traynor's generation.[114] Seven of Friendly's clerks serve in the federal judiciary. In addition to Roberts, Leval, and Boudin, his clerks include Circuit Judges A. Raymond Randolph, Jr., Merrick B. Garland, William C. Bryson, and Bankruptcy Judge Martin Glenn, as well as scores of law professors and prominent lawyers.

Judge Friendly's influence as a judge and scholar has been vast. His opinions have explained and clarified innumerable areas of law, including federal jurisdiction,[115] choice of law,[116] statutory interpretation,[117] libel and slander,[118] administrative law,[119] criminal conspiracy,[120] causation,[121] trademarks,[122] copyright jurisdiction,[123] class actions,[124] bankruptcy,[125] tax,[126] the application of the securities laws to partially foreign facts,[127] and admiralty,[128] to name a few. His scholarly writings influenced profound changes in the understanding of federal jurisdiction,[129] judicial discretion,[130] administrative law,[131] the common law process in the federal courts,[132] and the balance between the constitutional rights of criminal defendants and the needs of society.[133] His powerfully influential opinions and scholarly writings are far too numerous even to name in a brief biographical sketch.

Judge Friendly's opinions convey a sense of intellectual immediacy and offer a glimpse of his powerful mind at work. As Judge Leval put it, "He shunned rhetorical flourishes designed to make rulings look more obvious, indisputable, or necessary than they are. He presented the questions in their full complexity."[134] A good illustration is Judge Friendly's justly renowned opinion *Frigaliment Importing Company v. B.N.S. International Sales Corporation*,[135] which resolved a dispute over a chicken delivery. The opinion started with the famously prosaic statement: "The issue is, what is chicken?"[136] It then proceeded to show how complicated an issue it was. To the plaintiff, "chicken" meant "a young chicken, suitable for broiling and frying." But to the defendant, "chicken" meant "any bird of that genus . . . including what it calls 'stewing chicken' and plaintiff pejoratively terms 'fowl.'" Finding the contract to be little help in determining what the parties had meant by "chicken," Judge Friendly comprehensively surveyed the poultry marketplace. He considered: the difference between the English word "chicken" and the German word "Huhn," trade usage of "chicken," Department of Agriculture regulations governing chicken sales, and the comparative prices of broilers and stewing chickens. He ruled for the defendant, observing dryly: "Defendant's subjective intent would not be significant if this did not coincide with an objective meaning of 'chicken.'"[137] But, as Judge Friendly had unassailably demonstrated, it did.

During Richard M. Nixon's 1968 presidential campaign, he hinted that Friendly was "an ideal successor" to Supreme Court Chief Justice Earl Warren. And shortly after his election, Nixon identified Friendly as the "sort of judge" he would appoint to lead the high court.[138] Nixon, however, soon developed his "Southern strategy," and abandoned consideration of Friendly, ending his last, best chance at becoming a justice.[139]

According to Judge Boudin, Judge Friendly "did not bequeath to us an explicit philosophy of law," but his "effects on the legal landscape" included "crafting the template for the modern view of federal common law and . . . calling for a saner balance in criminal law between the interests of defendants and the needs of society."[140]

Judge Friendly kept his personal life personal. He deeply loved his wife, Sophie, the daughter of Chief Justice Horace Stern of the Supreme Court of Pennsylvania.[141] They had three children: Joan, David, and Ellen.[142] Judge Friendly struggled throughout his life with a detached retina[143] and a persistent melancholia.[144] In December 1984, Sophie learned that she had colon cancer; three months later, she died.[145] Judge Friendly was distraught. In addition, his eyesight failed. The inability to read deprived him of the most significant of his life's pleasures. On March 10, 1986, he died by his own hand, employing pills he had saved up for the purpose.[146] In 1989, the Court of Appeals commissioned sculptor Eliot Goldfinger to create a bronze bust of Friendly, to sit across the courtroom from the bust of Learned Hand. These busts commemorate those whom many would name as the two greatest judges never to sit on the Supreme Court.

Rick Sawyer

1. Paul Freund, *In Memoriam: Henry J. Friendly*, 99 HARV. L. REV. 1709, 1715 (1986) (quoting Frankfurter).

2. Herbert Wechsler, Remarks at the Extraordinary Session of the Court of Appeals for the Second Circuit, In Memoriam, Honorable Henry J. Friendly (Jun. 9, 1986) *in* 805 F.2d LXXXI, at C. Wechsler was a professor at Columbia Law School.

3. Richard A. Posner, *Forward* to DAVID M. DORSEN, HENRY FRIENDLY: GREATEST JUDGE OF HIS ERA at ix, xiii (2012).

4. Jon O. Newman, Letter to the Editor, *From Learned Hand to Henry Friendly*, N.Y. TIMES, Mar. 24, 1986, at A18.

5. Justice Thurgood Marshall, Remarks at the Extraordinary Session of the Court of Appeals for the Second Circuit, In Memoriam, Honorable Henry J. Friendly (Jun. 9, 1986) *in* 805 F.2d LXXXI, at LXXXVIII.

6. *See* Michael Norman, *Henry J. Friendly, Federal Judge in Court of Appeals, is Dead at 82*, N.Y. TIMES, Mar. 12, 1986, at B6.

7. DAVID M. DORSEN, HENRY FRIENDLY: GREATEST JUDGE OF HIS ERA 5 (2012).

8. *Id.* at 8-9.

9. *Id.* at 10.

10. *Id.* at 12.

11. *Id.* at 14.

12. *Id.*

13. *Id.* at 13.

14. *Id.* at 15-17.

15. *Id.* at 20.

16. *Id.* At the time Judge Mack sat on the Seventh Circuit, but he would later join the Second Circuit. *See generally* Julian Mack in this volume.

17. *Id.*

18. *Id.* at 21.

19. *Id.* at 21-22.

20. *Id.* at 26.

21. *Id.*

22. Paul A. Freund, Remarks at a Special Session of the United States Court of Appeals for the Second Circuit on the Occasion of the Unveiling of the Bust of Honorable Henry J. Friendly (Mar. 27, 1989) (transcript on file with the United States Courts Library for the Second Circuit). Freund was a professor at Harvard Law School.

23. DORSEN, *supra* note 7, at 23.

24. HENRY J. FRIENDLY, BENCHMARKS 196, 202 (1967).

25. DORSEN, *supra* note 7, at 25.

26. MARTIN MAYER, EMORY BUCKNER 149 (1968).

27. *Id.*

28. DORSEN, *supra* note 7, at 26.

29. *Id.* at 28.

30. *Id.* at 29 (quoting a letter from Frankfurter).

31. FRIENDLY, BENCHMARKS, *supra* note 24, at 198.

32. *Olmstead*, 277 U.S. 438, 471 (1928) (Brandeis, J., dissenting).

33. *See* Katz v. United States, 389 U.S. 347 (1967) (overruling *Olmstead*).

34. DORSEN, *supra* note 7, at 30.

35. *Id.*

36. *Id.* at 31-32.

37. LEO GOTTLIEB, CLEARY, GOTTLIEB, STEEN & HAMILTON: THE FIRST THIRTY YEARS 33 (1983).

38. DORSEN, *supra* note 7, at 34.

39. *Id.*

40. *Id.* at 285-86.

41. *Id.* at 291-92.

42. *Id.* at 292. *See* In re Valuation Proceeding under Reg. Rail Reorg. Act, 531 F. Supp. 1191 (R.R.R. Ct. 1981); In re Valuation Proceeding Under Reg. Rail Reorg. Act, 571 F. Supp. 1269 (R.R.R. Ct. 1983).

43. *See* TINSLEY E. YARBROUGH, JOHN MARSHALL HARLAN: GREAT DISSENTER OF THE WARREN COURT 42-44 (1992).

44. *Id.* at 45.

45. *Id.* at 45-46.

46. *Id.* at 46.

47. Stansbury v. Koss, 10 F.Supp. 477, 478-81 (S.D.N.Y. 1931).

48. Henry J. Friendly, *Mr. Justice Harlan, As Seen by a Friend and Judge of an Inferior Court*, 85 HARV. L. REV. 382, 382 (1971).

49. *Id.* at 383.

50. *Id.* at 383 n.6.

51. *Id.* at 383.

52. *Id.* at 384.

53. DORSEN, *supra* note 7, at 34.

54. *Id.* at 42-43.

55. *Id.*

56. *Id.*

57. *Id.* at 45-46.

58. *Id.*

59. *Id.* at 48.

60. *Id.*

61. GOTTLIEB, *supra* note 37, at 33.

62. Wells v. United States, 318 U.S. 257, 259-60 (1943).

63. United States v. New York Telephone Co., 326 U.S. 638 (1946).

64. GOTTLIEB, *supra* note 37, at 54-55.

65. DORSEN, *supra* note 7, at 50.

66. *Id.*

67. GOTTLIEB, *supra* note 37, at 55-56.

68. DORSEN, *supra* note 7, at 60.

69. *Id.*

70. GOTTLIEB, *supra* note 37, at 76.

71. *Id.* at 65.

72. *Id.* at 159.

73. DORSEN, *supra* note 7, at 71-72.

74. *Id.* at 74-75.

75. David M. Margolick, *Letters Show Frankfurter a Secret Voice of Brandeis*, N.Y. TIMES, Feb. 14, 1982, at 1, 58.

76. *Id.*

77. *Id.*

78. *Id.*

79. *Judge Hand Endorses Airline Aide for Bench*, N.Y. TIMES, Feb. 17, 1959, at 34.

80. DORSEN, *supra* note 7, at 75.

81. *Id.*

82. *See, e.g.*, *Mr. Friendly for the Bench*, N.Y. TIMES, Mar. 11, 1959, at 34.

83. DORSEN, *supra* note 7, at 76-77.

84. Henry J. Friendly, *In Praise of Herbert Wechsler*, 78 COLUM. L. REV. 974, 974 (1978).

85. *Id.*

86. DORSEN, *supra* note 7, at 77.

87. *Senate Confirms 13 as Federal Judges*, N.Y. TIMES, Sept. 10, 1959, at 16.

88. Freund, *supra* note 1, at 1715, 1719.

89. DORSEN, *supra* note 7, at 92.

90. Judge Pierre N. Leval, Remarks at the 91st Annual Meeting of the American Law Institute (May 21, 2014), *in* THE AMERICAN LAW INSTITUTE REMARKS AND ADDRESSES 105 (2014).

91. *Id.* at 106.

92. See Bruce A. Ackerman, *In Memoriam: Henry J. Friendly*, 99 HARV. L. REV. 1709, 1709 (1986).

93. Pierre N. Leval, *Remarks on Henry Friendly on the Award of the Henry Friendly Medal to Justice Sandra Day O'Connor*, 15 GREEN BAG 2D 257, 259-60 (2012).

94. DORSEN, *supra* note 7, at 92-93.

95. Judge Pierre N. Leval, Remarks, *supra* note 90, at 106.

96. Michael Boudin, *Judge Henry Friendly and the Mirror of Constitutional Law*, 82 N.Y.U. L. REV. 975, 981 (2007).

97. DORSEN, *supra* note 7, at 93.

98. Judge Pierre N. Leval, Remarks, *supra* note 90, at 106.

99. *Id.*

100. FRIENDLY, *supra* note 24, at 86, 87. The quotation is from Milton's description of Hell. PARADISE LOST, Book II, lines 592-94 ("A gulf profound as that Serbonian bog/Betwixt Damiata and Mount Casius old,/Where armies whole have sunk"). Justice Cardozo had previously used the phrase, somewhat less artfully, in a bitter dissent: "The attempted distinction between accidental results and accidental means will plunge this branch of law into a Serbonian Bog." Landress v. Phoenix Mut. Life Ins. Co., 291 U.S. 491, 499 (1934) (Cardozo, J., dissenting).

101. FRIENDLY, *supra* note 24, at 41, 47.

102. 384 U.S. 436 (1966).

103. FRIENDLY, *supra* note 24, at 266, 267-68.

104. *Id.*

105. *Id.* at 267 (quoting WILLIAM SHAKESPEARE, THE TEMPEST, act V, sc. 1).

106. *See, e.g.*, New York v. Quarles, 467 U.S. 649, 668-72 (O'Connor, J., concurring) (citing FRIENDLY, *supra* note 24, at 280).

107. *See* Henry J. Friendly, *Is Innocence Irrelevant? Collateral Attack on Criminal Judgments*, 38 U. CHI. L. REV. 142 (1970).

108. *See, e.g.*, Antiterrorism and Effective Death Penalty Act of 1996, Pub. L. No. 104-132, 110 Stat. 1214 (1996).

109. United States v. Miller, 411 F.2d 825, 830-32 (2d Cir. 1969).

110. DORSEN, *supra* note 7, at 100.

111. *Id.* at 106.

112. *Id.* at 107.

113. *Id.* at 109.

114. Henry J. Friendly, *Ablest Judge of His Generation*, 71 CAL. L. REV. 1039, 1039 n.1 (1983).

115. New York v. Galamison, 342 F.2d 255 (2d Cir. 1965); Colonial Realty Corp. v. Bache & Co., 358 F.2d 178 (2d Cir. 1966); Leather's Best, Inc. v. S. S. Mormaclynx, 451 F.2d 800 (2d Cir. 1971).

116. *E.g.*, Nolan v. Transocean Air Lines, 276 F.2d 280, 280 (2d Cir. 1960) ("Our principal task, in this diversity of citizenship case, is to determine what the New York courts would think the California courts would think on an issue about which neither has thought.").

117. Willheim v. Murchison, 342 F.2d 33 (2d Cir. 1965).

118. Pauling v. New Syndicate Co., 335 F.2d 659 (2d Cir. 1964); Cianci v. New Times Publ'g Co., 639 F.2d 54 (2d Cir. 1980).

119. *E.g.*, Toilet Goods Ass'n, Inc. v. Gardner, 360 F.2d 677 (2d Cir. 1966); *aff'd*, 387 U.S. 158 (1967); Hanly v. Kleindienst, 471 F.2d 823 (2d Cir. 1972).

120. *E.g.*, United States v. Borelli, 336 F.2d 376 (2d Cir. 1964); United States v. Geaney, 417 F.2d 1116 (2d Cir. 1969).

121. Petition of Kinsman Transit Co., 338 F.2d 708 (2d Cir. 1964).

122. *E.g.*, Polaroid Corp. v. Polarad Elec. Corp., 287 F.2d 492 (2d Cir. 1961); Abercrombie & Fitch Co. v. Hunting World, Inc., 537 F.2d 4 (2d Cir. 1976).

123. *E.g.*, T.B. Harms Co. v. Eliscu, 339 F.2d 823 (2d Cir. 1964).

124. *E.g.*, Nat'l Super Spuds, Inc. v. N.Y. Mercantile Exch., 660 F.2d 9 (2d Cir. 1981); N.Y. State Ass'n for Retarded Children, Inc. v. Carey, 706 F.2d 956 (2d Cir. 1983).

125. In re Gibralter Amusements, Ltd., 291 F.2d 22 (2d Cir. 1961).

126. Comm'r of Internal Revenue v. Ferrer, 304 F.2d 125 (2d Cir. 1962); Alperstein v. Comm'r of Internal Revenue, 613 F.2d 1213 (2d Cir. 1979); Druker v. Comm'r of Internal Revenue, 697 F.2d 46 (2d Cir. 1982).

127. Leasco Data Processing Equip. Corp. v. Maxwell, 468 F.2d 1326 (2d Cir. 1972); Bersch v. Drexel Firestone, Inc., 519 F.2d 974 (2d Cir. 1975); IIT v. Vencap, Ltd., 519 F.2d 1001 (2d Cir. 1975); IIT, an Int'l Inv. Trust v. Cornfeld, 619 F.2d 909 (2d Cir. 1980).

128. Hellenic Lines, Ltd. v. United States, 512 F.2d 1196 (2d Cir. 1975); Mitsui & Co. v. Am. Export Lines, Inc., 636 F.2d 807 (2d Cir. 1981).

129. HENRY J. FRIENDLY, FEDERAL JURISDICTION: A GENERAL VIEW (1973);

130. FRIENDLY, BENCHMARKS, *supra* note 24, at 1, 34.

131. *Id.* at 65, 86, 155.

132. *Id.* at 41, 155.

133. *Id.* at 235, 266; *Is Innocence Irrelevant?*, *supra* note 107.

134. Leval, *supra* note 93, at 261.

135. 190 F. Supp. 116 (S.D.N.Y. 1960). Judge Friendly heard *Frigaliment* while sitting by designation in district court.

136. *Id.* at 117.

137. *Id.* at 121.

138. DORSEN, *supra* note 7, at 136.

139. *Id.* (quoting the Nixon White House tapes).

140. Boudin, *supra* note 96, at 995.

141. DORSEN, *supra* note 7, at 36-37, 129.

142. *Id.* at 57, 128.

143. *Id.* at 46, 98.

144. *Id.* at xi-xii, 52-53.

145. *Id.* at 339.

146. *Id.* at 342-43.

# J. JOSEPH SMITH
## 1904-1980

District Court for the District of Connecticut:
1941-1960
Court of Appeals for the Second Circuit: 1960-1980

As the story goes, an attorney once argued that Judge J. Joseph Smith had to affirm the district court because the judge had ruled the same way in a factually identical case ten years earlier.[1] Judge Smith replied, "Counsel, what makes you think I haven't learned anything since then?"[2] Change would be a constant in Smith's career in public service. It began when Smith was elected to Congress prior to World War II and ended with his death in 1980 as a senior judge on the Second Circuit.[3]

John Joseph Smith was born on January 25, 1904 in Waterbury, Connecticut.[4] He went by J. Joseph Smith, or "Big

Joe" to his friends.[5] He attended Yale after receiving his early education in the public schools.[6] At Yale, he was an active member and officer in the Reserve Officers' Training Corps.[7] When a friend asked Smith why he spent so much time with ROTC, Smith answered, "They let you ride the horses!"[8]

Smith graduated from Yale in 1925.[9] During his final year, he was enrolled in a program that allowed him to simultaneously complete his senior year of college and the first year of law school.[10] Smith earned an LLB degree from Yale Law School in 1927.[11] An attack of appendicitis prevented him from completing the *Yale Law Journal* writing competition.[12] Nonetheless, he was selected for a prestigious research assistant position with Dean Charles Clark (who was later appointed to the Second Circuit).[13] This post led to a one-year fellowship after law school.[14] Smith published an article conducting a survey of how courts in 13 states assigned cases for trial.[15] He recommended that Connecticut adopt a system similar to that in Cleveland.[16]

After law school, Smith was a solo practitioner in Waterbury, Connecticut for more than ten years.[17] Judge Irving R. Kaufman later remarked that Smith could he considered a "country" lawyer.[18] During this time, he also served in the Field Artillery Reserves.[19] Over the years he befriended Governor Wilbur Cross, a former dean of the Yale Graduate School, and Senator Francis Maloney.[20] Out of these relationships grew Smith's candidacy for Congress.[21] Smith ran as a Democrat for Connecticut's fifth congressional district. His campaign was low key: he was described as "the reluctant candidate."[22] His approach, however, resonated with the farmers of the Litchfield hills; Smith handsomely defeated the Republican incumbent, Edward W. Goss.[23]

Smith was sworn into Congress in 1935, where he became an expert on military affairs.[24] He authored vital legislation to support the war effort during World War II.[25] He proposed additions to the Atlantic fleet, a progressive equipment replacement program, improved camouflage, new airfields, and an increase in anti-aircraft batteries.[26] Smith married Eleanor Murnane while in office.[27] They spent their honeymoon in Bermuda.[28] When they returned, Smith recommended building a military base in Bermuda.[29] The next year, the United States agreed to lease British military bases on Bermuda for 99 years.[30] Smith was reelected three times and served in Congress until 1941, when he resigned to take the bench.[31]

In 1941, President Franklin Delano Roosevelt nominated Smith to the District Court for the District of Connecticut.[32] Judge José A. Cabranes observed that "Judge Smith's appointment to the court completed a phase of the court's maturation."[33] Smith was the first Irish American and Roman Catholic to serve on a federal court in Connecticut.[34] He was the district's chief judge from 1953 to 1960.[35]

Smith's friends suspected he had an ulterior motive for returning to Connecticut to serve on the bench: to watch Yale football games.[36] Judge Andrew Hurwitz of the Court of Appeals for the Ninth Circuit, a Smith law clerk, described Smith's affinity for Yale football as "legendary."[37] As a judge, Smith never missed a game. Fridays in chambers during football season almost always included a discussion of the Eli's chances the next day.[38] Smith "never showed great disappointment over a loss," but he was "pleased by wins."[39]

Judge Cabranes observed that the cases Judge Smith handled on the district court "reflected the changing times."[40] Judge Smith was appointed during the initial surge in federal litigation caused by the adoption of the Federal Rules of Civil Procedure three years earlier.[41] His patience at trial, however, was "legendary."[42] Judge Smith oversaw high-profile criminal cases. One involved the prosecution of a prominent pastor, the Reverend Kurt Molzahn,[43] who was convicted of spying for the Nazis during World War II.[44] Molzahn arranged meetings between other spies to carry vital wartime information to Germany.[45] The trial helped "develop sensational disclosures of Axis operations in" the United States.[46]

Judge Smith swore in the actress Madeleine Carroll as a U.S. citizen.[47] Judge Smith told the new citizens that they "must do everything to support our government willingly and eagerly in order that enough guns, tanks, engines and ships go to our men who need them."[48] Carroll was so moved by Judge Smith's remarks that she found it "difficult to speak."[49]

President Dwight D. Eisenhower nominated Judge Smith to the Court of Appeals for the Second Circuit in August 1959.[50] Despite having the bipartisan support of Connecticut Senators Thomas Dodd and Prescott Bush, Judge Smith's nomination met with political gridlock.[51] Hearings began promptly but were mysteriously cut short.[52] It was later speculated that Dodd delayed the hearing until he had an agreement with the Justice Department over who would fill a new district court seat to be created by a pending bill.[53] The delay lasted more than a year; Judge Smith's nomination was confirmed in September 1960.[54]

Judge Smith authored 600 appellate decisions.[55] He became known for his deep commitment to individual liberties and the jury system. Judge Smith was one of the first to recognize a constitutional right to interstate travel.[56] Sitting on a three-member district court panel, he struck down a law that conditioned state aid on a residency requirement.[57] The plaintiff, who had moved from Boston to Hartford to be closer to her mother, was denied "Aid to Dependent Children" because she met all requirements but one: a year of Connecticut residency.[58] Although the "existence, source and dimensions of the right to travel have been the subject of much constitutional debate," Judge Smith concluded that the right existed—"whatever its source"—and that it "embodies not only the right to pass through a state but also the right to establish residence therein."[59] The Connecticut law's residency requirement had "a chilling effect on the right to travel" and was therefore unconstitutional.[60] The Supreme Court, recognizing the right to interstate travel for all, ultimately affirmed Judge Smith's opinion.[61]

In another case, Judge Smith wrote a dissenting opinion arguing that there was a right to a jury trial in a stockholders' derivative suit.[62] The majority opinion rested on the proposition that a shareholder traditionally had to sue in equity, where there was no jury right, to enforce the rights of a corporation.[63] Judge Smith opined that the "underlying claim is essentially 'a suit at common law,' an action for a money judgment for unlawful conversion, breach of fiduciary duty, fraud and gross negligence."[64] The Federal Rules of Civil Procedure merged law and equity, so, Smith argued, the "fact that historically it was necessary for the shareholder to resort to equity in order to step into the corporation's shoes should no longer bar jury trial of the corporate claim."[65] The Supreme Court reversed the majority and adopted Smith's point of view.[66]

Judge Hurwitz observed: "If you were to construct a judge around what the public perception of a good judge is—fair, dignified, and yet able to control the courtroom—Judge Smith would be the prototype. But more importantly, he understood the impact of the law on real people, had an incredibly analytic mind, and could explain outcomes in a way that all understood."[67]

Professor Martin Redish of Northwestern Law School, another Smith law clerk, recalled that Judge Smith "regularly tempered his keen intellect with compassion and common sense."[68] Judge Smith employed a "down home" sense of humor to make his points.[69] In a case concerning the First Amendment rights of high school students to distribute anti-war literature, Judge Smith's colleagues initially made derogatory comments about teenagers.[70] Judge Smith responded in a memorandum: "I think we should let the little stinkers get away with it this time."[71]

During his time on the Second Circuit, Judge Smith had lunch each day with District Judges Jon O. Newman and M. Joseph Blumenfeld and their clerks in Hartford at an entity styled "The Municipal Cafeteria."[72] Judge Smith ordered "milk," the local term for New England clam chowder.[73] Judge Smith was apparently trying to keep Judge Blumenfeld on a diet. If Judge Smith was out of town, Judge Blumenfeld would take the clerks "to some sort of greasy spoon or hamburger joint," and swore them to secrecy.[74]

Smith took senior status in 1971.[75] There was, however, little diminution in his caseload.[76]

At age 76, Judge Smith suffered a heart attack.[77] He died at St. Mary's Hospital in Waterbury, Connecticut on February 16, 1980.[78] He was survived by his wife, Eleanor, two sons, Joseph, Jr., and Richard, two daughters, Mary Lee McCarthy and Martha Murphy, and 12 grandchildren.[79] He was buried at Calvary

Cemetery in Waterbury, Connecticut.[80] A memorial scholarship was established in his name at Yale Law School.[81]

Daniel Principato

1. Email from Judge Jon O. Newman to Sally Pritchard (May 26, 2016, 1:22 EST) (on file with the United States Courts Library for the Second Circuit).

2. *Id.*

3. FEDERAL JUDICIAL CENTER, Biographical Directory of Federal Judges, John Joseph Smith, http://bioguide.congress.gov/scripts/biodisplay.pl?index=S000572.

4. *Id.*

5. *J. Joseph Smith 1904-1980*, 12 CONN. L. REV. 427, 428 (1980).

6. FEDERAL JUDICIAL CENTER, *supra* note 3.

7. *J. Joseph Smith 1904-1980*, *supra* note 5, at 428.

8. *Id.*

9. FEDERAL JUDICIAL CENTER, *supra* note 4.

10. Richard Joyce Smith, Remarks at a Joint Session of the United States Court of Appeals for the Second Circuit and the United States District Court for the District of Connecticut, Memorial Proceedings for the Honorable J. Joseph Smith LIX (Nov. 17, 1980), *in* 637 F.2d CV. Smith was a professor at Yale Law School and former partner at Whitman & Ransom.

11. FEDERAL JUDICIAL CENTER, *supra* note 3.

12. Smith, Remarks, *supra* note 10, at LX.

13. *Id.*

14. *Id.*

15. J. Joseph Smith, *The Assignment of Cases for Trial*, 12 AM. JUD. SOC'Y. 15 (1928).

16. *Id.*

17. FEDERAL JUDICIAL CENTER, *supra* note 4.

18. Martin Tolchin, *Vacancy in U.S. Court Stirs Dispute Between Weicker and Legal Establishment*, N.Y. TIMES, Oct. 12, 1973.

19. *Id.*

20. *J. Joseph Smith 1904-1980*, *supra* note 5, at 428.

21. *Id.*

22. *Id.*

23. *Id.*; *Connecticut Vote Likely to be Close*, N.Y. TIMES, Nov. 5, 1934.

24. *J. Joseph Smith 1904-1980*, *supra* note 6, at 428.

25. *Id.*

26. *Defense Key Urged for US in Bermuda*, N.Y. TIMES, July 12, 1940, at 6.

27. *Miss Murnane Wed to a Congressman*, N.Y. TIMES, Aug. 17, 1939, at 25.

28. *Id.*

29. *Defense Key Urged for US in Bermuda*, *supra* note 26.

30. *Bermuda Leases New Base to U.S.*, N.Y. TIMES, Jan. 23, 1941, at 9.

31. FEDERAL JUDICIAL CENTER, *supra* note 3.

32. *Id.*

33. José A. Cabranes, *Notes on the History of the Federal Court of Connecticut*, 57 CONN. BUS. J. 351, 369 (1983).

34. *Id.*

35. FED. BAR COUNCIL, SECOND CIRCUIT REDBOOK 1977, at 50 (1977).

36. *J. Joseph Smith 1904-1980*, *supra* note 5, at 428.

37. E-mail from Judge Andrew Hurwitz, former law clerk, to Sally Pritchard (June 30, 2015, 6:35 EST) (on file with the United States Courts Library for the Second Circuit). Judge Hurwitz also clerked for Judge Jon O. Newman.

38. *Id.*

39. *Id.*

40. Cabranes, *supra* note 33, at 369.

41. *Id.*

42. E. R. Shipp, *J. Joseph Smith, 76, a Senior Judge on U.S. Court in Connecticut, Dies*, N.Y. TIMES, Feb. 19, 1980, at BS.

43. *See* United States v. Molzahn, 135 F.2d 92 (2d Cir. 1943).

44. *Id.*

45. *Id.*

46. *Set to Try Pastor as Spy*, N.Y. TIMES, July 27, 1942, at 11.

47. *Madeleine Carroll Becomes a Citizen*, N.Y. TIMES, Feb. 27, 1943, at 10.

48. *Id.*

49. *Id.*

50. *Judges Nominated*, N.Y. TIMES, Aug. 28, 1959, at 47.

51. *Judgeship Moves Expected by Dodd*, N.Y. TIMES, June 27, 1960, at 21.

52. *Id.*

53. *Id.*

54. *2 Judges Confirmed*, N.Y. TIMES, Sept. 2, 1960, at 11.

55. Special Supplement, *Colleagues for Justice: One Hundred Years of the United States Court of Appeals for the Second Circuit*, 65 ST. JOHN'S L. REV. 937, 960 (1991).

56. Thompson v. Shapiro, 270 F. Supp. 331 (D. Conn. 1967).

57. *Id.* at 338.

58. *Id.* at 332-333.

59. *Id.* at 334-36.

60. *Id.* at 336.

61. Shapiro v. Thompson, 394 U.S. 618 (1969), *overruled in part on other grounds by* Edelman v. Jordan, 415 U.S. 651 (1974).

62. Ross v. Bernard, 403 F.2d 909, 915 (2d Cir. 1969) (Smith, J., dissenting).

63. *Id.* at 911.

64. *Id.* at 915.

65. *Id.* (internal citations omitted).

66. Ross v. Bernard, 396 U.S. 531 (1970).

67. E-mail from Judge Andrew Hurwitz, *supra* note 37.

68. Email from Martin Redish, former law clerk, to Sally Pritchard (Aug. 2, 2015, 10:25 EST) (on file with the United States Courts Library for the Second Circuit). Redish is the Louis and Harriet Ancel Professor of Law and Public Policy at Northwestern Pritzker School of Law.

69. *Id.*

70. *Id.*

71. *Id.*

72. Email from Judge Andrew Hurwitz, *supra* note 37; Note from Judge José A. Cabranes to author (on file with the United States Courts Library for the Second Circuit).

73. Email from Judge Andrew Hurwitz, *supra* note 37.

74. *Id.*

75. SECOND CIRCUIT REDBOOK, *supra* note 35.

76. Shipp, *supra* note 42.

77. *Id.*

78. *Id.*

79. *Id.*

80. FEDERAL JUDICIAL CENTER, *supra* note 3.

81. J. Joseph Smith Memorial Fund, Scholarship & Loan Forgiveness, https://www.law.yale.edu/info/alumni/giving-yls/gift-recognition.

# IRVING ROBERT KAUFMAN
## 1910-1992

District Court for the Southern District of New York: 1949-1961
Court of Appeals for the Second Circuit: 1961-1992

Irving Robert Kaufman is remembered both for his skill at judicial administration, results of which continue to benefit the Court of Appeals, and for his district court sentencing to death of Julius and Ethel Rosenberg, which dogged him for the rest of his life.

Kaufman was born in Brooklyn in 1910 to Rose and Herman Kaufman. His father owned a tobacco humidifier manufacturing company.[1] One of five children,[2] Kaufman entered Fordham College at fifteen and graduated at the top of his class from Fordham University School of Law. In his application, Kaufman explained why he wanted to study law: "So that I may become acquainted with the wonderful workings of the law and carry out these teachings in such a manner that I may be an asset to my community."[3] He was known as "Pope Kaufman" at Fordham because of his mastery of the religious courses of the Jesuit university, often outshining his Catholic classmates.[4] He graduated at twenty, before he was eligible to take the New York State bar examination.[5]

After school, he went to work in the law offices of Louis Rosenberg (unrelated to Ethel and Julius).[6] He married Louis Rosenberg's daughter, Helen, but waited until after he left the firm to avoid any appearance of impropriety.[7] They had three sons: James, Richard, and Robert.[8]

Kaufman left private practice to become an Assistant United States Attorney for the Southern District of New York.[9] Kaufman prosecuted notable cases involving financial conspiracy,[10] securities fraud,[11] and insurance disability fraud.[12] He often worked with chief of the Criminal Division, Gregory F. Noonan, in identifying insurance fraudsters.[13]

After five years, Kaufman returned to private practice.[14] With Noonan and a third partner, Kaufman formed Noonan, Kaufman & Eagan. The practice was "wide-ranging, lucrative, and politically tinged."[15] One of his notable clients was the comedian and actor Milton Berle.[16]

Kaufman was soon pulled back into public service, when he was asked to serve as a special assistant to U.S. Attorney General Tom Clark in 1947.[17] He spent two years organizing a new Justice Department division dedicated to controlling lobbying.[18]

President Harry S. Truman appointed Kaufman to the District Court for the Southern District of New York in 1949.[19] Kaufman served in the Southern District for 12 years.[20]

Judge Kaufman was known as a "staunch anti-communist."[21] But that was far from his only defining characteristic: he was "a mover of mountains, a man of broad vision [and] unbounded enthusiasm."[22] Judge Kenneth Starr remarked that he "was an extraordinarily able and energetic person" and "doggedly determined, tenacious, firm, tough, disciplined, fiercely principled, demanding of himself and others around him."[23] Julius

Rosenberg, who had a special perspective on Judge Kaufman, described him as looking like "a cross between a rabbinical student and an Army sergeant."[24] He was "an exacting taskmaster."[25] "[A]djectives such as humble, reticent, self-effacing, [did] not come readily to mind or trippingly on the tongue."[26]

Judge Kaufman conducted the 1950 trial of communists Abraham Brothman and Miriam Moskowitz for conspiracy to obstruct justice. According to the journalist Sam Roberts, Judge Kaufman then "lobbied vigorously for [the Rosenberg trial]. He got it. And he would never be rid of it."[27] The Rosenbergs were convicted of conspiring to deliver nuclear secrets to the Soviet Union.

After the jury returned a guilty verdict but without a recommendation as to punishment, Judge Kaufman "several times . . . went to his synagogue seeking spiritual guidance,"[28] and then sentenced the Rosenbergs to death. Judge Kaufman described their actions as "traitorous acts . . . of the highest degree" and "worse than murder."[29] Senator Carl Levin of Michigan, a friend of Judge Kaufman's, said that Kaufman had worried that any non-death sentence would fail to deter future Soviet spies.[30] In fact, Judge Kaufman had earlier called on Congress to "re-examine the penal provisions of the espionage statute" because the maximum period of incarceration that could have been ordered was 20 years.[31] The Rosenbergs are the only American civilians ever to be executed by the United States for espionage.[32]

The Rosenberg trial followed Judge Kaufman throughout his career. In 1975, he was forced to withdraw from delivering the commencement address at Pomona College after, as he described it, "a continuing pattern of harassment because of a trial I presided over more than 20 years ago."[33] Rallies were held for decades. The 1970s were particularly difficult as news stories reported that he had had private discussions with the prosecution before sentencing and that he asked the FBI to expedite the execution process.[34] Some degree of closure was attained in 1977 when an American Bar Association subcommittee found that Judge Kaufman had not committed any wrongdoing.[35]

Despite the distraction, Judge Kaufman remained busy on the bench. One of his last decisions as a district judge was *Taylor v. Board of Education*,[36] a desegregation case brought by a group of black students against the New Rochelle school board to enjoin the construction of a new school that, they alleged, would continue the city's segregation policy. Judge Kaufman ruled that the school district had run afoul of *Brown v. Board of Education* and ordered it to submit a desegregation plan that would comply with the Fourteenth Amendment.[37] The decision was one of the first to implement *Brown*. Judge Kaufman is reported to have often said that he wished this decision would be his legacy rather than the Rosenbergs' death sentences.[38]

Some historians think that the Rosenberg case delayed Judge Kaufman's elevation to the Second Circuit.[39] It may have affected his chances at the Supreme Court, too. As recounted by one of Justice Felix Frankfurter's law clerks, Justice Frankfurter considered Kaufman's visit to the synagogue before sentencing "unjudicial conduct" and suspected that it was part of Kaufman's plan to secure the "Jewish seat" on the Supreme Court.[40] In a letter to Judge Learned Hand, Justice Frankfurter wrote: "I despise a judge who feels God told him to impose a death sentence. . . . I am mean enough to try to stay here long enough so that K[aufman] will be too old to succeed me."[41]

Judge Kaufman was elevated to the Second Circuit in 1961 by President John F. Kennedy.[42] He was an active circuit judge for 26 years and a senior judge for five.[43] Though Judge Kaufman "knew the headline on his obituary would mention the Rosenbergs," his obituary quoted litigator David Boies saying that "if you asked 100 lawyers in the 40-year-old bracket what the significant cases of Judge Kaufman were, a relatively small number would think of the Rosenbergs."[44]

Judge Kaufman wrote one of the most widely cited antitrust decisions, *Berkey Photo v. Eastman Kodak*,[45] which some said allowed the camera company to leverage its dominant position using normal commercial methods.[46] Kodak had introduced a new version of its Instamatic photographic system that required a new type of film, but did not disclose that information until after its launch, catching suppliers flat-footed.[47] Judge Kaufman's opinion distinguished between a monopoly and that monopoly *monopolizing* its position to achieve an unfair advantage.[48] Judge Kaufman recognized a certain type of "paradox" in the Sherman Antitrust Act but warned, quoting Judge Learned Hand, ""The successful competitor, having been urged to compete, must not be turned upon when he wins.""[49]

In *Federal Election Commission v. Hall-Tyner Election Campaign Committee*,[50] Judge Kaufman wrote, in a "strongly worded" opinion, that the Communist Party did not have to comply with an FEC regulation that required disclosure of campaign contributors.[51] He criticized the FEC's application of the regulation to minority political groups as an "appalling disregard for the needs of the free and open political process."[52] Judge Kaufman concluded that the "agency charged with administering a comprehensive statute governing fundamental First Amendment freedoms should tread far more lightly."[53]

Judge Kaufman also contributed to the development of First Amendment jurisprudence and constitutional protections for journalists. In *United States v. New York Times*, better known as the *Pentagon Papers* case, the government sought to enjoin *The New York Times* (and in a parallel case, *The Washington Post*) from publishing embarrassing documents about the Vietnam War. Murray Gurfein, then a district judge, denied the government's request for injunctive relief but continued a temporary restraining order so that "the Government may seek a stay from a Judge of the Court of Appeals for the Second Circuit."[54] The case came to Judge Kaufman as a one-judge motion on a Saturday afternoon with just one narrow question: should the stay continue?[55] Judge Kaufman answered yes, pending a hearing by the full court. In a decision he filed just hours following argument, he cited "institutional considerations" in continuing the stay, but made clear that this result did not reflect his views of the merits.[56] He ultimately dissented from the court's *en banc* decision to remand the case to determine whether further publication would present a "grave and immediate danger to the security of the United States."[57] With two other judges, Kaufman said that he "would vacate the stay and affirm the judgment of the Court below."[58]

The Supreme Court reversed the Second Circuit, vindicating Kaufman.[59]

Judge Kaufman wrote about other press freedoms. In *Edwards v. National Audubon Society*,[60] he wrote that a publication could not be held liable for printing defamatory speech, even if the published statements were false. Judge Kaufman elaborated: "[T]he *New York Times* cannot, consistently with the First Amendment, be afflicted with a libel judgment for the accurate reporting of newsworthy accusations made by a responsible and well-noted organization."[61] In 1983, he wrote that a reporter did not commit libel for reporting in good faith on government proceedings.[62]

Judge Kaufman crafted his opinions with the help of his law clerks. A Kaufman clerkship began with "boot camp."[63] "The new clerks wrote bench memo after bench memo, and the Judge tore all of them to shreds and invited the old clerks to make them right."[64] This "breaking in" period lasted for two to three months.[65] During this time, he would dismiss his clerks' bench memos and draft opinions as "glib and superficial."[66] He did this so often that Judge Joseph McLaughlin once suggested that Judge Kaufman kept a "Glib and Superficial" stamp in his chambers.[67] Some incoming clerks did not make it through boot camp. One year, Judge Kaufman persuaded Dan Kelly, a seasoned clerk who was nearing the end of his term, to fill the temporary void after a new clerk quit.[68] Judge Kaufman then hired Kelly's wife for the position.[69]

Even after boot camp ended, life in chambers was intense. Judge Kaufman's clerks would encourage him to leave chambers and return to his Park Avenue apartment, where they would bring him memos and drafts in the evening.[70] They routinely worked seven days a week, but Judge Kaufman would not come in or call on weekends.[71] By the end of the year, the clerks "had been whipped into line" such that Judge Kaufman "had a little confidence" in them and they "worked pretty well with him."[72] "Judge Kaufman believed that [a] clerkship did not end after a year. Or two. Or ever." He was a "friend and supporter forever."[73] He was generous with advice. Once, word reached Judge Kaufman that a former clerk at a major law firm had let his hair grow long. One morning, the clerk found on his desk an envelope containing a $5 bill and "a handwritten note, unsigned but in the Judge's unmistakable handwriting. It read, in its entirety: 'Get a haircut.'"[74]

Judge Kaufman relished judicial administration beyond his chambers. As chief judge, a role he held from 1973 to 1980 (and sought to hold even longer),[75] Kaufman helped alleviate the pressures of the court's fast-growing civil docket. Between 1965 and 1974, the court saw its civil filings double.[76] Instead of substantially curtailing oral argument as other courts of appeals had done, Judge Kaufman focused on settling cases. In a test, Judge Kaufman selected five cases that lent themselves to "private dispute resolution" and, acting as a mediator, personally settled all five.[77] He then created the Civil Appeals Management Plan, or CAMP, and hired mediators to settle cases. CAMP was the first permanent implementation of Federal Rule of Appellate Procedure 33, which allows the court to "direct the attorneys . . . to participate in one or more conferences to address any matter that may aid in disposing of the proceedings."[78] To this day, mediation remains a fixture of the appellate process in the Second Circuit and nearly all other courts of appeals.[79]

In 1974, Judge Kaufman was awarded the Learned Hand Medal for "Excellence in Federal Jurisprudence."[80] In his acceptance speech, Judge Kaufman described the country as being "plunged in the midst of deep and troubled waters" with a faltering economy, the Watergate scandal, and President Richard M. Nixon on the verge of resigning.[81] He warned of the dangers of exclusively looking to the courts to safeguard freedom when another branch fails.[82]

In 1983, President Ronald Reagan appointed Judge Kaufman to lead a presidential Commission on Organized Crime.[83] Its goal was to study funding sources for national and regional organized crime groups and consider the effect of federal laws on their operations.[84] Many—including his fellow judges on the court, who had made private bets on this score[85]—thought that when he became a commissioner, Judge Kaufman would leave active service.[86] "Those who guessed correctly that Judge Kaufman would remain on active status counted on the fact that he ha[d] never been known to walk away from the action."[87]

Judge Kaufman did not take senior status until 1987.[88] That same year, President Reagan bestowed a Presidential Medal of Freedom on Judge Kaufman, lauding his "noble and heroic work" in "protecting the courts from political pressures."[89] Unfortunately, the award itself was tinged with political overtones: after the ceremony, the White House denied that it had given the medal to Judge Kaufman in exchange for his taking senior status so that the President could appoint a new judge to the Second Circuit.[90]

A celebration honoring Judge Kaufman's 40 years of service was held in a special *en banc* session in 1989. Chief Judge Oakes noted that Judge Kaufman had been on the bench for "a longer period of time than any circuit judge [then] sitting."[91]

Judge Kaufman died in 1992 after 43 years of service.

Greg Capobianco

1. JACKSON, ET AL., THE SCRIBNER ENCYCLOPEDIA OF AMERICAN LIVES, 1991-1993, http://www.encyclopedia.com/article-1G2-2874600164/kaufman-irving-robert.html.

2. SAM ROBERTS, THE BROTHER: THE UNTOLD STORY OF THE ROSENBERG CASE 300 (2001).

3. John Feerick, Remarks at a Special Session of the United States Court of Appeals for the Second Circuit, In Memoriam, Honorable Irving Kaufman (June 2, 1992), *in* 972 F.2d CV. Feerick is the former dean and current Norris Professor of Law at Fordham University School of Law.

4. *See, e.g.*, JACKSON, ET AL., *supra* note 1; ROBERTS, *supra* note 2, at 300; RONALD RADOSH & JOYCE MILTON, THE ROSENBERG FILE: A SEARCH FOR THE TRUTH 287 (1983).

5. Constantine N. Katsoris, *A Tribute to the Fordham Judiciary: A Century of Service*, 75 FORDHAM L. REV. 2303, 2316 (2007).

6. Marilyn Berger, *Judge Irving Kaufman, of Rosenberg Spy Trial and Free-Press Rulings, Dies at 81*, N.Y. TIMES, Feb. 3, 1992, at D10.

7. *Id.*

8. *Id.*

9. FEDERAL JUDICIAL CENTER, History of the Federal Judiciary, *The Rosenberg Trial*, http://www.fjc.gov/history/home.nsf/page/tu_rosenberg_bio_judge_kaufman.html.

10. *Government Says Drug Swindle is Work of Several*, KINGSTON DAILY FREEMAN, Mar. 8, 1940, at 1.

11. *Report Cops Aid Dope Racket, Indict 3 in $18,000,000 Drug Firm Conspiracy*, BROOKLYN DAILY EAGLE, Dec. 15, 1938, at 1.

12. JACKSON, ET AL., *supra* note 1.

13. *See 1938 Press Photo Irving R. Kaufman Gregory F. Noonan NYC*, http://outlet.historicimages.com/products/dfpy67739.

14. FEDERAL JUDICIAL CENTER, History of the Federal Judiciary, The Rosenberg Trial, *supra* note 9.

15. JACKSON, ET AL., *supra* note 1.

16. *Non Comprenevous*, BILLBOARD, Dec. 18, 1948 at 20.

17. JACKSON, ET AL., *supra* note 1.

18. *Id.*

19. *See* FEDERAL JUDICIAL CENTER, Biographical Directory of Federal Judges, Irving Robert Kaufman, http://www.fjc.gov/servlet/nGetInfo?jid=1231.

20. *See id.*

21. FEDERAL JUDICIAL CENTER, History of the Federal Judiciary, *The Rosenberg Trial*, *supra* note 9.

22. WILLIAM HUGHES MULLIGAN, JR., MULLIGAN'S LAW: THE WIT AND WISDOM OF WILLIAM HUGHES MULLIGAN 107–08 (1997).

23. Solicitor General Kenneth W. Starr, Remarks at a Special Session of the United States Court of Appeals for the Second Circuit, In Memoriam, Honorable Irving Kaufman (June 2, 1992), *in* 972 F.2d CV.

24. ROBERTS, *supra* note 2, at 300.

25. District Judge Leonard B. Sand, Remarks at a Special Session of the United States Court of Appeals for the Second Circuit, In Memoriam, Honorable Irving Kaufman (June 2, 1992), *in* 972 F.2d CV.

26. MULLIGAN, *supra* note 22, at 107.

27. ROBERTS, *supra* note 2.

28. *Id.* at 392 (quoting *Atom Spy Couple Sentenced To Die; Aide Gets 30 Years*, N.Y. TIMES, Apr. 6, 1951, at 1); *see also* RADOSH & MILTON, *supra* note 4, at 285.

29. United States v. Julius Rosenberg and Ethel Rosenberg, C 134–245 (S.D.N.Y. Jan. 1, 1953) (order denying clemency), *reprinted in Text of the Court Ruling Denying Clemency in Atom Spy Case*, N.Y. TIMES, Jan. 3, 1953, at 6.

30. Carl Levin, *Letter to the Editor*, N.Y. TIMES, Feb. 28, 1992, at A30.

31. *Atom Spy Couple Sentenced To Die; Aide Gets 30 Years*, *supra* note 28, at 1.

32. Berger, *supra* note 6.

33. Irving R. Kaufman, *A Free Speech for the Class of '75*, N.Y. TIMES MAG., June 8, 1975, at 37.

34. Berger, *supra* note 6.

35. *Id.* The A.B.A. subcommittee was organized by Kaufman's good friend Simon Rifkind "to counteract unwarranted criticism" of Kaufman. *A Judge Who Likes Action: Irving Robert Kaufman*, N.Y. TIMES, July 29, 1983, at A8.

36. 191 F. Supp. 181 (1961).

37. *Id.* at 192–97.

38. Berger, *supra* note 6.

39. *The New York Times* mentioned Kaufman's possible elevation as early as 1957, but he was not nominated until 1961. *See Big U.S. Court Job Hotly Contested*, N.Y. TIMES, Feb. 18, 1957, at 16 ("One of the main arguments being used in favor of Judge Kaufman is that his promotion would constitute an expression of Presidential and Senatorial approval for his conduct of the Rosenberg trial. During the trial and since the execution of the two convicted spies, he has been under heavy attack from left-wing groups."); *Thurgood Marshall Slated to Get Circuit Court Post*, N.Y. TIMES, Sept. 14, 1961, at 1 (noting that President Kennedy had announced his intention to nominate Judge Kaufman and that "[t]his had been widely expected").

40. Berger, *supra* note 6.

41. ROBERTS, *supra* note 2, at 489.

42. FEDERAL JUDICIAL CENTER, Biographical Directory of Federal Judges, Irving Robert Kaufman, *supra* note 19.

43. *Id.*

44. Berger, *supra* note 6.

45. 603 F.2d 263 (2d Cir. 1979).

46. *See* W. KIP VISCUSI, ET AL., ECONOMICS OF REGULATION AND ANTITRUST 265, 280 (2d ed. 1995).

47. *Id.* at 280.

48. *Berkey Photo*, 603 F.2d at 276.

49. *Id.* at 273 (quoting United States v. Aluminum Co. of Am., 148 F.2d 416, 430 (2d Cir. 1945)).

50. 678 F.2d 416 (2d Cir. 1982).

51. Arnold H. Lubasch, *Court Bars Rule on Contribution to Communists*, N.Y. TIMES, May 7, 1982, at B1.

52. 678 F.2d at 424.

53. *Id.*

54. United States v. New York Times Co., 328 F. Supp. 324, 331 (S.D.N.Y. 1971).

55. DAVID RUDENSTINE, THE DAY THE PRESSES STOPPED: A HISTORY OF THE PENTAGON PAPERS CASE 180–81 (1998).

56. *Id.*

57. United States v. New York Times Co., 444 F.2d 544 (2d Cir. 1971) (Kaufman, J., dissenting), *rev'd*, 403 U.S. 713 (1971).

58. *Id.*

59. New York Times Co. v. United States, 403 U.S. 713 (1971) (per curium).

60. 556 F.2d 113 (2d Cir. 1977).

61. *Id.* at 122.

62. *See* Reeves v. Am. Broad. Cos., *Inc.*, 719 F.2d 602 (2d Cir. 1983).

63. E-mail from Patrick Hanlon, former law clerk, to Guy Miller Struve (Apr. 21, 2015, 12:45 EST) (on file with the United States Courts Library for the Second Circuit). Hanlon is a Research Fellow at Stanford Law School. Struve is senior counsel at Davis, Polk & Wardwell, LLP.

64. *Id.*

65. E-mail from Daniel G. Kelly, Jr., former law clerk, to Guy Miller Struve (Apr. 8, 2015, 8:48 EST) (on file with the United States Courts Library for the Second Circuit). Kelly is senior counsel at Davis Polk & Wardwell, LLP.

66. *Id.*

67. Joseph M. McLaughlin, *The Second Circuit—Year in Revue*, 61 BROOK. L. REV. 347, 359 (1995).

68. E-mail from Daniel G. Kelly, *supra* note 65.

69. *Id.*

70. E-mail from Patrick Hanlon, *supra* note 63.

71. *Id*

72. *Id.*

73. *Id.*

74. E-mail from Jack C. Auspitz, former law clerk, to Guy Miller Struve (Apr. 13, 2015, 12:34 EST) (on file with the United States Courts Library for the Second Circuit). Auspitz is a retired partner of Morrison & Foerster, LLP.

75. *A Judge Who Likes Action: Irving Robert Kaufman, supra* note 35 ("Under Federal law, chief judges must yield their titles and administrative responsibilities at 70. Judge Kaufman lobbied for a change in the law.").

76. Irving R. Kaufman, *The Pre-Argument Conference: An Appellate Procedural Reform*, 74 COLUM. L. REV. 1094, 1094 n.1 (1974).

77. *Id.* at 1096.

78. FED. R. APP. P. 33; *see* JERRY GOLDMAN, FED. JUD. CENTER, AN EVALUATION OF THE CIVIL APPEALS MANAGEMENT PLAN: AN EXPERIMENT IN JUDICIAL ADMINISTRATION 3 (1977).

79. Craig A. Marvinney, *Mediation in the United States Circuit Courts of Appeals: A Survey*, 64 FDCC Q. 53, 56 (2014) (noting that "each circuit has instituted a formal mediation program" but the "program in the Eighth Circuit is currently suspended and is not likely to be reinstated").

80. Chief Judge Irving R. Kaufman, Remarks on the Occasion of Receiving the Learned Hand Medal for "Excellence in Federal Jurisprudence" at the Federal Bar Council Annual Dinner (May 1, 1974) (transcript on file with the United States Courts Library for the Second Circuit).

81. *Id.* at 2.

82. *Id.* at 5–6.

83. Leslie Maitland, *Reagan to Choose Crime Panel Soon, Officials Report*, N.Y. TIMES, May 4, 1983, at A1.

84. Exec. Order No. 12,435, 48 Fed. Reg. 37,635 (1983); *see also* Ronald Reagan, Executive Order 12435 - President's Commission on Organized Crime, July 28, 1983, http://www.presidency.ucsb.edu/ws/?pid=41647.

85. *A Judge Who Likes Action: Irving Robert Kaufman, supra* note 35.

86. Maitland, *supra* note 83.

87. *A Judge Who Likes Action: Irving Robert Kaufman, supra* note 35.

88. FEDERAL JUDICIAL CENTER, Biographical Directory of Federal Judges, Irving Robert Kaufman, *supra* note 19.

89. Ronald Reagan, Remarks on Presenting the Presidential Medal of Freedom to Irving R. Kaufman, (Oct. 7, 1987), http://www.presidency.ucsb.edu/ws/?pid=33515.

90. *See* Ruth Marcus and David Hoffman, *U.S. Judges Retires, Gets Reagan Award; Meese Denies Trade was made with 2nd Circuit's Kaufman*, WASH. POST, Sept. 19, 1987.

91. Chief Judge James L. Oakes, Remarks at an Extraordinary Session of the U.S. Court of Appeals for the Second Circuit sitting *in banc* to Commemorate Forty Years of Judicial Service by Honorable Irving R. Kaufman (November 1, 1989), *in* 895 F.2d LXXXIII.

# PAUL RAYMOND HAYS
# 1903-1980

Court of Appeals for the Second Circuit: 1961-1980

"[T]he allure of the law is as powerful as it is sometimes capricious. And it appears that budding classicists are, as a breed, no more immune to law's seduction than are lesser mortals."[1] Paul R. Hays was not immune. He graduated from Columbia College at 21, having majored in Latin and Greek, and became an instructor in classics at New York University and then at Columbia, where he taught Latin and Greek from 1926 to 1932.[2] Hays continued to teach classics while attending law school at Columbia; he earned an LLB degree in 1933 "with a high record notwithstanding the demands of college teaching."[3]

Hays was born in Des Moines, Iowa in 1903 to Everett Hollingsworth Hays and Fae Susan Hatch.[4] Hays's parents divorced sometime after 1904. His father, a drama critic in Chicago,[5] later remarried. He died in 1948.[6] Hays's mother remarried in 1919 to Philip Boland Lockwood, a banker in San Mateo County, California.[7] Hays had a younger sister, Marcia Susan Hays, born in 1904.[8] Both Hays and his sister lived in California after their mother's remarriage. In 1922, they were attending San Mateo Junior College; Hays was class president and the literary editor for the college annual, while Marcia was the manager of the women's baseball team.[9]

Hays married twice and had one child. His first marriage in 1924 to Eleanor Williams produced a son, Rhys Williams Hays, in 1926.[10] Rhys contracted polio at age seven, but survived and "[t]hanks in substantial part to the encouragement of his father, Rhys graduated from Union Theological Seminary, and received a Ph.D. in medieval history from Columbia."[11] He died in 1976 from internal injuries following a fall; he was 49.[12]

Hays and Eleanor Williams divorced in 1942.[13] In 1949, Hays married Elinor Rice, a best-selling novelist known for *The Best Butter*, published in 1938, and for biographies of suffragette Lucy Stone and the Blackwell family (which included Elizabeth Blackwell, the first woman to become an accredited physician in England).[14] Hays and Elinor traveled a great deal, generally taking two trips abroad each year. Their letters refer to travels to Europe (England, France, Spain, Italy), as well as to more far-flung locations (Penang, Kuala Lumpur, Tunisia, Morocco,[15] and India[16]). They also spent extended periods abroad in 1952 and 1961, while Hays took on teaching assignments in Berlin and Istanbul.[17] Although a seasoned traveler, Hays did occasionally run into some difficulties. He memorialized one in a letter to the New Winter Palace Hotel in Luxor, Egypt:

> On the final day of my stay I went to the cashier's desk to get my bill. The cashier borrowed my pen in order to complete some of the items on the bill. He kept the pen.
>
> Looking back on the episode I feel certain that the cashier's borrowing the pen and keeping it was no mistake and that it was a deliberate attempt at theft. This view of the matter is confirmed by the fact that you have failed to

> answer a letter which my wife wrote to you from Athens, Greece about two weeks ago.
>
> If I do not hear from you promptly with respect to this matter I plan to take it up with my friend who is the Egyptian Consul here in New York.[18]

The resolution of this mystery is lost to the ages.

Despite his Iowa origins and frequent travel, Hays was very much a New Yorker. After receiving his law degree, he spent a brief time in private practice at Cravath, de Gersdorff, Swaine & Wood[19] before leaving for Washington, DC, to serve as counsel to the Resettlement Administration of the National Recovery Administration from 1934 to 1935.[20] He returned to New York after only a year to join the faculty at Columbia Law School, first "assisting in the direction of the Legislative Drafting Research Fund," then teaching "labor law and civil procedure."[21] With the exception of brief periods, he taught full time at Columbia from 1936 to 1961; he continued to teach while on the bench.[22] The faculty at Columbia recognized him as "a dedicated and effective teacher, a pioneer in the development of labor law, an arbitrator of sustained preeminence, a potent force in redirecting legal education, a liberal in politics progressively increasing his participation in the effort to develop a third force, capable in times of close division of tilting the balance in this State toward liberty and social justice."[23] To this day, the Paul R. Hays prize at Columbia is "[a]warded annually to an outstanding first-year student in civil procedure."[24]

Although "[t]eaching and scholarship were . . . the dominant concerns" of Hays's pre-judicial legal career,[25] they were not his only concerns. Dean Michael Sovern of Columbia Law School commented that "the New York Times Index listed [Hays] as three different people—there was a Professor Hays, another fellow by the same name on the New York City Board of Health, and yet a third serving as Chairman of the Liberal Party."[26] In fact, Hays did appear to manage three careers simultaneously. As a professor, he authored "casebooks in administrative law, civil procedure, and labor law,"[27] as well as multiple articles, mainly addressing labor relations and labor arbitration and identifying what he believed to be the issue of the day, a "'constitutional crisis' arising out of the issue of the distribution between state and federal authority of power over labor relations."[28] Hays explained that in the field of labor relations, the federal-state preemption issue was compounded by a "question of whether the courts or the National Labor Relations Board have primary jurisdiction."[29] Hays's book, *Labor Arbitration—A Dissenting View*, contained the lectures Hays delivered at Yale Law School in 1965. It was a strong critique of labor arbitration. One reviewer described Hays's attack on labor arbitration and a Supreme Court decision in its favor as follows: "He launches a mopping-up exercise, pillories the enemy and finally parades him naked before the bar—virtue unmasked, halo removed and omniscience stripped away."[30] Another stated that Hays "treats labor arbitration as a genteel and lucrative form of prostitution."[31] Hays's criticism touched on the conflicts of professional arbitrators' (preservation of employability v. objective decision-making), corruption in the process, resolutions through compromise, lack of skilled arbitrators, and use of factors outside of the agreements they are meant to construe.[32]

Hays was a member of the State Board of Mediation and a private consultant who "helped fashion wage agreements in many industries since the 1940's."[33] Hays's career also had a political facet. "He headed the New York Chapter of Americans for Democratic Action,"[34] and was the vice chairman (1955-1960) and chairman (1960-1961) of the New York Liberal Party, until his judicial appointment.[35] In 1960, Hays was the first Liberal Party leader to be chosen as a member of the Electoral College.[36] Although generally allied with the Democratic Party, the Liberal Party was independent and sometimes supported Republican candidates or policies. In 1961, the party issued its approval of Governor Rockefeller's legislative program. Hays noted a disagreement with Rockefeller's proposed tax rebate, but praised the program for its attention to "medical programs for the aged," housing discrimination, "social welfare and juvenile delinquency and for the situation of migratory workers."[37] At the same time, Hays criticized Rockefeller's failure to recommend repeal of a law that allowed "the automatic dismissal of public employees who go on strike" and found his plans for employment and labor incomplete.[38]

Hays was emphatically anti-communist.[39] In 1960, he "resigned as one of 23 United States delegates" to the Inter-American Congress for Democracy and Freedom held in Venezuela.[40] Hays explained that the conference had condemned right-wing dictatorships in Spain (Franco) and Portugal (Salazar), but declined to do the same regarding communist dictatorships or to address the rise in communism in Central and South America.[41] Hays stated, "The prime obligation of anti-Communist liberals is to keep clear for those who do not have as thorough an understanding of contemporary politics, the reactionary and undemocratic character of communism."[42]

In 1960, with Hays as chairman, the Liberal Party endorsed John F. Kennedy for President.[43] After President Kennedy was elected, Hays's name was put forward for a vacancy on the Court of Appeals for the Second Circuit. Professor Herbert Wechsler of Columbia Law School commented that Hays's appointment was "not always looking too promising."[44] In May of 1961, Hays apparently had given up hope because he wrote to Attorney General Robert F. Kennedy to thank him for his "offer to recommend [his] appointment," and to say that although he "was naturally disappointed about the Court of Appeals," he would like to be considered for the district court.[45]

However, contemporaneous media reports reflect that Hays's appointment remained under consideration, but was viewed unfavorably by some as a quid pro quo for the Liberal Party's endorsement of President Kennedy. In June 1961, an article in *The New York Times* conceded that Hays was "a man of fine character," but prophesized that his appointment would "reduce[] the chances that the Liberal party will choose this year between Democratic and Republican candidates solely on the basis of their relative merits."[46] The Liberal Party was considering whether to back Democrats for mayor, city council president, and comptroller; Hays indicated "there was a 'serious possibility' the Liberals either would enter their own slate or form an alliance with Republicans or independent Democrats" rather than endorse the Democrats it had supported in 1957 (including the incumbent mayor, Robert F.

Wagner, Jr.).[47] The *Times* concluded that "judicial appointments should neither be made nor denied on a political basis. So far as the new crop of judges go, these first indications are not too good."[48] The article provoked a strong rebuke from Professor Wechsler, who penned a letter to the editor reprimanding the *Times* for failing to "practice what [it] preach[ed]" and consider Hays's merits; Wechsler compared Hays to others under consideration for judgeships and stated that "none can more confidently be asserted to possess the judicious disinterestedness and breadth of legal insight that are most required for success in high judicial office."[49]

In September 1961, shortly before President Kennedy appointed Hays to the Court, the *New York Post* expressed its support for Hays, noting that "Hays' appointment [would] be widely described as White House recognition of political services rendered by New York's Liberal Party," but opining that "it would be unjust to let his appointment be characterized as a political payoff."[50] The *Post* described Hays as "a scholarly, serious man, whose political activity has always been secondary to his preoccupation with the life of the law. He is a man of deeply liberal convictions; he is also a man who has served with distinction as an arbitrator in many rough conflicts. He possesses that rare combination of a passion for justice and a judicial temperament that is the mark of distinction in our courts."[51]

In October 1961, when President Kennedy, through use of a recess appointment,[52] named Hays to "the sorely pressed Second Circuit, all the members of the court were delighted," having heard of his reputation and knowing the esteem in which he was held by his students and colleagues.[53] Judge Hays was one of three judges appointed to fill new seats on the Second Circuit—the court grew from six to nine active judges—alongside Thurgood Marshall and Irving R. Kaufman.[54] At Hays's induction in November 1961, Judge J. Edward Lumbard remarked that it was "[s]urely . . . a matter for rejoicing that in Mr. Hays the President has selected a man so experienced and competent, and in the full height of his powers and his usefulness, to advise with us in the always difficult and demanding duties of decision."[55] Judge Lumbard emphasized Hays's experience in the areas of procedure and labor law, joking that he had the "temerity . . . to take over Professor Medina's course in procedure."[56] In a letter to Hays, Judge Harold R. Medina wrote, in a "masterpiece of understatement," that it was a "personal delight" to have Hays as a colleague. In Medina's view, the court needed Hays to make it "even greater than it has been in the past," noting that the court not only needed Hays's "unusual intelligence and tough mindedness and the frankness and candor with which [he] approach[ed] every problem, but also . . . the benefit of [his] expert knowledge and background in the labor field."[57] The Senate confirmed Hays in March 1962,[58] following a short hearing, at which Hays described the platform of the Liberal Party, emphasizing that it was formed in reaction to communist infiltration of the American Labor Party, and confirmed that he had resigned that and any other political affiliations upon learning of his nomination.[59]

Judge Hays retained the respect of his colleagues on the bench, based on "his devotion" and his adherence to the "unwritten rule, not always honored by other judges, that reaction to a colleague's opinion takes priority over writing one's own."[60] This discipline is even more impressive given, as reported by Hays's law clerk George A. Davidson, that Judge Hays did not use his law clerks to help prepare for sittings, only to aid in drafting opinions after cases were heard, and "placed great emphasis on completing all opinions from one sitting before the next sitting began."[61] Although Hays continued teaching part time after his appointment, his writing on the bench was not academic, but was "gaunt and spare."[62] According to Judge Henry Friendly, "[h]e sticks to the jugular; he believes the court's business is to decide the case, not to indulge in scholarly display that may haunt it in the future."[63] Although "no one [was] in the slightest doubt of his firmness and absolute integrity," he was "always ready to listen, and to yield when convinced that the other side ha[d] the better of the argument or even that the issue d[id] not warrant an expression of disagreement."[64]

Judge Hays was well known for his *Scenic Hudson Preservation Conference v. Federal Power Commission* opinions addressing challenges to the Federal Power Commission's license to Consolidated Edison for its Storm King project—a hydroelectric plant on the

Hudson River at Storm King Mountain that would have been the largest facility of its kind.[65] The project called for a 240-acre reservoir and a 125-foot wide path of transmission lines stretching 25 miles, and would pump more than a million cubic feet of water per minute in and out of the Hudson River.[66] Writing for a panel of Chief Judge Lumbard and Judge Sterry R. Waterman, Hays remanded the proceedings for the Commission to compile a more thorough record. He emphasized that the "project [was] to be located in an area of unique beauty and major historical significance. The highlands and gorge of the Hudson offer one of the finest pieces of river scenery in the world."[67] Judge Hays explained that the Federal Power Act required the Commission to consider "the conservation of natural resources, the maintenance of natural beauty, and the preservation of historic sites."[68] Judge Hays advised:

> [T]he Commission has claimed to be the representative of the public interest. This role does not permit it to act as an umpire blandly calling balls and strikes for adversaries appearing before it; the right of the public must receive active and affirmative protection at the hands of the Commission.[69]

The opinion also held that conservation groups had standing to challenge the agency's grant of a license "to protect their special interests," which included the effects of the plant on their trail systems in the area.[70]

In a second opinion addressing the grant of a license under a modified plan, Judge Hays upheld the Commission's decision, pointing out the "extensive powers delegated to the Commission and the limited scope of review entrusted to [the] court," and concluding "that the Commission ha[d] fully complied with [the Court's] earlier mandate and with the applicable statutes and that its findings [were] supported by substantial evidence."[71] Judge Friendly would later describe these opinions as holding the government and its agencies "to a high degree of responsibility in the performance of their duties," but declining to interfere if that responsibility was met.[72]

In addition to these cases addressing purported assaults on the natural environment, Judge Hays addressed an alleged assault on decency. In *United States v. A Motion Picture Film Entitled 'I am Curious-Yellow,'* Judge Hays overturned a jury verdict in favor of the United States, thereby allowing distribution of this Swedish film in the United States.[73] *The New York Times* described the film as the story of "an intensely serious (and funny) young woman who goes about Stockholm seeking to implement new answers to the social, political and sexual hang-ups that seem to her to have calcified Swedish life."[74] The film, in which the lead character is a young actress making a film, consists in large part of her interviewing people about class, unions, and politics, while also exploring her sexual identity through an affair. According to the *Times* reviewer, the sex scenes in locations "indoors and out, are explicit, honest and . . . unaffectedly frank"; "[b]y acknowledging the existence of genitalia and their function in the act of love, the movie salvages the depiction of physical love from the scrap heap of exploitation, camp and stag films."[75] Judge Hays described the film as follows:

> It would perhaps not be demonstrably wrong to say that it is concerned with that subject which has become such a commonplace in contemporary fiction and drama, the search for identity. It is the story of a young girl who is trying to work out her relationship to such political, social, and economic problems as the possibility of a classless society, the acceptance of the Franco regime, and the policy and practice of nonviolence. At one point the girl experiments with oriental religious ritual and meditation. The girl's inter-personal relationships are also pictured, including particularly her relation to her father, presented as an idealist who has become disillusioned and has given up meaningful activity. A fairly large portion of the film is devoted to the relations between the girl and her young lover.[76]

Judge Hays then addressed the definition of obscenity under the Tariff Act of 1930 and concluded that the film was entitled to First Amendment protection under Supreme Court law.[77] Judge Hays acknowledged that the "sexual content of the film [was] presented with greater explicitness than has been seen in any other film produced for general viewing," but concluded that the sexual content was not the "dominant theme," and that it was "clear that 'I am Curious' [was] not utterly without redeeming social value."[78] In overturning the jury verdict, Judge Hays explained that "obscenity . . . is not an issue of fact" but one "of constitutional law that must eventually be decided by the court."[79]

Judge Hays maintained active status until 1974. When he took senior status, Judge Wilfred Feinberg, who had been his student at Columbia, wrote that being his colleague had "been a source of great pride and satisfaction."[80] Judge Hays remained on the Second Circuit until his death in 1980, but contemplated retirement in 1979. In a letter to Judge Hays, Judge Medina expressed dismay to hear that Judge Hays was moving out of the courthouse, but understood that Judge Hays may "have been finding [his] health an obstacle to continue in [his] work." Judge Medina sympathized: "I am getting pretty near the end of my rope and seem to be getting these extremely difficult, complicated and controversial cases every time I sit."[81] Judge Hays died in February 1980 at the age of 76.[82]

Judge Feinberg presided over the Second Circuit memorial proceedings for Judge Hays. Professor Wechsler commented on Judge Hays's contributions to teaching, noting "his discerning, liberating view of the law and legal problems." He explained that Judge Hays believed that:

> . . . law teaching should be primarily legislative, meaning thereby that it should confront the inherent problems of a field of law as they would be confronted by a well-intentioned legislative body, charged with . . . improving the authoritative norms.[83]

Wechsler commented on Judge Hays's "great energy, self-discipline and capacity for speedy work" in relation to his role in reorganizing the curriculum at Columbia Law School after World War II.[84] Hays's law clerk, Columbia Law School Professor Harvey J. Goldschmid, described Hays as a "master" and "natural athlete" in the classroom. He used the words "direct," "concise," and "disciplined" to describe Judge Hays's preferred writing style, remarking that when he "asked Judge Hays what he expected in a draft opinion, he simply responded: 'Your best work and never in more than nine pages.'"[85]

The proceedings concluded with Judge Friendly, who described Judge Hays as "a steadying factor on our court," and explained that he was always willing to listen to the opinions of the other panel members and "would argue for his views firmly but not passionately." Judge Friendly acknowledged some of Judge Hays's sharply worded dissents, one of which questioned the ability of judges in their chambers to understand how an employee might feel threatened by statements of an employer.[86] Judge Friendly found it "really worth disagreeing with Paul to provoke him into" such a dissent, and pointed out that the Supreme Court often agreed with Judge Hays's dissenting positions.

Judge Hays believed that a good biography "not only gives a clear picture of [the subject's] life, including his contribution to the court and to the law, but presents a vivid impression of his character and personality. And all of this is woven into a picture rich in description of the time in which he lived."[87] This biography may not meet that mark, but Judge Friendly's description of Hays does:

> [S]imple in bearing, quiet in voice, courteous, reflective, cultivated in music and in literature, appreciating good food and wine and the cheer that they bring with them. . . . He spoke calmly save when a great principle was at stake. As a friend, he was always concerned and ready to help. He did not need to tell you this, it was implicit in the relation once that was formed.[88]

Elizabeth Duwe

1. Harold R. Medina, *Musings of a Humanist*, 72 COLUM. L. REV. 447, 448 (1972) (Judge Medina explaining his own love of Latin and implying some jealousy that Hays's education and early career were devoted to Greek and Latin).

2. *Id.* at 447.

3. *Resolution of the Faculty*, 72 COLUM. L. REV. 441, 441 (1972). Some sources report that Hays also earned a M.A. degree from Columbia in 1927. *See, e.g.*, FEDERAL BAR COUNCIL, SECOND CIRCUIT REDBOOK: 1977 42 (Marc White ed. 1977).

4. GENEALOGY OF THE JOHN BRIDGE FAMILY IN AMERICA 271 (Rev. William Dawson Bridge ed., rev. ed. 1924).

5. *Id.*

6. Letter from McLaughlin Law Offices to Paul R. Hays (Sept. 16, 1948) (copy on file with the United States Courts Library for the Second Circuit); Letter from Law Offices of White Ingram to Paul Hays (Aug. 9, 1948) (copy on file with the United States Courts Library for the Second Circuit);

Probate Document in the Matter of the Estate of Everett H. Hays, Moultrie County, Illinois (July 30, 1948) (listing heirs and date of death) (copy on file with the United States Courts Library for the Second Circuit).

7. GENEALOGY OF THE JOHN BRIDGE FAMILY IN AMERICA, *supra* note 4, at 271.

8. *Id.*

9. *Annual Staff Appointed by Editor Aliamus*; *Girls' Baseball*, 2 THE BARK, Dec. 11, 1922, at A1, B1 (Newspaper of San Mateo Junior College). Hays's sister Marcia went on to a distinguished career in medicine. She became the director of infant emergency and maternity services for the California Public Health Department in 1944 and later of the Crippled Children's Division; she "attained renown for her innovations and modernizations of therapy techniques" for the treatment of conditions including post-poliomyelitis. Dr. Hays contracted polio in 1958 upon her return from Japan as a consultant for the World Health Organization and spent 18 months on a respirator. She died in 1965 at the age of 61. *Dr. Marcia Hays Dies Here at 61*, S.F. CHRONICLE, Oct. 19, 1965, at 25.

10. GENEALOGY OF THE JOHN BRIDGE FAMILY IN AMERICA, *supra* note 4 (handwritten addendum).

11. William L. Cary, *Century Memorials: Paul R. Hays*, *in* THE CENTURY YEARBOOK 232 (1981).

12. *Dr. Rhys Williams Hays, 49, U. of Wisconsin Medievalist*, N.Y. TIMES, Feb. 15, 1976, at 67.

13. GENEALOGY OF THE JOHN BRIDGE FAMILY IN AMERICA, *supra* note 4 (handwritten addendum).

14. *Elinor Rice Hays, 92, Biographer of Women*, N.Y. TIMES, March 23, 1994, at B20.

15. Letter from Paul R. Hays to Salome Riber (a relative) (June 9, 1971) (copy on file with the United States Courts Library for the Second Circuit).

16. Letter from Paul R. Hays and his wife to Mr. and Mrs. Jacques de Kadt (July 9, 1973) (attempting to arrange plans to meet in Paris, and informing them that they would be spending 16 days on a houseboat in Kashmir) (copy on file with the United States Courts Library for the Second Circuit).

17. Herbert Wechsler, Remarks at a Special Session of the United States Court of Appeals for the Second Circuit, In Memoriam, Honorable Paul R. Hays (Oct. 21, 1980) (transcript on file with the United States Courts Library for the Second Circuit). Wechsler was a professor at Columbia Law School.

18. Letter from Paul R. Hays to New Winter Palace Hotel (Mar. 19, 1964) (on file with the United States Courts Library for the Second Circuit).

19. WHO WAS WHO IN AMERICA WITH WORLD NOTABLES, VOL. VII 1977-1981, at 262 (1981).

20. *Resolution of the Faculty*, *supra* note 3, at 441. The National Recovery Administration was created in 1933 to further the National Industrial Recovery Act, which was intended to promote industry cooperation, reduce unemployment, increase consumption and purchasing power, and eliminate unfair competition. *See* NIRA, tit. I, §1, Pub. L. No. 73-67, 48 Stat. 195 (1933).

21. *Resolution of the Faculty*, *supra* note 3, at 441.

22. *Id.*

23. *Id.*

24. *Academic Recognition*, COLUMBIA LAW SCHOOL, *http://*web.law.columbia.edu/prizes-awards.

25. Wechsler, Remarks, *supra* note 17, at 10.

26. Michael I. Sovern, *Professor Paul R. Hays*, 72 COLUM. L. REV. 450 (1972) (remarks by Dean of the Faculty of Law at Columbia University in an issue dedicated to Hays).

27. JEFFREY B. MORRIS, FEDERAL JUSTICE IN THE SECOND CIRCUIT 175 (1987).

28. Paul R. Hays, *Foreword*, 59 COLUM. L. REV. 1, 1-2 (1959) (writing for an issue of the Columbia Law Review addressing topics in the field of labor law); *see also* Paul R. Hays, *Federalism and Labor Relations in the United States*, 102 U. PA. L. REV. 959 (1954); Paul R. Hays, *State Courts and Federal Preemption*, 23 MO. L. REV. 373 (1958); Paul R. Hays, *The Future of Labor Arbitration*, 74 YALE L.J. 1019 (1965); Paul R. Hays, *The National War Labor Board and Collective Bargaining*, 44 COLUM. L. REV. 409 (1944).

29. Paul R. Hays, *The Supreme Court and Labor Law: October Term, 1959*, 60 COLUM. L. REV. 901, 902 (1960).

30. Alvin L. Goldman, *Book Review*, 19 J. LEGAL EDUC. 224, 226 (1966) (reviewing PAUL HAYS, LABOR ARBITRATION - A DISSENTING VIEW (1964)).

31. Bernard D. Meltzer, *Book Review*, 34 U. CHI. L. REV. 211, 211 (1966) (reviewing PAUL HAYS, LABOR ARBITRATION - A DISSENTING VIEW (1964)).

32. *Id.* at 212.

33. *Judge Paul R. Hays Is Dead at 76; Joined in Pentagon Papers Ruling*, N.Y. TIMES, Feb. 15, 1980, at D17.

34. *Id.*

35. MORRIS, *supra* note 27, at 175; Anthony Lewis, *Head of Liberals in Line for Bench*, N.Y. TIMES, June 1, 1961, at 32; *Liberals Release Paul Hays*, N.Y. TIMES, Sept. 28, 1961, at 44.

36. McCandlish Phillips, *Electors Will Find Brief Glory In Doing Bit for U.S. Politics*, N.Y. TIMES, Nov. 11, 1960, at 23.

37. Leo Egan, *Backing of Rockefeller's Program Lifts Hopes for Victory in '62*, N.Y. TIMES, Jan. 15, 1961, at 1, 2; *see also* Layhmond Robinson, *Hays Says That Support of Party Is Not Assured—Own Ticket 'Possibility'*, N.Y. TIMES, June 12, 1961, at 1.

38. Egan, *supra* note 37.

39. The Liberal Party was formed in 1943 by "President Franklin Delano Roosevelt and liberal members of the then communist-dominated American Labor Party." *Brief History and Platform of the Liberal Party*, LIBERAL PARTY OF NEW YORK, http://www.liberalparty.org/policies-and-platform/brief-history-and-platform-of-the-liberal-party/.

40. Arnold Beichman, *Communist Inroad Related by Liberal*, THE CHRISTIAN SCIENCE MONITOR, May 19, 1960, at 10B.

41. *Id.*

42. *Id.*

43. Leo Egan, *Liberal Party Formally Backs Democratic Presidential Ticket*, N.Y. TIMES, Sept. 4, 1960, at 28.

44. Wechsler, Remarks, *supra* note 17, at 10.

45. Letter from Paul R. Hays to Robert F. Kennedy (May 5, 1961) (sent from Istanbul, Turkey) (copy on file with the United States Courts Library for the Second Circuit).

46. *Politics and the Federal Bench*, N.Y. TIMES, June 3, 1961, at 22.

47. Robinson, *supra* note 37, at 1.

48. *Politics and the Federal Bench*, *supra* note 46, at 22.

49. Herbert Wechsler, *Basis for Naming Judges: Consideration of Professor Hays for Federal Bench Upheld*, N.Y. TIMES, June 8, 1961, at 34.

50. *Judge Paul R. Hays*, N.Y. POST, Sept. 22, 1961, at 48.

51. *Id.*

52. FEDERAL BAR COUNCIL, *supra* note 3, at 42.

53. Henry J. Friendly, *Judge Paul R. Hays*, 72 COLUM. L. REV. 445, 445 (1972).

54. MORRIS, *supra* note 27, at 175. Like Judge Hays, Thurgood Marshall was a recess appointment in October of 1961; he was not confirmed by the Senate until September of 1962. *See* FEDERAL JUDICIAL CENTER, Biographical Directory of Federal Judges, Thurgood Marshall, http://www.fjc.gov/servlet/nGetInfo?jid=1489&cid=999&ctype=na&instate=na.

55. Chief Judge J. Edward Lumbard, Remarks at the Proceedings Held on the Occasion of the Induction of the Honorable Paul R. Hays as United States Court of Appeals Judge for the Second Circuit 2 (Nov. 2, 1961) (transcript on file with the United States Courts Library for the Second Circuit).

56. *Id.*

57. Letter from Harold R. Medina to Paul R. Hays (Sept. 29, 1961) (copy on file with the United States Courts Library for the Second Circuit).

58. *New U.S. Judges Here*, N.Y. TIMES, Mar. 17, 1962, at 52.

59. *Nomination of Paul R. Hays to be United States Circuit Judge for the Second Circuit: Hearing Before the Senate Subcomm. of the Comm. on the Judiciary*, 87th Cong. 5-8 (1962) (statement of Paul R. Hays).

60. Friendly, *supra* note 53, at 445.

61. Email from George A. Davidson, former law clerk, to Sally Pritchard (July 17, 2015, 9:36 EST) (on file with the United States Courts Library for the Second Circuit). Davidson is senior counsel at Hughes Hubbard & Reed.

62. Friendly, *supra* note 53, at 445. George Davidson commented that Judge Hays could take his "habit of terseness to the extreme" by writing a dissent consisting only of the words, "I dissent," which was often to the annoyance of the writer of a majority opinion. Email from George Davidson, *supra* note 61.

63. Friendly, *supra* note 53, at 445.

64. *Id.*

65. 354 F.2d 608 (2d Cir. 1965).

66. *Id.* at 611-612, 611 n.3.

67. *Id.* at 613.

68. *Id.* at 614.

69. *Id.* at 620.

70. *Id.* at 615-16.

71. Scenic Hudson Preservation Conference v. Federal Power Commission, 453 F.2d 463, 467 (2d Cir. 1971). Judge Oakes dissented, in large part because the effects of the project on the Catskill Aqueduct, which provided (and still provides) a critical source of water for New York City, had not been sufficiently addressed. *Id.* at 482-94. Judge Oake's fear that the project could negatively affect the City's water supply did not come to pass. In 1980 Con Ed abandoned its Storm King project under pressure from environmental groups, in exchange for the groups not forcing Con Ed to close any facilities that used outdated cooling technology. *See Power Plant Cases*, RIVERKEEPER, http://www.riverkeeper.org/campaigns/stop-polluters/power-plants/.

72. Friendly, *supra* note 53, at 445-56.

73. 404 F.2d 196 (2d Cir. 1968). Judge Friendly concurred, noting that he was unhappy that the film was to be distributed in the United States, but remarking that "our individual happiness or unhappiness is unimportant, and [the decision] is dictated by Supreme Court decisions." *Id.* at 202. Chief Judge Lumbard dissented, *see infra* note 78.

74. Vincent Canby, *Screen: 'I Am Curious (Yellow)' From Sweden*, N.Y. TIMES, Mar. 11, 1969, at 42.

75. *Id.*

76. 404 F.2d at 198.

77. *Id.* at 199-200.

78. *Id.* at 198-99. Chief Judge Lumbard disagreed. He would have upheld the jury verdict given "the nature of this medium," the fact that "[t]he sexual aspect of the film does not arise from the plot, as that is nonexistent," and that "[t]he only impact [the film] was designed to have are the sexual scenes." *Id.* at 202-03. Judge Lumbard opined that, "[W]hen it comes to a question of what goes beyond the permissible in arousing prurient interest in sex, the jury verdict of twelve men and women is a far better and more accurate reflection of community standards and social value" than the opinion of "circuit judges in their middle sixties who cerebrate in the ivory towers of the judiciary." *Id.* at 204.

79. *Id.* at 199.

80. Letter from Wilfred Feinberg to Paul R. Hays (Sept. 13, 1974) (copy on file with the United States Courts Library for the Second Circuit).

81. Letter from Harold Medina to Paul R. Hays (Aug. 13, 1979) (copy on file with the United States Courts Library for the Second Circuit).

82. *Judge Paul R. Hays Is Dead at 76*, *supra* note 33.

83. Wechsler, Remarks, *supra* note 17, at 9.

84. *Id.* at 10.

85. Harvey J. Goldschmid, former law clerk, Remarks at a Special Session of the United States Court of Appeals for the Second Circuit, In Memoriam, Honorable Paul R. Hays 12, 12-13 (Oct. 21, 1980) (transcript on file with the United States Courts Library for the Second Circuit). Goldschmid was a professor at Columbia Law School.

86. Judge Henry Friendly, Remarks at a Special Session of the United States Court of Appeals for the Second Circuit, In Memoriam, Honorable Paul R. Hays 15, 15-16 (Oct. 21, 1980) (transcript on file with the United States Courts Library for the Second Circuit) (citing to Judge Hays's dissent in N.L.R.B. v. Golub Corp., 388 F.2d 921, 929 (2d Cir. 1967)).

87. Letter from Paul R. Hays to John P. Frank (June 8, 1964) (complimenting Frank on his biography of Supreme Court Justice Peter V. Daniel, who served on the Supreme Court from 1842 to 1860) (copy on file with the United States Courts Library for the Second Circuit).

88. Friendly, Remarks, *supra* note 86, at 18-19.

# THURGOOD MARSHALL
## 1908-1993

Court of Appeals for the Second Circuit: 1961-1965
Supreme Court: 1967-1991

Thurgood Marshall once said that if he could choose an epitaph for himself, it would be: "[H]e did what he could do with what he had."[1] Such an epitaph reflects a notable humility. As the most storied courtroom lawyer of his generation, he used his "combination of intelligence, strength, warmth, charm and earthiness"[2] to persuade courts to adopt his view that "the Constitution was the common person's sword in the enforcement of government's obligation to the individual, and a shield against governmental caprice."[3] After his legendary career as a civil rights lawyer, he served for four years on the Court of Appeals for the Second Circuit before becoming solicitor general of the United

States and then a Supreme Court justice. He was the first black American appointed to each of those posts.

Thoroughgood Marshall, as he was known at birth, was born in 1908 in Baltimore, the second son of William Marshall and Norma Marshall (Williams).[4] His grandparents owned two of the largest grocery stores in Baltimore: his paternal grandfather, Thorney Good Marshall (also born Thoroughgood), owned the T.G. Marshall Store, and his maternal grandfather, Isaiah Olive Branch Williams, owned two others.[5] His parents branched off: his father worked as a waiter and his mother became a teacher.[6]

After Thurgood's birth, the family moved in with Norma's sister and her husband in Harlem, where William worked for the New York Central Railroad.[7] They returned to Baltimore in 1913 and moved in with Norma's brother, Fearless Williams, so that Norma could care for her ailing mother. During Thurgood's childhood, both his grandmothers and his ten aunts and uncles also lived in the neighborhood. When Thurgood and his brother, William Aubrey Marshall, each reached the age of seven, they worked after-school and summer jobs.

Thurgood attended Henry Highland Garnett School 103, generally regarded as the best black elementary school in Baltimore's segregated school system.[8] In second grade, he grew tired of writing out his given name and shortened it to Thurgood. In 1948, when Thurgood was 40 years old, his father had the state records office cross out "Thoroughgood" on his birth certificate and write "Thurgood."[9]

Beginning in 1921, Marshall attended Baltimore's Colored High and Training School. He joined the nascent competitive debating team in ninth grade (collegiate competitive debate had only recently exploded in popularity and started spreading to the high school level); he was the team captain by year's end.[10] At age 16, having completed his graduation requirements, he left school to start raising money for college. He returned to graduate on the stage of Baltimore's Lyric Theatre, which would not allow black performers on its stage for another twenty years. He was one of 14 students to graduate with honors.[11]

Marshall followed his brother Aubrey to Lincoln University. But the family was continually in arrears on Aubrey's tuition payments, as they would be with Thurgood's payments. Each of the five years Thurgood went to Lincoln, his mother had to negotiate with the faculty to finance his return. Thurgood was the first freshman to make the varsity debate team. In a student survey at Lincoln, during his fourth year, he voted against integrating the university's all-white faculty.[12]

During the summer of 1929, and shortly before returning for his final semester, Thurgood married Vivian "Buster" Burey, an education student at the University of Pennsylvania.[13] He did not rejoin the debate team during his final year, focusing instead on trying to raise his grade point average and earning enough credits to graduate to avoid staying another semester. He wound up one credit shy of qualifying for graduation at the end of the semester, but the board of trustees waived the last credit and permitted him to graduate in January 1930.[14]

Thurgood and Buster moved in with his family in Baltimore. He commuted to law school at Howard University. Because classes started at 8:00 am, he had to wake up at 5:00 am to catch the train to Washington. He was part of the first full-time day law school program at Howard, which was rapidly changing to receive accreditation from the American Bar Association and the Association of American Law Schools. Students were discouraged from working nighttime jobs, and several were asked to leave because of low grades: Marshall's class shrank from 39 students to eight.[15]

Marshall had the highest grade point average of his law school class in all three years. William H. Hastie (who would become the first black federal district judge, and later the first black circuit judge) said Marshall was the best first-year law student he had ever taught.[16] His fellow students elected him associate justice and then chief justice of the Court of Peers, the student honor judiciary.[17]

When Marshall was a third-year law student, he began to work with Dean Charles Hamilton Houston on civil rights litigation. Houston had been retained by the NAACP to represent George Crawford, a black man from Boston accused of murdering two white women in Loudon County, Virginia. Crawford was fighting extradition to Virginia, where there was a strong possibility of lynching and little chance of a fair trial (no black American had ever served on a Loudon County jury).[18] Thanks in large part to Marshall's research, a federal judge blocked Crawford's extradition, finding that, because Loudon County unconstitutionally excluded blacks from service on grand juries, any conviction on his Virginia indictment would be reversed on appeal, so there was no purpose in sending him to Virginia.[19]

Marshall graduated law school *cum laude*, took the Maryland bar examination, and spent the early fall traveling with Houston through the deep south. On October 11, 1933, he became the sixtieth black person admitted to the Maryland bar, and only the thirty-fourth active black lawyer in the state.[20]

Marshall's first client was the organizer of Baltimore's "Buy Where You Can Work" campaign, in which Baltimore's black community boycotted and picketed stores that refused to hire black workers. He became the chief negotiator with Baltimore police regarding picketing. He also oversaw the demonstrators and served as a witness in a hearing on whether a temporary injunction against the picketing would be hardened into a permanent one.[21] It was.[22] According to his cousin, Charles Burns, this was the first time Marshall "really got charged up in the area of civil rights."[23] This representation also revealed several lifelong traits, such as an ability to work productively with opposing counsel and others who did not share his viewpoint.[24]

After establishing his practice in Baltimore, and working on more civil rights cases, Marshall founded the NAACP's Legal Defense and Educational Fund as a separate entity from the NAACP. He was its executive director from 1940 until his appointment to the bench in 1961.[25] In that capacity, he argued 32 cases before the Supreme Court, winning 29 of them. He tried a wide variety of cases, involving discriminatory treatment of blacks in the criminal law,[26] education law,[27] transportation law,[28] composition of juries,[29] and public recreational areas.[30] He most famously was counsel in *Brown v. Board of Education of Topeka*,[31] but he also worked on *Shelley v. Kraemer*,[32] and *Smith v. Allwright*.[33] He represented Autherine Lucy,[34] James Meredith,[35] and other pioneers of the civil rights movement, earning the nickname "Mr.

Civil Rights."[36] At trial, whether helping African-Americans avoid the electric chair or helping students trying to integrate schools, he displayed legendary litigation skills, a talent for working with others, tremendous physical courage,[37] and a spirit of optimism and humor in the face of oppression.[38]

Buster died of cancer in February 1955.[39] Marshall remarried in December of that year to Cecilia "Cissy" Suyat, who worked as a secretary in the NAACP headquarters.[40] Stories of his devotion to her are legion; according to one, Marshall, when filling out a judicial financial disclosure form, wrote under the category of "assets" what he believed was the complete list: "My Cissy."[41]

In September 1961, President John F. Kennedy nominated Marshall to one of three newly created seats on the Court of Appeals for the Second Circuit.[42] The Senate recessed the next week; however, in October 1961, he was given a recess appointment to the court.[43] After months of delays at the hands of Mississippi Senator and Judiciary Committee Chairman James O. Eastland, an ardent segregationist, Marshall was confirmed by the Senate in September 1962.[44] He served on the Second Circuit for four years. He was a remarkably informal figure who kept an open-door policy; each morning clerks from other judges' chambers would come by for coffee and to hear him talk in an atmosphere of "earthy stories, salty language, and booming laughter."[45]

Judge Marshall became an instant celebrity on the Second Circuit. District Judge John S. Martin, Jr., then a law clerk for Judge Leonard Moore, recalls "regularly fabricat[ing] reasons why [he] had to deliver something to Judge Marshall's chambers at 10:15 in the morning, because if you arrived at that time, the Judge would invite you to join him and [his clerk] Ralph Winter for coffee. . . . [and] tell the most marvelous stories."[46] He told anecdotes in an inimitable way, and supplied the material for new ones. Judge Ralph K. Winter, Marshall's first law clerk, recalls a group portrait of the Second Circuit judges, at a time when most of New York City's skilled unions refused to admit black workers. In setting up equipment in another judge's chambers, the photographer had blown a fuse. When Judge Marshall walked into the chambers, a secretary said, "You must be the electrician."

In recounting this story, he would remark, "Boy, that woman must be crazy if she thinks I could become an electrician in New York City."[47]

That same year, a rabidly pro-segregation southern governor was being considered for a federal appointment. The FBI asked Judge Marshall about the potential nomination; he "noted that he had irreconcilable differences with the man. However, he added, 'I have got to say, though, that he spent twenty-five years in politics in that state and never became rich. He must be one of the most honest men around.'"[48]

On the bench, Judge Marshall encountered securities cases, labor cases, and civil suits between corporations. In these areas, he found a new mentor in Judge Henry Friendly,[49] who admired Marshall's advocacy skills and accomplishments. Friendly's biographer, David Dorsen, notes that Friendly "went out of his way to assist Marshall, who was unfamiliar with many subjects of the court's work."[50] A Marshall biographer concurs: "For advice when he was over his head, he walked over to the chambers of J. Henry Friendly."[51]

While on the Second Circuit, Judge Marshall wrote 98 majority opinions, eight concurrences, and 12 dissents.[52] The Supreme Court did not reverse any of his majority opinions, and several of his dissents later became law.[53]

In *New York v. Galamison*,[54] civil rights activists prosecuted for civil disobedience during the 1964 World's Fair in Queens removed their criminal prosecutions to federal court, asserting jurisdiction on the ground that their protests constituted action "under color of authority derived from any law providing for equal rights,"[55] specifically the Equal Protection Clause of the Fourteenth Amendment. The district courts ordered all the cases remanded. On appeal, Judge Friendly wrote for the majority that a defendant seeking removal must "point to some law that directs or encourages him to act in a certain manner, not merely to a generalized constitutional provision."[56] Judge Irving R. Kaufman, concurring, clarified that he understood Judge Friendly to mean that removal is appropriate "where the persons seeking removal are being prosecuted for doing something which a specific federal law providing for equal rights gave them the impetus and authority to do."[57] Marshall, in what many regard as his most important opinion on the Second Circuit, dissented, advocating for a broad reading of the statute granting federal courts jurisdiction over civil rights cases.[58] He argued that the statutory phrase "under color of authority" included authority derived from "any law providing for equal rights."[59] He observed that under the majority's approach, removal might "be available to individuals peacefully protesting against segregated public accommodations," which was barred only by statute, but not "to individuals peacefully protesting against segregated public education," which was barred by the Fourteenth Amendment.[60]

He dissented in several other criminal cases, consistently advocating stronger protections for criminal defendants.[61] In others, he wrote majority opinions supporting criminal defendants' appeals or habeas petitions.[62]

Marshall wrote one significant free speech opinion on the Second Circuit. In *Keyishian v. Board of Regents of University of State of New York*,[63] faculty members sued SUNY Buffalo to challenge a New York law requiring all employees of public schools and colleges to sign loyalty oaths swearing that they had never been members of the Communist Party or any organization advocating for the violent overthrow of the government. The plaintiffs argued that the law was unconstitutionally vague and inhibited vital thought and speech.[64] Under federal law at the time, injunctions against state laws found unconstitutional had to be heard by three-judge panels. A district judge denied plaintiffs' motion to convene a three-judge panel, deeming their argument meritless.[65] Writing for the panel on appeal, Marshall ordered the case remanded and heard by a three-judge panel of the district court.[66] On remand, the district court found the statutes constitutional.[67] On direct appeal to the Supreme Court, the statutes were struck down as vague, restrictive of free expression, and overbroad.[68]

Marshall did not invariably come down on the side of the accused. In *United States v. Rickenbacker*,[69] he upheld the conviction of a man who refused to fill out a 1960 census questionnaire, concluding that "[t]he authority to gather reliable statistical data reasonably related to governmental purposes and functions is a necessity if modern government is to legislate intelligently and effectively." In *Seneca Nation of Indians v. United States,*[70] he upheld the government's power to condemn land given by treaty to a Native American tribe. He held that "[i]t is hard to see how a four-lane road will interfere with communication among the Senecas so much more than a two-lane road."[71] In dissent, Judge Leonard Moore quoted Justice Hugo Black's dictum, "Great nations, like great men, should keep their word."[72]

Judge Marshall resigned from the Second Circuit in 1965, when President Lyndon B. Johnson appointed him solicitor general. He served in that position from 1965 to 1967, and was appointed to a seat on the Supreme Court in 1967. He was the justice assigned to the Second Circuit from 1971 until his 1991 retirement, and remained involved with the Second Circuit in other ways, including speaking at the court's one hundredth anniversary in 1991.[73] He wrote one opinion for the Second Circuit after his retirement, in an antitrust case,[74] and served on four other Second Circuit panels.[75] He died of heart failure in 1993, survived by his wife, Cissy, and their two sons, Thurgood, Jr., and John W. Marshall. The Foley Square Courthouse was renamed in his honor in 2001.[76]

David Byowitz

1. William L. Taylor, *Thurgood Marshall,* 68 N.Y.U. L. REV. 205, 212 (1993).

2. District Judge John S. Martin, Jr., Remarks at a Special Session of the United States Court of Appeals for the Second Circuit, Honoring the Memory of Justice Thurgood Marshall XVIII (Apr. 14, 1993) (transcript on file with the United States Courts Library for the Second Circuit).

3. Robert L. Carter, *Thurgood Marshall,* 68 N.Y.U. L. REV. 205, 206 (1993).

4. LARRY S. GIBSON, YOUNG THURGOOD: THE MAKING OF A SUPREME COURT JUSTICE 41 (2012).

5. *Id.* at 36–41.

6. *Id.* at 41, 45.

7. *Id.* at 50.

8. JUAN WILLIAMS, THURGOOD MARSHALL: AMERICAN REVOLUTIONARY 28 (1998); GIBSON, *supra* note 4, at 56-59.

9. GIBSON, *supra* note 4, at 58-59.

10. WILLIAMS, *supra* note 8, at 34, 36.

11. *See* GIBSON, *supra* note 4, at 61-80; WILLIAMS, *supra* note 8, at 24-39.

12. *See* GIBSON, *supra* note 4, at 81-100; WILLIAMS, *supra* note 8, at 40-51. Apparently, opposition to integration was rooted in two rival black fraternities: students feared that black professors would display favoritism toward members of their own fraternity, whereas white professors would not. *See* WILLIAMS, *supra* note 8, at 48.

13. WILLIAMS, *supra* note 8, at 50.

14. GIBSON, *supra* note 4, at 101-03; WILLIAMS, *supra* note 8, at 50-51.

15. GIBSON, *supra* note 4, at 107–12.

16. GIBSON, *supra* note 4, at 112.

17. *Id.* at 114.

18. *Id.* at 120–21.

19. Comment, *Race Discrimination and Interstate Rendition – The Crawford Case*, 43 YALE L.J. 444, 444–45 (1934). The First Circuit reversed six weeks later; Crawford was extradited, convicted, and given a life sentence rather than the death penalty. GIBSON, *supra* note 4, at 120-23; WILLIAMS, *supra* note 8, at 58-59; *see also* Hale v. Crawford, 65 F.2d 739 (1st Cir. 1933).

20. GIBSON, *supra* note 4, at 123–25.

21. GIBSON, *supra* note 4, at 153–57.

22. Samuelson v. Green, Cir. Ct. Balt. City (1934), BALTIMORE DAILY RECORD, May 26, 1934, at 5; *aff'd* Green v. Samuelson, 178 A. 109 (Md. 1935).

23. GIBSON, *supra* note 4, at 165 (quoting interview by author).

24. *See generally id.* at 153–65; WILLIAMS, *supra* note 8, at 71–73.

25. FEDERAL JUDICIAL CENTER, Biographical Directory of Federal Judges, Thurgood Marshall, http://www.fjc.gov/servlet/nGetInfo?jid=1489&cid=999&ctype=na&instate=na.

26. *See, e.g.*, Lyons v. Oklahoma, 322 U.S. 596 (1944); Cooper v. Aaron, 358 U.S. 1 (1958).

27. *See, e.g.*, Sweatt v. Painter, 339 U.S. 629 (1950).

28. *See, e.g.*, Boynton v. Virginia, 364 U.S. 454 (1960).

29. *See, e.g.*, Patton v. Mississippi, 332 U.S. 463 (1947).

30. *See, e.g.*, Holmes v. City of Atlanta, 350 U.S. 879 (1955).

31. 347 U.S. 483 (1954).

32. 334 U.S. 1 (1948) (holding that courts lacked the authority to enforce restrictive racial covenants).

33. 321 U.S. 649 (1944) (invalidating the practice of *de jure* exclusion of black voters from the Democratic party primaries in the one-party south).

34. Lucy v. Adams, 134 F. Supp. 235 (D. Ala. 1955); *aff'd*, 350 U.S. 1 (1955).

35. Meredith v. Fair, 202 F. Supp. 224 (S.D. Miss. 1962); *rev'd*, 305 F.2d 343 (5th Cir. 1962). Marshall's associate counsel on the brief was Constance Baker Motley, who later became a judge on the District Court for the Southern District of New York.

36. MICHAEL D. DAVIS & HUNTER R. CLARK, THURGOOD MARSHALL: WARRIOR AT THE BAR, REBEL ON THE BENCH 121 (1992).

37. When Marshall would come to small southern towns, he would stay in the houses of local black families. "Later in the day, word would spread: 'Men are needed to sit up all night with a sick friend.' You'd hear it whispered everywhere. They'd all know what it meant. They were lining up armed guards to keep Marshall safe from night-riding Klansmen while he slept." GILBERT KING, DEVIL IN THE GROVE: THURGOOD MARSHALL, THE GROVELAND BOYS, AND THE DAWN OF A NEW AMERICA 5 (2012).

38. In handling a trial (of a case that resulted in the integration of the University of Oklahoma Law School), Marshall and his client, Ada Lois Sipuel, had to lunch on vending-machine peanuts in the courthouse basement, because no restaurants within walking distance would serve them. According to his client, after lunch, Marshall told her: "I'm gonna try this case for you, but as of tomorrow you're in charge of bologna sandwiches." *See* Sherrilyn A. Ifill, *Thurgood Marshall*, 68 N.Y.U. L. REV. 205, 224, 224 n.24 (1993). Marshall eventually won her case before the Supreme

Court, and Sipuel became the first black student at the University of Oklahoma Law School. *See* Sipuel v. Bd. of Regents of Univ. of Okla., 332 U.S. 631 (1948); *rev'g* 180 P.2d 135 (Okla. 1947); *see also About OU Law*, UNIV. OF OKLA. COLLEGE OF LAW, http://www.law.ou.edu/content/about-ou-law.

39. DAVIS & CLARK, *supra* note 36, at 45.

40. *Id.* at 181. While the short time period between Buster's death and Thurgood's marriage to Cissy led to speculation among their social circle, friends of both Thurgood and Cissy deny that their romance began before Vivian's death. *Id.* at 181-82.

41. District Judge John S. Martin, Jr., Remarks, *supra* note 2, at XIX.

42. GLENN L. STARKS & F. ERIK BROOKS, THURGOOD MARSHALL: A BIOGRAPHY 53–55 (2012); *see also* Act of May 19, 1961, Pub. L. No. 87-36, 75 Stat. 80 (1961) (increasing Second Circuit from six seats to nine).

43. FEDERAL JUDICIAL CENTER, *supra* note 25.

44. The nomination was further held up by Eastland's choice of South Carolina Senator Olin Johnston to chair the subcommittee handling Marshall's nomination; Johnston was in a bitter reelection campaign against his state's segregationist governor, Ernest Hollings, and he feared that Hollings would win the election if Marshall were confirmed before the Democratic primary in June. *See* WILLIAMS, *supra* note 8, at 298–99. For a more detailed picture regarding Marshall's confirmation, *see* Richard L. Revesz, *Thurgood Marshall's Struggle*, 68 N.Y.U. L. REV. 237 (1993).

45. Judge Ralph K. Winter, Remarks at the Proceedings of the Bar and Officers of the Supreme Court of the United States, In Memoriam, Honorable Thurgood Marshall XIII (Nov. 15, 1993) (transcript on file with the United States Courts Library for the Second Circuit); WILLIAMS, *supra* note 8, at 298.

46. District Judge John S. Martin, Jr., Remarks, *supra* note 2, at XVII–XVIII.

47. Ralph K. Winter, *TM's Legacy*, 101 YALE L.J. 25, 29 (1991).

48. *Id.* at 28.

49. WILLIAMS, *supra* note 8, at 304–05.

50. DAVID M. DORSEN, HENRY FRIENDLY: GREATEST JUDGE OF HIS ERA 115 (2012).

51. WILLIAMS, *supra* note 8, at 304-05. In later years, when Judge Friendly recommended a clerk for Justice Marshall, Marshall told the clerk, "If you're good enough for Friendly, you're good enough for me." DORSEN, *supra* note 50, at 407 n.16 (quoting Interview with Ira Feinberg (Nov. 20, 2006)).

52. RANDALL W. BLAND, PRIVATE PRESSURE ON PUBLIC LAW: THE LEGAL CAREER OF JUSTICE THURGOOD MARSHALL 120 (1993); DAVIS & CLARK, *supra* note 36, at 240.

53. HOWARD BALL, A DEFIANT LIFE: THURGOOD MARSHALL AND THE PERSISTENCE OF RACISM IN AMERICA 184 (1998).

54. 342 F.2d 255 (1965).

55. 28 U.S.C. § 1443 (2012).

56. 342 F.2d at 264.

57. *Id.* at 273 (Kaufman, J., concurring).

58. *Id.* at 277 (Marshall, J., dissenting).

59. *Id.*; *see also* 28 U.S.C. § 1443 (2012).

60. 342 F.2d at 278 (Marshall, J., dissenting); *cf.* Civil Rights Act of 1964, Pub. L. No. 88-352, 78 Stat. 241 (1964) (barring segregated public accommodations); Brown v. Bd. of Educ. of Topeka, 347 U.S. 483 (1954) (holding segregated public primary education unconstitutional).

61. *See, e.g.*, United States ex rel. Castillo v. Fay, 350 F.2d 400, 405 (2d Cir. 1965) (Marshall, J., dissenting) (exclusionary rule bars testimony about the fruit of an unconstitutional search); United States v. Aviles, 337 F.2d 552, 560 (2d Cir. 1964) (Marshall, J., dissenting) (dissenting from denial of new trial in light of the Government's failure to produce impeachment evidence); United States ex

rel. Angelet v. Fay, 333 F.2d 12 (2d Cir. 1964) (*en banc*) (Marshall, J., dissenting) (arguing that the exclusionary rule applied retroactively).

62. *See, e.g.*, Hetenyi v. Wilkins, 348 F.2d 844 (2d Cir. 1965) (holding that the Fourteenth Amendment bars a state from prosecuting a defendant multiple times for the same crime). Four years later he wrote a Supreme Court opinion to the same effect. *See* Benton v. Maryland, 395 U.S. 784 (1969).

63. 345 F.2d 236 (2d Cir. 1965).

64. *Keyishian*, 345 F.2d at 237.

65. Keyishian v. Bd. of Regents of Univ. of State of N.Y., 233 F. Supp. 752 (W.D.N.Y. 1964).

66. *Keyishian*, 345 F.2d at 238–39.

67. Keyishian v. Bd. of Regents of Univ. of State of N.Y., 255 F. Supp. 981 (W.D.N.Y. 1966).

68. Keyishian v. Bd. of Regents of Univ. of State of N.Y., 385 U.S. 589 (1967).

69. 309 F.2d 462 (2d Cir. 1962).

70. 338 F.2d 55 (2d Cir. 1964).

71. 338 F.2d at 57.

72. *Id.* at 57 (Moore, J., dissenting).

73. *See* Thurgood Marshall, *Introductory Remarks: Celebrating the Second Circuit Centennial*, 65 ST. JOHN'S L. REV. 645 (1991). When Marshall swore in his first law clerk, Ralph K. Winter, as a judge on the Second Circuit, "he reminded his new junior colleague that Justice Marshall was no longer to be an object of Winterian criticism." *See* District Judge Louis H. Pollack, Remarks at a Special Session of the United States Court of Appeals for the Second Circuit, Honoring the Memory of Justice Thurgood Marshall VIII (Apr. 14, 1993) (transcript on file with the United States Courts Library for the Second Circuit).

74. Trans Sport, Inc. v. Starter Sportswear, Inc., 964 F.2d 186 (2d Cir. 1992).

75. Morgan v. United States, 968 F.2d 200 (2d Cir. 1992); United States v. Butler, 970 F.2d 1017 (2d Cir. 1992); In re Grand Jury Subpoenas Dated Oct. 22, 1991, and Nov. 1, 1991, 959 F.2d 1158 (2d Cir. 1992); Sharpton v. Turner, 964 F.2d 1284 (2d Cir. 1992).

76. Act of August 20, 2001, Pub. L. No. 107-33, 115 Stat. 215 (2001).

# ROBERT PALMER ANDERSON
# 1906-1978

District Court for the District of Connecticut:
1954-1964
Court of Appeals for the Second Circuit: 1964-1978

Robert Palmer Anderson's ancestors were masters of sailing vessels and builders of ships.[1] A great lover of the sea himself, Anderson was a decorated veteran of the Coast Guard and, as a senior judge, kept his judicial chambers in his hometown coastal retreat of Noank, Connecticut, where he wrote dozens of admiralty decisions.[2]

Anderson was born in Noank on March 27, 1906, to Arthur Pickett and Jessie Palmer Anderson.[3] Following in his father's footsteps, Anderson, who went by Bob, attended Phillips Academy Andover, Yale College, and Yale Law School.[4] At Yale, he later served as a fellow of Jonathan Edwards College.[5] Anderson married Elizabeth Paffard of Brooklyn on January 5, 1935.[6] Together they had two sons, Robert Palmer Anderson, Jr., and Frederic Paffard Anderson.[7] "He was a devoted family man with a deep love for his [] wife, Libby, and his sons."[8]

After law school, Anderson went into private practice in the New London law firm of Waller, Waller, Avery & Gallup.[9] Anderson became a public defender, serving in New London County for eleven years.[10] He served as commissioner of the District Court for the District of Connecticut (predecessor to the magistrate) in 1936 and participated as a member of the Connecticut State Bar Examining Committee from 1936 to 1954.[11]

During World War II, at the age of 36, Anderson joined the Coast Guard, serving as a commander for the duration of the war.[12] Before he was deployed abroad, Anderson served as captain of the port of New London, Connecticut, "command[ing] the waters leading into the Long Island Sound."[13] He was soon reassigned to the 8th Amphibious Force of the Navy, participating in the North African Campaign, followed by the 11th Amphibious Force, stationed in London.[14] Anderson's "unit had the responsibility for all naval transport from England to the invasion beaches in Normandy."[15] At the war's end, he was awarded the Bronze Star, for "heroic or meritorious achievement or service," and the Order of the British Empire, an English honor given or conferred for "a significant achievement or outstanding service."[16] After the war, he served in the Coast Guard Reserve until 1957 and ended his tenure with the rank of captain.[17]

After the war, Anderson returned to practicing as a public defender in New London County. He became the state's attorney for New London County in 1947.[18] As state's attorney, Anderson was compassionate, yet he possessed a "strict honesty" and "devotion to duty"; "he never took unfair advantage and never was critical without lightening the criticism with delightful humor."[19] In the same year, Anderson was elected to the State Senate of Connecticut.[20] From 1952 until 1953, Anderson served on the Judicial Council for the State of Connecticut.[21] He was elected as a judge in Connecticut Superior Court in 1953.[22]

After Anderson had served for one year as a state court judge, President Dwight D. Eisenhower appointed him to the District Court for the District of Connecticut.[23] Representative Thomas J. Dodd of Connecticut remarked that Judge Anderson's confirmation "mean[t] that the Federal court in Connecticut [would] continue, as it has in the past, to be known for the outstanding ability and sterling character of its judges."[24] He went on to say that Judge Anderson had already earned an "enviable reputation in Connecticut as State's attorney for New London County and as a judge of our superior court" and that "Judge Anderson [was] young enough to be vigorous and enthusiastic and experienced enough to be moderate, careful, and scholarly. By temperament, by training, and by intellectual achievement he [was] well qualified to become one of the outstanding judges in our Federal system."[25]

Judge Anderson served as a district judge from 1954 to 1964, including four years as chief judge from 1960 to 1964.[26]

At the district court, Judge Anderson oversaw the reorganization of the bankrupt New Haven Railroad.[27] The railroad first declared bankruptcy in 1935.[28] For 12 years, District Judge Carroll C. Hincks oversaw the proceedings.[29] The railroad returned to bankruptcy in 1961, and Judge Anderson oversaw the proceedings for the following 17 years.[30] He kept the case after his appointment to the Second Circuit because he did not want to "saddle one of the District Judges with the task of learning all that had gone before and of handling all the ongoing problems of the receivership."[31] Over 17 years, he held 286 hearings on 850 petitions.[32] Anticipating the rough time ahead at the first case conference, Judge Anderson cried out, "Cling to the rigging!"[33] He often used this phrase, which "dripped of the sea he loved so well," and its "message came through to the landlubber, simple and clear: hang onto your saddle and don't fall off."[34] In the district court, he was an authority on admiralty law, displaying the silver oar of the admiralty on the bench, "although he never admitted to any expertise on the subject."[35]

In 1964, President Lyndon B. Johnson appointed Judge Anderson to the Court of Appeals for the Second Circuit.[36] Judge Anderson's varied legal experience gave him a "superlative background for the problems that came before him on the Court of Appeals."[37] The newly appointed appellate judge maintained an office at 40 Foley Square, but his principal chambers remained in Connecticut.[38] While Judge Anderson originally kept chambers in New Haven, he eventually moved them to his Noank property.[39] His chambers included "a complete federal law library overlooking the woods that was separate from and out of sight of his own residence."[40] Judge Anderson's longtime secretary, Phoebe Watrous, worked alongside him in the Noank chambers.[41] Every afternoon at four o'clock, Judge Anderson sat for tea and biscuits with Ms. Watrous and his law clerk, a habit cultivated during his military service in England during World War II.[42]

Judge Anderson's judicial work touched a wide variety of areas of law, including many controversial disputes. His opinions in *Berk v. Laird* and *Orlando v. Laird* upheld the constitutionality of the Vietnam War against challenges based on the absence of a declaration of war from Congress.[43] While other judges may have

> shirked this onerous burden relying on such convenient doctrines as political questions or nonjudiciable controversy, Judge Anderson proceeded to the merits. Such quality of mind enabled him to arrive at a conclusion he believed right, although it might be unpopular at the time, and was a clear demonstration of integrity and plucky decisiveness.[44]

Because of his seafaring past, Judge Anderson was "inevitably [] assigned any admiralty cases" that came before his panels.[45] In the words of Judge Irving R. Kaufman, "there were none who were [Anderson's] peers when he wrote of the sea."[46] Judge Anderson wrote 40 opinions involving maritime law.[47] His 1968 opinion in *Esso Standard Oil, S.A. v. S.S. Gasbras Sul*[48] was "frequently cited for its Conradesque description of wind, rain, and sea."[49]

> [I]t was raining. The current was setting from west to east at a rate slightly over a knot, and there were swells from the south. Darkness fell between 1830 and 1900,

> somewhat intensified by clouds and rain. The Master described the weather as 'up and down' all afternoon. The gentle-moderate wind had continued but the swells had gradually increased. . . . [T]he combination of wind and current and the increased swells were causing the vessel to yaw badly. A torrential rain had reduced visibility almost to zero. Under these circumstances the Master would have chosen to slip his moorings, take up his anchors and stand out to sea. What prevented him from doing so was the presence of the seven marker buoys and their chains, which were unlighted; one might be seen occasionally but only by chance. Some were heavy in the water from barnacles and the weight of the chains, and they rode so low in the water and were so poorly painted that they were hard to see. They could not be picked-up by flashlight beams which reflected back in the heavy rain.[50]

Judge Anderson's skills went well beyond admiralty. "[I]t was his capacity to view central issues and slough off nonessentials that made his opinions especially wise, clear and concise."[51] His "character was reflected in the language of his opinions," where his writing style "was not ornate, his preference was for clear and serviceable prose, which in its very simplicity often achieved eloquence."[52] His prior experience as a public defender, state's attorney, and a judge made him especially valuable to the court. Judge Kaufman stated, "If there was ever an individual who could see both sides of a dispute, it was Bob."[53] He had "an enlightened mind, not one darkened by prejudice or superstition, a mind filled with the simplest and finest source of illumination, common sense."[54]

Judge Anderson had two law clerks, one stationed at the Foley Square courthouse, and the other, "the fortunate clerk," with him in his Noank "chambers."[55] Once he felt that his law clerks had learned the ropes, he gave them "considerable latitude to express opinions" and "engage in debate on issues arising from the cases."[56] However, this had its limits. In one instance, Judge Anderson assigned one of his clerks to draft an admiralty opinion. The judge overheard his secretary explaining to the clerk, "now this is the bow, and this is the stern." Judge Anderson turned to the clerk and said, "On second thought, I will draft that opinion myself."[57]

Judge Anderson carried this "keen sense of humor" both on and off the bench.[58] A law clerk recalled an oral argument where the central issue was whether the appellant was a "responsible officer" as defined by the controlling statute.[59] Counsel began his argument by stating, "Your Honors, my client was not a responsible officer," to which Judge Anderson immediately countered, "Counsel, is it your position then that your client was an irresponsible officer?"[60] Another law clerk recalled a story that Judge Anderson told about swimming backstroke for Yale as an undergraduate: during one meet, he swam straight out from under his bathing suit. But without missing a beat, he finished the race.[61]

District Judge Robert C. Zampano clerked for Anderson at the district court and succeeded him as a district judge.[62] Judge Zampano described Anderson as combining "exceptional intellectual ability with compassion and understanding in all his dealings with human beings" with a "kindly twinkle in his eyes, and [a] courteous and refined demeanor."[63] Judge Anderson was a "truly outstanding trial judge" who "listened attentively to the testimony of the witnesses and the presentations of the lawyers."[64]

Judge Anderson was best remembered for his "unfailing good humor, his kindness and consideration."[65] He has been described by many as humble and kind, quick to put others at ease, and eternally patient.[66] He was a "teller of tales" and a "raconteur par excellence," always having "an anecdote for every occasion."[67] And, as to be expected, Judge Anderson loved to speak about sailing. "There was not much that he did not know about sailing vessels, not only his own but also the great sailing ships (on which he could tell you the proper name of each of the dozens of sails)."[68] But his stories of sailing, fishing, or naval operations never recounted his own decorations or achievements.[69]

Throughout his career, he maintained a close relationship with Noank. He served as director of the Marine Historical Association, and usually led the Noank Memorial Day parade in his Coast Guard uniform.[70] He fostered his "roots in both Yale College and Yale Law School," acting as a panel member for the Moot Court's final argument only weeks before he died.[71] Judge Anderson was also an active member of the Baptist Church in Noank; he even "once persuaded Judge Harold R. Medina to preach there."[72] His wife, Elizabeth, was a trustee of several colleges and was a "stalwart worker on various committees important to Connecticut."[73] Their sons became a doctor and a lawyer.[74]

Judge Anderson assumed senior status in 1971, largely due to his health.[75] However, "when the Chief Justice called on him to sit on the Temporary Emergency Court of Appeals, he took on that task as well as continuing to sit with the Second Circuit and in the New Haven case."[76] At one point, Judge Anderson took ill and was rushed to the hospital; his colleagues sent flowers to his room.[77] On realizing that he had been accidentally assigned to the gynecological wing of the hospital, Judge Anderson sent the court a memorandum, writing, "It occurred to me that if word of this got back to the court, a majority and an *in banc* sitting might very well vote to recall the beautiful tribute on the grounds that there had been a fraud in the inducement."[78]

Judge Anderson continued to serve as a Second Circuit judge until his death on May 2, 1978.[79] He was survived by his wife and two sons and their families.[80] A joint session of the Second Circuit and the District Court for the District of Connecticut was held to commemorate Judge Anderson's life; a host of renowned legal figures spoke at the service and recounted a man described principally as "a true gentleman, an outstanding jurist and a dear friend."[81]

Later that year, the *Brooklyn Law Review* dedicated its annual review of important cases to Judge Anderson, voicing hope that "this dedication will help to keep alive the memory of a great lawyer and jurist, a warm and compassionate man, who was admired and loved by all who knew him."[82] The dedication ended by claiming, "The lesson to be learned from this brief review of Judge Anderson's career can be summarized in a verse from Henry Wadsworth Longfellow's *Psalm of Life*:

Lives of great men all remind us
We can make our lives sublime,
And, departing leave behind us
Footprints on the sands of time."[83]

Abigail Dwyer Maltz

1. Leonard P. Moore, *Dedication: Robert Palmer Anderson*, 45 BROOK. L. REV. xvii, xvii (1978-1979).

2. *Id.*

3. HAROLD CHASE ET AL., BIOGRAPHICAL DICTIONARY OF THE FEDERAL JUDICIARY 7 (1976).

4. CHASE ET AL., *supra* note 3, at 7.

5. *Id.* at 8.

6. *See* CHASE ET AL., *supra* note 3, at 7; Moore, *Dedication: Robert Palmer Anderson, supra* note 1, at xvii.

7. Moore, *Dedication: Robert Palmer Anderson, supra* note 1, at 3.

8. District Judge Robert Zampano, Remarks at a Joint Session of the United States Court of Appeals for the Second Circuit and the United States District Court for the District of Connecticut, In Memory of the Honorable Robert P. Anderson 16 (June 19, 1978) *in* 581 F.2d LIX.

9. 1 JUDGES OF THE UNITED STATES 11 (2d ed. 1983).

10. CHASE ET AL., *supra* note 3, at 7.

11. *Id.*; 1 JUDGES OF THE UNITED STATES, *supra* note 9, at 11.

12. CHASE ET AL., *supra* note 3, at 8; E-mail from Michael A. Varet, former law clerk, to Sally Pritchard (June 30, 2015, 2:57 EST) (on file with the United States Courts Library for the Second Circuit).Varet is a partner at DLA Piper.

13. Email from Michael A. Varet, *supra* note 12.

14. Allyn L. Brown, Jr., Remarks at a Joint Session of the United States Court of Appeals for the Second Circuit and the United States District Court for the District of Connecticut, In Memory of the Honorable Robert P. Anderson 12-13 (June 19, 1978) *in* 581 F.2d LIX. Brown is a past president of the Connecticut State Bar Association.

15. *Id.* at 13.

16. CHASE ET AL., *supra* note 3, at 8; *U.S. Air Force Fact Sheet: Bronze Star*, DEP'T A.F., http://www.afpc.af.mil/library/factsheets/factsheet_print.asp?fsID=7771&page=1; *The Honours System*, GOV.UK., https://www.gov.uk/honours/types-of-honours-and-awards.

17. FEDERAL JUDICIAL CENTER, Biographical Directory of Federal Judges, Robert Palmer Anderson, http://www.fjc.gov/servlet/nGetInfo?jid=49&cid=999&ctype=na&instate=na.

18. *Id.* at 7.

19. Brown, Jr., Remarks, *supra* note 14, at 13.

20. FEDERAL JUDICIAL CENTER, *supra* note 17.

21. *Id.*

22. *Id.*

23. *Id.*

24. *Extension of Remarks of Hon. Thomas J. Dodd*, 100 CONG. REC. 5802 (1954) (statement of Rep. Dodd).

25. *Id.*

26. FEDERAL JUDICIAL CENTER, *supra* note 17.

27. Special Supplement, *Colleagues for Justice: One Hundred Years of the United States Court of Appeals for the Second Circuit*, 65 ST. JOHN'S L. REV. 938, 961 (1991); *see also The New Haven Railroad Reorganization Proceedings, or the Little Railroad that Couldn't*, 78 HARV. L. REV. 861, 861 (1965).

28. *A Brief History of the New Haven Railroad*, NEW HAVEN RAILROAD HIST. AND TECHNICAL ASS'N, INC., http://www.nhrhta.org/htdocs/history.htm.

29. *Carroll Hincks, U.S. Judge, Dead*, N.Y. TIMES, Oct. 1, 1964, http://www.nytimes.com/1964/10/01/carroll-hincks-us-judge-dead.html.

30. Judge J. Joseph Smith, Remarks at a Joint Session of the United States Court of Appeals for the Second Circuit and the United States District Court for the District of Connecticut, In Memory of the Honorable Robert P. Anderson 19 (June 19, 1978) *in* 581 F.2d LIX.

31. *Id.*

32. *Id.*

33. James William Moore, Remarks at a Joint Session of the United States Court of Appeals for the Second Circuit and the United States District Court for the District of Connecticut, In Memory of the Honorable Robert P. Anderson 6 (June 19, 1978) *in* 581 F.2d LIX. Moore is the Sterling Professor Emeritus of Law at Yale Law School.

34. *Id.*

35. Judge J. Joseph Smith, Remarks, *supra* note 30, at 22.

36. FEDERAL JUDICIAL CENTER, *supra* note 17.

37. Moore, *Dedication: Robert Palmer Anderson, supra* note 1, at xvii.

38. E-mail from Josette Jones, to Sally Pritchard (Feb. 16, 2016, 5:29 EST) (on file with the United States Courts Library for the Second Circuit). Jones serves as interior architect for the Second Circuit.

39. *See* E-mail from Dale E. Thomas, former law clerk, to Sally Pritchard (July 14, 2016, 12:04 EST) (on file with the United States Courts Library for the Second Circuit). Thomas is a senior counsel at Sidley Austin, LLP in Chicago; *see also* E-mail from Michael A. Varet, *supra* note 12.

40. E-mail from Dale E. Thomas, *supra* note 39.

41. E-mail from Michael A. Varet, *supra* note 12.

42. *Id.*

43. *See* Orlando v. Laird, 443 F.2d 1039, 1043 (2d Cir. 1976); Berk v. Laird, 429 F.2d 302, 305–07 (2d Cir. 1970).

44. Chief Judge Irving R. Kaufman, Remarks at a Joint Session of the United States Court of Appeals for the Second Circuit and the United States District Court for the District of Connecticut, In Memory of the Honorable Robert P. Anderson 23-24 (June 19, 1978) *in* 581 F.2d LIX.

45. Email from Dale E. Thomas, *supra* note 39.

46. Chief Judge Irving R. Kaufman, Remarks, *supra* note 44, at 24.

47. *Colleagues for Justice, supra* note 27, at 962.

48. 387 F.2d 573 (1968).

49. *Id.*

50. *Esso Standard Oil S. A.*, 387 F.2d at 575.

51. Moore, *Dedication: Robert Palmer Anderson, supra* note 1, at xvii.

52. Chief Judge Irving R. Kaufman, Remarks, *supra* note 44, at 24.

53. *Id.* at 23.

54. *Id.*

55. E-mail from Dale E. Thomas, *supra* note 39.

56. *Id.*

57. *Id.*.

58. E-mail from Michael A. Varet, *supra* note 12.

59. *Id.*

60. *Id.*

61. E-mail from Dale E. Thomas, *supra* note 39.

62. District Judge Robert Zampano, Remarks, *supra* note 8, at 13.

63. *Id.* at 14.

64. *Id.* at 16.

65. Moore, *Dedication: Robert Palmer Anderson, supra* note 1, at xviii.

66. *See* James William Moore, Remarks, *supra* note 33, at 6.

67. Moore, *Dedication: Robert Palmer Anderson, supra* note 1, at xviii; James William Moore, Remarks, *supra* note 33, at 7.

68. E-mail from Michael A. Varet, *supra* note 12.

69. *See* James William Moore, Remarks, *supra* note 33, at 7.

70. CHASE ET AL., *supra* note 3, at 8; Moore, *Dedication: Robert Palmer Anderson, supra* note 1, at xviii.

71. James William Moore, Remarks, *supra* note 33, at 7.

72. Moore, *Dedication: Robert Palmer Anderson, supra* note 1, at xviii.

73. *Id.*.

74. *Id.*

75. FEDERAL JUDICIAL CENTER, *supra* note 17; Judge J. Joseph Smith, Remarks, *supra* note 30, at 21.

76. Judge J. Joseph Smith, Remarks, *supra* note 30, at 21.

77. Chief Judge Irving R. Kaufman, Remarks, *supra* note 44, at 25.

78. *Id.*

79. *See* Judge J. Joseph Smith, Remarks, *supra* note 30, at 19.

80. Moore, *Dedication: Robert Palmer Anderson, supra* note 1, at xviii.

81. Retired Chief Justice of the Connecticut Supreme Court Charles S. House, Remarks at a Joint Session of the United States Court of Appeals for the Second Circuit and the United States District Court for the District of Connecticut, In Memory of the Honorable Robert P. Anderson 23-24 (June 19, 1978) *in* 581 F.2d LIX.

82. Moore, *Dedication: Robert Palmer Anderson, supra* note 1, at xvii.

83. *Id.* at 3.

## WILFRED FEINBERG
## 1920-2014

District Court for the Southern District of New York: 1961-1966
Court of Appeals for the Second Circuit: 1966-2011

Wilfred Feinberg was a judge who "regard[ed] judicial office as a way to serve justice, not as a chance to wield power."[1] Born June 22, 1920 in New York City to Jack and Eva Feinberg,[2] who owned a hosiery company,[3] he and his family moved to Mount Vernon, New York, when he was nine.[4]

Feinberg completed high school in 1936, at age 16, and was elected to Phi Beta Kappa at Columbia College.[5] Unsure what to do next, Feinberg enrolled in Columbia Law School.[6] Feinberg was "scared to death" in his first year, but his father convinced him to finish the year (for which he had already paid the tuition), and at year's end, he was asked to join the *Columbia Law Review*.[7]

Feinberg left Columbia after two years to join the Army at the outbreak of World War II.[8] He served in the U.S. Signal Corps, decoding and encoding messages, and participated in the invasions of Sicily and mainland Italy.[9] He often recalled that he was on a troop transportation in the Pacific destined for the invasion of Japan when the war was ended by the dropping of the atomic bombs.[10] While in the Army, Feinberg became interested in writing fiction: a few of his short stories were published in *Yank, the Army Weekly*.[11]

In the summer of 1945, while staying in Mount Vernon before returning to law school, Feinberg met and became engaged to Shirley Marcus; they were married the following June, and remained together until his death, 68 years later.[12] Both were skilled tennis players.[13] They had three children: Jack, Susan, and Jessica.[14]

Feinberg returned to Columbia Law School in the fall of 1945, was elected editor-in-chief of the *Columbia Law Review*,[15] and graduated in 1946.[16] Feinberg's association with Columbia University would remain important to him all his life.[17] At least one law clerk was always a Columbia Law School graduate.[18] Feinberg also served on the board of visitors for both Columbia College and Columbia Law School, and was president of the law school's alumni association from 1974 to 1976.[19] In 1990, the law school awarded Feinberg its highest honor, the Medal for Excellence.[20] Every year, Columbia's Wilfred Feinberg Prize, created in 1998, is presented to "a student who does the best work in an area related to federal courts," and the Wilfred Feinberg Scholarship in Law, created in 2010, "is awarded to students based on academic accomplishment and financial need."[21]

After law school, Feinberg clerked for District Judge James P. McGranery in Philadelphia,[22] and then worked as an associate at Kaye, Scholer, Fierman, Hays & Handler.[23] In 1953, he became a partner at McGoldrick, Dannett, Horowitz & Golub,[24] where his practice focused on corporate reorganization.[25] He left private practice in 1958 to serve as New York deputy superintendent of banking.[26]

In 1961, when he was 41 years old,[27] Feinberg received a recess appointment from President John F. Kennedy to fill a newly created position on the Southern District of New York.[28] He would serve on the bench for 50 years.[29] He "quickly gained a reputation as a wise, industrious, and thoroughly capable trial judge."[30] Judge Feinberg's courtroom was "a place of dignity without stuffiness," and he "presided with a light hand: unfailingly courteous, even-tempered, considerate, and always gently in command."[31] Judge Pierre N. Leval once noted, when he was a law clerk to Judge Henry Friendly, the young Judge Feinberg was "obviously destined for a brilliant future."[32]

During his five years on the district court, Judge Feinberg wrote several important decisions.[33] In *Zippo Manufacturing Company v. Rogers Imports, Inc.*, a trademark and unfair competition case, Judge Feinberg ruled that consumer surveys were admissible, reasoning that: (a) they were not hearsay because they were not offered to prove the truth of the matter asserted, and regardless, (b) they fell under the exception for evidence offered to prove the declarant's state of mind.[34] *Zippo* became one of the most widely cited cases on the admissibility of consumer surveys.[35]

In *In re Chin Thloot Har Wong*, Judge Feinberg overruled the Immigration and Naturalization Service, which had refused to grant citizenship to an eleven-year-old orphan from China because the statute required a petition by "the adoptive parent or parents," and the adoptive father did not join the petition.[36] Judge Feinberg found that the INS ruling was inconsistent with the statute's purpose to bring noncitizen orphans to the United States.[37]

In 1965, Supreme Court Chief Justice Earl Warren appointed Judge Feinberg to the Advisory Committee on the Federal Rules of Civil Procedure—the first of Judge Feinberg's contributions to judicial procedure and administration.[38]

Soon after, in January 1966, President Lyndon B. Johnson nominated Judge Feinberg to the Court of Appeals for the Second Circuit.[39] Judge Feinberg served as chief judge of the Second Circuit from 1980 to 1988.[40]

While on the Court of Appeals, Judge Feinberg wrote for the panel in *Goetz v. Ansell*, which invalidated a regulation requiring a high school student who refused to salute the flag to either stand silently or leave the classroom.[41] He reasoned that the state "cannot punish non-participation," and that "being required to leave the classroom during the pledge may reasonably be viewed by some as having that effect."[42] He observed that such behavior could be disruptive, noting that "the argument is sound," but there was no evidence of disruption.[43] Judge Feinberg then added: "[w]hile we do not share plaintiff's resistance to pledging allegiance to this nation, his reservations of belief must be protected. In time, perhaps, he will recognize that such protection is sound ground for a firmer trust in his country."[44] In *United States v. Miller*, Judge Feinberg upheld the constitutionality of a federal law that made it illegal to burn a draft card, reasoning that the gesture was not purely symbolic.[45]

More famously, Judge Feinberg was also one of three Second Circuit judges who dissented from the court's *en banc* opinion in *United States v. New York Times Company*, commonly known as the *Pentagon Papers* case, which allowed the government to restrain *The New York Times* from printing classified government documents related to the Vietnam War.[46] In about one week, the Supreme Court reversed,[47] thus vindicating Judge Feinberg's position.

Judge Feinberg authored opinions and dissents in a number of other notable cases. He presided over *National Labor Relations Board v. J.P. Stevens & Company*,[48] which required a North Carolina textile company to allow its employees to unionize, and inspired the 1979 movie *Norma Rae.*[49] He vigorously dissented in *United States v. McCord*, a conscientious-objector case, in which the majority upheld a criminal sentence that Judge Feinberg believed was unjustly severe and warranted an evidentiary hearing.[50]

Judge Feinberg also wrote a number of decisions about the finality and appealability of district court cases (usually against widening the collateral order doctrine), establishing himself as a leading expert in that area.[51] Also "an internationally known authority on arbitration,"[52] Judge Feinberg was author of *Matter of the Arbitration between Andros Compania Maritima, S.A., and Marc Rich*

*& Company, A.G.*,[53] which held that an arbitration award should be enforced as long as arbitrators "explain their conclusions in terms that offer even a barely colorable justification for the outcome reached": in such cases, "confirmation of the award cannot be prevented by litigants who merely argue, however persuasively, for a different result."[54]

Judge Feinberg wrote over 1,000 published appellate opinions.[55] He exhibited a "taste for brevity."[56] His opinions were direct and to the point, exhibiting "no effort to create a mystery story aura of suspense."[57] Chief Judge Robert A. Katzmann has remarked that Judge Feinberg's opinions were "invariably clear, concise, thorough in their consideration of the complexities, careful, and illuminating. They were balanced so that each side felt at the end of the day that its position was taken seriously."[58] His writing has been praised frequently for its care and craft.[59] Professor Richard L. Revesz of New York University School of Law once said of his clerkship, "What my co-clerks and I learned through this process was the enormous power of craft."[60] Judge Feinberg was "always willing to consider the possibility that his initial view was wrong"—although "it wasn't often."[61]

Judge Feinberg was "[o]ne of the most thoughtful observers of developments in federal judicial administration."[62] As a member of the Judicial Conference of the United States, he served on the Subcommittee on Supporting Personnel; the Subcommittee on Judicial Statistics; the Federal Judicial Center's Advisory Committee on Experimentation in the Law; and the Committee to Study the Judicial Conferences, among others.[63] He often wrote and commented on judicial administration, which he referred to as "the stepchild of the law,"[64] including the customs and practices of the Second Circuit,[65] of allowing oral argument in nearly every appeal, using voting memos, and requiring trial counsel in criminal cases "to continue to represent [the] appellant until relieved by the appellate court."[66]

When he became chief judge in 1980, Judge Feinberg approached the role with "trepidation": "His primary love was the law and the judge's role in resolving cases; he had no desire for any kind of power, and no apparent taste for or experience in management."[67] Judge Feinberg never moved to the bigger office that came with the post. According to Chief Judge Katzmann, he said of his chambers: "if it was good enough for Thurgood Marshall, it's good enough for me."[68]

Although Judge Feinberg was proud of his court's success in managing a rapidly growing caseload,[69] he looked for other solutions. He testified before the Senate Judiciary Committee's Subcommittee on the Courts regarding the "Omnibus Judgeship Bill," which would authorize two new judgeships for the Second Circuit and new judgeships for three of its district courts.[70] He defended the use of summary orders against the backlash of public opinion, explaining why they were necessary to efficiently manage the court's docket.[71] He urged Congress to put an end to diversity jurisdiction: historically, it "was necessary to protect out-of-state citizens from possible local bias in state courts," but the "advent of increased mobility and the mass media ma[de] it 'unlikely that such local bias persists.'"[72]

In honor of his persistent efforts to improve administration of justice—particularly his work with the Judicial Conference of the United States[73]—Judge Feinberg received the 2004 Edward J. Devitt Distinguished Service to Justice Award,[74] which "honors a judge whose career includes significant contributions to the administration of justice, the advancement of the rule of law, and the improvement of society as a whole."[75]

Judge Feinberg was beloved by his law clerks. At one law clerk reunion, Judge Feinberg remarked, "movingly," that "[t]he relationship between a federal judge and his or her law clerks has been one of the most interesting and rewarding aspects of being a federal judge . . . I regard you all, as well as your spouses or significant others, as good friends."[76] The feeling was mutual. Professor Rochelle Dreyfuss of New York University School of Law once remembered that Judge Feinberg was a man who "adored" his family, and "basically treated his law clerks as part of the brood."[77] There were trips to his home in Mount Vernon and cream-cheese-and-jelly sandwich runs; and his wife, Shirley, "remembered every single one of [them]."[78]

Another Feinberg clerk, Judge Gerard Lynch, has described Judge Feinberg as "an admired mentor and role model" who worked closely with his clerks on opinions: together, they "would go line by line through the opinion making sure that everything in it was well supported," and he was "gentle in correcting his clerks' mistakes."[79] "[H]e was cautious to a fault" and his comments on current events were "carefully hedged or uncontroversial."[80] As Judge Lynch reflected,

> When your first full-time job in your chosen profession is working for a man who is so able, so generous, so thoughtful, so gentle, so dedicated to his job, and so happy and fulfilled in his work, that can't help but plant a seed to tell you that it would be a wonderful thing to have the opportunity to do that kind of work yourself. And if you are some day privileged to have that opportunity, you promise yourself to try every day to live up to his example.[81]

Having assumed senior status in 1991,[82] Judge Feinberg continued to serve with the Second Circuit until 2011. He died in July 2014, at age 94.[83]

Emily Seiderman

1. Maurice Rosenberg, *Chief Judge Wilfred Feinberg: A Twenty-Fifth Year Tribute*, 86 COLUM. L. REV. 1505, 1505 (1986).

2. JEFFREY B. MORRIS, FEDERAL JUSTICE IN THE SECOND CIRCUIT 181 (1987).

3. William Yardley, *Wilfred Feinberg, Federal Appeals Court Judge and Mentor, Dies at 94*, N.Y. TIMES, Aug. 4, 2014, at A16.

4. Interview by Jeffrey Morris with Judge Wilfred Feinberg, in New York, NY (Dec. 20, 1996), at 1 (transcript on file with the United States Courts Library for the Second Circuit).

5. *Id.* at 2, 5; Chief Judge Robert A. Katzmann, Remarks at a Meeting of the United States Court of Appeals for the Second Circuit in Memory of the Honorable Wilfred Feinberg 1 (Dec. 10, 2014) (transcript on file with the United States Courts Library for the Second Circuit).

6. Ned McCormack, *From Ping Pong Champ to Judge Seat*, DAILY ARGUS, Feb. 1, 1982.

7. *Id.*

8. Interview with Judge Wilfred Feinberg, *supra* note 4, at 2.

9. *Id.* at 2-3.

10. Note from Judge Gerard E. Lynch, to Emily Seiderman, Staff Attorney, Court of Appeals for the Second Circuit (Aug. 17, 2015) (on file with the United States Courts Library for the Second Circuit).

11. Interview with Judge Wilfred Feinberg, *supra* note 4, at 20.

12. *Id.* at 4.

13. Tania Karas, *Obituary: Wilfred Feinberg*, N.Y. L.J., Aug. 5, 2014 (referencing a comment by Chief Judge Loretta Preska of the District Court for the Southern District of New York).

14. *Id.*

15. Interview with Judge Wilfred Feinberg, *supra* note 4, at 4-5.

16. Rosenberg, *supra* note 1, at 1505.

17. Chief Judge Robert A. Katzmann, Remarks, *supra* note 5, at 3.

18. Interview with Judge Wilfred Feinberg, *supra* note 4, at 7.

19. Rosenberg, *supra* note 1, at 1506.

20. Press Release, Columbia Law School, Wilfred Feinberg, Venerable Federal Jurist and Distinguished Law School Alumnus, Dies at Age 94, http://www.law.columbia.edu/media_inquiries/news_events/2014/august2014/judge-wilfred-feinberg-tribute.

21. *Id.*

22. Rosenberg, *supra* note 1, at 1505-06; Interview with Judge Wilfred Feinberg, *supra* note 4, at 14. McGranery would later serve as attorney general under President Harry S. Truman. McGranery, James Patrick, (1895-1962), BIOGRAPHICAL DIRECTORY OF THE UNITED STATES CONGRESS, http://bioguide.congress.gov/scripts/biodisplay.pl?index=M000454.

23. Chief Judge Robert A. Katzmann, Remarks, *supra* note 5, at 4.

24. MORRIS, *supra* note 2, at 181.

25. Press Release, *supra* note 20.

26. MORRIS, *supra* note 2, at 181; *Attorney is Appointed N.Y. State Banking Aide*, N.Y. TIMES, Feb. 3, 1958, pg. 35.

27. Interview with Judge Wilfred Feinberg, *supra* note 4, at 33.

28. Karas, *supra* note 13; *New U.S. Judges Here: Senate Confirms Hays, Bonsal, Feinberg and Rosling*, N.Y. TIMES, Mar. 17, 1962.

29. Chief Judge Robert A. Katzmann, Remarks, *supra* note 5, at 4.

30. Rosenberg, *supra* note 1, at 1506.

31. *Id.*

32. Judge Pierre N. Leval, Remarks at a Meeting of the United States Court of Appeals for the Second Circuit in Memory of the Honorable Wilfred Feinberg 15-16 (Dec. 10, 2014) (transcript on file with the United States Courts Library for the Second Circuit).

33. Rosenberg, *supra* note 1, at 1506.

34. 216 F. Supp. 670, 683-84 (S.D.N.Y. 1963).

35. Interview with Judge Wilfred Feinberg, *supra* note 4, at 41. *See, e.g.*, Marvin L. Longabaugh, *The Z-Test for Percentages: A Statistical Tool to Detect Pretextually Neutral Juror Challenges*, 13 RICH J.L. & TECH. 1, 22 (2006); Shashank Upadhye, *Trademark Surveys: Identifying the Relevant Universe of Confused Consumers*, 8 FORDHAM INTELL. PROP. MEDIA & ENT. L.J. 549, 559 (1998).

36. 224 F. Supp. 155 (S.D.N.Y. 1963).

37. *See generally id.*; *see also U.S. Judge Breaks Precedent to Grant Chinese Citizenship*, N.Y. TIMES, Dec. 12, 1963, at 64.

38. Rosenberg, *supra* note 1, at 1506.

39. FEDERAL JUDICIAL CENTER, Biographical Directory of Federal Judges, Wilfred Feinberg, http://www.fjc.gov/servlet/nGetInfo?jid=742&cid=999&ctype=na&instate=na.

40. *Id.*

41. 477 F.2d 636 (2d Cir. 1976).

42. *Id.* at 638.

43. *Id.*

44. *Id.* at 638-39; *see also* Rosenberg, *supra* note 1, at 1508 (discussing case).

45. 367 F.2d 72 (2d Cir. 1966).

46. *See generally* New York Times Co. v. United States, 403 U.S. 713 (1971).

47. *New York Times*, 403 U.S. at 713.

48. 563 F.2d 8 (2d Cir. 1977).

49. *See* Yardley, *supra* note 3, at A16; Press Release, *supra* note 20.

50. 466 F.2d 17, 21-24 (2d Cir. 1972) (Feinberg, J., dissenting).

51. Rosenberg, *supra* note 1, at 1510 (discussing cases).

52. MORRIS, *supra* note 2, at 181.

53. 579 F.2d 691 (2d Cir. 1978).

54. *Id.* at 704.

55. Chief Judge Robert A. Katzmann, Remarks, *supra* note 5, at 6.

56. Rosenberg, *supra* note 1, at 1509.

57. Id. at 1507.

58. Chief Judge Robert A. Katzmann, Remarks, *supra* note 5, at 6.

59. *See, e.g., id.* at 7 ("If you have read WF's opinions, you many have discerned his extraordinary craftsmanship"); Judge Gerard E. Lynch, Remarks at a Meeting of the United States Court of Appeals for the Second Circuit in Memory of the Honorable Wilfred Feinberg 26-27 (Dec. 10, 2014) (transcript on file with the United States Courts Library for the Second Circuit) ("Judge Feinberg had an abiding respect for the craft of law and of judging.")

60. Richard L. Revesz, former law clerk, Remarks at a Meeting of the United States Court of Appeals for the Second Circuit in Memory of the Honorable Wilfred Feinberg 39 (Dec. 10, 2014) (transcript on file the United States Courts Library for the Second Circuit). Revesz is the Lawrence King Professor and Dean Emeritus at New York University School of Law.

61. Judge Gerard E. Lynch, Remarks, *supra* note 59, at 28.

62. MORRIS, *supra* note 2, at 181.

63. Rosenberg, *supra* note 1, at 1506.

64. Wilfred Feinberg, *Unique Customs and Practices of the Second Circuit*, 14 HOFSTRA L. REV. 297, 298 (1986).

65. *See id.*; *see also, e.g.*, Wilfred Feinberg, *Expediting Review of Felony Convictions*, 59 A.B.A. J. 1025 (1973) (commenting on the "urgent need to accelerate the determination of criminal appeals" and providing recommended procedures); *Second Circuit Note, 1976 Term; Forward: Judicial Administration: Stepchild of the Law*, 52 ST. JOHN'S L. REV. 187 (1976) (discussing the "astounding developments in the way the eleven circuit courts of appeals decide cases," the growing appellate caseload, en banc procedures, and the appellate court structure and jurisdiction).

66. *See generally* Wilfred Feinberg, *Unique Customs and Practices of the Second Circuit*, *supra* note 64.

67. Judge Gerard E. Lynch, Remarks, *supra* note 59, at 32.

68. Karas, *supra* note 13; *New U.S. Judges Here*, *supra* note 28 (quoting Chief Judge Robert Katzmann).

69. Wilfred Feinberg, *Chief Judge Feinberg Explains Second Circuit's Success in Managing Heavy Caseload*, THE THIRD BRANCH, vo. 16, no. 6 (June 1984).

70. *Circuit Judicial Conference Focuses on Court Improvement*, SECOND CIRCUIT NEWSLETTER, vol. 6, no. 2, (Summer 1981), at 1.

71. Wilfred Feinberg, *Letter to the Editor: U.S. Appeals Court: Separating the Significant from the Trivial*, N.Y. TIMES, Feb. 22, 1983, at A14.

72. *NY County Bar Dinner: Chief Judge Feinberg Urges End to Diversity Jurisdiction; Ct of Appeals Clerk Fusaro Honored*, Second Circuit Newsletter (Winter 1982); *see also* Wilfred Feinberg, *Is Diversity Jurisdiction an Idea Whose Time has Passed?*, 61 N.Y. St. B. J. 14 (1989).

73. Judge Gerard E. Lynch, Remarks, *supra* note 59, at 32-33.

74. Press Release, *supra* note 20.

75. *Id.*

76. Revesz, Remarks, *supra* note 60, at 45-46.

77. Rochelle Dreyfuss, former law clerk, Remarks at a Meeting of the United States Court of Appeals for the Second Circuit in Memory of the Honorable Wilfred Feinberg 53 (Dec. 10, 2014) (transcript on file with the United States Courts Library for the Second Circuit). Dreyfuss is the Pauline Newman Professor of Law at New York University School of Law.

78. *Id.*

79. Judge Gerard E. Lynch, Remarks, *supra* note 59, at 22, 29.

80. *Id.* at 31.

81. *Id.* at 22.

82. Press Release, *New Scholarship Honors Judge Wilfred Feinberg '43*, Columbia Law School Magazine, Fall 2010, http://www.law.columbia.edu/magazine/54730/new-scholarship-honors-judge-wilfred-feinberg-43.

83. Karas, *supra* note 13.

# JAMES LOWELL OAKES
## 1924-2007

District Court for the District of Vermont: 1970-1971
Court of Appeals for the Second Circuit: 1971-2007

It was his humanity, thought Supreme Court Justice Ruth Bader Ginsberg, that made Judge James L. Oakes "the very model of what a great judge should be—learned in the law, but ever mindful of the people law exists to serve."[1]

An adoptive son of Vermont, Oakes was born in Springfield, Illinois on February 21, 1924.[2] Oakes's parents met there as college students at the University of Illinois, where his father (also James Lowell Oakes) went on to law school.[3]

When Oakes's mother, Della Kuykendall Oakes, died six months after his birth, his maternal grandparents took over his care.[4] Oakes's grandmother, the daughter of Springfield's chief of police in the 1890s, was president of the Illinois chapter of the Women's Christian Temperance Union.[5] Her husband was neither as godly nor as temperate as she. He owned a large Springfield insurance firm and, much to his wife's disapproval, always kept his "medicinal spirits" close at hand.[6] The young Oakes "dearly loved" his grandparents.[7]

When Oakes was six, his father remarried and moved the family to Philadelphia, Pennsylvania.[8] There Oakes completed most of his schooling at the Haverford School, a preparatory school for boys.[9]

At his father's urging, Oakes attended Harvard College,[10] but admitted that he "totally wasted" his freshman year.[11] A roommate thought "Jim ought to be a professional poker player because he's taught us all how to play."[12] Oakes lost his Harvard scholarship and left after one year.[13] Although he participated in Army ROTC, a "misdiagnosed" medical condition prevented him from passing the physical examination for service in World War II.[14] Oakes worked on a farm "to assist the war effort."[15]

Oakes returned to Harvard after a 13-month stint on the farm.[16] This time, he "really applied" himself academically, while at the same time working night shifts as a cable spooler at the Simplex Wire and Cable Company as part of the war effort.[17] He graduated *cum laude* in 1945 with a degree in American History and Literature.[18]

Again at his father's recommendation, Oakes continued on to Harvard Law School.[19] According to Oakes, he "lucked out" and, to his "utter astonishment," was made a member of the *Harvard Law Review* his first term, an honor he attributed as much to the law review's being "very shorthanded" as to the "A" he earned on his first exam.[20] Oakes served as articles editor and book review editor.[21] He graduated *cum laude* in 1947.[22]

Oakes's 1946 marriage to Rosalyn Landon,[23] which later ended in divorce, produced three children: Cynthia, Elizabeth, and James.[24] After Oakes's elevation to the Second Circuit, he married Evelena (Deede) Stevens Kenworthy in 1973.[25] Two years after Deede's death in 1997, Oakes married Mara Williams, who survived him.[26] Karen McAndrew, one of Oakes's first law clerks, recalled that he told her shortly before his own death "how lucky he was to have been married to three such intelligent, interesting, beautiful women."[27]

After graduating law school, Oakes and Rosalyn moved to Brattleboro, Vermont where he clerked for Second Circuit Judge Harrie B. Chase at the recommendation of Erwin Griswold, dean of Harvard Law School.[28] Oakes adored Judge Chase and loved his clerkship. He described the judge as the "most decent of men,"[29] who would be a "shining light on any court" but who was particularly integral to the Second Circuit, where, in Oakes's view, he served as the "balance wheel" of a court defined by Chief Judge Learned Hand.[30] Oakes's clerkship regularly took him from Judge Chase's Brattleboro chambers to 40 Foley Square, a route he would retrace years later as a judge. His first day in New York also brought his first encounter with the formidable Hand.[31] As Oakes tells it, he boarded the elevator to find Hand already on board. Both were wearing hats. When a woman entered several floors later, Oakes removed his; Hand did not. Torn between following his father's teaching or Hand's example, Oakes left his hat off, hoping that Hand would not notice. He was not so lucky. When the elevator reached the ground floor and the woman passed out of earshot, Hand rounded on Oakes. "Young man," Hand said firmly, "in New York we take our hats off for ladies above Fourteenth Street; below Fourteenth Street we do not."[32]

When at 40 Foley Square with Judge Chase, Oakes would "skip across Pearl Street to the New York State Supreme Court" to watch the trial lawyers in action—"some flamboyant, others mediocre, all interesting."[33] Back in Brattleboro, Oakes met and befriended Robert T. Gannett, a local trial attorney.[34] Immediately struck by Oakes's "brilliant mind," Gannett told Oakes to give him a call if ever Oakes wanted to go into practice together.[35]

Other than a desire to become a trial lawyer, Oakes had "no idea" what he would do when his clerkship ended in 1948.[36] He moved to San Francisco and landed an associate position with the firm of McCutcheon, Thomas, Matthews, Griffith & Greene.[37] Oakes soon tired of the job, which mainly consisted of "writing footnotes" for a brief in a large tax case.[38] Realizing that he would not become a full-fledged trial attorney at McCutcheon for at least five years, and missing Vermont, Oakes began planning his return to Brattleboro six months after arriving in San Francisco.[39] He sent a series of letters to his Vermont connections, asking Judge Chase if he would take him back as a clerk for one year while he studied for the Vermont bar, and asking Bob Gannett if his offer to partner still stood.[40] Both said yes, and the Oakes family returned to Vermont in 1949.[41]

In 1950, after completing a second clerkship with Judge Chase, Oakes joined Gannett to form Gannett & Oakes, the Brattleboro firm where he would practice for the next 16 years.[42] Oakes soon "built a reputation throughout the state as a successful and reliable trial attorney,"[43] and credited much of his success to the mentorship of Harold O'Brien, a "commanding" veteran attorney from Rutland, Vermont,[44] who taught the "flatlander" Oakes "what he needed to know to convince a jury of Vermonters."[45]

Oakes's most memorable case from this time was his successful defense of Ingeborg Lorenz, a postmistress from Marlboro, Vermont, in an administrative trial before the U.S. Postal Service Loyalty Board.[46] The basis for the charge was her marriage to a bookstore owner who "had probably been a Communist" in the 1930s.[47] Oakes said the case taught him more about "what is really due process of law than [he] ever learned in [his] constitutional law class" at Harvard.[48]

In 1961, Oakes successfully ran for state senator (Windham County) on the Republican ticket and won election handily.[49] Oakes spent some of his time in the state senate on utilities reform, working to increase telecommunications service to rural areas, and pushing for local and municipal ownership of electrical lines.[50] This work helped make Oakes a "favorite" of George Aiken, the soft-spoken but powerful Republican U.S. senator from Vermont and a staunch supporter of public power.[51]

He was defeated in a bid to be lieutenant governor in 1965,[52] but the next year he was elected attorney general, the only Republican to win a statewide race that year.[53] Even though he was a Republican, Oakes worked well with, and was respected by, the Democratic governor, Phillip H. Hoff.[54] Oakes's two-year tenure as attorney general gave him some of his first in-depth exposure to the complexities of environmental law and regulation, which would become prominent in his later jurisprudence.

Oakes's 1968 run for governor was derailed by a racially charged incident that summer in the small town of Irasburg, in Vermont's northeastern corner. The Irasburg Affair, as the incident became known, began in July 1968 when the Reverend David Johnson, a black minister, his wife, and their children moved there to live in a home with Barbara Lawrence, a white woman, and her children.[55] When Oakes learned that shotgun blasts were fired into the walls and windows of the Johnson home,[56] Oakes and his wife travelled to Irasburg to show their support for the Johnsons.[57] He also ordered 24-hour protection for the family.[58]

Oakes's show of support triggered a backlash in northern Vermont, where racial resentment was already simmering against Governor Hoff's Vermont-Harlem "educational interchange of young people."[59] The state police investigation into the shooting was half-hearted and focused on the Johnsons themselves, running background investigations of the Reverend Johnson and then, three days after the incident, accusing him and Lawrence of adultery.[60] Oakes "laughed . . . off" requests to prosecute the adultery charge, observing that there had been no adultery prosecution in the county for some 15 years.[61] With the state police's shooting investigation going nowhere, Oakes assigned a deputy attorney general who brought charges against the prime shooting suspect within a day.[62] A board of inquiry absolved Oakes of wrongdoing and faulted the state police.[63] Nevertheless, Oakes was savaged in the press for his refusal to prosecute the adultery charge,[64] and he was soundly defeated in the Republican gubernatorial primary later that year, losing the vote in "every town" in the northern half of Vermont.[65]

Oakes returned to private practice until, in 1970, President Richard M. Nixon nominated him to the District Court for the District of Vermont.[66] Oakes attributed his appointment to the efforts of two men: District Judge Ernest Gibson, Jr., who on his deathbed named Oakes as his preferred successor,[67] and Senator Aiken.[68] When Aiken caught wind that the Nixon administration favored another lawyer for the nomination, Aiken convinced the chairman of the Senate Judiciary Committee, Senator James O. Eastland of Mississippi, to "send word to the White House that only one candidate would be confirmed by the Senate, and that was James Oakes."[69] Years later, Aiken explained that his old friend Learned Hand had once told the senator that "there was a young fellow . . . coming to [his] neighborhood to practice law" who could have "gone into almost any law firm in New York City, but wanted to go to Vermont and make his own way."[70]

As he had loved being a trial attorney, Oakes loved the work of a trial judge. By his account, he "knew every lawyer in the state,"[71] and during trials in his Brattleboro courtroom, he would send notes to his clerks predicting that one would "persuade the jury that his client's habitual drunkenness is just an endearing human foible," or that another would "skewer this expert witness on cross."[72]

Less than one year later, Judge Sterry R. Waterman, who held the "Vermont seat" on the Court of Appeals for the Second Circuit, decided to take senior status, and invited Oakes to take his place.[73] Oakes urged Judge Waterman to call him back in "six or seven years," but Oakes could not resist returning as a judge to the court where he had clerked.[74] Senator Aiken again gave his full support, contingent on a letter from Oakes pledging that he would never change his residency from Vermont to New York and would always remember his "responsibilities" as a Vermonter.[75] Oakes was "more than delighted" to comply.[76]

Judge Oakes's first month on the Second Circuit in June 1971 brought with it one of his most important cases: *United States v. New York Times Company*, also known as the *Pentagon Papers* case.[77] He soon grew to love the appellate process.[78] He described the work as "a cycle, a pipeline, truly to be cherished by anyone interested in intellectual challenge, with an inspirational sense of political-social-historical American values, aims, and aspirations, but also with a deep moderating sense of the constraints of logic, intellectual candor, practicality, and the evolutionary process of law."[79] He wrote most of his own opinions, and did so with "astonishing speed."[80] William Treanor, dean of Georgetown Law Center and one of Judge Oakes's law clerks, remembered:

> Judge Oakes was a master of precedent and legal reasoning. It was humbling, as a clerk, to witness the brilliance and rapidity with which he analyzed the legal issues presented in the cases. He wrote the opinions by himself and didn't seem to need the bench memos my co-clerks and I produced. Indeed, my co-clerks and I often debated whether we made any meaningful contributions to the work of the chambers at all. I should add that we never broached this topic with him; we were afraid, I think, of putting him in the awkward position of having to acknowledge that we were unnecessary.[81]

Judge Oakes's law clerks also recall his empathy and respect for the litigants who appeared before him. Professor Bruce Green of Fordham Law School recounted:

> One morning in the beginning of our clerkship (Fall 1981), the Judge came back to chambers after oral argument. There had been a pro se appellant named Frank Forrester who was given five minutes to argue along with the Judge's customarily courteous attention. Afterward, the Judge was certain that he had heard the same man argue his own appeal previously, but that the man had a different name. It seemed improbable, but the Judge called over to . . . the pro se clerks' office[, which] . . . confirmed that, yes, the same man, originally named Ernest Boruski, had argued before the Judge in 1973. At the time, I was most impressed by the Judge's great memory, which I assume contributed to his success as a politician as well as a trial lawyer. Later, I reflected that he couldn't have remembered if he did not truly listen to and take seriously everyone who appeared in front of him.[82]

Although Judge Oakes made contributions in many fields of law, the two for which he is known are individual rights and environmental law. In both, he advocated an active judicial role. As to the former, Judge Oakes wrote that the purpose of the federal courts was to serve not only as a check on the power of the legislative and executive branches, but also as a bulwark "protecting individuals and minorities against 'the community,' the majority."[83] He believed that legislatively-created "imbalances" (like Jim Crow laws) and "legislative inaction" (like the failure of the federal and state governments to remedy school segregation) "invited" and, indeed, required "judicial intervention."[84] In *North Haven Board of Education v. Hufstedler*,[85] he held—contrary to every other circuit that had considered the issue—that Title IX of the Education Amendments Act of 1972 could be reasonably interpreted to prohibit sex discrimination in educational employment, not just discrimination against students.[86] The Supreme Court agreed.[87]

His positions led some to cast him as the consummate judicial activist,[88] though he preferred to think of himself as "old fashioned—fashioned from the thirties of the Great Depression, the forties of war and the Holocaust and fascism, the fifties of the cold war and McCarthyism and Little Rock, and the sixties of the civil rights movement, the assassinations, and the would be Great Society—who . . . still believes that a federal judge *can* make a difference and . . . should make a difference when the rest of our political structure bogs down."[89]

Judge Oakes became chief judge in January 1989.[90] In that role, he oversaw the start of construction on a new federal courthouse in Manhattan, the automation of the Second Circuit's docket, and the Second Circuit's centennial celebration in 1991.[91] He held the "firm belief" that, as chief judge, he "should be the leader in terms of promoting collegiality" on the court.[92] To that end, he stepped down in June 1992, after only three years at the post, so that Judge Thomas Meskill could have an opportunity to serve as chief before he became ineligible for the position at age 65.[93]

Later that year, Judge Oakes took senior status. Consistent with the pledge he made to Senator Aiken, he did so only after being convinced that his seat would be filled with a Vermonter.[94] The person chosen, he advised, should be someone with "a basic underlying commitment to Vermont and its history," which he thought brought with it a unique and necessary viewpoint to a court otherwise filled with judges from New York and Connecticut.[95] His seat was filled in 1994 by Fred I. Parker, whom Judge Oakes later described as "one great judge, and a true Vermonter."[96] Judge Oakes himself remained committed to the state and its legal profession throughout his time on the Second Circuit, serving for nearly 20 years on the board of the Vermont Law School, where the "primary classroom" is named in his honor.[97]

Judge Oakes continued his service as a senior judge until early 2007, when he retired at the age of 83.[98] He died on October 13 that same year, at his home on Martha's Vineyard.[99] During a memorial service held for him at the Second Circuit, Judge Robert A. Katzmann, quoting Judge Jon O. Newman, remarked that although many judges are respected, "only a few judges are loved; the judges of the Court of Appeals loved Jim Oakes, and we always will."[100]

In 1991, when Judge Oakes was presiding over the Second Circuit's centennial celebration, he observed that the court lacked an official motto.[101] In its absence, he proposed a toast to his Second Circuit colleagues, past and present:

> To excellence, to craftsmanship, to collegiality and to the spirit of liberty: may the next hundred years bring us more of the same.[102]

Lucas C. Buzzard

1. Justice Ruth Bader Ginsberg, Remarks at a Special Session of the United States Court of Appeals for the Second Circuit In Memoriam for the Honorable James L. Oakes, at 7 (Feb. 4, 2008), *in* 531 F.3d XXVII.

2. Fran Lynggaard Hansen, *Former AG James Oakes Dead at 83*, RUTLAND HERALD, Oct. 16, 2007, http://www.rutlandherald.com/apps/pbcs.dll/article?AID=/20071016/NEWS04/710160394.

3. Audio CD Recording: Oral History Interview by Stephen Young and Frederick S. Nathan with Judge James L. Oakes, Brattleboro, Vt., Disc 1, Track 2, at 3:15–3:39, 13:41–13:44 (June 12, 2003) (on file with the United States Courts Library for the Second Circuit).

4. *Id.* at 0:24–0:40.

5. *Id.* at 1:00–1:30.

6. *Id.* at 4:43–4:56.

7. *Id.* at 1:30–1:45.

8. *Id.* at 2:37–2:46.

9. *Id.* at 2:46–2:56, 8:48–8:56.

10. *Id.* at 10:49–11:10.

11. *Id.* at 11:12–12:18.

12. *Id.*

13. *Id.*

14. *Id.* at 12:18–12:55.

15. *Id.*

16. *Id.*

17. Fran Lynggaard Hansen, *James Oakes Was Federal Judge Appointed by President Nixon*, VINEYARD GAZETTE, Oct. 18, 2007, at 2; Oral History Interview, *supra* note 3, at 12:54–13:17.

18. Hansen, *supra* note 17, at 1.

19. Oral History Interview, *supra* note 3, Disc 1, Track 2, at 11:00–11:07, 13:29–13:55.

20. *Id.* at 15:53–17:40.

21. Hansen, *supra* note 17, at 1.

22. *Id.*

23. *Id.*

24. *Id.*

25. *Id.*

26. *Id.*

27. Karen McAndrew, Esq., *James L. Oakes Eulogy*, Delivered at Marlboro College, Vermont (Oct. 27, 2007) (transcript on file with the United States Courts Library for the Second Circuit).

28. Oral History Interview, *supra* note 3, Disc 1, Track 2, at 27:25–27:52.

29. *Id.* at 28:00–28:13.

30. James L. Oakes, Introduction, *Colleagues for Justice: One Hundred Years of the United States Court of Appeals for the Second Circuit*, 65 ST. JOHN'S L. REV. 647, 650 (1991).

31. James Oakes, *Personal Reflections on Learned Hand and the Second Circuit*, 47 STAN. L. REV. 387, 389 (1994).

32. *Id.* (internal quotation marks omitted).

33. James L. Oakes, *Five from the Bench and Five from the Bar* (unfinished work), *in* A TRIBUTE TO JAMES L. OAKES 19, 19 (Carl A. Yirka ed., 2007) (transcript on file with the United States Courts Library for the Second Circuit).

34. Oral History Interview, *supra* note 3, Disc 1, Track 2, at 31:10–32:15.

35. Elizabeth A. York, *The Honorable James L. Oakes: A Tribute*, 33 VT. B.J. 33, 33 (2007) (internal quotation marks omitted).

36. Oral History Interview, *supra* note 3, Disc 1, Track 2, at 28:00–29:30.

37. *Id.*

38. *Id.*

39. *Id.*

40. *Id.* at 31:10–32:21.

41. *Id.*

42. *Id.*

43. District Judge J. Garvan Murtha & Nicole Y. Murtha, Remarks, In Memoriam for Hon. James L. Oakes, Delivered at the Second Circuit Judicial Conference 2 (2008) (on file with the United States Courts Library for the Second Circuit).

44. Oakes, *supra* note 33, at 20.

45. District Judge J. Garvan Murtha & Murtha, *supra* note 43, at 2 (internal quotation marks omitted).

46. Oakes, *supra* note 33, at 21.

47. *Id.*

48. *Id.*

49. Oral History Interview, *supra* note 3, Disc 1, Track 4, at 0:05–1:00.

50. Oral History Interview, *supra* note 3, Disc 1, Track 3, at 10:25–11:10.

51. *Id.* at 11:13–11:38.

52. Oral History Interview, *supra* note 3, Disc 1, Track 4, at 1:00–1:27.

53. Hansen, *supra* note 2.

54. *Id.*

55. BOARD OF INQUIRY, FINDINGS AND RECOMMENDATIONS OF BOARD OF INQUIRY INVESTIGATING THE SO-CALLED IRASBURG AFFAIR 5 (1968) (on file with the United States Courts Library for the Second Circuit).

56. *Id.* at 6.

57. Oakes, *supra* note 33, at 23.

58. *Id.*

59. *Id.*

60. BOARD OF INQUIRY, *supra* note 55, at 23–24.

61. Oakes, *supra* note 33, at 23.

62. *Id.*

63. BOARD OF INQUIRY, *supra* note 55, at 29 (concluding that the "failure of the Attorney General . . . to vigorously investigate th[e] case would have been a dereliction of duty on his part" and that the perpetrator of the shooting "might not have been convicted . . . had it not been for the activity of the Attorney General's office").

64. Oral History Interview, *supra* note 3, Disc 1, Track 5, at 11:33–12:15.

65. *Id.* at 13:35–14:02.

66. *See* Oakes, *supra* note 33, at 25.

67. Oral History Interview, *supra* note 3, Disc 2, Track 1, at 0:03–0:35.

68. *Id.* at 3:48–4:43.

69. Sally Johnson, *Vermonter of the Year: Judge James L. Oakes*, VT. SUNDAY MAGAZINE, Dec. 27, 1992, at 4, 13 (internal quotation marks omitted).

70. *Id.* (internal quotation marks omitted).

71. Oral History Interview, *supra* note 3, Disc 2, Track 1, at 7:40–7:46.

72. McAndrew, *supra* note 27, at 2 (internal quotation marks omitted).

73. Oral History Interview, *supra* note 3, Disc 2, Track 2 at 0:03–0:38.

74. *Id.*

75. Audio CD Recording: Interview by John Kristensen with Judge James L. Oakes, in Brattleboro, Vt., Disc 1, Track 3, 6:56–7:31 (transcript on file with the United States Courts Library for the Second Circuit); Johnson, *supra* note 69, at 13.

76. Kristensen Interview, *supra* note 74, Disc 1, Track 3, at 7:25–7:31; *see also* Johnson, *supra* note 69, at 13.

77. 444 F.2d 544 (2d Cir. 1971) (en banc), *rev'd*, 403 U.S. 713 (1971) (per curiam); *see id.* (Oakes, J., dissenting); *see also supra* discussion in the biography of Wilfred Feinberg.

78. McAndrew, *supra* note 27, at 2.

79. James L. Oakes, *On the Craft and Philosophy of Judging*, 80 MICH. L. REV. 579, 581 (1981) (internal quotation marks omitted) (reviewing FRANK M. COFFIN, THE WAYS OF A JUDGE (1980)).

80. William Treanor, Remarks at a Special Session of the United States Court of Appeals for the Second Circuit In Memoriam for the Honorable James L. Oakes, at 22-23 (Feb. 4, 2008), *in* 531 F.3d XXVII. Treanor is the executive vice president and dean of the Georgetown University Law Center.

81. Email from William Treanor, former law clerk, to Sally Pritchard (Aug. 24, 2015, 15:49 EST) (on file with the United States Courts Library for the Second Circuit).

82. Email from Bruce Green, former law clerk, to Sally Pritchard (Aug. 25, 2015, 11:17 EST) (on file with the United States Courts Library for the Second Circuit). Green is the Lewis Stein Chair of Law at Fordham Law School.

83. James L. Oakes, *The Proper Role of the Federal Courts in Enforcing the Bill of Rights*, 54 N.Y.U. L. REV. 911, 916 (1979).

84. James L. Oakes, *The Role of Courts in Government Today*, 14 AKRON L. REV. 175, 183 (1980).

85. 629 F.2d 773 (2d Cir. 1980).

86. *Id.* at 785.

87. North Haven Bd. of Educ. v. Bell, 456 U.S. 512, 535–36 (1982) (affirming *Hufstedler*).

88. *See* Adam Liptak, *James L. Oakes, 83, Nixon Choice for Federal Bench*, N.Y. TIMES, Oct. 16, 2007, at C13.

89. James L. Oakes, *Jack Weinstein and His Love-Hate Relationship with the Court of Appeals*, 97 COLUM. L. REV. 1951, 1957 (1997).

90. Deborah Pines, *Meskill to Succeed Oakes as 2d Circuit Chief Judge*, N.Y. L.J., Apr. 8, 1992, at 1.

91. *Id.*

92. James L. Oakes, *Judges on Judging, Grace Notes on "Grace Under Pressure,"* 50 OHIO ST. L.J. 701, 707 (1989).

93. Pines, *supra* note 90.

94. Kristensen Interview, *supra* note 74, Disc 1, Track 1, at 6:15–7:02.

95. Kristensen Interview, *supra* note 74, Disc 1, Track 3, at 4:35–4:50.

96. Judge James L. Oakes, Remarks at a Special Session of the United States Court of Appeals for the Second Circuit In Memoriam for the Honorable Fred I. Parker, at VII (Dec. 7, 2003) (transcript on file with the United States Courts Library for the Second Circuit).

97. Geoffrey B. Shields, *Introduction*, *in* A TRIBUTE TO JAMES L. OAKES, *supra* note 33, at 3.

98. Kathleen M. Sullivan & William Treanor, *Tribute to James Oakes*, N.Y. L.J., Mar. 19, 2007, at 2.

99. Hansen, *supra* note 17, at 1.

100. Judge Robert A. Katzmann, Remarks at a Special Session of the United States Court of Appeals for the Second Circuit In Memoriam for the Honorable James L. Oakes (Feb. 4, 2008) *in* 531 F.3d XXVII.

101. Oakes, *supra* note 30, at 651.

102. *Id.*; *see also* LEARNED HAND, THE SPIRIT OF LIBERTY (1944).

# WALTER ROE MANSFIELD
## 1911-1987

District Court for the Southern District of New York: 1966-1971
Court of Appeals for the Second Circuit: 1971-1987

Walter Roe Mansfield's high school magazine predicted that ten years after graduation he would be a criminal lawyer.[1] He was underestimated: ten years later, Mansfield was an Assistant United States Attorney for the Southern District of New York. Fifteen years later, he was parachuting behind enemy lines in World War II. And 40 years later, Mansfield was a judge on the Court of Appeals for the Second Circuit.

Mansfield was the only child of Irish immigrants, Fredrick W. and Helen Roe.[2] Fredrick was a prominent Massachusetts lawyer who became the mayor of Boston.[3] Mansfield attended the Notre

Dame Academy and Roxbury Latin School, where he played basketball and football, before earning his undergraduate and law degrees at Harvard University.[4] He graduated from law school in 1935 near the top of his class and chose to practice law outside Boston, lest his job be attributed to his father's political influence.[5] He moved to New York and joined Donovan Leisure Newton & Lumbard with a starting annual salary of $1,800.[6] When Mansfield married his first wife, Dorothy,[7] he sought a raise, but the senior partner observed that "it was [Mansfield] who married his wife, not the firm."[8] Mansfield had one son with Dorothy, Matthew; after Mansfield and Dorothy divorced, he married Gertrude Rient, who also had a son, Peter. Together, they had a daughter, Trina.[9] Following Gertrude's death, Mansfield married Elizabeth Bergfeld in 1979, who survived him.[10]

Mansfield was "serene, placid, and soft-spoken."[11] He brought a "quiet style and grace" to his work.[12] "His total modesty made the man eschew self-seeking."[13] Even in his later years, Mansfield did not consider himself "one of the great Second Circuit Judges who could dispense justice through the sheer force of monumental intellect, but just an ordinary guy who needed all the help he could get from his so-called assistant judges."[14]

After about four years of practice, Mansfield became an Assistant United States Attorney for the Southern District of New York,[15] a position he "keenly desire[d]" to gain trial experience.[16] In a letter to fellow Bostonian Joseph P. Kennedy, Frederick Mansfield's friend, Walter Mansfield remarked that "there is a dearth of able trial counsel in downtown New York, and I would like to make my mark in that field."[17] He got the job, but had to relinquish his membership at the Harvard Club because he could no longer afford the dues.[18]

After two years at the United States Attorney's Office, Mansfield returned to Donovan Leisure. His time at the firm was cut short by World War II. Months before the attack on Pearl Harbor, founding partner William J. Donovan had been appointed the director of Intelligence Information by President Franklin Delano Roosevelt.[19] As Donovan began developing an intelligence service to support the war effort, Donovan turned to

Mansfield, who had already enlisted with the Marines because "[i]f [he] didn't go voluntarily, [he was] certainly going to be going involuntarily."[20] Donovan asked him to join the newly created Office of Strategic Services, the predecessor to the CIA.[21] While at the OSS, Mansfield met Murray Gurfein; the two would sit together in the 1970s as judges on the Second Circuit.[22]

Mansfield's niche in the OSS was parachuting behind enemy lines, "one of the most daring and unique assignments of any marine during this war."[23] With self-deprecation, Mansfield explained: "[P]arachuting doesn't mean a damned thing. All they do is throw you out of airplanes. Do five jumps, and you're a parachutist. And then all you do is throw other people out five times. They're parachutists."[24] He made a total of 23 jumps.[25]

Mansfield's first training assignment was teaching the Norwegian and French how to parachute into German-occupied territory.[26] Then, in July 1943, it was Mansfield's turn to jump into a battlefield. Donovan assigned him to enter Yugoslavia and ascertain whether Chetnik soldiers, Serbian forces detached from the regular Yugoslav army, were Nazi collaborators, as the British suspected.[27] After spending time on the ground, Mansfield escaped through mountainous terrain, was picked up by a Navy boat at night, and went to Cairo to share his findings with American intelligence officials: the Chetniks whom he encountered were not, according to Mansfield's report, sympathetic to the Nazis.[28] Later in the war, Mansfield was sent to northern China to train recruits behind Japanese lines; he also commanded teams that parachuted into Chinese prison camps.[29] The harsh winter, short rations, and the difficulties of guerilla warfare took a significant physical toll.[30] Mansfield's time in China ended with several rescue missions, followed by his safe return home.[31]

Mansfield attained the rank of major,[32] was awarded the Bronze Star, the Legion of Merit, and the White Eagle Award of Yugoslavia (by the Yugoslav government in exile).[33] Welcomed home as a hero, he found that civilian life was not so easy. On New York's severe housing shortage, Mansfield remarked: "Peace is sure hell . . . finding a place to live in New York is more nerve-racking than anything the Japanese or Nazis had to offer."[34]

He returned to Donovan Leisure, becoming a partner in 1949.[35] In 1961 when members of the American Bar Association asked Mansfield if he would be interested in an appointment to the Southern District of New York,[36] he declined: he did not want to leave his clients "in the lurch," and he had to pay for his children's education.[37] But in 1966, when all but one of his children were out of school,[38] New York Senator Robert F. Kennedy recommended that Mansfield be appointed to the Southern District of New York,[39] and President Lyndon B. Johnson appointed him.[40] At his confirmation hearing, the Senate Judiciary Committee asked no questions.[41]

Judge Mansfield heard several high-profile cases, "often issu[ing] opinions protecting the rights of individuals."[42] When the New York State Boxing Commission denied Muhammad Ali a boxing license because he had been convicted of draft dodging, Judge Mansfield ruled that the commission had violated Ali's equal protection rights because the state did not deny licenses to others who had been convicted of more serious offenses.[43] He also ordered McSorleys' Ale House in New York City to serve women.[44] The bar had been open only to men for its 114-year history; within one year of Mansfield's ruling, the city adopted ordinances requiring public restaurants to serve people regardless of sex.[45] In his final months on the district court, Judge Mansfield ruled that the Immigration and Naturalization Service could not block citizenship on the ground of sexual orientation.[46]

President Richard M. Nixon elevated Judge Mansfield to the Court of Appeals in 1971. Because he had been nominated to the district court by a Democratic president, administration officials asked Mansfield to prove his Republican bona fides.[47] Luckily, he found an inscribed photo of Nixon from 1956.[48] At his induction ceremony to the Second Circuit, Judge Henry J. Friendly noted that, while "Judge Mansfield has been a Judge of the Southern District of New York for five years, [i]t seem[ed] longer,"[49] in the sense that it was remarkable Judge Mansfield "produced work of such quantity and quality" in so short a time.[50]

Judge Mansfield was sworn in by Judge J. Edward Lumbard, his former partner at Donovan Leisure.[51] In his first month, the court sat *en banc* in the *Pentagon Papers* case.[52] Also early in his appellate career, Judge Mansfield wrote a strongly worded opinion about the New York State prison uprising at Attica, concluding that injunctive relief against prison officials should have been granted because of the prison abuse that took place.[53] He described the prison officials' conduct as "barbarous," "beyond any force needed to maintain order," and "exceeded[ing] what our society will tolerate on the part of officers of the law in custody of defenseless prisoners."[54]

In *Engblom v. Carey*, Judge Mansfield wrote for a divided court in one of the few applications of the Third Amendment prohibition against soldier quartering.[55] When corrections officers at a New York State facility went on strike, National Guardsmen were quartered in their staff housing buildings. The court held that National Guardsmen qualified as soldiers and the Amendment was incorporated against the states.[56] (The case was remanded to the district court, which ultimately found the defendants protected by qualified immunity.)[57] Less than a year before his death, he wrote for a unanimous court affirming a district court decision that enjoined a Texas law and allowed Texaco to appeal a state court case without posting a nearly 12 billion dollar bond.[58] Mansfield wrote that enforcement "would rapidly produce a catastrophe of major proportions" such that Texaco's due process rights would be violated.[59] The Supreme Court heard oral argument days after Judge Mansfield's death in 1987 and reversed, in a fractured decision that spawned five concurrences.[60]

Judge Mansfield "knew how to judge. He was decisive—he did not agonize or equivocate."[61] During his first years as a federal judge, Judge Mansfield acted "like a kid in a candy store" because "everything was a new and breathtaking journey into unknown waters."[62] He usually did without bench memoranda because "he could read faster than [law clerks] could write."[63] Judge Mansfield was a productive and efficient lawyer.[64] He aimed to finish his assigned opinions from one sitting before the next. "He abhorred unnecessary delay."[65] By 1980, Judge Mansfield had "served gratuitously and generously on more [rule-making and regulatory] committees than any other judge on the bench."[66]

He rarely lost his temper. One hot day in June 1980, another judge delivered "a lengthy harangue" from the bench to an air conditioning repairman, warning that he "should be prepared to show cause why he should not be held in contempt" if the courtroom was not cool by the next day.[67] Judge Mansfield wrote to all chambers explaining that "it does not help our objectives when a [judge] shoots off his mouth to a defenseless employee."[68] The next day, the show-cause order was vacated.[69]

In late 1971, Judge Mansfield was considered for a seat on the Supreme Court by President Nixon, who had appointed him to the Court of Appeals only months earlier.[70] However, Attorney General John Mitchell thought Mansfield "was a weak character." Nixon ultimately appointed William Rehnquist instead.[71]

In 1980, Judge Mansfield was awarded the Learned Hand Medal by the Federal Bar Council. Presenting the award, Judge William Hughes Mulligan observed that Judge Mansfield was "never unprepared for argument" and praised him as "an able and scholarly jurist"[72] with a penchant for obsessing over the record, often demanding litigants answer "where does it say that?" during oral argument.[73] At the voting conference, Judge Mansfield's primary response to his fellow panel members' thoughts was: "take another look at the record."[74]

Judge Mansfield spent his free time playing tennis[75] and windsurfing into his 70s.[76] He skied.[77] "In his later years, [he] developed an interest in pottery and took certain mornings off from work to attend a pottery class."[78] He also knew "many people in the theater world" and at Judge Friendly's eightieth birthday party, served as "the producer, director, and master of ceremonies."[79] One of the skits featured Judge Friendly going "to heaven and correcting Gibbon and other great historians about errors in their work."[80]

At 70, Judge Mansfield took senior status.[81] His letter to President Ronald Reagan noted that there were other vacancies on the court and that "prompt replacements [were] essential."[82] He remained committed as a judge: at 74, he wrote more opinions than six of the active judges.[83] At his death, Chief Judge Wilfred Feinberg reported that Judge Mansfield had "continued to discharge nearly the full workload of his active colleagues."[84]

Judge Mansfield died at 75, while on vacation in Christchurch, New Zealand.[85] In his honor, a red oak tree from the home of the first chief justice of the Supreme Court, John Jay, was transplanted to Foley Square. The inscription read in part: "He was always unstinting of self, the first to volunteer, the first to get his job done. Leader, collator, adjuster of conflict. Flexible except in matters of principle, he enjoyed the universal respect and affection of bench and bar."[86]

Greg Capobianco

1. FEDERAL BAR COUNCIL, GLIMPSES OF WALTER MANSFIELD 2 (1995).
2. *Id.* at 1.
3. *Id.*
4. *Id.* at 2.
5. *Id.* at 4–5.
6. *Id.*
7. *See id.* at 19.
8. Samuel W. Murphy, Remarks at the Extraordinary Session of the United States Court of Appeals for the Second Circuit, In Memoriam, Honorable Walter R. Mansfield (Apr. 7, 1987), *in* 827 F.2d LXXI. Murphy was a colleague at Donovan Leisure.
9. GLIMPSES OF WALTER MANSFIELD, *supra* note 1, at 19.
10. *Id.*
11. WILLIAMS HUGHES MULLIGAN, MULLIGAN'S LAW: THE WIT AND WISDOM OF WILLIAMS HUGHES MULLIGAN 133 (1996).
12. *Id.* at 134.
13. Judge James L. Oakes, Remarks at the Extraordinary Session of the United States Court of Appeals for the Second Circuit, In Memoriam, Honorable Walter R. Mansfield (Apr. 7, 1987), *in* 827 F.2d LXXI.
14. John S. Kiernan, former law clerk, Remarks at the Extraordinary Session of the United States Court of Appeals for the Second Circuit, In Memoriam, Honorable Walter R. Mansfield (Apr. 7, 1987), *in* 827 F.2d LXXI. Kiernan is a partner at Debevoise & Plimpton, LLP.
15. GLIMPSES OF WALTER MANSFIELD, *supra* note 1, at 8–9.
16. *Id.* at 9–10.
17. *Id.*
18. *Id.* at 10.
19. *Id.* at 11.
20. *Id.* at 92.
21. *Id.* at 11.
22. *See* Henry B. Hyde, Remarks at the Memorial Proceedings for the Honorable Murray I. Gurfein, Judge, United States Court of Appeals (Sept. 15, 1980), *in* 634 F.2d LXXXVI. Hyde was a colleague in the OSS during World War II.
23. Ronald D. Rotunda, *Remembering Judge Walter R. Mansfield*, 53 BROOK. L. REV. 271, 271 (1987) (quoting The Marine Corps Gazette: The Professional Magazine for United States Marines, Jan. 1946, at 1.).
24. GLIMPSES OF WALTER MANSFIELD, *supra* note 1, at 11.
25. MULLIGAN, *supra* note 11, at 132.

26. GLIMPSES OF WALTER MANSFIELD, *supra* note 1, at 11.

27. *Id.* at 13–14.

28. *Id.* at 15–16. The goals and allegiances of the Chetniks were, and continue to be, controversial. *See generally* MATTEO J. MILAZZO, THE CHETNIK MOVEMENT & YUGOSLAV RESISTANCE (1975).

29. GLIMPSES OF WALTER MANSFIELD, *supra* note 1 at 17.

30. *Id.*

31. *Id.* at 17–18.

32. Rotunda, *supra* note 23, at 271.

33. GLIMPSES OF WALTER MANSFIELD, *supra* note 1, at 18.

34. *Id.*

35. *Id.* at 19.

36. *Id.* at 107.

37. *Id.*

38. GLIMPSES OF WALTER MANSFIELD, *supra* note 1, at 107.

39. Warren Weaver, *Kennedy Backing G.O.P. Judgeship*, N.Y. TIMES, May 16, 1966, at 44.

40. *Mansfield Is Confirmed as Federal Judge Here*, N.Y. TIMES, June 30, 1966, at 34.

41. *Id.*

42. Dennis Hevesi, *Walter R. Mansfield, Federal Judge, Is Dead at 75*, N.Y. TIMES, Jan. 8, 1987, at B12.

43. *Id.* at 112; *see also generally* MICHAEL MELTSNER, THE MAKING OF A CIVIL RIGHTS LAWYER 144–45 (2006).

44. GLIMPSES OF WALTER MANSFIELD, *supra* note 1, at 112.

45. *Id.*

46. Hevesi, *supra* note 42.

47. GLIMPSES OF WALTER MANSFIELD, *supra* note 1, at 114.

48. *Id.*

49. Chief Judge Henry J. Friendly, Remarks at the Proceedings Held on the Occasion of the Induction of the Honorable Walter R. Mansfield as United States Court of Appeals Judge for the Second Circuit 3 (June 10, 1971) (transcript on file with the United States Courts Library for the Second Circuit).

50. *Id.*

51. *Id.* at 2.

52. GLIMPSES OF WALTER MANSFIELD, *supra* note 1, at 115 (describing his "first week of hearing appeals"); *see also* New York Times Co. v. United States, 403 U.S. 713, 713 (1971) (Mansfield voting with the majority of the en banc court to continue a stay of the district court's order and remand the case for further *in camera* proceedings).

53. Inmates of Attica Corr. Facility v. Rockefeller, 453 F.2d 12 (2d Cir. 1971).

54. *Id.* at 22.

55. 677 F.2d 957 (2d Cir. 1982); *see also* Tom W. Bell, *The Third Amendment: Forgotten but Not Gone*, 2 WM. & MARY BILL RTS J. 117, 142–43 (1993).

56. *Engblom*, 677 F.2d at 966.

57. Engblom v. Carey, 572 F. Supp. 44, 45 (S.D.N.Y.), *aff'd*, 724 F.2d 28 (2d Cir. 1983).

58. Texaco Inc. v. Pennzoil Co., 784 F.2d 1133, 1136 (2d Cir. 1986), *rev'd*, 481 U.S. 1 (1987).

59. *Id.*

60. *See* Pennzoil Co. v. Texaco, Inc., 481 U.S. 1 (1987).

61. GLIMPSES OF WALTER MANSFIELD, *supra* note 1, at 142 (remembrance of Allen R. Bentley, former law clerk).

62. *Id.* at 136 (remembrance of John H. Wilkinson, former law clerk).

63. Rotunda, *supra* note 23, at 273.

64. *Id.*

65. *Id.* at 274.

66. MULLIGAN, *supra* note 11, at 134.

67. GLIMPSES OF WALTER MANSFIELD, *supra* note 1, at 157–58 (remembrance of Charles E. Davidow, former law clerk).

68. *Id.* at 158.

69. *Id.*

70. *See* JOHN W. DEAN, THE REHNQUIST CHOICE 307 n.2 (2001).

71. *Id.*

72. MULLIGAN, *supra* note 11, at 134.

73. *Id.*

74. *Id.*

75. *See, e.g.*, GLIMPSES OF WALTER MANSFIELD, *supra* note 1, at 151, 161 (remembrances of Steven M. Schatz and Davison M. Douglas, former law clerks).

76. Kiernan, Remarks, *supra* note 14; *see also* GLIMPSES OF WALTER MANSFIELD, *supra* note 1, at 161 (remembrance of Thomas P. Olson, former law clerk).

77. Rotunda, *supra* note 23, at 275.

78. GLIMPSES OF WALTER MANSFIELD, *supra* note 1, at 161.

79. DAVID M. DORSEN, HENRY FRIENDLY, GREATEST JUDGE OF HIS ERA 116 (2012).

80. GLIMPSES OF WALTER MANSFIELD, *supra* note 1, at 160.

81. Arnold H. Lubasch, *Retirement Creates a 3d Vacancy on Federal Appeals Court in City*, N.Y. TIMES, Mar. 31, 1981, at B10.

82. *Id.*

83. Rotunda, *supra* note 23, at 275.

84. Hevesi, *supra* note 42.

85. *Id.*

86. GLIMPSES OF WALTER MANSFIELD, *supra* note 1, at 196.

# WILLIAM HUGHES MULLIGAN
# 1918-1996

Court of Appeals for the Second Circuit: 1971-1981

William Hughes Mulligan "was a true Gaelic giant."[1] Born March 5, 1918, Mulligan was the only son of Stephen Mulligan and the former Jane Donahue.[2] His great-grandfather, Patrick Mulligan, had emigrated from Ireland in 1844.[3]

Mulligan was raised in the Bronx. A devout Catholic,[4] he attended primary school at Our Lady of Refuge, followed by Cathedral Preparatory, a high school that prepared young men to become priests.[5] The priesthood was not for Mulligan; he enrolled at Fordham College,[6] thus beginning a long association with that institution as an undergraduate, law student, professor, and dean. In 1939, Mulligan graduated *cum laude* from Fordham College,[7] where he sang in the glee club, served on the student council, and was a sports editor for the school newspaper.[8] When the Depression dashed his ambition of becoming a sports writer,[9] Mulligan enrolled at the law school. He was an editor of the *Fordham Law Review*[10] and graduated *cum laude* in 1942.[11]

For three years after graduation, Mulligan served as a special agent in the counterintelligence corps of the Army during World War II.[12] "I was shipped overseas—to Staten Island," he said.[13] During his service, he met a colonel's secretary named Roseanna Connelly, whom he married on October 20, 1945. They settled in Bronxville.[14] Each of Mulligan's children followed in his footsteps: Anne became a teacher, while William, Jr., and Stephen earned law degrees at Fordham.[15]

In 1946, Mulligan returned to Fordham Law as a professor, teaching criminal law, equity, trade regulation, and insurance law, among other courses.[16] One of his criminal law students was Joseph M. McLaughlin, who, like Mulligan, would become dean of Fordham Law School and a judge of the Court of Appeals for the Second Circuit.[17] Until he was promoted to assistant dean of the law school in 1954, Mulligan practiced law at Manning, Hollinger & Shea, where he was a partner.[18]

In 1956, Mulligan was named dean of Fordham Law School.[19] During his 15-year deanship, the law school was transformed from a regional trade school into an institution of national prominence.[20] He oversaw the law school campus's move from downtown Manhattan to its current location at Lincoln Center, added over 21 new courses, recruited faculty of diverse religious and educational backgrounds, and insisted that faculty members publish legal scholarship.[21] Professor Constantine Katsoris, whom Mulligan taught and later hired, observed: "To the modern day Fordham Law School, Bill Mulligan was its father."[22] Fordham's annual moot court competition is named in Mulligan's honor.

While dean, Mulligan was engaged in government service. After the Supreme Court ruled that the apportionment of seats in the New York State legislature violated the "one man, one vote" rule,[23] Governor Nelson Rockefeller chose Mulligan to chair the Citizens' Committee on Reapportionment, which recommended structural changes.[24] He served on the New York State Law Revision Commission; he was counsel to the Republican delegation at the New York State Constitutional Convention; and he was appointed chairman of the Examining Board of the Manhattan and Bronx Surface Transit Operating Authority.[25]

Mulligan resigned as dean on June 15, 1970.[26] According to Judge McLaughlin, Mulligan "'had just had it with the student revolutions in the late '60s,'" and was particularly exasperated after students picketed Fordham, demanding exemptions from final exams in the wake of the Kent State shootings.[27] In a speech before the Vinson Club later that year, Mulligan reflected on his deanship and young people of that era:

> I look upon them with mitigated enthusiasm not because of their views or even their clothes or their hair, but rather because of their arrogant, humorless, monotonous group psychosis that theirs is the only approach, the only solution to all of the ills of mankind, their acceptance of all the material benefits of our generation and their failure to comprehend our own history of conquest over depression and oppression.[28]

Mulligan intended to rejoin the faculty full time the following academic year,[29] but in April 1971, President Richard M. Nixon nominated him to the Court of Appeals for the Second Circuit.[30] Judge Mulligan joked that, because he was appointed to a seat vacated by Judge J. Edward Lumbard, who was "a Chief Judge, it seemed crystal clear to me that I become the new Chief Judge. My mother who didn't even have the benefit of a legal education had the same understanding."[31]

Judge Mulligan's Second Circuit caseload reflected the controversies of the day, including the Vietnam War and the war on drugs. *Holtzman v. Schlesinger*[32] was an appeal from an order enjoining the President and military personnel from continuing combat operations in Cambodia on the ground that, absent renewed Congressional authorization, those operations exceeded executive authority, given a ceasefire in Vietnam, the withdrawal of American troops, and the release of American prisoners of war.[33] Reversing, Judge Mulligan's majority opinion held that the question whether the war had so changed as to require additional Congressional authorization was not for the judiciary to decide:

"While we as men may well agonize and bewail the horror of this or any war, the sharing of Presidential and Congressional responsibility particularly at this juncture is a bluntly political and not a judicial question."[34] The bombing of Cambodia ceased one week after the Second Circuit issued its opinion,[35] and the Supreme Court later denied a petition for writ of certiorari.[36] One historian called *Holtzman* Judge Mulligan's "most celebrated opinion."[37]

In *Carmona v. Ward*, a divided panel reversed a grant of habeas corpus relief to two women who received mandatory maximum sentences of life imprisonment for narcotics offenses under New York State's Rockefeller drug laws.[38] Judge Mulligan's majority opinion rejected the Eighth Amendment claim, emphasizing that it is the role of the legislature, not the court, to determine the appropriate punishment for a crime, and citing "the extraordinary crisis faced by the State of New York, caused by the crime of drug trafficking."[39] Justice Thurgood Marshall's dissent from the denial of certiorari questioned whether the circuit opinion "abdicate[d] the function conferred by the Eighth Amendment, to determine whether application of a given legislative judgment results in punishment grossly out of proportion to specific offenses."[40]

In February 1981, after almost ten years of service on the Court of Appeals, Mulligan resigned from the bench.[41] Although he enjoyed being a judge, he said that "inflation has rendered continued judicial service inequitable" and observed that, if he had died in the year before he resigned, his wife would receive an annuity of only $8,700 per year.[42] He remarked of the compensation, "You can live on it, but you can't die on it."[43] He later served as a nonjudge member of the Committee on the Judicial Branch of the United States Judicial Conference.[44] He testified before the Senate about the inadequacies of judicial compensation, and, due in part to his efforts, federal judges received a pay raise and improved survivors' benefits.[45]

After his resignation, Mulligan returned to private practice as a member of Skadden, Arps, Slate, Meagher & Flom.[46] Colleagues who asked how they should address him in light of his varied career were told that they could call him "Your Worship."[47] He took up keeping a diary. Former colleagues Barry H.

Garfinkel and Timothy Reynolds remember Mulligan describing that task:

> I had not kept a diary since I was in grammar school. After a few weeks, a partner came in and closed the door behind him which was an ominous sign in itself. He said "Your Worship." I said "You may approach the bench." The firm, he said, is really not interested in your reports on the weather, the antics of grandchildren or the problems of the New York Giants backfield. He said do you know about Billable Hours? I said yes—I think he is running in the fifth at Belmont.[48]

Mulligan's practice focused on appellate advocacy and arbitration, including high-profile litigation.[49] Overall, Mulligan enjoyed success in private practice and found the work satisfying. After the Second Circuit affirmed a district court's decision in his favor, he said that he "experienced a sense of exhilaration greater than I ever did on the bench, greater than having the Supreme Court reverse when you had written a dissenting opinion."[50]

Mulligan's sense of humor was legendary. Bar associations and other civic organizations sought him out as a guest speaker.[51] A recurring theme of his speeches was his Irish heritage. At the Society of the Friendly Sons of Saint Patrick dinner in 1972, Mulligan recounted a little-known fact of Irish history: that Christopher Columbus was really an Irish navigator named Lynch.[52] Mulligan made his case:

> I discovered to my dismay that Lynch's name does not appear on the list of the crew of any of the three vessels. This in turn led me to a somewhat spectacular discovery which I must share with you tonight in the privacy of this room. [A historian's] book gives a physical description of Columbus which was provided by his own contemporaries . . . "He was more than middling tall, aquiline nose, blue eyes, complexion light and tending to bright red, beard and hair red. When he was angry, he would exclaim 'May God take you.' In matter of religion he was so strict that for fasting and saying all the canonical offices he might have been taken for a member of a religious order." Gentlemen, in all honesty and frankness, how

> many religious, blue-eyed, red-faced, red-haired Italians have you met in your life?

Much of his humor was also self-deprecating:

> Some time ago I was introduced as a man who had, in a short time, won the respect and attention of his fellow judges. I responded that this reminded me of the story of the cross-eyed javelin thrower—although [he] never won any contests while he was competing, he always won the respect and attention of all the other contestants.[53]

William, Jr., published a posthumous book of Mulligan's speeches, *Mulligan's Law.*[54]

Mulligan's wit was not reserved for social gatherings. One of Judge Mulligan's law clerks recalled that a lawyer, who was underprepared and had exceeded his allotted time, ended his oral argument by pounding the podium and shouting, "What I demand from you is that you follow the immortal words above the doors of the Supreme Court and give my clients 'Equal Justice Under the Law.'"[55] Judge Mulligan, in kind, slapped the bench and responded, "And what I demand from you, sir, is that you follow the immortal word above the door at the Loew's Paradise: 'Exit.'"[56]

Judge Mulligan's final opinion—not-so-coincidentally handed down on St. Patrick's Day—is another well-remembered example of his humor. *United States v. Byrnes* involved a defendant indicted for smuggling rare birds from Canada into the United States.[57] Mulligan's opinion began:

> Who knows what evil lurks in the hearts of men? Though the public is generally aware of the sordid trafficking of drugs and aliens across our borders, this litigation alerts us to a nefarious practice hitherto unsuspected even by this rather calloused bench—rare bird smuggling. This appeal is therefore accurately designated as *rara avis.* While Canadian geese have been regularly crossing, exiting, reentering and departing our borders with impunity, and apparently without documentation, to enjoy more salubrious climes, those unwilling or unable to make the flight either because of inadequate wing

> spans, lack of fuel or fear of buckshot, have become prey to unscrupulous traffickers who put them in crates and ship them to American ports of entry with fraudulent documentation in violation of a host of federal statutes.[58]

He ended: "Justice has triumphed and this is my swan song."[59]

In August 1989, Mulligan suffered a stroke while on vacation in Bridgehampton, New York.[60] The stroke ended his career, and, as his son remarked, he was never quite the same.[61] A second stroke followed in July 1995.[62] He died on May 13, 1996, survived by his wife, three children, and six grandchildren.[63]

Emer M. Stack

1. John D. Feerick, *Dedication to the Honorable William Hughes Mulligan*, 7 FORDHAM INTELL. PROP. MEDIA & ENT. L.J. 1, 1 (1996).

2. William Hughes Mulligan, Jr., *Introduction* to MULLIGAN'S LAW, at xiii (William Hughes Mulligan, Jr., ed., Fordham University Press 1997).

3. William Hughes Mulligan, Address at the Annual Dinner of the Society of the Friendly Sons of Saint Patrick of Westchester County (Mar. 12 1976), *in* MULLIGAN'S LAW, *supra* note 2, at 88.

4. *Id.* at 90; William Hughes Mulligan, Jr., *Eulogy to William Hughes Mulligan*, 65 FORDHAM L. REV. 27, 28 (1996).

5. Mulligan, Jr., *Eulogy to William Hughes Mulligan, supra* note 4, at 30.

6. *Id.*

7. Mulligan, Jr., MULLIGAN'S LAW, *supra* note 2, at xiii.

8. *Founder's Relative Heads Fordham's Senior Week*, N.Y. TIMES, Mar. 30, 1939, at 11; *Dean of Districting*, N. Y. TIMES, July 13, 1964, at 21; Constantine N. Katsoris, *In the Service of Others: From Rose Hill to Lincoln Center*, 82 FORDHAM L. REV. 1533, 1577 (2014).

9. Paul Leventhal, *Profile: William Hughes Mulligan*, NEWSDAY, July 17, 1964, at 39.

10. *Fordham Editors Named*, N.Y. TIMES, Dec. 5, 1940, at 27.

11. Mulligan, Jr., MULLIGAN'S LAW, *supra* note 2, at xiii.

12. Wolfgang Saxon, *William Hughes Mulligan, 78, Judge and Dean of Law School*, N.Y. TIMES, May 14, 1996, at B6.

13. Mulligan, Jr., *Eulogy to William Hughes Mulligan, supra* note 4, at 29.

14. *Dean of Districting, supra* note 8; *Michael Hartmere Weds Anne Mulligan*, N.Y. TIMES, Oct. 22, 1972.

15. William H. Mulligan, Jr., BLEAKLEY PLATT, http://www.bpslaw.com/attorneys/william-h-mulligan-jr.aspx; Katsoris, *supra* note 8, at 1578.

16. Katsoris, *supra* note 8, at 1578; John Feerick, Remarks at a Special Session of the United States Court of Appeals for the Second Circuit, In Memoriam, Honorable William Hughes Mulligan VIII (Oct. 23, 1996), *in* 165 F.3d LXXXV. Feerick is the former dean of Fordham University School of Law and currently serves as the Norris Professor of Law there.

17. Joseph M. McLaughlin, *In Memoriam: William Hughes Mulligan*, 65 FORDHAM L. REV. 15, 15 (1996).

18. *Dean of Districting, supra* note 8.

19. *New Dean Is Appointed At Fordham Law School*, N.Y. TIMES, Aug. 19, 1956, at 53.

20. John D. Feerick, *Remarks Delivered on the Occasion of the Presentation of the Fordham-Stein Award to the Honorable William Hughes Mulligan*, 59 FORDHAM L. REV. 479, 480 (1990).

21. *Fordham Visitors See New Building: 2,000 Attend Open House at Lincoln Sq. Law Unit*, N.Y. TIMES, Oct. 8 1961, at 84; Katsoris, *supra* note 8, at 1580; ROBERT J. KACZOROWSKI, FORDHAM UNIVERSITY SCHOOL OF LAW: A HISTORY 215, 223 (2012).

22. Katsoris, *supra* note 8, at 1579.

23. *See* WMCA Inc. v. Lomenzo, 377 U.S. 633 (1964).

24. Leventhal, *supra* note 9.

25. Michael P. Walsh, *Dean William Hughes Mulligan—A Tribute*; 39 FORDHAM L. REV. xxvi (1970).

26. KACZOROWSKI, *supra* note 21, at 262.

27. *Id.*

28. William Hughes Mulligan, Address at the Annual Dinner of the Vinson Club (Nov. 19, 1970), *in* MULLIGAN'S LAW, *supra* note 2, at 38.

29. KACZOROWSKI, *supra* note 21, at 262; Walsh, *supra* note 25, at xxvii ("We are happy and pleased that he intends to remain as a Professor where he will be given even more opportunities to relate closely and intimately with students.")

30. Richard L. Madden, *Nixon Names 4 as Judges on Local Federal Benches*, N.Y. TIMES, Apr. 27, 1971, at 1.

31. Judge William Hughes Mulligan, Address to the New York County Lawyers Association (Dec. 9, 1971), *in* MULLIGAN'S LAW, *supra* note 2, at 44.

32. 484 F.2d 1307 (2d Cir. 1973), *cert. denied*, 416 U.S. 936 (1974).

33. 361 F. Supp. 553, 563–66 (E.D.N.Y. 1973).

34. *Id.* at 1311.

35. *See Justiciability of Presidential War Power (Holtzman v. Schlesinger)*, 48 ST. JOHN'S L. REV. 309, 315 (1973) (noting that bombing ceased on August 15, 1973).

36. 416 U.S. 936 (1974).

37. JEFFREY B. MORRIS, FEDERAL JUSTICE IN THE SECOND CIRCUIT 180 (1987).

38. 576 F.2d 405, 406 (2d Cir. 1978).

39. *Id.* at 409–10, 416–17.

40. Carmona v. Ward, 439 U.S. 1093–97 (1979).

41. Arnold H. Lubasch, *U.S. Appellate Judge Quits Over His Salary and Benefits*, N.Y. TIMES, Feb. 5, 1981, at B1.

42. *Id.*

43. *Id.*

44. Judge Thomas J. Meskill, Remarks at a Special Session of the United States Court of Appeals for the Second Circuit, In Memoriam, Honorable William Hughes Mulligan VII (Oct. 23, 1996), *in* 165 F.3d LXXXV.

45. *Surviving Justice*, N.Y. TIMES, Jan. 10, 1983, at A18.

46. Judge Thomas J. Meskill, *supra* note 44, at VII; Lubasch, *supra* note 41.

47. Barry H. Garfinkel, *William Hughes Mulligan at Skadden Arps*, 65 FORDHAM L. REV. 25 (1996); *see also* Timothy Reynolds & Barry H. Garfinkel, *Some Thoughts on Judge Mulligan's Presence at Skadden, Arps* (Aug. 13, 2015) (unpublished) (on file with the United States Courts Library for the Second Circuit).

48. Reynolds & Garfinkel, *supra* note 47.

49. Katsoris, *supra* note 8, at 1584; Reynolds & Garfinkel, *supra* note 47.

50. Mulligan, Jr., MULLIGAN'S LAW, *supra* note 2, at xv.

51. *See generally id.*

52. Judge William Hughes Mulligan, Address at the Annual Dinner of the Society of the Friendly Sons of Saint Patrick in the City of New York (Mar. 12, 1972), *in* MULLIGAN'S LAW, *supra* note 2, at 53.

53. *Epigram* to MULLIGAN'S LAW, *supra* note 2, at vii.

54. MULLIGAN'S LAW, *supra* note 2.

55. *See* E-mail from Charles Carberry, former law clerk, to Sally Pritchard (July 13, 2015, 12:03 EST) (on file with the United States Courts Library for the Second Circuit). Carberry is a partner at Jones Day.

56. *See id.*

57. 644 F.2d 107 (2d Cir. 1981).

58. *Id.* at 108–09.

59. *Id.* at 112.

60. Mulligan, Jr., MULLIGAN'S LAW, *supra* note 2, at xv.

61. *Id.*

62. Donna Greene, *Son Remembers Judge's Humor and Wit*, N.Y. TIMES, Apr. 12, 1998, at WE3.

63. *Id.*; Saxon, *supra* note 12.

# WILLIAM H. TIMBERS
# 1915-1994

District Court for the District of Connecticut:
1960-1971
Court of Appeals for the Second Circuit: 1971-1994

Jurist, outdoorsman, and dog lover: "Whispering Willie" Timbers was all of these things and more. Born in Yonkers, New York on September 5, 1915,[1] Timbers grew up in Glen Ridge, New Jersey, just a few miles west of Newark.[2] In 1937, he graduated from Dartmouth College and began law school at Yale, graduating in 1940.[3] The next year, Timbers and his wife, Charlotte, moved to Darien, Connecticut,[4] where they lived for the rest of their lives.

After law school, Timbers mixed private practice with government service. He began his career as an associate at Davis,

Polk, Wardwell, Sunderland & Kiendl; in 1948, he moved to the Connecticut firm of Cummings & Lockwood, where he handled litigation in Connecticut's state and federal courts for five years.[5] In 1953, Timbers began his long career of public service by joining the Securities and Exchange Commission as general counsel—at the time, a unique move because the SEC had never before appointed a general counsel from outside the agency.[6]

While at the SEC, Timbers stated that he wanted to argue a case in every court of appeals in the country.[7] He did not succeed, but the job did send him far and wide across the United States on behalf of the government. In fact, it nearly sent him to jail.

The SEC was trying a case in federal court in Detroit, and the district court had threatened two agency employees with contempt for refusing to disclose records of an open SEC investigation that the agency believed contained privileged information.[8] Timbers flew to Detroit to defend the employees against any contempt charges.[9] The district court had reassured the SEC and Timbers that if it decided to hold any of the attorneys in contempt for refusing to disclose, it would give them access to counsel and a stay so that they could take the matter to the Court of Appeals for the Sixth Circuit.[10] When Timbers arrived, the district court required him to take the stand and answer questions for several days about the documents; Timbers steadfastly refused to submit the documents to the court.[11] The court then held Timbers in contempt, denied him access to counsel or a stay, and issued a written order fixing his sentence at 60 days.[12] Timbers was in the custody of the U.S. marshal for four hours until the Sixth Circuit stayed his sentence.[13]

On appeal, Warren Burger, then an assistant attorney general, defended Timbers against the contempt charge.[14] The Sixth Circuit wrote that the district court "abused all justifiable discretion" and ordered that Timbers "be completely absolved from any punishment for his alleged contempt."[15] According to one of his law clerks, the entire experience informed Timbers's sympathetic approach to prisoners' rights cases—as he was fond of reminding his clerks, he had actually been to jail.[16]

Timbers's time at the SEC was short—only three years. However, he made a strong impression; as his friend and colleague Irving Pollack stated, his departure was "a great loss for us and a great regret."[17] In 1956, he joined the recently formed firm of Skadden, Arps, Slate, Meagher & Flom.[18] Timbers was the firm's third partner; the firm had five associates.[19] (It now employs over 1,600 lawyers and is the most profitable law firm in the United States.)[20] He immediately brought the firm something it had yet to obtain: access to the Wall Street financial community, which was drawn to Timbers's reputation from the SEC.[21]

Timbers developed a unique schedule at Skadden. Every morning, he would take the train from Darien to Manhattan, but he would not go straight to the firm's offices.[22] Instead, he would go to the Yale Club, where his secretary would be waiting for him, mail in hand.[23] She would stay while he dictated his responses, after which he would leave the club, go to meetings around the city, and then come to the office.[24] Timbers's devotion to the Yale Club never wavered after he became a judge; if he was in New York for a sitting, he did much of his work there, and he urged all Connecticut judges to stay at the club when they were in New York, even if they never attended Yale.[25]

In 1960, Timbers was appointed to the District Court for the District of Connecticut.[26] His sense of humor and loyalty to that court was illustrated by his frequent public references to it as the nation's oldest federal trial court—needling the Southern District of New York for its claim to be the "Mother Court." Because of a priority of one day, he would facetiously call the District Court of Connecticut "the grandmother court."[27]

His devotion to Connecticut and its district court was nowhere more evident than in his tenacious advocacy to save the beautiful pre-World War I United States Courthouse on the New Haven Green from the designs of local urban planners. They intended to destroy it as part of a design that would move the court facilities into a new, modern federal office building.[28] His only half-serious threats to have the U.S. marshals arrest anyone who attempted to deploy a wrecking ball in the vicinity of the courthouse,[29] and his mobilization of Yale art historians (including, most notably, the eminent Vincent Scully) and New Haven preservationists, are generally credited with saving the courthouse that had been designed by James Gamble Rogers and built in 1914.[30]

Judge Timbers served on the district court for eleven years prior to his appointment, by President Richard M. Nixon, to the Court of Appeals for the Second Circuit in 1971.[31]

Throughout his judicial career, Judge Timbers voiced concern about organized crime, especially in Connecticut. In 1965, while presiding over the trial of 50 men accused of failing to obtain gambling tax stamps, he delivered a speech from the bench on gambling and organized criminal activity in the state, lambasting the state courts for handing out lax sentences and urging the state to create a commission to deal with gambling crimes in the state.[32] The commission was formed a year later.[33] In 1972, after appointment to the Court of Appeals, he urged Connecticut Governor Thomas Meskill (a future colleague on the bench) to block a bill to expand gambling beyond a lottery.[34] And, in 1985, he wrote an opinion holding that defendants in racketeering cases may be required to disclose attorneys' fees when those fees are paid on behalf of other members of a racketeering ring.[35] This ruling helped federal prosecutors prove the existence of the ring itself. Finally, he joined the court in holding that the government may use the federal racketeering statute (RICO) to prosecute terrorists even if financial gain was not the primary motive for their crimes.[36]

Like almost all Second Circuit judges, Judge Timbers also issued decisions affecting New York City. In 1990, he joined the majority in upholding the city's ban on begging on the subways.[37] In 1991, he upheld the city's sale of urban renewal land in Williamsburg to the Satmar Hasidic organization.[38] The battle over the land was intense, with multiple Hispanic groups objecting that the Hasidic organization bought the land in an attempt to set up an unconstitutional Hasidic enclave, but Judge Timbers found that argument unpersuasive.[39]

Judge Timbers was known for his tremendous work ethic.[40] A law clerk noted that, while he had a lighter side that he regularly showed to his clerks and friends, he was generally a serious, stern individual who took great pride in his role as a judge; he spent most of his time working, either in chambers or in his cabins in Connecticut and Maine.[41] He exhibited a perfectionism well known to those on the court, to the point where he regularly amassed a backlog of cases rather than rush through them at the expense of accuracy and thorough consideration. His motto was, "No opinion will be circulated before its time."[42] His attention to detail was intense: when drafting an opinion involving a ship that had run aground, he made sure to use proper nautical terminology, but his clerk changed "port" to "left" and "starboard" to "right," presumably for the benefit of the reader ignorant of maritime vocabulary.[43] Judge Timbers—a sailor himself—disapproved.[44]

This portrait of Judge Timbers—stern, uncompromising, even intimidating—is incomplete, however, for he was also eccentric and wily. As Chief Judge Jon O. Newman stated, "Bill Timbers was as distinctive an individual as I have ever known."[45] He always spoke in a soft whisper—his nickname was "Whispering Willie."[46] He had no love for quarterly court meetings, which led to a long-running ruse that allowed him to miss them.[47] In the spring, Judge Timbers would tell Chief Judge Irving R. Kaufman that the tide in Surry, Maine, where he had a second home, was just right for him to launch his sailboat; he would miss the sailing season otherwise.[48] In the fall, he would say that he had to get the boat out of the water before the winter weather hit.[49] Chief Judge Kaufman almost certainly knew a tall tale when he heard one, but he always played along.[50]

In general, Judge Timbers disdained formalities. Even in the 1970s—when business attire was universal among lawyers throughout the profession—Judge Timbers wore a green hiking outfit under his robes.[51] One afternoon in the late 1970s, an attorney mistook him for a janitor and asked him for directions to a courtroom.[52] Judge Timbers obliged. When the attorney arrived for oral argument, he found Judge Timbers waiting behind the bench.[53]

Judge Timbers's time away from the court was devoted to his family, his dogs, and the outdoors. Indeed, the urge to be outside the confines of an office remained constant throughout Judge Timbers's career. As a judge, he did much of his work in his two log cabins, which he had built on the grounds of his homes in Darien and Surry.[54] The latter was built from the trees of the forests surrounding his Maine home, and he considered it a refuge from interruption, where he could work unimpeded by any other demands.[55] During construction, he sent status updates to a group of friends he titled "Society of Friends of Log Cabin Justice."[56] After it was built, he referred to the cabin as his "Main(e) chambers."[57] In the early 1980s, his Surry cabin hosted meetings of the Judicial Statistics Committee, leading Chief Justice Warren Burger to note that it was the first time in over a century that judges had met in a log cabin.[58] Judge Timbers would bring his law clerks to the cabin, housing them in his large home in Surry while they all worked on cases in peace and tranquility.[59] Timbers had a feeling for the outdoors that could best be described as moral: he belived that time spent in nature strengthened the character and was essential to a life fully lived.[60]

Judge Timbers's love for dogs—in particular, Norwegian elkhounds—was profound. He was president of the Elkhound Association of America, which funded research into canine blindness that Judge Timbers hoped would lead to a medical breakthrough for human blindness as well.[61] He bred and trained the elkhounds for show, where they won several awards.[62] His first elkhound, bought in 1958 after an encounter with the breed on a trip to Vermont, was named Champion Lief of Dragondell and won several honors.[63] A younger dog was named Lieflet. Judge Timbers was a member of the Ox Ridge Kennel Club in Darien, where he served as delegate to the American Kennel Club.[64] For years, he was the head of the New York trial board of the American Kennel Club, and he was eventually named chairman of the board of the American Kennel Club after he took senior status.[65] Judge Timbers was rarely without his dogs; he brought them to the courthouse regularly, and they sat in with him during judicial proceedings[66] and swearing in of new judges.[67] Judge Timbers even judged the elkhounds at the Westminster Dog Show.[68] As befit Judge Timbers's streak of mock-seriousness, he wore a barrister's wig to the show, where he judged the dogs in what was surely a manner appropriate to his attire.[69]

Judge Timbers served as an active judge for 21 years, taking senior status in 1981. He spent his later years surrounded by his wife, Charlotte, their four children—John, Dwight, William, Jr. ("Nick"), and Nancy—and his ten grandchildren.[70] His sons remained in Connecticut throughout their lives, while his daughter resides in Palo Alto, California.[71] When he took senior status, his desire to see more of his family was the primary reason he cited for doing so.[72] His son William, speaking at a memorial for his father, provided a fitting and poignant tribute:

> [R]egardless of the name we used for him—Judge or Bill, Dad or Granddad . . . we all carry a little bit of him in us. We felt his tenacity. We were affected by his strong beliefs and convictions. His good judgment and quiet counsel hopefully will live through us. . . . [T]he extension of my father's character and traits carried forward in all of us is the most enduring legacy of all.[73]

He continued to handle cases until his death in 1994 at age 79.[74]

Stephen Strother

1. FEDERAL JUDICIAL CENTER, Biographical Directory of Federal Judges, William Homer Timbers, www.fjc.gov/servlet/nGetInfo?jid=2389&cid=999&cytpe=na&instate=na.

2. Donald Marchione, *Judge William H. Timbers: Applying the Basic Principles*, N. HAVEN J.-COURIER, Oct. 9, 1965.

3. *Id.*

4. *Id.*

5. Barry H. Garfinkel, Remarks at a Special Session of the United States Court of Appeals for the Second Circuit, In Memoriam, Honorable William H. Timbers XCI–XCII (Apr. 17, 1995) (transcript on file with the United States Courts Library for the Second Circuit). Garfinkel is a senior member of the Skadden, Arps, Slate Meagher & Flom international litigation and arbitration group.

6. *Id.* at XCII; Irving M. Pollack, Remarks at a Special Session of the United States Court of Appeals for the Second Circuit, In Memoriam, Honorable William H. Timbers XCIV (Apr. 17, 1995) (transcript on file with the United States Courts Library for the Second Circuit). Pollack served as commissioner and assistant general counsel of the SEC for over 30 years.

7. Pollack, Remarks, *supra* note 6, at XCIV.

8. Appeal of U.S. Secs. & Exch. Comm'n, 226 F.2d 501, 502 (6th Cir. 1955); Pollack, Remarks, *supra* note 6, at XCV.

9. 226 F.2d at 502.

10. Pollack, Remarks, *supra* note 6, at XCV.

11. 226 F.2d at 511–15 (Timbers' testimony).

12. *Id.* at 512, 515–16.

13. *SEC Attorney Fights Sentence for Contempt*, IRONWOOD DAILY GLOBE, Mar. 3, 1955, at 20.

14. 226 F.2d at 501.

15. *Id.* at 520.

16. Telephone Interview with Filiberto Agusti, former law clerk (Apr. 29, 2015) (notes on file with the United States Courts Library for the Second Circuit). Agusti is a partner at Steptoe & Johnson LLP.

17. Pollack, Remarks, *supra* note 6, at XCV.

18. Garfinkel, Remarks, *supra* note 5, at XCII.

19. *Id.*

20. *Skadden, Arps, Slate, Meagher & Flom LLP and Affiliates*, VAULT, http://www.vault.com/company-profiles/law/skadden,-arps,-slate,-meagher-flom-llp-and-affiliates/company-overview.aspx.

21. Garfinkel, Remarks, *supra* note 5, at XCII.

22. *Id.* at XCIII.

23. *Id.*

24. *Id.*

25. *Id.*; Judge Thomas J. Meskill, Remarks at a Special Session of the United States Court of Appeals for the Second Circuit, In Memoriam, Honorable William H. Timbers XCVII (Apr. 17, 1995) (transcript on file with the United States Courts Library for the Second Circuit).

26. *William H. Timbers, 79*, N. HAVEN REG., Nov. 29, 1994.

27. *See* José A. Cabranes, *Notes on the History of the Federal Court of Connecticut*, 57 CONN. B.J. 351, 355 (1983) ("Thus, by a span of some twenty-four hours, it could be said that the District of Connecticut is our 'Mother Court,' or as Judge Timbers suggests in moments of exaltation, our 'Grandmother Court.'"); *see also* José A. Cabranes, *On the Mythology of "The Mother Court,"* 88 CONN. B.J. 226, 233 (2015).

28. *See* William H.H. Rees, *How We Saved the Post Office—& the Library*, N. HAVEN INDEP., http://www.newhavenindependent.org/index.php/archives/entry/how_we_saved_the_post_office_—_the_library/ ("Among the structures slated to vanish was the elegant 1910 post office and federal courthouse, by James Gamble Rogers, later the architect for a dozen Yale buildings as colonial or medieval clones.")

29. Interview with Judge José A. Cabranes (Apr. 15, 2014) (notes on file with the United States Courts Library for the Second Circuit).

30. *See* Rees, *supra* note 28 ("[O]n Oct. 24, 1966, Judge William H. Timbers, chief judge of the [District Court of Connecticut], announced that the six federal judges unanimously agreed to keep their court in its present location in its elegant, Vermont marble building. . . . Thus, the General Services Administration ('GSA') had to agree to keep the oldest court in the nation on the Green where it had been for 177 years."); *see also* Charles C. Goetsch, *Ceremony of Rededication, United States District Courthouse, New Haven, Connecticut*, www.ctd.uscourts.gov/sites/default/files/forms/REDEDICATION%20BOOKLET.pdf ("The New Haven Preservation Trust quickly joined forces with the judges in this battle, and on October 19, 1966, Professor Vincent J. Scully, Jr. galvanized public opinion against the proposed demolition during a 90 minute address to an overflow crowd at the Yale Law School auditorium. Comparing the historical importance of buildings such as the Courthouse to the Acropolis, he concluded, 'the new project is like an act of undeniable vandalism so gross that one cannot believe it was proposed without irony.'")

31. *William H. Timbers, 79*, *supra* note 26.

32. *Bridgeport Raids Shock U.S. Judge*, N.Y. TIMES, Jan. 14, 1965; Marchione, *supra* note 2.

33. Marchione, *supra* note 2.

34. Judge Thomas J. Meskill, Remarks, *supra* note 25, at XCVI.

35. Gerald McKelvey, *Supreme Court Adds Weapon to War on Organized Crime*, NEWSDAY, Apr. 8, 1986, at 5.

36. Arnold H. Lubasch, *Court Shuts Gap in Past Decisions on Rackets Law*, N.Y. TIMES, Apr. 15, 1983, at B4.

37. Craig Wolff, *U.S. Appeals Court Upholds Ban on Begging in New York Subways*, N.Y. TIMES, May 11, 1990, at A1.

38. Bob Liff, *Court Backs B'klyn Yeshiva*, NEWSDAY, Mar. 30, 1991, at 11.

39. *Id.*

40. *See* Telephone Interview with Filiberto Agusti, *supra* note 16; Pollack, Remarks, *supra* note 6, at XCIV; Carroll W. Brewster, former law clerk, Remarks at a Special Session of the United States Court of Appeals for the Second Circuit, In Memoriam, Honorable William H. Timbers XCVIII (Apr. 17, 1995) (transcript on file with the United States Courts Library for the Second Circuit). Brewster was former dean of Dartmouth and former president of Hobart and William Smith college.

41. Telephone Interview with Filiberto Agusti, *supra* note 16.

42. Judge Thomas J. Meskill, Remarks, *supra* note 25, at XCVII.

43. *Id.*

44. *Id.*

45. Chief Judge Jon O. Newman, Remarks at a Special Session of the United States Court of Appeals for the Second Circuit, In Memoriam, Honorable William H. Timbers XCI (Apr. 17, 1995) (transcript on file with the United States Courts Library for the Second Circuit).

46. Marchione, *supra* note 2; Interview with Judge José A. Cabranes, *supra* note 29.

47. Judge Thomas J. Meskill, Remarks, *supra* note 25, at XCVI.

48. *Id.*

49. *Id.* at XCVII.

50. *Id.*

51. Telephone Interview with Filiberto Agusti, *supra* note 16.

52. *Id.*

53. *Id.*

54. *Id.*

55. Judge Thomas J. Meskill, Remarks, *supra* note 25, at XCVII.

56. *Id.*

57. *Id.*

58. Walter R. Fletcher, *Dog-Loving Judge Leads Kennel Club*, N.Y. TIMES, Apr. 4, 1982, at CN19.

59. Telephone Interview with Filiberto Agusti, *supra* note 16.

60. *Id.*

61. Fletcher, *Dog-Loving Judge Leads Kennel Club*, *supra* note 58; Marchione, *supra* note 2.

62. Fletcher, *Dog-Loving Judge Leads Kennel Club*, *supra* note 58; Marchione, *supra* note 2.

63. Walter R. Fletcher, *The Judge Rules for Elkhounds*, N.Y. TIMES, Oct. 24, 1974, at 58; Fletcher, *Dog-Loving Judge Leads Kennel Club*, *supra* note 58.

64. *About Us*, OX RIDGE KENNEL CLUB, oxridgekc.org/aboutus.html.

65. Fletcher, *Dog-Loving Judge Leads Kennel Club*, *supra* note 58.

66. Interview with Judge José A. Cabranes, *supra* note 29.

67. Fletcher, *Dog-Loving Judge Leads Kennel Club*, supra note 58; Judge Thomas J. Meskill, Remarks, *supra* note 25, at XCVI.

68. Telephone Interview with Filiberto Agustis, *supra* note 16.

69. *Id.*

70. *William H. Timbers, 79*, *supra* note 26.

71. *Id.*

72. Arnold H. Lubasch, *Judge Timbers Leaving U.S. Appeals Court Post*, N.Y. TIMES, July 17, 1981, at B3.

73. William H. Timbers, Jr., Remarks at a Special Session of the United States Court of Appeals for the Second Circuit, In Memoriam, Honorable William H. Timbers CI (Apr. 17, 1995) (transcript on file with the United States Courts Library for the Second Circuit). William H. Timbers, Jr., is the son Judge Timbers.

74. FEDERAL JUDICIAL CENTER, *supra* note 1.

# MURRAY IRWIN GURFEIN
## 1907-1979

District Court for the Southern District of New York: 1971-1974
Court of Appeals for the Second Circuit: 1974-1979

"[I]n his relatively short tenure as a judge, he published 315 opinions covering the whole spectrum of criminal and civil litigation, in which . . . he judged in the grand manner and demonstrated his judicial integrity and temperament as well as his ability to reason and to fairly balance the equities of the case."1 These words were spoken by District Judge John R. Bartels in remembrance of his friend Murray Gurfein.

Murray Irwin Gurfein was born in New York City on November 17, 1907, to Louis Gurfein and the former Rosa Feld.[2] He graduated Phi Beta Kappa from Columbia College in 1926 and *magna cum laude* from Harvard Law School in 1930.[3]

He and his wife, Eva Hadas, had two daughters, Abby and Susan.[4] The family divided their time between two homes. Their Manhattan apartment, at 530 Park Avenue, was where they resided on weekdays.[5] Nearly every weekend and summer, the family escaped to their country home in Putnam Valley, New York. Gurfein was said to spend most of his leisure time in the expansive law library he kept at this home.[6] A lover of the woods and countryside, Gurfein regularly went on a three-mile walk on Sundays along his favorite country dirt road, Bell Hollow Road. His neighbors instantly recognized him based on his usual outfit of "country slacks, a colorful sport shirt, . . . hiking shoes, a bizarre cap and sometimes a sweater," and practice of carrying a cane or walking stick.[7] Gurfein, convivial and personable, was popular among his neighbors.[8] Judge Bartels recalled, "His common sense and his unique sense of humor added to his reputation," and "one might describe him as the squire of Putnam Valley."[9]

In the 1930s, Gurfein served as an Assistant United States Attorney in Manhattan; he later worked as an assistant district attorney in the Rackets Bureau under Manhattan District Attorneys Thomas E. Dewey and Frank S. Hogan.[10] In this capacity, Gurfein exposed labor racketeering along New York City's waterfront.[11] Among his many prosecutions, he secured the theft conviction of George Scalise, the head of the International Building Service Employees Union, and the extortion conviction of Edward S. Moran, Jr., a Brooklyn Democratic assemblyman.[12]

When the United States joined World War II, Gurfein resigned from his post as assistant district attorney to join the staff of Colonel William J. Donovan.[13] In 1942, President Franklin Delano Roosevelt had secretly granted Donovan (who was perhaps better known by his moniker, "Wild Bill") authority to assemble, in the President's words, "that heterogeneous outfit of intellectuals, dilettantes and footpads which came to be known as OSS," or the Office of Strategic Services.[14] The OSS was America's "first organized nonmilitary espionage and sabotage agency," and was the forerunner to the CIA.[15] During his time with the OSS, Gurfein was introduced to Walter Mansfield.

Although their professional careers diverged after they left the OSS, they were reunited in the 1970s when both men sat as judges on the Second Circuit.[16]

Gurfein was given OSS assignments in London, Glasgow, and Istanbul. Toward the end of the war, he was reassigned to the Supreme Headquarters for the Allied Expeditionary Force, where he worked for the Psychological Warfare Branch. After three and a half years in the military, he left military service with the rank of lieutenant colonel.[17] He held the Legion of Merit and the Croix de Guerre, and he was named an Honorary Officer of the British Empire.[18]

In November 1945, Gurfein was selected as one of a special panel of nine attorneys who would assist the United States counsel at Nuremberg.[19] Gurfein's duties included "keeping check on points of evidence as proofs are advanced against individual prisoners," and keeping "charge of documents to make certain that those to be used in each day's proceedings are ready at hand, as well as similar chores designed to expedite the presentation of the prosecution's case."[20]

Beginning in 1946, and for the next 25 years, Gurfein was a partner at several New York law firms, including his own, Goldstein, Judd & Gurfein.[21] His OSS service seemed to influence his practice of law. One of his colleagues recalled Gurfein's "extreme security consciousness" and how, in corporate takeover cases, Gurfein "gave code names to the corporations his clients sought to acquire, and to the clients too, and stuck to them in the office and on the phone." Gurfein was also known to "lock up the relevant papers in his desk every night before going home."[22]

During his years of private practice, Gurfein also made his mark as a leader of Jewish organizations; he served as the president of the United Hebrew Immigration Aid Society, an international migration and resettlement agency, for ten years.[23] In 1970, the American Jewish Committee awarded Gurfein its Learned Hand Human Relations Award for his contributions to the Jewish community.[24]

In 1971, on the recommendation of Senator Jacob K. Javits, Gurfein was appointed to the District Court for the Southern

District of New York by President Richard M. Nixon.[25] The beginning of his judicial career was steeped in irony. For his first week as a district judge, Gurfein was assigned the "motions calendar," which consisted of "a melange of matters mostly procedural, matters that seldom determine the outcome of specific cases but have their importance nevertheless and present an ideal starting point for a newly appointed judge."[26] For Gurfein, however, his first case on the motions calendar generated his most famous decision.

On Sunday, June 13, 1971, *The New York Times* published a series of articles and descriptions of secret documents created by the Pentagon and Department of Defense concerning the Vietnam War and the alleged attack on Navy warships by North Vietnamese forces in the Gulf of Tonkin.[27] The following day, June 14, the *Times* published its next installment in the series.[28] June 14 also happened to be Gurfein's first day on the job as a district judge, during which he presided over a naturalization ceremony.[29] On Tuesday, June 15, the *Times* published its third installment of the Pentagon's study on Vietnam.[30] That day, Gurfein received a telephone call from Whitney North Seymour, Jr., the United States Attorney for the Southern District of New York, who planned to move for an injunction to stop the *Times* from publishing sensitive government documents.[31] Over the next week, Gurfein presided over "a heated struggle between his favorite newspaper and the President who named him a judge."[32]

The case was extraordinary, and Gurfein knew it. In his own words, "Never before had there been such a single massive breach of security or so unprecedented a request by the executive for a restraint prior to publication. There was no clear precedent to serve as a guide. All that existed were generalizations in a handful of cases."[33] After hearing oral argument, Gurfein denied the government's motion for a preliminary injunction. In his June 19, 1971 decision, Gurfein explained that "Congress[,] recognizing the Constitutional problems of the First Amendment with respect to free press, refused to include a form of precensorship even in war time."[34] He explained that, while the government had a right to injunctive relief "against a newspaper that is about to publish information or documents absolutely vital to current national security," he did not "find that to be the case here."[35] Acknowledging that the government might suffer some embarrassment from the security breach, Gurfein advised that "we must learn to live with it." "The security of the Nation is not at the ramparts alone. Security also lies in the value of our free institutions," he said. "A cantankerous press, an obstinate press, an ubiquitous press must be suffered by those in authority in order to preserve the even greater values of freedom of expression and the right of the people to know."[36] Gurfein concluded his decision by writing:

> These are troubled times. There is no greater safety valve for discontent and cynicism about the affairs of Government than freedom of expression in any form. This has been the genius of our institutions throughout our history. It is one of the marked traits of our national life that distinguish us from other nations under different forms of government.[37]

The government appealed. On June 22, 1971, the Second Circuit heard the appeal *en banc* and issued a five-to-three decision the following day, continuing a stay of Judge Gurfein's order and remanding the case for further *in camera* proceedings.[38] Days later, on June 26, the Supreme Court heard argument and issued a decision reversing the Second Circuit, remanding "with directions to enter a judgment affirming the judgment of the District Court for the Southern District of New York."[39]

After three years as a district court judge, Gurfein was appointed by President Nixon to the Court of Appeals for the Second Circuit in 1974.[40] Although he was a circuit judge for only five years, he wrote over 100 opinions on diverse areas of law, including tax, securities, criminal, and civil rights.

In *Parent Association of Andrew Jackson High School v. Ambach*, parents and students sought an injunction forcing Andrew Jackson High School in Queens to implement a desegregation plan. At issue in the case was the commissioner of education's July 1976 plan that provided that the school's minority students could attend any New York City high school in which the majority of students were white, and that the school's white students could attend any New York City high school in which the majority of students were minorities.[41] The district court ruled there was no intentional segregation, but found the 1976 plan unconstitutional and ordered the school district to develop a plan for the desegregation of the Andrew Jackson High School.[42]

On appeal, Gurfein wrote an opinion affirming in part and reversing in part. Gurfein explained that, having correctly determined "that there had been no intentional segregation, the [district court] judge lacked authority under [c]ontrolling law to compel the school authorities to implement an affirmative plan designed to achieve racial balance at Jackson."[43] Gurfein analyzed the constitutionality of the 1976 plan under a strict scrutiny test and determined that remand was appropriate, as there was insufficient evidence.[44]

Gurfein also wrote an opinion in a case that likely piqued his interest in light of his work with the OSS during World War II. In *Birnbaum v. United States*, a suit under the Federal Tort Claims Act, an appeal was taken from a district court order awarding damages and requiring government apologies to the plaintiffs. The plaintiffs alleged that agents of the CIA had covertly opened mail that was either sent to or received from the Soviet Union; this mail was photocopied by CIA agents and then turned over to postal employees for delivery.[45] Gurfein concluded that the plaintiffs had sustained a "personal injury" under state law, and that the government's conduct fell outside any exception to the waiver of immunity provision of the FTCA[46] The court reasoned that the opening of letters did not fall under the "postal exception," because that waiver of immunity was premised on negligent conduct, whereas the CIA's conduct was intentional; it also did not fall under the "discretionary function exception" because "the CIA was acting so far beyond its authority that it could not have been exercising a function which could in any proper sense be called 'discretionary.'"[47] The only remaining issue was whether the district court's judgment of money damages and apologies was proper. Because the injury to the plaintiffs was minimal, "the question of damages [was] close," but the court affirmed the money judgments for $1,000 per plaintiff "with the feeling that they represent the upper limit of allowable compensation in these cases." As to the government's letter of apology to the plaintiffs, Gurfein wrote, "[T]hough such letters might some day achieve monetary value as collectors' items, we do not view them as 'money damages,' the only form of relief provided in the Act."[48]

In December 1979, Gurfein died of a sudden heart attack at his New York City apartment at the age of 72.[49] He was survived by his wife, two daughters, and six grandchildren.[50] Although the many memorials paying tribute to Gurfein focused on his decision in the *Pentagon Papers* case, those who were most familiar with his 50-year legal career appreciated the larger scope of Gurfein's contributions to the law. In the words of Morton Hamburg, who worked at Gurfein's law firm and watched Gurfein litigate many cases,

> Judge Gurfein was much more than just the author of one district court decision, however significant it was in the annals of constitutional or communications law, or the law in general. He was . . . one of the most brilliant men ever to enter our profession, and his contributions to the law and our society throughout his life were many and will be remembered.[51]

Molly Guptill Manning

1. District Judge John R. Bartels, Remarks at a Special Session of the United States Court of Appeals for the Second Circuit, Memorial Proceedings for the Honorable Murray I. Gurfein (Sept. 15, 1980), *in* 634 F.2d LXXXVI.

2. Robert D. McFadden, *Judge M.I. Gurfein, Who Allowed Pentagon Papers' Publication, Dies*, N.Y. TIMES, Dec. 18, 1979, at B16.

3. District Judge John R. Bartels, Remarks, *supra* note 1, at LXXXVI; James L. Oakes, *Judge Gurfein and the Pentagon Papers*, 2 CARDOZO L. REV. 5, 5 (1980).

4. District Judge John R. Bartels, Remarks, *supra* note 1; Henry B. Hyde, Remarks at a Special Session of the United States Court of Appeals for the Second Circuit, Memorial Proceedings for the Honorable Murray I. Gurfein (Sept. 15, 1980), *in* 634 F.2d LXXXVI, XC. Hyde was a colleague in the OSS and partner at the firm currently known as Wormser, Kiely, Galef & Jacobs; *see also* McFadden, *supra* note 2, at B16.

5. McFadden, *supra* note 2, at B16.

6. District Judge John R. Bartels, Remarks, *supra* note 1, at LXXXVII.

7. *Id.*

8. *Id.*

9. *Id.*

10. McFadden, *supra* note 2, at B16; *M. I. Gurfein Resigns as Prosecutor's Aide*, N.Y. TIMES, May 29, 1942, at 19.

11. McFadden, *supra* note 2, at B16.

12. *M. I. Gurfein Resigns as Prosecutor's Aide*, *supra* note 10, at 19.

13. *Id.*

14. *Fighter for Liberty William J. Donovan*, N.Y. TIMES, Nov. 19, 1956, at 10.

15. Irvin Molotsky, *World War II Spies Plan Symposium on O.S.S.*, N.Y. TIMES, Nov. 11, 1985, at A16.

16. Hyde, Remarks, *supra* note 4, at LXXXVIII–XCI; *see also* FEDERAL BAR COUNCIL, GLIMPSES OF WALTER MANSFIELD 11–18 (1995) (describing Mansfield's experience in the O.S.S.).

17. Hyde, Remarks, *supra* note 4, at LXXXVIII–XCI.

18. McFadden, *supra* note 2, at B16.

19. *Prosecution Adds Procedural Staff for Nuremberg War-Crimes Trials*, N.Y. TIMES, Nov. 7, 1945, at 10.

20. *Id.*

21. Hyde, Remarks, *supra* note 4; Judge William H. Mulligan, Remarks at a Special Session of the United States Court of Appeals for the Second Circuit, Memorial Proceedings for the Honorable Murray I. Gurfein (Sept. 15, 1980), *in* 634 F.2d LXXXVI, XC, XCII; McFadden, *supra* note 2, at B16. Nathaniel Goldstein was New York's attorney general from 1943 until 1954; Orrin Judd, who had been New York's solicitor general, was appointed to the District Court for the Eastern District of New York in 1968.

22. Hyde, Remarks, *supra* note 4, at XC–CI.

23. Morton I. Hamburg, *Judge Gurfein*, N.Y. L.J., Jan. 16, 1980, at 4; McFadden, *supra* note 2, at B16.

24. McFadden, *supra* note 2, at B16.

25. Oakes, *supra* note 3, at 5.

26. *Id.*

27. Neil Sheehan, *Vietnam Archive: Pentagon Study Traces 3 Decades of Growing U.S. Involvement*, N.Y. TIMES, June 13, 1971, at 1, 35–40.

28. Oakes, *supra* note 3, at 7.

29. *Id.* at 6.

30. Neil Sheehan, *Vietnam Archive: Study Tells How Johnson Secretly Opened Way to Ground Combat*, N.Y. TIMES, June 15, 1971, at 1, 22.

31. Murray I. Gurfein, *Nathaniel Goldstein Memorial Lecture*, 2 CARDOZO L. REV. 15, 16 (1980); Oakes, *supra* note 3, at 6, 8.

32. *Judge Gurfein's First Case*, N.Y. TIMES, Dec. 18, 1979, at A18.

33. Gurfein, *supra* note 31, at 16.

34. United States v. New York Times Co., 328 F. Supp. 324, 329 (S.D.N.Y. 1971).

35. *Id.* at 330.

36. *Id.* at 331.

37. *Id.*

38. United States v. New York Times Co., 444 F.2d 544 (2d Cir. 1971) (per curiam).

39. New York Times Co. v. United States, 403 U.S. 713, 714 (1971).

40. Chief Judge Feinberg, *supra* note 1, at LXXXV.

41. Parent Assoc. of Andrew Jackson High School v. Ambach, 598 F.2d 705, 711 (2d Cir. 1979).

42. Parent Assoc. of Andrew Jackson High School v. Ambach, 451 F. Supp. 1056, 1077–82 (E.D.N.Y. 1978).

43. *Parent Assoc. of Andrew Jackson High School*, 598 F.2d at 715.

44. *Id.* at 721.

45. 588 F.2d 319, 321 (2d Cir. 1978).

46. *Id.* at 321–25.

47. *Id.* at 328–32.

48. *Id.* at 335.
49. McFadden, *supra* note 2, at B16.
50. *Id.*
51. Hamburg, *supra* note 23, at 1, 4.

# ELLSWORTH ALFRED VAN GRAAFEILAND
## 1915-2004

Court of Appeals for the Second Circuit: 1974-2004

Ellsworth Alfred Van Graafeiland's life began and ended in Rochester, New York. The second of three children, he was born on May 11, 1915, afflicted with scoliosis. He had to wear a full body cast until he was in the fifth grade.[1] When it was time to start kindergarten at the local grammar school (a block from where Van Graafeiland was born), his teacher agreed that if Van Graafeiland's older brother would bring him to school "on a cart," she would take care of him.[2] The cast shaped Van Graafeiland's spine and mind: because he was rendered physically inactive as a child, he "did a great deal of reading," which helped him "tremendously in school."[3] In Van Graafeiland's words, "I decided I wanted to be a lawyer when I was five years old."[4]

The Great Depression delivered a hard blow to the Van Graafeiland family. The father had worked as a clothing cutter for Fashion Park, a local clothing manufacturer: he cut the patterns for suits using "great big shears."[5] By the time Van Graafeiland graduated from Benjamin Franklin High School in 1932, his father had been unemployed for three years.[6] He called it "pretty tough sledding": today, the family would be "classified as poor persons," but "[t]here was no such a thing as welfare in those days. You just managed."[7] The family ran up a debt with the local dairy man, but when Van Graafeiland's father went back to work, he repaid every cent, just as "the dairy man knew he would."[8]

Economics altered the course of Van Graafeiland's education. After high school he enrolled at Cornell's School of Agriculture. He went to Ithaca with $15 in his pocket and rented an apartment for $2 a week. Van Graafeiland returned to Rochester, enrolled at the University of Rochester, where he lived at home, and worked nights and Sundays as a cashier at Walgreens.[9] He graduated from college in 1937 and returned to Cornell for law school, graduating in 1940.[10]

During one law school summer, Van Graafeiland worked as a lifeguard at a Rochester pool, where he met Rosemary "Rhody" Vaeth, a fellow Rochester native.[11] They married in 1945 and had five children: Gary, Sue, Joan, Jack, and Anne. Van Graafeiland selected their names to remedy past ills: "My first name I detested it all my life and I made up my mind that if we ever had any children," their names "would be short. . . . The last name is bad enough."[12]

After graduating from Cornell Law School, Van Graafeiland joined the Rochester firm of Mann, Strang, Bodine & Wright, where he would spend the next 35 years. At the firm (now known as Harter Secrest & Emery LLP), Van Graafeiland learned to be a trial lawyer. He was in court on a weekly basis defending insurance companies in fender-bender litigations.[13] He had a ferocious work ethic. One of his partners recalled that even at the height of his practice, Van Graafeiland "always wanted to do the research and thinking himself, and we could never get him out of the library, even though some people felt that the head of the firm's Litigation Department should leave the research to others."[14] A judicial colleague noted, as an illustration of Van Graafeiland's "reputation for rectitude—and the great regard Van's colleagues in law practice accorded him—that he was the partner all the others agreed should be charged with distributing profits at his law firm."[15]

Van Graafeiland built a reputation as a top insurance litigator. However, he lost one of his most significant cases, *Babcock v. Jackson*,[16] in which the New York State Court of Appeals held that the location of a tort did not necessarily dictate the choice of law governing the litigation. Ms. Babcock and the Jacksons, all three New York residents, were driving in Ontario when Mr. Jackson crashed into a stone wall. Ontario had a so-called "guest statute" that barred a passenger from recovering from the owner or driver; New York did not. Van Graafeiland, representing Jackson, pressed the guest statute as a defense. The Court of Appeals rejected his argument, reasoning that New York had more substantial contacts with, and interests in, the tort.[17] Van Graafeiland recalled, "I got clobbered which I knew I would."[18] The case was the source of some teasing. For 50 years, Van Graafeiland regularly had coffee with a group of fellow Rochester lawyers. Whenever he made "a very powerful statement or something, one of the guys [would] say 'weren't you the losing lawyer in that case of *Bobcock* something or other.'"[19]

Van Graafeiland did "very little criminal defense work."[20] But the work he did was remarkable. In 1971, a special grand jury convened by Governor Nelson Rockefeller indicted Hobart College for having recklessly tolerated the criminal offense of first degree coercion. The facts: one June morning, "500 students vandalized two police cars and kept policemen hostages inside the cars until three youths arrested in an early morning raid on drug charges were freed and granted amnesty from prosecution."[21] The disturbance began after students "learned the drug raid had been engineered by Sheriff Ray O. Morrow of Ontario County with the aid of an undercover agent, M.L. Singkata Thomas Tongyai, known as 'Tommy the Traveler.'"[22] At trial, the Ontario County district attorney testified that the police and university officials gave in to the rabble's demands because "almost certainly somebody would be hurt," particularly Tommy the Traveler.[23] Hobart was believed to be the first college ever indicted on criminal charges relating to a campus disorder.[24] It was an innovative but losing theory: Van Graafeiland, defending Hobart, persuaded the state trial judge to direct the jury to acquit.[25]

Van Graafeiland was deeply connected to the bar. He was a fellow of the American College of Trial Lawyers and president of the Monroe County Bar Association. He was also active in the New York State Bar Association, serving as its vice president and president, chairman of its House of Delegates, and chairman of its Negligence Compensation and Insurance Section.[26] And he was a member of the Committee on Character and Fitness of the Seventh Judicial District in New York State.[27]

Van Graafeiland confessed that he "never planned or dreamed of being a judge."[28] His oral advocacy seems to have paved the way: after arguing several cases before the New York State Court of Appeals, Judge John Van Voorhis, a member of both that court (a dissenter in *Babcock*) and of Senator James L. Buckey's committee on judicial nominees, recommended Van Graafeiland for a post on the Court of Appeals for the Second Circuit.[29] When Van Graafeiland was 59 years old, President Gerald Ford nominated him. The confirmation process was not without its bumps—literally. Here is the tale of Van Graafeiland's meeting with Senator Jacob Javits, a liberal Republican, as told by Van Graafeiland himself:

> Of course it's no secret that I have quite a conservative background so I was a little concerned about going to see Javits. . . . In preparation for this august meeting I got my best suit and [a] new pair of shoes, I was all slicked up. New shoes come with leather heels on them and I can't wear leather heels. I don't know if it's any connection with my back but I can't walk with leather heels. So I was nonchalantly talking with Senator Javits when he came out of the chambers leaning against the wall and all of a sudden my feet went out from under me and I went down. People came running from all over and poor Senator Javits got so upset he forgot to ask me any questions. So I passed.[30]

One of Van Graafeiland's law partners had his own interpretation of the incident: "I know what happened, Senator Javits said are you a liberal or a conservative and you said if I'm not a liberal may God strike me dead and down you went."[31]

On the bench, Judge Van Graafeiland advocated judicial restraint. He "was clear in how he saw his job and the role of courts: not to favor a view of what the law 'should' be, however close that view was to his personal beliefs, but rather to identify the relevant legal principles and apply them to the case before him."[32]

That philosophy permeated his decisions on equal protection. In *Kirkland v. New York State Department of Correctional Services*, Judge Van Graafeiland, writing for the majority, upheld the district court's finding that a New York State civil service examination discriminated against blacks and hispanics, but reversed its order that the state institute race-based quotas.[33] "It seems to us," he wrote for the panel, "that the judiciary should act with great reluctance in undermining traditional civil service concepts; and, if a decision is to be made to subordinate the social purposes of civil service to those of equal employment opportunity, that decision should be made by the people speaking through their legislators."[34] Similarly, he dissented from the court's *en banc* decision in *Turpin v. Mailet*, which held that a municipality could be liable under 42 U.S.C. § 1983 for its police officers' constitutional violations. The majority reasoned that a cause of action could be implied from the Fourteenth Amendment because "courts have the power to fashion common law remedies for constitutional wrongs,"[35] and that doing so "opens a dialogue with Congress" about individual rights.[36] Judge Van Graafeiland, joined by three of his colleagues, expressed disbelief that "a decision of such incalculable impact as the one they now make can be justified as simply the opening of a 'dialogue with Congress' or that it comports with this Court's constitutional role in a democratic society."[37] He cautioned that under the majority's approach, "the only restraint upon the power of the federal judiciary is that which is self-imposed."[38]

Judge Van Graafeiland was a prolific dissenter. He explained, "I never argue with my fellow judges, try to change their mind or anything like that. I tell them what I think and I say you're entitled to your opinion and I'm entitled to mine."[39] And opinions he had. In 1994, the *New York Law Journal* reported that dissents in the Second Circuit were rare, with one exception: Judge Van Graafeiland, who "wrote dissents in 7 percent of his cases in which a published decision was issued, more than triple the circuit average."[40] In one memorable case dealing with how to weigh LSD for the purpose of sentencing, Van Graafeiland's dissent began: "My colleagues' entry into the field of judicial legislation undoubtedly will elicit huzzahs from those who traffic in illegal narcotics. However, I cannot join in this applause."[41]

Although Judge Van Graafeiland "enjoyed something of a folkloric reputation for irascibility on the bench and for his occasionally tart dissenting opinions—he wrote about one hundred dissenting opinions in his years on this Court—no one could ever accuse him of bombast, in person or in prose."[42] He was, however, notoriously tough from the bench. During one oral argument, Judge Van Graafeiland challenged an outstanding appellate lawyer with a series of hostile questions. The lawyer calmly responded to each one with a persuasive answer. That provoked Judge Van Graafeiland to ask his next question with increasing vehemence and visible agitation. After the lawyer's fifth thoughtfully worded response, Van Graafeiland, thoroughly exasperated, exclaimed, "Oh, counsel. you have an answer to every question I ask!"[43]

Law clerk Susan Palmer recounted the following tale of a hapless advocate:

> I remember an insurance case involving a building that had collapsed under the snow load of a Vermont winter. The building collapsed in two stages, leading to a dispute over whether the policy ought to pay the limits once or twice. Had there been two separate collapses, or one extended one? The Judge was inclined toward the policyholder's position, and during oral argument the attorney for the insurance company, who I could tell was aggravating the Judge with an unfocused presentation, slipped up by referring to "these occurrences" – plural. The Judge leaned forward, cupping his hand around his

> ear in his best imitation of an old man, saying "Eh? What's that you said?" The attorney helpfully repeated her statement, louder this time. The Judge sat back with satisfaction. "Occurrences. I thought that's what you said." Her case was over.[44]

His colleagues had deep admiration for Judge Van Graafeiland. According to Judge McLaughlin, "No one reads a record as carefully as Judge Van Graafeiland."[45]

Judge Van Graafeiland's law clerks adored him. One, Professor Charles Whitehead, described him as "a modest, unassuming person in chambers—a mentor, a role model, and a teacher to his many law clerks."[46] Professor Whitehead relates the following learning experience:

> On my first day in chambers, the Judge asked me to draft a short memorandum for an upcoming oral argument. In hindsight, he was throwing me a soft ball—there were no less than eight (!) Second Circuit decisions on point, each in favor of the appellee. Although not briefed, I noticed that the first of the eight cases had drawn on a D.C. Circuit analysis that judges in that court had modified over time. There was now a split between the circuits and, on balance, I thought the D.C. Circuit made a good case. So, fresh from law school, I argued for a switch—the kind of analysis that would have received an "A" as a student. I remember the Judge popping into my office, memorandum in hand, with a puzzled look on his face. "So, let me get this straight," he said. "You're telling me there are eight cases on point, going back over a decade." "Yes," I said. "Seven of them authored by Judge Friendly (someone whom the Judge admired)," he continued. "Yes," I said. "And now, based on your analysis, you want me to come out the other way? . . . Bah," he said as he threw both hands down and walked back to his office. (I learned later that a "two-handed bah" was a rare occurrence, much less on the first day of work.)[47]

Judge Van Graafeiland's mentoring extended beyond the law. Later in Professor Whitehead's clerkship, Judge Van Graafeiland remarked, "I've noticed from my window that, over the past few weeks, you've started walking down the street every day for lunch with the same young woman. Since your parents aren't here, I think it would [be] good for me to meet her."[48] Whitehead duly brought the young woman to chambers, where Judge Van Graafeiland spent about 20 minutes speaking with her. Afterwards, Judge Van Graafeiland told Whitehead, "She's very nice . . . You should take more time for lunch, take 90 minutes or two hours."[49] Whitehead and the young woman later married.[50]

In addition to writing dissents, Judge Van Graafeiland found time to write articles.[51] In one, he chided his colleagues for holding that "under the Due Process Clause, a prison inmate's application for conditional release" from the detention facility on Rikers Island "must be processed within ninety days of his arrival at the Island."[52] Judge Van Graafeiland confessed that the decision left him "in a state of 'ninety-day wonder,'" asking why "does a hearing held on the ninetieth day meet constitutional requirements when one held on the ninety-first day does not? I read and reread the [F]ourteenth [A]mendment, yet I could not find the answer."[53] He described the result of "modest research" into how his "colleagues were able to find precise figures, such as ninety days, in the constitution when they were completely hidden from my view."[54] He catalogued the federal courts' work in what one might call quantitative constitutional construction. Courts had dictated the number of: days of notice required for a proposed prisoner classification; days a prisoner can be in segregated confinement without a hearing; hours of notice that such a hearing will take place; and days a prisoner can be held in segregated confinement altogether. Judge Van Graafeiland protested: "Constitutionality simply cannot be measured by the tick of a clock."[55] To him, the problem was not the courts' efforts to restrain state actors in the name of constitutional rights; it was the courts' refusal "to admit that they are no longer interpreting the Constitution, but are, instead, 'legislating under the guise of judging.'"[56] He counseled intellectual honesty—that judges concede that they rule based on "their own concepts of what is fair and practical," so that future students can "enter upon their labors without a calendar in one hand and a pocket calculator in the other."[57]

Judge Van Graafeiland had similar—and prescient—criticism for the Sentencing Guidelines. The Sentencing Commission aimed to reduce disparities between similarly situated offenders. Judge Van Graafeiland wrote: "Reacting perhaps to the modern generation's fascination with numbers, the Commission seeks to attain this goal by means of mathematical computations."[58] He predicted that "a completely new body of sentencing law is almost certain to result" from challenges to those computations.[59] Aside from that practical concern, Judge Van Graafeiland voiced a philosophical one: "whether judges, who deal with human beings, not numbers, are prepared to operate on the theory that disparity is 'shameful' and to apply the sentencing guidelines in the literal fashion that the Commission apparently intends."[60]

Judge José A. Cabranes has remarked that "[l]ike many of his generation, Van endured much, he accomplished much, and he bragged not at all. He did not indulge in that cliché of modern American politics whereby potential appointees to office are celebrated by their 'story' of overcoming disadvantage. Van preferred his career to be a tale of hard work and love of the law—and he personified both until his very last days."[61] After taking senior status in 1985, Judge Van Graafeiland continued to sit with the court. He issued his last published opinion in May 2004.[62] Six months later, on November 20, 2004, he died at the age of 89 in Rochester. He was survived by his wife, five children, nine grandchildren, and one great-granddaughter.[63]

Sally Pritchard

1. Interview by Jodi Balsam with Judge Ellsworth A. Van Graafeiland, in New York, N.Y. 1 (Apr. 25, 1996) (transcript on file with the United States Courts Library for the Second Circuit).

2. *Id.* at 1.

3. *Id.* at 2.

4. *Id.* at 9.

5. *Id.* at 3.

6. *Id.*

7. *Id.* at 7.

8. *Id.*

9. *Id.* at 4.

10. FEDERAL JUDICIAL CENTER, Biographical Directory of Federal Judges, Ellsworth Alfred Van Graafeiland, http://www.fjc.gov/servlet/nGetInfo?jid=2443&cid=999&ctype=na&instate=na.

11. Interview, *supra* note 1, at 10–12.

12. *Id.* at 12.

13. *Id.* at 14–15.

14. Peter L. Faber, Remarks at a Special Session of the United States Court of Appeals for the Second Circuit In Memoriam for the Honorable Ellsworth Van Graafeiland 4 (Mar. 9, 2005) (transcript on file with the United States Courts Library for the Second Circuit). Faber and Van Graafeiland worked together at the firm now known as Harter, Secrest & Emery.

15. Judge José A. Cabranes, Remarks at a Special Session of the United States Court of Appeals for the Second Circuit In Memoriam for the Honorable Ellsworth Van Graafeiland 2 (Mar. 9, 2005) (transcript on file with the United States Courts Library for the Second Circuit).

16. 191 N.E.2d 279 (N.Y. 1963).

17. *Id.* at 283–84.

18. Interview, *supra* note 1, at 22.

19. *Id.*

20. *Id.*

21. William E. Farrel, *Rules at Hobart Entered at Trial: Prosecutor Asserts College Ignored Its Regulations*, N.Y. TIMES, Feb. 4, 1971, at 15.

22. *Hobart Is Indicted by a Special Jury In Student Disorder*, N.Y. TIMES, Dec. 19, 1970, at 23.

23. *Rules at Hobart Entered at Trial*, *supra* note 21.

24. *Hobart College Acquitted In Riot: Court Directs Verdict—Says Evidence Is Insufficient*, N.Y. TIMES, Feb. 9, 1971, at 1.

25. *See id.*

26. FED. BAR COUNCIL, SECOND CIRCUIT REDBOOK 1975-76, at 42 (Marc White ed., 1975).

27. *Ex-President Of State Bar Named Judge*, N.Y. L. J., Dec. 23, 1974, at 1, 3.

28. Interview, *supra* note 1, at 18.

29. *Id.*

30. *Id.* at 18–19.

31. *Id.* at 19.

32. Charles K. Whitehead, *Dedication: Ellsworth A. Van Graafeiland*, 97 CORNELL L. REV. vii (2012).

33. 520 F.2d 420 (2d Cir. 1975).

34. *Id.* at 429.

35. 579 F.2d 152, 156 (2d Cir. 1978).

36. *Id.* at 158.

37. *Id.* at 172.

38. *Id.* at 173.

39. Interview, *supra* note 1, at 35.

40. Edward A. Adams, *Judges Most Likely To Write, Dissent*, N.Y. L. J., Aug. 3, 1994, at 5.

41. United States v. Acosta, 963 F.2d 551, 557 (2d Cir. 1992).

42. Judge José A. Cabranes, Remarks, *supra* note 15, at 4.

43. Memorandum from Judge Jon O. Newman, to Sally Pritchard (July 28, 2015) (on file with the United States Courts Library for the Second Circuit).

44. Susan Palmer, former law clerk, Remarks at a Special Session of the United States Court of Appeals for the Second Circuit In Memoriam for the Honorable Ellsworth Van Graafeiland (Mar. 9, 2005) (transcript on file with the United States Courts Library for the Second Circuit). Palmer is the associate dean for student affairs at the University of South Carolina School of Law.

45. Joseph M. McLaughlin, *Foreword: The Second Circuit—Year in Revue*, 61 BROOK. L. REV. 347, 354 (1995).

46. Whitehead, *supra* note 32, at vii.

47. Memorandum from Charles Whitehead, former law clerk, to Sally Pritchard (May 23, 2015) (on file with the United States Courts Library for the Second Circuit). Whitehead is the Myron C. Taylor Alumni Professor of Business Law at Cornell Law School.

48. *Id.*

49. *Id.*

50. *Id.*

51. In addition to the articles discussed above, Judge Van Graafeiland wrote: *Foreword: A Lawyer's Observations on* Hochfelder, 51 ST. JOHN'S L. REV. 239 (1977); *Forward: The Proposed Model Rules of Professional Conduct and the Mail Fraud Statute*, 48 BROOK. L. REV. 653 (1982); *Foreword: Attorneys' Fees from Uncompensated Class Members: Fleecing the Lost Sheep*, 47 BROOK. L. REV. 605 (1981); and *RICO and the Rule of Lenity*, 9 N. ILL. U. L. REV. 331 (1989).

52. Ellsworth A. Van Graafeiland, *Foreword: The Constitution and the Numbers Game*, 44 BROOK. L. REV. 747, 747 (1978).

53. *Id.*

54. *Id.* at 748.

55. *Id.* at 755.

56. *Id.* at 756.

57. *Id.*

58. Ellsworth A. Van Graafeiland, *Some Thoughts on the Sentencing Reform Act of 1984*, 31 VILL. L. REV. 1291, 1292 (1986).

59. *Id.* at 1295.

60. *Id.* at 1297.

61. Judge José A. Cabranes, Remarks, *supra* note 15, at 1.

62. United States v. Vargas, 369 F.3d 98 (2d Cir. 2004).

63. Wolfgang Saxon, *Ellsworth Van Graafeiland, 89, Appellate Judge*, N.Y. TIMES, Nov. 25, 2004, at B11.

# THOMAS JOSEPH MESKILL
## 1928-2007

Court of Appeals for the Second Circuit: 1975-2007

"Where is the person who has served in high office in all three branches of government, who served in high office in the local, state and national levels, who lived his life in his Connecticut hometown while exercising his benign power and influence in New York City and Washington, D.C.?"[1] The answer: Thomas Joseph Meskill. And the story of his ascent to those posts reveals a person of remarkable mettle.

Meskill was born in New Britain, Connecticut, on January 30, 1928. His mother was a homemaker; his father was a purchasing agent for the Stanley Works.[2] He had two sisters, Ruth and Laura Marie. Meskill spoke fondly of his father. In a speech given late in his judicial career, he recalled his father coming home from work visibly upset. A salesman had "passed a small package across" the elder Meskill's desk; "[i]nside was a lady's wristwatch."[3] Meskill said, "My father pushed the box back saying, 'I can't accept this.' The salesman responded, 'Who is going to know?' My father's reply was, '*I'm* going to know.' The salesman didn't laugh at his response, neither did we. I never forgot this lesson."[4]

After attending New Britain Senior High School and Saint Thomas Seminary, he enrolled at Trinity College intending to become a doctor, but "found dissecting a fetal pig in biology lab pretty hard to take."[5] He earned a BS degree in 1950, the first in his family to graduate from college. He then enlisted in the U.S. Air Force, serving for three years in the Korean War. He reached the rank of first lieutenant.[6]

After his military service, Meskill returned to his home state and enrolled at the University of Connecticut Law School, graduating in 1956. He was chairman (the equivalent of editor-in-chief) of the law review. While in law school, he married Mary Grady. They would have five children: Eileen, Maureen, John, Peter, and Thomas.

After spending two years in private practice, Meskill launched a political career that would be marked with setbacks and success. His first race was for the Connecticut State Senate, which he lost in a landslide.[7] For the next two years, he worked as an assistant corporation counsel for New Britain.[8] In 1960, he ran for mayor of New Britain and lost by only 115 votes.[9] In 1962, he ran for mayor again and won by a margin of 5,500 votes. He held the post for two years, only to lose his race for reelection in 1964.[10] Meskill was undeterred: that same year, he ran for the U.S. House of Representatives seat for the Sixth Congressional District in Connecticut, "a largely rural district, ranging from the shade-tobacco fields of the Connecticut River valley to the apple farms and cattle ranches along the border of Dutchess County, N.Y."[11] He lost. Between political races, he served as New Britain's corporation counsel and was a Republican delegate to Connecticut's constitutional convention, which drafted a new constitution after the Supreme Court struck down the state's apportionment scheme for electing state legislators.[12] In 1966, he again ran for Congress and won. He was the youngest member of the state's delegation and its only Republican.[13] Contemporary accounts of Meskill's two congressional campaigns reveal dogged dedication. One reporter watched Meskill crossing "lawns still wet with dew to ring doorbells in a suburban neighborhood" as he tried to reach "a goal of 1,000 handshakes a day."[14] When he successfully ran for reelection to Congress in 1968, "he covered the campaign trail in his Chevrolet station wagon."[15] He "move[d] through factories giving a firm handshake, smiling and passing out ballpoint pens inscribed with 'Meskill cares.'"[16]

After two terms in Congress, Meskill returned to Connecticut in 1970 to run for governor. He won by a margin of nearly seven percent, or 80,000 votes.[17] The first Republican governor in Connecticut in 16 years, at the age of 42 he became the "dominant political figure in the state."[18] He faced a budget deficit of $244 million.[19] His efforts to cut that deficit earned him the nickname "Tough Tommy." He cut appropriations to state agencies, imposed a freeze on hiring state employees, and introduced tuition at the University of Connecticut.[20] He established a state lottery.[21] And he set a record for vetoes: 227 vetoes from 1971 to 1972 as he locked horns with the state's Democratically controlled legislature.[22] He did not, however, veto the state's first income tax, a move that was met with predictable public outrage. Meskill took it in stride. When he and his wife attended Connecticut Day at Yankee Stadium, the "announcer introduced him and asked him to stand. As he did so, 55,000 booed him, and Mary said, 'Oh, Tom, this is awful.' Tom said, 'what do you mean? Six months ago none of these people had even heard of me.'"[23] Tough Tommy's efforts paid off for the people of Connecticut; by the end of his term, he had converted the $244 million budget deficit into a surplus of $65 million.[24]

Despite these accomplishments, Meskill's governorship came to be remembered for an ice storm. When the storm hit, in December 1973, Meskill was in New Jersey. He returned to order the National Guard to clear fallen trees, and left a day later for his ski house in Vermont. Meanwhile, residents across the state were without power. As Judge Ralph K. Winter has observed, although Meskill's "ability to give routine orders to move snow was as great in Vermont as it was in Hartford, the most obligatory duty a governor in Connecticut has during blizzards is to appear on screens in our living rooms personally ordering the state highway department to plow snow."[25] The predictable uproar ensued. The *Hartford Courant* wrote, "Where was the governor when the lights went out? Everywhere, it seems, but where he should have been: [i]n effective and reassuring command of the recovery efforts from Monday's massive ice storm and power failure."[26] The author of a letter to the editor of the *Courant* griped: "He skis. We freeze."[27]

In later years, conventional wisdom would hold that Meskill chose not to seek reelection because of the ice storm.[28] But Meskill said that he stepped down because he did not want his five children, then between the ages of two and 13, to grow up in the governor's mansion. "It's a very unreal life for very young children to be brought to school by a state trooper," he explained. "I didn't want to continue that lifestyle for them."[29] While the ice storm was swirling in the press, so were rumors that Meskill had his eye on "another line of work," that is, "a federal judgeship."[30]

In his final hours in office, President Richard M. Nixon nominated Meskill to the Court of Appeals for the Second Circuit.[31] Controversy erupted: the American Bar Association's Committee on the Federal Judiciary opposed the nomination on the ground that Meskill did "not have the legal background or expertise as a lawyer to be a judge of the U.S. Court of Appeals for the Second Circuit" because his resume included neither "legal scholarship" nor "courtroom experience."[32] The Association of the Bar of the City of New York followed suit.[33] A group of 35 law professors in Connecticut, including 21 from the University of Connecticut, Meskill's alma mater, published a letter to the Senate Judiciary Committee protesting the nomination; they argued that as governor, Meskill had "shown himself insensitive to the rights of the poor and the disadvantaged, and indifferent to civil and political liberties."[34] The Senate declined to act on the nomination.[35] In January 1975, President Gerald Ford renominated Meskill to the Second Circuit.[36] The American Bar Association and City Bar Association maintained their opposition on the ground that Meskill "lacked legal qualifications for the post."[37] Later that spring, with the support of Connecticut's liberal Republican senator, Lowell P. Weicker, the Senate Judiciary Committee voted to approve the nomination,[38] and the full Senate confirmed it a month later.[39] Judge Meskill received his commission on April 23, 1975.

Many judges are sworn in at marble-lined courthouses. Judge Meskill's ceremony was held in the gymnasium of the New Britain High School. Four of his new colleagues, numerous district judges, state court judges, and the mayor of New Britain packed the room. His former campaign aide quipped, "Tom, if we'd had as many people at our [p]olitical [r]allies as are here today, we never would have lost an election!"[40]

Judge Meskill kept his permanent chambers in his hometown. One law clerk recalled him saying, "The chambers are in a building that used to be the post office. And actually, I used to work there when I was in high school. So, my whole life, I really only moved up one floor."[41]

Judge Meskill reflected on his bruising journey with characteristic humor. When he was introduced as a new member of the court at its annual judicial conference, he unbuttoned his jacket to reveal an apron with a play on the advertising slogan of his harshest detractor: "'I did not get my job through The New York Times.'"[42] Years later, Judge Meskill reflected, "One of the good things about politics is you get used to being maligned. While you never get to like it, your skin gets a little thicker."[43]

Though politics inured him to the attacks of critics, by all accounts it did not influence his work on the bench. In the words of Judge Jon O. Newman, "Some might have wondered when the politician would begin to act like a judge. The answer turned out to be the moment he was sworn in."[44] One of his law clerks recalled, "[I]n deciding cases, he never pursued a personal or political agenda. He simply tried to decide each case correctly based on the law, the facts, and the equities."[45] Another Meskill law clerk, Judge Jeffrey Sutton of the Court of Appeals for the Sixth Circuit, echoed that sentiment, remarking that Judge Meskill's decisions "eschewed pretense and lofty theories. He spoke and wrote in a straightforward and authentic manner. He listened to both sides of an argument."[46] Judge Meskill's law clerk family was diverse: he "was not an elitist" and "had a cooler spot in his heart for those who were."[47] He hired "a surprising number of Democrats" and "even a few Radicals" as law clerks.[48] When asked why, Judge Meskill would joke, "I see it as a mission," but speaking more seriously, he would say, "[t]o keep me honest."[49]

Those who had opposed Judge Meskill's appointment would change their tune soon after he joined the court. Lawrence E. Walsh, who had led the charge as president of the American Bar Association, described Meskill as a "hardworking, able judge," conceding, "I certainly changed my mind and I publicly acknowledged my error within a year."[50] With good reason: Judge Meskill "could speak the language of a precise lawyer, a seasoned public official and a middle-class American, a set of perspectives that few judges have combined so favorably or so well."[51]

Eight years after his appointment, the Association of Trial Lawyers of America named Judge Meskill the Outstanding Federal Appellate Judge in 1983. The Federal Bar Council awarded him the Learned Hand Medal for Judicial Excellence in 1994. In his acceptance speech, Judge Meskill implored the audience to stop looking to the government to stop violent crime and instead turn to "the most basic unit of government, the family."[52] He presented a stark choice: "[u]nless we highlight the importance of family, and each parent's individual responsibility in it for teaching children right from wrong, we may face a future where, as one wag put it, half the population will be behind bars and the other half will be guarding them."[53] Of course, Judge Meskill was himself a dedicated family man, as evidenced by his decision not to run for reelection as governor. A law clerk remarked that Judge Meskill taught him "that it is possible to achieve at the highest levels while still honoring your commitments as a spouse and as a parent."[54]

During his three decades on the bench, Judge Meskill dissented from 68 panel decisions. As Judge Newman observed, "his language in dissent was never harsh" and revealed "the work of a careful thinker," who often took care to dissent in part in order to note "a precise issue on which he thought a more limited view of the law's reach was appropriate."[55] Judge Sutton distilled

Judge Meskill's philosophy: "Disagreement over a legal issue was just that, and nothing more."[56] Judge Meskill preserved that civility in his chambers. His law clerks said, "[W]e tried to think if we ever heard him utter a harsh word about any of his colleagues," but the only thing they could recall was the occasional comment "that a colleague with whom he disagreed had made 'an annoyingly good point.'"[57] One law clerk recalled that the judge taught that "we can be tough adversaries and civil human beings at one and the same time."[58] Yet another said this: "He was a gentleman and a kind soul, through and through; and that kindness found its way into every aspect of his life."[59]

Judge Meskill's civility and common sense were reflected in his dissent from the panel decision in *Herbert v. Lando*.[60] Colonel Anthony Herbert captured the nation's attention when he accused his superiors of having covered up war crimes in Vietnam. After a lengthy investigation, Barry Lando, a producer at CBS news, put together a program that presented viewers with "a fallen hero," casting doubt on Herbert's accusations and reporting that Herbert himself "had countenanced the commission of war crimes."[61] Herbert sued Lando and others for defamation. The issue before the court was whether the First Amendment protected Lando from having to answer certain questions about "his beliefs, opinions, intent and conclusions in preparing the program" to air on CBS.[62] The majority opinion traced the development of the First Amendment since the Sedition Act of 1789 and concluded that Herbert's proposed line of questioning would chill the editorial process of journalists. In dissent, Judge Meskill argued that Herbert should have been permitted to ask the questions. He took this clear-eyed approach:

> After *New York Times v. Sullivan* . . . judicial review of the editor's thought process is what a libel action is all about. The mere existence of a libel cause of action chills the exercise of editorial judgment. That is the whole idea. It is exactly this kind of chill that *New York Times v. Sullivan* condones.[63]

The Supreme Court reversed, vindicating Judge Meskill's view.[64]

Judge Meskill's Connecticut roots were on display in his concurrence in *United States v. Various Articles of Obscene Merchandise,*

*Schedule No. 2102,*[65] which affirmed Judge Robert W. Sweet's finding that various pornographic films were not "obscene" in light of community standards in the Southern District of New York. Obscenity is one component of the test set out in the Supreme Court's decision in *Miller v. California.*[66] The majority in *Various Articles of Obscene Merchandise* wrote that "the trier's finding that the material is non-obscene is virtually shielded from appellate scrutiny" because *Miller* leaves the trier "unchecked by any definition of the relevant community (except that it may not extend to the entire nation) or by any more precise benchmarks."[67] Applying this standard, the majority declined to disturb Judge Sweet's finding that the pornographic materials "were not patently offensive under contemporary standards in the New York area."[68] Judge Meskill concurred in the result, but voiced his disbelief "that our hands are tied nearly as tight as the majority thinks" with respect to the standard of review.[69] Judge Meskill conceded, "I am not a resident of nor as well acquainted with New York City as is Judge Sweet, and I am not well versed in the varieties and types of pornography which circulate there."[70] He therefore reluctantly concurred, advising that "[h]ad this case originated in the District of Connecticut, in a community whose standards are familiar to me, I would not hesitate to reverse."[71]

His decision in *Phillips v. Girdich*, written late in his career, marks a counterpoint to the legal academy's critique of him three decades earlier. The *Phillips* panel reversed a district judge's *sua sponte* dismissal of a pro se inmate's complaint. The district court had held that Phillips's complaint (and two amended versions of it) "failed to comply with the Federal Rules of Civil Procedure" because, among other failings, they were not "sequentially paginated," and his claims were not "separated into numbered paragraphs."[72] Judge Meskill began his analysis with the precept that "the Rules command us never to exalt form over substance."[73] A court must "therefore excuse technical pleading irregularities as long as they neither undermine the purpose of notice pleading nor prejudice the adverse party."[74] Phillips's "allegations were not neatly parsed and included a great deal of irrelevant detail," but "that is not unusual from a pro se litigant. As long as his mistakes do not prejudice his opponent, a plaintiff is entitled to trial on even a tenuous legal theory, supported by the thinnest of evidence."[75]

In 1991, Judge Meskill wrote an article about the Second Circuit's efforts to handle its growing caseload. He observed that many people instinctively blame the rise in filings on the "litigious nature" of society; a "close second in the blame department seems to be 'too many lawyers.'"[76] Judge Meskill set out to dispel those assumptions. He explained that some of the rise was fueled by drug prosecutions and bankruptcy filings; but much of it came from Congress. OSHA, ERISA, Title VII, and various environmental statutes all "spurred litigation in the federal courts."[77] And that litigation did not simply require the straightforward application of law to fact; rather, the federal courts must "seek to discover and to implement congressional intent. . . . Unfortunately, the search for congressional intent is often in vain" by virtue of "scant" or "inconclusive" legislative history.[78] That puts the courts in an uncomfortable position: "When we are unsure of a district judge's reasoning, we can remand for clarification. Unfortunately, we do not have the same avenue open to us when interpreting the language of a statute."[79] Some had suggested that the court could ease its docket pressure by denying oral argument for all pro se appellants. Judge Meskill acknowledged that "most of these appeals are without merit and many are frivolous," but hoped that oral arguments would continue because even pro se cases "offer a surprise once in a while."[80] He closed the article on an egalitarian note: "If we must abandon our present policy on oral argument, I would hope that the decision to deny oral argument would be based on the briefs, the issues and the record on appeal, and not on the status of the advocate."[81]

Meskill served as chief judge from 1992 to 1993, when he took senior status. He continued to hear cases until his death, in Florida, at the age of 79. He was survived by his wife, five children, and seven grandchildren.[82] In 2008, the University of Connecticut Law School named its library in his honor.

Sally Pritchard

1. Chief Judge Dennis Jacobs, Remarks at a Special Session of the United States Court of Appeals for the Second Circuit, In Memoriam, Honorable Thomas J. Meskill (May 20, 2008), *in* 588 F.3d XIII.

2. Deborah Pines, *New Chief Judge Meskill Won Them Over*, N.Y. L. J., June 29, 1992, at 1.

3. Judge Thomas J. Meskill, Address Delivered on the Occasion of the Award of the Federal Bar Council's Learned Hand Medal for Excellence in Federal Jurisprudence (May 3, 1994), *in* FED. BAR COUNCIL, SECOND CIRCUIT REDBOOK 1994-1995 SUPPLEMENT 291, 293 (Vincent C. Alexander, ed., 1995).

4. *Id.*

5. Suzanne Zack, *Thomas J. Meskill, Jr. '50: Rising to the Top of the World of Politics and Jurisprudence*, TRINITY COLLEGE MOSAIC (Dec. 1997).

6. Almanac of the Federal Judiciary, vol. 2, 2nd Circuit 41 (2007).

7. *Thomas J. Meskill, 79, Ex-Congressman, Connecticut Governor and Federal Judge*, N.Y. TIMES, Oct. 30, 2007, at D8.

8. Almanac of the Federal Judiciary, *supra* note 6, at 41.

9. *Thomas J. Meskill, 79, Ex-Congressman, Connecticut Governor and Federal Judge, supra* note 7.

10. *Id.*

11. William Borders, *Meskill Bases Hopes on Grabowski Ties with President*, N.Y. TIMES, Oct. 17, 1966, at 40.

12. Pinney v. Butterworth, 378 U.S. 564, 564 (1964) (affirming district court injunction against the state of Connecticut and remanding for further proceedings consistent with *Reynolds v. Sims*); *see also* Reynolds v. Sims, 377 U.S. 533 (1964) (striking down, as violation of Equal Protection clause, Alabama apportionment scheme that was not based on population). Pinney was decided by a three-judge district court panel made up of District Judge William H. Timbers, District Judge Robert P. Anderson, and Circuit Judge J. Joseph Smith.

13. *Tom Meskill Takes Seat in Congress*, MORNING RECORD, Jan. 5, 1967, at 17.

14. Borders, *supra* note 11.

15. David Bird, *Sharaf, a Democrat, Seeks Meskill's Seat in 6th*, N.Y. TIMES, Oct. 17, 1968, at 40.

16. *Id.*

17. Joseph B. Treaster, *Meskill Victory Puts Republicans in Power in Connecticut After 16 Lean Years*, N.Y. TIMES, Nov. 5, 1970, at 40.

18. *Id.*

19. *Meskill Years: Deficit Gone, but His Popularity Wanes*, THE DAY, Mar. 12, 1974, at 1.

20. *Id.*

21. *Thomas J. Meskill, 79, Ex-Congressman, Connecticut Governor and Federal Judge, supra* note 7.

22. Christopher Keating, *Former Governor Meskill Dies Suddenly in Florida*, HARTFORD COURANT, Oct. 29, 2007.

23. Ralph K. Winter, *In Memoriam—Judge Thomas J. Meskill*, 40 CONN. L. REV. 3 (2008).

24. *Thomas J. Meskill, 79, Ex-Congressman, Connecticut Governor and Federal Judge, supra* note 7.

25. Winter, *supra* note 23.

26. *Our Absent Governor*, HARTFORD COURANT, Dec. 22, 1973, at 26.

27. Rita S. Jaworski, *The People's Forum, Meskill's Mania*, HARTFORD COURANT, Dec. 27, 1973, at 30.

28. Keating, *supra* note 22.

29. *Id.*

30. Stan DeCoster, *Political Pitch: A One-Term Governor?*, THE DAY, Dec. 29, 1973, at 6.

31. *Meskill Named Judge*, N.Y. TIMES, Aug. 9, 1974, at 1.

32. *Bar Panel Opposes Meskill Judgeship*, N.Y. TIMES, Aug. 16, 1974, at 11; *Nomination of Thomas J. Meskill To Be United States Circuit Judge: Hearing Before a Subcommittee of the Committee on the Judiciary of the United States Senate*, 93rd Cong. 23 (1974) (statement of John A. Sutro, past chairman, American Bar Association Standing Committee on the Federal Judiciary).

33. *Meskill Facing More Opposition: Law Professors Add Voices to Dissent on Judgeship*, N.Y. TIMES, Sept. 14, 1974, at 22.

34. *Id.*

35. *Federal Judgeship Hits New Snag*, N.Y. L. J., Dec. 18, 1974, at 2.

36. *Ford Nominations Re-sent to Senate*, N.Y. TIMES, Jan. 16, 1975, at 33.

37. Marjorie Hunter, *New A.B.A. Head Calls Meskill Unqualified for Appeals Bench*, N.Y. TIMES, Jan. 24, 1975, at 37.

38. Martin Tolchin, *Meskill Nomination as Judge Approved by a Senate Panel*, N.Y. TIMES, Mar. 22, 1975, at 1.

39. *Meskill is Confirmed as U.S. Appeals Judge*, WALL ST. J., Apr. 23, 1975, at 23.

40. J. Brian Gaffney, Remarks at the Induction of the Honorable Thomas J. Meskill as United States Circuit Judge of the Court of Appeals for the Second Circuit 11 (Apr. 30, 1975) (transcript on file with the United States Courts Library for the Second Circuit). Gaffney was a longtime friend and colleague of Meskill's who later served as state chair of the Republican Party.

41. Tom Sheridan, former law clerk, Remarks at a Special Session of the United States Court of Appeals for the Second Circuit, In Memoriam, Honorable Thomas J. Meskill (May 20, 2008), *in* 588 F.3d XXXI. Sheridan is a shareholder at Simmons, Hanly, Conroy in the complex litigation department.

42. Judge Jon O. Newman, Remarks at a Special Session of the United States Court of Appeals for the Second Circuit, In Memoriam, Honorable Thomas J. Meskill (May 20, 2008), *in* 588 F.3d XXXI.

43. Pines, *supra* note 2, at 3.

44. Judge Jon O. Newman, Remarks, *supra* note 42.

45. Tom Nelson, former law clerk, Remarks at a Special Session of the United States Court of Appeals for the Second Circuit, In Memoriam, Honorable Thomas J. Meskill (May 20, 2008), *in* 588 F.3d XXXI. Nelson is a partner at Stinson, Leonard, Street.

46. Judge Jeffrey S. Sutton, *A Tribute to the Honorable Thomas J. Meskill*, 40 CONN. L. REV. (2008).

47. *Id.*

48. Sheridan, Remarks, *supra* note 41.

49. *Id.*

50. Pines, *supra* note 2, at 1.

51. Sutton, *supra* note 46.

52. Judge Thomas J. Meskill, *supra* note 3, at 294.

53. *Id.*

54. Robert J. Deichert, *A Tribute to the Honorable Thomas J. Meskill*, 40 CONN. L. REV. (2008).

55. Judge Jon O. Newman, Remarks, *supra* note 42.

56. Judge Jeffrey S. Sutton, *supra* note 46.

57. Sheridan, Remarks, *supra* note 41.

58. *Id.*

59. Nelson, Remarks, *supra* note 45.

60. 568 F.2d 974 (2d Cir. 1977).

61. *Id.* at 981.

62. *Id.* at 982-83.

63. *Id.* at 997 (Meskill, J., dissenting).

64. Herbert v. Lando, 441 U.S. 153 (1979).

65. 709 F.2d 132 (2d Cir. 1983).

66. 413 U.S. 15, 24 (1973).

67. *Various Articles of Obscene Merchandise*, 709 F.2d at 136.

68. *Id.* at 137.

69. *Id.* at 138.

70. *Id.*
71. *Id.*
72. 408 F.3d 124, 126 (2d Cir. 2005).
73. *Id.* at 128.
74. *Id.* at 128.
75. *Id.* at 128.
76. *Thomas J. Meskill, Caseload Growth: Struggling To Keep Pace*, 57 BROOK. L. REV. 299, 300 (1991).
77. *Id.*
78. *Id.* at 301.
79. *Id.* at 303.
80. *Id.* at 305.
81. *Id.*
82. *Thomas J. Meskill, 79, Ex-Congressman, Connecticut Governor and Federal Judge, supra* note 7.

# RICHARD J. CARDAMONE
# 1925-2015

New York State Supreme Court: 1962-1971
New York Appellate Division, Fourth Department: 1971-1981
Court of Appeals for the Second Circuit: 1981-2008

Judge Richard J. Cardamone believed that a collegial temperament is a defining trait of an appellate judge. He lived that definition in his 37 years of service on both state and federal appellate courts.

Cardamone was born in Utica, New York on October 10, 1925 to Joseph J. and Scala Cardamone, both of whom emigrated from Italy.[1] His father, who had only an eighth grade education, turned a corner grocery store, A. Cardamone & Sons Wholesale Food & Liquor, into one of Utica's most successful businesses.[2]

Young Richard Cardamone attended public schools until enrolling at Northwood Lake School in Lake Placid. After graduation, he joined the Navy at the height of World War II. He rose to become the commanding officer of a submarine chaser in the Pacific theater.[3]

After returning home from the war, Cardamone and a friend went on a double date. Although Cardamone had been matched with one young woman, he craftily emerged from the evening with the phone number of the other, Catherine Baker Clarke, known as Kate. According to Cardamone family lore, the two had met before, when five-year-old Dick snuck onto the playground of the Utica Country Day School and was promptly thrown off the jungle gym by Kate.[4] When they met 15 years later, Kate did not throw him off. Instead, she agreed to marry him. Before the wedding, however, Cardamone had to prove his mettle to Kate's skeptical older brothers by jumping into a freezing cold natural spring at the Clarke family home in Blue Barn Bend in Barneveld. He passed the test. He and Kate were married for 69 years and had ten children: Richard, Josephine, Catherine, Ceceila, Mary Brian, Ann, Margaret, Roderick, Amy, and William.

Cardamone enrolled at Harvard College, graduating in 1948. He returned to upstate New York to attend Syracuse University College of Law. He then worked at the law firm that would eventually be called Ferris Kehoe Cardamone & Tenney.[5]

At the same time, Cardamone became active in Oneida County Republican politics, which, in his words, "had been run by mossbacks."[6] He served as the county Republican chairman for three years, from 1959 to 1962, when Governor Nelson Rockefeller appointed him to the New York State Supreme Court. Judge Cardamone remained on that court for nine years until 1971, when Governor Rockefeller elevated him to the Appellate Division, Fourth Department.

On the appellate court, Judge Cardamone played a role in the landmark Fourth Amendment case *People v. Dunaway.* The facts of *Dunaway* are familiar to any criminal practitioner: in March 1971, the owner of a Rochester pizzeria was killed during an attempted robbery. Nearly five months later, a policeman told a detective that a jailhouse informant could implicate Dunaway in the crime. The detective questioned the informant, who did not provide "enough information to get a warrant" for Dunaway's arrest.[7]

The detective nonetheless had Dunaway brought in for questioning. Detectives found Dunaway at a neighbor's house early one morning, drove him to the police station in a police car, put him in an interrogation room, gave him his *Miranda* warnings, and then questioned him about the robbery and killing. Dunaway, who was 18 years old, waived counsel and implicated himself in the crime.[8] The Fourth Department twice held that the police did not violate Dunaway's Fourth Amendment rights and that the incriminating statements need not be suppressed.[9] Judge Cardamone dissented. He highlighted the critical facts: as the prosecutor had conceded, "there was no distinction between the pickup of this defendant and an arrest, except for the absence of the word 'arrest,'" and Dunaway "did not voluntarily accompany the detectives to police headquarters."[10] Rather, "[t]his small Black youth was confronted by two very large white detectives who, according to him grabbed him and took him to the police car."[11] To Judge Cardamone, this was plainly a seizure—one made "solely for investigatory purposes" based on "stale rumors and triple-hearsay"—and Dunaway's Fourth Amendment rights "should not turn upon the use or failure to use the word 'arrest' where that, in fact, was his status."[12] The Supreme Court agreed.[13]

Judge Cardamone served as an associate justice on the Fourth Department until 1981, when President Ronald Reagan appointed him to the Court of Appeals for the Second Circuit. His children nearly derailed the appointment. Given the size of the Cardamone clan, someone was nearly always using the phone. When President Reagan called the house, he got a busy signal. Fortunately, he tried again later.[14]

When he was appointed, Judge Cardamone was the first sitting New York state court judge in over a century to join the Second Circuit. Three more would soon follow: Judges Frank X. Altimari, Rosemary S. Pooler, and Richard C. Wesley. In an interview with *The New York Times*, Judge Cardamone said that his diminutive appearance meant he was "seldom mistaken for a judge," but that he was not surprised by the nomination for one reason: "I work very hard."[15] At his induction ceremony, Chief Judge Wilfred Feinberg observed that Judge Cardamone was not the first from Utica to join the Second Circuit: Judge Alexander Smith Johnson, who was appointed to the Court of Appeals for the Second Circuit in 1875, also hailed from the upstate city.[16] Because Judge Cardamone came from state court, one might think that he had never been reviewed by the Second Circuit. But Chief Judge Feinberg discovered that the Second Circuit had agreed with Judge Cardamone's dissent in a state habeas case. Chief Judge Feinberg joked, "[C]andor requires me to disclose further that the United States Supreme Court overruled us both—unanimously. . . . That augers well for our compatibility if not our infallibility."[17]

The following decades would demonstrate that Judge Cardamone was perfectly compatible with his new colleagues. Judge Rosemary S. Pooler said, "In my mind's eye, I always see RJC smiling and laughing. He was a happy man, and it showed in his work, in his life, and in how he treated his colleagues and his law clerks."[18] Similarly, Justice Sonia Sotomayor remarked that she remembered him with "a smile and a twinkle in his eyes."[19] His son William recalled that his father viewed his decades on the Second Circuit as his and Kate's "New York years."[20] Each time they arrived in Manhattan, they dove into new restaurants, museums, the symphony, and Yankees games.[21] Harry Sandick, a law clerk, said that Judge Cardamone once remarked, "I'm always happy to travel to New York City for argument and to see my colleagues and my friends in the city. And I'm always happy when it's time to return home."[22] Waiting for him in Utica was an idyllic life filled with touch football games, which were fiercely competitive and followed by parties around the fireplace listening to the music of the 1960s and 1970s; watching Giants games, which were often not fiercely competitive; his rose garden, a hobby inherited from his mother; and Ol' Boy, the skiff that took the Cardamone family on cruises among the thousand islands of the St. Lawrence River.[23]

In 1999, after serving on the court for nearly two decades, Judge Cardamone wrote an article about the impact of growing caseloads on federal appellate procedures. He observed that "the decline of collegiality seems to be the most pervasive" result of the federal courts' burgeoning dockets.[24] In his view, this was a dangerous trend. He suggested amending Lord Chancellor Lyndhurst's definition of a "good judge" to include collegiality. (The other attributes: "honest, industrious, courageous, courteous; and, if he or she knows some law, it will help.")[25] He defined collegiality as the "give-and-take in the discussion of how to dispose of a case the panel is called upon to decide. It is predicated on respect for a colleague's intellectual integrity, knowledge of the law, capacity to engage in insightful analysis of the legal problems presented, and exercise of sound judgment in reaching a satisfactory resolution of an appeal."[26] Put another way, it "means being able to disagree with a colleague without loss of civility."[27] He referred to the "apocryphal tale of a feud between Judges Charles Clark and Jerome Frank that prevented the active judges of the court from convening for a group picture for 12 years," and noted with gratitude that "those days are long gone."[28]

On the bench, Judge Cardamone's "judicial philosophy was that of a common law judge: examine the facts very carefully and then look at all the possible sources of authority – statutes, prior decisions, scholarly comment—and figure out the right result."[29] His opinions were careful and thoughtful, and often began with a quotation from literature. A study conducted in 2008 found that among federal opinions, "Judge Cardamone accounted for more than 50 percent of all references to Shakespeare."[30] If Shakespeare had not spoken on the theme, Judge Cardamone began with an elegant turn of phrase that encapsulated the tensions laid bare by the parties' dispute. His decision on a foreign sovereign's immunity, in which the result seemed unjust but mandated by law, began with this: "How one wishes to decide a case comes lightly to mind, on a wing; but often how one must decide it comes arduously, weighed down by somber thought."[31] His decision in the so-called *Westway* case, which effectively condemned the highway project "to oblivion," began with this: "A change in something from yesterday to today creates doubt. When the anticipated explanation is not given, doubt turns to disbelief. This case is capsulized in that solitary simile."[32]

Sandick, explained that, "[o]ut of respect for his colleagues" and for the court, Judge Cardamone "dissented rarely, only when he believed that it was absolutely required."[33] Ironically, Judge Cardamone is perhaps best known for his dissents in a series of decisions that narrowed civil liability under the Racketeer Influenced and Corrupt Organizations Act. Three district judges, in three unrelated cases, dismissed civil RICO complaints, variously reasoning that the defendants had not been convicted of any crimes and the plaintiffs failed to allege a distinct RICO injury.[34] All three cases went up on appeal simultaneously and were argued within months of each other. Judge Cardamone was on all three panels. He lost the battle, but won the war.

The first panel held that, to be civilly liable under RICO, the defendant must have "criminal convictions on the underlying predicate offenses," and that to have standing, the plaintiffs must have suffered a "racketeering injury," which the court described as harm to the market or competition rather than mere injury from the racketeer's predicate acts.[35] The following day, the second panel issued a decision agreeing that "racketeering injury" was needed.[36] The day after that, the third panel wrote that it was compelled to follow those two controlling decisions, but cited with approval Judge Cardamone's dissents.[37] In those dissents, Judge Cardamone traced RICO's legislative history and read the statutory language to support neither of the requirements the court had imposed.[38] In his view, the majority approach "pulled the teeth from the statute," "reduced its effectiveness nearly to zero," and "trespassed in an area of law-making exclusively reserved to Congress."[39] Judge Cardamone's view was later vindicated by the Supreme Court, in what Judge Pooler has described as one of the "how great it is" moments of a judicial career.[40]

Judge Cardamone was kind and collegial to everyone in his life, from fellow judges to courthouse staff to his law clerks. Fridays in chambers began with donuts.[41] Lunch was to local restaurants in Utica and neighboring towns.[42] When it came to work, Sandick and his co-clerk recalled "that it often felt like we had a dad as opposed to a boss in the other room."[43] Christopher Cole, a law clerk, particularly remembered a criminal appeal involving a sting operation of a suspected cocaine trafficking ring in Queens. After following the defendant for a few days, DEA agents saw "him driving his Cadillac to a stop near another expensive car, and finally followed a guy on foot into an elevator, where the DEA agent observed, in a bag the guy was carrying, a 'rectangular object wrapped in tape.' The DEA agent decided this was enough for him and based on his experience seized the object which, lo and behold, turned out to be contraband."[44] Judge Cardamone and his law clerk "went at it hammer and tong for days" over whether the search was permissible under the plain view doctrine.[45] The panel upheld the seizure, in an opinion drafted by Cole. After it issued, Judge Cardamone said to Cole,

> You know Chris, this is the way it's supposed to work. . . [Y]ou're supposed to challenge my thinking on these cases, and keep me and the whole of the NYPD and DEA on the straight and narrow, and that's what you did here – and you should be proud of yourself." . . . Almost 30 years later, I still remember his socks and feet on my desk, his kindliness and smile . . . and the gentlemanly way he told me I was dead wrong.[46]

The judge "was always steady, always polite, always fatherly and considerate" of his law clerk's views, "however much he disagreed with them."[47]

Judge Cardamone retired from the bench in 2008. He died on October 16, 2015, at the age of 90. He was survived by his wife, ten children, 22 grandchildren, and 13 great-grandchildren.[48]

Sally Pritchard

1. Mark Hamblett, *Longtime Second Circuit Judge Richard J. Cardamone Dies*, N.Y. L.J., Oct. 23, 2015, at 2.

2. William Cardamone, Remarks at a Special Session of the United States Court of Appeals for the Second Circuit, In Memoriam, Honorable Richard J. Cardamone 2 (Mar. 2, 2016) (transcript on file with the United States Courts Library for the Second Circuit).

3. Hamblett, *supra* note 1.

4. Cardamone, Remarks, *supra* note 2, at 2.

5. Hamblett, *supra* note 1.

6. E.J. Dionne, Jr., *New York Judge Picked for U.S. Court*, N.Y. TIMES, Oct. 1, 1981, at B8.

7. Dunaway v. New York, 442 U.S. 200, 203 (1979).

8. *Id.*

9. People v. Dunaway, 42 A.D.2d 689, 689 (4th Dep't 1973); *vacated by*, Dunaway v. New York, 422 U.S. 1053, 1053 (1975); People v. Dunaway, 61 A.D.2d 299, 302–03 (4th Dep't 1978); *rev'd sub nom.*, *Dunaway*, 442 U.S. at 200.

10. *Dunaway*, 61 A.D.2d at 306 (Cardamone, J., dissenting).
11. *Id.*
12. *Id.* at 307.
13. *Dunaway*, 442 U.S. at 216.
14. William Cardamone, Remarks, *supra* note 2, at 3.
15. Dionne, Jr., *supra* note 6.
16. Chief Judge Wilfred Feinberg, Remarks at the Proceedings Held on the Occasion of the Induction of Honorable Richard J. Cardamone as United States Circuit Judge of the United States Court of Appeals for the Second Circuit 1, 2 (Nov. 18, 1981) (transcript on file with the United States Courts Library for the Second Circuit).
17. *Id.*
18. Judge Rosemary S. Pooler, Remarks at a Special Session of the United States Court of Appeals for the Second Circuit, In Memoriam, Honorable Richard J. Cardamone 1 (Mar. 2, 2016) (transcript on file with the United States Courts Library for the Second Circuit).
19. Telephone Interview with Justice Sonia Sotomayor (Mar. 3, 2016).
20. William Cardamone, Remarks, *supra* note 2, at 4.
21. *Id.*
22. Harry Sandick, former law clerk, Remarks at a Special Session of the United States Court of Appeals for the Second Circuit, In Memoriam, Honorable Richard J. Cardamone 2 (Mar. 2, 2016) (transcript on file with the United States Courts Library for the Second Circuit). Sandick is a partner at Patterson Belknap.
23. Cardamone, Remarks, *supra* note 2, at 5.
24. Hon. Richard J. Cardamone, *How an Expanding Caseload Impacts Federal Appellate Procedures*, 65 BROOK. L. REV. 281, 282 (1999).
25. *Id.*
26. *Id.*
27. *Id.*
28. *Id.*
29. Sandick, Remarks, *supra* note 22, at 4.
30. M. Todd Henderson, *Citing Fiction*, 11 GREEN BAG 2d 171, 175–76 (2008).
31. *De Letelier v. Republic of Chile*, 748 F.2d 790, 791 (2d Cir. 1984).
32. *Sierra Club v. U.S. Army Corps of Engineers*, 772 F.2d 1043, 1046 (2d Cir. 1985).
33. Sandick, Remarks, *supra* note 22, at 6.
34. Bankers Trust Co. v. Feldesman, 566 F. Supp. 1235 (S.D.N.Y. 1983); Sedima S.P.R.L. v. Imrex Co., Inc., 574 F. Supp. 963 (E.D.N.Y. 1983); Furman v. Cirrito, 578 F. Supp. 1535 (S.D.N.Y. 1985).
35. Sedima, S.P.R.L. v. Imrex Co., 741 F.2d 482, 496 (2d Cir. 1984); *rev'd*, 473 U.S. 479 (1985).
36. Bankers Trust Co. v. Rhoades, 741 F.2d 511 (2d Cir. 1984); *cert. granted, judgment vacated sub nom.*, Bankers Trust Co. v. Rhoades, 473 U.S. 922 (1985).
37. Furman v. Cirrito, 741 F.2d 524 (2d Cir. 1984); *cert. granted, judgment vacated sub nom.*, Joel v. Cirrito, 473 U.S. 922 (1985).
38. *Sedima*, 741 F.2d at 504–10; *Bankers Trust Co.*, 741 F.2d at 518–24.
39. *Bankers Trust Co.*, 741 F.2d at 518.
40. *Sedima*, 473 U.S. at 479; Judge Rosemary S. Pooler, Remarks, *supra* note 18, at 2.
41. Sandick, Remarks, *supra* note 22, at 1.
42. *Id.*
43. *Id.*
44. Email from Christopher Cole, former law clerk, to Sally Pritchard (Feb. 28, 2016, 10:25 EST) (on file with the United States Courts Library for the Second Circuit). Cole is a shareholder at Sheenan, Phinney, Bass & Green, PA.

45. *Id.*
46. *Id.*
47. *Id.*
48. Hamblett, *supra* note 1.

# ROGER J. MINER
# 1934-2012

New York State Supreme Court, Third Judicial District, Columbia County: 1976-1981
District Court for the Northern District of New York: 1981-1985
Court of Appeals for the Second Circuit: 1985-2012

"Upon the conclusion of any contested litigation, there is a winner and a loser. My goal simply is this—that the loser leave this courtroom without the slightest doubt that justice abides here."[1]

Roger J. Miner was born in Hudson, New York on April 14, 1934.[2] He was the son of Abram Miner, a local Hudson attorney, and Anne Goldshlager, a housewife.[3] Abram Miner was his son's principal mentor throughout his life. The son of Polish immigrants who ran a small grocery in Hudson, Abram Miner graduated from New York Law School in 1926 and returned to Hudson as a private practitioner.[4]

Miner attended public schools in Hudson and played clarinet and saxophone in the school band;[5] he even considered a career in music,[6] but finally followed in his father's footsteps and enrolled at New York Law School, where he was the first managing editor of the *New York Law School Law Review*.[7]

Upon receiving an LLB degree in 1956, Miner was drafted into the Army as a member of the Judge Advocate General's Corps, attaining the rank of first lieutenant.[8] While in the JAG Corps, he served in Japan and Korea, and he was awarded the Commendation Ribbon with Medal Pendant for his revision of the Manual for Courts-Martial.[9]

After his military service, Miner returned to Hudson in 1959 to practice law with his father.[10] He was active in Columbia County politics as president of the Columbia County Young Republican Club and as counsel to the New York Association of Young Republican Clubs and the Columbia County Republican Committee.[11] He was also the campaign manager for Samuel T. Wheeler during his campaign for reelection as mayor of Hudson.[12] In 1961, Miner became corporation counsel for the city of Hudson, and in 1964, he became an assistant district attorney for one year.[13] In 1968, he was elected district attorney of Columbia County.[14] He was reelected twice, and served as the district attorney for seven years.[15] Between 1959 and 1976, Miner always maintained a private practice with his father because his public posts were part-time jobs.[16]

Miner's time as a prosecutor influenced his approach to criminal cases on the bench. In his jury instructions, he always advised the jury as follows: "Ladies and Gentlemen, the question here is not whether the government wins or loses in this case. The government always wins when justice is done."[17] Apparently, some prosecutors did not appreciate this instruction, preferring that the judge maintain the adversarial atmosphere of the trial.[18] Judge Miner would have none of it. Instead, he lamented excesses in the adversarial system, and he saw these instructions as a contribution to an idea of justice that existed independently of winners and losers.[19]

In 1976, Miner won a seat on the New York State Supreme Court, Third Judicial District,[20] becoming the first judge elected from Columbia County in half a century.[21] His father told him that, now that he was a judge, he must never forget that he was a lawyer; apparently, every time Abram received an adverse decision from a judge, he would remind his son of this fact in order to garner sympathy for his plight.[22]

The experience was a positive one, and Judge Miner lamented its end when President Ronald Reagan appointed him to the District Court for the Northern District of New York in 1981.[23] Judge Miner commented candidly that the appointment process was unavoidably political because a prospective judge must know a senator in some fashion in order to be considered for the job.[24] In Miner's case, his wife, Jackie, had a personal friendship with Senator Alfonse D'Amato, the Republican senator from New York.[25] Judge Miner was therefore able to have his name brought to the attention of the senator and secure the appointment (after the Reagan administration's extensive vetting process).[26]

Sitting in Albany, Judge James T. Foley became Judge Miner's mentor.[27] They had lunch together every day,[28] and Judge Miner was continually struck by Judge Foley's passion for learning and his devotion to the work of the court.[29] This love of learning characterized Judge Miner's time on the Northern District; he said that he had to learn multiple areas of law he had never before encountered in his career, which ensured that his job remained exciting and interesting.[30]

Judge Miner issued an important and controversial decision as a district judge. In *Washburn v. Abrams*,[31] he refused to appoint a legal guardian for Baby Jane Doe, an infant born with an open spine whose parents decided to forgo surgery for their daughter because the surgery would have provided her with only a few years of a life filled with pain and suffering.[32] A Vermont attorney, A. Lawrence Washburn, Jr., filed suit to have a legal guardian appointed who would authorize the surgery.[33] Washburn argued that any hospital policy allowing parents to refuse life-saving medical care for their child was unconstitutional because it violated the child's right to life.[34] Judge Miner refused to appoint the guardian on the "assumption that parents are concerned about the welfare of their children" and sanctioned Washburn under Rule 11 of the Federal Rules of Civil Procedure.[35]

Judge Miner became fascinated with the history of the Northern District. He was the head of the court's historical committee, and he gave a lecture on its history that was later published.[36] In that lecture, Judge Miner, tongue firmly in cheek, traced the history of the Northern District to the Pleistocene Era, one and a half million years ago, when glaciers moved from what is now northern New York to an area just north of New York City, leaving the Northern District covered with "deep rivers, clear lakes, magnificent mountains, rolling hills, lush valleys, and verdant meadows."[37] He gave a complete history of the geographical region comprising the Northern District, from Native American settlements through the Dutch West India Company to the Revolutionary War and beyond.[38]

In 1985, President Reagan appointed Judge Miner to the Court of Appeals for the Second Circuit.[39] Judge Miner authored hundreds of opinions as a circuit judge, several of which were reviewed by the Supreme Court. Perhaps the most controversial was Judge Miner's opinion in *Quill v. Vacco*,[40] holding that a New York statute banning assisted suicide through the administration of medication, but allowing a patient to order the removal of life-support systems, violated the Equal Protection Clause.[41] Judge Miner reasoned that there was no rational distinction between the choice to withdraw life-support treatment and the decision to request prescribed medications causing death; the state had no legitimate interests in treating those choices differently.[42]

The Supreme Court reversed,[43] holding that New York's statute bore a rational relationship to the legitimate goals of "prohibiting intentional killing and preserving life; preventing suicide; maintaining physicians' role as their patients' healers; protecting vulnerable people from indifference, prejudice, and psychological and financial pressure to end their lives, and avoiding a possible slide toward euthanasia."[44] The Supreme Court identified a rational distinction between withdrawal of life support and assisted suicide: in one, the underlying disease caused death, whereas in the other, the physician did.[45]

Judge Miner wrote several important First Amendment opinions. *Loper v. New York City Police Department*[46] held that New York's statute criminalizing loitering in a public place for the purpose of begging violated the First Amendment.[47] According to Judge Miner, no "compelling state interest is served by excluding those who beg in a peaceful manner from communicating with their fellow citizens."[48] *Lamb's Chapel v. Center Moriches Union Free School District*[49] held that a public school was a limited public forum not open to religious use and that a school district could deny access to a church seeking to show a religious film series at the school.[50] The Supreme Court reversed,[51] holding that the school district's denial of access to the church outside of school hours violated the Freedom of Speech Clause.[52] *Good News Club v. Milford Central School*[53] held that a public school reasonably denied a Christian club access to a meeting room because the school worried that students would think the school officially sanctioned the club's views.[54] Again, the Supreme Court reversed,[55] holding that the school engaged in unconstitutional viewpoint discrimination in barring the Christian club from using school facilities.[56]

Judge Miner was considered a candidate for elevation to the Supreme Court in the late 1980s and early 1990s. After both Robert Bork and Douglas Ginsburg failed to be confirmed in 1987, Judge Miner was frequently mentioned as a possible nominee.[57] One night, Judge Miner reportedly received a call from a Republican senator asking for his position on abortion.[58] Judge Miner said that he would decide each case on its merits.[59] His wife, Jackie, was said to have heard his answer and called out that he should give a "more delicate answer."[60] He refused, saying, "My reputation is too big a price to pay for a seat on the Supreme Court."[61]

Later, Judge Miner published a controversial critique of the confirmation process for federal judges, alleging that the process did not function as it was envisioned by the founders.[62] Judge Miner's evaluation was scathing: "The President has abdicated his duty to nominate, the Senate provides no advice whatsoever, and the function of senatorial consent is a mere formality in most instances."[63] He argued that merit no longer played a significant role in the choice of federal judges; instead, personal friendship, ideological compatibility, and the ability to be confirmed were paramount.[64] Judge Miner placed much of the blame on the use of presidential staff in vetting nominees suggested by senators, a system he termed "nomination by a Senator and advice and consent by the Presidential staff," and that elevated political considerations above those of judicial ability.[65]

Apart from his work on the Second Circuit, Judge Miner wrote many articles, with a particular focus on appellate practice and the lawyer's role in society. Judge Miner thought that appellate practitioners had lost their sense of professional ethics, bringing frivolous appeals, challenging precedent without good faith arguments for their overruling, refusing to disclose adverse precedent when it might hurt the client's chance of winning, and submitting exceedingly poor briefs.[66] He suggested several changes to the rules of professional responsibility, including a change requiring "government lawyers to exercise special care when arguing for the elimination of an established right," a rule requiring lawyers to "cite pertinent authority from other jurisdictions to help the court in its labors, even if the adversary fails to do so," and elimination of a prejudice requirement for clients seeking to show ineffective assistance by appellate counsel.[67]

Judge Miner argued that lawyers have a professional duty to criticize the courts if it could improve the administration of justice.[68] However, he contended that they do not do so out of fear of reprisal in cases before the judges they have criticized.[69] Judge Miner also thought that judges should not publicly respond to such criticism but instead should improve the courts.[70]

According to his clerks, Judge Miner was a mentor and teacher of great kindness, integrity, and wit. His clerks attested to the joy of working for him.[71] Senator Kirsten E. Gillibrand, who clerked for Judge Miner, stated that "[t]here was no matching the degree of honor that he brought to the Court."[72] According to the senator, Judge Miner "owned a clarity of conscience that will be truly missed in American life."[73] Another clerk, Lori Sherman, spoke of Thursday nights in chambers, when the clerks and Judge Miner worked late as a team.[74] Every Thursday, they would go to

Pagliacci's, an Italian restaurant in Albany, where Judge Miner would order seafood fra diavolo and a glass of Lambrusco.[75] Judge Miner would then grill the clerks on their memos; over the course of the year, the clerks would become more confident, and the debates would intensify.[76] In the words of a Miner law clerk, "Thursday nights were a lot of fun."[77] So was life in chambers: "We were all fairly green when we walked into chambers. The Judge knew all this, but he was never negative, and he never put you down. And the sense of humor was always just under the surface . . . when he was training the clerks."[78]

Judge Miner's sense of humor was one of his defining qualities. Chief Judge Dennis Jacobs recalled that, as toastmaster, "he once had the Second Circuit Judicial Conference convulsed as he piled on joke on joke, witticism on witticism—without himself cracking a smile."[79] Ms. Sherman recalled that his sense of humor "was a wonderful thing about the Judge. It infused the whole atmosphere in which we worked. It was there to lift you at the right moment, push you forward and to make you enjoy the experience."[80]

Judge Miner's wife, Jackie, played a pivotal role in his career. An activist within the Republican Party for years, Jackie Miner held a devotion to Judge Miner and his career that was unceasing.[81] Judge Miner stated that he owed her his life because she insisted he seek medical care after a cardiac arrest, and that he owed her his career because "[h]er political skills have guided me through my years of public service."[82] According to Judge Miner:

> it was her talent and knowledge of the workings of the national government that brought me to the attention of the senator who recommended my nomination to the District Court. And it was her talent and knowledge of the workings of the White House and its staff and her participation in those operations that brought me to the attention of those who zealously guarded the process by which President Reagan chose Circuit Court appointees.[83]

Judge Miner said that "[s]he has been, is, and as long as I live, will be, my everything."[84]

Judge Miner was also a father and grandfather. He had four sons, Larry, Ron, Ralph, and Mark.[85] His son Mark recalled that, after he became a campaign advisor to Governor Rick Perry of Texas during his 2012 run for President, Judge Miner was irked by Perry's call for term limits for federal judges.[86] However, according to Mark, "We both had our jobs to do. He truly understood that with a sense of humor."[87] Mark also recalled his love for his grandchildren, stating, "Later in life, as we got married and had children, his greatest love was reserved for his grandchildren. . . . In the final days, he could either play student and my daughter Sydney would play teacher and [he] watched more children's movies than any adult should ever have to watch in a lifetime."[88] And his son Ralph reminisced, "His sense of play and imagination with his grandchildren was inspiring: he could make the house basement seem like a place to hunt for monsters and mysteries with his grandson; or it could be a classroom, to play class or teacher with his granddaughter."[89]

It is fitting to give the final word to Ron Carmichael, Judge Miner's stepson, who attested to Judge Miner's passion and love for life: "A flame that once burned with such passion and vitality flickered for just a short while and then quietly went out, and finally today he lives in the minds and hearts of those he touched."[90]

Judge Miner died of "heart-related problems" in his home in Hudson on February 17, 2012.[91] He was 77 years old.[92]

Stephen Strother

1. District Judge Roger J. Miner, Remarks at the Induction of the Honorable Roger J. Miner as a United States District Judge for the Northern District of New York 37 (Oct. 10, 1981) (transcript on file with the United States Courts Library for the Second Circuit).

2. State of New York Birth Certificate for Robert Jeffrey Miner (Issued Apr. 27, 1934) (copy on file with the United States Courts Library for the Second Circuit).

3. *Id.*

4. District Judge Roger J. Miner, Remarks, *supra* note 1, at 33–34.

5. DVD: A Conversation with Roger J. Miner, Volume I, United States Court of Appeals and the Federal Bar Council at 3:53-3:55 (2003) (transcript on file with the United States Courts Library for the Second Circuit).

6. *Id.* at 4:00–4:02.

7. *Dedication: Roger J. Miner*, 30 N.Y.L. SCH. L. REV. 693, 693 (1986).

8. 2 ALMANAC OF THE FEDERAL JUDICIARY 42 (2007).

9. Chief Judge Dennis Jacobs, Remarks at the United States Court of Appeals for the Second Circuit Memorial Service for the Honorable Roger J. Miner 5 (June 22, 2012) (transcript on file with the United States Courts Library for the Second Circuit).

10. 2 ALMANAC OF THE FEDERAL JUDICIARY, *supra* note 8, at 42.

11. *Id.* at 42–43.

12. A Conversation with Roger J. Miner, *supra* note 5, at 44:10–44:15.

13. 2 ALMANAC OF THE FEDERAL JUDICIARY, *supra* note 8, at 42.

14. *Id.*

15. *See* A Conversation with Roger J. Miner, *supra* note 5, at 47:05–47:12.

16. *Id.* at 40:20–41:45.

17. Roger J. Miner, *Professional Responsibility in Appellate Practice: A View From the Bench*, 19 PACE L. REV. 323, 326 (1999).

18. *See id.* at 326–27.

19. *See id.* at 330.

20. 2 ALMANAC OF THE FEDERAL JUDICIARY, *supra* note 8, at 42.

21. A Conversation with Roger J. Miner, *supra* note 5, at 49:53–50:00.

22. Judge Roger J. Miner, Remarks at the Investiture of the Honorable Roger J. Miner as a Circuit Judge of the United States Court of Appeals for the Second Circuit 44 (Sept. 14, 1985) (transcript on file with the United States Courts Library for the Second Circuit).

23. District Judge Roger J. Miner, Remarks, *supra* note 1, at 34–35.

24. A Conversation with Roger J. Miner, *supra* note 5, at 1:00:05–1:01:00.

25. *Id.* at 1:03:00–1:04:00.

26. *Id.*

27. *Id.* at 1:13:00–1:14:05.

28. *Id.* at 1:14:25.

29. *Id.* at 1:13:00–1:14:05.

30. *Id.* at 1:16:30–1:16:35.

31. No. 83-cv-1711 (N.D.N.Y. Jan. 20, 1984). Unfortunately, no written order was issued in this case.

32. *Suit by Lawyer Over Baby Jane Doe is Thrown Out*, N.Y. TIMES, Jan. 21, 1984, at 24.

33. *Id.*

34. *Id.*

35. *Id.*

36. *See* Roger J. Miner, *United States District Court for the Northern District of New York: Its History and Antecedents*, *in* SECOND CIRCUIT HISTORY LECTURES 62 (1984).

37. *Id.* at 63.

38. *Id.* at 63–68.

39. 2 ALMANAC OF THE FEDERAL JUDICIARY, *supra* note 8, at 42.

40. 80 F.3d 716 (2d Cir. 1996), *rev'd*, 521 U.S. 793 (1997).

41. *Id.* at 726–31.

42. *Id.* at 729–30.

43. *See Vacco*, 521 U.S. 793.

44. *Id.* at 808–09.

45. *Id.* at 800–01.

46. 999 F.2d 699 (2d Cir. 1993).

47. *Id.* at 705–06.

48. *Id.* at 705.

49. 959 F.2d 381 (2d Cir. 1992), *rev'd*, 508 U.S. 384 (1993).

50. *Id.* at 386–89.

51. 508 U.S. 384 (1992).

52. *Id.* at 394–97.

53. 202 F.3d 502 (2d Cir. 2000), *rev'd*, 533 U.S. 98 (2001).

54. *Id.* at 509–11.

55. 533 U.S. 98 (2000).

56. *Id.* at 107–12.

57. *See, e.g.*, David A. Kaplan & Ann McDaniel, *Campaigning for the High Court: Merit Alone Won't Win a Seat on the Bench*, NEWSWEEK, July 2, 1990, at 61.

58. Justice Sonia Sotomayor, Remarks at the United States Court of Appeals for the Second Circuit Memorial Service for the Honorable Roger J. Miner 14 (June 22, 2012) (transcript on file with the United States Courts Library for the Second Circuit).

59. *Id.* at 14.

60. *Id.*

61. *Id.* at 15.

62. *See* Roger J. Miner, *Advice and Consent in Theory and Practice*, 41 AM. U. L. REV. 1075, 1075 (1992).

63. *Id.* at 1075.

64. *Id.* at 1079–80.

65. *Id.* at 1081.

66. Miner, *supra* note 17, at 324–38.

67. *Id.* at 327, 331, 336–37.

68. Roger J. Miner, *Should Lawyers Be More Critical of Courts?*, 71 JUDICATURE 134, 134–35 (1987).

69. *Id.*

70. *Id.* at 172.

71. *See, e.g.*, Senator Kirsten Gillibrand, Remarks at the United States Court of Appeals for the Second Circuit Memorial Service for the Honorable Roger J. Miner 16-18 (June 22, 2012) (transcript on file with the United States Courts Library for the Second Circuit); Paul Silver, Remarks at the United States Court of Appeals for the Second Circuit Memorial Service for the Honorable Roger J. Miner 34-37 (June 22, 2012) (transcript on file with the United States Courts Library for the Second Circuit). Silver is an assistant United States attorney for the Northern District of New York. *See also* Lori Sherman, former law clerk, Remarks at the United States Court of Appeals for the Second Circuit Memorial Service for the Honorable Roger J. Miner 38-41 (June 22, 2012) (transcript on file with the United States Courts Library for the Second Circuit). Sherman practices antitrust law at Wachtell, Lipton, Rosen & Katz.

72. Senator Kirsten Gillibrand, Remarks, *supra* note 71, at 16.

73. *Id.*

74. Sherman, Remarks, *supra* note 71, at 40.

75. *Id.*

76. *Id.*

77. *Id.*

78. *Id.* at 38.

79. Chief Judge Dennis Jacobs, Remarks, *supra* note 9, at 7.

80. Sherman, Remarks, *supra* note 71, at 39.

81. *'My Everything,' Says Judge: Jackie Miner Shares Spotlight*, REGISTER-STAR, Sept. 16, 1985.

82. Jim Hellegaard & Michael Roffer, *Law School Honors Judge Rober J. Miner '56*, N.Y.L. SCH. IN BRIEF, Fall/Winter 2003, at 11.

83. *Id.*

84. *Id.*

85. Chief Judge Dennis Jacobs, Remarks, *supra* note 9, at 3.

86. Mark Miner, Remarks at the United States Court of Appeals for the Second Circuit Memorial Service for the Honorable Roger J. Miner 29-30 (June 22, 2012) (transcript on file with the United States Courts Library for the Second Circuit). Miner is Judge Miner's youngest son.

87. *Id.* at 30.

88. *Id.* at 31.

89. Ron Carmichael, Remarks at the United States Court of Appeals for the Second Circuit Memorial Service for the Honorable Roger J. Miner 27 (June 22, 2012) (transcript on file with the United States Courts Library for the Second Circuit). Carmichael is Judge Miner's stepson.

90. *Id.*

91. Kris Fischer & Mike Pquette, *Second Circuit Judge Miner Dies at 77*, N.Y. L.J. ONLINE, Feb. 18, 2012, http://www.newyorklawjournal.com/id=1202542916704/Second-Circuit-Judge-Miner-Dies-at-77.

92. *Id.*

# FRANK X. ALTIMARI
## 1928-1998

New York State Supreme Court, Tenth Judicial District, Nassau County: 1974-1982
District Court for the Eastern District of New York: 1982-1985
Court of Appeals for the Second Circuit: 1985-1998

Judge Roger J. Miner once said that he could hear Judge Altimari speak to him when writing opinions: "The people, Roger, what about the people? They are all that truly matters."[1]

Born in Ridgewood, Queens in 1928,[2] Francesco Xaverio Altimari was the son of Antonio and Elvira,[3] two Italian immigrants.[4] He was baptized at St. Mathias Roman Catholic Church, was raised in Brooklyn, and attended public schools.[5] He graduated from St. Francis College in 1948 and Brooklyn Law School in 1951. A few months after law school, he married

Angelina Scavuzzo.[6] They had three sons, Anthony, Nicholas, and Michael, and one daughter, Vera.[7] They lived in Old Westbury, New York.[8]

After law school, Altimari worked for Austin & Dupont in Jamaica, Queens.[9] The firm "handled everything from wills and estates to real estate closings and criminal trials."[10] He was an associate from 1951 until the mid-1950s.[11] Altimari left the firm to start his own practice with a partner, Ted Hoffman; they opened Hoffman & Altimari in Mineola, New York, the heart of suburban Long Island.[12] Business in the early days of the new firm was slow, but "before [their] patience and financial resources were exhausted, [they] started to develop a client base."[13] Altimari gained "experience as a busy negligence-trial lawyer" and was a partner with the firm until 1965, when he left for the bench.[14] During this time, he was also an associate professor of law at St. Francis College.[15]

Altimari's "ambition in life was to be a judge."[16] In 1963, he met with local Republican leaders to discuss running for a district court judgeship in Nassau County.[17] He was sponsored by Sol Wachtler, who had worked with him at Hoffman & Altimari and who was active in local Republican politics.[18] Altimari earned the party's nomination.[19]

His path to the bench was not easy. As Wachtler described it, 1964 was a bad year for Republicans, with presidential candidate Barry Goldwater's presence at the top of the ticket adversely affecting all candidates down the ballot.[20] Still, Altimari seemed to have bested his Democratic opponent, Julius R. Lippman, to become the third Nassau County district court judge.[21] Although Altimari appeared "to have won comfortably" on election night 1964,[22] the Board of Elections later declared Lippman the winner by just one vote.[23] An elections commissioner called it "the closest [vote] in county history."[24] During the recount, ten absentee ballots were uncovered; they were split five to five.[25] Following the full recount, however, Altimari ended up on top by five votes.[26] Lippman challenged the result in court, taking the case to the New York State Court of Appeals. After months of back and forth about the validity of a handful of absentee ballots, the race ultimately ended in a tie: 53,371 votes for Altimari and

53,371 for Lippman.[27] Although *The New York Times* had earlier reported that if "a tie ensues, it is the consensus that a special election would have to be held,"[28] the Nassau County executive had the authority to appoint a judge in the event of a tie. The executive, a Democrat, selected Lippman.[29]

Altimari's dream of becoming a judge was not denied, only deferred; "[t]he following year, sympathy dictated that [Altimari] receive bipartisan endorsement, which he got, and he became a county district court judge."[30] After his election in 1965, Altimari served in various state judicial roles: in 1970, he was elected to Nassau's County Court; in 1973, he served as the administrative judge of that court;[31] and in 1974, he was elected to the New York State Supreme Court, Nassau County.[32]

Eight years later, on the recommendation of New York Senator Alfonse D'Amato,[33] President Ronald Reagan nominated Altimari to the District Court for the Eastern District of New York in 1982.[34] He served there until 1985 when, again on the recommendation of Senator D'Amato,[35] President Reagan elevated Altimari to the Court of Appeals for the Second Circuit.[36] At Altimari's induction, Chief Judge Wilfred Feinberg remarked that the court had "affirmed most of Judge Altimari's decisions . . . [and t]hrough the magic of Westlaw, . . . [we] have determined that [the court had] even affirmed several of his decisions as a state judge, which came before [the court] on habeas petitions."[37]

On the bench, Judge Altimari focused on how his decisions would affect ordinary people. In the words of Judge Miner, "People mattered to Frank Altimari."[38] Running throughout his decisions were compassion and an understanding of human nature. Judge Altimari "empathized with those without power or position and sought to make the Constitution a living document for the ordinary person."[39] The "law was not an abstract tool, but rather was an instrument of justice."[40] He believed that "justice was not always found in case law, a statute, or a rule or regulation."[41] "He loved the 'underdog,' regular people who he understood needed the protection of the law, and for whom a fair, independent, credible judiciary was essential."[42]

Judge Altimari's judicial philosophy was on display in his most well-known decision,[43] *Young v. New York City Transit Authority*, better known as the New York City subway panhandling case.[44] Writing for a divided panel, Altimari reversed the district court, which had reasoned that beggars on the subway had a First Amendment right to panhandle.[45]

> In language unusually strong for a Court of Appeals ruling, [Altimari] . . . said that 'whether intended as so, or not, begging in the subway often amounts to nothing less than assault, creating in the passengers the apprehension of imminent danger.' He also chastised the lower court for deferring to the rights of the beggars while overlooking the concerns of the system's millions of riders.[46]

"The phrase 'common good' appears three times in the opinion, signaling [Judge Altimari's] notion of the weight to be given to this objective in the adjudicatory process."[47]

One of Judge Altimari's law clerks during the panhandling case, Michael A. Gerstenzang, remembers the "many long discussions about the merits of [the] case, and [how] . . . hardly a single one of our discussions ended without the Judge reminding us to think about what the individuals—the commuters and the beggars—were actually experiencing in their interactions in the subway."[48] For Judge Altimari, "[j]urisprudence was important. But the people whose lives were affected by the jurisprudence was paramount."[49]

Other cases also demonstrated Judge Altimari's concern for "human dignity." In *Doe v. City of New York*, the plaintiff

> had filed a complaint with the City of New York Human Rights Commission accusing an airline of refusing to hire him because he was a single gay male suspected to be HIV seropositive. . . . A confidentiality clause was made part of the agreement, but the Commission issued a press release. . . . [T]he release did not identify the plaintiff, [but] the plaintiff considered that the release included information that allowed him to be identified.[50]

Altimari wrote that "[i]ndividuals who are infected with the HIV virus clearly possess a constitutional right to privacy regarding their condition."[51] Judge Miner later remarked that Judge Altimari's opinion "demonstrated his understanding of human nature as well as the part (albeit small) that courts can play in promoting societal concepts of human ethical conduct."[52]

In *Ayala v. Speckard*, a habeas petitioner brought a Sixth Amendment challenge based on the closure of the courtroom during testimony of an undercover officer.[53] Judge Altimari ordered that the writ be issued, stressing the importance of the right to a public trial and concluding the police officer's fear of public testimony was not particularized enough to justify closure. "Judge Altimari felt very strongly . . . [that] 'trial courts are under an absolute duty to consider possible alternatives to complete courtroom closure.'"[54] This time, when an *en banc* was called, the full court did not agree with his position: the court concluded that the prosecution sufficiently justified the courtroom closure.[55]

Judge Ralph K. Winter described Judge Altimari as "the salt of the earth, a deeply religious man devoted to his family, a man from what has unfortunately come to be known as the old school."[56] Father John Coughlin added: "He loved to attend early morning Mass at St. Andrew's Church located adjacent to [the Thurgood Marshall United States Courthouse]."[57] He would visit the church to pray when a troubling case was before the court.[58]

Judge Altimari once observed, in a civil rights case about a judge's dismissal of a law clerk, "The working relationship between a judge and her law clerk . . . is unique."[59] Such was the case with Judge Altimari and his clerks. When law clerks went to talk with the judge about a case, they would notice a small sign "[a]bove the door to his chambers . . . that read 'Strive for Perfection, Settle for Excellence.'"[60] Beyond the sign, clerks would then get to sit "in one of the big leather chairs in front of the Judge's desk, listening to him analyze cases, or talk on the phone with other judges, former clerks or members of his family—until he kicked you out of his office and told you to get back to work."[61] Judge Altimari "enjoyed discussing the cases before him with his law clerks and listened attentively to different points of view."[62] "Ultimately, such discourse would yield to reason and fairness; and the judicial process (and usually the Judge) would win."[63]

When Judge Altimari did not "win" with his colleagues on the court, he was not reluctant to voice his opinion through a dissent.[64] In a law review article about his decision writing, he acknowledged that he broke from his fellow panel members more often than most—about ten percent of the time.[65] That discovery didn't bother him, because he believed that while "dissenting merely for the sake of dissenting is pointless . . . when a member of a panel disagree[d] over deeply felt values, he or she ha[d] a duty to articulate his or her disagreement."[66] He added: "[T]he writing of a principled dissent is one of the most important obligations of an appellate judge," because "often times the dissent serves as the blueprint for a new majority opinion."[67]

Two cases illustrate his approach to dissenting. In *Bellamy v. Cogdell*, a prisoner sought a writ of habeas corpus, arguing that he had received ineffective assistance of trial counsel.[68] Even though his attorney admitted he was incapacitated prior to trial and was suspended after trial by the disciplinary committee, the district court denied relief.[69] On appeal, a divided panel concluded that counsel was *per se* ineffective and reversed and remanded the case; Judge Altimari dissented, reasoning that the attorney's performance neither fell into the limited categories of *per se* ineffectiveness nor qualified as ineffective under *Strickland v. Washington.*[70] An *en banc* panel was called and Judge Altimari "got his revenge."[71] Writing for a closely divided seven-to-six *en banc* court, Altimari wrote that the attorney was not ineffective and that the conviction stood.[72] Judge Feinberg, who had been on the original three-member panel, argued in dissent that the new majority simply did not like the panel decision and that use of the court's *en banc* power in this case was a waste of time.[73]

In *Pro-Choice Network v. Schenck*,[74] Judge Altimari joined the opinion of a divided panel that struck down provisions of an injunction regulating abortion clinic protests. The injunction created a "buffer zone" around the building, where only two "sidewalk counselors" could patrol. Those sidewalk counselors were required to cease and desist if a patient asked to be left alone.[75] The court, sitting *en banc*, reversed the panel decision and concluded that the injunction burdened no more speech than necessary to achieve the state's significant interests.[76] Judge Altimari dissented from the *en banc* decision, arguing that the majority had "departed from a proud tradition of zealously protecting the most fundamental of the freedoms bequeathed to us by our forefathers—the right to speak freely."[77] In his view, had abortion not been at issue, the panel decision "would have occasioned little interest and no notoriety."[78] The Supreme Court ruled that the buffer zone violated the First Amendment, but the "cease and desist" provision did not.[79]

Away from the bench, Judge Altimari was a passionate New York Giants football fan.[80] Later in his life, he became a sculptor.[81] He made busts of family members and created many religious works. When the Touro Law School Jewish Law Students Association wanted to establish a Holocaust memorial, the school's dean enlisted Judge Altimari.[82] The judge created a sculpture based on a picture he had found of "a young boy in the Warsaw Ghetto, with a Star of David on his chest and his arms upraised as he was being rounded up."[83] The work, titled "Zachor" (which means "Remember" in Hebrew), is on display at Touro.[84]

In 1998, Judge Altimari died of brain cancer at age 69 at his Old Westbury home.[85] He was buried at the Holy Rood Cemetery.[86]

Gregory Capobianco

1. Roger J. Miner, *Frank X. Altimari – Humanist Judge*, 15 TOURO L. REV. 1411, 1422 (1999).

2. *See* Wolfgang Saxon, *Frank X. Altimari, 69, Judge Who Affirmed Ban on Begging*, N.Y. TIMES, July 21, 1998, at D21.

3. 21 THE AMERICAN CATHOLIC WHO'S WHO, BICENTENNIAL EDITION 6 (A.E.P. Wall ed., 1975).

4. Father John Coughlin, former law clerk, Remarks at a Special Session of the United States Court of Appeals for the Second Circuit, In Memoriam, Honorable Frank X. Altimari 12 (Dec. 9, 1998) (transcript on file with the United States Courts Library for the Second Circuit). Coughlin serves as Global Distinguished Professor of Religious Studies and Law at New York University School of Law.

5. *Id.*

6. *See* THE AMERICAN CATHOLIC WHO'S WHO, *supra* note 3.

7. Chief Judge Ralph K. Winter, Remarks at a Special Session of the United States Court of Appeals for the Second Circuit, In Memoriam, Honorable Frank X. Altimari 3 (Dec. 9, 1998) (transcript on file with the United States Courts Library for the Second Circuit).

8. Saxon, *supra* note 2, at D21.
9. *See* THE AMERICAN CATHOLIC WHO'S WHO, *supra* note 3.
10. SOL WACHTLER, AFTER THE MADNESS: A JUDGE'S OWN PRISON MEMOIR 144 (1997).
11. THE AMERICAN CATHOLIC WHO'S WHO, *supra* note 3.
12. WACHTLER, *supra* note 10.
13. *Id.*
14. Saxon, *supra* note 2, at D21; THE AMERICAN CATHOLIC WHO'S WHO, *supra* note 3.
15. THE AMERICAN CATHOLIC WHO'S WHO, *supra* note 3.
16. WACHTLER, *supra* note 10, at 145.
17. *Id.*
18. *Id.*
19. *Id.*
20. *Id.*
21. R.W. Apple Jr., *Court Rules Vote in Nassau Is a Tie*, N.Y. TIMES, May 28, 1965, at 35.
22. *Id.*
23. Roy R. Silver, *Nassau Judgeship is Won by One Vote*, N.Y. TIMES, Nov. 17, 1964, at 1.
24. *Nassau Republican Who 'Lost' by 1 Vote Wins Recount by 5*, N.Y. TIMES, Dec. 18, 1964, at 22.
25. *Id.*
26. *Id.*
27. Apple Jr., *supra* note 21, at 35.
28. Silver, *supra* note 23, at 23.
29. *Id.* at 1; WACHTLER, *supra* note 10, at 145.
30. WACHTLER, *supra* note 10, at 145.
31. *See* THE AMERICAN CATHOLIC WHO'S WHO, *supra* note 3.
32. *Id.*
33. *D'Amato Recommends 3 to Be U.S. District Judges*, N.Y. TIMES, Aug. 19, 1982, at B6.
34. Saxon, *supra* note 2, at D21.
35. Arnold H. Lubasch, *D'Amato Suggests Several as Judges*, N.Y. TIMES, Feb. 24, 1985, at 37.
36. Saxon, *supra* note 2, at D21.
37. Chief Judge Wilfred Feinberg, Remarks at the Proceedings Held on the Occasion of the Induction of Honorable Frank X. Altimari 2 (Jan. 27, 1986) (transcript on file with the United States Courts Library for the Second Circuit).
38. Miner, *supra* note 1, at 1422.
39. Linda Johnston, former law clerk, Remarks at a Special Session of the United States Court of Appeals for the Second Circuit, In Memoriam, Honorable Frank X. Altimari 11 (Dec. 9, 1998) (transcript on file with the United States Courts Library for the Second Circuit). Johnston is currently a novelist.
40. *Id.*
41. Magistrate Judge Michael Orenstein, Remarks at a Special Session of the United States Court of Appeals for the Second Circuit, In Memoriam, Honorable Frank X. Altimari 6 (Dec. 9, 1998) (transcript on file with the United States Courts Library for the Second Circuit).
42. E-mail from Michael A. Gerstenzang, former law clerk, to Sally Pritchard (Aug. 20, 2015, 2:24 EST) (on file with the United States Courts Library for the Second Circuit). Gerstenzang is currently partner at Cleary, Gottlieb, Steen & Hamilton, LLP.
43. Miner, *supra* note 1, at 1411.
44. 903 F.2d 146 (1990).
45. *Id.*
46. Craig Wolff, *U.S. Appeals Court Upholds Ban on Begging in New York Subways*, N.Y. TIMES, May 11, 1990, at A1.
47. Miner, *supra* note 1, at 1413–14 (footnote omitted).

48. Gerstenzang, *supra* note 42.
49. *Id.*
50. Miner, *supra* note 1, at 1416–17 (footnotes omitted).
51. Doe v. City of New York, 15 F.3d 264, 266 (2d Cir. 1994).
52. Miner, *supra* note 1, at 1418.
53. 89 F.3d 91 (2d Cir. 1996), *vacated on reh'g*, 131 F.3d 62 (2d Cir. 1997).
54. Miner, *supra* note 1, at 1419 (quoting *Ayala*, 89 F.3d at 96).
55. *Speckard*, 131 F.3d at 72.
56. Chief Judge Ralph K. Winter, Remarks, *supra* note 7, at 3.
57. Coughlin, Remarks, *supra* note 4, at 14.
58. *Id.*
59. Sheppard v. Beerman, 18 F.3d 147, 152 (2d Cir. 1994).
60. Email from Michael A. Gerstenzang, *supra* note 42.
61. *Id.*
62. Johnston, Remarks, *supra* note 39, at 11.
63. *Id.*
64. *See* Magistrate Judge Michael Orenstein, Remarks, *supra* note 41, at 6.
65. Frank X. Altimari, *The Practice of Dissenting in the Second Circuit*, 59 BROOK. L. REV. 275 (1993).
66. *Id.* at 280.
67. *Id.* at 279, 284.
68. 952 F.2d 626 (2d Cir. 1991), *vacated on reh'g*, 974 F.2d 302 (2d Cir. 1992).
69. *Id.*
70. *Id.* at 631–32 (Altimari, J., dissenting); 466 U.S. 668 (1984).
71. David Margolick, *When a Convict Says His Lawyer Was Too Sick, a Federal Appeal Panel Replies, in Effect, Too Bad.*, N.Y. TIMES: AT THE BAR, Sept. 18, 1992, at A22.
72. *Bellamy*, 974 F.2d at 309.
73. *Id.* at 309–13 (Feinberg, J., dissenting).
74. 67 F.3d 359 (2d Cir. 1994), *vacated in part on reh'g*, 67 F.3d 377 (2d Cir. 1995) (en banc), *aff'd in part, rev'd in part sub nom.* Schenck v. Pro-Choice Network, 519 U.S. 357 (1997).
75. *Id.* at 371.
76. *Pro-Choice Network*, 67 F.3d 377, *affd in part, revd in part*, 519 U.S. 357.
77. *Id.* at 409 (Altimari, J., dissenting).
78. *Id.*
79. *Schenck*, 519 U.S. 357.
80. Chief Judge Ralph K. Winter, Remarks, *supra* note 7, at 3.
81. Magistrate Judge Michael Orenstein, Remarks, *supra* note 41, at 8.
82. Howard Glickstein, Remarks at a Special Session of the United States Court of Appeals for the Second Circuit, In Memoriam, Honorable Frank X. Altimari 17 (Dec. 9, 1998) (transcript on file with the United States Courts Library for the Second Circuit). Glickstein is the dean of Touro Law School.
83. *Id.*
84. *Id.*
85. Saxon, *supra* note 2, at D21.
86. Chau Lam, *Obituary of Frank X. Altimari*, NEWSDAY (July 22, 1998).

# JOHN DANIEL MAHONEY
# 1931-1996

Court of Appeals for the Second Circuit: 1986-1996

"It may seem trite to describe someone as a man of principle, but Dan virtually defined the phrase."[1]

John Daniel Mahoney was born in Orange, New Jersey in 1931 to an Irish Catholic family.[2] A friend recalled: "Dan was one of the most religious people I have ever known, a daily communicant. I think he spent more time in church than many priests I know."[3] Mahoney graduated *magna cum laude* from St. Bonaventure University in 1952 and went to Columbia Law School, where he was a Kent Scholar.[4] He graduated in 1955.[5] Mahoney married Kathleen O'Doherty that same year.[6] They had six children, Daniel, Kieran, Francis, Mary, Eileen, and Elizabeth.[7]

After law school, he served three years as a lieutenant in the Coast Guard during the Korean War.[8] He "liked to remark that he had protected the country from invasion by the Koreans in the soft underbelly of Mobile, Alabama."[9]

After leaving the service, Mahoney joined Simpson, Thacher & Bartlett in 1958 as an associate in the tax department.[10] A friend at the firm recalled: "Dan and I had grown up with people named Tom, Dick, Harry, Mike, Tony and Sid. At Simpson, Thacher we encountered people with first names like Bay, Burr, East, Fifield, Courtland and Whitney."[11] Mahoney, nevertheless, adapted quickly.[12]

In 1962, Mahoney left the firm to found the Conservative Party of New York with Kathleen's brother, Kieran O'Doherty.[13] Mahoney's colleagues reacted with skepticism to this "quixotic enterprise."[14] Mahoney recalled, "It was as if I had announced an intention to take nine months off and become an opera star."[15] The Conservative Party was founded in response to the policies of Governor Nelson Rockefeller and Senator Jacob Javits, both "liberal" Republicans, and as a counterweight to New York's Liberal Party. When Mahoney first announced to Kathleen that he and Kieran were going to found the party, she asked, "Have you got time for dinner first?"[16] The news could hardly have been a shock: the "O'Doherty family had always had a consuming interest in politics and conservatism" and was active in efforts to get conservative Republicans elected against liberal Republicans.[17]

Mahoney outlined the Conservative Party's plans in a "political prospectus": "We envision the creation of a fourth political party in New York State, the Conservative Party. Like the present Liberal Party, it would exercise leverage upon the major political parties by endorsing and working for candidates from either party whose views paralleled its own, and running its own candidates where acceptable major party candidates were not put forth."[18] In Mahoney's view, the Republican ticket, topped by Governor Rockefeller and Senator Javits, threatened to destroy the two-party system by foreclosing an alternative to Democratic policies. Mahoney stated, "We're struggling toward an honest two-party system between liberals and conservatives on a national level."[19]

The Conservative Party began with a targeted mailing that elicited the support of many influential professionals, including law professors at New York University School of Law and senior editors of the *National Review*.[20] The Conservative Party opened its headquarters in Manhattan on April 1, 1962, a date Mahoney "hoped . . . would not prove symbolic."[21] Kathleen worked at headquarters full time, and became, as Mahoney observed, "indispensable to a successful organizing effort."[22] The first Conservative Party candidate for governor was David Jaquith, who received 141,877 votes.[23]

Mahoney announced during a television interview that the Conservative Party intended to run a candidate for mayor of New York City in 1965.[24] The candidacy of Bill Buckley, "one of the biggest figures in American conservatism," thereafter "simply dropped into the lap of the Conservative Party."[25] Buckley garnered 341,226 votes, 13.4% of the vote, in the election that sent the Republican candidate, John V. Lindsay, to City Hall.[26] In the Conservative Party's only state-wide victory, James Buckley, Bill's brother, was elected a U.S. senator.[27] He is now a senior judge on the Court of Appeals for the District of Columbia.[28]

Mahoney resumed the practice of law in 1966 as a partner at Wormser, Kiely, Alessandroni, Mahoney & McCann.[29] He switched his focus to litigation and corporate work, "apparently having buried his tax knowledge with the Conservative Party."[30] Mahoney continued as the Conservative Party's state chairman part time.[31]

Buoyed by strong election showings, the Conservative Party sought to wrest Row C on the ballot from the Liberal Party.[32] In New York, the ballot positions were determined by the performance in the preceding gubernatorial election.[33] The Conservative Party selected Paul Adams as its gubernatorial candidate for the 1966 election.[34] The goal was simply to get more votes than the Liberal Party. Mahoney observed that the Liberal Party's choice of Franklin Delano Roosevelt, Jr. (who "stunned many political observers" by breaking from the Democrats) as its candidate for governor "lengthened the odds against our winning Row C immeasurably."[35] The unofficial tally had Roosevelt leading Adams. But the official numbers came in a few weeks later: Adams had 510,023 votes to Roosevelt's 507,234.[36] Mahoney remarked, "We had won the contest by 2,789 beautiful votes"—and Row C along with it.[37]

Mahoney's book chronicling the early years of the Conservative Party, *Actions Speak Louder: The Story of the New York Conservative Party*, ended by predicting that Ronald Reagan's 1966 gubernatorial victory in California was a sign of things to come.[38] Mahoney called for "maximum support" of Reagan in a presidential bid.[39] The Conservative Party complied, endorsing Reagan in 1976 against incumbent Gerald Ford, and again in 1980, giving Reagan Row C in addition to the Republican line on the ballot.[40] The Conservative Party endorsement provided Reagan's margin of victory in New York in 1980.[41]

Mahoney, who had by then joined Windels, Marx, Davies & Ives, left private practice and resigned from the chairmanship of the Conservative Party in 1986, when President Ronald Reagan appointed him to a seat on the Court of Appeals for the Second Circuit.[42]

Mahoney's ascent to the Second Circuit paralleled that of Judge Paul Hays, the former chairman of the Liberal Party nominated by President John F. Kennedy, who had enjoyed the Liberal Party's endorsement. On that account, Hays's nomination had generated some controversy.[43] By contrast, Mahoney's "Senate Judiciary Committee hearings consisted of mild questioning . . . and an endorsement by [New York's] Democratic Senator, Daniel Patrick Moynihan."[44] Mahoney complained that he "seem[ed] to be insultingly noncontroversial."[45] Mahoney preemptively declared his judicial independence: "It's not a question of ideology; it's understanding that a judge is supposed to be impartial and should not use the judiciary as a platform for proselytizing any personal views."[46] Mahoney analogized himself to an "umpire . . . interpret[ing] other people's rules."[47]

Judge Jon O. Newman remarked: "[T]he measure of Dan Mahoney as a judge is the fact that his work was informed by his talent for law, not his philosophy of politics. He brought to every issue an inquiring mind, a readiness—even an eagerness—to consider all points of view. . . . Dan Mahoney epitomized an open-minded approach to the judicial role. For him, every appeal was an occasion to think about the law. He brought to the task not ideology but ideas."[48] At the same time, Judge Mahoney remained a man of conviction. His law clerks observed, "As befits the founder of the Conservative Party, his approach to judging was a conservative one, by which we mean cautious and restrained, with fidelity to text and tradition."[49] Judge Mahoney "was tenacious in discussions" with other members of the Second Circuit.[50] Judge Ralph K. Winter recalled, "More than once he caused me to change my mind about the outcome [of an appeal] and frequently persuaded me to alter the reasoning of an opinion."[51] Judge Winter wondered why "Rockefeller and Javits hadn't simply given up rather than have to deal with him."[52] Judge Mahoney's tenacity was never divisive; he "was well known for his collegiality with his fellow members of the court," and "even the occasional dissenting drafts were respectful and exchanged without discord."[53]

Judge Mahoney took his job seriously, but not himself. He would often talk of the "massive exception to the democratic principle" that a federal judgeship entailed.[54] A law clerk observed that Judge Mahoney "was a total stranger to self-importance."[55] His clerks would joke with him "that whenever he picked up a ballpoint pen, the pen suddenly became, in Winston Churchill's phrase, 'heavy with destiny.'"[56] Judge Mahoney's "spring-loaded" laugh "filled the room, raised the rafters, and turned heads."[57]

Judge Mahoney "agonized over detail and sought to eliminate all doubt in his mind as to the proper disposition of a case."[58] His editing of law clerks' drafts was legendary. One morning he found a mock *New York Times* headline pinned to his door that read: "ENRAGED JUDGE SAVAGES LAW CLERK'S DRAFT."[59] Judge Mahoney's article discussing the role of law clerks explained, "The key to good writing is rewriting."[60]

Judge Mahoney wrote the opinion in *United States v. Salerno*, upholding 100-year sentences for the ruling "Commission" of the notorious La Cosa Nostra organization.[61] The opinion held that the evidence was sufficient to establish that the defendants, bosses of the various New York mafia families, violated RICO with three schemes: extortion and labor bribery in which the defendants demanded two percent of all New York City concrete construction contracts over $2 million; loansharking in Staten Island; and a plot to murder three mafia members to end internal strife within the Bonanno family.[62]

In another case, Judge Mahoney held that a "freeze out" merger, effectuated to take a company private, does not constitute a "purchase or sale of any security" for purposes of section 10(b) of the Securities Exchange Act of 1934 and Rule 10b-5 of the Securities and Exchange Commission. In *Gelles v. TDA Industries, Inc.,* three insiders, who together owned 82% of TDA Industries, agreed to acquire the remaining 18% of publicly owned stock through a private merger with the public shareholders.[63] The insiders formed a holding company, transferred their shares to it, and then merged it with TDA, buying out the public shareholders with cash.[64] One of the insiders claimed securities fraud when the new concern did not keep him on as a director and senior executive.[65] Judge Mahoney reasoned that the transactions were not "purchase[s] or sale[s]" of a security because the merger was effectively "an internal corporate management decision which only incidentally involve[d] an exchange of shares."[66] Judge Mahoney analogized the merger to "[s]ubstantially similar rearrangements of internal corporate governance . . . that would not even arguably have involved any purchase or sale of Gelles' shares," such as a tender offer or reverse stock split at a sufficiently high ratio to eliminate the public shares.[67]

Judge Mahoney died on October 23, 1996.[68] He was 65. Judge Mahoney had gone home after evening mass to work on an address he was scheduled to give at the University of Notre Dame Law School.[69] Minutes after telling Kathleen that he "finally [had] the Notre Dame speech exactly the way [he] want[ed] it," Judge Mahoney collapsed and died of a brain hemorrhage.[70] His speech was published posthumously by the *Notre Dame Law Review.*[71]

Daniel Principato

1. Judge Ralph K. Winter, Remarks at a Special Session of the United States Court of Appeals for the Second Circuit, In Memoriam, Honorable J. Daniel Mahoney VI (Apr. 30, 1997) (transcript on file with the United States Courts Library for the Second Circuit).

2. FEDERAL JUDICIAL CENTER, Biographical Directory of Federal Judges, John Daniel Mahoney, http://www.fjc.gov/servlet/nGetInfo?jid=1466&cid=999&ctype=na&instate=na.

3. John J. McDermott, Remarks at a Special Session of the United States Court of Appeals for the Second Circuit, In Memoriam, Honorable J. Daniel Mahoney X (Apr. 30, 1997) (transcript on file with the United States Courts Library for the Second Circuit). McDermott was a partner at Windels, Marx, Davies & Ives.

4. FEDERAL BAR COUNCIL, SECOND CIRCUIT REDBOOK 1993-1994 59 (Vincent C. Alexander ed. 1993).

5. *Id.*

6. Lawrence Van Gelder, *Judge J. Daniel Mahoney, 65, Founder of Conservative Party*, N.Y. TIMES, Oct. 26, 1996, at 13.

7. *Id.*

8. *Id.*

9. McDermott, Remarks, *supra* note 3, at X.

10. *Id.*

11. *Id.*

12. *Id.*

13. Van Gelder, *supra* note 6.

14. J. DANIEL MAHONEY, ACTIONS SPEAK LOUDER: THE STORY OF THE NEW YORK CONSERVATIVE PARTY 42 (1968).

15. *Id.*

16. *Id.* at 19.

17. *Id.*

18. *Id.* at 23.

19. Van Gelder, *supra* note 6.

20. MAHONEY, *supra* note 14, at 29.

21. *Id.* at 43.

22. *Id.* at 45.

23. *Id.* at 59-60, 118.

24. *Id.* at 267.

25. *Id.* at 269.

26. *Id.* at 301.

27. Clayton Knowles, *Buckley Will Ask Senate Listing as Conservative-Republican*, N.Y. TIMES, Jan. 18, 1971, at 10; Thomas P. Ronan, *Conservatives Endorse Buckley, Liberal Party Picks Stern for U.S. Senate Race*, N.Y. TIMES, June 13, 1976, at 35.

28. FEDERAL JUDICIAL CENTER, Biographical Directory of Federal Judges, James Lane Buckley, http://www.fjc.gov/servlet/nGetInfo?jid=309&cid=999&ctype=na&instate=na.

29. FEDERAL BAR COUNCIL, *supra* note 4, at 59.

30. McDermott, Remarks, *supra* note 3, at XI.

31. MAHONEY, *supra* note 14, at 265.

32. *Id.* at 307; Clayton Knowles, *'Line C' is Sought by Conservatives*, N.Y. TIMES, July 31, 1966, at 38.

33. MAHONEY, *supra* note 14, at 307.

34. *Id.* at 326.

35. *Id.* at 325; John T. McQuiston, *Franklin Roosevelt Jr., 74, Ex-Congressman, Dies*, N.Y. TIMES, Aug. 18, 1988, at D22.

36. MAHONEY, *supra* note 14, at 337-39.

37. *Id.* at 339. Rockefeller won the general election with more than 2,650,000 votes; *see also* Frank Lynn, *Rocky Wins by 400,000*, NEWSDAY, Nov. 9, 1966, at 1.

38. MAHONEY, *supra* note 14, at 346.

39. *Id.*

40. Maurice Carroll, *Conservatives Give Reagan Line on the New York Ballot*, N.Y. TIMES, Sept. 16, 1980, at B5; Frank Lynn, *Conservative Party to Support Reagan Over Ford for 1976*, N.Y. TIMES, Oct. 21, 1975, at 1.

41. *NY Conservative Eyed for Court*, NEWSDAY, Nov. 3, 1985, at 17.

42. FEDERAL BAR COUNCIL, *supra* note 4, at 59.

43. *Nomination of Paul R. Hays to be United States Circuit Judge for the Second Circuit: Hearing Before the Subcomm. of the S. Comm. on the Judiciary*, 87th Cong. 5-8 (1962) (statement of Judge Paul R. Hays); *Politics and the Federal Bench*, N.Y. TIMES, June 3, 1961, at 22.

44. Frank Lynn, *Conservative Chief Sees Himself an 'Umpire' as Federal Judge*, N.Y. TIMES, Apr. 28, 1986, at 22.

45. *Id.*

46. *Id.*

47. *Id.*

48. Chief Judge Jon O. Newman, Remarks at a Special Session of the United States Court of Appeals for the Second Circuit, In Memoriam, Honorable J. Daniel Mahoney V (Apr. 30, 1997) (transcript on file with the United States Courts Library for the Second Circuit).

49. E-mail from Michael S. Fried & Christian G. Vergonis, former law clerks, to Sally Pritchard (Sept. 1, 2015, 4:46 EST) (on file with the United States Courts Library for the Second Circuit). Fried and Vergonis are both partners at Jones Day.

50. Judge Ralph K. Winter, Remarks, *supra* note 1, at VI.

51. *Id.*

52. *Id.*

53. Email from Fried & Vergonis, *supra* note 49.

54. John P. McConnell, former law clerk, Remarks at a Special Session of the United States Court of Appeals for the Second Circuit, In Memoriam, Honorable J. Daniel Mahoney IX (Apr. 30, 1997) (transcript on file with the United States Courts Library for the Second Circuit). McConnell served as a speechwriter for President George W. Bush and Vice President Dick Cheney.

55. *Id.*

56. *Id.*

57. *Id.*

58. *Id.* at VI.

59. *Id.*

60. J. Daniel Mahoney, *Law Clerks: For Better or For Worse?*, 54 BROOK. L. REV. 321, 343 (1988).

61. 868 F.2d 524 (2d Cir. 1989).

62. *Id.* at 528-34.

63. 44 F.3d 102 (2d Cir. 1994).

64. *Id.* at 103.

65. *Id.*

66. *Id.* at 104 (internal quotation marks omitted).

67. *Id.* at 105.

68. Charles E. Rice, *This Was a Man*, 72 NOTRE DAME L. REV. 1221, 1221 (1997).

69. *Id.*

70. *Id.*; Van Gelder, *supra* note 6.

71. *See* J. Daniel Mahoney, *Thoughts on Originalism*, 72 NOTRE DAME L. REV. 1225 (1997).

# JOSEPH MICHAEL MCLAUGHLIN
# 1933-2013

District Court for the Eastern District of New York:
1981-1990
Court of Appeals for the Second Circuit: 1990-2013

Judge Joseph M. McLaughlin had an intimidating wit, but as Justice Sonia Sotomayor has recalled, his "bigger-than-life personality and his deadpan face in delivering a joke were always softened by the twinkling in his eye."[1] Judge McLaughlin achieved renown as a scholar and institution-building dean at Fordham Law School before joining the federal bench, where his intellect and wit enlighted the Eastern District, and later, the Second Circuit.

McLaughlin was born on March 20, 1933 in Flatbush, Brooklyn to Irish immigrants Joseph and Mary McLaughlin.[2] As a youth, he attended St. Teresa of Avila Church, where bells bearing the names of Irish saints summoned the faithful to Mass.[3] A staunch Brooklynite, he once took a job operating the Coney Island Parachute Jump.[4] He attended the Brooklyn Preparatory School, a Jesuit high school, and majored in classics at Fordham University.[5] He mastered Latin and Greek and could teach their intricacies even to language scholars. At Fordham, he was a drum major, an announcer at the school's radio station, and a cadet in the Reserve Officer Training Corps.[6] After 16 months of active duty in Korea, McLaughlin plunged into study at Fordham Law School. He was editor-in-chief of the *Fordham Law Review*,[7] and graduated with the highest average in his section.[8] He then did a brief stint with Cahill, Gordon, Reindel & Ohl, where he helped defend NBC in the rigged game-show cases.[9] (The scandal was later portrayed in the film *Quiz Show*.)[10]

In 1961, at the request of his mentor, Dean William Hughes Mulligan, McLaughlin returned to Fordham to teach New York civil practice.[11] The following year, the New York legislature rejected calls to adopt the federal counterpart rules and significantly revised the state's civil practice law, thereby ensuring perpetual employment for specialists in New York procedure.[12] McLaughlin and David Siegel published the definitive early commentaries on the Civil Practice Law and Rules.[13] McLaughlin also co-wrote a leading casebook on New York practice, cementing his authority.[14] His other area of commanding authority was evidence; he served as editor-in-chief of *Weinstein's Federal Evidence*. Students loved McLaughlin. Professor Gail Hollister recalled McLaughlin as "the greatest teacher I ever met. Learning and laughter flourished in his class, and so much of what he taught us lingers in my mind."[15] Another student recalled, "Studying New York Practice can be like reading the phone book. . . . Judge McLaughlin made the phone book sing."[16] McLaughlin nurtured "scrappy, smart lawyers who were ethical and engaged."[17] He taught through humor, illustrating difficult legal concepts with the annals of Del Vermo, a colorful murderer he created "to keep the students focused."[18] McLaughlin introduced Del Vermo to at least two federal judges: Second Circuit Judge Denny Chin, who attended

Fordham,[19] and Southern District Judge John Koeltl, one of many future judges who took McLaughlin's popular bar study course.[20]

When Dean Mulligan joined the Second Circuit in 1971, McLaughlin succeeded him as dean of Fordham Law School.[21] Answering Mulligan's erstwhile office phone, McLaughlin told a caller, biblically, "He is not here . . . for he is risen as he said he would."[22]

Dean McLaughlin was "a master builder" of Fordham Law School,[23] who inherited his post at a time of social and political upheaval.[24] Dean McLaughlin responded constructively to student discontent by introducing the *Fordham Urban Law Journal* and authorizing Fordham's first clinical programs.[25] At the same time, he oversaw a tenfold increase in alumni giving, established elective courses and an employment placement office, and intensified on-campus recruiting by law firms.[26] He also hired some of the faculty's first women.[27] He foresaw the demand for increased legal specialization, but insisted that law schools should emphasize essential skills: "A sound legal education is what is left after what has been learned has been forgotten."[28]

McLaughlin's influence extended beyond Fordham. In 1961, he served on the New York City Charter Revision Commission, which proposed strengthening the mayor's office and expanding the City Council.[29] From 1975 until 1982, he chaired the New York State Law Revision Commission, a standing body of the New York State government, which, among other things during McLaughlin's tenure, helped recodify the Insurance Law, and suggested revisions to parts of the New York Uniform Commercial Code, the Public Officers Law, and the Criminal Code.[30] In 1976, he mediated labor misconduct claims against picketing New York City police.[31]

In 1981, President Ronald Reagan appointed McLaughlin to the District Court for the Eastern District of New York, on the recommendation of the newly elected Senator Alfonse D'Amato.[32] Judge McLaughlin's appointment put a Queens resident on the Eastern District bench, a fact that Judge José A. Cabranes would later surmise had not been lost on Senator D'Amato.[33] Despite Judge McLaughlin's manifest qualifications for appointment, he had a noticeable lack of federal trial experience. At Judge McLaughlin's induction ceremony, Chief Judge Jack B. Weinstein quipped, "Dean McLaughlin is a living example of misspent scholarship. We both trained to be expert on New York practice and evidence, and, as a result, we were appointed to the Federal bench, where this knowledge is largely useless."[34]

As soon as Judge McLaughlin joined the Eastern District, he came close to leaving it. In December 1982, the State Commission on Judicial Nomination recommended Judge McLaughlin, along with three others, to fill a vacancy on the New York State Court of Appeals,[35] which was ultimately filled by Richard D. Simons.[36]

Judge McLaughlin oversaw two high-profile trials involving the Lucchese crime family. Both hinged on testimony from mobster Henry Hill, the subject of the film *Goodfellas*.[37] In the first trial, Lucchese lieutenant Paul Vario was convicted of fraud for arranging a fake job for Hill so that he could get federal probation.[38] In the second, corrupt Teamsters were convicted of extorting air transportation companies at the behest of Vario and other gangsters.[39] The latter case resonated with Judge McLaughlin. As a law clerk recalled, during sentencing Judge McLaughlin

> told the union leader about how his father was an immigrant and got a job as a trolley car conductor, how the union movement enabled his father to support his family, how one of his father's proudest days was introducing his son the federal judge to legendary union leader Mike Quill, and how one of the worst things you could do was sell out working people in order to line your own pockets.[40]

Judge McLaughlin dabbled in international affairs when the mayor of Glen Cove, Long Island banned Soviet diplomats from the town's beach—even though the Soviets owned a beach estate.[41] Judge McLaughlin ordered the town to let the eight Glen Cove residents use the beach, but upheld the ban against the 250 Soviets who lived in Manhattan.

In 1990, President George H.W. Bush nominated Judge McLaughlin to the Court of Appeals for the Second Circuit.[42] At his induction, Judge McLaughlin confessed that he would "miss ruling on outrageous objections, silly interrogatories, and the general shenanigans that are woven into the fiber of every trial."[43]

He waxed, "[T]rial judges finish the fight and go on to the next battle whereas appellate judges come down from the observation tower, prowl the quiet battlefield, and shoot the survivors."[44] Still, he was ready for the challenge. Adopting the words of the corrupt Medici Pope Leo X, he intoned, "God has given us the Papacy. Let us now enjoy it."[45]

Judge McLaughlin once reflected, "[W]e Irish never hesitate to give a serious thought the benefit and halo of a laugh."[46] He distributed his halos freely. Early in his time on the Second Circuit, a panel reversed his district court opinion affirming the legitimacy of the 1990 U.S. census.[47] When the Supreme Court unanimously reversed the Second Circuit, Judge McLaughlin circulated the following memorandum to his colleagues:

> When you strike at a king, you must kill him.
>
> Magnanimous in victory, Joe.[48]

Judge McLaughlin's warm and beautiful eulogy of Judge Mulligan—his friend, mentor, and predecessor at Fordham and the Second Circuit—was marked with characteristic wit: William Hughes Mulligan "adopted the clerical middle name when he learned that he was a collateral descendent—in those days the clergy did not acknowledge direct descendants—of John Hughes, the first Archbishop of New York."[49]

Judge McLaughlin's memorable speeches were delivered at the annual dinner of the Society of the Friendly Sons of St. Patrick and other civic events.[50] Once, Senator D'Amato asked Judge McLaughlin to give spontaneous remarks at a gathering.[51] The theme was immigration. Rising to the occasion, Judge McLaughlin told the story of how his Uncle Mike, upon arrival on these shores, was asked by an immigration official, "Do you advocate the overthrow of the government of the United States by force or by arms?" Uncle Mike gave the question some thought, and responded, "By force!" Judge McLaughlin did not have an Uncle Mike.

As one of his sons understood it, Judge McLaughlin's humor was "his way of reminding lawyers that they are keepers of a noble profession with an old and grand mystique, invested in honor."[52] Accordingly, he spared the nonlawyers. When a pro se litigant nervously sprinted through her oral argument, Judge

McLaughlin slowed her down, smiled, and politely asked her to explain why she thought the trial court had reached the wrong decision. One law clerk, District Judge Cathy Seibel, recalled the "humility and connection to everyday people" that Judge McLaughlin brought to naturalizations: "He would swear in the new citizens and then tell them his own story."[53]

As another law clerk put it, "The day I reported aboard, the Judge told me that I needed only two things to work for him: a sense of loyalty and a sense of humor. He neglected to tell me that most of the humor would be at my expense."[54] The kidding was Judge McLaughlin's way of treating his clerks like family. Fridays, he took them out to the local red sauce joint, where he knew the owner and all the regulars.[55] St. Patrick's Day began in chambers with a screening of John Ford's Irish idyll *The Quiet Man*, progressed to a local pub for Irish stout and Irish song, and concluded at Judge McLaughlin's home, where his wife served corned beef and cabbage.[56]

In one appeal, Judge McLaughlin weighed the First Amendment rights of a law clerk in a judge's chambers.[57] Brian Sheppard, a law clerk to a New York State Supreme Court justice, had been fired after calling his judge "corrupt" and a "son of a bitch."[58] Sheppard sued, arguing that the firing had violated his right to free speech. Reversing the district court's judgment against Sheppard, Judge McLaughlin acknowledged that "[i]f a judge cannot believe that his clerk is competent, loyal, and discreet, the working relationship between the two is not just injured, it is nonexistent."[59] "But," he added, "the First Amendment protects the eloquent and insolent alike."[60] Despite his own misgivings, Judge McLaughlin allowed the disloyal law clerk his day in court. (Sheppard ultimately lost.)[61]

Judge McLaughlin, the procedure expert, made a significant contribution to class action law with *In re Drexel Burnham Lambert Group, Inc.*[62] Drexel, which had made a fortune selling junk bonds, declared bankruptcy.[63] The SEC and hundreds of former customers filed claims with the bankruptcy court arising from Drexel's illegal securities sales, and those claims threatened to overwhelm Drexel's assets. To save the bankruptcy proceedings, the district court withdrew the securities claims from the bankruptcy court and established mandatory subclasses, which negotiated a global settlement of the claims. Federal Rule of Civil Procedure 23(b)(1)(B) authorizes a mandatory class to settle claims on a limited fund, but it does not plainly authorize a mandatory class to settle claims in bankruptcy.[64] Writing for the panel, Judge McLaughlin approved the settlement. He held that because the claimants had voluntarily submitted their claims to the district court, the district court had jurisdiction to settle them as it saw fit. Judge McLaughlin also deferred to the district court's finding that the claimants had been fairly represented in the settlement negotiations. In the words of a later panel, Judge McLaughlin authorized an "adventuresome use of a class action settlement" that inspired further productive experiments in settling complex cases.[65]

In another case arising from 1980s Wall Street, Judge McLaughlin reversed the conviction of John Mulheren, an associate of the infamous Ivan Boesky.[66] The case turned on whether Boesky had asked Mulheren to manipulate a stock's price when he told Mulheren "it would be great" if the stock "traded at 45."[67] Judge McLaughlin concluded that a criminal conviction based on that "threadbare phrase . . . defies reason and a sense of fair play."[68]

In *Karibian v. Columbia University*, Judge McLaughlin held that a victim of sexual harassment could sue her employer even if she had suffered no economic harm.[69] Karibian, a fundraiser for Columbia University, submitted to her supervisor's sexual advances in exchange for favorable work conditions.[70] The district court dismissed her discrimination suit on the ground that the sexual relationship had not harmed her economically, but rather had led to promotions and other benefits. Judge McLaughlin reversed. He wrote, "We do not read Title VII to punish the victims of sexual harassment who surrender to unwelcome sexual encounters. Such a rule would only encourage harassers to increase their persistence."[71]

*United States v. Cutler* reunited Judge McLaughlin with the mob.[72] During John Gotti's trial, his lawyer Bruce Cutler told the press that the government had "thrown the Constitution out the window," compared the trial to McCarthyism, and leaked inaccurate details about trial evidence.[73] The district court ordered Cutler to stop making public comments about the case. When Cutler kept giving interviews, the court held him in contempt. Judge McLaughlin affirmed the conviction:

> Trial practice, whether criminal or civil, is not a contact sport. And, its tactics do not include eye-gouging or shin-kicking. In this case, a conscientious trial judge tried mightily to limit the lawyers to press statements that were accurate and fair. The defendant's statements were dipped in venom and were deliberately couched to poison the well from which the jury would be selected.[74]

In 2013, Judge McLaughlin succumbed to pneumonia in a Queens nursing home.[75] He left behind his wife, Frances, three sons, a daughter, and 13 grandchildren. His namesake, Joseph M. McLaughlin, Jr., a partner at Simpson Thacher & Bartlett, follows in his father's scholarly footsteps as the author of *McLaughlin on Class Actions*.[76]

Rick Sawyer

1. Chief Judge Robert A. Katzmann, Remarks at a Special Session of the United States Court of Appeals for the Second Circuit, In Memoriam, Honorable Joseph M. McLaughlin (Dec. 11, 2013), *in* 757 F.3d XXXI at XXXIV (quoting Justice Sotomayor).

2. Paul Vitello, *Joseph M. McLaughlin, Judge and Fordham Law Dean, Dies at 80*, N.Y. TIMES, Aug. 14, 2013, at B7.

3. Constantine N. Katsoris, *In the Service of Others: From Rose Hill to Lincoln Center*, 82 FORDHAM L. REV. 1533, 1585 (2014); N.Y.C. CHAPTER OF THE AM. GUILD OF ORGANISTS, ST. THERESA OF AVILA CHURCH, http://www.nycago.org/Organs/Bkln/html/StTeresaAvila.html.

4. Joseph M. McLaughlin, Jr., Remarks at a Special Session of the United States Court of Appeals for the Second Circuit, In Memoriam, Honorable Joseph M. McLaughlin (Dec. 11, 2013), *in* 757 F.3d XXXI at L.

5. John D. Feerick, Remarks at a Special Session of the United States Court of Appeals for the Second Circuit, In Memoriam, Honorable Joseph M. McLaughlin (Dec. 11, 2013), *in* 757 F.3d XXXI at XXXV-VI. Feerick was a personal friend of Judge McLaughlin and succeeded him as dean of Fordham University School of Law.

6. Katsoris, *supra* note 3, at 1586.

7. *See* John D. Feerick, *The Fordham Law Review and Dean Joseph M. McLaughlin: A Combined Tribute*, 50 FORDHAM L. REV. v, vi (1981).

8. *Fordham to Hold Exercises Today*, N.Y. TIMES, June 10, 1959, at 34.

9. Katsoris, *supra* note 3, at 1586; *see, e.g.*, *Clark v. Nat'l Broadcasting Co.*, 22 Misc. 2d 319, 319 (Sup. Ct. N.Y. Cnty. 1960) (including McLaughlin as counsel).

10. QUIZ SHOW (Hollywood Pictures 1994).

11. Feerick, Remarks, *supra* note 5, at XXXV.

12. *See generally* Jack B. Weinstein, *CPLR's Genesis*, 16 N.Y.U. J. LEGIS. & PUB. POL'Y 647 (2013).

13. Katsoris, *supra* note 3, at 1587.

14. HERBERT PETERFREUND & JOSEPH M. MCLAUGHLIN, NEW YORK PRACTICE: CASES AND OTHER MATERIALS (4th ed. 1978).

15. Feerick, Remarks, *supra* note 5, at XXXV.

16. *Fordham Law Mourns Passing of Hon. Joseph M. McLaughlin '59*, FORDHAM UNIVERSITY SCHOOL OF LAW NEWSROOM, http://law.fordham.edu/30521.htm.

17. Katsoris, *supra* note 3, at 1587 (quoting Matthew T. McLaughlin).

18. John D. Feerick, *In Memoriam of Hon. Joseph M. McLaughlin*, 83 FORDHAM L. REV. 1711, 1716 (2015); *see also* Joseph M. McLaughlin, *Objectionable Objections*, 10 LITIG. 32, 33 (1984) (using Del Vermo in examples of evidence problems). Del Vermo's namesake was convicted by spontaneous declaration: "Del Vermo stabbed me with a knife!" People v. Del Vermo, 85 N.E. 690, 692, 696 (1908).

19. Chief Judge Robert A. Katzmann, Remarks, *supra* note 1, at XXXII.

20. Feerick, *In Memoriam*, *supra* note 18, at 1716; *see also* Tom Goldstein, *Summertime Is Cram Time for Students Preparing for Bar Exam*, N.Y. TIMES, July 19, 1976, at 46 (describing McLaughlin's bar study course).

21. Katsoris, *supra* note 3, at 1587, 1589.

22. Joseph M. McLaughlin, *In Memoriam: William Hughes Mulligan*, 65 FORDHAM L. REV. 15, 16 (1996); *see Matthew* 28:6.

23. Feerick, Remarks, *supra* note 5, at XXXVI.

24. Katsoris, *supra* note 3, at 1588-89.

25. *Id.* at 1590-91.

26. *Id.* at 1591.

27. Vitello, *supra* note 2.

28. Joseph M. McLaughlin, *The Future of Fordham Law School*, 49 FORDHAM L. REV. xlvi, xlvii (1980).

29. Peter Kihss, *Stronger Mayor, More Councilmen Asked in Charter*, N.Y. TIMES, July 13, 1961, at 1.

30. NEW YORK STATE LAW REVISION COMMISSION, HONORABLE JOSEPH M. MCLAUGHLIN MEMORIAM, https://lawrevision.state.ny.us/honorable-joseph-w-mclaughlin-memoriam/.

31. *A Fair Proposal*, N.Y. TIMES, Oct. 23, 1976, at 24.

32. John Caher, *Second Circuit Senior Judge McLaughlin Dies at 80*, N.Y. L.J., Aug. 12, 2013.

33. Judge José A. Cabranes, Remarks at a Special Session of the United States Court of Appeals for the Second Circuit, In Memoriam, Honorable Joseph M. McLaughlin (Dec. 11, 2013), *in* 757 F.3d XXXI at XLI.

34. *Id.* (quoting Judge Weinstein).

35. Frank Lynn, *Panel Said to Suggest 4 for Appeals Court Seat*, N.Y. TIMES, Dec. 15, 1982, at B3.

36. Michael Oreskes, *Cuomo Appoints a G.O.P. Judge to Appeals Seat: Upstate Man is Sworn in for State's Top Court*, N.Y. TIMES, Jan. 4, 1983, at A1.

37. GOODFELLAS (Warner Bros. 1990).

38. Pete Bowles, *Reputed Mob Boss Guilty of Fraud*, NEWSDAY, Feb. 10, 1984, at 4.

39. Jesus Rangel, *Trial Starts in Airport Extortion Case*, N.Y. TIMES, Oct. 1, 1986, at B3. The conviction of one Teamster was later reversed on procedural grounds. *See* United States v. Davidoff, 845 F.2d 1151 (2d Cir. 1988).

40. Cathy Seibel, *In Memoriam of Hon. Joseph M. McLaughlin*, 83 FORDHAM L. REV. 1723, 1725 (2015).

41. Pete Bowles, *Judge Opens Glen Cove Sands to 8 Soviets*, NEWSDAY, Sept. 2, 1983, at 6.

42. Vitello, *supra* note 2.

43. Judge Joseph M. McLaughlin, Remarks at the Proceedings Held on the Occasion of the Induction of Honorable Joseph M. McLaughlin as United States Circuit Judge of the United States Circuit Court of Appeals for the Second Circuit 9 (Oct. 26, 1990) (transcript on file with the United States Courts Library for the Second Circuit).

44. *Id.* at 12.

45. *Id.* at 13.

46. McLaughlin, *In Memoriam: William Hughes Mulligan*, *supra* note 22, at 19 (citing Sean O'Casey).

47. *See* City of New York v. U.S. Dep't of Commerce, 34 F.3d 1114 (2d Cir. 1994); *rev'g* 822 F. Supp. 906 (E.D.N.Y. 1993).

48. McLaughlin, Jr., Remarks, *supra* note 4, at LII.

49. McLaughlin, *William Hughes Mulligan*, *supra* note 22, at 15.

50. *See* Judge José A. Cabranes, Remarks, *supra* note 33, at XL.

51. T. Edward Tighe, former law clerk, Remarks at a Special Session of the United States Court of Appeals for the Second Circuit, In Memoriam, Honorable Joseph M. McLaughlin (Dec. 11, 2013), *in* 757 F.3d XXXI at XLVIII (quoting Judge McLaughlin). Tighe is vice president of labor relations to the National Football League.

52. McLaughlin, Jr., Remarks, *supra* note 4, at LII-LIII.

53. Seibel, *supra* note 40, at 1725.

54. Tighe, Remarks, *supra* note 51, at XLV.

55. Seibel, *supra* note 40, at 1724.

56. Tighe, Remarks, *supra* note 51, at XLVII.

57. Sheppard v. Beerman, 94 F.3d 823 (2d Cir. 1996).

58. *Id.* at 826.

59. *Id.* at 829.

60. *Id.*

61. *See* Sheppard v. Beerman, 317 F.3d 351 (2d Cir. 2003).

62. 960 F.2d 285 (2d Cir. 1992).

63. *Id.* at 288.

64. *Id.* at 291-92.

65. In re Joint E. & S. Dist. Asbestos Litig., 982 F.2d 721, 737 (2d Cir. 1992).

66. United States v. Mulheren, 938 F.2d 364 (2d Cir. 1991).

67. *Id.* at 369.

68. *Id.* at 370.

69. 14 F.3d 773, 779 (1994).

70. *Id.* at 776-77.

71. *Id.* at 778.

72. 58 F.3d 825 (2d Cir. 1995).

73. *Id.* at 829, 831.

74. *Id.* at 840.

75. *See* Vitello, *supra* note 2.

76. JOSEPH M. MCLAUGHLIN, MCLAUGHLIN ON CLASS ACTIONS: LAW AND PRACTICE (12th ed. 2015).

# FRED I. PARKER
## 1938-2003

District Court for the District of Vermont: 1990-1994
Court of Appeals for the Second Circuit: 1994-2003

Two days before President Bill Clinton nominated Vermont District Judge Fred I. Parker, a Republican, to the Second Circuit, Parker ruled unconstitutional one of President Clinton's major legislative accomplishments—the Brady Handgun Violence Prevention Act.[1] When asked why he had not waited a mere two days to issue the opinion, Parker replied that such delay would not have been "honest" and, if it would cost him the nomination, then "so be it."[2] Luckily, Clinton was impressed by Parker's "guts," and as a result, the Second Circuit gained (and then prematurely lost) an honest man, an avid sailor, and "one great judge"[3] who "used a ladle to savor life, [but] brought a scalpel to the law."[4]

Parker, born in Boston on February 2, 1938, had humble roots.[5] The son of Geraldine and Walter Parker—a homemaker and a "hard-working plumber who refused to allow his combat injuries to get in the way of making a living"[6]—Parker started out with "little expectation of attending college."[7] He made his way nevertheless: after high school, he served in the Marine Corps Reserve, attended trade school for two years, and worked for a time at an electronics firm before enrolling at the University of Massachusetts, where he graduated *cum laude* in 1962.[8] He carried the lessons of his working-class background with him for his entire life. Many years later, after being appointed to the federal bench, he would describe his hoped-for central character trait as "humility."[9] He attributed it to his father, who advised Parker when he was "feeling indispensable," to "put [his] fist in a bucket of water and then see how much of a hole [he left]."[10]

After college, Parker attended Georgetown University Law Center, where he was classmates with Patrick Leahy, the future Democratic senator from Vermont.[11] Leahy, who would later back Parker's nomination to the Second Circuit, was immediately struck by Parker's "brilliance and wry sense of humor."[12] Parker graduated from Georgetown Law in 1965, after serving as managing editor of the law review.[13]

Parker went to work in Boston as an associate with the firm Lyne, Woodworth & Evarts.[14] After one year, he moved to Burlington, Vermont to join Yandell & Page.[15] Though short, his time in Boston had been eventful: he became engaged to, and married, Barbara (Barbie) Cain, a Cornell graduate who was the director of advertising and promotion for children's books at the Houghton Mifflin publishing company.[16] The couple had two sons: Hawkeye and Bruce.

Parker soon caught the attention of James Jeffords, the newly elected Republican attorney general of Vermont, who hired Parker as one of his deputies in 1969.[17] As part of Jeffords's team, Parker developed and implemented stringent land-use regulations for the areas surrounding Vermont's ski slopes.[18] His most important achievement, however, was as lead attorney in a suit brought by Vermont against New York and the International Paper Company, which owned a mill on the New York side of

Lake Champlain that regularly deposited "mercury-laden sludge" into the lake.[19] Parker successfully convinced the Supreme Court to accept the case under its original jurisdiction, thus advancing a novel argument that the company, by depositing the sludge on the lake floor, had essentially altered the border between New York and Vermont.[20] The case "dragged on for years," but New York and International Paper eventually agreed to a deal under which the company would "abide by the toughest pollution standards" and pay Vermont to monitor its compliance.[21]

Parker returned to private practice in 1972 after Jeffords ran for governor.[22] Parker joined the Middlebury office of Langrock, Sperry, Parker & Wool.[23] A "public-spirited" man, Parker served on numerous professional associations, including the Vermont Criminal Justice Training Council, the Vermont Professional Conduct Board, the Judicial Conduct Board of Vermont, and the Vermont Bar Association's Special Committee for the Reform of the Jury.[24] Aside from his many legal achievements, Parker was also an accomplished sailor, a skill he perfected during his time through many voyages on Lake Champlain, the North Atlantic, and the Caribbean.[25] On one such trip to Bermuda, Parker and his shipmate were caught in a nor'easter that buffeted the ship for some 13 hours and drove it well off course.[26] Parker's only words to his shipmate when he was finally able to get a fix on their position: "Willy, you'll be pleased to know you will not have to shorten the rum ration."[27]

In the late 1980s, Jeffords, who had been elected to the Senate, recommended his former protégé to fill a vacancy on the bench for the District of Vermont.[28] Parker, an "independent, moderate Republican," also had the support of Vermont's Democratic senator—his old law school classmate Patrick Leahy.[29] The administration of President George H.W. Bush reportedly had other plans, however, especially after Parker refused to disclose his views on *Roe v. Wade.*[30] Bucking the tradition of allowing the senator of the president's party to select the nominee for a federal judicial vacancy in the state, the Bush administration nominated another candidate.[31] Incensed, Jeffords blocked all of the administration's other judicial nominees from receiving Senate confirmation.[32] The standoff lasted for 18 months, after which the administration relented and Parker was easily confirmed.[33]

Parker served four years as a district judge, three of them as chief judge.[34] He "relished" the job.[35] As Bernie Lambek, one of Judge Parker's first law clerks, recalled, "He was so patient and calm on the bench, so intelligent, so considerate of the women and men whose dramas unfolded before him."[36]

In 1994, President Clinton nominated Judge Parker to fill the "Vermont seat" on the Second Circuit. This time, it was Vermont's Democratic senator, Patrick Leahy, who recommended him for the post. Convincing Clinton to nominate a Republican was not easy. Senator Leahy recalled a conversation with Judge Parker after his first meeting with the President:

> I called Fred and he asked me how it went. I said, "Fred, I told the President you had three strikes against you. First, you look like an oversized, unmade bed. Secondly, you're a Republican. And thirdly, you're a conservative Republican." There was a stunned silence on the other end of the line. And then Fred said, "I really resent that description. I'm not that conservative."[37]

Clinton overcame his misgivings about nominating a Republican judge who had just invalidated one of his major legislative accomplishments, and Parker was confirmed by the Senate in a unanimous vote.[38]

Judge Parker brought no "ideological baggage" with him to the Second Circuit and strove to make his opinions accessible to "everyday Americans" through his "clear, precise prose."[39] Judge John M. Walker, who described Judge Parker as a "gentle, kind bear of a man," recalled that colleagues "admired the way [he] went about deciding a case," and that he was "[a]lways receptive to new arguments and new ways of looking at a case, never suffer[ing] from the debilitating conceit that he had nothing to learn from others."[40]

Judge Parker was on the panel that affirmed the convictions of those responsible for the 1993 bombing of the World Trade Center, including the blind cleric Abdul Rahman.[41] Each judge on the panel wrote one-third of the per curiam opinion.[42] In another opinion, he wrote that a district judge, exercising the inherent power of the court, need not make a specific finding of bad faith before fining a lawyer who returned late for a jury verdict.[43]

In three habeas appeals, Judge Parker dissented from the court's *en banc* decision upholding courtroom closures during testimony of undercover police officers.[44] The majority reasoned that the state had "an extremely substantial interest" in the continued effectiveness of undercover police, an interest that was likely to be prejudiced by testimony in open court. A trial judge was not obliged to consider *sua sponte* alternatives to the closures at issue. Joined by two of his colleagues (the original panel in one of the cases), Judge Parker contended that a trial judge must *sua sponte* consider alternatives to closing the courtroom.[45] In a case with some risible aspects, he was on a panel that ruled a Muppet character named "Spa'am" did not infringe nor dilute Hormel's lunch meat trademark.[46]

On August 12, 2003, after only nine years on the Second Circuit, Judge Parker died unexpectedly in Burlington while undergoing a procedure to adjust his pacemaker.[47] He was 65. Shortly after his death, Judge Parker's family and friends deposited his ashes into the Lake Champlain waters that he loved so well and had worked so hard to protect.[48]

Lucas Buzzard

1. Chief Judge John M. Walker, Remarks at the Special Session of the United States Court of Appeals for the Second Circuit In Memoriam, Honorable Fred I. Parker (Dec. 17, 2003) *in* 390 F.3d XXIX, at XXXIX (reading letter from Senator Patrick Leahy).

2. *Id.*; Wolfgang Saxon, *Judge Fred I. Parker, 65; Served on the Second Circuit*, N.Y. TIMES, Aug. 14, 2003, at B8.

3. Chief Judge John M. Walker, Remarks, *supra* note 1, at XXXVIII (reading letter from Sen. Patrick Leahy); Judge James L. Oakes, Remarks at the Special Session of the United States Court of Appeals for the Second Circuit In Memoriam, Honorable Fred I. Parker (Dec. 17, 2003) *in* 390 F.3d XXIX, at XXXIII.

4. Bernie Lambek, former law clerk, Remarks at the Special Session of the United States Court of Appeals for the Second Circuit In Memoriam, Honorable Fred I. Parker (Dec. 17, 2003) *in* 390 F.3d XXIX, at XXXVII. Lambek is a partner at Zalinger, Cameron & Lambek.

5. Judge James L. Oakes, Remarks, *supra* note 3, at XXXII.

6. James Jeffords, *Please Join Me in Saying, 'Thanks Fred'*, 8 VT. LAWYER, July 31, 2003, at 7.

7. Christopher Graff, *Parker, Federal Judge, Dies at 65*, RUTLAND HERALD, Aug. 13, 2003, at 1.

8. *Id.*; Judge James L. Oakes, Remarks, *supra* note 3, at XXXII.

9. Jeffords, *supra* note 6, at 7.

10. *Id.*

11. Chief Judge John M. Walker, Remarks, *supra* note 1, at XXXIX (reading letter from Senator Patrick Leahy).

12. *Id.*

13. Judge James L. Oakes, Remarks, *supra* note 3, at XXXII.

14. *Id.*

15. *Id.*

16. *Fred Parker Fiance of Barbara Cain*, N.Y. TIMES, Nov. 21, 1965, at K105.

17. Jeffords, *supra* note 6, at 7.

18. *Id.*

19. *Id.*

20. *Id.*; *see* Vermont v. New York, 406 U.S. 186 (1972).

21. Jeffords, *supra* note 6, at 7.

22. Peter Langrock, Remarks at the Special Session of the United States Court of Appeals for the Second Circuit In Memoriam, Honorable Fred I. Parker (Dec. 17, 2003) *in* 390 F.3d XXIX, at XXXIV. Langrock was Judge Parker's law partner from 1972-1990 and is currently parter at Langrock, Sperry & Wool.

23. Judge James L. Oakes, Remarks, *supra* note 3, at XXXII; Saxon, *supra* note 2, at B8.

24. Judge James L. Oakes, Remarks, *supra* note 3, at XXXII.

25. Bill Dunn, *Fred Parker*, THE BINNACLE: MONTHLY NEWSLETTER OF THE LAKE CHAMPLAIN YACHT CLUB, Aug.-Sept. 2003, at 1.

26. *Id.*

27. *Id.*

28. Jeffords, *supra* note 6, at 7.

29. Saxon, *supra* note 2, at B8.

30. Judge James L. Oakes, Remarks, *supra* note 3, at XXXII.

31. Jeffords, *supra* note 6, at 7.

32. *Id.*

33. *Id.*

34. Judge James L. Oakes, Remarks, *supra* note 3, at XXXIII.

35. Lambek, Remarks, *supra* note 4, at XXXVI.

36. *Id.*

37. Chief Judge John M. Walker, Remarks, *supra* note 1, at XXXVIII-XXXIX (reading letter from Senator Patrick Leahy).

38. *Id.* at XXXIX.

39. *Id.* at XXXVIII.

[39] *Id.* at XXX, XXXII.

41. *Id.* at XXXIII; *see* United States v. Rahman, 189 F.3d 88 (2d Cir. 1999) (*per curiam*).

42. *Rahman*, 189 F.3d at 88.

43. United States v. Seltzer, 227 F.3d 36 (2d Cir. 2000).

44. Ayala v. Speckard, 131 F.3d 62 (2d Cir. 1997) (*en banc*).

45. *Id.* at 75.

46. Hormel Foods Corp. v. Jim Henson Prod., 73 F.3d 497 (2d Cir. 1996).

47. Graff, *supra* note 7, at 1.

48. Dunn, *supra* note 25, at 1.

# THE CURRENT COURT

The following pages document the life and work of each current member of the Court of Appeals for the Second Circuit. Many of the biographies were written by the judges themselves.

# JON O. NEWMAN
# 1932-

District Court for the
District of Connecticut: 1972-1979
Court of Appeals for the Second Circuit: 1979-

Jon O. Newman was born to Harold W. Newman, Jr., and Estelle Ormond on May 2, 1932, in New York City. After living for brief intervals in Summit, New Jersey, Washington, D.C., and New York City, he moved with his family to Connecticut at age eight and, except for a brief return to New York City, lived in Connecticut for the next 72 years.

Newman went to the Hotchkiss School in Lakeville, Connecticut, and graduated from Princeton University and Yale Law School. He was a law clerk for Judge George T. Washington at the Court of Appeals for the District of Columbia Circuit and senior law clerk to Chief Justice Earl Warren.

Returning to Connecticut, Newman combined law practice with state government. He served as counsel to the majority at the Connecticut General Assembly and then a series of positions with Abraham Ribicoff: special counsel to the governor, executive assistant to the secretary of Health, Education, and Welfare, and administrative assistant to the Senator.

Back in Connecticut, Newman was United States Attorney for the District of Connecticut from 1964 to 1969. For the next three years he practiced law in Hartford in his own law office.

In 1971, President Richard M. Nixon, on the recommendation of Senator Ribicoff, appointed Newman to the District Court for the District of Connecticut, where he served from 1972 to 1979. In 1977, President Jimmy Carter committed himself to selecting nominees for circuit judgeships from lists sent to him by citizen commissions established in each circuit. For the Second Circuit, the commission consisted of seven lawyers and six nonlawyers. In 1978, the Court of Appeals for the Second Circuit was expanded from nine to eleven judges. The commission was asked to submit a list of eight names. Newman and Amalya L. Kearse were on the list, and, in 1979, President Carter appointed them to the Second Circuit.

Judge Newman was chief judge of the Court of Appeals from 1993 to 1997, when he became a senior judge.

Throughout his judicial career, Judge Newman has been heavily involved in community activities. He continues as a longtime member of the board of regents of the University of Hartford, of which he was chairman for five years. He served on the boards of the Hartford Foundation for Public Giving and Hartford's Jewish Community Foundation. In earlier years, he founded Hartford's Neighborhood Legal Services and the Hartford Institute of Criminal and Social Justice.

For many years, he chaired the board of the Friends of the Library of the Friends of the Supreme Court of Israel, which arranged for English translations of the opinions of the Israeli Supreme Court. He has consulted on law reform in China, Russia,

Hungary, Colombia, and Israel. As a consultant to the Ford Foundation, he proposed what became the Police Foundation.

A man of varied interests, Judge Newman compiled (with his father) A GENEALOGICAL CHART OF GREEK MYTHOLOGY,[1] a 263-page book linking 3,673 named figures into one family tree of 20 generations, with citations to ancient sources for every relationship. The book is in libraries throughout the world.

Judge Newman's marriage to Martha G. Silberman ended after 51 years when she died in 2005. They had three children and two grandchildren. In 2007, he married Ann Z. Leventhal. They now live in Sarasota, Florida, spending several months in New York City for court assignments in the spring and fall.

1. HAROLD NEWMAN & JON O. NEWMAN, A GENEALOGICAL CHART OF GREEK MYTHOLOGY (1st ed. 2003).

## AMALYA L. KEARSE
## 1937-

Court of Appeals for the Second Circuit: 1979-

Judge Kearse was born and raised in Vauxhall, New Jersey. Her father, Robert Kearse, was Postmaster of Vauxhall and her mother, Dr. Myra Smith Kearse, was a physician. When Kearse was ready for high school, her parents paid tuition to send her to the highly regarded public high school in a neighboring town, Columbia High School in Maplewood. Many years later Kearse and the actor Roy Scheider became the inaugural inductees in the Columbia High School Hall of Fame.

Kearse's father's ambition to become a lawyer had been thwarted by the Great Depression, and in her undergraduate years as a philosophy major at Wellesley College, Kearse decided that she would become a trial lawyer. Graduating from Wellesley in

1959, Kearse entered the University of Michigan Law School, where she won the freshman moot court competition, became an editor of the *Michigan Law Review*, and graduated *cum laude* in the class of 1962.

At the time that Kearse was looking for a job following law school, there was overt discrimination against women lawyers and there were no black lawyers at all in the Wall Street firms. Nonetheless, Kearse was hired as an associate by Hughes Hubbard & Reed and in 1969 became a partner in the firm. She was a litigator throughout her time in private practice, handling a variety of antitrust, banking, commercial and product liability cases, and concluding her private practice career with a successful argument of an antitrust case in the Supreme Court. In 1979, Kearse became the first woman to be inducted as a fellow of the American College of Trial Lawyers.

President Jimmy Carter appointed Kearse to the Court of Appeals for the Second Circuit in June 1979, the centennial year of the admission of the first woman to the bar in the United States. Judge Kearse is the first woman to serve as a judge of the Second Circuit.

A former competitor in national and international contract bridge tournaments with several national championships and one world championship in pairs or team events, Judge Kearse has written, edited, or translated from the French several books on contract bridge.

Judge Kearse was a member of the University of Michigan Law School Committee of Visitors from 1971 to 1979. Judge Kearse has received, among other honors, the Learned Hand Medal for Excellence in Federal Jurisprudence from the Federal Bar Council. She is a member of the American Law Institute, the Association of the Bar of the City of New York, and the American Academy of Arts and Sciences.

## RALPH K. WINTER
## 1935-

Court of Appeals for the Second Circuit: 1982-
Foreign Intelligence Surveillance Court of Review
(by designation of the
Chief Justice of the United States): 2003-2010

Ralph K. Winter was born on July 30, 1935, in Waterbury, Connecticut. He grew up there and attended the Taft School in Watertown, a few miles away. For college he moved a little farther south, to Yale College, where he received an A.B. degree in 1957.

He remained in New Haven to attend Yale Law School, where he not only received a LL.B. degree in 1960, but also met his wife, the former Kathryn Higgins, a New Haven native who was working in the law school's library.

Winter spent his first two years after law school as a federal judicial law clerk. The first year, from 1960 to 1961, he moved to Wilmington, and served as a law clerk to Chief Judge Caleb M. Wright, of the District Court for the District of Delaware.

The following year, from 1961 to 1962, Winter clerked for a new judge on the Second Circuit, the court on which he would ultimately serve. The new judge was Judge (and later, of course, Justice) Thurgood Marshall, with whom Winter would form a close, lifelong friendship. Judge Marshall was a recess appointment, southern Senators had balked at his nomination, and in late 1961 entered service in sudden and immediate need of help.

Winter came highly recommended by two Yale professors, Louis H. Pollak and Charles L. Black, Jr. It was a Wednesday or Thursday in October when Judge Marshall offered Winter the job. Winter thanked his new boss and mentioned as casually as he could that he was getting married to Kate on Friday. That was fine, Judge Marshall replied, Winter could come in on Tuesday, which he did.

And thus Winter became Thurgood Marshall's first law clerk. Winter had moved back to Connecticut, but as Justice Marshall would recall two decades later at Winter's induction, Winter "commuted from New Haven to New York daily to serve me," something for which Justice Marshall always felt "indebted" to Winter.[1]

After clerking, Winter returned to Yale Law School, turning down offers to practice corporate law in Wilmington. Instead he would teach corporate law and a whole lot more. He served as a full-time member of the Yale Law faculty from 1962 until he entered judicial service in 1982, and at the time of his nomination as a judge was the William K. Townsend Professor of Law, a chair named in honor of an earlier Yale law professor who served on the Second Circuit.

As a law professor, Winter was a jack-of-all-trades—teaching not only corporations, but also torts, constitutional law, antitrust, labor law, and evidence, among other subjects. But as Dean Harry Wellington later observed, "Unlike many jacks of all trades, . . . Ralph [was] master of most. In almost all of his teaching fields he has committed original and important scholarship. His writings [were] stylish but, where appropriate, they reject[ed] conventional wisdom. His scholarship show[ed] his conservative bent, but it also demonstrat[ed] his receptivity to a good idea," and "helped many . . . in the many areas of law he has illuminated, to understand better the relationship between good law and economic reality, and to comprehend the limits of all law in a free society."[2]

Any good corporate law class today, for example, will teach its students about something called the "Cary-Winter debate." There was no debate until Professor Winter came along: a Columbia law professor and former SEC Chairman, William Cary, had written an article in 1974 arguing that states had been engaging in a "race to the bottom" in corporate law: a competition to provide legal regimes that put managers' interests over shareholders'—and urging the federalization of corporate law. Professor Winter responded in 1977 with the then-contrarian contention that regulatory competition was actually producing a race to the *top*: that corporations were economically incentivized to charter themselves in states providing legal regimes that lowered the cost of raising capital by maximizing shareholder value, and that states, seeking corporate franchise fees, responded accordingly.[3] Almost four decades later, the debate continues, with legal empiricists continuing to conduct economic event studies on the efficiency of state corporate law. Most scholars today agree with Professor Winter's remarkable and original insight. Judge Frank Easterbrook of the Court of Appeals for the Seventh Circuit has described the article expounding this insight as "the single most important contribution to the economic analysis of corporate law since Ronald Coase published The Nature of the Firm in 1937."

In the realm of labor law, Professor Winter joined forces with Dean Wellington in 1971 to write a seminal Brookings Institution book on public-sector unionism, *The Unions and the Cities.* The book's thesis: that government was not just another industry, and that politically powerful government-employee unions, through the use of a legal regime designed for private-sector labor, could distort the political process and divert public resources to their members to the detriment of the public.[4]

Professor Winter loved the intellectual give-and-take of the classroom, once telling a reporter, "Part of the fun is to be the devil's advocate and say outrageous things and let them drive you back."[5] And he took great pride in his role as a teacher and scholar. At the hearing on his nomination to the Second Circuit, the chairman of the Senate Judiciary Committee asked, "Mr. Winter, you are a dean?" The nominee responded, "No. A professor." That apparently disappointed the chair: "Oh, merely a professor? Not a dean?" To which Professor Winter replied, "No sir. A professor, not merely a dean."[6]

Still, during his academic years, Winter did not confine himself to the ivory tower. He worked as a consultant to the Senate Judiciary Committee's Subcommittee on Separation of Powers from 1968 to 1970. He was a senior fellow at The Brookings Institution from 1968 to 1970. And he served at the American Enterprise Institute as a John Simon Guggenheim fellow from 1971 to 1972, and as an adjunct scholar there from 1972 to 1981.

Winter even took time out from teaching and scholarship to actually practice law. Nearly a decade and a half after graduating from law school, he finally decided to take the bar examination. He had a client who needed his help in an important case. The client was James L. Buckley, then the junior United States senator from New York, and today a senior judge on the D.C. Circuit. The case was *Buckley v. Valeo,* the landmark First Amendment challenge to numerous provisions of the Federal Election Campaign Act of 1971.[7] Winter passed the Connecticut bar, argued the case in the Supreme Court of the United States—and won.

On November 18, 1981, President Ronald Reagan nominated Winter to serve on the Court of Appeals for the Second Circuit, and the Senate that day unanimously confirmed him.[8] Judge Winter entered judicial service on January 5, 1982. From July 1, 1997 to September 30, 2000, he served as chief judge of the Second Circuit. He took senior status on October 1, 2000.

Judge Winter served from 1987 to 1992 as a member of the Judicial Conference Advisory Committee on the Rules of Civil Procedure. In that capacity, he played a critical role in crafting important discovery reforms: most notably, the revolutionary 1993 amendments to the Federal Rules of Civil Procedure that require parties to exchange relevant information with adversaries at the outset of civil cases.

Judge Winter also served as chair of the Judicial Conference Advisory Committee on the Rules of Evidence from 1992 to 1996. In 1998, he was appointed to the Executive Committee of the United States Judicial Conference, and in 1999 and 2000, was appointed chair of that Executive Committee by Chief Justice William Rehnquist. And from 2003 to 2010, Judge Winter served by appointment of Chief Justice Rehnquist as a member of the three-judge Foreign Intelligence Surveillance Court of Review. Judge Winter also served as chair of the United States Judicial Conference Committee to Review Circuit Council Conduct and Disability Orders from 2005 to 2008. During his tenure, the Committee promulgated extensive rules governing misconduct and disability proceedings that brought about a uniformity in practice and vitalized the scheme governing the federal judiciary's regulation of judicial misconduct and disability.

Meanwhile, he continued to teach. During his judicial tenure, he served as an adjunct professor at Yale Law School—teaching corporations, securities regulation, antitrust, evidence, and sports law. He also served for many years as a trustee of Brooklyn Law School. In 1996, Judge Winter received the Federal Bar Council's Learned Hand Medal for Excellence in Federal Jurisprudence. He has also received the Yale Law School Association's Award of Merit, the Connecticut Law Review Award, and honorary degrees from Brooklyn Law School and New York Law School.

Judge Winter's marriage to Kate Winter ended after 50 years when she passed away in 2012. They have a son, Andrew, and a granddaughter, Kiersten.

1. Circuit Justice Thurgood Marshall, Remarks at the Proceedings Held on the Occasion of the Induction of Honorable Ralph K. Winter as a United States Circuit Judge of the United States Court

of Appeals for the Second Circuit 11 (Jan. 5, 1982) (transcript on file with the United States Courts Library for the Second Circuit).

2. Harry Wellington, Remarks at the Proceedings Held on the Occasion of the Induction of Honorable Ralph K. Winter as a United States Circuit Judge of the United States Court of Appeals for the Second Circuit 9 (Jan. 5, 1982) (transcript on file with the United States Courts Library for the Second Circuit). Wellington was dean of Yale Law School.

3. Ralph K. Winter, Jr., *State Law, Shareholder Protection, and the Theory of the Corporation,* 6 J. LEGAL STUD. 251 (1977).

4. RALPH K. WINTER, JR., & HARRY H. WELLINGTON, THE UNIONS AND THE CITIES: STUDIES OF UNIONISM IN GOVERNMENT (1971).

5. Richard L. Madden, *A Yale Professor of Law Sworn In as U.S. Judge*, N.Y. TIMES, Jan. 6, 1982, at B2.

6. Wellington, Remarks, *supra* note 2, at 8.

7. 424 U.S. 1 (1976).

8. *PN843 — Ralph K. Winter Jr. — The Judiciary,* U.S. CONGRESS, http://www.congress.gov/nomination/97th-congress/843.

# JOHN M. WALKER
## 1940-

District Court for the Southern District of New York: 1985-1989
Court of Appeals for the Second Circuit: 1989-

John M. Walker, Jr., was appointed first by President Ronald Reagan to the District Court of the Southern District of New York in 1985, and then by President George H.W. Bush to the Second Circuit in 1989.

Walker was born in New York City on December 26, 1940, the first of seven children of Dr. John M. Walker and Louise Mead Walker. After some years at different residences during and immediately after World War II, in which Dr. Walker served in the Army, the family settled in Greenwich, Connecticut.

Dr. Walker, who graduated from Yale University and Columbia Medical School, was a successful surgeon and a scratch golfer when he was struck by polio at age 40. Unable to perform surgeries (which was why he entered medicine), he joined the New York brokerage firm G.H. Walker & Co., then being run by his older brother G.H. Walker, Jr., and later was managing partner. The firm had been started early in the twentieth century by Walker's grandfather, G.H. Walker. His grandfather was also a president of the United States Golf Association and in 1922 donated a trophy for an amateur golf competition between the United States and Great Britain that is today known as the "Walker Cup." His six children, in addition to Dr. Walker and G.H. Walker, Jr., included Dorothy Walker Bush, who was the mother of George H.W. Bush, the 41$^{st}$ President of the United States.

Walker's mother, Louise Mead Walker, the oldest child of George and Elsie Mead, grew up in Dayton, Ohio. She studied music and attended Sarah Lawrence College until her marriage and the family dislocations during World War II intervened. She later served on the board of Sarah Lawrence and ultimately graduated from the College. Devastated by the loss of her brother George, who as a young Marine was killed on Guadalcanal in World War II, she worked throughout her life for numerous public interest organizations primarily dedicated to reducing international conflict.

Walker graduated from Phillips Exeter Academy, Yale University, and then Michigan Law School. He served in the U.S. Marine Corps Reserve from 1963 to 1968. In 1966, following law school, Walker spent two years on a public fellowship program as state counsel in the attorney general's chambers in Botswana, Africa, where he drafted a codification of tribal law and was the country's principal prosecutor in the regular (non-tribal) courts.

Starting in 1969, Walker resided in New York City. After less than two years in private practice, he joined the Criminal Division of the United States Attorney's Office for the Southern District of New York, where he prosecuted drug and business fraud cases. Following that, he became a litigation partner on Wall Street at Carter Ledyard and Milburn. In 1980, he was elected from New

York's Upper West Side as a delegate to the Republican National Convention. The election went smoothly because Republicans were so few in number on the Upper West Side that he was able to reach most of them by phone. He joined the Reagan campaign after his cousin George H.W. Bush, for whom he had campaigned, lost the nomination.

From 1981 to 1985, Judge Walker served in the Reagan administration as assistant secretary of Treasury for enforcement and operations with supervisory and regulatory authority over Treasury's enforcement bureaus: the Secret Service, the Customs Service, the Bureau of Alcohol, Tobacco and Firearms, the Federal Law Enforcement Training Center and the Office of Foreign Assets Control. Significant events that occurred on then-Assistant Secretary Walker's watch were the Department of Treasury's implementation of the Algiers Accords that unfroze Iranian assets upon the release by Iran of 52 American hostages, the Department's review of the Secret Service's response to the attempted assassination of President Ronald Reagan by John Hinckley, and the development of Treasury's drug interdiction and financial enforcement programs. For his Treasury service, Judge Walker received the Alexander Hamilton Award, Treasury's highest honor. Walker's work caught the attention of New York Senator Alfonse D'Amato who supported him for the position of district judge.

During his four years as a district judge, Judge Walker handled the wide variety of motions and trials in different legal areas typically presented to busy trial judges in the Southern District of New York. Judge Walker's most notable trial was that of billionaire hotel magnate Leona Helmsley, who was convicted of tax fraud.[1]

Throughout his judicial career on the Court of Appeals, Judge Walker has written several hundred opinions in the various areas of federal law, including securities, anti-trust, copyright, criminal law, criminal and civil procedure, bankruptcy, and constitutional law. He also has taught Constitutional Litigation, first with Judge Pierre Leval at New York University Law School, and later, after he moved his family to Connecticut in 1998, with Judge Guido

Calabresi at Yale Law School where he has been a lecturer in law. He has also authored numerous papers and law review articles.

Judge Walker was chief judge of the Court of Appeals for the Second Circuit from 2000 to 2006. As chief judge, in addition to his normal administrative duties, he faced several unique challenges. First, dislocations resulting from the September 11, 2001 terrorist attacks required cleaning the Foley Square building, restoring the telephone system and temporarily holding court at the New York City Bar Association. Then, in 2005, the court was inundated by a flood of more than 5,000 alien petitions from the Department of Justice (after Attorney General John Ashcroft had directed their summary administrative disposition). This required establishing a non-argument immigration calendar, alongside the court's regular argument calendar. Judge Jon O. Newman, picked by Judge Walker to lead the effort, worked tirelessly on this successful backlog reduction project. Finally, Judge Walker had to address the severe physical deterioration of the Cass Gilbert-designed courthouse at Foley Square. He secured $200 million in federal funding for a major courthouse renovation that required vacating the building for several years and led the project until he stepped down as chief judge. The renovation continued into the term of his successor, Judge Dennis Jacobs, who obtained supplemental funding from the major stimulus package that followed the 2008 financial collapse and led the project through to its completion.

Judge Walker took an interest in judicial administration beyond the chief judge's required duties. At various times, at the request of the chief justice of the United States Supreme Court he served on the Executive, Budget, and International Judicial Relations Committees of the Judicial Conference of the United States, and was chair of the Conference's Committee on Judicial Conduct and Disability.

Starting with a trip to China in 2002 as part of a judicial delegation that was requested by the Chinese Supreme People's Court and led by Supreme Court Justice Sandra Day O'Connor, Judge Walker resumed his interest in the legal systems of developing countries. Aided by his experience in court administration, Judge Walker thereafter worked on rule of law projects for various judiciaries in Eastern Europe, Asia, the Middle East and Africa. He helped establish a governing structure for the courts in Albania, for which that country's President, Alfred Moisiu, awarded him a Medal of Merit. He has trained judges in countries such as Poland, Thailand, Iraq, Tunisia and the Republic of Georgia.

Judge Walker, as a member of the International Judicial Relations Committee, was the liaison from the U.S. Courts to the Chinese judiciary. This took him frequently to China, where he worked on various law projects and lectured to law students, lawyers and judges. Even though China has no common law tradition of *stare decisis*, Judge Walker has assisted the Supreme People's Court in developing a system of precedent—the so-called "Guiding Cases" system. He has also been a regular participant in an ongoing track-two dialogue on rule of law and human rights development in collaboration with noted Chinese law scholar Professor Jerome Cohen of New York University, which meets in China and the United States.

Judge Walker was also instrumental in organizing the Conference of Chief Justices of Central and Eastern Europe. The Conference first met in 2011 at the CEELI Institute in Prague with the participation of Supreme Court Chief Justice John G. Roberts, Jr. The Conference includes the chief justices of the supreme courts of 24 countries from the Baltic Sea to the Caucasus, including the Balkan Peninsula, that were formerly republics within the Soviet Union or under the Soviet sphere of influence. The Conference, which Judge Walker has continued to advise, meets annually in a different country in Central and Eastern Europe. It provides a confidential forum in which the chief justices in these developing democracies are able to learn from one another by sharing ideas and discussing issues of common concern. In 2015, in Brijuni, Croatia, with Judge Walker's assistance, the Fifth Conference issued an extensive Statement of Principles of Judicial Independence.[2]

Judge Walker's awards for judicial service include the Learned Hand Medal for Excellence in Federal Jurisprudence (Federal Bar Council), the Robert L. Haig Award for Distinguished Public Service (New York State Bar Association), the J. Edward

Lumbard Award for Outstanding Service (United States Attorney's Office), and honorary L.L.D. degrees from Brooklyn Law School, Quinnipiac Law School, and Capital Law School.

In 1987, Judge Walker married Katharine B. Kirkland. To her three boys, the couple added a daughter, Katie, in 1992. The family includes five grandchildren and two great grandchildren.

1. *See* United States v. Helmsley, 941 F.2d 71 (2d Cir. 1991).

2. *See* CEELI INSTITUTE, *The Conference of Chief Justices of Central and Eastern Europe Undertakes Landmark Step in Approving The Statement of Principle of the Independence of the Judiciary*, http://ceeliinstitute.org/the-conference-of-chief-justices-of-central-and-eastern-europe-undertakes-a-landmark-step-in-approving-the-statement-of-principle-of-the-independence-of-the-judiciary-at-the-2015-meeting-in-brijuni/.

# DENNIS JACOBS
## 1944-

Court of Appeals for the Second Circuit: 1992-

Dennis Jacobs is a life-long New Yorker, born during an air raid blackout on February 28, 1944, raised on the Upper West Side, and educated in City schools from kindergarten through college. His paternal grandfather came to the United States from Poland before the First World War and settled in Belair, Ohio. His father, Harry N. Jacobs (1910-93), came to the United States in 1920.

His parents met in Toledo, and settled in New York in 1936, where his father opened a linens and domestics shop on Broadway at 95th Street. An older brother, Barry Jacobs (1940-2012), practiced ophthalmology in Boston.

The Jacobs family moved to Queens in 1955. Jacobs attended Forest Hills High School (class of 1960), where he worked on the school newspaper; the faculty adviser of *The Beacon*, James J. Kernan, was teacher, mentor and a lifelong influence on his writing. At Queens College (class of 1964), he majored in English and realized in his French and Latin classes that he would always be monolingual. When he was a teenager, a summer job as a messenger in Manhattan took him all over the island and inspired a continuing interest in the City's history and buildings.

He was awarded a master's degree in English literature by New York University (1965), and worked there toward a doctorate, but did not complete a dissertation. He concentrated on early English prose and Victorian novels.

In a brief first career, he taught in the English Department of Queens College and at the Nassau Police Science Academy, and for a summer at Prairie View A&M College in Texas. In a talk delivered long afterward to a bar association, Judge Jacobs complained that his time as a graduate student and English teacher had rendered him a compulsive proofreader, and morbidly sensitive to solecisms and mixed metaphors. He cited one lawyer, who told a judge that his question had hit the nail on the coffin; and another lawyer, who gloated that his adversary had inflicted this self-inflicted wound on himself.

In 1970, he enrolled at New York University School of Law, where he became a Pomeroy Scholar and a member of the Law Review. A particular influence was his first-year contracts teacher, Professor Sylvester Petro. On graduation in 1973, he joined Simpson Thacher & Bartlett as an associate. The following year, he married Judith Weissman, who was then a preceptor in French at Columbia College, and who went on to a career in university development.

At Simpson Thacher, he started as a corporate transactional lawyer, but soon came to the conclusion that he was not cut out to update utility bond indentures. He then joined the litigation department, and dealt over the ensuing years chiefly with cases involving securities, antitrust, contracts, insurance and reinsurance. He was elected to partnership in 1980.

In March 1992, President George H.W. Bush nominated Judge Jacobs to the Second Circuit. He was confirmed in September and assumed office on December 8.

Judge Jacobs was appointed a member of the United States Judicial Conference Committee on Judicial Resources in 1997, and was chair from 1999 to 2004. In 2006, he became chief judge of the Second Circuit for a seven-year term. The chief judgeship largely coincided with the six-year renovation of the 1935 Thurgood Marshall United States Courthouse at 40 Foley Square, a project suited to Judge Jacobs's interest in New York City and its landmarks. For that work, the judge was awarded the 2014 Chairman's Award of the New York Landmarks Conservancy.

Judge Jacobs was honored by the *Green Bag* for his John F. Sonnett Memorial Lecture, delivered at Fordham Law School in 2007. The lecture, The Secret Life of Judges, identified an insidious judicial bias in favor of the legal profession and in favor of legal proceedings and legal principles as solutions for everything. Another lecture, Lawyers at War, cited the estrangement between elite law and the military professions, and warned of the resulting danger to national security and effective civilian control of the military. In The Pardon Power: The Power Nobody Wants, a speech first delivered in 2003 and several times thereafter, the judge deplored the neglect of the pardon power as a corrective when the judicial system misfires.

In 2009, St. John's University conferred on him the honorary degree of Doctor of Laws.

# PIERRE N. LEVAL
# 1936-

District Court for the Southern District of New York:
1977-1993
Court of Appeals for the Second Circuit: 1993-

Pierre N. Leval was appointed by President Bill Clinton to the Second Circuit in 1993 after serving nearly 17 years as a district judge in the Southern District of New York.

Leval was born in New York City in 1936 in a French-speaking family. His father was a Swiss-born, naturalized American citizen of an Alsatian Jewish family, which had moved from France to Switzerland as a result of the Franco-Prussian war. In his youth in the early years of the twentieth century, Leval's father was sent from Paris to New York to tend to the U.S. affairs of a French international grain-trading firm and made his career in the United States as an executive of the firm. Leval's mother, the daughter of Romanian and Russian immigrants, was born in New York but educated largely in Europe and fluent in French. During Leval's childhood in the war years from 1939 to 1945, his New York home was a regular meeting place of French refugees from the Nazi occupation of France.

After the War, his family regularly traveled to France during his summer vacations from school, reuniting with Leval's aunt (his father's sister) and her son, Edouard Louis (Loulou) who, together with his older brother, served as a Resistance fighter against the Nazi occupation of France in hiding in the Free Zone, and who used his Resistance resources to arrange and guide his mother's escape into Switzerland. The older brother was captured, tortured, and executed. Loulou escaped capture, sometimes narrowly, and survived. He and Leval remained close for nearly 70 years until his death at age 94.

Leval attended grade school at the Allen Stevenson School in New York, high school at Phillips Exeter Academy in New Hampshire, and college at Harvard. After college, he served in the Army and then got an internship in a Swiss bank in Geneva, learning something of international banking while awaiting the start of his first year of law school. He entered Harvard Law School in 1960.

He found his first law school year, taught at Harvard with commitment to the Socratic method (some professors rarely uttered a sentence that did not end with a question mark), to be the most exciting, mind-stretching year of his education. In those days, the course curriculum was largely prescribed, with limited opportunity for choice in the last year. Leval had heard that the best and most delightful course the school had to offer was Copyright, taught by the great Professor Ben Kaplan. He was tempted but resisted, making what he believed was the mature decision to choose "a course that would be useful to me in the future." It was a bad decision. Fifteen years later, he began a career as a federal judge, exercising exclusive (but bewildered) jurisdiction over puzzling copyright matters.

Leval served on the Harvard Law Review as notes editor and graduated *magna cum laude*. In his estimation, the most important ingredient of his legal education was the time he spent working with Judge Richard Posner, who was the first ranking student and president of the law review in the preceding class. When Leval was a second-year junior editor and Posner was president, Posner took charge of editing all of Leval's law review writings. Leval recalls with delight how he and Posner would spend endless hours late into the night, meticulously examining hypothetical variations to test the practical efficacy of every possible governing rule. In Leval's view, these exchanges with so brilliant a mentor afforded him a glimpse of the fabled School of Athens.

His first law job was a summer internship after his first year of law school, working for Thurgood Marshall and Jack Greenberg at the NAACP Legal Defense and Education Fund, Inc., colloquially known as the Inc Fund. Barely six years after Marshall's groundbreaking victory in Brown v. Board of Education, the Inc Fund was still a tiny, intimate office of six or seven lawyers, which meant a rewarding experience for a summer intern. He was assigned to write a cert petition for Ruth Tinsley, the wife of a Richmond, Virginia NAACP official, who had been convicted of loitering in a civil rights demonstration. The petition was assigned to the student-intern because the office's lawyers believed that the case, taken as a courtesy, had no chance of success. Leval prided himself that his petition won an affirmative vote from Justice Douglas, until his bosses explained to him that the mere fact the petition sought to overturn the conviction of a civil rights demonstrator and was signed by the Inc Fund was sufficient to guarantee Justice Douglas's vote.[1]

The judge's first job as a law graduate was in this court, to which he would return as a judge 30 years later. He had the immense good fortune to be selected as the clerk to the great Judge Henry J. Friendly, the generally acknowledged genius of the federal judiciary. In those days, the judges left the selection of their clerks largely to trusted professors. Court of Appeals judges had only one clerk (as compared with four today), which was one more than Friendly needed. As law jobs go, it was in some ways easy work. Friendly carried virtually all of law in his head, hardly ever needed research, and wrote his opinions himself. Little was required of the law clerk, whose only significant utility to Friendly was to confront the judge occasionally with cogent disagreement on some aspect of the judge's analysis. Friendly instantly understood all the implications of a criticism, as well as whether he liked the suggestion (in which case he loved it and glowed with pride in his clerk), or, as was more frequently the case, had no use for it. In that event, his indecipherable growl meant that the subject was closed. Leval remembers having heard a number of such growls. Although easy in some ways, the Friendly clerkship did present difficulties: Friendly was a gruff man, who had little tolerance for imperfection and made scant effort to conceal his displeasure when he encountered it. Notwithstanding occasional bruises during the clerkship, Leval developed a warm, filial relationship with the great judge, who, in his late years, often dined in the Leval household.

Clerking for Friendly was an amazing education because the judge brought to bear on every judicial decision a profound, organic understanding of the meaning, function, and limits of every legal doctrine. His decisions were a teaching tool. Every subject he addressed emerged better explained and better understood. During the clerkship, Leval turned down offers to clerk the next year on the Supreme Court. The decision was motivated in part by impatience, after three years of scholarly remoteness in law review work and clerkship, to get into the rough-and-tumble of criminal prosecution as an Assistant United States Attorney, and in part because of the sense that no Supreme Court justice was the equal of the judge for whom he had already clerked. He later recognized that it was foolish and arrogant to pass up the Supreme Court experience (even accepting the correctness of his assessment of the relative merits of the judges).

But, as the path of his life could scarcely have been more fortunate, he does not regret even his silliest decisions along the way. As an example, had he chosen the Supreme Court clerkship, he thinks it unlikely his path would have led to the Second Circuit.

Following the advice of one of our most famous savants—that one who comes on a fork in the road should take it—Leval instead became an Assistant United States Attorney prosecuting criminal cases under the inspiring leadership of United States Attorney Robert M. Morgenthau. Within his first weeks in the office, arrests were made in the most sensational case of its day, a plot to blow up the Statue of Liberty. The case was assigned to Stephen E. Kaufman, then chief of the Criminal Division and one of the office's outstanding and universally respected lawyers.

Kaufman chose the two most junior assistants, Leval and his officemate, the super-talented Franklin A. Thomas (who later became president of the Ford Foundation), to assist him in the prosecution. Kaufman was a great teacher and a generous mentor. The trio's intense work together on the case led to a deep and lifelong three-way friendship. Leval worked for four years in the Morgenthau office, eventually serving as chief of appeals. Like many others who served in that office, he thinks the job may have been the best and most exciting of his career.

In 1969, he entered private practice at Cleary Gottlieb Steen & Hamilton, which had been cofounded in the late 1940s by Judge Friendly. He practiced six years with the firm, three as an associate, three as a partner. He worked primarily on matters of international finance and business litigation. While he derived immense pleasure and pride from working with the firm's congenial and superb lawyers, he ultimately decided (oddly) that he got greater pleasure from the meager rewards of public service than the copious rewards of private practice. In 1974, Leval's old boss, Morgenthau, who was famed as a person to whom it was impossible to say no, made Leval "the kind of offer you can't refuse"—to take a leave from his well-compensated law partnership to work instead as unpaid campaign manager, directing Morgenthau's bid to follow in the fabled Dewey-Hogan succession as district attorney of New York County. After Morgenthau's election victory, Leval joined him in the D.A.'s office, where he worked for three years as first assistant and chief assistant. It was an exciting time, as Morgenthau, at the start of what became a 34-year career as D.A., modernized the outdated structures and procedures of the office.

The 1976 national elections brought a new Democratic President Jimmy Carter and a new Democratic New York Senator Daniel Patrick Moynihan. Although appointments to the federal courts are technically made by the President, with the advice and consent of the Senate, for many years the effective power to select district judges has lain with the home State's senators of the President's party. Traditionally, senators had approached this function through procedures veiled in secrecy, taking whispered advice from undisclosed confidants. The newly elected Moynihan did an unheard-of thing—appointing a bipartisan committee that would accept applications, interview candidates, and recommend to the senator. On learning that Moynihan had instituted this open procedure, Friendly called Leval to urge him to apply. Leval put in his application, backed by supporting letters from Friendly and Morgenthau, and had the good luck to emerge with Moynihan's blessing as Carter's first appointee to the District Court for the Southern District of New York.

He served in the district court for over 16 years, writing close to 1000 opinions. Cases are distributed among the judges in the Southern District at random, by the spin of the wheel in the Clerk's office. Over a period of years, every judge will inevitably receive a share of cases that attract public attention. Leval's most widely publicized cases were General William Westmoreland's libel suit against CBS and Mike Wallace, based on a telecast that accused the general of manipulating intelligence reports to underrepresent the enemy strength in Vietnam, so as to guarantee White House support for the war effort; the 17-month-long Pizza Connection trial of 22 Sicilian Mafiosi involving a ten-year conspiracy to import drugs from South America; and J.D. Salinger's suit for copyright infringement, seeking to enjoin publication of a biographical book by Ian Hamilton, which took extensively from Salinger's letters. That case had a tortuous history. The publisher's defense, that the quotations were justified as *fair use*, prevailed before Leval in the district court, but Leval's ruling was overturned by the Court of Appeals. Then, in response to an outcry from the publishing industry, Congress amended the copyright statute to reject the theory underlying the Court of Appeals decision.

In 1993, the newly elected President Clinton named Leval to the Second Circuit where he has served for 23 years, most recently in senior status. Like all judges, he has drawn responsibility for, and written opinions on, a wide variety of subjects, including torts, contracts, criminal law, securities markets, insurance, constitutional law, antitrust, taxation, copyright, trademark, and human rights.

The judge is perhaps most known for his writings on copyright. When he was in the district court, random distribution sent him a statistically improbable number of fascinating cases involving claims of fair use, including, in addition to Salinger's suit, claims by the heirs of Igor Stravinsky and L. Ron Hubbard against biographical books that quoted from their letters, and a suit by the publisher of a scientific journal against a major oil exploration company, protesting the defendant corporation's practice of repeatedly photocopying articles relevant to the research of its nearly 90 geologists. His work on these cases led Leval to recognize that neither statutory nor decisional law explained how to identify fair use, and to write an article proposing standards. His proposals were largely adopted by the Supreme Court in *Campbell v. Acuff-Rose Music, Inc.*[2] His article, *Toward a Fair Use Standard*, published in the *Harvard Law Review*,[3] is identified by a Harvard statistical study as the most frequently cited law review article on a private law subject in 25 years.[4] Another of his publications, *Dicta about Dicta*,[5] originally delivered as New York University School of Law's James Madison Lecture, helped persuade the Supreme Court to abandon its recently adopted mandate that the inferior courts, when considering a claim of a constitutional tort, were required to first answer the potentially difficult question whether the complaint stated a constitutional claim, before turning to the often easy, decisive question whether the case needed to be dismissed on grounds of qualified immunity because the specific right asserted was not clearly established at the time.[6] Leval argued, and the Supreme Court eventually agreed, that the obligation often compelled courts to sow confusion in the law and in the administration of governmental agencies by declaring the unconstitutionality of governmental practices in dictum that would have no effect on the case, where the merits of that question had been poorly briefed—in part because the defendant had no practical interest in it. In another widely noted article published in the wake of his *Westmoreland v. CBS* trial,[7] Leval argued that the essential elements of a claim of libel, brought by a public figure who renounces any claim for a monetary award and seeks only a ruling that the defamatory publication was false, should not include an obligation to satisfy the *actual malice* standard adopted by the Supreme Court in *New York Times Co. v. Sullivan.*[8]

The judge has often been invited to lecture at law schools – most frequently on issues of intellectual property law and human rights. He is an emeritus member of the Council of the American Law Institute. Awards to him have included honorary degrees of the Vermont Law School and New York Law School, the Learned Hand Medal for Excellence in Federal Jurisprudence of the Federal Bar Council, and the Henry J. Friendly Medal of the American Law Institute.

1. Judge Leval recently attended a talk by Risa Goluboff, Dean of the Virginia Law School and a former clerk of Judge Calabresi, on her new book "Vagrant Nation," which examines the widespread use of vagrancy laws to suppress civil rights demonstrations in the 1960s, and the eventual invalidation of these laws. After the talk he told Dean Goluboff of his summer job with the Inc Fund and the Tinsley cert petition, he was amazed to learn that her book discusses the unsuccessful cert petition and reveals that, a few years later, the Virginia statute under which Ruth Tinsley was convicted was held unconstitutional and was repealed by the Virginia Legislature.

2. 510 U.S. 569 (1994).

3. Pierre N. Leval, *Toward a Fair Use Standard*, 103 HARV. L. REV. 1105 (1990).

4. Ted Sichelman, *Most Cited Private Law Articles Published in the Last 25 Years*, NEW PRIV. L. (Apr. 22, 2015), https://blogs.harvard.edu/nplblog/2015/04/22/most-cited-private-law-articles-published-in-the-last-25-years/.

5. Pierre N. Leval, *Judging Under the Constitution: Dicta About Dicta*, 81 N.Y.U. L. REV. 1249 (2006).

6. Saucier v. Katz , 533 U.S. 194 (2001); *abrogated by* Pearson v. Callahan, 555 U.S. 223 (2009).

7. 752 F.2d 16 (2d Cir. 1984); *see also* Pierre N. Leval, *The No-Money, No-Fault Libel Suit: Keeping* Sullivan *in Its Proper Place*, 101 HARV. L. REV. 1287 (1988).

8. 376 U.S. 254 (1964).

# GUIDO CALABRESI
# 1932-

Court of Appeals for the Second Circuit: 1994-

Guido Calabresi was born in Milan, Italy on October 18, 1932 to Bianca Maria Finzi-Contini and Massimo Calabresi. His family—both sides of which traced themselves back to Roman times and were very well off—could not seem to be more insiders. One grandfather had been an early student of Charcot, Freud's teacher; the other was a leading industrialist and noted patriot-philanthropist during World War I. One grandmother came from a family with centuries-old intellectual roots; the other from extremely large landowners. Yet, the family's fierce opposition to fascism would soon put this comfortable status into peril. His paternal grandfather's anti-fascism had caused him to be excluded from his home city of Ferrara, and his father, having been beaten and jailed by the fascists as early as 1924, had become a key member of "Giustizia e Libertà" (Justice and Liberty), a small group of anti-fascists who were democrats, with a small "d."

When Guido (as he is universally called) was born, his father, already a leading professor of cardiology, had made plans to leave Italy, but relented when his father told him that one should stay and fight. Still, under a fascist but not yet fully totalitarian regime, everyday life remained unbelievably comfortable for Guido and his family. Nevertheless, in early 1937, when Guido's grandfather had died and the two leaders of Justice and Liberty had been murdered by the fascists, his father decided to flee. This turned out to be especially fortunate as the soon to be enacted racial laws would have changed the family's position drastically. And, on September 16, 1939, Guido, his brother, Paolo, and his parents arrived, penniless, in New York.

Guido knew French and German, but only three words of English: yes, no, and briefcase. On September 18, he was in public school in New York, where he was bullied because he could not speak the language. When in January 1940, his father was given a fellowship at the Yale Medical School and the family moved to New Haven, life improved. But, in that New Haven and Yale, being Italian-Catholic-Jewish, meant being an outsider.

Some old New Haveners took a liking to Guido and his family, and as a result of what today would be called affirmative action, Guido and his brother (now called Paul) received scholarships to private day schools. They did well and went on to Yale College, where Guido received a BS degree in Analytical Economics, *summa cum laude.* He won a Rhodes Scholarship and got a BA degree (and then an MA degree) degree in Politics, Philosophy, and Economics, from Magdalen College, Oxford, with First Class Honours. He returned to New Haven and graduated from Yale Law School in 1958, first in his class.

After clerking for Justice Hugo Black, of the Supreme Court, Guido began teaching at Yale Law School in 1959. He became a full professor (the youngest in the school's history) in 1962, and has been teaching there ever since. He married Anne Gordon Audubon Tyler, a friend since childhood, and a deeply rooted New Havener, in May 1961. They have three children, Bianca

Finzi-Contini, a literature scholar, Anne Oldshue, a psychiatrist, and Massimo Franklin Tyler, a journalist, and four grandchildren. Guido's wife, a graduate of Radcliffe (Harvard), is a cultural anthropologist, and his soul mate. She writes about Tuscan sharecroppers (mezzadri), and is at the center of virtually every cause to better New Haven and its neediest.

Guido is considered one of the founders of the modern Law and Economics movement. He has written seven books and innumerable articles in that and other fields of law, including especially the role of courts in an age of statutes. Some of these rank among the most cited in the legal canon. As a result, he has received honorary degrees and other awards, too numerous to list, from scholarly and bar groups, as well as leading universities in America and throughout the world. Most of all, he has always viewed himself as a teacher who loves his students. He has taught Torts to first year students consistently for nearly 60 years.

In 1985 he became dean of the Yale Law School and is credited with cementing its place as one of the leading law schools in the world. His appointments were ideologically and personally diverse, and uniformally regarded as the intellectual leaders of their generation. His mantra was "Excellence, but with Humanity and Decency."

In early 1994, President Bill Clinton nominated Guido to the Court of Appeals, and in July the U.S. Senate confirmed him unanimously. He was formally sworn in on September 16, 1994, 55 years to the day of his landing in America. Before their deaths, his parents had become successful Professors of Cardiology and of Literature in New Haven. His brother was the Chief of Medicine at Brown University Medical School, and a founder of cancer chemotherapy. They had all overcome difficulties and had done well here. So, on taking office, Guido thanked America for all it had done for him and his family; this made him profoundly patriotic. But he also emphasized what America had not done for many others. And, he dedicated himself and his judgeship, under the law, to them. He reiterated that the most important part of his legal education was that he was a refugee and an immigrant. Having been and remaining an outsider after having been born an insider would, he hoped, continue to characterize him and his judgeship.

Guido loves to talk, and some scholars have described his legal philosophy as rooted in conversation – with other courts, and with members of the executive, legislative, and administrative branches, both federal and state. Hence, his particular support of certification of state law questions to state courts.

As a senior judge, Guido teaches 2/3 time, judges 2/3 time, and makes many trips to Italy where he frequently lectures on American Law and where, with his wife, he makes olive oil. This, Anne and Guido give to their friends, often together with homemade American raspberry jam, a symbol, perhaps, of their now-joint background.

# JOSÉ A. CABRANES
## 1940-

Court of Appeals for the Second Circuit: 1994-
United States District Court for the District of Connecticut: 1979-1994
Foreign Intelligence Surveillance Court of Review (by designation of the Chief Justice of the United States): 2013-

José A. Cabranes was appointed a judge of the Court of Appeals for the Second Circuit in 1994. At the time of his appointment, he was chief judge of the District Court for the District of Connecticut, a court to which he was appointed in 1979. In August 2013, he was appointed by the chief justice of the United States to serve also a seven-year term on the three-judge United States Foreign Intelligence Surveillance Court of Review.

Cabranes was born in 1940 in Mayagüez, Puerto Rico, into a family of educators; both his mother and father were originally school teachers. His parents were part of the first generation of Puerto Ricans educated under the American flag, following the Spanish-American War (1898). Born and reared in rural hamlets, they were educated in the public schools of Puerto Rico in the early decades of the twentieth century, and later at the newly-founded University of Puerto Rico. His father, Manuel Cabranes, was also one of the island's first professionally-trained social workers. Manuel Cabranes undertook advanced studies in social work at Fordham University in the early 1930s, and, upon returning to the island, helped found its system of probation and parole, later serving as the chief probation officer of the District Court for the District of Puerto Rico.

José Cabranes moved with his family to the South Bronx at the age of five, when his father was recruited to direct a settlement house there (Melrose House); the settlement house had served Jewish immigrants for decades and, after the Second World War, was increasingly devoted to helping Puerto Rican newcomers who, as U.S. citizens, freely migrated in large numbers to the mainland after the war. Manuel Cabranes later headed the Government of Puerto Rico's Office in New York City and then served in the municipal administrations of New York City Mayors Vincent R. Impelliteri and Robert F. Wagner. His mother, Carmen López Cabranes, was production editor of the journals of the American Society of Mechanical Engineers in New York.

After attending public schools in New York City, José Cabranes graduated from Columbia College (A.B. 1961), Yale Law School (J.D. 1965) and the University of Cambridge, Cambridge, England (M.Litt. in International Law, 1967). He studied at Cambridge under a Kellett Research Fellowship from Columbia College and the Humanitarian Trust Studentship in Public International Law awarded by the Faculty Board of Law of the University of Cambridge.

Cabranes was serving as general counsel of Yale University when appointed to the federal bench in 1979; he was the first

Puerto Rican appointed to the federal bench in the continental United States. Previously he had practiced in a New York City law firm; taught administrative law, conflicts of law and international human rights law on the full-time faculty of Rutgers University Law School and courses on the law of westward expansion and international human rights on the adjunct faculty of Yale Law School; and served as special counsel to the governor of Puerto Rico and as head of the Commonwealth of Puerto Rico's office in Washington, D.C. He is the author of CITIZENSHIP AND THE AMERICAN EMPIRE (Yale University Press, 1979), a legislative history of the United States citizenship of the people of Puerto Rico, and co-author (with Kate Stith) of FEAR OF JUDGING: SENTENCING GUIDELINES IN THE FEDERAL COURTS (University of Chicago Press, 1998) (Certificate of Merit of the American Bar Association, 1999), and articles in various law journals.

Cabranes's principal avocational activity after his appointment to the federal bench has been university trusteeship. He served successively as a trustee of Colgate University from 1981 to 1989, and at the two universities of which he is a graduate: as a successor trustee of Yale University (Fellow of the Yale Corporation) from 1987 to 1999 and as a trustee of Columbia University from 2000 to 2012. (At Yale he was the first Roman Catholic to serve on the university's governing board.) He has been elected a member of the Council on Foreign Relations, the American Academy of Arts and Sciences and the American Law Institute, and as a fellow of the American Bar Foundation.

In 1988, Cabranes was one of five federal judges appointed by Chief Justice Rehnquist to the 15-member Federal Courts Study Committee created by Act of Congress "to examine problems facing the Federal courts and develop a long-range plan for the future of the Federal judiciary."[1]

He was the recipient of the Learned Hand Medal for Excellence in Federal Jurisprudence of the Federal Bar Council in 2000.

Before his appointment to the federal bench, Cabranes served as chairman of the Board of Directors of two major Hispanic civil rights organizations: Aspira of New York, an educational agency helping inner-city Hispanic youth prepare for college, and the Puerto Rican Legal Defense and Education Fund (now LatinoJustice), of which he was a founding member.

Cabranes is married to Kate Stith, a former federal prosecutor in New York who is the Lafayette S. Foster Professor of Law at Yale Law School. Kate Stith is a graduate of Dartmouth College and Harvard Law School and served for more than a decade as a Dartmouth trustee. She and Cabranes are the parents of four children: Jennifer Cabranes Braceras, a lawyer in Massachusetts, and Amy Cabranes, a development professional in Los Angeles, both born to José Cabranes's first marriage, to Susan Feibush; Alejo Cabranes, a lawyer in New York City, and Benjamin José Cabranes, a recent graduate of Dartmouth College also residing in New York.

1. Pub. L. No. 100-702, 102 Stat. 4644 (1988) (codified at 28 U.S.C.A. § 331).

## CHESTER J. STRAUB
## 1937-

Court of Appeals for the Second Circuit: 1998-

Chester J. Straub was born to Chester and Ann Straub (née Majewski) on May 12, 1937, in Greenpoint, Brooklyn—a neighborhood so famously Polish-American that the two bridges connecting it to Queens are named for Kazimierz Pulaski and Tadeusz Kościuszko, the Polish military commanders and American Revolutionary War heroes.

As a teenager, Judge Straub's father had moved to Brooklyn from upstate New York with a one-way railroad ticket and instructions to drive a truck for his uncle at Straub Beverages in Greenpoint. Thereafter, Straub, Sr., started his own business with a one-room store to sell butter and eggs. It was in this family undertaking that Judge Straub worked until he had completed two years of law school. At his Second Circuit induction ceremony, Judge Straub would remember his father's business as the epitome of Brooklyn's melting-pot culture, recalling a store full of "gentlemen in yarmulkes dealing with the problems of the local yeshiva," "bodega owners from Williamsburg trying to determine how they might get the Sanitation Department to respond," Polish-American women "buying eggs and . . . babkas," and Italian-Americans "from another part of the community seeking our finest ricotta."[1] Judge Straub's father used this "atmosphere" to teach his son "the importance of the inclusiveness of our society and . . . how important it [is] to participate in the public process"—lessons that he would put to good use during a long and distinguished career in the public and private sectors.[2]

Judge Straub attended St. Stanislaus Kostka School in Greenpoint, followed by Brooklyn Preparatory School, known as Brooklyn Prep. Now defunct, Brooklyn Prep was a prestigious Jesuit high school that attracted studious, ambitious boys from all over New York—including Judge Straub's future colleague on the Second Circuit, Judge Joseph McLaughlin.

Judge Straub continued his education in the Jesuit tradition at St. Peter's College in Jersey City, New Jersey, where he received a B.A. degree in 1958. From St. Peter's, he went on to the University of Virginia School of Law, where he was a contemporary of three future U.S. senators (Edward "Ted" Kennedy of Massachusetts, John Tunney of California, and Christopher "Kit" Bond of Missouri) and two future federal judges (Eugene Siler, Jr., of the Court of Appeals for the Sixth Circuit and G. Kendall Sharp of the District Court for the Middle District of Florida). Judge Straub had been guided to the law by his "Babcia, [his] Polish immigrant grandmother," who had laid out three potential paths for him to follow: priest, doctor, or lawyer.[3] "The spirit didn't move [him] to the cloth," and he was "hardly a scientist at any stage of [his] development," but "her advice about the law stuck with [him]."[4]

After his graduation from law school in 1961, Judge Straub served as a first lieutenant in U.S. Army Intelligence and Security for two years, before entering private practice at the venerable Wall Street law firm of Willkie Farr & Gallagher, where he made partner in 1971. It was during his time at Willkie Farr that he entered politics, becoming one of the last citizen-lawyers to combine practice at a major national law firm with service in elected office.

Running as a Democrat, Judge Straub won a seat in the New York State Assembly in 1966, and he represented his home district of Greenpoint there until 1972. During his time in the Assembly, he served as the chair of the Assembly's Democratic Policy Committee and as a member of the Committees on the Judiciary, Ways & Means, and Ethics & Guidance. In 1972, he was elected to the New York State Senate, where he served as the ranking Democrat on the Committee on Corporations, Authorities & Public Utilities and as a member of the Committees on the Judiciary, Health, Civil Service & Pensions, Housing & Urban Development, and Transportation. Throughout his service in the legislature, Judge Straub and his family continued to reside in Greenpoint, in an apartment above his father's store, moving to Bronxville in Westchester County only after his retirement from active electoral politics.

Judge Straub's Senate term was not without controversy. In the wake of the Watergate scandal, he triggered a "bitter debate" on the Senate floor when he introduced a petition requesting that the U.S. House of Representatives impeach President Richard Nixon.[5] Judge Straub explained to his colleagues that Section 603 of Thomas Jefferson's *Manual of Parliamentary Practice*—adopted by the House as its rules of procedure in 1837—permitted impeachment proceedings to be initiated through "charges transmitted from the legislature of a state."[6] Republican Senate Majority Leader Warren Anderson was not amused. He referred Judge Straub's petition to the Finance Committee, "which the Democratic minority view[ed] as a burial ground for its ideas."[7] Undeterred, Straub eventually "managed to read his statement in support of his petition under cover of a debate over another bill."[8] Anderson made known, on the legislative floor, his continued displeasure by forewarning Judge Straub that he "ha[d] [his] ways" of dealing with such matters.[9] At the coming legislative reapportionment, the lines of Judge Straub's legislative district were sufficiently altered so as to make the next legislative election somewhat more challenging. Nevertheless, upon Judge Straub's nomination to the Second Circuit, Anderson would be the first Republican to encourage Senator Orrin Hatch, the chairman of the U.S. Senate Judiciary Committee, to act favorably.

Judge Straub resigned from the Senate in 1975, in part "to prevent a conflict of interest between his law practice" at Willkie Farr, "which involved state bonds and notes, and his elective post."[10] But his involvement in politics was far from over. The following year, he became counsel to the Moynihan Committee, the campaign to elect Daniel Patrick Moynihan of New York to the U.S. Senate. Judge Straub had previously worked for Moynihan in his unsuccessful effort to become the Democratic nominee for president of the New York City Council (an office that no longer exists). In addition to his participation in the successful Senate effort, Judge Straub would chair Senator Moynihan's re-election campaigns in 1982, 1988, and 1994. Judge Straub later characterized his "participation with and for Pat Moynihan over the years" as one his life's great opportunities "to do something of significance, perhaps have an impact, and take satisfaction from it."[11] Judge Straub learned from Senator Moynihan "to put principle above party, and . . . that the public interest is more significant than public approval of the moment."[12]

Senator Moynihan, a political scientist and student of international relations by training, would in turn credit Judge Straub (along with another of his closest advisors, Leonard Garment) with informing him "that United States Senators choose District Judges. I didn't know that. I thought bishops did perhaps."[13] According to Senator Moynihan, it was Judge Straub and Mr. Garment who "suggested that we create a Judicial Selection Committee" to make the judicial appointment process more transparent and bipartisan.[14] Following their advice, Senator Moynihan and his Republican counterpart, Senator Jacob Javits, instituted an arrangement pursuant to which the senator whose political party did not control the White House would make every fourth "designation" of a prospect for appointment. In Senator Moynihan's words, "In the history of the Republic, nothing of the kind had ever happened. And I think it has been emulated around the country. . . . It was that level of openness and of sharing that so distinguished [Judge Straub's political] career in so many ways . . . ."[15] Judge Straub would also play a crucial role in judicial appointments at the state level, serving as the chair of Governor Mario Cuomo's Statewide Judicial Screening Committee from 1988 to 1994. Judge Straub had also served as a member of the Democratic National Committee.

In 1998, President Bill Clinton nominated Judge Straub to the Second Circuit. The U.S. Senate confirmed him by voice vote the same year. But even in Judge Straub's new judicial role, issues of political significance continued to arise before him. In one of the many notable opinions that he authored, Judge Straub's majority held that certain Vermont campaign-finance laws were "supported by [the state's] compelling interests in safeguarding [its] democratic process from (1) the corruptive influence of excessive and unbridled fundraising and (2) the effect that perpetual fundraising has on the time of candidates and elected officials."[16] Similarly, Judge Straub led a unanimous panel in striking down New York State's system of nominating its Supreme Court Judges via political boss control of judicial convention delegates rather than by direct voter expression at the ballot box.[17] The Supreme Court disagreed in both cases.

During his time on the bench, Judge Straub has also become well-known for his measured dissents. A law review article devoted to that subject described one of their "over-arching themes" as his "ever-watchful eye on the boundaries of the judicial role and the jurisdiction of the Second Circuit," and noted that they "placed heavy emphasis on not only maintaining clarity in jurisprudence, but also keeping the lines of precedent well-defined and the interpretation of such precedents uncomplicated."[18]

Prior to joining the Second Circuit, Judge Straub served as a mediator in the District Courts for the Eastern and Southern Districts of New York and a special master in the New York County Supreme Court. Judge Straub was also a longtime trustee of the Lenox Hill Hospital, a member of the Cardinal's Committee for the Laity of the Catholic Charities of the

Archdiocese of New York, and a member of the Knights of Columbus.

Judge Straub took senior status in 2008.

He resides in Bronxville with his wife of 57 years, Pat, with whom he raised four sons—the late Chet, Jr., (assistant secretary of commerce for economic development under President Clinton), Mike (a lawyer in Vermont), Chris (a director at Bank of America Merrill Lynch in New York), and Robert (a doctor in Georgia). Judge Straub and Mrs. Straub also have seven grandchildren—Mira, Christopher, Jr., Nicholas, Robert, Jr., Daphne, Lindsey, and Jack.

1. Judge Chester J. Straub, Remarks, at the Induction Proceedings for Chester J. Straub 18 (July 27, 1998) (transcript on file with the United States Courts Library for the Second Circuit).

2. *Id.*

3. *Id.* at 17–18.

4. *Id.* at 18.

5. Linda Greenhouse, *Impeachment Debate Argued and Scuttled in Albany*, N.Y. TIMES, Mar. 26, 1974, at 30.

6. *Id.*

7. *Id.*

8. *Id.*

9. Francis X. Clines, *The Political Hopefuls Are Squaring Off*, N.Y. TIMES, June 9, 1974, at 101.

10. *Special Elections Slated To Fill 2 Legislature Seats*, N.Y. TIMES, Jan. 8, 1976, at 37.

11. Judge Chester J. Straub, Remarks, *supra* note 1, at 16.

12. *Id.*

13. Senator Daniel Patrick Moynihan, Remarks at the Induction Proceedings for Chester J. Straub 8 (July 27, 1998) (transcript on file with the United States Courts Library for the Second Circuit).

14. *Id.*

15. *Id.* at 9.

16. Landell v. Sorrell, 382 F.3d 91, 97 (2d Cir. 2004).

17. Lopez Torres v. New York State Board of Elections, 462 F.3d 161 (2d Cir. 2006).

18. Danielle L. Levine, *Staying True to the Ideals of Fundamental Fairness: An Empirical Study of the Dissents of Judge Straub*, 75 ALB. L. REV. 1163, 1173, 1184 (2012).

## ROSEMARY S. POOLER
## 1938-

New York State Supreme Court,
Fifth Judicial District, Onondaga County: 1991-1994
District Court for the Northern District of New York:
1994-1998
Court of Appeals for the Second Circuit: 1998-

Rosemary S. Pooler received a B.A. degree from Brooklyn College in 1959, a M.A. degree in History from the University of Connecticut in 1961, and a J.D. degree from the University of Michigan Law School in 1965. Following law school, she worked in private practice from 1966 to 1972, when she became director of the Consumer Affairs Unit of the Syracuse City Corporation Counsel. She was elected a Syracuse City common councilor in 1974. Beginning in 1976, she served as chair and executive director of the New York State Consumer Protection Board, which included being the statutory intervenor in rate cases pending before the Public Service Commission. In 1978, she received a graduate certificate in Regulatory Economics from the State University of Albany. Judge Pooler was appointed to a "consumer" seat as a commissioner of the New York State Public Service Commission. She also served as a visiting professor of law at Syracuse University College of Law and as the vice president of Legal Affairs for Atlantic States Legal Foundation, Inc.

In 1991, Pooler became the first woman elected to the New York State Supreme Court for the Fifth Judicial District. Four years later, she was appointed by President Bill Clinton to the District Court for the Northern District of New York, becoming the first woman to serve on that bench. President Clinton elevated Judge Pooler to the Court of Appeals for the Second Circuit, where she assumed duty on June 19, 1998.

Judge Pooler was honored with the Women's Bar Association of the State of New York Doris S. Hoffman Medal in 2012; the Onondaga County Bar Association William C. Ruger Award in 2009; and the National Council of Jewish Women's Hanna G. Solomon Award in 1998. She is a member of the Onondaga County and New York State Bar Associations, the Women's Bar Associations of the State of New York and Central New York, and is an honorary member of the Board of Advisors for the Syracuse University College of Law. Judge Pooler is married to retired Syracuse University Professor William Pooler. They have two grown children.

# ROBERT D. SACK
1939-

Court of Appeals for the Second Circuit: 1998-

In November 1997, Robert D. Sack was nominated for a seat on the Court of Appeals for the Second Circuit by President Bill Clinton. He was confirmed on June 15, 1998, and entered into service on August 6 of that year. He was an active judge for eleven years. He took senior status in August 2009. He maintains his chambers on the twenty-eigth floor of 40 Foley Square. He is the author of some 300 opinions for the court and several dozen concurrences and dissents.

Sack attended elementary school, junior high school, and high school (Midwood) in Brooklyn, leaving for the University of Rochester in 1956. He graduated from that institution with a B.A.

degree (history) in 1960, and then returned to New York in 1960, enrolling in Columbia Law School.

Upon graduation from Columbia in 1963 with an LL.B degree, followed by a successful encounter with the New York State bar examination, he clerked for District Judge Arthur S. Lane, in Trenton, New Jersey. Judge Lane introduced the young Mr. Sack to Robert S. Potter, a partner at what was then the downtown New York law firm of Patterson, Belknap & Webb. In September 1964, Sack signed on as an associate.

When Sack joined Patterson, Belknap, specialization was the exception, not the rule. Sack was a generalist, spending some years as a litigator, counselor, *and* corporate lawyer, both as an associate and, beginning in late 1970, as a partner in the firm.

Thus, early in his tenure, he assisted partners Chauncey Belknap and Robert Pennoyer in addressing the aftermath of the notorious "Salad Oil" swindle, perpetrated by one Tino DeAngeles, the Bernie Madoff of his day, which involved the raising of funds from financial institutions through the use of fraudulent warehouse receipts. The scam left a major brokerage firm in ruins and inflicted many millions of dollars of damages on some of the most prominent banks and commodity trading companies in the country.[1] American Express Co., caught in the middle, put up more than $100 million to settle the matter. For the better part of a decade, Patterson, Belknap represented Chemical Bank as the holder and disburser of the settlement funds.

During the same general time period, Sack, as an associate and then partner, represented U.S. Industries, Inc., an active "conglomerate" located in New York City, in its purchase of a number of smaller northeastern U.S.-based companies.

In the 1970s, by contrast, with his partner and close friend D. Robert Owen and several other Patterson, Belknap lawyers, Sack participated in the defense of Bangkok Bank, Ltd., in a civil suit brought in the Southern District of New York by a New York-based commodities firm.[2] The plaintiff attributed the collapse of its ambition to become the dominant player in maize trading in Thailand—a venture supported by the U.S. Agency for International Development—to the failure of Bangkok Bank to make good on a particular promise to provide $1 million in financing. The Bank prevailed in a bench trial before District Judge Richard Owen in 1979.

By the early 1980s, at about the time of the publication of his treatise *Libel, Slander and Related Problems*, Sack's practice became focused largely on the provision of legal services to Dow Jones & Company, Inc., publisher of, among other media, *The Wall Street Journal,* and to other authors and publishers. His representation included pre-publication counseling and defense of suits brought on libel and related theories. But he also participated in representing Dow Jones in, among other things, its litigation with the Chicago Board of Trade with respect to the latter's ultimately unsuccessful efforts to develop a futures market based on unauthorized use of the Dow Jones Averages;[3] a variety of antitrust-law related counseling and litigation involving distribution arrangements for the *Wall Street Journal*; and allegations of insider trading related to articles published by Dow Jones publications, most notably the conviction in the Southern District of New York of a *Wall Street Journal* reporter and two co-defendants for trading on advance knowledge of the content of the reporter's columns.[1]

Beginning in the mid-1980s, Sack also spent a significant portion of his professional time representing Dow Jones with respect to its publishing presence abroad. The challenge facing the company was to publish news and commentary meeting high standards of American journalism under legal conditions in one way or another hostile to that effort. Sack, with leading professionals from the U.K. and other local bars, engaged in proceedings in Hong Kong, Singapore, Malaysia, and the U.K., meeting with some, if not overwhelming, success.[5]

Meanwhile, in 1974, at the suggestion of Bob Owen, Sack took a seven-month leave from Patterson, Belknap, moving to Washington, D.C. to join the U.S. House of Representatives [Richard M. Nixon] Impeachment Inquiry staff headed by former Department of Justice Civil Rights Division Chief John Doar. (Owen had been Doar's deputy during his days at the Division.) There, ultimately as senior associate special counsel, Sack participated in a wide variety of facets of the Inquiry.[6]

Returning to New York in the late summer of 1974 after the President's resignation, Sack resumed his career with Patterson, Belknap—by now ensconced in "30 Rock," then known as the RCA Building. Twelve years later, he left for a partnership with the New York office of the global firm, Gibson, Dunn & Crutcher, where he remained until he took the federal bench another 12 years thereafter.

Both before and after taking the bench, Sack has been a frequent author, lecturer, and teacher, largely on topics related to legal matters affecting the institutional press. His 1980 book, now entitled *Sack On Defamation: Libel, Slander, and Related Problems* (4th ed. 2014)—a fifth edition is contemplated for the near future—is, according to a *Lexis* search, the most often cited defamation treatise in the nation's courts. Sack also co-wrote with his friend P. Cameron DeVore, of the Seattle-based Davis, Wright firm, the first edition of *Advertising and Commercial Speech: A First Amendment Guide* (1999). Before and after becoming a judge, he has also written occasional law review articles, more often than not on press-law topics.[7]

In the mid-70s through the mid-80s, Sack was a frequent panelist on coast-to-coast "Media and the Law" seminars associated primarily with Fred Friendly and originally sponsored by the Ford Foundation. And beginning in 1973, he has lectured or appeared as a commentator in nearly every annual Practising Law Institute communications law program, which was chaired from the beginning and for several decades by James C. Goodale. Soon after taking the bench, Judge Sack began co-teaching, as a lecturer at law and then an adjunct professor, a course titled "The First Amendment and the Institutional Press" at Columbia Law School. More recently, he has, often with his colleague Debra Ann Livingston, participated in a Second Circuit judicial extern program and an associated seminar for Columbia Law School students. The program had been inaugurated by now-Justice Sotomayor when she was a Second Circuit judge.

Judge Sack was Columbia Law School's commencement speaker in 2007. He was adjunct professor of Political Science and special guest lecturer at the University of Rochester in 2012, and a Distinguished Visiting Jurist at the University of Chicago

Law School in 2013. In 2008, Judge Sack was awarded the Federal Bar Council's Learned Hand Medal for Excellence in Federal Jurisprudence.

Judge Sack has also served not-for-profit organizations, including the William F. Kerby and Robert S. Potter Fund, which provided funding to the legal defense of journalists abroad; the Bureau of National Affairs' *Media Law Reporter*; and the ABA Forum Committee's *Communications Lawyer*. He is a member of the Board of Visitors of Columbia Law School. He is also a member of the American Bar Association, the New York City Bar Association (chair, Communications Law Committee, 1986 to 1989), and the American Judicature Society, and is a fellow of the American Bar Foundation.

Judge Sack's grandparents on both his mother's and father's sides were early twentieth-century immigrants from Eastern Europe to the United States. His mother's parents arrived separately in New York City, where they met and married. His father's father, a glove cutter by training and trade, settled in the upstate New York city of Gloversville. His family soon followed. He met, and five years after reaching the States married, Sack's Russian-born grandmother. Her death preceded Sack's birth.

Sack's father, Yehuda (then Anglicized to Julius, then Americanized to Eugene), was born in Gloversville in 1912. Sponsored by a local businessman and philanthropist, he left for the University of Cincinnati at the age of 16. Thereafter, he enrolled in Hebrew Union College, also in Cincinnati. Upon graduation, he was ordained as a rabbi. Meanwhile, his only sibling, Rose, had been a student at Hunter College in New York City. Her roommate, Sylvia Rivlin, not long thereafter became Mrs. Sack, the wife of Eugene and mother of Sack and his brother, Steven.

Shortly after Pearl Harbor, Eugene, by then a junior rabbi with a large Reform Jewish Synagogue in Philadelphia, volunteered for the Army. Some of Sack's most vivid childhood memories are of his family's odyssey during the War. Eugene, family in tow, moved to Macon, Georgia in 1942, where he trained for the chaplaincy. Then, during the 18 months he was serving in the Pacific Theater, most of the time in New Guinea,

Sack and his mother lived with relatives in California and then Brooklyn. Upon Eugene's return to the States in 1944, he was stationed in Fort Knox, Kentucky, where he and his family were residents on "VJ Day"—August 15, 1945—marking the end of the War.

After Eugene's discharge from service and a relatively brief stay back in Philadelphia, the family moved to a modest Victorian-style house on East 16th Street in Ditmas Park, Brooklyn. Eugene took the pulpit at Congregation Beth Elohim, in Park Slope, Brooklyn, where he served for more than 30 years.

Judge Sack is married to Anne K. Hilker (Anne Hilker Sack). He has three children who now reside in various parts of the country, working as officers of not-for-profit organizations, and living with families of their own.

Anne was a prominent trusts and estates lawyer in California and New York (where she chaired the City Bar's Trusts, Estates, and Surrogate's Courts Committee). In 1995, both she and Sack were named in New York Magazine's list of "Best Lawyers in New York." Late-diagnosed Lyme disease forced her to leave the practice of law in 2002. As part of a long recovery, she has pursued part-time graduate studies in the history of decorative arts and material culture.

Judge Sack quips that now that he has taken senior status, he has been able to reduce his workweek to seven days. His somewhat abbreviated sitting schedule has, however, allowed him time to sit annually by designation on the Ninth Circuit, and for Anne and him to spend a bit more time travelling. They have visited, toured, or cruised in six continents, with a seventh in sight.

1. NORMAN C. MILLER, THE GREAT SALAD OIL SWINDLE (1966).

2. Calabrian Co. v. Bangkok Bank Ltd., 55 F.R.D. 82 (S.D.N.Y. 1972) (outlining the plaintiff's allegations; denying the defendant's motion to dismiss on forum non conveniens grounds).

3. Bd. of Trade of Chi. v. Dow Jones & Co., Inc., 456 N.E.2d 84 (Ill. 1983).

4. Carpenter v. United States, 484 U.S. 19 (1987).

5. Robert D. Sack, *New York Times Co. v. Sullivan—50-Year Afterwords*, 66 ALA. L. REV. 273, 274-76 (2014).

6. TIMOTHY NAFTALI, AN ORAL HISTORY INTERVIEW WITH ROBERT SACK (2011), https://www.nixonlibrary.gov/virtuallibrary/documents/histories/sack-2011-09-27.pdf (a video-taped interview for the Richard M. Nixon Library and the National Archives).

7. Sack, *supra* note 5; *see also, e.g.*, Robert D. Sack, *Protection of Opinion Under the First Amendment: Reflections on Alfred Hill, "Defamation and Privacy Under the First Amendment,"* 100 COLUM. L. REV. 294 (2000) (published in the 100th Anniversary issue of the Columbia Law Review); Robert Sack, *Hearing Myself Think: Some Thoughts on Legal Prose*, 4 SCRIBBS J. LEGAL WRITNG 93 (1993); Robert D. Sack, *Reflections on the Wrong Question: Special Constitutional Privilege for the Institutional Press*, 7 HOFSTRA L. REV. 629 (1979); Robert D. Sack, *Principle and* Nebraska Press Ass'n v. Stuart, 29 STAN. L. REV. 411 (1977).

# ROBERT A. KATZMANN
## 1953-

Court of Appeals for the Second Circuit, 1999-

A proud graduate of New York City's public schools, Robert A. Katzmann, born in Manhattan, grew up in Queens. His father, John, was a refugee from Nazi Germany, and is now a retired engineer; his mother, Sylvia, a homemaker, is a Brooklyn-born daughter of Russian immigrants. In 1999, Katzmann was appointed to the Court of Appeals for the Second Circuit and on September 1, 2013 became its chief judge.

Katzmann's interest in government and law began as a child, when he and his twin brother, also now a judge, devoured biographies of presidents and history accounts of the United States, and his family took trips to Washington, D.C. Although he was always interested in a career in the law, a chance comment from a college professor, concerned that Katzmann as a commuting student had not had a real campus experience, led him to apply to graduate school before law school.

After receiving his AB degree *summa cum laude* from Columbia College, Katzmann obtained his AM and Ph.D degrees in government from Harvard University, where he studied with and worked for then-professor Daniel Patrick Moynihan, and also with James Q. Wilson and Richard E. Neustadt. Katzmann then attended Yale Law School; he was an article and book review editor of the *Yale Law Journal.* After clerking for Judge Hugh H. Bownes of the Court of Appeals for the First Circuit, Judge Katzmann joined the Brookings Institution. In Washington, D.C., where he lived and worked from 1981 to 1999, projects at Brookings, teaching at Georgetown, government projects, and writing consumed his energies. Much of his pre-bench work focused on the challenges of governing, on the way that our institutions operate, and steps towards the more effective functioning of government. At the time of his judicial appointment in 1999, Katzmann was Walsh Professor of Government, Professor of Law, and Professor of Public Policy at Georgetown University; a fellow of the Governmental Studies Program of the Brookings Institution, having served a term as acting director; and president of the Governance Institute.

In 1993, Senator Moynihan asked then-professor Katzmann to serve as special counsel on the confirmation of Justice Ruth Bader Ginsburg; it was an assignment Katzmann greatly enjoyed although his labor was hardly needed, so prepared was she. Senator Moynihan also appointed him to his advisory committee on federal district court and United States attorney appointments, and as special counsel pro bono to the Commission on Protecting and Reducing Government Secrecy.

Reflecting his law and political science background – he is the first judge of the federal courts with a doctorate in government -- Katzmann has long had an interest in judicial-legislative relations. That interest deepened in 1984 when Judge Frank M. Coffin, then chair of the United States Judicial Conference Committee on the Judicial Branch, asked him to help examine those relations. In time, he and Judge Coffin created, with some colleagues, the

Governance Institute as the vehicle for that work. As editor and contributing author, Katzmann produced *Judges and Legislators.* Before joining the federal bench, he wrote *Courts and Congress.* His involvement in legislative-judicial relations continues as a judge, as a former chair, by appointment of Chief Justice John Roberts, and still member of the Judicial Conference Committee on the Judicial Branch. More recently, his experience as a judge led him to write *Judging Statutes* (Oxford University Press, 2014; paperback, 2016), which offers a succinct critique of a purely textualist approach to the interpretation of legislation.

In his early years on the bench, Judge Katzmann witnessed the inadequate legal representation of non-citizens and its adverse impact on the fair and effective administration of justice. Greatly concerned, in 2007 he delivered the Marden Lecture of the New York City Bar Association, "The Legal Profession and the Unmet Needs of the Immigrant Poor," and, inspired by the enthusiastic response, soon after organized an interdisciplinary Study Group on Immigrant Representation. He sparked the creation, in 2014, of the non-profit Immigrant Justice Corps, the country's first fellowship program for recent law school and college grauates, dedicated to meeting the need for high-quality legal assistance for immigrants.

A project of his tenure to date as chief judge is the year-long commemoration of the 125th anniversary of the Second Circuit, chaired by Judge Richard C. Wesley. Judge Katzmann has also launched a circuit-wide initiative involving all federal courts – "Justice For All: Courts and the Community" -- to increase public understanding of the federal judiciary The initiative, which he cochairs with Southern District Judge Victor Marrero, encompasses a variety of activities and programs and is principally intended for students of all ages.

In addition to his books on judicial-congressional relations, Judge Katzmann is the author of: *Regulatory Bureaucracy; Institutional Disability*; co-editor of *Managing Appeals in Federal Court*; editor and contributing author of *The Law Firm and the Public Good*; and editor and contributing author of *Daniel Patrick Moynihan: The Intellectual in Public Life.*

Since 2001 he has taught an administrative law class at New York University School of Law.

His honors include the Learned Hand Medal for Excellence in Federal Jurisprudence of the Federal Bar Council, the Green Bag award for legal writing, the Charles E. Merriam Award of the American Political Science Association, and honorary degrees. He has served on many judicial and governmental committees, and on law school boards.

His wife, Jennifer, is a filmmaker and writer/editor.

## BARRINGTON D. PARKER, JR.
## 1944-

District Court for the Southern District of New York: 1994-2001
Court of Appeals for the Second Circuit: 2001-

Barrington D. Parker, Jr., was appointed a Judge of the United States Court of Appeals for the Second Circuit by President George W. Bush in October 2001. At the time of his appointment, he was a Judge of the United States District Court for the Southern District of New York having been appointed to that Court by President Clinton. Judge Parker was President Bush's first judicial nominee.

Parker was born in Washington, D.C. in 1944 into a family that includes four generations of lawyers as well as educators and clergy. His father Barrington Parker (Chicago, J.D. 1947) was a Judge of the United States District Court for the District of Columbia. He was appointed by President Nixon in 1970 and served until 1992. His mother Marjorie Parker (Chicago Ph.D, 1951) was a college professor. His grandfather George A. Parker practiced law in the District of Columbia for many years. He was the founder and Dean of the Robert H. Terrell Law School a night law school for African American students. Dean Parker's clients included W.E.B. Dubois and Paul Robeson.

After attending public schools in Washington, D.C., Judge Parker graduated from Yale College (A.B. 1965) and Yale Law School (J.D. 1969). He served as law clerk for the Judge Aubrey E. Robinson, Jr., of the United States District Court for the District of Columbia. He was an associate at Sullivan and Cromwell and in 1977 founded Parker Auspitz Neesemann and Delehanty. In 1987 Parker Auspitz merged with Morrison and Foerster and Parker was a partner there until his appointment to the Southern District. He argued cases in numerous courts of appeal. On a pro bono basis he briefed and argued cases in the United States Supreme Court both by certorari and by special appointment by that Court.

Throughout his professional and judicial career he has been heavily involved in community and educational activities. From 1999 until 2011 he was a Successor Trustee of Yale University (Fellow of the Yale Corporation). For many years he served as President of the Harlem School for the Arts and as Vice President of the NAACP Legal Defense and Educational Fund, Inc. He was an original trustee of the Central Park Conservancy and a member of the Board of Directors of the Yale New Haven Hospital.

He was the recipient of the Learned Hand Medal for Excellence in Federal Jurisprudence of the Federal Bar Council in 2013.

Judge Parker is married to Anne D. Connelly. His previous wife of 33 years, Toni Trent, died in 2005. He and Anne are parents to three children born to Toni: Christine, Kathleen and Jennifer. They are parents to two children born to Anne and Michael (died 2007): Jennifer and Meredith. They have seven grandchildren.

# REENA RAGGI
# 1951-

District Court for the Eastern District of New York:
1997-2002
Court of Appeals for the Second Circuit: 2002-

Reena Raggi was appointed a judge of the Court of Appeals for the Second Circuit in 2002. At the time of her appointment, she was a judge of the District Court for the Eastern District of New York, where she had served for 15 years.

Raggi was born in Jersey City, New Jersey, the eldest of three sisters. Her father, Edward Raggi, served in the United States Army during World War II and was awarded the Purple Heart and Bronze Star in the final Allied offensive in Europe. He earned his college degree *magna cum laude* at night while working full time to support his young family. For most of his adult life, he was employed as an industrial engineer. Judge Raggi credits her father with giving his daughters a love of language and with encouraging them to pursue "professions" to ensure their independence.

Raggi's mother, Santina ("Tina") Navarchi Raggi, was born in Terrinca, Italy, and emigrated to the United States in 1930 at age seven with her brother and deaf mother. She was the first member of her family to graduate high school, by which time she had thoroughly mastered English grammar and spoke the language without a trace of accent even though only Italian was spoken at home. She won a scholarship to secretarial school and went on to work as executive secretary to the heads of two international companies. Judge Raggi credits her mother with giving her daughters faith, ambition, and a hunger for advanced education. All three sisters would earn professional graduate degrees.

Judge Raggi was educated through twelfth grade in Catholic schools. She earned a B.A. degree with honors from Wellesley College, where she was elected to Phi Beta Kappa. At Wellesley, she studied early American legal history with one of the leaders in that field, Kathryn Preyer. Raggi graduated *cum laude* from Harvard Law School and clerked for the Judge Thomas E. Fairchild, then chief judge of the Court of Appeals for the Seventh Circuit. Together with her fellow clerks, Judge Raggi helped institute the Fairchild Lecture at the University of Wisconsin Law School and, in 2004, was privileged to deliver the fifteenth such lecture, entitled "In Praise of District Courts."

In 1979, after two years as an associate at a major New York firm, Raggi became an Assistant United States Attorney in the Eastern District of New York. She was the first assistant hired by United States Attorney (now District Judge) Edward Korman, who would become her life-long mentor. In her seven-year tenure as an Assistant United States Attorney, Judge Raggi would head the office's Narcotic Unit and its Special Prosecutions Unit, the latter focusing on official corruption cases. Fluent in Italian, she frequently worked on collaborative investigations with Italian authorities, including the successful extradition to Milan of financier Michele Sindona. In 1986, the Eastern District Board of

Judges unanimously appointed Judge Raggi as the district's interim United States Attorney, making her the first woman to head a federal prosecutor's office in New York State. Judge Raggi credits the Board of Judges' action with prompting another that followed later that same year, soon after her return to private practice: her nomination by President Ronald Reagan as a district judge for the Eastern District of New York. She was then 35, one of the youngest persons nominated to any federal judgeship, and the first woman to serve on the Eastern District bench. Fifteen years later, President George W. Bush nominated Judge Raggi to fill the Second Circuit seat vacated when Amalya Kearse, a fellow Wellesley alumna, took senior status.

During her judicial tenure, Judge Raggi has served as a member of the Judicial Conference Committee on Judicial Resources and the Judicial Conference Committee on the Federal Rules of Procedure. From 2011 to 2015, she chaired the Conference's Advisory Committee on the Rules of Criminal Procedure.

In 2007, the Federal Bar Council awarded Judge Raggi its Learned Hand Medal for Excellence in Federal Jurisprudence. In accepting the Medal, she spoke on the importance of jury trials to the administration of justice. Judge Raggi has also received the New York State Bar Association's Haig Award for Distinguished Public Service, Wellesley's Alumnae Achievement Award, and an honorary Juris Doctor degree from Brooklyn Law School, where she taught trial practice and served on the Board of Trustees. From 2008 to the present, Judge Raggi has taught Federal Trial and Appellate Advocacy at New York University School of Law. She also serves on the Board of the William Nelson Cromwell Foundation, which awards grants to scholars working in the field of legal history.

Judge Raggi was married for 24 years to David W. Denton, a distinguished New York attorney who died prematurely in 2007 from brain cancer. Early in his career, Denton had served for 15 years as an Assistant United States Attorney in the Southern District of New York, where he rose to the positions of chief of the Criminal Division and executive United States Attorney. Judge Raggi and Mr. Denton have one son, David W. Denton, Jr., who followed in his mother's footsteps by attending Harvard Law School and is following in his father's footsteps as an Assistant United States Attorney in the Southern District of New York.

# RICHARD C. WESLEY
## 1949-

New York State Supreme Court, Seventh Judicial District, Monroe County: 1986-1994
New York State Supreme Court, Appellate Division, Fourth Department: 1994-1997
New York State Court of Appeals: 1997-2003
Court of Appeals for the Second Circuit: 2003-

Richard C. Wesley was born to Charles and Beatrice Wesley on August 1, 1949 in Canandaigua, New York. He grew up in Hemlock, a hamlet in the town of Livonia, New York, in a house built by his father and uncles.

Wesley attended Livonia Central School, where he played football (he was the team captain his senior year), basketball, and baseball. He also sang in the All-State chorus. After high school, Wesley attended the State University of New York at Albany, graduating in 1971 *summa cum laude*, with a B.A. degree. He then attended the Cornell Law School, where he was on the *Cornell Law Review*. Upon his graduation in 1974, he worked as an associate at the firm of Harris, Beach & Wilcox. He left to join Welch, Streb, and Porter, where he became a name partner in 1977.

In 1982, he was elected to the New York State Assembly for the 136th Assembly District. He was reelected in 1984 without opposition.

After four years in the legislature, Wesley was elected to a 14-year term as a justice of the New York Supreme Court in 1986. In January 1991, Wesley was appointed by the chief administrator of the courts to serve as the supervising judge of the criminal courts in the Seventh Judicial District, which covers Monroe, Wayne, Livingston, Ontario, Seneca, Cayuga, Steuben, and Yates counties. In this capacity, Judge Wesley supervised the operation of over 280 criminal courts. On March 25, 1994, Governor Mario Cuomo appointed Judge Wesley to the Appellate Division of the Supreme Court for the State of New York for the Fourth Department, which hears appeals of trial decisions from central and western New York. On December 3, 1996, Governor George Pataki nominated Judge Wesley to the New York State Court of Appeals. Judge Wesley was confirmed by a unanimous vote of the New York State Senate on January 14, 1997. On March 5, 2003, President George W. Bush nominated Judge Wesley to the Court of Appeals for the Second Circuit; the Senate unanimously confirmed him on June 11, 2003, and on June 12, 2003, President Bush signed his commission. Judge Wesley currently serves on the Standing Committee on Rules of Practice and Procedure.

In 1978, Wesley married Kathryn Rice, who hails from Auburn, New York. He and Kathy raised their two children, Sarah and Matthew, in Livonia, just a few miles from the house where Wesley grew up. Both of the Wesley children followed their father's path to the law. After graduating from Cornell, Sarah attended the University of Buffalo Law School, graduating in 2006. She served as an associate at White & Case LLP and an assistant district attorney in the Monroe County District Attorney's Office, and now practices criminal defense law at the firm of Wesley, Clark & Bates LLP in Rochester, New York. Matthew received both his undergraduate and law degrees from Cornell. He served as an associate in Sullivan & Cromwell LLP's New York City office, and now works as a transactional attorney at Coller Capital, a private equity firm in New York City.

For many years, Judge Wesley was a dedicated recreational runner. He ran two marathons: the Wineglass, finishing at a respectable 3:52:39, and the Chicago, finishing at an impressive 3:39:30. Various ailments have limited him to a five-mile walk each morning.

Judge Wesley remains an active participant in his hometown community. For seven years, he drove the Livonia volunteer ambulance. He has been a board member of the Trustees of the United Church of Livonia, Chances and Changes (a community-based organization in Livingston County that provides safe housing to battered women), the Charles Settlement House, the Center for Dispute Resolution, and the Pre-Trial Service Corporation. Judge Wesley currently serves on the board of the Myers' Foundation, the Cornell Law School Advisory Council, and the Cornell University Council. Judge Wesley is also a fellow of the New York Bar Foundation. In 1997, Judge Wesley was awarded the Distinguished SUNY Alumni Award by the SUNY Alumni Association. In 1999, Judge Wesley was named a Distinguished Alumni of SUNY at Albany. Judge Wesley is also active in a number of local youth sports programs. Although he has been on the bench for 30 years, in Livonia he is known as Dick Wesley.

## PETER W. HALL
## 1948-

Court of Appeals for the Second Circuit: 2004-

Peter W. Hall was appointed to the Court of Appeals for the Second Circuit by President George W. Bush in 2004. During the nomination process, the ABA deployed Lorna Schofield (now a judge on the Southern District of New York) to vet Hall. When they met she declared, "I have been checking you out on the internet. You are the least interesting person I have ever had to investigate." This biography makes only a modest attempt to alter that impression.

Hall's great-great-grandfather, Peter Washburn, a lawyer, was the reporter of Vermont Supreme Court decisions. Washburn also served as adjutant general for Vermont during the Civil War, after which he was elected governor of the state. He died of pneumonia while in office. His portrait hangs in Hall's chambers.

Although his ancestral Vermont roots run deep, Hall is technically not a native son of the state. When he was born, his parents were living part-time in Vermont on a 70-acre farm. His grandmother insisted that his mother give birth at the Hartford, Connecticut hospital where his grandfather was chief of staff. The Halls would go on to have four other children, only of one whom was lucky enough to be born in Vermont.

Hall's father was an educator. His career took the family from the Hotchkiss School in Lakeville, Connecticut, where he taught science; to Harvard, where he earned a master's degree in education; and then to Montclair Academy in New Jersey, where he served as headmaster. When Hall was eleven years old, the family returned to Vermont full-time. Hall was put to work cutting pulpwood and haying for the cattle, and spent his free time hunting and fishing, cultivating a lifelong love of the outdoors. He left home for boarding school at Hotchkiss, followed by a year studying at the Westminister School in London on an English Speaking Union exchange.

After his stint abroad, Hall attended the University of North Carolina at Chapel Hill as a Morehead Scholar. He received an A.B. degree, with honors, in English in 1971. In a foreshadowing of his future career as a prosecutor, his honors paper addressed prisons in literature. After graduating a semester early, he taught English at a high school in Sanford, North Carolina. He then returned to the university, working as an assistant dean of students in charge of the fraternity system and liaison to the student government. He also studied for a master's degree in student personnel administration, which he earned in 1975.

The call to public service took Hall to Cornell Law School. His first class was taught by Professor G. Robert Blakey, widely considered the "father" of RICO. Blakey fostered Hall's lifelong interest in criminal justice and constitutional criminal procedure, selecting him as a research assistant to study gambling laws nationwide, among other matters. While in law school, Hall also served as student president of Cornell's Legal Aid clinic. He graduated in 1977.

Hall then served as a law clerk to Judge Albert W. Coffrin of the District Court for the District of Vermont. After his clerkship, Hall joined the United States Attorney's Office for the District of Vermont and was posted to Rutland. The office had four attorneys (including the United States Attorney). After three years, the office had grown to eight attorneys, and Hall was promoted to first Assistant United States Attorney. Among his other notable cases, Hall helped investigate Raymond Luc Levasseur, the leader of a New England-based revolutionary group responsible for killing a New Jersey state trooper and robbing numerous banks.

After eight years as a prosecutor, Hall left the government to form a law firm that became Reiber, Kenlan, Schwiebert, Hall & Facey P.C., and eventually grew to have 14 attorneys—a large firm by Vermont standards. Hall's private practice included commercial and tort litigation, attorney malpractice defense, representation of state prosecutors accused of ethical violations, and in the last three years a significant mediation practice. During this time, he was a member of the Board of Managers of the Vermont Bar Association, serving as its president from 1995 to 1996. In 1997, he was inducted into the American College of Trial Lawyers.

Just days after the September 11 attacks, Hall was confirmed by the Senate as the United States Attorney for the District of Vermont. During his three-year tenure in that post, he increased community outreach in the state's efforts against heroin addiction and helped lead efforts to strengthen cargo container security through the Operation Safe Commerce program.

Hall has lived in Chittenden, Vermont since 1978. His wife, Rebecca (Maria) Dunton, is a veterinarian. Between them, they have one dog, one horse, five cats, and five human children: Sam, Clyde, Susan, Anna, and Elizabeth. In 2015, they welcomed their first grandchild, Simon Washburn Firth.

# DEBRA ANN LIVINGSTON
# 1959-

Court of Appeals for the Second Circuit: 2007-

Debra Ann Livingston was appointed to the Second Circuit in 2007. At the time of her appointment, she was the Paul J. Kellner Professor of Law at Columbia Law School, where she also served as vice dean.

Livingston, the older sister of two brothers, was born in Waycross, Georgia, and moved throughout the South—Georgia, Alabama, Tennessee, Kentucky, and Florida—during her youth. She attended eight schools in six different cities before graduating from Hialeah Miami Lakes High School in Miami, Florida, where she was editor-in-chief of her school newspaper and worked summers as a clerical assistant in the Miami-Dade County State Attorney's Office. Livingston's mother, Sarah Livingston, was a homemaker, while her father, Robert Livingston, began his career as a technician with AT&T and retired (many moves later) as the director of Corporate Labor Relations. Judge Livingston remarked at her induction that she had been blessed with two wonderful parents and that she and her brothers, Robert and Mitchell, grew up in a family "where there was lots of love, lots of humor, where we were surrounded at all times by warmth, affection and support."

Livingston was a member of Phi Beta Kappa at Princeton University, where she graduated *magna cum laude* in 1980 after only three years. At Princeton she was a member of the University Press Club, serving as a stringer for the Associated Press and writing news, reviews, and feature stories for local newspapers. She graduated from Harvard Law School *magna cum laude* in 1984, after spending a year between her second and third years of law school in Bangkok, Thailand, where she worked as a legal consultant to the Office of the United Nations High Commissioner for Refugees, which was then involved in the resettlement of displaced Cambodians. At Harvard, Livingston was an editor on the *Harvard Law Review*. She also worked as a teaching assistant for Professors Clark Byse, Archibald Cox, and Lloyd Weinreb.

Following law school, Judge Livingston clerked for Second Circuit Judge J. Edward Lumbard in the very courthouse in which she now serves. Judge Lumbard, a distinguished jurist and former United States Attorney for the Southern District of New York, first pointed her in the direction of his former office. Thereafter, following a stint as an associate at a major New York firm, Judge Livingston became an Assistant United States Attorney in the United States Attorney's Office for the Southern District of New York in 1986, serving in the Criminal Division as a line assistant and as deputy chief appellate attorney. In 1992, following another short stint at the firm, Judge Livingston entered academia, moving to Ann Arbor to join the faculty of the University of Michigan Law School and winning Michigan's L. Hart Wright Award for excellence in teaching her first year there.

Livingston returned to New York City and joined the faculty at Columbia Law School in 1994. Following her return, Mayor

Rudolph Giuliani appointed her as a commissioner to the New York City Civilian Complaint Review Board, where she served from 1994 to 2003. At Columbia, Livingston has taught evidence, criminal law, and continues regularly to teach criminal procedure. Her scholarship has centered on the Fourth Amendment and on the police function. She is a co-author, with Ronald Allen, Joseph Hoffmann, Andrew Leipold, and Tracey Meares, of COMPREHENSIVE CRIMINAL PROCEDURE, a widely respected casebook now in its fourth edition. Livingston has received Columbia's Wein Prize for Social Responsibility. In 2014, Chief Justice John Roberts appointed Judge Livingston to the Judicial Conference Advisory Committee on Evidence Rules.

Judge Livingston is married to John McEnany, a Columbia Law School graduate and the long-serving Associate United States Attorney for the Southern District of New York. They have a teenage son.

## GERARD E. LYNCH
## 1951-

District Court for the Southern District of New York: 2000-2009
Court of Appeals for the Second Circuit: 2009-

Gerard E. Lynch was appointed to the Court of Appeals for the Second Circuit by President Barack Obama in 2009. From 2000 through 2009 he served on the District Court for the Southern District of New York, to which he was appointed by President Bill Clinton. Before his appointment, Lynch was both an academic and a practitioner, teaching at the Columbia University School of Law and practicing criminal law as both a prosecutor and defense lawyer.

Judge Lynch is a life-long New Yorker. The son of an airline mechanic and a homemaker, he was born in Brooklyn and raised in Ridgewood, Queens. He graduated first in his class from Manhattan's Regis High School, an all-scholarship Jesuit school where he was introduced to classical languages and literature, and majored in Greek and Latin at Columbia Colleges, where he was elected to Phi Beta Kappa and was class valedictorian. Seeking greater engagement with social issues, he went on to Columbia Law School, again graduating first in his class. At Columbia, Lynch benefitted from the outstanding academic faculty, including such luminaries as Herbert Wechsler, E. Allan Farnsworth, and Willis Reese, but was also inspired by the pathbreaking litigation of another of his teachers, Ruth Bader Ginsburg, and was intrigued by a clinical course that introduced him to the practical skills and challenges of litigation.

After graduation, Lynch's first job brought him to the Second Circuit, and to what is now the Thurgood Marshall United States Courthouse at Foley Square, as law clerk to one of the court's greatest judges, Judge Wilfred Feinberg. The following year, he clerked for Justice William J. Brennan, Jr., at the Supreme Court. Better apprenticeships for a future judge would be hard to find.

In 1977, upon completing his clerkships, Lynch joined the faculty of Columbia Law School, where he has taught ever since, as assistant professor of law. Over the years, he rose through the academic ranks, being appointed full professor in 1986 and named the first Paul J. Kellner Professor of Law in 1996. From 1992 to 1997 he served as vice dean of the Law School, with responsibility for curriculum, adjunct faculty and student services. Lynch has taught a wide range of courses including constitutional law, criminal procedure, federal criminal law, criminal litigation, criminology, sentencing, contracts, advanced civil procedure and appellate advocacy, but his primary responsibility has been the first-year course in criminal law, which he taught some 30 times from 1979 to 2015. He received the student-voted Willis Reese Award for Excellence in Teaching in 1994, and in 1997 he became the first member of the Faculty of Law to receive the university-wide President's Award for Outstanding Teaching. Judge Lynch is the author of various academic and popular articles about criminal law and procedure, constitutional law, and legal ethics, most notably a book-length study of criminal RICO, an influential account of our de facto administrative process of criminal adjudication, and a number of articles about sentencing.

Lynch took a public service leave from Columbia in 1980, to become an Assistant United States Attorney for the Southern District of New York. He held that position until 1983, investigating and trying white-collar criminal cases and serving as deputy chief and later chief appellate attorney. After returning to Columbia, he served on a part-time basis as counsel to several commissions and independent counsel investigating allegations of misconduct in office, including the Iran/Contra investigation, in which he managed the motion practice in the prosecution of Oliver North and argued appeals in the Fourth and District of Columbia Circuits, including the appeal from North's conviction. From 1990 to 1992, he returned to the United States Attorney's Office for the Southern District of New York as chief of the Criminal Division, where he supervised all of the office's criminal litigation.

Upon returning to Columbia after that assignment, in addition to teaching he became counsel to the New York law firm Howard Darby & Levin (later named Howard Smith & Levin and eventually merging into Covington & Burling), where he represented individuals and corporations in criminal and regulatory investigations. His assignments also included appeals before the Second Circuit; among those appeals, he won reversal of the mail fraud conviction of the president of the nation's largest aviation insurer, and successfully defended a malpractice judgment against a major New York law firm. On a pro bono basis, he has also briefed and argued cases in the Supreme Court and the Second Circuit.

Judge Lynch has received various awards, including the Wien Prize in Social Responsibility from Columbia Law School (2008), the Edward Weinfeld Award for Distinguished Contributions to the Administration of Justice from the New York County Lawyers' Association (2009), and the Learned Hand Medal for Excellence in Federal Jurisprudence from the Federal Bar Council (2016).

He has been married for more than 40 years to Dr. Karen Marisak, a clinical psychologist and psychoanalyst. He takes great pride and delight in his son, Chris, who is a lawyer, and his granddaughter, Olivia.

# DENNY CHIN
# 1954-

District Court for the Southern District of New York:
1994-2010
Court of Appeals for the Second Circuit: 2010-

Denny Chin was born in Hong Kong in 1954. He immigrated with his family to the United States in 1956 and was raised in New York City.

Chin attended public schools in New York, including Stuyvesant High School, where he played football. He received a B.A. degree *magna cum laude* in 1971 from Princeton University, where he was managing editor of *The Daily Princetonian*, and a J.D. degree 1978 from Fordham Law School, where he was managing editor of the *Fordham Law Review*.

Chin clerked for Judge Henry F. Werker of the Southern District of New York from 1978 to 1980. He was associated with Davis Polk & Wardwell from 1980 to 1982. In 1982, Chin was appointed an Assistant United States Attorney for the Southern District of New York and served in that position until 1986, when he and two colleagues from the United States Attorney's Office started a law firm, Campbell, Patrick & Chin. In 1990, he became counsel to Vladeck, Waldman, Elias & Engelhard, P.C., where he specialized in labor and employment law. He became a partner at that firm in 1991.

In 1994, Chin was appointed a district judge for the Southern District of New York. He became the first Asian American appointed to a district court outside the Ninth Circuit. He served in that capacity for almost 16 years, presiding over a number of significant and high-profile cases, including cases involving Megan's Law, the Million Youth March, the Naked Cowboy, the Google Books project, and the United Nations Oil for Food Program. He also presided over the trial of Bashir Noorzai, the leader of an Afghan tribe charged with conspiring to import heroin, and the guilty plea and sentencing of financier Bernard L. Madoff.

In 2010, Judge Chin was appointed to the Court of Appeals for the Second Circuit. He became, at the time, the only active Asian American circuit judge in the country.

Judge Chin has taught legal writing at Fordham Law School since 1986. He is a member of the American Bar Association, the New York City Bar Association, the New York County Lawyers Association, the Federal Bar Council Inn of Court, the American Law Institute, the National Asian Pacific American Bar Association, and the Asian American Bar Association of New York. He served as president of the Asian American Bar Association of New York from January 1992 through January 1994. Before his appointment to the bench, he served on the boards of numerous not-for-profit and professional organizations, including Hartley House, Care for the Homeless, the Prospect Park Environmental Center, the Clinton Housing Association, and the National Employment Lawyers Association. He is presently a member of the boards of trustees or advisors of Princeton University, the Fordham Law School Alumni Association, the Feerick Center for Social Justice, the Fordham Center for Law and Information Policy, and the Sonia and Celina Sotomayor Judicial Internship Program.

Judge Chin has received numerous awards and honors, including: honorary doctorate degrees from Fordham University and CUNY Law School; the Woodrow Wilson Award from Princeton University; the Spirit of Excellence Award from the American Bar Association; the Edward Weinfeld Award from the New York County Lawyers Association; the Leadership Award from the Korean American Lawyers Association of Greater New York; the Lifetime Achievement Award from Judicial Friends; the Abely Award for Leading Women and Children to Safety from Sanctuary for Families; the Lifetime Achievement Award from the New York State Division of Human Rights; the Trailblazer Award from the National Asian Pacific American Bar Association; and the National Football Foundation Scholar-Athlete Award. He has given the commencement address to graduating classes at Cardozo Law School, Fordham Law School (twice), Boston University Law School, St. John's Law School, the University of Miami Law School, and Packer Collegiate Institute.

Judge Chin is married to Kathy Hirata Chin, a partner at Cadwalader, Wickersham & Taft, LLP, a law firm in New York City. They have two sons; one is an educator in a charter school in New York City and the other is a college student. Judge Chin and his wife are the principal writers for a number of reenactments of historic cases presented by the Asian American Bar Association of New York, including "The Vietnamese Fishermen v. The Ku Klux Klan," "Justice Denied: Wards Cove v. Atonio," and "22 Lewd Chinese Women: Chy Lung v. Freeman." His teams on the Federal Bar Council Inn of Court have also presented a number of historic reenactments, including "The Amistad Case," "The Trial of Lizzie Borden," and "The Trial of Ethel Rosenberg: Criminal Justice In A Time of National Crisis."

Judge Chin has completed four New York City marathons, in 2000, 2001, 2002, and 2003.

## RAYMOND J. LOHIER, JR.
## 1965-

Court of Appeals for the Second Circuit: 2010-

Raymond J. Lohier was appointed to the Court of Appeals for the Second Circuit by President Barack Obama in 2010.

Lohier is an immigrant and the son of immigrants from the Caribbean. His mother left Haiti to become a nurse in Canada. His father, a doctor, fled to Canada to avoid the dictatorship in Haiti, returning to his birthplace only once during the remainder of his life in exile. Lohier was born in Montreal, Canada. In 1972, he and his family moved to the United States, settling in Philadelphia.

In 1988, Lohier received an A.B. degree from Harvard College, where he concentrated in philosophy and was taught by some of the most influential philosophers of the twentieth century. Although he considered pursuing a doctorate in philosophy,

Lohier instead enrolled in law school. In 1991 he received a J.D. degree from New York University School of Law, where he was a recipient of the Vanderbilt Medal and pursued courses in legal philosophy and jurisprudence with Ronald Dworkin, among other professors. He also served as a research and teaching assistant to Chief Judge A. Leon Higginbotham, Jr., of the Court of Appeals for the Third Circuit, who was completing his seminal work on the history of race in the American legal process. Lohier's exposure to that work sparked his interest and involvement in legal history and civil rights.

After graduation, Lohier enjoyed a brief initial stint as an associate with the law firm Cleary, Gottlieb, Steen & Hamilton. From 1992 to 1993, he served as a law clerk for Judge Robert P. Patterson, Jr., of the Southern District of New York, whose father, Robert P. Patterson, had been a circuit judge on the Second Circuit from 1938 to 1939.[1] Lohier's relationship with the younger Judge Patterson, an important mentor, ended only with the latter's death in 2015.

Upon completing his clerkship, Lohier returned to Cleary, Gottlieb, where he worked as both a litigator and a corporate transactional lawyer from 1993 to 1997, while also serving on the firm's diversity and pro bono committees.

From 1997 to 2000, Lohier lived in Washington, D.C., and served as a senior trial attorney with the Employment Litigation Section of the Civil Rights Division of the United States Department of Justice, where he spearheaded employment discrimination-related litigation and worked on other civil rights matters of importance to the federal government throughout the United States. During his tenure at the Civil Rights Division, Lohier was the vice-chairperson of the Department of Justice Association of Black Attorneys.

For the decade prior to his appointment to the federal bench, Lohier served in the United States Attorney's Office for the Southern District of New York, where he was special counsel to the United States Attorney, chief of the Securities and Commodities Fraud Task Force, and chief of the Narcotics Unit. Lohier was the first African American to serve in each of these positions. As chief of the Securities and Commodities Fraud Task Force,

Lohier oversaw the investigations and prosecutions related to Bernard Madoff and Marc Dreier, the Galleon and other hedge fund insider trading cases, and several other high-profile securities and commodities fraud cases and investigations.

Judge Lohier currently serves as Chair of the Judicial Conference Committee on Defender Services and on the New York State-Federal Judicial Council. He is a member of the Council of the American Law Institute and the Federal Bar Council American Inn of Court, as well as a member of the Board of Trustees and an adjunct professor of law at New York University School of Law. He is also an advisory board member of Law Alumni of Color Association and a lifetime director of the New York University Law School Alumni Association. From 2007 until his appointment, he also served as first vice-chairperson of Brooklyn Community Board 6. Judge Lohier is the recipient of several awards, including the New York University Alumni Association's Eugene J. Keogh Award for Distinguished Public Service.

Judge Lohier's wife, Donna Lee, is a professor of law at the City University of New York School of Law. They met in law school and married in 1999. They have two sons.

1. Judge Patterson, Jr., gave his father's judicial robes to Judge Lohier upon his appointment to the Second Circuit.

## SUSAN L. CARNEY
## 1951-

Court of Appeals for the Second Circuit: 2011-

Susan L. Carney became a federal circuit judge in June 2011, following her nomination to the Court of Appeals by President Barack Obama. The granddaughter of Greek immigrants who worked in the mills of Manchester, New Hampshire, she was born and grew up in the suburbs of Boston, the oldest child and only girl in a family of six children. Her Greek-American mother, Cleopatra Olgas Carney, and her father, John Robert Carney, Jr., of Irish and Swedish descent, found each other in Boston after the end of World War II. Both were Navy veterans able to get a college education with the help of the GI Bill. They met in the library line at Boston University, waiting to borrow books.

John Carney became a trial lawyer in Boston, practicing law with a partner in a small firm with an office that looked out on the Old Granary Burying Ground. A photograph of Judge Learned Hand hung prominently in his office. Cleo Carney stayed home caring for the children until the youngest went off to school. She then began to work part-time in a retail clothing store, a setting in which she continued to work until age 88, only a few years before she died in 2015.

At age ten (in 1961), Carney began to study the cello, and classical music became a lifelong interest. When she was 15 years old, her hometown of Weston, Massachusetts, chose her to live in France and attend school there through a local exchange program. She did so, from August 1967 through August 1968. After returning to Weston and finishing high school, she enrolled in Radcliffe College (soon to become part of Harvard College), where she continued to play the cello and majored in Russian History and Literature. She graduated *cum laude* in 1973. She then worked for a year as a Teaching Fellow and instructor in French and Russian at Phillips Academy in Andover, Massachusetts.

After her fellowship, she attended the University of Chicago Law School for her first year of law school. She then returned to Cambridge to complete her J.D. studies, joining the women who made up approximately 15 percent of the class at Harvard Law School. Following her graduation from law school *magna cum laude* in 1977, she clerked in Boston for Judge Levin H. Campbell of the Court of Appeals for the First Circuit. The model set by Daniel Steiner, Esq., as counsel to Harvard President Derek Bok—then a novel role, and one that Carney found compelling—prompted her after her clerkship to join Ropes & Gray, which represented many colleges, universities, and large not-for-profit organizations in New England.

Not long after she arrived at the firm, however, her husband, Lincoln Caplan, received a fellowship that led them to take a "one-year detour" from Boston to Washington, D.C. The detour turned into 19 years in the nation's capital. Ropes & Gray had no Washington office then, so Carney joined a small labor-oriented litigation firm, about half of whose lawyers were women. She became a partner there. Over the following years, she worked at other firms, including Bredhoff & Kaiser, and pursued a varied path in the law that included engagements for Georgetown University and George Washington University, a project on court funding prepared for the Bar Association of the District of Columbia, and almost two years as associate counsel for the Peace Corps, based in Washington.

In 1998, she and her husband (with their daughter, then age ten) moved to her husband's native New Haven, and Carney began work as associate, then deputy general counsel at Yale University, serving as acting general counsel from June through December 2008. Her work at Yale included advising on federal regulatory regimes concerning the conduct of research, negotiating research funding transactions and intellectual property matters, participating in the management of certain litigation, and handling a broad array of other legal matters.

Throughout her time at Yale, she was active in the National Association of College & University Attorneys, serving on the Board of Directors of that organization from 2007 through 2010. She also served on the boards of the bipartisan Women Organizing Women Political Action Committee and the New Haven Youth Soccer League, among other Connecticut organizations. Since assuming her position on the bench, she has also taught at Yale Law School and become a member of the American Law Institute. In 2013, she was elected to a six-year term as a member of the Board of Overseers of Harvard University.

# CHRISTOPHER F. DRONEY
## 1954-

District Court for the District of Connecticut:
1997-2011
Court of Appeals for the Second Circuit: 2011-

Christopher F. Droney was born in Hartford, Connecticut on June 22, 1954. He attended the public schools in West Hartford and then graduated *magna cum laude* from the College of the Holy Cross, where he also played lacrosse. Among his academic awards at Holy Cross was his election to Alpha Sigma Nu, the national Jesuit honor society.

While in college, Droney spent a semester as an intern for the U.S. House of Representatives Committee on Education and Labor, chaired by the legendary Carl D. Perkins of Kentucky. During that time, Droney attended the first State of the Union

Address by President Gerald R. Ford, following the resignation of President Richard M. Nixon for the Watergate scandal.

Droney graduated from the University of Connecticut School of Law in 1979, where he was a notes and comments editor of the *Connecticut Law Review.*

Droney then went into the private practice of law in Hartford and became a partner in the firm of Reid & Riege, P.C., and specialized in trial work, including trials as a Criminal Justice Act panel member.

At the same time, Droney became active in Connecticut politics. He was elected mayor of West Hartford at the age of 31, the youngest mayor in the town's history. He also was a member of the Connecticut Democratic State Central Committee, chaired the Al Gore for President campaign in Connecticut in 1988, and was a delegate for Bill Clinton at the Democratic National Convention in New York City in 1992.

Following the election of President Clinton, Droney was appointed United States Attorney for the District of Connecticut. He concentrated the efforts of the United States Attorney's Office on gang violence in Hartford, New Haven, and Bridgeport, and received numerous community and law enforcement awards for those efforts. In 1996, he addressed President Clinton and Attorney General Janet Reno in the East Room of the White House on strategies to address gang violence.

As United States Attorney, Judge Droney personally tried cases, including one involving the Ku Klux Klan. He also argued appeals before the Court of Appeals for the Second Circuit on the constitutionality of the Violence Against Women Act, the Child Support Recovery Act, and the National Firearms Act. Droney was also a member of Attorney General Reno's Advisory Committee of United States Attorneys.

In 1997, Judge Droney was appointed by President Clinton as a district judge for the District of Connecticut. He served as a district judge for 14 years.

In 2011, President Barack Obama appointed Judge Droney to the Court of Appeals for the Second Circuit, to the seat previously held by Judge Guido Calabresi. Judge Droney was confirmed by the Senate unanimously, as he had been for United States Attorney and district judge.

Judge Droney has received numerous awards, including the University of Connecticut School of Law Distinguished Graduate Award, the Connecticut Law Review Award, and an honorary degree from the University of Connecticut.

Judge Droney lives in West Hartford with his wife, Elizabeth. They have three adult daughters: Sarah, Emily and Katherine. Elizabeth is a history teacher in West Hartford. Sarah is an attorney, Emily is a nurse-practitioner, and Katherine is a special education teacher.

## FORMER MEMBERS

These three judges are no longer members of the Court of Appeals for the Second Circuit. They specifically approved their entries.

# LAWRENCE WARREN PIERCE
# 1924-

District Court for the Southern District of New York:
1971-1981
Court of Appeals for the Second Circuit: 1981-1995

Judge Lawrence Warren Pierce was appointed United States circuit judge for the Second Circuit in November 1981. He assumed senior status in 1990 and retired in 1995. Prior to his appointment to the Second Circuit, Judge Pierce served as a district judge for the Southern District of New York from 1971 to 1981, including two years of dual service as a member of the Foreign Intelligence Surveillance Court, from 1979 to 1980. During the 1970s, he was chairman of the Southern District's History Committee and served on the Second Circuit Bicentennial Committee.

Pierce entered Saint Joseph's University in Philadelphia in 1942, but after one year left to serve in the Army in Italy as an infantry sergeant. Returning after World War II, he resumed his studies at Saint Joseph's, and graduated in 1948. He went on to study law at Fordham Law School in New York City, and graduated in 1951. He is the recipient of honorary degrees from Fordham, Saint Joseph's, Fairfield, and Saint John's Universities and Hamilton College.

Pierce has spent almost his entire career in public service. Upon graduation from law school, he joined the Legal Aid Society of New York for three years as a staff attorney in the civil branch, followed by six years as an assistant district attorney for Kings County (Brooklyn). From 1961 to 1963, he was a deputy commissioner for the New York City Police Department. He entered New York State government in 1963 as director of the New York State Division for Youth. From 1966 to 1970, he was chairman of the New York State Narcotics Addiction Control Commission. From 1970 to 1971, he served as a visiting professor at the Graduate School of Criminal Justice at the State University of New York at Albany.

Judge Pierce is a member of the American Bar Association and the National Bar Association. For two years, he served as the ABA's Alternate Observer at the United States Mission to the United Nations. He was a member of the Board of Fellows of the Institute of Judicial Administration and a trustee of the Practising Law Institute. He has served on a number of civic organizations, including: the Board of Directors of CARE, USA; the Board of Managers of the Havens Relief Fund Society; the Board of Trustees of Saint Joseph's and Fordham Universities; and the Board of Managers of Lincoln Hall for Boys. He is the former vice president of the New York chapter of the Sons of the Revolution and is a founding member of 100 Men. Early in his career, he was chairman of the New York and Brooklyn Catholic Interracial Councils. From 1965 through 1995, he served on several delegations studying criminal justice systems in England, Sweden, China, Japan and Africa. In 1970, he was a member of the secretary of the Army's Special Civilian Committee to Study Army Confinement Facilities in the United States, Europe and

Asia. In recent years, he has been a member of the Council on Foreign Relations. In retirement, Judge Pierce became the director of the USAID-funded Cambodian Court Training Project.

He was married to the late Wilma Taylor and Cynthia Straker. He enjoys time with his three sons and their families.

# GEORGE C. PRATT
## 1928-

District Court for the Eastern District of New York:
1976-1982
Court of Appeals for the Second Circuit: 1982-1995

Judge Pratt was appointed circuit judge for the Second Circuit on June 29, 1982, having served as a district judge for the Eastern District of New York since May 24, 1976. He took senior status on May 22, 1993, and retired on January 31, 1995. He came from a long line of judges. His father, grandfather, and great-grandfather all served as state-court judges in upstate Steuben County, New York.

Since 1952, Judge Pratt has been married to Carol Hoffman Pratt, who is one of Long Island's best duplicate bridge players. They have two sons, two daughters, five grandchildren, and four great-grandchildren. Their two sons, one granddaughter, and one grandson are all lawyers.

He received a B.A. degree from Yale College in 1950, a JD degree from Yale Law School in 1953, and an honorary Doctor of Laws Degree from Hofstra Law School. After serving a clerkship with Judge Charles W. Froessel of the New York Court of Appeals, Pratt practiced law as a trial and appellate attorney on Long Island, and served as attorney for several Nassau County villages, school attorney for the Syosset Central School District, and special counsel for the Nassau County Board of Supervisors, defending its weighted-voting representation, a system upheld ultimately in the Supreme Court.

From 1993 to 2002, he was a professor at Touro College, Jacob D. Fuchsberg Law Center, teaching civil procedure, civil rights litigation, federal courts, and appellate advocacy. With Professor Martin A. Schwartz, he co-authored "Jury Charges in § 1983 Cases," and he is the name author of volumes 19, 20, and 20A of *Moore's Federal Practice*, covering appeals in the federal courts.

From 1989 to 1996, Judge Pratt served on the Standing Committee on the Rules of Practice and Procedure of the United States Judicial Conference, and from 1964 to 1976 he was a member of the New York State Judicial Conference's Committee to Advise and Consult with the Judicial Conference on the Civil Practice Law and Rules.

In 2001 Judge Pratt returned as special counsel to Farrell Fritz, PC, the firm he helped organize before going on the bench. The firm had grown from ten to 80 lawyers. At Farrell Fritz, he works primarily as an expert witness and consultant, and as an arbitrator of complex commercial matters in domestic and international disputes.

## SONIA SOTOMAYOR
## 1954-

District Court for the Southern District of New York: 1992-1998
Court of Appeals for the Second Circuit: 1998-2009
Supreme Court: 2009-

Justice Sonia Sotomayor's career on the bench began in 1992, when President George H.W. Bush appointed her to the District Court for the Southern District of New York. In October 1998, President Bill Clinton elevated her to the Court of Appeals for the Second Circuit. President Barack H. Obama appointed her to the Supreme Court in 2009. She is the only sitting Supreme Court justice who has served as both a district and circuit judge.

Sotomayor is a native New Yorker, born and raised in the South Bronx. Her parents, Celina and Juan Luis ("Juli") Sotomayor, both migrated from Puerto Rico. They arrived in New

York within only days of each other, just before Christmas of 1944, she as a cadet in the Women's Army Corps and he aboard a U.S. Army transport ship ferrying workers from the Caribbean.

Celina had grown up on a farm near the village of Lajas, the youngest of six siblings. Her father abandoned the family when she was young; her mother died when she was nine years old. Celina then moved in with an older sister in the then-small city of San Germán. Eager to escape poverty and explore life beyond the island, at the age of 17, Celina enlisted in the Women's Army Corps, claiming to be 18. She would spend the rest of her life in New York City. She and Juli met at a party in the Bronx, and married soon thereafter at city hall. They had two children: Sonia and Juan Luis, Jr.

The Sotomayor household spoke Spanish and maintained close ties to a sprawling network of aunts, uncles, and cousins in the Bronx. When Justice Sotomayor was three years old, the family moved from a crowded tenement building to the Bronxdale Houses, a 28-building public housing project in the Soundview neighborhood. Juli worked in a mannequin factory and then a radiator factory. Despite having only a sixth-grade education, he had a talent with numbers and took on bookkeeping work for the factory. He died of heart disease and alcohol-related complications at the age of 42 years old when Sotomayor was only nine. From then on, Celina raised the children as a single mother. She worked the evening shift (and many weekends) as a practical nurse at Prospect Hospital, earning just enough money to pay her children's tuition at Blessed Sacrament School and then Cardinal Spellman High School. Celina earned her nursing degree in 1972. Juan (whose older sister still calls him "Junior") is an allergy and asthma physician practicing in Liverpool, New York, with his three children, Kiley, Conner, and Corey.

Sotomayor left the Bronx at age 18 for Princeton University on a full scholarship. She graduated *summa cum laude*, Phi Beta Kappa, in 1976 with a bachelor's degree in history. She won the Pyne Prize, given for excellent scholarship and effective support of the best interests of Princeton University. Sotomayor graduated from Yale Law School in 1979, where she served as an editor of the *Yale Law Journal* and managing editor of *Yale Studies in World Public Order.*

Sotomayor began her legal career as an assistant district attorney in New York County, working for the legendary "Boss" of the office, Robert M. Morgenthau. As a prosecutor, Sotomayor spent five years trying everything from petty misdemeanors to high-profile felony cases. During that time, she also joined the board of the Puerto Rican Legal Defense and Education Fund (now known as LatinoJustice), a civil rights organization that litigates and advocates on behalf of Latino Americans. Sotomayor served on the board for 12 years. In 1984, she left the DA's office to practice civil litigation with the law firm Pavia & Harcourt, as an associate and then partner. Her focus at the firm was on intellectual property and international litigation and arbitration of commercial and commodity export trading cases. She practiced there until her 1992 appointment to the bench in the Southern District of New York.

The list of Justice Sotomayor's community service activities is long. She serves on the board of iCivics, a non-profit founded by Justice Sandra Day O'Connor that provides video games to educators to use as a teaching aid for civics instruction. Along with the Puerto Rican Legal Defense and Education Fund, she has served on the boards of the State of New York Mortgage Agency, the New York City Campaign Finance Board, and the Maternity Center Association. She was also a trustee of Princeton University. Justice Sotomayor regularly devotes time to the Sonia & Celina Sotomayor Judicial Internship Program, which seeks to increase diversity in the legal profession by placing promising high school and law school students in internships in the state and federal judicial systems; Dream Big Day, sponsored by the Bronx Children's Museum for students participating in their summer program; the Cissy Marshall National Capital Lawyers Auxiliary Law Day Essay Contest at the Supreme Court, an event for middle school students; the Sphinx Medal of Excellence, given to emerging black and Latino leaders in classical music; and College Bound, an after-school mentoring program for high school students. She also helped create the Judicial Studies Institute in Puerto Rico, which, in collaboration with the Department of State and Department of Justice, educates Latin American judges about the American adversarial legal system. She has been a member of numerous organizations, including the American Bar Association, the New York City chapter of the Women's Bar Association, the Hispanic National Bar Association, the Puerto Rican Bar Association, the Association of Judges of Hispanic Heritage, the American Philosophical Society, the National Association of Women Judges, and Phi Alpha Delta. She has received honorary degrees from Herbert H. Lehman College (1999), Princeton University (2001), Brooklyn Law School (2001), Pace University (2003), Hofstra University (2006), Northeastern University School of Law (2007), Université Paris Ouest (2010), Howard University (2010), St. Lawrence University (2010), the University of South Carolina (2011), Ramapo College of New Jersey (2011), New York University (2012), Yale University (2013), Fordham University (2014), the University of Puerto Rico (2014), the Icahn School of Medicine at Mount Sinai (2015), and the University of Rhode Island (2016). For many years, she taught as an adjunct professor at New York University School of Law and a Lecturer-in-Law at Columbia Law School. She is a frequent speaker at conferences and university and law school events, and has made two appearances (as herself) on Sesame Street. In 2010, the Bronxdale Houses development was renamed the Justice Sonia Sotomayor Houses and Community Center.

In 2013, Justice Sotomayor authored a memoir titled *My Beloved World*, which recounts her path to the bench. Although she now resides happily in Washington, DC, she misses New York City and her brilliant and caring Southern District and Second Circuit colleagues, and remains a devoted New York Yankees fan.

# The Judges of

# THE SECOND CIRCUIT

CPSIA information can be obtained
at www.ICGtesting.com
Printed in the USA
LVOW05*2242051217
558745LV00012B/205/P